PHILOSOPHY

A GUIDE THROUGH THE SUBJECT

EDITED BY

A. C. GRAYLING

OXFORD UNIVERSITY PRESS

Oxford University Press, Walton Street, Oxford OX2 6DP
Oxford New York
Athens Auckland Bangkok Bombay
Calcutta Cape Town Dar es Salaam Delhi
Florence Hong Kong Istanbul Karachi
Kuala Lumpur Madras Madrid Melbourne
Mexico City Nairobi Paris Singapore
Taipei Tokyo Toronto
and associated companies in
Berlin Ibadan

Oxford is a trade mark of Oxford University Press

Published in the United States by
Oxford University Press Inc., New York

First published in hardback and paperback 1995
Reprinted in paperback 1995, 1996

This work was originally produced for the use of students of the
External Programme of the University of London

British Library Cataloguing in Publication Data
Data available

Library of Congress Cataloging in Publication Data
Data available
ISBN 0-19-875156-7
ISBN 0-19-875157-5 (Pbk)

Printed in Great Britain
on acid-free paper by
Bookcraft (Bath) Ltd,
Midsomer Norton, Bath

Preface

If you intend a journey, you do well to consult a map. And if the terrain to be crossed promises forests and mountains, rivers and ravines—wonderful to behold, but demanding more than an afternoon's stroll—then the map should be detailed enough, and of the right kind. With a suitable map one always travels more hopefully, and arrives sooner.

This book is a map of the central provinces of philosophy. It is an introduction, a guide, a companion, and a survey all in one, and it aspires to be so by addressing philosophy's chief questions clearly and in some detail. It consists of eleven extended essays, each providing an account of the main topics in the field of philosophy it covers. The essays, although introductory, are not elementary, because they are aimed at those who wish to take more than a superficial look at philosophy. They therefore seek to give the full character of inquiry into its most important questions.

Nor do the essays try to be comprehensive. The fields they cover are large, so they aim instead to identify and discuss the core questions, so that readers will be well equipped to continue their exploration of those fields independently.

The eleven essays are self-contained discussions of the philosophical subjects they introduce. But philosophy is a pursuit in which there are many overlaps and interconnections, and therefore the chapters cross each other's territory frequently; as the reader reads more of them, so their internal connections become apparent. (More is said of this in the Introduction.) Different authors take different views of the same matter; the reader will at times see those contrasts here, and is invited to reflect on them.

This volume originated in work done on behalf of the University of London in commissioning material to accompany undergraduate studies in philosophy. London has arguably one of the best single-subject degrees in philosophy offered by any university in the world. When the opportunity arose to put together a collection of essays to serve as a companion to London's philosophy degree, the missionary possibility immediately suggested itself of promoting the university's conception of what is central to philosophical study. This volume is the result.

Almost all the contributors to this volume either teach at or have taught at the University of London; and almost all have also had experience of teaching elsewhere—at Oxford, Cambridge, and universities elsewhere in Britain, North America, and Australasia. The resulting combination of philosophical interest with pedagogical experience drawn from this wide range finds expression in this book in two forms—in the choice of subjects considered to be the ground-work of philosophy, and in the level at which the subjects are introduced.

The choice of subjects regarded as the basis of a philosophical education is: epistemology, metaphysics, philosophical logic, elementary philosophy of science (here called 'methodology'), ethics, the history of ancient Greek philosophy, and the history of modern philosophy from Descartes to Kant. These form the basis for further studies, of such subjects as philosophy of mind, aesthetics, political philosophy, philosophy of language, medieval philosophy, continental philosophy from Hegel, twentieth-century analytic philosophy, and a number of others.

This volume covers all the core subjects, and two of the more widely studied additional subjects, namely philosophy of mind and aesthetics. A second volume will cover the remaining fields of philosophy.

Much might be said about the doubtful value of too simple or too pedagogical an approach to introductory philosophy. The essays in this volume do not try to simplify what is not an elementary subject. They instead aim at clear but unflinching examination of the central topics. The level at which the volume is pitched is that of a discussion which regards its readers not only as capable of tackling philosophy seriously, but as wishing to do so. It is therefore also a companion; the reader can return to it often in the course of his or her study of philosophy. And it is also a survey: anyone interested to know what is at the centre of each major area of philosophical inquiry will find these essays thoroughly informative.

Apart from the contributors themselves, whom I warmly thank for their endeavours, a number of others were also helpful in the preparation of this volume: I especially thank my colleagues in the Department of Philosophy at Birkbeck College, University of London; Alex Orenstein and Jonathan Dancy; Jude Brooks, Jane van der Ban, and M. C. Black at Senate House, University of London; Peter Momtchiloff and the readers of Oxford University Press; and Elizabeth Cotton and Marylois Chan.

A.C.G.

Contents

List of Contributors

TIM CRANE is Lecturer in Philosophy, University College, London.

MARTIN DAVIES is Wilde Reader in Mental Philosophy in the University of Oxford.

SEBASTIAN GARDNER is Lecturer in Philosophy, Birkbeck College, London

A. C. GRAYLING is Lecturer in Philosophy, Birkbeck College, London, and Senior Research Fellow, St Anne's College, Oxford.

CHRISTOPHER JANAWAY is Senior Lecturer in Philosophy, Birkbeck College, London.

HUGH LAWSON-TANCRED is Departmental Fellow in Philosophy, Birkbeck College, London.

M. G. F. MARTIN is Lecturer in Philosophy, University College, London.

DAVID PAPINEAU is Professor of the History and Philosophy of Science, King's College, London.

MARK SAINSBURY is Stebbing Professor of Philosophy, King's College, London.

ROGER SCRUTON is Professor of Philosophy, Boston University, and Visiting Professor of Philosophy, Birkbeck College, London.

SCOTT STURGEON is Lecturer in Philosophy, Birkbeck College, London.

DAVID WIGGINS is Wykeham Professor of Logic in the University of Oxford, and Visiting Professor of Philosophy, Birkbeck College, London.

BERNARD WILLIAMS is White's Professor of Moral Philosophy in the University of Oxford, and Deutsch Professor of Philosophy at the University of California, Berkeley.

EDITOR'S INTRODUCTION

A. C. Grayling

The aim of philosophical inquiry is to gain insight into questions about knowledge, truth, reason, reality, meaning, mind, and value. Other human endeavours, not least art and literature, explore aspects of these same questions, but it is philosophy that mounts a direct assault on them, in the hope of clarifying them and, where possible, answering them.

'Philosophy' is derived from a Greek word literally meaning 'love of wisdom'. But it is better and more accurately defined as 'inquiry' or 'inquiry and reflection', allowing these expressions their widest scope to denote thought about general features of the world and human experience within it.

In its earliest days, at a time when few distinctions were drawn between the pursuits we now label 'natural science', 'social science', the 'humanities', and the 'arts', philosophy was the study of almost everything. The Greeks of the classical period are credited with the beginnings of Western philosophy, in this sense, because they inquired freely into all aspects of the world and humankind, starting not from religious or mystical principles, but from the belief that human reason is competent on its own account to formulate the right questions, and to seek answers to them, concerning every matter of interest or importance to humanity.

The Greeks speculated about the origins, composition, and functioning of the physical universe. They discussed the ethical and political circumstances of mankind, and proposed views about their best arrangement. They investigated human reason itself, and the nature of truth and knowledge. In doing so they touched upon almost every major philosophical question, and their legacy to subsequent thought is vast.

For a very long period—roughly from the fourth to the seventeenth centuries AD—thought in the West was dominated by Christianity. This does not mean that there was no philosophy; far from it; but much of it served theology, or at least (except in such cases as logic) it was constrained by theological considerations. In the seventeenth century, as a result of the complex events which for convenience are collected under the labels 'Renaissance' and 'Reformation' and which took place during the preceding two centuries, there occurred a powerful renewal of philosophical inquiry. It was connected with the rise of modern science, and began by asking fundamentally important questions about the nature of knowledge. This same freedom of thought prompted renewal of debate about moral and political questions also.

According to a certain view of recent intellectual history, one can see philosophy as having given birth in the seventeenth century to natural science, in the eighteenth century to psychology, and in the nineteenth to sociology and linguistics; while in the twentieth century it has played a large part in the development of computer science, cognitive science, and research into artificial intelligence. No doubt this oversimplifies the role of philosophical reflection, but it does not much exaggerate it, because in effect philosophy consists in inquiry into anything not yet well enough understood to constitute a self-standing branch of knowledge. When the right questions and the right methods for answering them have been identified, the field of inquiry in question becomes an independent pursuit. For example: in the suppositious history just sketched, as soon as philosophical reflection on the nature and properties of the physical universe identified appropriate ways of asking and answering questions—chiefly, in this case, by empirical and mathematical means—it ceased to be philosophy and became science.

Philosophy accordingly remains a pursuit which—to put the point as a seeming paradox—tries to bring itself to an end either by solving its problems or by finding ways of transforming them into special inquiries like physics, psychology, or history. On the 'divide and conquer' principle, the systematic study of philosophy has come to organize itself into fields of philosophical inquiry: 'ethics', 'political philosophy', and 'logic' are more or less self-explanatory as to their subject-matter, while 'epistemology' (inquiry into the nature of knowledge) and 'metaphysics' (inquiry into the ultimate nature of reality) need more explanation on first mention. (There are also philosophical inquiries into particular subjects—the philosophy of science, the philosophy of law, the philosophy of history, and so forth—in which philosophers reflect on the assumptions, methods, aims, and claims of the special pursuits.)

It is the aim of what follows to introduce philosophy's central fields of inquiry. There are so many connections and overlaps between them that to separate them under different labels in the way just indicated is somewhat artificial. But not entirely so; for there are problems distinctive to each, and a preliminary grasp of what they concern offers a first step towards understanding them.

Each of the chapters that follow is devoted to a major area of philosophical endeavour. They are their own introductions to the questions they discuss, and therefore need little supplementary introduction here. But a preliminary note about what each chapter contains will help with orientation, as follows.

Chapter 1: Epistemology. Epistemology—sometimes called 'theory of knowledge'—concerns the nature and sources of knowledge. The questions asked by epistemologists are, What is knowledge? How do we get it? Are all our means of seeking it equally good? To answer these questions we need to define knowledge if we can, examine the means we employ in seeking it, and confront sceptical challenges to our claims to have it.

Each of the three parts of Chapter 1 takes up one of these tasks. The first considers the problem of giving an adequate definition. The second examines one major means to knowledge—sensory perception—and the third surveys sceptical arguments and efforts to counter them.

Chapter 2: Philosophical Logic. Philosophical logic is in many respects the workshop of philosophy, where a set of related and highly important concepts come in for scrutiny, among them reference, truth, existence, identity, necessity, and quantification. These concepts are fundamental not just to philosophical inquiry but to thought in general. This chapter examines these concepts by focusing upon the question of reference. The first two sections look at what seem to be the most obvious examples of referring devices, names and descriptions. The third concerns a problem about existence; the fourth examines identity statements and the fifth considers the question whether, when true, such statements are 'necessarily' true. The final section examines some views about truth.

Chapter 3: Methodology. Epistemological discussions of the kind pursued in Chapter 1 concern the concept of knowledge in general. A more particular application of it concerns science, one of the major fields of knowledge-acquiring endeavour. Philosophical investigation into the assumptions, claims, concepts, and methods of science raises questions of great philosophical importance. The elementary part of this inquiry, here called Methodology, focuses largely on questions about the concepts and methods used in investigating the physical world. Each of the sections concerns a major topic: induction and its problems; the concept of laws of nature; realism, instrumentalism, and under-determination of theory by evidence; confirmation and probability; and the concept of explanation.

Chapter 4: Metaphysics. All the foregoing branches of philosophy share certain problems about what ultimately exists in the universe. These problems are the province of Metaphysics. Its primary questions are, What is there, and what is its nature? These questions immediately prompt others, so many indeed—and so important—that some of them have now come to constitute branches of philosophy in their own right, for example, philosophy of mind and philosophical theology.

In addressing questions about the nature of reality, the metaphysician has to examine concepts of time, free will, appearance and reality, causality, universals, substance, and a number of others besides. Here four of these topics are considered: causation, time, universals, and substance.

Note that questions about causality also come up in the chapters on Methodology and Mind, and the discussion of substance connects with the discussion of Aristotle in the chapter on Greek philosophy (see below)—thus exemplifying the interconnectedness of philosophical inquiry.

Chapter 5: The Philosophy of Mind. Questions about the nature of mind were once usually included in metaphysics, but their great importance has led to so much debate, and to such significant use of materials from the neighbouring fields of psychology and brain physiology, that the philosophy of mind is now treated separately. Chief among the points requiring discussion are the relation of mind and brain, the nature of intentionality and consciousness, and the question whether mental phenomena have causal powers or are merely in some sense by-products of brain activity. The sections in this chapter take up each point in turn.

Chapters 6–9: The History of Philosophy. Because the problems of philosophy are ancient and persistent, studying the history of philosophy is an important part of a philosophical education. It is not simply, or even very largely, that this study is interesting for its own sake—although it certainly is—but rather, it is that the outstanding philosophers of the past made contributions to philosophy which we must grasp in the interests of our current work. To study the history of philosophy is to study philosophy, for almost all the great questions were formulated and explored by our predecessors.

Two main periods of the history of Western thought are discussed in this volume: Greek philosophy from about 600 BC until 322 BC (the date of Aristotle's death), and Modern philosophy from Descartes to Kant (the seventeenth and eighteenth centuries AD).

The Greeks initiated all of philosophy's major fields, and identified their basic questions. Two of them, Plato and Aristotle, are especially important. They and their forerunners, known as the Pre-Socratics, are the subject of Chapters 6 and 7.

The philosophers of the Modern period who have done so much to shape philosophical discussion since their day are Descartes, Spinoza, Leibniz, and Kant (discussed in Chapter 8) and Locke, Berkeley, and Hume (discussed in Chapter 9). They are grouped in this way because the first three are usually described as 'Rationalists' and the last three 'Empiricists' (Kant occupies a position apart), some important differences between rationalism and empiricism being at stake. But perhaps the best order in which to read them, and to read about them, is: Descartes, Locke, Berkeley, Hume, Spinoza, Leibniz, Kant.

Chapter 10: Ethics. The supreme importance of critical reflection on the values by which we live is unquestionable. Our values are the basis of our judgements about others, and of our decisions about how to act and live. Ethics is the study of theories about moral values, and of the concepts we use in identifying and asserting them. An important distinction is required here: a theory which prescribes how we should live is called a 'first-order' or 'normative' morality. Reflective enquiry into the assumptions, concepts, and claims of such first-order moralities is often called 'metaethics'. Both are of crucial interest in the study of ethics, as this chapter shows. It discusses theories of ethics, examines some of the most important ethical concepts, and investigates aspects of 'moral psychology'.

Chapter 11: Aesthetics. Aesthetics in contemporary philosophy concentrates upon discussion of the experience of appreciating artistic and natural beauty, and investigates whether there is an underlying unity in the nature of such experience. In this chapter the three sections successively examine aesthetic experience and judgement, fundamental concepts of the philosophy of art, and theories about the nature of art.

The kind of philosophy introduced in these chapters is often called 'Analytic Philosophy'. Analytic philosophy is not so much a school of thought as a style or method. It is a style of philosophizing which seeks to be rigorous and careful, which at times makes use of ideas and techniques from logic, and which is aware of what is happening in science. It is, in particular, alert to linguistic considerations, not because of an interest in language for its own sake, but because it is through language that we grasp the concepts we use, and it is by means of language that we express our beliefs and assumptions. One of the principal methods of analytic philosophy is analysis of the concepts we employ in thinking about ourselves and the world: not surprisingly, this is called 'conceptual analysis'.

Most philosophy done in the English-speaking world is analytic philosophy. The chapters in this book well display both its character and its methods. The name 'analytic philosophy' is sometimes used to distinguish the rigorous style of philosophizing just described from other styles of philosophizing, for example from so-called 'Continental Philosophy', by which is meant—variously— the philosophical work done in France, Germany, and elsewhere in continental Europe since the beginning of the twentieth century. Thus the thought of Husserl, Heidegger, Merleau-Ponty, Sartre, the Frankfurt School, Foucault, Derrida, and others (a highly various assortment which it is not at all helpful to collect under a single label) is so named. There are indeed substantial differences both of interest and method between analytic and 'Continental' philosophy, but there is also some overlap. In just the same way as a certain amount of

'Continental' philosophy is done in the English-speaking world, so there is increasing interest in analytic philosophy in continental Europe.

The order of the chapters is intended to aid the reader who is making a systematic study of philosophy. A recommended approach is to read the essays in each of Parts I and II sequentially, and to read Parts I and II simultaneously. Upon turning to the two essays in Part III the reader should again, for preference, read them in sequence. But this is a suggestion for systematic students; the ordering is not intended to be coercive.

1

EPISTEMOLOGY

Scott Sturgeon, M. G. F. Martin,
and A. C. Grayling

INTRODUCTION

A. C. Grayling

Epistemology, or theory of knowledge, is the branch of philosophy which examines questions about the nature of knowledge and how we get it. It attempts to answer the questions 'What is knowledge?' and 'What are the best and most secure ways of acquiring knowledge?' These questions, as the following discussions show, are connected, but attempts to answer them can be made in different ways.

One helpful approach to answering the first question is to consider a suggested definition of knowledge. In the tradition of debate on these matters knowledge is standardly defined as *justified true belief*, because at very least it seems that to know something one must believe it, one's belief must be true, and one's reason for believing it must be satisfactory in the light of some standard, because one could not be said to know something if one had, say, arbitrarily or haphazardly decided to believe it. So each of the three parts of the definition appears to express a necessary condition for knowledge. The claim is that taken together they are sufficient for knowledge.

But as the first of the following discussions shows, there are difficulties with this idea, especially about the kind of justification required for a true belief to count as knowledge. Competing theories have been put forward to deal with this difficulty, and the first discussion explores them.

While the debate about how to define 'knowledge' goes on, another flourishes about how we get knowledge. In the history of epistemology there have been (speaking, for convenience, very roughly) two principal schools of thought: the 'rationalist' school, which holds that the chief route to knowledge is the exercise of reason; and the 'empiricist' school, which holds that the chief route to knowledge is perception (the use of the five senses of sight, hearing, smell, taste, and touch, and their extension by means of such instruments as telescopes, microscopes, and the like). The model for the rationalists is mathematics and logic, where necessary truths are arrived at by rational inference. The model for empiricists is any of the natural sciences where observation and experiment are the chief motor of inquiry. The history of science in the last few centuries has lent strength to the empiricist case; but for that very reason philosophical questions about perception have become more important, and the second discussion below examines the problems that arise in that connection.

For both traditions in epistemology, however, one of the central concerns is to investigate whether our means of getting knowledge are trustworthy. A sharp way to identify the problems that require to be addressed in this connection is to examine the challenge posed by scepticism. The third and final discussion below surveys the nature and point of sceptical arguments, and some of the responses to them which epistemologists have suggested.

Together these three discussions give an introduction to the chief concerns of epistemology. There are other debates in epistemology besides—e.g. memory, judgement, introspection, reasoning, the 'a priori–a posteriori' distinction, scientific method—but a grasp of the three central topics discussed below constitutes a basis for understanding these other debates, and serves as a preface to them.

KNOWLEDGE

Scott Sturgeon

1.1. Introduction

Consider the following sentences:

(1) John knows London.
(2) John knows how to get to London from Manchester.
(3) John knows that London is south of Manchester.

Sentence (1) captures what philosophers call 'acquaintance knowledge'. Intuitively, this consists in first-hand acquaintance with a person, a place, an event, and so on. We gain acquaintance knowledge of people by meeting them; we gain acquaintance knowledge of places by going there; and we gain acquaintance knowledge of events by witnessing them. Sentence (2) captures what philosophers call 'ability knowledge'. Intuitively, this consists in knowing how to perform various actions. For example, we gain ability knowledge by learning how to speak a language, by learning how to ride a bicycle, and by learning how to prepare a meal. Sentence (3) captures what philosophers call 'propositional knowledge'. This will be the subject of our inquiry.

Suppose there are three cups on a table in front of you. This would be a situation you might know about. The question we shall address is this: what is it to know about situations like this? Or more generally: what are the conditions in virtue of which someone knows such situations?[1]

1.2. Structuring the Task

Situations in the world are described by true propositions. Returning to our cups: the proposition asserting that there are three cups on the table describes

---

[1] We shall restrict our attention to empirical situations, and thus to empirical knowledge. Ethical knowledge, mathematical knowledge, and logical knowledge raise further problems which are beyond the scope of this essay. See BonJour (1985), Dancy (1987), and Pollock (1986) for further discussion.

the situation accurately. It is thus a true proposition. The reason philosophers call knowledge of situations 'propositional knowledge' is because situations are described by true propositions. So, whatever it comes to precisely, propositional knowledge is a special relationship between a person and a true proposition. Our task is to determine what that relationship is.

We may structure this task by asking how to complete the following schema:

(K) S knows P iff (if and only if) S and P have features F_1, F_2, ...

By completing (K) we uncover the essence of propositional knowledge. To see how this works notice that (K) is a *biconditional*. This means (K) is two claims asserted in tandem. The word 'and' signals that (K) is a conjunction of two claims. Specifically, (K) is a conjunction of two if–then statements, or conditionals. There is a left-to-right direction of (K), and a right-to-left direction of (K).

The left-to-right direction of (K) asserts this:

If S knows P, then S and P have features F_1, F_2, ...

The important idea here is that features F_1, F_2, etc. are each *necessary for propositional knowledge*. In general, when you find something on the end of an if—then statement, it is necessary for whatever is at the beginning of the statement. End conditions are what philosophers call 'necessary conditions'. Just as one might think sugar necessary for a proper cup of tea, the left-to-right direction of (K) asserts that F_1, F_2, etc. are *each* necessary for propositional knowledge.

On the other hand, the right-to-left direction of (K) asserts this:

If S and P have features F_1, F_2, ... , then S knows P.

Here we have the previous claim turned around. Now the idea is that features F_1, F_2, etc. are together *sufficient for propositional knowledge*. In general when you find something at the beginning of an if–then statement, it is sufficient for whatever is at the end of the statement. Beginning conditions are what philosophers call 'sufficient conditions'. Just as one might think love sufficient for happiness, the right-to-left direction of (K) asserts that F_1, F_2, etc. are *jointly sufficient for propositional knowledge*.

Now, (K) is the conjunction of its left-to-right direction and its right-to-left direction. (K) therefore claims that features F_1, F_2, etc. are separately necessary and jointly sufficient for propositional knowledge. This is why completing (K) is important. If we can do so, we will have found the conditions which are individually necessary for propositional knowledge, and which together are sufficient for propositional knowledge.

Here is how we proceed:[2] first, we look for conditions to complete (K). Next

---

[2] The method of looking for necessary and/or sufficient conditions is standard in analytic philosophy. But it should not be presupposed, however, that every philosophical problem can be usefully addressed in this way.

we *test* a proposed completion by checking whether it agrees with our firmly held intuitions about knowledge. This is done by constructing thought experiments. A thought experiment is a fictional story we compose. We shall use thought experiments to see whether completions of (K) are adequate. We do this by constructing a fictional scenario, judging whether knowledge is present in the scenario, and then checking to see whether the proposed completion of (K) agrees with us.

There are two ways a completion of (K) could fail such a test:

1. If a completion of (K) implies that knowledge is present in a thought-experiment scenario, when we are sure that it is absent, then the completion is inadequate. In such a case we discover that the right-hand side of the completion is not sufficient for the left-hand side. For a completion of (K) will imply that knowledge is present because its right-hand side is fulfilled, and because its right-to-left direction says that its right-hand side is sufficient for knowledge. Thus, if a completion of (K) implies that knowledge is present, when we are sure that it is not, this means that its right-hand side is not sufficient for knowledge.

2. If a completion of (K) fails to imply that knowledge is present in a thought-experiment scenario, when we are sure that it is present, then the completion is also inadequate. In such a case we discover that the right-hand side of the completion is not necessary for the left-hand side. For a completion of (K) will fail to imply that knowledge is present because its right-hand side is not fulfilled. But if we are sure that knowledge is present, then we can be sure that the completion's right-hand side is not needed for knowledge. Thus, if a completion of (K) fails to imply that knowledge is present, when we are sure that it is, this means its right-hand side is not necessary for knowledge.

When, in light of a particular thought experiment, a completion of (K) falls into categories (1) or (2), that completion will be *refuted by the thought experiment*. Such a thought experiment is known as a 'counter-example' to the completion of (K). Obviously, this method for testing theories of knowledge relies on our ability to determine when knowledge is present in thought-experiment scenarios.

1.3. Decomposing Knowledge

We have already found one condition needed to complete (K), namely, the proposition in question must be true. Thus we have:

(K1) *S* knows *P* iff (*a*) *P* is true,
                    (*b*) *S* and *P* have features F_1, F_2, etc.

Further, when we have knowledge, we believe the world to be a specific way, namely, we believe it to be the way a true proposition *describes* it as being. This amounts to a second condition needed for our completion of (K): we have knowledge only when we believe the true proposition in question.

Together these points generate a very simple theory of knowledge:

(K2) *S* knows *P* iff (*a*) *S* believes *P*,
                  (*b*) *P* is true.

Unfortunately, (K2) is extremely inadequate. The problem is with its right-to-left direction. Note what this says:

If *S* believes a true proposition *P*, then *S* knows *P*.

This cannot be right. Let us construct a thought experiment and use it to refute (K2).

Suppose you wake up one morning and find yourself believing something outlandish. Let it be the proposition that Plato and Aristotle were one and the same person. You realize that this is a ridiculous proposition, but you cannot shake your conviction. No matter how hard you try to be reasonable, you find yourself believing that Plato and Aristotle were one. Suppose, further, that you believe this because a friend has hypnotized you and 'planted' the idea as a joke. But suppose, finally, that unbeknownst to your friend, Plato and Aristotle really were the same person. In such a case you would believe a true proposition, and thus, by (K2), it would follow that you knew that proposition. But it is obvious that in this case you would not know that Plato and Aristotle were the same person. Therefore, this thought experiment is a counter-example to (K2).

Often a thought experiment will not only show that a given theory is unacceptable; it will also suggest ways to modify the refuted theory. Our previous thought experiment is good in this respect. For what seems obvious about that thought experiment is this: you fail to have knowledge because your belief about Plato and Aristotle is not based on evidence. For this reason it is what philosophers call an *unjustified* belief.

This suggests a third condition is needed to complete (K):

(K3) *S* knows *P* iff (*a*) *S* believes *P*,
                  (*b*) *S*'s belief in *P* is justified,
                  (*c*) *P* is true.

Now, (K3) is a plausible suggestion about knowledge. But it tells us little until we better understand the notion of justification it employs. And there are two questions we need to ask: first, what is the strength of justification needed for knowledge? and second, what is the underlying nature of justification itself?

The first question focuses on the relationship between (*b*) and (*c*) of (K3). The issue is whether the justification mentioned in (*b*) must imply the truth mentioned in (*c*) (i.e. whether (*b*) implies (*c*)). If so, then (*c*) is a redundant clause

in the definition. For if justification implies truth, then knowledge is simply justified belief. On the other hand, if justification does not imply truth, then truth
is an *extra* ingredient needed in addition to belief and justification. We shall
address this question in the next section.

The second question focuses on justification. The demand is to construct a
theory of justification just as we are now constructing a theory of knowledge.
We shall address this question in Section 5.

1.4. The Strength of Justification

What is the connection between justification and truth? For our purposes we
may focus on two options: either justification implies truth or it does not.

The view that justification implies truth is known as *infallibilism*. This view
holds that justified beliefs cannot be mistaken. According to the infallibilist, it is
impossible to have a false-but-justified belief. *Fallibilism* is the view that this situation is possible. According to the fallibilist, justified mistakes are possible.
(See BonJour (1985), Dancy (1987), Descartes (1979), and Pollock (1986).)

So which position is correct?

There is a tempting argument for infallibilism. It begins by noticing the plausibility of this claim:

(*) If *S* knows *P*, then *S* cannot be mistaken about *P*.

The argument proceeds as follows:

(ARG) Since *S* cannot be mistaken about *P* when *S* knows *P*, this means that
        S's justification guarantees that *P* is true. Thus, (*) implies that justi-
        fication guarantees truth. In other words, (*) implies infallibilism.

Now, this argument is fallacious. The fallacy in question springs from an ambiguity in (*). Though plausible, (*) can be understood in *two* different ways. One
of them is highly plausible but does not imply infallibilism. The other implies
infallibilism but is not very plausible.

To uncover the ambiguity in (*) notice that it is a conditional statement of
this form:

(C) If *X*, then it cannot be that *Y*.

Statements of this form admit two readings. They do so because the word
'cannot' may be understood to have what logicians call 'greater or lesser scope
within the statement'. This means the word 'cannot' may be understood to
cover the *entire conditional*, or it may be understood to cover merely the *consequent* of the conditional. The former understanding is known as the 'wide-
scope' reading of (C), and the latter is known as the 'narrow-scope' reading of
(C). By explicitly marking the scope of 'cannot' with brackets, we may display
the wide- and narrow-scope readings of (C):

(WSC) It cannot be that {if *X*, then *Y*}.

(NSC) If *X*, then it cannot be that {*Y*}.

The wide-scope reading asserts the impossibility of the *consequence* (i.e. the impossibility of the entire conditional). The narrow-scope reading asserts the impossibility of the *consequent* (i.e. the impossibility of *Y* by itself).

Now, since (*) is a conditional statement of form (C) it inherits the ambiguity of this form. This means (*) has a wide- and narrow-scope reading. Here are the two readings:

(WS*) It cannot be that {if *S* knows *P*, then *S* is mistaken about *P*}.

(NS*) If *S* knows *P*, then it cannot be that {*S* is mistaken about *P*}.

(WS*) says that it is impossible to know something false. And this seems right. For propositional knowledge is knowledge of a real situation in the world. It thus involves belief in a true proposition. This trivial point implies the wide-scope reading of (*).

On the other hand, (NS*) says that if one knows something, then one is in a position which rules out the possibility of error. But this is not at all obvious. For example, we take ourselves to know many things about our external environment. You know, for instance, that you are reading. But your evidence certainly does not rule out the possibility of error. As Descartes famously emphasized, you could be dreaming that you are reading (Descartes 1979). So, if we understand (*) along the lines of (NS*) the claim looks to be false.

The point then is this: the narrow-scope reading of (*) is the reading we need to make sense of (ARG). But that reading seems false. The reason (ARG) looks convincing is because (*) has one reading which is trivially true: the wide-scope reading. But (ARG) does not use that reading. Rather, it uses the suspicious narrow-scope reading. So we still need a persuasive argument for or against infallibilism.

Infallibilism has several theoretical advantages. Notice, for example, that infallibilism permits a very concise definition of knowledge:

(K4) *S* knows *P* iff (*a*) *S* believes *P*,
                    (*b*) *S*'s belief in *P* is infallibly justified.

If justification implies truth then condition (*c*) of (K3) will be implied by condition (*b*) of (K4). So there will be no need to add a third condition to (K4) asserting that *P* is true. The truth of *P* will be guaranteed by the infallible justification of *S*'s belief in *P*. Further, infallibilism would explain why the wide-scope reading of (*) is true. For if infallible justification is necessary for knowledge, as the left-to-right direction of (K4) asserts, and such justification implies truth, then it follows that one cannot know something false. This latter claim is what the wide-scope reading of (*) asserts.

But as we began to notice three paragraphs back, infallibilism makes knowledge *extremely* difficult to obtain. The view implies that one is justified in believing *P* only when one has gained sufficient evidence to rule out the possibility that *P* is false (Dretske 1971). But for most of our beliefs we have no such evidence. Consider once again whether you know you are reading. What is your evidence for this? Well, you seem to be reading. You have certain perceptual evidence of a page in front of you. You seem to see a book, and perhaps also to feel pages. This is the evidence which makes you justified in believing that you are reading. Hence this is the evidence on the basis of which you know that you are reading. This much is undeniable. But does your evidence rule out the *possibility* that you are not reading?

Certainly not. Perhaps you are dreaming that you are reading, or perhaps hallucinating that you are reading, or perhaps your brain has been placed in a machine by evil scientists and manipulated to make you think you are reading. None of these possibilities is ruled out by the evidence on the basis of which you now believe that you are reading. But this doesn't mean that you actually fail to know whether you are reading. *Of course* you know that you are reading. That you know this is one of the most obvious things in the world. Our job, then, is to construct a theory of knowledge consistent with this fact. In other words, we need a theory of knowledge which will explain how you know that you are reading on the basis of your present evidence.

Notice that your present situation is a counter-example to (K4). For you know that you are reading despite the fact that your belief is not infallibly justified. Hence your present situation shows that infallible justification is not necessary for knowledge. But the left-to-right direction of (K4) implies that infallible justification is necessary for knowledge. Thus, your present situation shows that (K4) is false.

This suggests that we retain the structure of (K3) and employ a fallible notion of justification:

> (K5) *S* knows *P* iff (*a*) *S* believes *P*,
> (*b*) *S*'s belief in *P* is fallibly justified,
> (*c*) *P* is true.

Notice here that we need condition (*c*). For condition (*b*) fails to entail truth, and we know that it is impossible to know something false. This means that truth is an extra ingredient of knowledge in addition to belief and fallible justification.

The idea behind (K5) is very simple: knowledge consists in fallible justification for propositions which are in fact true. This is an appealing idea. Unfortunately, there is a well-known problem with this idea. The problem was first made famous by Edmund Gettier, and has become known as the Gettier Problem. (See Dancy (1987), Gettier (1963), Pollock (1986), and Shope (1983).) Let us construct our second thought experiment to expose the Gettier Problem.

Suppose you drive your car to work and park it in your usual parking-space. Suppose further that, unbeknownst to you, someone breaks into your car, takes it for a drive, and coincidentally parks it back in your space. Now suppose you agree to loan your car to someone for an errand. They ask you where your car is, and you tell them what you believe, namely, that your car is in your parking-space. Naturally, you are right. The car *is* in your parking-space. For the thief has put it back there. Moreover, your belief that your car is in your parking-space is fallibly justified. After all, you always park your car there, and it is always there when you go down to use it. You have terrific-but-fallible evidence that your car is in your parking-space. And since your car *is* in your parking-space, you have a fallibly justified true belief. (K5) thus implies that you know your car is in your parking-space. But do you?

Certainly not. It is an accident that your car is where you think it is. For this reason you do not know where your car is. Thus (K5) is inadequate. The right-hand side is not sufficient for the left-hand side. In other words, fallibly justified true belief is not sufficient for knowledge.

What we need, then, is some way to rule out cases in which two things happen: first, in which one is led to believe a true proposition on the basis of fallible evidence, and second, in which the fact that one ends up believing a true proposition is merely an accident. Intuitively at least, one's fallible evidence should ensure that one has not accidentally come to believe a true proposition. This means that a proper definition of knowledge will expand the following idea:

(K6) *S* knows *P* iff (*a*) *S* believes *P*,
           (*b*) *S*'s belief in *P* is fallibly justified,
           (*c*) *P* is true,
           (*d*) (*b*) ensures that (*a*)-and-(*c*) are not jointly an accident.

Now, philosophers have investigated many ways to complete (K6). The literature on this topic is voluminous. (See Shope (1983) for a survey.) But we need not worry about the details. For, despite its incompleteness, (K6) provides good insight into the nature of propositional knowledge. In a nutshell, propositional knowledge consists in believing true propositions on the basis of fallible evidence which ensures that one has not accidentally believed the truth.

1.5. The Nature of Justification

We turn now to an issue which philosophers have investigated at length, namely, what is the nature of epistemic justification? Basically, we need to do for justification what (K6) does for knowledge: we need to locate the underlying nature of epistemic justification.

Once again we may structure our task by seeking to complete a schema:

(J) S's belief in P is justified iff S's belief in P has features F_1, F_2, ...

Just as before, we are looking for necessary and sufficient conditions. But now we are looking for features which are each necessary, and which together are sufficient, for epistemic justification. These will be features which make a belief justified. What could they be?

There are two broad schools of thought about this question. There are so-called 'internalist' theories of justification, and there are so-called 'externalist' theories of justification. As the labels indicate, internalist theories try to complete (J) through appeal to internal features of S; and externalist theories try to complete (J) through appeal to external features of S. Thus, we need to understand what makes a feature count as internal rather than external to a thinker. (See Brueckner (1988), Dancy (1987), Descartes (1979), Goldman (1979; 1986), and Pollock (1986).)

The issue turns on what kind of *access* a thinker has to the feature in question. For instance, suppose a thinker S consciously believes that snow is white. This is a feature of S *we* may come to recognize. We would do so, for example, if S were to tell us he consciously believes that snow is white. But there is an obvious sense in which S can recognize this feature more directly than we can. This is because there is an obvious sense in which S can be 'directly aware' of this feature. We, on the other hand, can only be indirectly aware of this feature.

The distinction between direct and indirect awareness is the distinction needed to understand the difference between internalist and externalist theories of justification. Internalist theories try to complete (J) through appeal to features which are directly accessible to S. Externalist theories relax this constraint. In the next two sections we shall investigate internalist theories of justification. Externalist theories will be the topic of Section 8.

1.6. Internalist Theories of Justification

Traditionally there are two types of internalist theory of justification. They differ most readily in how they view *the structure* of justified thought. For reasons that will be clear in a moment, the first view is called 'foundationalism' and the second is called 'coherentism'. (See BonJour (1985), Chisholm (1977), Dancy (1987), Harman (1973; 1984), Lehrer (1974), Moser (1985), Pollock (1986), and Sosa (1981).)

1.6.1. *Foundationalism*

Foundationalist theories of justification distinguish two kinds of justified belief: one the one hand, foundationalist theories maintain that some beliefs are justified *independently* of their relationship to other beliefs; on the other, they recognize that many beliefs are justified *because of* their relationship to other beliefs. The first sort of belief is called 'foundational' and the second sort is called 'non-foundational'.

According to this picture, the structure of justified thought is like a building. The foundation of the building consists in foundational beliefs. These beliefs are said to be justified because of their intrinsic character. Higher levels of the building consist in non-foundational beliefs. These beliefs are said to be justified because of their relationship to other beliefs. Specifically, non-foundational beliefs are said to be justified by their relationship to foundational beliefs. Just as the upper reaches of a building rest on its foundation, so, according to the foundationalist, do non-foundational beliefs rest on foundational beliefs.

Foundationalist theories of justification complete (J) as follows:

(FJ) *S*'s belief in *P* is justified iff either (*a*) *S*'s belief in *P* is a foundational belief, or

(*b*) *S*'s belief in *P* rests on foundational beliefs.

This raises two new questions: what is the nature of foundational beliefs and how do non-foundational beliefs 'rest on' foundational beliefs?

Foundational beliefs are thought justified because of their intrinsic nature. (See Alston (1983), BonJour (1985), Chisholm (1977), Dancy (1987), Lehrer (1974), Moser (1985), Pollock (1986), Price (1936), and Shope (1983).) This means that foundational beliefs have some intrinsic 'justification-making' property. This property must be sufficient to guarantee that foundational beliefs are justified *independently* of their relationship to other beliefs. Unfortunately, it is difficult to see what this property could be. Typically foundationalists claim that beliefs about our perceptual states are 'self-evident' or 'indubitable' or 'infallible'. But these notions are not particularly convincing. Infallibility, for example, is usually claimed to be a feature of beliefs which guarantees we have them just when they are true. The problem is that we do not seem to have any beliefs like this. On the face of it, *all* our beliefs could turn out to be false. On the other hand, if we have any indubitable beliefs, then they are so few in number that they could not provide a foundation for the rest of what we obviously know. This means that clause (*a*) of (FJ) is suspect.

Moreover, there is a problem about the way non-foundational beliefs are said to rest on foundational beliefs. Here the foundationalist has just two options: she might require foundational beliefs logically to imply non-foundational beliefs, or she might relax this requirement. But neither option seems to work.

A group of propositions $P_1, ..., P_n$ logically imply another proposition C when it is impossible for $P_1, ..., P_n$ to be true while C is false. For example, the following two propositions,

> Socrates is a man,
> All men are mortal,

logically imply this proposition:

> Socrates is mortal.

For it is impossible that the first two propositions are true while the third is false.

But notice: if the foundationalist requires foundational beliefs logically to imply non-foundational beliefs, then most beliefs turn out to be unjustified. Consider, for example, your belief that you are reading. We have already accepted that you know you are reading, and, hence, that you are justified in believing that you are reading. We have also accepted that you might doubt this given your evidence, for you might be dreaming. This means your belief that you are reading is not a foundational belief. But your evidence concerning this belief is fallible. It thus fails logically to imply that you are reading. So once again your situation is a counter-example. Specifically, it is a counter-example to the view which interprets (*b*) of (FJ) in terms of logical implication. For your belief that you are reading is a justified non-foundational belief which fails to be logically implied by your evidence.

The foundationalist, then, must claim that foundational beliefs need not logically imply non-foundational beliefs. This means that foundational beliefs can be non-logical evidence for non-foundational beliefs.

Philosophers call non-logical evidence 'defeasible' evidence. (See Harman (1973; 1984), Lehrer (1974), and Pollock (1979; 1986).) The reason is this: if E is non-logical evidence for some proposition C, then it will be possible to 'defeat' E's support for C by adding more information. For example, suppose you go into a room and face a wall which looks red to you. This will be evidence for the belief that the wall is red. But it will be non-logical evidence. That the wall looks red does not logically imply that it is red. If, for example, you learn that the room is bathed in red light, then you should no longer count the way the wall looks as good evidence for the wall being red. If you continue to believe the wall is red despite knowing how it is lit, this belief will cease to be justified. For your new information about the lighting will defeat your perceptual evidence about the colour of the wall.

But now the foundationalist is in trouble. For if foundational beliefs are defeasible evidence for non-foundational beliefs, then non-foundational beliefs will be justified *only if* the foundational beliefs upon which they rest are themselves undefeated. In other words, a non-foundational belief will be justified only if two things happen: first, it must rest upon foundational beliefs, and second, those foundational beliefs must not be defeated by other things one believes. But this second condition makes trouble for the foundationalist. For it implies that non-foundational beliefs depend for their justification on more than the foundational beliefs upon which they rest. In particular they depend on the *global* condition that no defeater be present for those foundational beliefs. This means the right-to-left direction of (FJ) is false. For condition (*b*) is not sufficient for justification.

Thus, there are problems with both (*a*) and (*b*) of (FJ). In brief: it is not obvious that we have beliefs which are indubitable, incorrigible, or in any sense intrinsically justified; and hence it is not obvious that we have any beliefs which should count as foundational. Moreover, even if we admit foundational beliefs, those beliefs will be defeasible evidence for the rest of what we believe. And this ensures that the rest of what we believe is justified because of the way our evidence globally fits together. But global requirements of this sort are the hallmark of *coherence* theories of justification.

1.6.2. Coherentism

Coherence theories of justification recognize one sort of justified belief. According to coherence theories, *all* beliefs are justified through their relationship to other beliefs. This view has no room for foundational beliefs. Rather, coherence theories maintain that all beliefs are justified through *coherence* with other beliefs.

Coherence theories complete (J) as follows:

(CJ) *S*'s belief in *P* is justified iff *S*'s belief in *P* coheres with the rest of what *S* believes.

But this raises a new question: what is it for a belief to cohere with the rest of what one believes?

There are three options:

(1) coherence can be understood in a purely negative way,
(2) coherence can be understood in a purely positive way,
(3) coherence can be understood in both a positive and a negative way.

Option (1) generates a *negative* coherence theory, option (2) a *positive* coherence theory, and option (3) a *mixed* coherence theory. These views are distinguished by the role they give evidence within justified thought. (See Harman (1973; 1984), Pollock (1979; 1986), and Sosa (1981).)

Negative coherence theories give evidence a purely negative role. This means beliefs are justified until and unless one has evidence *against* them. On the face of it, however, this seems wrong. If we find ourselves believing something for no reason at all, then our belief will not be justified. This is because beliefs should be adopted, and maintained, *on the basis of* evidence.

This is very important. Not only must a theory of justification give evidence a positive role, it must do so very carefully. In particular, we must distinguish between having good evidence for a given belief and holding that belief *on the basis of* the evidence. For example, suppose Sherlock Holmes and his assistant Watson uncover evidence pointing to the butler's guilt. And suppose they believe the butler is guilty. But suppose Holmes believes on the basis of the evidence while Watson believes because he hates the butler. In such a case Holmes's belief would be justified. Watson's would not. And this would be true despite the fact that each has the very same evidence. In short: there is a crucial distinction between justifi*able* beliefs and justifi*ed* beliefs. The former exist when one has good evidence for one's beliefs. The latter exist when one holds one's beliefs *on the basis of* good evidence.

Now, since positive coherence theories can recognize this distinction, they have an advantage over negative coherence theories. But positive coherence theories face a difficulty of their own, namely, they fail to make room for the defeasibility of evidence. Recall that evidence is normally defeasible. This means the evidential support which comes from information can be overridden by new information. The new information will be a defeater for the original evidence. But the defeater will play a negative role. In effect, the defeater will cancel the support provided by the original evidence. The problem is that positive coherence theories only recognize positive evidential support. Yet evidence plays a positive and a negative role. When we adopt a new belief on the basis of evidence, that evidence plays a positive role. When we retract a belief in light of new evidence, that evidence plays a negative role.

If a coherence theory is to succeed, then, it must be a mixed coherence theory. According to such a view, coherence is a matter of positive evidential support which fits one's background beliefs. Specifically,

(C) *S*'s belief in *P* coheres with the rest of what *S* believes iff
   (*a*) *S*'s belief in *P* is based on adequate evidence *E*, and
   (*b*) *E* is undefeated relative to the rest of what *S* believes.

By plugging the right-hand side of (C) into the right-hand side of (CJ), we generate a plausible mixed coherence theory:

(MCJ) *S*'s belief in *P* is justified iff
   (*a*) *S*'s belief in *P* is based on adequate evidence *E*, and
   (*b*) *E* is undefeated relative to the rest of what *S* believes.

What should we make of this theory?

Note first the similarity between (MCJ) and foundational theories of justification. Both approaches recognize lines of positive evidential support tracing through justified thought; and each recognizes that such lines can be defeated by background evidence. Both views, therefore, give evidence a positive and a negative role. And this seems right. The views differ solely in whether they recognize foundational beliefs. Foundational theories do, and mixed coherence theories do not.

Mixed coherence theories have the best of both worlds: they incorporate what seems right about foundational theories, and also what seems right about coherence theories. They do so by utilizing lines of evidential support which, to be effective in producing justified belief, must fit properly into the background setting of one's other beliefs. This makes justification not only a local matter, but a global matter as well.

1.7. Problems for Internalist Theories of Justification

Unfortunately, internalist theories of justification face two problems. The first concerns the role of perception in justified thought. The second concerns the way internalist theories explain the nature of justified thought.

1.7.1. The Input Problem

Notice that internalist theories claim justification is determined by other *beliefs*. Internalist theories thus exclude perceptual states from contributing to justification. But this seems wrong.

When we perceive the world around us, through sight or touch, for example, we gain new evidence about our environment. Foundational theories try to finesse this issue by postulating beliefs *about* perceptual states, and by taking those beliefs to be basic. This is how foundational theories get perceptual experience into the picture. The problem, however, is that we do not normally have beliefs about perceptual experience. Normally we base beliefs about the world directly on perceptual experience, thereby *using* experience in a positive evidential way. But since perceptual states are not beliefs, it follows that the justification of certain beliefs is not determined solely by other beliefs. Specifically, the justification of perceptually based belief is determined, at least in part, by perceptual experience itself.

Now, explaining how perceptual experience plays such a role is not our present task. (But see the next section of this chapter, on perception.) The point is simply that it does, and that any correct theory of justification must be consistent with this fact. As we have seen, however, internalist theories of justification are inconsistent with this fact. For this reason such theories are unacceptable as they stand.

1.7.2. The Essence Problem

Recall that (K6) is a plausible suggestion about the nature of knowledge. (K6) specifies necessary and sufficient conditions for knowledge, *and none of the conditions it mentions are knowledge-like in themselves*. (K6) puts certain notions together in a way which intuitively adds up to knowledge. This is why it tells us what knowledge is. Our present task is to construct a theory of justification like this. Both foundationalism and coherentism purport to do for justification what (K6) does for knowledge.

But internalist theories do not fully explain the nature of justification. For internalist theories use the notion of non-logical (or defeasible) evidence, and this notion amounts to little more than epistemic justification itself. Intuitively, at least, we have no grip on the notion of defeasible evidence independently of that notion's role in producing justification. This means internalist theories explain justification through a notion which itself presupposes an understanding of justification.

One way to appreciate this problem is to contrast our understanding of defeasible evidence with our understanding of logical evidence. As we saw in Section 1.6, logical evidence can be understood independently of justification via the notion of truth. A conjunction P & Q, for example, is logical evidence for P because it is impossible for P & Q to be true while P is false. We do not need to understand epistemic justification in order to understand the notion of logical evidence. But the notion of defeasible evidence is not like this. Our only pre-theoretic grip on the notion of defeasible evidence is via its role in fixing justified belief.

On the other hand, this point about logical evidence suggests a solution to the problem about defeasible evidence. Specifically, we might try to understand the notion of defeasible evidence, and hence justification, in terms of truth. As we are about to see, however, this approach generates an externalist theory of justification.

1.8. Reliabilism

When forming beliefs on the basis of evidence, we should try to believe what is true and avoid believing what is false. In a sense, truth is the goal. A natural thought then suggests itself, namely, define justification in terms of this goal.

Any approach like this will be an externalist approach to justification. For whether our beliefs are true, or whether they render one another likely to be true, is not a feature to which we have direct access. So by placing this sort of feature at the heart of our epistemic theory we generate an externalist approach.

The most common version of externalism is *reliabilism*. (See Dancy (1987),

Goldman (1979; 1986), and Pollock (1986).) The idea is to ground justification in the reliability of belief-forming processes. Specifically:

(R) *S*'s belief in *P* is justified iff *S*'s belief in *P* is produced by a reliable process.

There are three main reasons why this is a plausible suggestion.

First, by defining justification in terms of truth we make clear why justified belief is epistemically valuable. Since truth is our epistemic goal, reliable belief-forming mechanisms are a means to this goal. Beliefs produced by them will therefore be epistemically valuable.

Second, reliability and justification both come in degrees. Just as beliefs may be more or less justified, so mechanisms which produce them may be more or less reliable. Consider, for example, the fact that the more evidence we gain for a proposition, the greater our justification will be for believing it. This mirrors the fact that processes which produce beliefs on the basis of large amounts of evidence will be more reliable than those which use lesser amounts of evidence. So the graded nature of justification matches the graded nature of reliability. This is further reason to suppose that (R) is correct.

Finally, the belief-forming procedures we think rational are also procedures we think reliable. Consider vision: we use vision in normal circumstances to produce beliefs about our environment, and we take those beliefs to be justified. But we also think visual mechanisms are reliable. Indeed, there is something strange about the idea of an unreliably-produced-but-justified belief. This points to a close intuitive connection between epistemic justification and reliability.

(R) is thus a plausible theory. It does, however, have problems. Not surprisingly, there are problems with the left-to-right direction of (R), and with its right-to-left direction. (See BonJour (1985), Dancy (1987), Feldman (1985), and Pollock (1984; 1986).)

1. *Is reliability necessary for justification?* The left-to-right direction of (R) says this: if a belief is justified, then it is produced by a reliable process. This means reliability is necessary for justification. But is it?

Suppose that while you sleep aliens remove your brain and place it in a fancy machine. Suppose they have taken you to their planet and are now simulating earth conditions through the machine. Naturally, to keep you from learning what happened they mimic the conditions you would have faced had they not stolen your brain. So it seems to you that you are reading.

Two things seem clear: first, since you have no indication of what has happened, your belief that you are reading is justified. This is exactly what you *ought* to believe given your evidence. But second, you are not reliable about what you are doing, or about your surroundings. This indicates that reliability is not necessary for justification, and hence that the left-to-right direction of (R) is false.

2. *Is reliability sufficient for justification?* The right-to-left direction of (R) says this: if a belief is produced by a reliable process then it is justified. This means reliability is sufficient for justification. But is it?

Suppose you see a ball which is illuminated by a lamp on a table. And suppose the ball looks red. But suppose you believe there are red lights in the lamp, and that red lights distort the colour objects appear to have. What should you believe about the colour of the ball? Intuitively, you should suspend judgement until you can look at the ball in normal light. But now suppose three further things about this scenario: first, you are wrong about the lights in the lamp. They are normal lights. Secondly, in normal light vision is a reliable method for forming beliefs about the colour of objects; and thirdly, you form the belief that the ball is red on the basis of how it looks *despite* your beliefs about the lights in the lamp. Given all this, would your belief about the colour of the ball be justified? Intuitively, it would not. Since you believe the lights in the lamp distort the way the ball looks, you should disregard how it looks and suspend judgement about the colour of the ball. And this seems true despite your having used a reliable mechanism in forming your belief. This indicates that reliability is not sufficient for justification, and hence that the right-to-left direction of (R) is false.

1.9. Conclusion

We have reached three main conclusions:

1. Propositional knowledge is a complex relation between a person and a true proposition. To have knowledge a person must be fallibly justified in believing a true proposition, and it should be no accident that what the person believes is true.

2. The structure of justified thought is that of a mixed coherence theory. This means that justified belief is produced by positive lines of evidential support which remain undefeated relative to one's background beliefs (and perceptual states).

3. Since internalism does not fully explain the nature of justification, externalism is motivated. But the problems surrounding reliabilism indicate that explaining justification in terms of truth is not a straightforward matter.

PERCEPTION
M. G. F. Martin

2.1. Introduction

To use any of the five senses—seeing, hearing, feeling, tasting, and smelling—is to perceive. It is through the use of these senses that we explore the world around us and gain knowledge of it. It should be of no surprise, then, that the theory of knowledge should take an interest in the nature of perception.

Yet the five senses are also objects of study in physiology and psychology. We are increasingly becoming aware of the various conditions under which our senses operate, their powers of discrimination, and the manner in which they operate. Do these disciplines remove the need for philosophers to study perception?

Whatever the advances in understanding provided by the sciences, the deepest problems in epistemology and metaphysics remain central to the issue of perception for philosophers, as they have since earliest times: those of the relation between appearance and reality. For we do not always perceive things as they really are: the page before you may look white, but under certain abnormal lighting conditions it can look blue instead of white. The page would then appear to be a way that it is not. But now, if things do not always appear as they in fact are, how can I know how things really are simply on the basis of appearance? To answer this question, we need first to turn to an even deeper and more puzzling question: Given that things can sometimes appear as they are, and other times not, what is it for things to appear to one at all?

In this section, on perception, we shall review the attempts of some philosophers to answer this latter question, and also see how the various answers to it bear on the former question, of how we can gain knowledge through perception. Section 2.2 asks what makes an object the object we are perceiving; 2.3 addresses the nature of perceiving and experience; while 2.4 turns to the relation between appearance and perceptual knowledge.

2.2. The Objects of Perception

There are two aspects to the act of perceiving: the objects perceived—the things we see, hear, or feel; and the perceiving of them—the seeing, hearing, or feeling. When I look at the vase on the table, the vase is the thing which I see—it is an object of perception; my seeing of the vase, on the other hand, is a perceptual experience. More exactly it is a visual experience, and for each of the senses there is a corresponding kind of perceptual experience: auditory, tactual, olfactory, and gustatory experiences.

It is natural to think that there is a two-way independence between objects of perception and the perceptual experiences of them. One cannot determine how an object appears to someone from knowledge of how it is; and one cannot determine from how things appear to someone how the object of perception actually is. The vase has many properties, not all of which are apparent to me. I can see that the vase is turquoise, but I cannot see that it was made in Italy. Some properties of the vase are visible to me when I look at it from one point of view, while others are apparent from another: from one side the vase does not appear cracked, while from the other it does. And certain properties of the vase are visible only under some conditions and not others: in twilight I can still determine the shape of the vase, but I cannot tell what colour it is. So, even if one did know all the properties an object possesses, one cannot determine how it looks to an observer without also knowing which of those properties are visible ones, and what conditions and from what perspective a perceiver views it.

There is, of course, a further reason why one cannot determine how things appear from how they look, and, vice versa, determine how they are from how they look: that is that objects can appear to be other than they really are. Under normal lighting, the walls of my office appear off-white, and that is their colour; under certain abnormal lighting conditions the walls can look not off-white, but pink or blue. In such circumstances I am still perceiving the walls, but they do not appear to me to be the way that in fact they are. So, from knowing that the walls are off-white, one could only determine that they looked to me to be off-white if one knew that I was not misperceiving them. Likewise, from knowing that it looks to me as if the walls are pink, one cannot infer that they are pink unless one knows that I am perceiving them as they are.

In addition to illusions, where someone perceives a thing although it appears to be other than it really is, we need to consider hallucinations. Under the influence of narcotics, or by suitable electrical stimulation of parts of my brain, I could be so affected that it would look to me as if there were a pink elephant in front of me, even if there were nothing there at all. In contrast to cases of illusion, I do not perceive something in front of me which looks other than it is; rather it is just that things look to me a certain way, even if I do not see anything at all. From the subject's point of view, an illusion or hallucination may be indistinguishable from a veridical perception. So we can talk of having a perceptual experience in all three kinds of case and hence allow that one can sometimes have a perceptual experience without perceiving. In terms of this we can set out two kinds of problem that a theory of perception may address: the first is to determine when a perceptual experience is a perception of a particular object rather than the perception of another object, or simply a hallucination; the second is to determine what the nature of perceptual experiences themselves is.

What ties an object to the perceiving of it? Imagine that it looks to you as if the Eiffel Tower is in front of you, when in fact all that is there is a small orange. Are you seeing the orange, but misperceiving it as the Eiffel Tower? Or are you having a hallucination of the Eiffel Tower and not seeing the orange at all? Perhaps the answer here is not clear, but if you have the feeling that this cannot really be a case of seeing the orange, then you are liable to accept that there must be some link between the properties an object actually has, and how it appears to be, in order for it to be perceived. If there is such a link, it is difficult to determine exactly how it should be formulated. For instance, it does not seem right to say that one can perceive something only if one perceives its shape or location correctly: we are happy to suppose that we can still perceive something even if we see it in a fairground mirror, where neither shape nor location need be as they seem.

Even if appearing to have some property that an object does actually have is a necessary condition of being perceived, it is certainly not sufficient for perception. Imagine the following case: an experimenter blindfolds you and stimulates part of your brain so that it appears to you as if an orange has been placed in front of you, even though no orange is there. This seems clearly to be a case of hallucination and not a case of perception. Suppose now that the experimenter, while continuing to stimulate your brain, places an orange in just that position where it appears to you an orange must be present. The experimenter has not thereby overridden the effect of his machine, so you are still hallucinating. But now, how things appear to you matches how things actually are, so it cannot be sufficient for being the object of perception that an object perfectly matches how things appear to the subject: the orange matches exactly how things look to you, but the orange is not seen by you.

What, then, is the difference between this case and a normal case of perception? The causal theory of perception claims that the object must cause the perceiving of it. In support one might point out that in this case the orange in front of you which matches your experience is not responsible for that experience. Things look to you that way because the experimenter has turned on his machine, and not because the orange is in front of you. If you were genuinely seeing the orange, then it would look to you as if there were an orange there because an orange was there, and light had been reflected from the orange's skin into your eyes.

On the other hand, the orange's causing one's experience would not seem sufficient to guarantee that one was genuinely perceiving and not hallucinating. Suppose now that the experimenter's machine is connected to a light-sensitive switch which turns the power on only if an object the shape of the orange and the same shade of colour is placed on a spot in front of you. In this case it will look to you as if there is an orange in front of you because an orange is there and has caused the switch to turn on the machine causing your experience. Intuitively this is still not a case of perception, but the orange is a cause of the experience nevertheless.

One response to this is to assume that the object must not only cause the perceiver's experience, but also cause it in the right way. According to this view, the causal claim must be supplemented by further conditions which will enable us to distinguish between normal and deviant causal processes. Various attempts have been made over the last few years to spell out what such further conditions might be, but with only limited success. One serious problem with the task is that it would not be sufficient simply to discover some difference or other between the deviant and normal case: the relevant difference must be one which explains how we are already capable of sorting the cases as falling into either the deviant or the normal category even though we are ignorant of the more obscure facts of physics and physiology concerning the ways in which sense perception is brought about.

An alternative response is to be sceptical about the way the reasoning above has developed. The appeal to the causal difference between the case described above and a case of genuine perception might be justified if there were no other salient difference between them. One might assume so, because you, the subject, in this situation would not be able to tell whether you were being stimulated by the experimenter, and having a hallucination, or genuinely seeing the orange in front of you. This suggests that you are having exactly the same experience in the two cases—any difference must then be one concerning how that experience is brought about. But one might question this assumption. On one point of view, we cannot describe what your perceptual experience is like, in the case of perceiving, without mentioning the very objects that you can see. It is that orange, in front of you, which looks a certain way. And if we did have to mention particular objects in describing how things appear to someone, then we could not assume that appearances are the same in the two cases, even though they are indistinguishable.

This may appear a somewhat defeatist position to adopt. If we cannot assume that we can pick out a perceptual experience independently of determining whether it is a perception, then no interesting answer can be given to what makes a perceptual experience a case of perception. So, this view would not show that the causal theory of perception is wrong, but it would defeat the point of the debate. The real interest in this challenge is rather that it raises questions about the nature of perceptual experience which are central to the problems of perception. We cannot really answer the question 'What makes an object the object of perception?' until we are clear about what a perceptual experience is.

2.3. Perceptual Experience

2.3.1. *The Problem of Perception*

Perceptual experiences are conscious states of mind (not all perception need be conscious—unconscious perception will not involve experience in the sense I am using it here), and the task in giving an account of perceptual experiences is to give an account of their conscious character or what may be called their phenomenological character. Thomas Nagel pointed out that a key difference between conscious entities and non-conscious things is that with the former one can always ask, 'What is it like to be that thing?' The same kind of question can be asked about particular types of conscious state: we can ask what it is like to be seeing, rather than feeling, some object; or what it is like to see a vase of flowers rather than see an ice-cream cone.

If I am asked to describe the world around me now, as I can see it to be, I will offer a description of the things on my desk and the qualities that they possess. What should I do if I am asked to describe not the objects themselves, but my state of mind, my experience of them? As P. F. Strawson points out, it seems difficult to do justice to my experience unless I describe it in the very same terms that I would be inclined to apply to describing the objects on my desk. But of course there is a distinction between my state of mind and the objects in the world around me. This is most manifest in cases of illusion or hallucination: in such cases, I would still be inclined to describe my experience in terms appropriate to the world around me, but in that case such a description of my surroundings might well be false. In order to indicate that I am describing my state of mind rather than the world, we might indicate it by saying something like, 'It is as if there is a vase of roses and a piece of paper in front of me', or even 'It looks to me as if there is a vase . . .'. These descriptions may be true even if the unhedged claim that there is a vase etc. is false, and we may take the descriptions to indicate that the subject is telling us about his or her state of mind rather than the world.

Now we can pose the ancient problem of perception, that is, that of the contrast between appearance and reality, in the following way. In order to do justice to our experiences, we need to describe them in terms appropriate to the physical world. But, in cases of illusion or hallucination, the corresponding descriptions of the physical world would be false. One's state of mind can hardly be vase-shaped or pink, so what is one describing when one asserts that it looks to one as if there is a vase before one? What is the nature of one's experience that should make it appropriate to describe it in terms of the physical world, even when the physical world doesn't match one's description of one's experience?

Now it is tempting to think that this raises a general problem for perceptual experience as a kind of mental state, to be solved in the same way for cases of perception, illusion, and hallucination. That assumption is made by two of the approaches which we shall consider: the sense-datum theory of perception and the intentional theory. But, in accord with the sceptical point of view at the end of the last section, there is a further account of experience which denies that any such general account of perceptual experience is possible, and which insists that the case of perception has to be treated as special. In order to assess the merits of these approaches, we shall need to look at each in more detail.

2.3.2. The Sense-Datum Theory of Perception

Some philosophers take the possibility of illusions and hallucinations to show that we do not perceive physical objects at all, or at least that we do not perceive them in any direct or immediate manner. This somewhat surprising view we can understand in terms of the aim of explaining the nature of perceptual appearances.

Suppose it looks to me as if there is a pink rectangle in front of me, but I am in fact hallucinating and no such physical object is present. The description of my experience, that it looks to me as if there is such a shape before me, is not made true by how things are in my physical environment. According to the sense-datum theory it has to be taken as a description of something. Since there is no appropriate physical candidate, the description must be of something non-physical. Indeed, if the description must be of something in any case in which I have a perceptual experience, even when hallucinating, then there must be some guarantee that such a state of affairs will obtain whenever I have such an experience.

Sense-data are introduced as entities which are not only non-physical but are also assumed to exist just in case one has an appropriate experience, and are assumed to have just those properties which they appear to have. With respect to sense-data, there is no possibility of misperception, and hence a description of the sense-datum one is perceiving will also suffice as a description of how things appear to one.

If sense-data are taken to explain perceptual appearances, what is the supposed connection between perceptual experience and the physical objects of perception? There are two traditional options here. On one view, normally called 'representative' or 'indirect' realism, sense-data, being mind-dependent, are taken to be distinct from the physical objects we perceive and to stand in for or represent those physical objects we are perceiving. On the other view, labelled 'phenomenalism', the existence of a mind-independent world is called into question, and mind-dependent sense-data are held not to represent distinct physical objects, but partly to constitute them.

In order to assess either approach we need to know the kinds of property sense-data may be taken to possess. On the one hand, they must clearly have properties which match how things appear to us; on the other, they can only have those properties it makes sense to ascribe to non-physical objects. It is not immediately clear that these two demands are reconcilable. For example, it is common for a defender of the sense-datum theory to assume that each sense has its own private data, unshared with any other sense. In the case of vision, visual data are commonly assumed to possess figure and colour, but not other properties. Arguably, this does not accord with how we would most naturally describe the appearance of, say, a vase of flowers. How things look to me in that case would seem to involve the kind of object which would be perceptible not only by sight, but also by smell or touch. Even if we can make sense of the idea of non-physical colour-patches, we can hardly make sense of non-physical flowers, yet it does seem to me as if there are a number of roses in front of me.

What this shows is that the sense-datum theory needs to make distinctions within our descriptions of perceptual experience. The narrowest description of experience will be in terms of the properties possessed by the sense-data apparent to one, but in addition one may describe one's experiences in terms of the kinds of physical object which the sense-data may be taken normally to represent.

How plausible is this as an account of perceptual experience? At one time the theory almost had the status of orthodoxy among philosophers, but it is now almost universally rejected. (An entertaining and scathing attack on the traditional view is to be found in J. L. Austin's *Sense and Sensibilia*.) There seem to be two predominant grounds for rejecting it. One persistent worry has been with the consequences that the truth of the theory would have within the theory of knowledge. For, at least since Berkeley and Hume, philosophers have been worried that representative realism might lead to an inescapable scepticism concerning the existence of a mind-independent world. This appears to be one of the reasons Berkeley gives for embracing idealism, according to which we cannot contrast the physical world perceived as standing independently of our perceptions of it, as representative realism seems to require. As mentioned above, proponents of the sense-datum theory may reject representative realism and embrace instead phenomenalism, the view that experience constitutes the external world, a view often taken to be a descendant of Berkeley's idealism. Critics of phenomenalism often accuse it of being little more than a denial of the existence of an external world, and so, faced with the choice of embracing representative realism or phenomenalism, those critics have instead elected to reject the sense-datum theory itself. However, a recent defender of the sense-datum theory, Frank Jackson, has robustly rebutted the arguments for supposing that representative realism has these sceptical consequences.

The second worry concerns the theory's commitment to the existence of non-physical objects. Do we really want to accept that, in addition to rocks, trees, tables, and chairs, there are non-physical objects presented to each of us in perceiving these physical things which stand for and represent them? How is the existence of such non-physical entities to be reconciled with a scientific approach to the world and the neurophysiological underpinnings of perception? This worry has led some philosophers to endorse an adverbial account of sensory experience. While otherwise accepting the sense-datum theory's claims about the nature of experience, they have questioned whether our descriptions of experience genuinely commit us to the existence of inner objects of perception. When one dances a polka, no entity, a polka, exists over and above one's dancing; rather, one dances in the manner of a polka. Likewise, according to the adverbialist, when one has a red after-image, or indeed any visual experience of a red thing, there is no non-physical object which one is aware of; rather, one is just sensing in a red manner.

There is quite general support among philosophers for the view that sensory experiences do have qualities which account for their conscious character which are not to be attributed to any object of perception, but are, rather, qualities of the experience itself. These are often known as subjective qualities, or 'qualia'. Just like the alleged qualities of sense-data, experience is assumed to possess these qualities whenever it has a certain conscious character so that there can be no mismatch between how things appear in experience and what qualities the experience has. An adverbialist theory of sense experience may simply be claiming that our experiences have such subjective qualities, and that such qualities alone are sufficient to explain the phenomenological character of experience, without one having to commit oneself to the existence of subjective objects in addition.

However, a purely adverbial, or qualia-based, theory of perceptual experience faces even greater difficulties in explaining the terms in which we describe our experiences than does a sense-datum theory. For, if it is difficult to see how a non-physical object could be square or pink, it is even more difficult to see how a state of mind could have those qualities. This approach must respond to this difficulty by denying that the qualities in terms of which we normally describe what our experiences are like really capture the quality of the experience itself. For example, when we call a certain kind of pain a nettle sting, we do not mean to say that it has a nettle-ish quality, but only that it is that type of pain normally caused by contact with nettles. Likewise the adverbial, or qualia-based, theory will claim that a description of one's visual experience as of something pink indicates only that it is the type of experience normally caused by pink objects. But this suggestion does not really do justice to Strawson's point, mentioned above, that the natural expression of what our perceptual experiences are like must make reference to concepts of objects in the world.

A more radical response to the sense-datum theory than simply rejecting its commitment to the existence of non-physical objects would be to question its assumption that one's experience can have a certain phenomenological character only if some object has the appropriate quality corresponding to what the experience is like. For while the views discussed in the last paragraph reject the existence of such inner objects, by appealing to subjective qualities, or qualia of the experience, in order to explain its phenomenological character, they still accept that experience can only be a certain way for one if there is a corresponding instance of the relevant quality. This leads us to the intentional theory of perception.

2.3.3. The Intentional Theory of Perception

The intentional theory of perception stresses the close analogy between the case of perception and that of other mental states, such as beliefs and desires or intentions and judgements. These latter kinds of mental state possess what philosophers call an intentional content. One can believe that things are a certain way, whether or not they are that way; and one can desire that things should be a certain way, when they are not yet that way, and may never be so.

For example, imagine a child opening a tube for sweets and expressing surprise at finding only pencils there. The child believed that there were sweets in the tube, but on opening the tube discovered his belief to be false. The case of belief provides us with an analogue for the problem of perception. If asked what the child believed before opening the tube, we would have to answer that he believed that the tube contained sweets. The tube did not contain sweets, so why was it appropriate to describe the child's state of mind, his belief, in terms appropriate to how the world was not?

It would be a bizarre thing to insist that, if there are no sweets in the physical world, then some non-physical tube of sweets must exist which the child's belief is really about. The right thing to say instead is that his belief represented the world as being a certain way, namely, that it represented the world as being such that there were sweets in the tube in front of him. How the belief represents the world to be is what we call its intentional content. If the world is as someone believes it to be, then the intentional content of their belief is true, or correct. That content may also be expressed by the sentence we would use to say what someone believes. It is simply in the nature of belief, as it is the nature of language, that one can believe the world to be a certain way, or say that it is a certain way, even when it is not. Whether or not one's belief is correct, that belief is still about the world and not about some inner replica of the world.

This intentionality of belief and other mental states—that is, their possession of intentional contents, or equivalently their properties of representing or being about things—is a topic of central concern within philosophy today. Franz Brentano (1838–1917) claimed that intentionality was the mark of the mental, which is to say that all and only mental states possess intentionality; and he claimed that the mind's possession of intentionality showed that no scientific or naturalistic account of the mind could be given. Many philosophers have responded to Brentano by attempting to show how we can accommodate intentionality within a purely natural world. We do not have space here to pursue the various problems associated with intentionality, or to assess the debate between Brentano and his critics. We can only note that the problems raised in connection with intentionality, thinking about the non-existent, or thinking things which are not the case are completely general problems which arise for almost all mental states. So, if we claim that perceptual experiences are intentional states just like beliefs, or desires, hopes, wishes, intentions, judgements, then whatever general account of intentionality we adopt, we shall apply it equally to the case of perception.

The intentional theory of perception applies the same account to experience as to belief, claiming that one's perceptual experience represents the world as being a certain way. The experience has an intentional content, and if the world matches the intentional content, then the experience is veridical, otherwise it is illusory. My experience is the way it is in virtue of the intentional content it has. When I describe my visual experience by saying that it looks as if there is a vase of flowers in front of me, I simply describe how my experience represents the world to be, namely, how the world would have to be in order for my experience to be veridical.

But this does not really explain how this is different from the sense-datum theory of perception. The latter, in the form of indirect realism, also claims that sense-data represent the world as being a certain way. This can be brought out in the following way: according to the sense-datum theory those qualities which we must mention in giving an account of what our experiences are like must actually be possessed by something—namely the sense-datum of which one is aware. While that sense-datum may also represent the physical world to be a certain way, that fact about the sense-datum plays no role in determining what the experience is like. According to the intentional theory, however, the qualities which we must mention in giving an account of experience need not be possessed by anything; they need only to be represented as being possessed by something. In this way, one's experience can still be of the physical world even in cases of illusion and hallucination, in virtue of representing that world to be a certain way. The intentional theory, just like the adverbial theory, avoids the commitment to the existence of non-physical objects of perception. It also has an account of why the terms we use to characterize the world should also be the terms we use to characterize what our experiences are like.

But does the intentional theory really take enough account of the difference between sensory experiences and other mental states—the difference, as David Hume put it, between feeling and thinking? One difference is that I can say what I believe by using a sentence, and there is no sense that I need have left something out. But the description of what my experience is like does not seem capable of doing justice to how things seem to me, just as I cannot completely capture what a picture displays in words. So, if perceptual experiences have an intentional content, it may be a different kind of content from that possessed by beliefs and desires.

One might still feel a certain resistance to the thought that all there is to a conscious experience is how it represents the world to be. One reason for this resistance may be the thought that there is a difference between what it is like to see something and what it is like to feel something where the difference is not simply a matter of what one is perceiving. Surely one can tell whether one is seeing a round coin or feeling it, even where in both cases one is perceiving that the object is round. For this and related reasons, many philosophers reject a purely intentional theory of perception and embrace one aspect at least of the sense-datum or related subjectivist accounts of perceptual experience. That is to say that they claim that perceptual experiences not only have intentional content, but also possess subjective qualities, or qualia, which partly account for what the experience is like.

2.3.4. Disjunctive Theories

Both of the above approaches appeal to the difficulty of accounting for illusions and hallucinations in support of their claims. For the sense-datum theory first assumes that the qualities which one mentions in describing one's experience must be possessed by something. In looking to cases of illusion and hallucination, the theory aims to show that whatever it is that possesses these qualities, it cannot be the physical object in front of the perceiver, and hence must be a sense-datum. On the other hand, the intentional theory shows that the qualities by which we characterize appearances are represented in experience, rather than possessed by anything, by pointing to cases of illusion and hallucination where there is no appropriate physical object to possess the qualities.

As we noted in discussing the causal theory of perception, some philosophers question whether these two approaches are right simply to assume that the kind of mental state one has when veridically perceiving is the sort of state which one could have when hallucinating. When we describe how things look to us, we need not be talking about a state of mind common to the three cases, but rather we may be being non-committal as to which of three kinds of situation we are in: either I am veridically perceiving, or having an illusion to that effect, or having a hallucination. If that doubt is justified, then we would have no reason to suppose that, in giving an account of perceptual appearances in the case of veridical perception, we would also thereby have to be giving the same sort of account for cases of illusion or hallucination.

Why insist on this distinction between veridical perception and mere illusion or hallucination? One might agree with the sense-datum theory that if one's perceptual experience is as of a certain quality, of something's being pink, say, then something must really be pink, while also agreeing with Strawson that one's experience is as of objects in the physical world. These two claims are only consistent if one rejects the assumption, common to both the sense-datum theory and the intentional theory, that perceptual experience forms a common kind among the three cases of veridical perception, illusion, and hallucination. For then one may claim of the case of veridical perception that things must really be that way if one has such an experience while denying that this is also true of illusion and hallucination. Only in this way, the advocate of the disjunctive view may claim, can we really make sense of the way in which perceptual experience gives us immediate contact with the objects of perception in a way that mere thought or imagination do not.

Whether or not this is sufficient justification to reject the assumption that perceptual experience is a kind of mental state in common among perception, illusion, and hallucination, does it even make sense to deny this? After all, to the subject an illusion or hallucination can be indistinguishable from a veridical perception. There is a sense, then, in which the three kinds of state all seem to be the same. Surely we are giving an account of appearances; hence if the three seem to be the same, then they all involve the same state of appearing? This is certainly a powerful consideration, but it may not be decisive. The opponent might claim that, in the case of veridical perception, what one is conscious of are the very objects in front of one which one is perceiving, and the qualities that they actually have. One's experience does not merely represent the presence of these things; rather, these things are 'present' in the experience and a part of it. Clearly they cannot be a part of it in the case of hallucination, and perhaps not even in the case of illusion. In the sense of 'something being present to consciousness' the illusion and hallucination would be different from the veridical perception. This would not be to deny that when one has an illusion or hallucination one is deceived by one's state of mind into supposing that one is veridically perceiving the world. The key thought is that there is no common conscious state present in all three cases which accounts for things so appearing to one, even though that is how things seem. As a consequence, therefore, the view must claim that, when having an illusion or hallucination, unknowingly one will be as deceived about one's own state of mind as one will be about the world.

But the sense-datum theory and intentional theory can offer another argument in their support. This turns on the causal history of the mental states. When the experimenter stimulates your brain to cause a hallucination of an orange, he need only bring about the same kind of neural activity as in other cases will produce a veridical perception of an orange. Furthermore, a hallucination of an orange is just as liable to produce orange-directed physical behaviour as is a perception. This suggests that the very same immediate causes may bring about a hallucination in the one case and a veridical perception in the other, while the two states also seem to have the same powers to produce physical effects in the world. So in this case it looks not only as if the states are subjectively indistinguishable, but—from the perspective of their places in the causal order—they are objectively indistinguishable also. Both thoughts strongly support the hypothesis that we are dealing with the same kind of mental state in all three cases.

This argument may not be decisive either. According to many philosophers, we need to recognize that many biological kinds and even mental states need to be counted as different even where their causal powers are identical. In the case of biological kinds, it is plausible that what makes a given lump of tissue part of an organ is its biological function. According to many philosophers of biology, biological function is to be explained in terms of evolutionary history. So intrinsically indistinguishable lumps of tissue may fall under different biological kinds in worlds where history is different. While, in the case of mental states, externalists about the content of thought claim that one can think of particular objects or particular kinds of stuff only if the objects in question or the stuffs actually exist. On this view of thought, the same consequence follows that episodes of thinking may be causally indistinguishable and yet concern different objects. So too, in the case of perceptual states, it might be that we simply have to accept the same consequences when looking to the case of perception.

In the end, are there good reasons to reject the assumption made by both the sense-datum theory and the intentional theory? One might claim that doing so avoids the major objections to the other two views. In agreement with the intentional theory, and in contrast to the sense-datum theory, the view accords with introspective evidence that our perceptual experiences are to be described in terms of the physical world. In agreement with the sense-datum theory, and in contrast to the intentional theory, the view supports the intuition that there is something distinctive about sensory states in contrast to pure thought—that sensory states involve the immediate presence or presentation of what is experienced in a way that mere representation cannot.

Whether one can settle the disputes here is something that we must leave aside for the moment. In the final section of this part of the chapter we should simply look to the consequences that these views may have for the theory of perceptual knowledge.

2.4. Perceptual Knowledge

How does perceiving an object lead to knowledge? Perceiving an object involves having a perceptual experience. When one has a perceptual experience of an object, the object appears some way to one. In the case of a veridical perception, how the object appears coincides with how it actually is. So does veridical perception that the vase is turquoise amount to knowledge that the vase is turquoise?

Perceiving that things are a certain way does not amount to believing that they are that way. Inasmuch as knowledge involves belief, therefore, perceiving need not be knowing. To see that perceiving need not be believing consider a familiar example of visual illusion. In the example of the Müller-Lyer illusion shown in the figure the two horizontal lines appear to be unequal in length, even though they are in fact of exactly the same length. If you did not know this previously, you do now. Yet while you will no longer believe that they are unequal in length (if you do not trust me or the printer, please apply a measure) this will not affect how the lines look to you. In this case, you do not believe that the lines are unequal, but they still appear unequal. Of course, this is not a case

of perceiving something to be the case which you do not believe, since the
Müller-Lyer is an illusion. But nothing about the example turns essentially on
its actually being an illusion. Suppose, for instance, that someone you trust as
an authority tells you that a room you are about to enter has strange lighting so
that the white walls look pink. In fact, the person is misleading you: the lighting is normal and the walls really are pink. In this case, it looks to you as if the
walls are pink, you perceive them to be the way they in fact are, but you fail to
believe that they are pink.

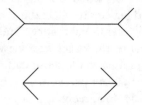

If perceiving is not simply believing, what is the transition involved from perceptual experience to belief? The simplest view here would be that the perceptual experience is just a stage along the causal process leading to belief. It is a
more immediate cause than the stimulation of the retinas, but has no more special status than that. Just such a view has been propounded by the American
philosopher Donald Davidson, among others. The view is likely to appeal particularly to those who conceive of perceptual experiences as not being intentional in character but rather purely subjective in nature. For then it might seem
that there was no intrinsic link between the conscious character of the experience and the perceptual belief which results concerning the physical world, and
hence that the only link would be causal.

One might feel that this story ignores the tight connection between things
looking this way to me and my coming to believe that they are so, or my tasting the object this way and my then coming to believe that it is so. Surely the
fact that this is the way it looks has an intrinsic link to my believing that it is so.
According to a causal story, this cannot be so: the tightest link will merely be a
lawlike connection between the various qualities of experience and the beliefs
we form. Our impression that there is a tighter link will simply turn on the close
association of our beliefs that our experience has a certain character and our
beliefs that the world is a certain way. Furthermore, in support of the merely
causal story, one might consider various alternatives to normal conscious perception. We can imagine reliably forming beliefs about the world on the basis
of some mechanism that we know nothing about; someone might simply have
a hunch that there is a table in front of him when there is; and so on. Indeed
some philosophers appear to believe that the pathological condition of blindsight is just such a case: someone suffering from blindsight will commonly deny

that he can see in a certain area of the visual field, but upon being forced to guess will guess reliably when an object is located within that blind area. Such people seem to have access to information about the world around them without thereby having conscious visual experience. Whether this is the correct description of the case is highly controversial among cognitive neurophysiologists as well as philosophers, but it is at least suggestive of a kind of case that we can imagine.

If one is to reject the merely causal story we need a further argument. Here our initial case for the possibility of disbelief in perception provides us with a reason. People do not just happen to fail to believe that things are as they appear. Rather, an explanation of why they fail to believe things to be that way may be because how things appear to them is inconsistent with how they believed things to be prior to experiencing them that way. Indeed, appearances may be so intrinsically incredible that a cautious judge can do no more than suspend judgement: for example, were it suddenly to appear to me now as if a ten-foot-high green cat had walked into the room, then I would be inclined to mistrust my senses. Here my mistrust, and hence failure to acquire the relevant beliefs, is to be explained by how things appeared to me. But the explanation does not appear to be merely causal—it was quite reasonable for me to distrust my senses, given how things appeared to me.

The alternative to the mere causal account is to suppose that there is some rational or justificatory relation between sensory experience and perceptual belief. Exactly which account is adopted will depend on the account of experience that the theorist favours.

On a traditional sense-datum theory of experience, having an experience is to be aware of, or presented with, a non-physical object which has a certain character. This confrontation of this state of affairs by the subject is supposed to place him in a position to form an epistemically favourable belief about the state of affairs in question. One way of putting the point is to say that such states of affairs are self-intimating to the subject upon whom their existence depends, and hence that the state of affairs in question is given to the subject in experience. There is less agreement about the epistemic properties of the belief formed. According to one form of traditional foundationalism, the belief in question is incorrigible—no other belief can give one reason to correct it—or even infallible—guaranteed to be true. But a weaker link may be claimed: the belief may be taken simply to have a high degree of justification which may nevertheless be overturnable by sufficient weight of other beliefs.

Even if the belief about the non-physical state of affairs presented to the perceiver would be justified, as yet no account has been given of the justification of the perceiver's belief about the physical world. Here the bridge may be made by supposing that the perceiver has various general beliefs about the kinds of situation in which this type of experience is caused by a particular physical state of affairs. The non-physical state of affairs given to the subject in experience can then act as a sign for the physical state of affairs he comes to form a belief about.

This view is a form of traditional foundationalism, and it claims for itself the virtue of basing our knowledge of the external world on secure foundations of our beliefs about what we experience in the world. Whatever its status as an account of the justification of belief, the story is implausible as an account of the psychological process of forming perceptual beliefs. In the normal course of things, we do not reflect on some non-physical state of affairs and then infer the presence of a physical object on the basis of general causal principles. Rather, when you see a ball heading straight for you, you immediately put your hands up or just duck. If there is any form of inference involved in the transition from perception to action, it is unconscious.

The point is not only one about the causal transition from perception to belief. The kinds of causal principle that this view will rely upon—that experiences of this type are caused by physical objects of that kind—must, on this view, be taken to have a justification independent of one's perceptual belief that an object of that kind is before one. However, if we inquire into our reasons for believing that certain kinds of object are normally responsible for certain kinds of experience, then we cannot avoid appealing to past perceptual beliefs concerning our encounters with particular objects of that kind as part of our justification for these beliefs. If this is so, it suggests that perceptual belief about particular objects must ground our general beliefs about the causal connections between types of experience and the types of things in the world which cause them, rather than vice versa.

This suggests that any intuitively appealing link between experience and belief requires that the experience be physical-world-involving. One way in which this might be claimed, consistent with a form of modified foundationalism, would be to adopt the disjunctive approach to perception discussed earlier. On this view, what is given to the perceiver, at least in the case of veridical perception, just is an aspect of the physical world. The perceiver is then in a position to form a justified belief on the basis of so being presented with an aspect of the world. As with traditional foundationalism, the subject stands in some relation to a state of affairs which then leads his beliefs to be justified. Traditional foundationalism has commonly led to a more radical reaction. According to the reaction, self-intimating states of affairs and experiences cannot justify any beliefs—only beliefs can stand in justificatory relations to other beliefs. This view seems too extreme in the light of earlier discussion, for it does seem as if experiences can stand in some justificatory relation to beliefs. A modified version of the principle would not be flouted by this example: one might claim that only states with an intentional content, mental states which represent the world to be some way, can stand in justificatory relations.

If one adopts an intentional theory of perception, perceptual experiences are claimed to have intentional contents, and hence one may claim that they stand in justificatory relations to beliefs, as we have seen reason to endorse. Furthermore, because the content of such experiences concerns the nature of the external world, the beliefs which they can directly justify will not be beliefs about some non-physical state of affairs, nor beliefs about one's mental state, but rather beliefs about that feature of one's environment which is represented to be a certain way by the content of one's perceptual experience. Unlike the case of traditional foundationalism, it cannot be claimed that the perceptual beliefs which result will be incorrigible or infallible: an illusion or hallucination is just as liable to lead to perceptual belief as is a veridical perception. The belief may at the least be accorded a defeasible warrant.

This raises two difficult questions. The first is to inquire exactly what beliefs about the external world are supported directly by one's perceptions. On one restrictive view, only beliefs about the strictly observational properties of objects will be justified: so someone would be justified in supposing the object before them is red, but not that it is a tomato (since one cannot tell by looking whether a given fruit is begotten by the right sort of plant or tree). The distinction here between observational and non-observational is tied to the idea that one's experience will be illusory where something apparently red is not red; but it need not be illusory if something apparently a tomato is not a tomato. The second problem arises in relation even to the strictly observational: a perceptual experience supports one's perceptual beliefs only where the experience is veridical. Does the subject have to have positive reason to suppose his experiences on a given occasion are veridical? Is he instead allowed a certain presumption that his experiences are veridical unless he has specific reason to question this? Or, even more weakly, does the justification merely depend upon the fact that he is veridically perceiving, regardless of whether he has reason to believe this or not? However, the pursuit of these questions takes us away from the study of perception proper and back into the theory of knowledge.

SCEPTICISM
A. C. Grayling

3.1. Introduction

In both the ordinary and the philosophical senses, a sceptic is one who, at least unless he is shown satisfactory reason why he should do otherwise, doubts some proposition, belief, or theory. Sceptical considerations are immensely important for philosophical inquiry into questions about knowledge. For these purposes the characterization just given is too general as it stands, so a more careful explanation of scepticism is needed, together with an account of the reasons that prompt it.

In the general business of life a sceptical attitude is healthy when it aims at testing the grounds for claims upon our credence, by whomever they are made. It is of course impractical to be sceptical about everything; ordinarily we have to take on trust a great deal of what others say. Society could not function unless most people were taken to be honest, and most information reliable, most of the time. But there are cases where it is appropriate, even necessary, to be sceptical; where the responsible course is to question a given claim and to assess the case offered in its support. A barrister in a court of law, or a voter listening to politicians on the hustings, has a duty to do so.

In philosophy the study and use of sceptical arguments belongs to epistemology, and in one sense might be said to define it. One of the chief concerns of epistemology is to determine how we can be sure that the means we employ to acquire knowledge are adequate. A powerful way to show what is required is to look carefully at sceptical challenges to our knowledge-acquiring endeavours, challenges which reveal or allege ways in which they can go wrong. If we are able to identify and meet them, we will have achieved a primary epistemological aim.

Scepticism is often described as the claim that nothing is—or, more strongly, can be—known. But this is a bad characterization, because if we know or can know nothing, then we do not or cannot know that we know nothing, and so the claim is trivially self-defeating. It is more telling to premise the view of scepticism given in the previous paragraph: as a challenge directed at knowledge-claims made in some field of inquiry, the form and nature of the challenge varying with the field in question, but in general taking the form of a request for the justification available in support of the knowledge-claims at issue, together with the reasons that motivate such a request—standardly, that certain considerations indicate that the assumed justification might be inadequate to its task. To conceive of scepticism like this is to see it as more philosophically troubling than if it is described as a positive thesis asserting our ignorance or incapacity for knowledge.

If therefore scepticism consists in asking 'How do you know?', and if it advances points which suggest that ordinary standards of justification for our epistemic claims are vulnerable in various ways, then it makes a serious demand on us. But if it consists in assertions that we do not know this or that, then it is a positive claim in need of a supporting case, about which we are entitled to be sceptical in our turn. And if it consists in a denial that we know anything at all, it is merely self-defeating and ignorable.

3.2. A Historical Sketch

Pessimism about the prospects for scientific progress—using 'science' in the broadest sense to mean theoretical knowledge of the world—so infected some among the philosophers of antiquity that they developed distinctive sceptical viewpoints. Pyrrho of Elis (*c.*360–270 BC) and his followers argued that because inquiry is both unproductive and vexing, given the difficulty of determining whether the arguments for any proposition are better or worse than those against, one should suspend judgement altogether, for only thus will the important goal—shared by most philosophical schools of the time—of achieving *ataraxia* (peace of mind) be realizable.

Less radically, the successors of Plato in his Academy, although they agreed with Pyrrho that certainty must elude us, tempered this view with a recognition of the need to accept life's demands, and therefore argued that we should accept whatever proposition or theory is more probable than its competitors. They did not think it a practical possibility to 'suspend judgement', as the Pyrrhonists recommended. The various views of these thinkers are collectively known as Academic scepticism.

In the later part of the Renaissance, with religious certainties under attack and new ideas abroad, some of the sceptical considerations discussed by the Academics and Pyrrhonians acquired a special significance, most notably in the work of René Descartes (1596–1650); for they proved useful as tools in the highly consequential matter of investigating the nature of knowledge and the proper means of getting it. In Descartes's day practitioners of astronomy and astrology, chemistry and alchemy, medicine and magic were often the same people in each or all cases, so there was an urgent need for a way of distinguishing those inquiries that might yield genuine knowledge from those that merely yield nonsense. In his *Meditations* Descartes accordingly identified epistemology as an essential preliminary to science, and sought to establish the grounds of certainty as a preparation for the study of physics and mathematics. As a sharp way of effecting that task Descartes adapted some of the traditional sceptical arguments. His contribution in this respect is so significant that, until recently, epistemology—and in particular the task of refuting scepticism—has occupied a central place in philosophy. The arguments he used are discussed later.

3.3. The Nature of Sceptical Arguments

Sceptical arguments exploit certain contingent psychological facts about the ways we acquire, test, remember, and reason about our beliefs. Since knowledge consists in belief which at very least is true and, in a way to be defined, properly justified, any problem which infects the acquisition and employment of beliefs about a given subject-matter threatens our claims to knowledge in respect of that subject-matter.

The contingent psychological facts in question are those relating to the nature of perception, the normal human vulnerability to error, and the existence of states of mind—for example, dreaming and delusion—which can be subjectively indistinguishable from those we take to be appropriate for acquiring knowledge, but which are not so. By appealing to these considerations the sceptic aims to show that there are significant questions to be answered about the degree of confidence we are entitled to repose in our standard ways of getting knowledge.

The considerations appealed to by the sceptic between them pose problems for epistemologists of both the 'rationalist' and the 'empiricist' schools of thought. This division into competing views about knowledge is somewhat crude, but is a useful way of marking the difference between those who hold that the main instrument in the acquisition of knowledge is reason, and those who hold that it is experience. A rationalist might typically emphasize reason because in his view the objects of knowledge are propositions which are eternally, immutably, and necessarily true, for example the propositions of mathematics and logic; and these, he says, can only be arrived at by thought. An empiricist might typically hold that all genuine knowledge of the world must be learned through empirical experience, by means of the five senses (and their extension via telescopes, microscopes, and other instruments). The rationalist need not deny that empirical awareness is an important adjunct of our rational faculties, nor the empiricist that reason is an important adjunct of empirical investigation; both will, however, hold that the primary, chief, or final means to knowledge is respectively one or the other.

The refinements and details of debates about these matters merit more detailed examination than can be given here. For present purposes the point is that scepticism is a problem for both schools of thought. For both, possibilities of error and delusion pose a challenge. For the empiricist in particular, to these must be added problems about perception and perceptual consciousness.

3.4. Sceptical Arguments: Error, Delusion, and Dreams

The arguments from error and delusion are simply stated. Consider the error argument first. We are fallible creatures; we sometimes make mistakes. If, however, we are ever to be able to claim to know some proposition p, we must be able to exclude the possibility that at the time of claiming to know p we are in error. But since we typically or at least frequently do not realize, as we make an error in claiming to know p, that we are indeed making an error, we are not justified in making such a claim.

The same applies when a person is the subject of delusion, illusion, or hallucination. Sometimes one who experiences one or other of these states does not know that he is doing so, and takes himself to be having veridical experiences. But although he thinks he is in a state which lends itself to his being justified in claiming to know a given *p*, he is not so. In such a case he does not know what he claims to know. So in order for anyone to claim knowledge of some *p*, he must be able to exclude the possibility that he is the subject of such states.

This pattern of argument is at its most familiar in the 'dream argument' of Descartes. One way of sketching it is as follows. When I sleep I sometimes dream, and when I dream I often do not know I am dreaming. So I can have experiences which appear to be veridical waking experiences on the basis of which I take myself to be entitled to claim knowledge of such-and-such. But because I am dreaming, I do not in fact know such-and-such; I merely dream that I do. Might I not be dreaming now? If I cannot exclude the possibility that I am now, at this moment, dreaming, I am unable to claim knowledge of the things I at this moment take myself to know. For example, it seems to me that I am writing this at a pair of French windows opened to a garden, with recorded music playing in the room behind me. But because I might be dreaming that this is so, I cannot claim to know it.

In these arguments the possibility of error, delusion, or dreaming acts as a 'defeater' to knowledge-claims. The pattern is: If one knows *p*, then nothing is acting to subvert one's entitlement to know it. But one can seem to oneself fully entitled to claim to know some *p*, and in fact not be so, as the foregoing considerations show. So our claims to knowledge are in need of better grounds than we standardly take ourselves to have. We must find a way of defeating the defeaters.

3.5. Sceptical Arguments: Perception and Perceptual Relativities

The arguments sketched in the preceding paragraphs equally threaten both rationalist and empiricist views about the sources of knowledge. Further considerations which trouble the empiricist arise from the nature and limitations of sensory experience.

Our best current model of perception tells us something like the following. Light reflects from the surfaces of objects in the physical environment and passes into the eyes, where it irritates the cells of the retinas in such a way that impulses are triggered in the optic nerves. The nerves convey the impulses to the part of the cerebral cortex which processes visual data, where they stimulate certain sorts of brain activity. As a result, in ways yet mysterious to science and philosophy, coloured motion pictures arise in the consciousness of the subject of these events, representing the world outside his head. This remarkable transaction, *mutatis mutandis*, is repeated in the other sensory pathways of hearing, smell, taste, and touch, although in these cases it is not of course coloured motion pictures which result from the impingement of the world upon the subject's sensitive membranes, but music and conversation, flavours and scents, textures and temperatures.

The sceptic can use this model to make another application of the defeater argument. He points out that the complex causal story thus told is one which might be interrupted at any point along its length in problematic ways. The experiences which we say result from the interaction of our sense organs and the world might occur in us for other reasons. They might occur when, as noted above, we dream or suffer hallucinations; or, to take fancy further, they might be produced in us by a deity, or by a mad scientist who has wired our brains to a computer. From the subjective point of view there might be no way of telling the difference. So unless we find means of excluding these possibilities, says the sceptic, we are not entitled to claim knowledge of what we standardly take ourselves to know.

But these same considerations about perception might prompt sceptical challenge by a different route. Only a little reflection shows that some of the properties we seem to perceive in objects are in fact not 'in the objects themselves' but are the artefact of the perceptual relation. The colour, taste, smell, sound, and texture of objects vary according to the condition of the perceiver or the conditions under which they are perceived. The standard examples are legion. Grass is green in daylight, grey or black at night; tepid water feels warm to a cold hand, cool to a hot hand; objects look large from close by, small from far away; the sides of a table look parallel from above, but converge when looked at from one end. And so on. These perceptual relativities are invoked by the sceptic to raise questions not just about whether perception is a reliable source of information about the world, but, further, whether the world can properly be said to exist independently of perception at all. For what if the properties by whose means we detect the presence of objects—their colours, textures, shapes, and the rest—cannot be described apart from their being objects of perception? Only consider the old conundrum whether a sound is made by something that falls to the ground with no sentient beings present to hear it do so. If there is no ear to hear, there is no sound, only at best the conditions—vibrating airwaves—which might cause sound to be heard if there were eardrums, aural nerves, and the rest to be affected by them.

What these considerations suggest to the sceptic is that perceivers are in something like this case: Imagine a person wearing a helmet of the type worn by motorbike-riders, with the big difference that it has no visor, so that the wearer cannot see out. And imagine that a camera, a microphone, and other sensors affixed to the top of the helmet transmit pictures, sounds, and related information to the helmet's interior. And suppose finally that it is impossible for the wearer to remove the helmet to check whether the information passed to its interior faithfully represents the exterior world; the wearer has to rely on the intrinsic character of the information available inside the helmet to judge its reliability. He knows that the information sometimes comes from sources other than the exterior world, as in dreams and delusions; he has deduced that the equipment affixed to the helmet works upon the incoming data and changes it, for example adding colours, scents, and sounds to its picture of what intrinsically has none of these properties (at very least, in those forms); and he knows that his beliefs about what lies outside the helmet rest on the inferences he draws from the information available inside it, and that his inferences are only as good as his fallible, error-prone capacities allow them to be. Given all this, asks the sceptic, have we not a job of work to do to justify our claims to knowledge?

3.6. Methodological and Problematic Scepticism

Before reflecting on these arguments and inspecting some ways of responding to them, it is helpful to note one fact and to draw one distinction. The fact is that sceptical arguments are not best dealt with by attempts at direct refutation on a one-by-one basis. The distinction is one between—broadly speaking—two ways in which scepticism can be employed in epistemology. It is important to note both this fact and this distinction because otherwise the prima-facie implausibility of most sceptical arguments will mislead one into ignoring their significance.

Attempted refutation of sceptical arguments singly and directly is futile for two very good reasons. One is that they are at their strongest not when they seek to prove an agniological result—that is, one which positively affirms that we are ignorant about some subject-matter—but when they ask us to justify our claims to knowledge. A challenge to justify is not a claim or a theory, and cannot be refuted; it can only be accepted or ignored. Since the sceptic offers reasons why justification is needed, the response might be to inspect those reasons to see whether the challenge needs response. This indeed is one good response to scepticism. Where the reasons are cogent, the next good response is to try to meet the challenge thus posed.

The second good reason is that the whole range of sceptical arguments taken together has maieutic status. Literally 'maieusis' means midwifery, that is, the practice of aiding childbirth. Whatever has maieutic status is whatever helps something else into being. To say that sceptical considerations are maieutic is to say that they together bring into the light what is needed for a satisfactory theory of knowledge. If one could refute, or show to be ungrounded, one or another particular sceptical argument, it would leave others in place still demanding that we give a positive account of knowledge.

These points can be simply illustrated by a consideration of Gilbert Ryle's attempt to refute the argument from error by a 'polar concept' argument. There cannot be counterfeit coins, Ryle observes, unless there are genuine ones, nor crooked paths unless there are straight paths, nor tall men unless there are short men. Many concepts come in pairs which are polar opposites of one another, and these conceptual polarities are such that one cannot grasp either pole unless one grasps its opposite at the same time. Now, 'error' and 'getting it right' are conceptual polarities. If one understands the concept of error, one understands the concept of getting it right. But to understand this latter concept is to be able to apply it. So our very grasp of the concept of error implies that we sometimes get things right.

Ryle takes the error sceptic to be claiming that, for all we know, we might always be in error. Accordingly his argument—that if we understand the concept of error, we must sometimes get things right—is aimed at refuting the intelligibility of claiming that we might always be wrong. But of course the error sceptic is not claiming this. He is simply asking how, given that we sometimes make mistakes, we can rule out the possibility of being in error on any given occasion of judgement—say, at this present moment. But the sceptic need not concede to the more general claims Ryle makes, namely, that for any conceptual polarity, both poles must be understood, and, further, to understand a concept is to know how to apply it, and for it to be applicable is for it actually to be applied (or to have been applied). This last move is question-begging enough, but so is the claim about conceptual polarities itself. For the sceptic can readily cite cases of conceptual polarities—those denoted, for example, by the expressions 'perfect–imperfect', 'mortal–immortal', 'finite–infinite'—where it is by no means clear that the more exotic poles apply to anything, or even that we really understand them (taking a term and attaching a negative prefix to it does not guarantee that we have grasped an intelligible concept).

These thoughts suggest that sceptical arguments, even if singly they appear implausible, jointly invite a serious response; which is what, in large measure, epistemology seeks to offer. But there is still the matter of the distinction to be explained, and here a brief rehearsal of Descartes's use of sceptical arguments proves useful.

Descartes's aim is to find something of which he can be certain as a basis for knowledge. To find certainty he needs to exclude whatever admits of the least taint of doubt, however absurd that doubt, for only then will what is truly indubitable be revealed. In the first *Meditation* he embarks on this task by borrowing some sceptical arguments from antiquity. First he cites the fact that we can be misled in perception. But this is not a thoroughgoing enough scepticism, for even if we make perceptual mistakes, there is much that we can still claim to know. So he next considers the possibility that on any given occasion of taking oneself to know something, one might be dreaming. This sceptical consideration catches more in its net, but is still not enough, for even in dreams we can know things; arithmetical truths, for example. So to get as swingeing a consideration as possible Descartes introduces the 'evil demon' hypothesis, in which the supposition is that, with respect to everything about which one can possibly be misled, an evil demon is indeed misleading one. Famously, what such a being cannot mislead one about is that, whenever one thinks 'I exist', this proposition is true.

It is vital to note that Descartes's use of these arguments is purely methodological. The remainder of the *Meditations* is devoted to showing that we know a great deal, because the fact (as he unsuccessfully attempts to prove) that there is a good deity ensures that, providing we use our faculties correctly, whatever we clearly and distinctly perceive to be true will indeed be true—for a good deity, unlike an evil one, would not wish us to embrace ignorance. So Descartes is by no means a sceptic, nor does he think the sceptical arguments, least of all the one employed as a device to set aside as many beliefs as possible, are persuasive. The 'method of doubt' is merely a tool.

Descartes's successors, however, were far more impressed by the sceptical arguments he employed than by the response he gave to them. They accepted his diagnosis of the problem, but not the cure. So for the tradition of epistemological thinking after his time these and allied sceptical arguments were not mere methodological devices, but problems requiring solution. Hence the distinction I draw between methodological and problematic scepticism.

It is clear that there are sceptical considerations which have merely methodological utility, and are not genuinely problematic, because they do not represent a stable and cogent challenge to our ordinary epistemological standards. The 'evil demon' device is a case in point. Since the hypothesis that there is such a thing is about as arbitrary and groundless as a hypothesis can get, it does not merit being taken seriously otherwise than as a tactic to make a point. But considerations about perception, error, delusion, and dreams raise more interesting and troubling general issues, and it is these which merit examination.

Two things might be noted about Descartes's discussion. First, his quest for certainty is arguably misconceived. Certainty is a psychological state that one can be in independently of whether one is right or wrong. For example, one can be certain that such-and-such a horse will win the Derby, and yet lose one's money. The falsity of a belief is no bar to one's feeling certain that it is true. Descartes's intention was of course to identify means of recognizing which of our beliefs are true, but he led himself into talking of certainty because—and this is the second point—he assumed that epistemology's task is to provide individuals with a way of knowing, from their own subjective viewpoints, that they are in possession of knowledge rather than error. His inquiry begins from the private data of an individual consciousness and attempts to work outward to knowledge of what lies beyond, securing a guarantee for itself *en route*. Almost all of Descartes's successors in epistemology, up to and including Bertrand

Russell and A. J. Ayer in the twentieth century, unquestioningly accepted this perspective upon their task. In this respect at least they are all Cartesians. And, as we shall see below, it is for this reason that they all found it difficult to meet the sceptical challenge.

3.7. Some Responses to Scepticism: The 'Gap'

The general effect of sceptical challenges is to suggest that we suffer an epistemic plight, which is that we can possess the very best possible evidence for believing some p, and yet be wrong. Stated more formally, scepticism comes down to the observation that there is nothing contradictory in the conjunction of statements s embodying our best grounds for a given belief p with the falsity of p: schematically, (s & $\sim p$) is not a contradiction.

Scepticism thus epitomized can informatively be represented as the opening of a gap between, on the one hand, the evidence any putative knower has for the knowledge-claims he makes, and, on the other hand, those claims themselves. Responses to scepticism variously take the form of attempts either to bridge that gap or to close it. The standard perceptual model, in which our beliefs are formed by sensory interaction with the world, postulates a causal bridge across the gap; but that bridge is alleged to be vulnerable to sceptical sabotage, so without support a causal story is insufficient. Descartes, as noted, identified the epistemological task as the need to identify a guarantee—call it X—which, added to our ordinary grounds for belief, renders them proof against scepticism and thus transforms belief into knowledge. His candidate for X was the goodness of a deity; rejecting this candidate sets us the task of finding an alternative. If an X cannot be found to support a bridge across the sceptical gap, an option is to try closing the gap—or more accurately, to show against the sceptic that there is in fact no gap at all. Both the quest for X and the closing of the gap have constituted major epistemological endeavours against scepticism in modern philosophy. In brief, some of these endeavours are as follows.

Descartes's immediate successors, as mentioned, were unpersuaded by his attempt to bridge the gap by appeal to a theistic X. John Locke made covert use of a weaker version of Descartes's view by saying that sceptical threats to the causal story can be ignored because 'the light that is set up in us shines bright enough for all our purposes'. For Locke's own purposes it does not matter whether the light was set up by God or nature; the point is that there is something X—the light—that provides a ground for regarding our ordinary knowledge-acquiring means as adequate.

Others, not content with such unsatisfactory moves, looked elsewhere for X, and claimed to find it in the thought that our system of beliefs has foundations in the form of basic self-justifying or self-evident beliefs which, in conjunction with the evidence we ordinarily have for making knowledge-claims, secure them against sceptical attack. This approach has given rise to a debate in which some participants attempt to make the notion of 'foundations' plausible, while others reject it in favour of so-called 'coherence' theories of knowledge, which have it that beliefs mutually support one another without resting on a privileged base, the ground for rejecting which is that no satisfactory candidate for foundations can, so it is claimed, be identified.

3.8. Kant and Transcendental Arguments

One stimulating way of making something like a foundationalist case was offered by Immanuel Kant in the *Critique of Pure Reason*. He regarded failure to refute scepticism a 'scandal' to philosophy, and offered the *Critique* as a solution. His thesis is that our minds are so constituted that they impose upon incoming sensory data a framework of concepts, among them those of the independent existence and the causal interactivity of the objects of perception, which transforms the data into experience properly so called. Our faculties are such that when the raw data come under the shaping influence of these concepts, they have already been given a spatial and temporal character by the nature of our sensory capacities; all our experience, considered as relating to an external world, is experience of a world arrayed in space, and all our experience, considered as relating to its received character in our minds, is arrayed in time. Upon the spatio-temporal data thus brought before our minds we stamp the 'categories'—the concepts which make experience possible by giving it its objective and determinate character. A humble analogy is afforded by the cook's dough and the pastry-cutters he uses to cut patterns in it before baking: the raw shapeless dough is the spatio-temporal sensory data, the pastry-cutters are the categorial concepts. Experience is the result of applying the latter to the former. If a sceptic asks us to justify our claims to knowledge, we do so, Kant claims, by pointing to these facts about the way experience is constituted.

Kant said that it was Hume who had suggested to him these ideas, for Hume had argued that although philosophical reason is impotent to refute scepticism, this does not matter because human nature is so constituted that we cannot help but believe the things scepticism challenges us to justify—for example, that there is an external world, that causal relations obtain between events in the world, that inductive reasoning is reliable, and so on. From this hint Kant built his view that the concepts challenged by the sceptic are constitutive features of our capacity to have any experience at all.

The style but not the substance of Kant's argument has prompted interest in more recent philosophy. The argument he employs is called a 'transcendental argument', most conveniently characterized as one which says that because *A* is a necessary condition for *B* (which means that there could be no *B* unless there were *A*), and because *B* is actually the case, it follows that *A* must be the case also. An example of such an argument in use against scepticism is as follows. One thing scepticism challenges us to do is to justify our belief in the unperceived continued existence of objects, for how do we know, the sceptic asks, that things remain in existence when we are not perceiving them? The transcendental arguer responds by saying that because we take ourselves to occupy a single unified world of spatio-temporal objects, and because on this view spatio-temporal objects have to exist unperceived in order to constitute the realm as single and unified, a belief in their unperceived continued existence is a condition of our thinking about the world and our experience of it in this way. Now, we do indeed think this way; so the belief which the sceptic challenges us to justify is thereby justified. A contemporary writer who has used something like this style of argument is P. F. Strawson.

3.9. Idealism and Phenomenalism

Parallel to these more or less Kantian ways of refuting scepticism has been another approach to arguing that there is no gap of the kind the sceptic alleges. The salient figures in this camp are George Berkeley (1685–1753) and the 'phenomenalists' of more recent times, who—allowing for differences among them, and for the fact that the two latter held these views only for part of their respective careers—include John Stuart Mill, Bertrand Russell, and A. J. Ayer.

Berkeley argued that scepticism arises from thinking that behind or beyond our sensory experiences there lies a material world. In the phrase 'material world' the word 'material' means 'made of matter', and 'matter' is a technical philosophical term supposed to denote an empirically undetectable substance believed by Berkeley's philosophical predecessors to underlie the sensorily detectable qualities of things, such as their shapes and colours. Berkeley denied the existence of matter thus conceived—it is a common misreading of him to take it that he thereby denied the existence of the world of physical objects; he did no such thing—arguing that because objects are collections of sensible qualities, and because sensible qualities are ideas, and because ideas can only exist if perceived, the existence of objects therefore consists in their being perceived; if not by finite minds such as our own, then everywhere and at all times by an infinite mind. (He thought that his refutation of scepticism was at the same time a new argument for the existence of God.) Note that Berkeley thought that this way of explaining the existence of the world is just another way of stating the traditional theological view that God creates the universe and keeps it in existence by his activity. Berkeley's way of saying that things exist 'in the mind' has led uncritical readers to suppose he means that objects exist only in one's head, which is what a subjective idealist or solipsist might try to hold. Berkeley's idealism, whether independently defensible, is not quite as unstable a view as that.

For present purposes the point to note is that Berkeley sought to refute scepticism by denying that there is a gap between experience and reality, on the grounds that experience and reality are the same thing. (He had a theory of how, despite this, we can nevertheless make mistakes, dream, and imagine.) The phenomenalists, with one very important difference, argued likewise. Their view, briefly stated, is that all our beliefs about the world are derived from what appears to us in experience (the words 'appearances' and 'phenomena' are synonyms). When we analyse the phenomena, we see that they are built out of the basic data of sense—the smallest visible colour-patches in our visual field, the least sounds in our auditory field. Out of these sense-data we 'logically construct' the familiar objects of the everyday world—chairs and tables, rocks and mountains. An alternative but equivalent way of putting this point is to say that statements about physical objects are merely convenient shorthand for longer and more complicated statements about how things seem to us in the course of employing our sensory capacities. And to say that objects continue to exist unperceived is to say that they are (in Mill's phrase) 'permanent possibilities of sensation', meaning that one would experience them if certain conditions were fulfilled.

Berkeley said that things remain in existence when not perceived by finite minds because they are perceived by a deity. The phenomenalists argue that what it means to say that things exist unperceived is to say that certain 'counterfactual conditionals' are true, namely, those that assert that those things would be perceived if any perceiver were in a position to perceive them. Counterfactuals are statements of if–then form whose verbs are in the subjunctive mood: 'If so-and-so *were* the case, such-and-such *would be* the case also'. Such conditionals are philosophically problematic because it is not clear how we should understand them. What, in particular, makes them true when they are (or seem quite obviously to be) true? We cannot invoke, say, laws of nature or other supposed regularities to explain them, for these are usually interpreted in terms of counterfactuals rather than the reverse. It is not, in short, clear that we make an advance over Berkeley's ubiquitous deity by substituting barely true counterfactuals in its place ('barely' here meaning 'true in their own right'). Berkeley's view has the modest attraction that everything in the world is actual—anything that exists *is* perceived—whereas in the phenomenalist's universe most of what exists does so as a possibility rather than an actuality, namely, a possibility of perception.

It is clear at least that one does not get phenomenalism simply by subtracting the theology from Berkeley's theory. One has to substitute a commitment to the existence of barely true counterfactuals, with, therefore, an accompanying commitment to a metaphysics of possibilia. Both Berkeley's theory and phenomenalism thus exact high prices for closing the sceptical gap.

3.10. Sceptical Epistemology versus Anti-Cartesianism

Some epistemologists, among them a number of people now working in philosophy, do not attempt to refute scepticism for the good reason that they think it (or more accurately, what it implies: either lack of knowledge, or false beliefs, in some sphere) is true or at least irrefutable. Their view might be summed up as stating that scepticism is the inevitable result of attempts to think about knowledge, so we must accept either that we are only ever going to have imperfectly justified beliefs, always subject to revision in the light of experience, or that we have to recognize that what scepticism implies, despite being irrefutable, is not a practical option, and therefore we have to live as most people anyway do, namely, by simply ignoring it. Some commentators on Hume read him as taking this latter view, and consequently label it the 'Humean' attitude to scepticism. In the books by Stroud and Michael Williams cited in the bibliography, and in the later of the two cited books by P. F. Strawson, variants of the Humean view are adopted.

Less concessive approaches are taken by others in the recent debate, among them John Dewey and Ludwig Wittgenstein. Despite large differences, these two thinkers share an interesting common view, namely, that scepticism is a product of accepting the Cartesian starting-point, that is, a starting-point among the private data of individual consciousness. If instead we start in the public world, with considerations relating to facts about the essentially public character of human thought and language, a different picture emerges.

Dewey argued that on the Cartesian model the putative knower is seen as a passive recipient of experiences, like someone sitting in the dark of a cinema watching the screen. But, he pointed out, ours is in fact a participant perspective; we are engaged in the world, and our acquisition of knowledge is the result of our activity there.

Wittgenstein argued against the very legitimacy of the Cartesian approach by showing that a private language—one that is logically available only to one speaker, which is what a Cartesian subject would need in order to begin discoursing about his private inner experience—is not possible. This is because language is a rule-governed activity, and one only succeeds in speaking a language if one follows the rules for the use of its expressions. But a solitary would-be language-user would not be able to tell the difference between actually following the rules and merely believing that he is doing so; so the language he speaks cannot be logically private to himself, but must be sharable with others. Indeed Wittgenstein argues that language can only be acquired in a public setting (he likens language-learning to the training of animals; to learn a language is to imitate the linguistic behaviour of one's teachers), which similarly weighs against the idea that a Cartesian project is even in principle feasible.

In a draft essay on the subject of scepticism and knowledge that he was writing in the last months of his life, and which was later published under the title *On Certainty*, Wittgenstein offers a response to scepticism which is not dissimilar to that offered by Hume and Kant, namely, that there are some things we have to accept in order to get on with our ordinary ways of thinking and speaking. Such propositions as that there is an external world, or that the world came into existence a long time ago, are simply not open to doubt; it is not an option for us to question them. And therefore, says Wittgenstein, neither can we say that we *know* them, because knowledge and doubt are intimately related, in that there can only be knowledge where there can be doubt, and vice versa. The propositions which cannot be doubted are the 'scaffolding' of our ordinary discourse, or, varying the metaphor, they are like the bed and banks of a river, down which the stream of ordinary discourse flows. In this sense the beliefs which scepticism attempts to challenge are not open to negotiation; which, says Wittgenstein, disposes of scepticism.

These views are suggestive; but one of the problems with the way Wittgenstein puts them is that he uses foundationalist concepts in describing the relation of 'scaffolding' propositions to ordinary ones, but repudiates foundationalism as such, and seems to allow a version of relativism by doing so (the bed and banks of the river, he says, might in time be worn away). But relativism is simply scepticism in disguise—perhaps, indeed, it is the most powerful and troubling form of scepticism; for it is the view that knowledge and truth are relative to a point of view, a time, a place, a cultural or cognitive setting: and knowledge and truth thus understood are not the *knowledge* and *truth* we are most ambitious to possess.

3.11. Concluding Remarks

Two points in this brief survey of scepticism merit special emphasis. Scepticism defines one of the central problems in epistemology, namely, the need to demonstrate how knowledge is possible. This is done—if it can be done—by meeting the challenge to show that sceptical considerations do not after all defeat our best epistemic endeavours. Implicit in this characterization are two important claims: first, that scepticism is best understood as a *challenge*, not as an agniological *claim* that we do or can know nothing; and secondly, that the best way to respond to scepticism is not by attempting to refute it on an argument-by-argument basis, but by showing how we know.

BIBLIOGRAPHY

GENERAL BIBLIOGRAPHY

Some useful general texts are these: R. Nozick, *Philosophical Explanations* (Cambridge, Mass., 1981); J. Dancy and E. Sosa, *A Companion to Epistemology* (Oxford, 1992); B. Williams, *Descartes: The Project of Pure Enquiry* (London, 1978); K. Lehrer, *Knowledge* (Oxford, 1974); L. BonJour, *The Structure of Empirical Knowledge* (Cambridge, 1985); P. F. Strawson, *Scepticism and Naturalism: Some Varieties* (London, 1985); G. Pappas and M. Swain, *Knowledge and Justification* (Ithaca, NY, 1978).

The classic texts in epistemology include Plato's *Meno* and *Theaetetus*, Descartes's *Meditations*, John Locke's *Essay Concerning Human Understanding*, Bishop Berkeley's *Principles of Human Knowledge* and *Three Dialogues between Hylas and Philonous*, David Hume's *Treatise of Human Nature* and *Enquiry Concerning Human Understanding*, and Immanuel Kant's *Critique of Pure Reason*.

One of the best short elementary books remains Bertrand Russell's *The Problems of Philosophy*.

KNOWLEDGE

ALSTON, WILLIAM (1983), 'What is Wrong with Immediate Knowledge?', *Synthese*, 55: 257–72.

BONJOUR, LAURENCE (1985), *The Structure of Empirical Knowledge* (Cambridge, Mass.).

BRUECKNER, ANTHONY (1988), 'Problems with Internalist Coherentism', *Philosophical Studies*, 54: 153–60.

CHISHOLM, RODERICK (1977), *Theory of Knowledge* (Englewood Cliffs, NJ).

DANCY, JONATHAN (1987), *Introduction to Contemporary Epistemology* (Oxford).

DESCARTES, RENÉ (1979), *Meditations on First Philosophy* (Indianapolis).

DRETSKE, FRED (1971), 'Conclusive Reasons', *Australasian Journal of Philosophy*, 49: 1–22.

FELDMAN, RICHARD (1985), 'Reliability and Justification', *Monist*, 68: 159–74.

GETTIER, EDMUND (1963), 'Is Justified True Belief Knowledge?', *Analysis*, 23.

GOLDMAN, ALVIN (1979), 'What is Justified Belief?', in George Pappas (ed.), *Justification and Knowledge* (Dordrecht).

—— (1981), 'The Internalist Conception of Justification', *Midwest Studies in Philosophy*, 5: 27–51.

—— (1986), *Epistemology and Cognition* (Cambridge, Mass.).

HARMAN, GILBERT (1973), *Thought* (Princeton, NJ).

—— (1984), 'Positive versus Negative Undermining in Belief Revision', *Nous*, 18: 39–49.

LEHRER, KEITH (1974), *Knowledge* (Oxford).

MOSER, PAUL (1985), *Empirical Justification* (Dordrecht).

POLLOCK, JOHN (1979), 'A Plethora of Epistemological Theories', in George Pappas (ed.), *Justification and Knowledge* (Dordrecht).

—— (1984), 'Reliability and Justified Belief', *Canadian Journal of Philosophy*, 14: 103–14.

—— (1986), *Contemporary Theories of Knowledge* (Totowa, NJ).

PRICE, H. H. (1936), *Truth and Corrigibility* (Oxford).

SHOPE, ROBERT (1983), *The Analysis of Knowing* (Princeton, NJ).

SOSA, ERNEST (1981), 'The Raft and the Pyramid: Coherence versus Foundations in the Theory of Knowledge', *Midwest Studies in Philosophy*, 5: 3–25.

PERCEPTION

Two useful collections of articles about perception are J. Dancy (ed.), *Perceptual Knowledge* (Oxford, 1988) and Tim Crane (ed.), *The Contents of Experience* (Cambridge, 1992). These contain two of the best introductory essays to the topics covered in this chapter: P. F. Strawson's 'Perception and its Objects', in the Dancy, and Tim Crane's introduction to the book edited by him.

R. Swartz (ed.), *Perceiving, Sensing and Knowing* (Berkeley, Calif., 1965) is also a useful collection of papers on perceiving and perceptual knowledge from earlier in this century. In particular, the papers in section II of this volume are a good survey of the debates surrounding the sense-datum theory of perception in the middle of the century.

The causal theory of perception is argued for in H. P. Grice's paper of that name, reprinted in an abridged form in the Dancy, and in a complete form in Swartz. A comprehensive discussion of recent attempts to solve the problem of causal deviancy can be found in chapter 7 of David Owens, *Causes and Coincidences* (Cambridge, 1992). A critical assessment of the argument can be found in P. F. Snowdon's 'Perception, Vision and Causation', reprinted in the Dancy.

For an extended defence of the sense-datum theory of perception, see Frank Jackson, *Perception* (Cambridge, 1977). For an adverbialist variant on Jackson's view, one might look to Moreland Perkins, *Sensing the World* (Indianapolis, 1983).

An early version of the intentional theory can be found in 'Perception and Belief', by D. M. Armstrong in the Dancy collection. The Dancy also contains a fine piece criticizing Armstrong, by Fred Dretske, 'Sensation and Perception'. A very sophisticated version of the intentional theory is presented in Christopher Peacocke's paper 'Scenarios, Concepts and Perception', in Crane.

For the disjunctive view of perception, see the Snowdon article mentioned above and 'Criteria, Defeasibility and Knowledge' by John McDowell, also reprinted in Dancy.

On the relation between perception and belief, see the paper by Roderick Chisholm in the Swartz collection, or alternatively his *The Theory of Knowledge*, 3rd edn. (Englewood Cliffs, NJ, 1989), the paper by Anthony Quinton, 'The Problem of Perception', reprinted in Swartz, and Alvin Goldman, 'Discrimination and Perceptual Knowledge', in Dancy, for a very different approach. The McDowell paper mentioned above is also highly relevant.

SCEPTICISM

The best elementary introduction to sceptical arguments remains Bertrand Russell's *The Problems of Philosophy*, chs. 1–4 (reference above). But it is essential to see the arguments in a classic setting, and for this one must read René Descartes, *Meditations on First Philosophy*, trans. J. Cottingham (Cambridge, 1986), especially the First Meditation. Useful discussions of sceptical arguments and the sense-datum theory are to be found in A. J. Ayer, *The Problem of Knowledge* (London, 1956) and J. L. Austin, *Sense and Sensibilia* (Oxford, 1961), although one should also look at Ayer's reply, 'Has Austin Refuted the Sense-Datum Theory?', *Synthese*, 17 (1967), 117–40. For responses to scepticism influenced by Kant one should see P. F. Strawson, *Individuals* (London, 1959) and *Scepticism and Naturalism: Some Varieties* (London, 1985), and A. C. Grayling, *The Refutation of Scepticism* (London, 1985). An allied line of thought is to be found in G. E. Moore, *Philosophical Papers* (London, 1959) and Ludwig Wittgenstein, *On Certainty* (Oxford, 1969). Two more recent discussions are Barry Stroud, *The Significance of Philosophical Scepticism* (Oxford, 1984) and Michael Williams, *Unnatural Doubts* (Oxford, 1991), and there is an Aristotelian Society symposium of interest: Ernest Sosa, 'Philosophical Scepticism and Epistemic Circularity' and Barry Stroud, 'Scepticism, "Externalism" and the Goal of Epistemology', in *Proceedings of the Aristotelian Society*, supp. vol. 68 (1994), 291–307. Scepticism, foundationalism, and coherence theories of knowledge are discussed in Keith Lehrer, *Knowledge* (Oxford, 1974), in useful papers collected by G. S. Pappas and Marshall Swain, *Knowledge and Justification* (Ithaca, NY, 1978), and in Marjorie Clay and Keith Lehrer (eds.), *Knowledge and Scepticism* (Boulder, Colo., 1989). For a distinctive approach to the sceptical problem which draws on Dewey and Wittgenstein, see R. Rorty, *Philosophy and the Mirror of Nature* (Princeton, NJ, 1979). A textbook which surveys the field and provides a useful bibliography is J. Dancy, *A Contemporary Introduction to Epistemology* (Oxford, 1985). For the history of scepticism, see M. Burnyeat (ed.), *The Sceptical Tradition* (Berkeley, Calif., 1983) and R. Popkin, *The History of Skepticism* (Berkeley, Calif., 1979).

2

PHILOSOPHICAL LOGIC

Mark Sainsbury

INTRODUCTION

If we know that all rich people are happy and that John is rich, we can infer that John is happy. If we know that the potatoes have been boiling for twenty minutes, we can infer that they are cooked.

These are examples of apparently different kinds of inference. The first we can call a *deductively valid* inference, marked by the fact that if what we infer *from* is true, it is quite impossible for what we infer *to* to be false. The second we can call an *inductively strong* inference, marked by the fact that, although what we infer *from* gives a good reason for what we infer *to*, it is not a conclusive reason. At high altitudes, water boils at a lower temperature, and cooking-time is prolonged; and even at normal altitudes, some potatoes are very tough!

This essay concerns reasoning of the first kind: reasoning that aspires to be deductively valid. One group of questions relates to the nature of the concepts used by logicians: truth, logical truth, validity, entailment. Of these, we will be dealing just with the first, in Section 6.

Another group of questions concerns the analysis of idioms which are important in reasoning, for example, conditionals. An especially important feature of reasoning is reference; and it is this feature which is the main topic of this essay. A connected topic, to be discussed in Section 5, is necessity.

A logician studies one feature of reasoning which makes it worth while: that it be truth-preserving, or *valid*. (For a more detailed account, see Sainsbury 1991, ch. 1.) Typically a piece of reasoning moves from one or more statements which are, at least provisionally, taken for granted to some other statement. The starting-points are called the *premisses*, the end-point the *conclusion*. A set of statements consisting of some premisses and a conclusion is called an *argument*. A standard definition of the validity of an argument is this:

> An argument is valid if and only if it is impossible for all the premisses to be true, yet the conclusion false.

The study of validity involves studying reference. Here is an example to show this. Is the argument from the premiss 'Napoleon was dynamic' to 'Someone was dynamic' valid? That is, is it impossible for the premiss to be true, yet the conclusion false? We are inclined to answer 'Yes'. In that case, should we not give the same answer when the question is asked about the argument from the premiss 'The greatest prime number does not exist' to the conclusion 'Something does not exist'? We ought to have some unease about answering 'Yes' in this second case: for the premiss is true, and validity preserves truth, so the answer would commit us to the view that something does not exist; which seems at best strange and at worst crazy.

One thing you should be able to do after studying logic is steer your way through the quite complex issues raised in the preceding paragraph. It is some advantage to be familiar with elementary formal logic, as expounded in such books as Guttenplan (1988); Hodges (1978); Lemmon (1964).

The first section of this chapter looks at what appear to be the most obvious examples of words whose job is to refer, names like 'Napoleon' and 'France'. You will need to understand the theories of John Stuart Mill (1843), Gottlob Frege (1892*a*), Bertrand Russell (1912), and Saul Kripke (1972).

The second section looks at definite descriptions, expressions of the form 'The so-and-so', for example 'The first Emperor of France'. These appear to be expressions whose job is to refer, but Bertrand Russell, in his 'theory of descriptions', argued that they are not. You need to be familiar with Russell's theory (1905, 1919), with his arguments for it, and with objections to it (the main ones are reviewed in Sainsbury (1979, ch. 4), but you will also need to look at some of the original sources of the objections).

The third section examines a problem about existence. If we say that something does not exist, we seem thereby to presuppose that it does exist. You will need to understand a well-known theory on this which stems from Russell (1918–19, lecture 5), and also a recent new theory (Evans 1982, ch. 10).

Section 4 concerns identity statements, and in particular whether true ones are invariably necessarily true. This introduces the concept of necessity, which is studied in more detail in Section 5. The main texts are: Gibbard (1975); Kripke (1972); Lewis (1986). The going gets quite rough in places (especially 5.2–4), but bear in mind that you don't have to have detailed knowledge of all the topics discussed here.

Section 6 is about truth. Here I have been a guide in the most superficial sense. I have tried to give an account of where some of the main debates lie, without taking you at all far in any of them. If one of the aspects arouses your interest, it will be essential to follow up some of the suggested reading.

A good number of the articles you need, especially for the first three sections, are reprinted in Moore (1993).

One of the most important reasons to study philosophy is to learn how to form and defend views of your own. A view of your own does not have to be a view no one has ever held before. In logic, new views are hard to come by. A view counts as your own if you believe it and are willing to defend it. In what follows, you will find many opposing views presented; you will have to decide which to make your own.

Sometimes, especially early in one's studies, one does not feel able to decide which of two opposed theories is correct. However, one should be able to make lesser decisions: does this argument decisively establish or refute this theory? Could an objection be avoided by some modification of the theory? Can one not distinguish at least two versions of the doctrine that so-and-so? Asking and answering these questions is essential, if studying philosophy is to be worth while.

1. NAMES

1.1. Mill

Mill (1843, book 1, chapters 1, 2)

Names like 'Napoleon' and 'France' seem to be the clearest cases of expressions whose job is to refer to things in the world. The most straightforward theory is that this is all that needs be said: 'Napoleon' refers to Napoleon, 'France' to France. More or less this straightforward theory was advanced by John Stuart Mill.[1]

Mill distinguished between general names, like 'white' as it occurs in 'This rose is white', and singular names, like 'Dartmouth' and 'The present Prime Minister of Great Britain'. A singular name is meant to apply to, or denote, just one thing, whereas a general name may, and typically does, apply to, or denote, many. Some names, like 'white' and 'The present Prime Minister of Great Britain', are *connotative*: they connote an attribute, and they denote all and only those things which possess the attribute. Thus 'white' denotes all the white things: and it denotes each one in virtue of that thing possessing the attribute which 'white' connotes, namely, whiteness.

A *proper name*, for Mill, is a non-connotative singular name, like 'Dartmouth'. We may, indeed, have had a reason for calling something by one name rather than another. We may call a man 'John' because that was his father's name, and we may call Dartmouth 'Dartmouth' because it stands at the mouth of the river Dart.

> But it is no part of the signification of the word John that the father of the person so called bore the same name, nor even of the word Dartmouth, to be situated at the mouth of the Dart. If sand should choke up the mouth of the river, or an earthquake change its course, and remove it to a distance from the town, the name of the town would not necessarily be changed. . . . Names are attached to the objects themselves, and are not dependent on the continuance of any attribute of the object. (Mill 1843: 26)

Mill is making two points against the suggestion that proper names are connotative. One is that the candidates for being the attributes connoted do not determine the name's denotation. The other is that one can understand a name without knowing the candidates for its connotation. (Which of the two examples, 'John', 'Dartmouth', is best fitted to make which of these two points?)

Mill's specific points seem good: the purported connotations of 'John' and 'Dartmouth' are unsatisfactory. But in order to establish that proper names are not connotative, Mill has two generalizations to make. First, he needs to show

---

[1] John Stuart Mill (1806–73), British philosopher, politician, and social reformist, arrested for distributing birth-control literature. Best known for his political writings (esp. 1859, 1861, 1863), and as the father of liberalism.

that there are no other and better candidates for the connotation of 'John' and 'Dartmouth'. (Can you think of one?) Second, he would then have to show that this holds for proper names generally, and not just for the chosen examples.

One might offer Mill the following more general argument: two people who use a name may associate quite different bodies of information with it, so that there might be nothing common to each which could serve as a shared connotation. This point is effective only if knowledge of connotation needs to be common to successful communicators. (Is Mill committed to this?)

Mill's theory faces two conspicuous problems: dealing with names like 'Zeus' or 'Santa Claus' which don't refer; and dealing with 'Frege's puzzle'.

A name which doesn't refer doesn't have a denotation. Given Mill's account, a name doesn't have a connotation either. So on Mill's theory a name without denotation has no semantic properties. This means that it ought not to be intelligible as part of a language. Yet it would seem that bearerless names have a perfectly intelligible use in our language.

Frege's puzzle concerns identity, and led to the development of his theory of sense (*Sinn*) and reference (*Bedeutung*).

1.2. Frege

Frege (1892a)

Frege[2] claimed that there is no guarantee that two names for the same thing can be used interchangeably; yet this ought to be guaranteed if the only relevant feature of a name is its reference. Let's suppose that 'Hesperus' and 'Phosphorus' refer to the same heavenly body. The story is that 'Hesperus' was a name given to the planet Venus on the basis of its being conspicuous in the evening; and 'Phosphorus' was a name given to the same planet on the basis of its being conspicuous in the morning (in a different part of the sky, at a different time of year).[3] The phrases 'the Evening Star' and 'the Morning Star' serve similar purposes. The ancient astronomers didn't realize that there was a single heavenly body (a planet rather than a star) which appeared in different ways.

Now compare the statements:

(1) Hesperus is Hesperus.
(2) Hesperus is Phosphorus.

---

[2] Gottlob Frege (1848–1935), mathematician at Jena University. Worked all his life as an academic. Espoused 'logicism' (the view that mathematics is reducible to logic) but in a form that Russell, in 1903, showed to be contradictory. (Russell wrote to tell Frege, who was shattered by the news.) Now regarded as one of the greatest philosophers of recent times. Dummett says (1973a, preface) that he was shocked to discover that Frege was a racist (anti-Semite).

[3] It's hard to remember which is which! I'm told that there is an etymological connection between 'Hesperus' and 'vespers'. Whether or not this is correct, I personally find it helpful.

These seem to say something different. (1) is trivial, but (2) could express valuable new information: the two statements 'obviously differ in cognitive value'. Yet they differ only in that 'Phosphorus' has replaced one occurrence of 'Hesperus'. Frege concluded that two names for the same thing cannot be used interchangeably, and that there is therefore something more to how a name functions than what it refers to.

Frege called this additional feature of names their sense (*Sinn*). In his article 'Über Sinn und Bedeutung', he starts by characterizing the sense of a name as 'the mode of presentation of the thing designated'. He goes on to suggest that 'the sense of a proper name is grasped by everybody who is sufficiently familiar with the language' (1892*a*: 158). There are further theses: sense determines reference (that is, expressions which agree in their sense must also agree in their reference) and both sense and reference can be extended to whole sentences: the sense of a whole sentence is a thought, and its reference is a truth-value, the True or the False, as the case may be.

Frege's argument about 'Hesperus' and 'Phosphorus' establishes that there is something more to a name than its reference, but this leaves open that the additional feature, rather than being Fregean sense, is merely syntactic, or that it is something which varies from person to person in a way which is inconsistent with its being a stable public feature of language. This point is urged by Salmon (1986). We need to see Frege's initial argument as establishing the smaller point, that there is something more to a name than its reference; the article as a whole is intended to lend support to the larger claim that the something more is sense.

Frege tells us that he had earlier (1879) held a view which he now rejects. The argument comes in the second part of the first page of the article, and the first part of the second page. It is not easy to follow, but here is one interpretation.

Frege's earlier theory is that an identity sentence like 'Hesperus is Phosphorus' can be regarded as saying that the two names 'Hesperus' and 'Phosphorus' refer to the same thing. On this view, the 'metalinguistic view', identity is a relation between names ('the signs themselves would be under discussion'). Arguably, this view allows for a difference in cognitive value between 'Hesperus is Hesperus' and 'Hesperus is Phosphorus'; for perhaps it is trivial that 'Hesperus' and 'Hesperus' refer to the same object but more interesting that 'Hesperus' and 'Phosphorus' refer to the same object. This metalinguistic view, however, is unacceptable. It would entail that in identity statements we are not really talking about the world, but about language, and so the view could not explain our ability to use such statements to express proper knowledge of the world ('In that case the sentence $a = b$ would no longer refer to the subject-matter, but only to its mode of designation; we would express no proper knowledge by its means'). Moreover, the relevant facts about names are 'arbitrary': it is just a matter of convention that we use 'Hesperus' and 'Phosphorus' to refer to the same thing, but it is not a matter of convention that Hesperus is Phosphorus.

On my interpretation, then, Frege takes his earlier view to be the metalinguistic one, and he now rejects it for the reasons given: it makes identity statements contingent and arbitrary and about matters that are fixed by linguistic convention, rather than about the world.

For Frege, a name which refers (has *Bedeutung*) also has sense. Does every name which has sense also have *Bedeutung*? Frege's answer appears clear: 'The expression "the least rapidly convergent series" has a sense but demonstrably nothing is its *Bedeutung*' (1892a: 159). This interpretation has been challenged by Gareth Evans[4] (1982), who argues that, although Frege definitely allowed for sense without reference in fictional contexts, we should not use this to infer that sense without reference is genuinely possible. To say that a fictional name like 'Odysseus' lacks reference is to say that it lacks any *real* reference; the name was certainly supposed to have a reference in the story. However, one might also suggest that the name lacks any *real* sense: rather, to tell the story is to pretend that the name has sense. The view which Evans attributes to Frege is thus that sense and reference always go together: if you have fictional or pretended sense, you have fictional or pretended reference; if you have real sense, you have real reference.

The view is certainly of interest; and perhaps it is what Frege should have said. However, at the very least he did not say it all the time, as the quote about the least rapidly convergent series shows.[5]

We can now see how Frege's theory addresses the two puzzles we raised in connection with Mill. Frege used the distinction between sense and reference to explain the puzzle of identity: truth or falsehood is settled by reference, but cognitive value by sense; and, on the orthodox interpretation offered here, the possibility of sense without reference explains how names lacking denotation may none the less have a sound semantic role.

One could accuse Frege of treating sense as whatever is needed to explain the identity puzzle; in which case the explanation is inadequate, being a mere relabelling of the problem. For Frege's explanation to be satisfactory, he must give an account of sense which goes beyond characterizing it as whatever explains the puzzle.

Frege certainly does specify independent features of sense. As noted, he starts by saying that the sense of a name is the way in which it presents its reference, and goes on to say, among other things, that the sense of a name is grasped by everyone who understands the language. However, these features generate a

---

[4] Probably the best philosopher of his generation. Taught at Oxford during the 1970s, and died of cancer in 1981 when still in his early thirties; a tragedy, and a great loss to the subject.

[5] On other occasions, Frege's words give more support to Evans, for example: 'A sentence containing a proper name lacking *Bedeutung* is neither true nor false; if it expresses a thought at all, then that thought belongs to fiction' (1979: 194). In other words, if a sentence contains a name without *Bedeutung*, then it lacks *Sinn* (except for the pretend thoughts of fiction); which can only be explained by the fact that a name lacking *Bedeutung* lacks *Sinn*.

worrying tension. The same thing may well be presented differently to different people; yet, intuitively, what one must grasp, in order to understand a name, is the same for everyone who understands it. Mode of presentation thus tends to become idiosyncratic, whereas what must be grasped, it seems, ought not to be.

Frege notes this in 'On Sense and Reference' (compare also the somewhat more agonized discussion in Frege 1918):

in the case of an actual proper name such as 'Aristotle' opinions as to the sense may differ. It might, for instance, be taken to be the following: the pupil of Plato and teacher of Alexander the Great. Anybody who does this will attach another sense to the sentence 'Aristotle was born in Stagira' than will a man who takes as the sense of the name: the teacher of Alexander the Great who was born in Stagira. (1892*a*: 158)

Frege goes on to say that these variations can be tolerated, so long as there is no variation in reference, but that they ought to be eliminated from a perfect language. The tolerant first part of this remark entails either that some names, like 'Aristotle', have no unequivocal use, or else that for these names understanding them is not to be identified with grasping their sense.

I believe that Frege never resolved this tension adequately.[6] The crucial thing at the moment is to feel the different pulls; you might find it useful to try to state them to yourself as clearly as you can.

1.3. Russell

Russell (1912, 1918–19)

Russell[7] has a theory of names which promises release from the tension. In order to tell you what it is, I must give a little background.

To Russell it seemed obvious that a name ought to behave in the way Mill described. (I don't think he mentions Mill in this connection; but we know he read his work.) He says: 'the name itself is merely a means of pointing to the thing' (1918–19: 245); and he rushes with enthusiasm for two of the 'problems' which, we have noted, arise for this view: existence and identity.

'If ["Romulus"] were really a name, the question of existence could not arise, because a name has got to name something or it is not a name' (1918–19: 243). Russell concludes that 'Romulus', despite appearances, isn't a name, since the question whether Romulus existed does arise (he is a mere legend). We thus

---

[6] A standard thing to say is that Frege had no need to worry about it, given his overall concerns with mathematics and artificial languages, rather than natural languages. There is something in this, but not enough to explain the depth of Frege's concern in his (1918).

[7] Bertrand Russell (1872–1970), British philosopher and mathematician, popular writer, Nobel prize-winner for literature, impish radio personality, outspoken champion of good causes, imprisoned for pacifism (1918) and for demonstrating against nuclear weapons (1961). Never had a permanent teaching-post in a university. As unlike the cloistered and academic Frege as could be imagined.

have a new kind of theory: names are divided into at least two categories, and 'Romulus' does not belong with those which function in the way Mill envisaged.

We find a similar structure in the case of identity: 'If one thing has two names, you make exactly the same assertion whichever of the two names you use.' Hence, if 'Hesperus' and 'Phosphorus' were really names, you would make exactly the same assertion whether you said 'Hesperus is Hesperus' or 'Hesperus is Phosphorus'. This would give us a fresh class of expressions to exclude from the category of names; or rather from the category of 'names in the narrow logical sense of a word whose meaning is a particular' (1918–19: 201)—as I shall say, following custom, 'logically proper names'.

This test will exclude just about everything we count as a name from the category of logically proper names. Even if something has only one name at the moment, we could easily enough introduce another, and arrange matters so that Frege's puzzle could arise. This little piece of social engineering, it seems, should not have altered the original character of the name. So, even before the rival name was introduced, the name was not a logically proper one. Going down this route, it seems one would be forced to say that there are no logically proper names at all.

Russell comes close: 'The only words one does use as names in the logical sense are words like "this" or "that"' (1918–19: 201). Discussing these words leads to a whole new range of issues. But we must return to our original track: words like 'Aristotle', concerning which Frege's view leads to a certain tension from which, I claimed, Russell could release us.

To see how, we need to turn our back on the logically proper names 'this' and 'that' in order to understand Russell's theory of 'ordinary proper names'. (Again following custom, I use 'ordinary' to mark these names out from the logically proper ones.) On the question of what Russell's theory was, a myth has grown up. In this section I will tell the real story, with occasional indications of what the myth is; in the next I will describe the myth.

'Common words, even proper names, are usually really descriptions' (Russell 1912: 29). Russell cannot have meant this literally. A description, that is, a definite description, is a phrase of the form 'the so-and-so'; but it is obvious that, for example, 'Aristotle' is not a phrase of this form (its first letter is an 'a', not a 't', etc.). The myth is that we should read Russell as holding that names are synonymous with definite descriptions. However, the next sentence in the text sows doubts about whether this was what Russell intended: 'That is to say, the thought in the mind of a person using a proper name correctly can generally only be expressed explicitly if we replace the proper name by a description.' The 'meaning' of a proper name ought to be something public and common to all users of the name. We cannot tell from the sentence just quoted whether Russell thinks that 'the thought in the mind' of the user of a name will have analogous features: whether all users of a name will have thoughts which are the same in the relevant respect. However, the subsequent sentence makes Russell's position unequivocal: 'Moreover the description required to express the thought will vary for different people, or for the same person at different times. The only thing constant (so long as the name is rightly used) is the object to which the name applies' (1912: 29–30).

So Russell's theory is that a name is associated with a variety of different descriptions: the various descriptions needed explicitly to report the thoughts of the various users of the name. This variability shows that the descriptions cannot, for Russell, give the public meaning of the name, for meaning should be common through the linguistic community.

I promised that Russell's theory would do something to resolve the tension we found in Frege: associated descriptions, which are useful for explaining differences in cognitive value and other features of use, appear to be idiosyncratic, whereas the sense or meaning of a name ought to be constant among speakers. The role Russell envisages for descriptions is entirely idiosyncratic. It does justice at best to one side of the tension.

However, Russell indicates in an ingenious way how the constant aspect of names can be integrated with the variable one. We have already seen the first hint: 'The only thing constant (so long as the name is rightly used) is the object to which the name applies.'

A name can be said to have a public reference in a community provided that something satisfies all (or most) of the descriptions the users of the name associate with it. Given this notion, we can say that people succeed in communicating, through the use of a name, provided they are both parties to a community in which it has a public reference; and we can say that someone who utters a sentence of the form '*n* is so-and-so', for some name, *n*, where object *o* is the public reference of *n*, speaks truly iff[8] *o* is so-and-so.

For example, suppose I utter the words 'Bismarck was an astute diplomat'. As I use the name 'Bismarck', the thought in my mind may be best described as that *the first Chancellor of Germany* is an astute diplomat. However, I realize that you may associate the name with a different description, perhaps 'the most powerful man in Europe'. So when I utter my sentence, I am not trying to get you to share my thought; rather I am trying to get you to have a thought, concerning Bismarck (however you think of him), that he is an astute diplomat. My intentions would be satisfied if you realized that I had tried to say, of the most powerful man in Europe, that he was an astute diplomat. I think this is how we should interpret the somewhat obscure passages on and near p. 31 of Russell (1912).

Russell does justice to the tension we saw in Frege in the following way: the

---

[8] 'Iff' abbreviates 'if and only if'.

idiosyncratic elements are allowed to be just that, and are not required to have any semantic role of their own; however, they are connected with public reference, and this has the stability and constancy to be the meaning of a proper name.

Russell's view may be able to do justice to Frege's puzzle (about identity and cognitive value) but it is less well placed to deal with issues about existence and bearerless names.

On the first of these points, Russell can explain the difference between 'Hesperus is Hesperus' and 'Hesperus is Phosphorus' in terms of the different descriptions associated with the two names. The explanation need not run at the level of truth or reference, but can just be that the sentences will typically be associated with different thoughts. (Indeed, Russell can allow for a way of hearing 'Paderewski is Paderewski' as having cognitive value, which is as it should be: cf. Kripke 1979.)

In Russell's account, the public reference is the stable element, and a bearerless name will not have a public reference. This means that we cannot guarantee that any one thing will be said by two utterances of 'Moses did not exist'. We cannot guarantee that there is an object in common, because we cannot guarantee that there is a public reference (we cannot guarantee that anyone satisfies associated descriptions like 'uniquely led the Israelites out of Egypt'); and we cannot guarantee that there is a description in common, because descriptions may vary from speaker to speaker. So such an utterance may have no public semantics.

It is not obvious that this is a decisive objection, for it is not obvious that in such cases there has to be a semantic account. We could say that if the associated descriptions do not anchor the name to the world, its use is defective (unless intended as fictional, which raises different issues).

Frege, as here interpreted, can classify bearerless names simply as cases of sense without reference; but this puts pressure on the positive nature of sense. It's supposed to be a way of thinking of something; but, as we've already seen, it is not easy to cut ways of thinking coarsely enough to ensure a single way for each apparently unequivocal name like 'Moses'. So although there are some difficulties here for Russell, it is not as if Frege's alternative is obviously better.

1.4. Kripke

Kripke (1972, lectures 1, 2)

Kripke[9] has made an important and widely accepted claim about names: he says that they are 'rigid designators': they designate the same through possible

---

[9] Saul Kripke (b. 1940). Child prodigy, published brilliant formal logical results in his teens, took the world by storm with his lectures 'Naming and Necessity' in the 1960s.

changes in circumstances. He writes rather as if this entails that a view he calls the description theory of names, and which he attributes to Frege and to Russell, is wrong. I will start by looking at the positive claim, and will then turn to the criticisms of Frege and Russell.

When Kripke gave the lectures 'Naming and Necessity', many philosophers, under Quine's influence, regarded modal notions (of necessity, of possibility, and so on) with suspicion. Quine had called them creatures of darkness. Kripke's early work offers a possible worlds formal semantics for a modal language (see Section 5 below). The lectures, among other more explicit agenda, put modality back on the map.

In particular, the notion of a rigid designator is a modal notion. The description 'the first Emperor of France' designates Napoleon. But things might have been otherwise. Had the French Revolution never broken out, there might have been no French emperor, or if there had been one it might well not have been Napoleon. In the one case, the description 'the first Emperor of France' would designate no one; in the other case, the other person. The description is thus not rigid, since what it designates may vary with possible changes of circumstance, even holding the meaning of the expression constant.

By contrast, 'Napoleon' seems to be a rigid designator. We could describe a situation in which Napoleon exists but is not designated by 'the first Emperor of France'; but we seem not to be able to describe a situation in which he exists but is not designated by 'Napoleon'. We can imagine a situation in which he had another name, but that is not the point: we need to imagine using our expression 'Napoleon' as we do, yet, because of altered circumstances, it not designating Napoleon. We can even use his name to describe a possible situation in which no one bears that name, thus: it might have been that Napoleon was called Jean-Michel, and that no one in the Bonaparte family was called Napoleon.

The phenomenon is claimed to apply quite generally to names, and we can express it more generally (cf. Peacocke 1973). A singular term, s, counts as a rigid designator as it occurs in an utterance of '. . . s . . .' iff for some object o, necessarily the utterance is true iff o satisfies '. . . ζ . . .'. We will work through this definition, showing first how it rules 'the first Emperor of France' non-rigid, and 'Napoleon' rigid; in doing this, the technicalities will be explained.

Consider my utterance now of 'The first Emperor of France was born in Corsica'. To find out whether the singular term (fit to be the subject of a verb) 'the first Emperor of France' is a rigid designator, we need to find whether there is an object upon which its truth-condition depends (to use a somewhat metaphorical phrase). The utterance is in fact true, thanks to Napoleon's having been born in Corsica, so if there is an object upon which the truth-condition depends, it must be Napoleon. So Napoleon would have to satisfy the condition (expressed on the variable o in the definition) that, necessarily, the utterance is true iff Napoleon satisfies 'ζ was born in Corsica'. But he does not satisfy this condition, for if he had not become Emperor, as he certainly would not had he been killed at the Battle of Mondovi, the truth or falsehood of the utterance would have had nothing to do with him. So 'the first Emperor of France' is not a rigid designator. (Should we count the utterance false, if France never had an Emperor?)

Now consider an utterance of 'Napoleon was born in Corsica'. Is there an object upon which the truth-condition of this sentence depends? The answer appears to be yes: Napoleon. Necessarily, the utterance is true iff he was born in Corsica. With respect to no circumstance could the truth of the utterance be dependent on anyone else.[10]

To say that a name is a rigid designator leaves a good deal unsaid or unexplained. We have to explain Frege's puzzle about identity. We have to explain bearerless names: even if they count, trivially, as rigid designators, they must differ in some not merely syntactic way. However, Kripke writes as if the claim that names are rigid designators should come as bad news for theorists such as Frege and Russell. Why is this? The short Kripkean answer seems to be as follows: Frege and Russell believe that, for each proper name, there is some description which gives its meaning, or at least, fixes its reference; and that this description is a non-rigid designator. But the meaning of a rigid designator could never be identified with that of a non-rigid designator. So the theory of Frege and Russell is wrong.

The problem with the argument is that it is doubtful if anyone has held the view attacked. We saw that Frege toys with descriptions to illustrate the sense of 'Aristotle', but he does not say that a name's sense could be given only by a description. Perhaps the only way to express the sense of a name is to use the name itself. It is true that 'Hesperus' designates Phosphorus, but in order to say what it designates in a way which reveals its sense we should say that it designates Hesperus. If we use this rule to interpret speakers (treat them as using 'Hesperus' to designate Hesperus) we will get correct results; better results than if we tried to interpret them as using 'Hesperus' to designate Phosphorus. The differences would emerge in, for example, the contrasting cases of Frege's puzzle. We should not say of someone who has uttered the words 'Hesperus is Phosphorus' that he has said that Hesperus is Hesperus.[11]

If an account of this kind can be made to work, Fregean sense can be liberated from descriptions, and so Kripke's argument would become irrelevant.

Kripke's argument is also irrelevant to Russell's position. Russell's main idea

---

[10] At this point it might be worth considering whether the view of ordinary proper names which I attributed to Russell in the previous section rules them rigid designators: 'someone who utters a sentence of the form "n is so-and-so", for some name, n, where object o is the public reference of n, speaks truly iff o is so-and-so'.

[11] I have in mind McDowell's version of Frege's position in McDowell (1977).

was that descriptions are related to names in that they can be used to make more explicit what is in the thinker's mind when using a name. This is not the relation of synonymy. The very brief account Russell gives of how names contribute to truth-conditions suggests that he is treating them, in effect, as rigid designators. The truth-conditions of an utterance of 'Bismarck was an astute diplomat' are supposed to depend on the public reference of 'Bismarck', which is in fact Bismarck. Using the language as it now is, 'Bismarck' will refer to Bismarck even with respect to a situation in which he is not first Chancellor. Thus Russell can allow for the truth of the supposition that even if the French had won the Franco-Prussian war, so that no German Empire was formally constituted, and thus there was no first Chancellor, Bismarck would still count as an astute diplomat.

Kripke's lecture reads as if an objection to the thesis that each proper name is synonymous with some definite description is that definite descriptions are not rigid designators. The point I have mostly been making so far is that neither Frege nor Russell can be credited with the thesis in question, and in particular Russell's view has logical features which ought to appeal to Kripke: he treats proper names as, in effect, rigid designators. However, Kripke has other points to make against theories which, like Russell's, make use of descriptions at some point in the account of names, and I will consider two of them.

'The man in the street ... may ... use the name "Feynman". When asked he will say: well he's a physicist or something. He may not think that this picks out anyone uniquely. I still think he uses the name "Feynman" as a name for Feynman' (Kripke 1972: 292). The objection is that some users may fail to associate a name with any description. Hence such users cannot be having the kinds of thought which Russell envisaged.

Russell does best to deny that such cases are possible; and he makes a particular suggestion for finding a description which is likely to be applicable in a wide range of cases:

in order to discover what is actually in my mind when I judge about Julius Caesar, we must substitute for the proper name a description made up of some of the things I know about him. (A description which will often serve to express my thought is 'the man whose name was *Julius Caesar*'. For whatever else I may have forgotten about him, it is plain that when I mention him I have not forgotten that that was his name.) (Russell 1911: 160)

It seems reasonable to me to say that if Kripke's ignorant speaker could not even attain some description like 'the person (or famous physicist) called "Feynman"', he cannot be regarded as someone who really understands this name.

Kripke objects to this manœuvre on grounds of circularity. Certainly it would be circular to say that every speaker understands a name through grasp of such a description. But there is no need for Russell or anyone else to say this.

Another of Kripke's objections is more serious. Gödel is known to many of us as the person who first proved the incompleteness of arithmetic; so it is simply a psychological fact that this name is, for many, associated with that description. Kripke asks us to suppose that Schmidt first proved the incompleteness of arithmetic, and that Gödel passed off the proof as his own. Given that we associate the name 'Gödel' with the description 'the person who discovered the incompleteness of arithmetic', then an utterance by us of 'Gödel was born in Vienna' would be true iff Schmidt was born in Vienna. Yet intuitively we have referred to Gödel, not Schmidt, and we speak truly just in case Gödel was born in Vienna; Schmidt's birthplace is irrelevant. (Cf. Kripke 1972: 294.)

This raises difficult issues. Russell allows that there might be interesting distinctions to be made among users of a name. Thus he suggests that Bismarck might be able to use the name 'Bismarck' for himself, without benefit of descriptions, whereas we are not so favourably placed. This is not far removed from a distinction made by Evans between 'producers' and 'consumers' in the practice of using a name (cf. Evans 1982, ch. 11). Producers have contact with the named object; consumers have no such contact, and thus have to defer in their usage to producers. For names of the long dead, we are all consumers; for names of contemporary fame, some of us are producers but most are consumers. For names of contemporary nobodies, there are producers but few consumers.

In terms of this distinction, it is not unreasonable to require that consumers show a special deference in their usage. Returning to Kripke's Gödel–Schmidt case, we consumers in the practice of using the name 'Gödel' might be described as allowing the description 'the person called "Gödel"' to *dominate* any other descriptions they associate with the name in the following sense: if there were to be a divergence of reference, the description just mentioned should be regarded as giving the correct reference. Here the notion of being *called* 'Gödel' would be unpacked in terms of the distinction between consumers and producers: the practices of producers would trump those of consumers in determining who is called so-and-so.

Such an account goes well beyond anything which can be found in Russell, and would require detailed fine-tuning before it could be seriously assessed. It shows, however, that despite misunderstanding Russell on some points, Kripke does provide an important and substantive objection to Russell's theory; but an objection which someone who adopted Russell's basic standpoint, in which names are associated with descriptions but are not their meanings, might be able to accommodate.

FURTHER READING: Evans (1982, chs. 1, 2, 11); McCulloch (1989).

2. DESCRIPTIONS

2.1. Russell's Theory

Russell (1905; 1919, ch. 16); Sainsbury (1979)

Russell thought that although definite descriptions, phrases of the form 'the so-and-so', look as if they function rather like names, to refer to things, their real function is quite different: they are quantifier phrases, not referring ones. A sentence like 'The first Emperor of France was born in Corsica' does not function at all like 'Napoleon was born in Corsica'. Its function is more similar to a sentence like 'No Emperor was born in Corsica'. It is a kind of generalization.

More exactly, a sentence of the form 'The so-and-so is *F*' (for arbitrary predicate '*F*') is to be analysed as follows:

(1) There is at least one so-and-so.
(2) There is at most one so-and-so.
(3) Whatever is so-and-so is *F*.

It is important that the word 'the' does not occur in this analysis. It is equivalent to the more compact:

There is exactly one so-and-so and it is *F*.[12]

Russell thought that 'exists' is not a predicate (for reasons to be examined in Section 3 below), so that a sentence of the form 'The so-and-so exists' requires a different analysis, namely:

(1) There is at least one so-and-so.
(2) There is at most one so-and-so.

In the more compact form:

There is exactly one so-and-so.

'The present King of France is bald' is true iff there is exactly one King of France at present and he is bald; it is false, since there is no present King of France. 'The inhabitant of London is prosperous' is true iff there is exactly one inhabitant of London and that person is prosperous; it is false, since there is more than one inhabitant of London.[13] 'The golden mountain does not exist' is true iff it is not the case that there is exactly one thing which is both a mountain and made of gold; it is true, since it is not the case that there is at least one such thing. Russell gave these as examples of how his theory delivered intuitively correct results.

---

[12] In symbols, replacing 'so-and-so' by '*G*': $\exists x(Gx \,\&\, \forall y(Gy \rightarrow y = x) \,\&\, Fx)$.

[13] These inferences depend upon equating 'false' with 'not true'. Arguably, this is not always acceptable, e.g. in the case of vagueness.

As far as I am aware, Russell gave only one direct argument for his theory. (The other arguments are indirect: they show that the theory can solve certain puzzles, or that other theories run into difficulties. We'll be discussing some of these in a subsequent section, 2.3.) The direct argument is simple: Russell claims that the only difference between 'a' and 'the' is that the latter implies uniqueness (1919: 176). Since 'a' is to be understood in terms of the existential quantifier, so that 'I met a man' is analysed as 'There is something human which I met', 'the' must be the existential quantifier with uniqueness added; which is indeed just what Russell's theory offers.

As an argument, this will not persuade the main source of opposition. Opponents see definite descriptions as really referring expressions, so they would not agree that the only difference between 'a' and 'the' is that 'the' implies uniqueness.

2.2. Names and Descriptions Contrasted

Russell (1918–19, lecture 6)

> The first thing to realize about a definite description is that it is not a name.
>
> (Russell 1918–19: 244)

In the context, Russell means by 'name' a logically proper name, in other words, 'this' or 'that'. The point of his claim here is to insist that descriptions are not referring expressions. To establish this, he uses the following arguments.

2.2.1. *Understanding*

> If you understand the English language, you would understand the mean-ing of the phrase 'The author of *Waverley*' if you had never heard it before, whereas you would not understand the meaning of 'Scott' if you had never heard it before because to know the meaning of a name is to know who it is applied to.
>
> (Russell 1918–19: 245)

Russell's point here is, I believe, correct for at least some descriptions. Names are semantically simple: understanding them is not a function of understanding their parts, for their parts do not contribute to their meaning. (There is indeed an occurrence of the letters 'rat' in 'Socrates', but this has no bearing on the mean-ing of 'Socrates'.) By contrast, descriptions are by definition semantically com-plex, and in at least some cases (e.g. 'the greatest prime number') it is plain that we understand them purely in virtue of understanding the words of which they are composed. Nothing like acquaintance with the denotation (if any) is required.

2.2.2. Stipulation

We can assign a name by stipulation; but no stipulation can make 'The author of *Waverley*' denote Scott; rather, Scott has to take up his pen, and write the novel without a collaborator (Russell 1918–19: 245). This point again appears correct, and is a corollary of the semantic simplicity of names as contrasted with the semantic complexity of descriptions.

2.2.3. Identity

> If one thing has two names, you make exactly the same assertion whichever of the two names you use.
>
> (Russell 1918–19: 245)

But the assertion 'Scott is *c*', where '*c*' is any name for Scott, is not the same as the assertion 'Scott is the author of *Waverley*', for the former is an uninformative tautology and the latter is not. So 'the author of *Waverley*' is not a name.

Russell assumes that names which name the same mean the same, whereas one could take Frege's argument to disprove this. So this is at best a controversial basis for Russell's conclusion.

2.2.4. Existence

> You can have significant propositions denying the existence of 'the so-and-so' . . . [e.g.] 'The greatest finite number does not exist'.
>
> (Russell 1918–19: 248)

But since a name must name something, any such proposition would be false, and indeed you could tell it was false just on the basis of understanding the sentence. This certainly establishes that at least some descriptions differ from names, if a name is something which has to refer.

2.3. Russell's 'Puzzles'

Russell (1905: 47–8, 51–4)

> A logical theory may be tested by its capacity for dealing with puzzles, and it is a wholesome plan, in thinking about logic, to stock the mind with as many puzzles as possible, since these serve much the same purpose as is served by experiments in physical science.
>
> (Russell 1905: 47)

Such a method will not be decisive, for it would remain a possibility that some other theory could also solve the puzzles. However, as in science, we have good reason to believe a theory which survives tests, so long as we are aware of no rivals which also survive the tests.

2.3.1. *The Law of Identity*

> If *a* is identical with *b*, whatever is true of the one is true of the other, and either may be substituted for the other in any proposition without altering the truth value of that proposition. Now George IV wished to know whether Scott was the author of *Waverley*; and in fact Scott *was* the author of *Waverley*. Hence we may substitute *Scott* for *the author of 'Waverley'*, and thereby prove that George IV wished to know whether Scott was Scott. Yet an interest in the law of identity can hardly be attributed to the first gentleman of Europe.
>
> (Russell 1905: 47–8)

When Russell talks of substituting one thing (as opposed to word) for another, he means what he says. For him, a proposition is a sequence of things, the meanings of the words of a sentence expressing the proposition.[14] To the sentence 'Scott is human' there corresponds a proposition involving the actual things Scott and humanity. This conception of a proposition makes it impossible for Russell to distinguish the proposition expressed by 'Hesperus is Hesperus' from the proposition expressed by 'Hesperus is Phosphorus', assuming that both 'Hesperus' and 'Phosphorus' are logically proper names.

The premiss about the substitutability of identicals is sometimes known as Leibniz's law of the indiscernibility of identicals. It requires careful formulation. For example, if Frege is right, it would be incorrect to formulate it as follows: If '*a* = *b*' is true, then '. . . *a* . . .' has the same truth-value as '. . . *b* . . .'. (The dots represent any way of forming a sentence using the name.) For we have as true 'Hesperus is Phosphorus', yet, according to Frege, the following sentences, in which 'Phosphorus' replaces 'Hesperus', differ in truth-value: 'The ancients believed that Hesperus is Hesperus'; 'The ancients believed that Hesperus is Phosphorus'. (Would the same point hold against Russell's formulation of Leibniz's law, in terms of substituting things rather than expressions?)

Russell's solution to the puzzle is that 'Scott was the author of *Waverley*' does not express an identity proposition, so we do not have what we need in order legitimately to invoke Leibniz's law. It does not express an identity, because the definite description does not introduce a constituent of the proposition, as Russell would put it; that is, its role is not to refer. This is revealed by the analy-

---

[14] He is not consistent in his usage. Thus he also says, quite inconsistently with the view just attributed to him, 'A proposition is just a symbol' (1918–19: 185).

sis, which is: There is exactly one author of *Waverley*, and Scott is that person. This is an existential generalization (it tells you that there is something uniquely meeting a certain condition) and not an identity.

Although Russell is right that sentences with definite descriptions are not, on his analysis, identity sentences, some scepticism ought to attend the way this puzzle is set up, since there is a real question, made vivid by Frege, whether identity would in any case support substitution in indirect contexts, those generated by expressions like 'The ancients believed that . . .'.

2.3.2. *The Law of Excluded Middle*

> By the law of excluded middle, either '*A* is *B*' or '*A* is not *B*' must be true. Hence either 'the present King of France is bald' or 'the present King of France is not bald' must be true. Yet if we enumerated the things that are bald, and then the things that are not bald, we should not find the present King of France in either list.
>
> (Russell 1905: 48)

The law of excluded middle, expressed more generally, says that every instance of '*A* or not-*A*' is true, where 'not-*A*' is the negation of '*A*'. Yet, Russell says, we are inclined both to regard 'The present King of France is bald' and 'The present King of France is not bald' as false, so that their disjunction is false, and to regard the second as the negation of the first.

Russell's solution involves a distinction of *scope*.[15] ('Scope' is the modern word; Russell expresses the distinction in terms of primary and secondary occurrence.) We must distinguish between, for example, 'Some men are not happy' and 'It is not the case that some men are happy'. The latter rules out there being any happy men, but the former does not. The distinction doesn't seem to arise from the meaning of any word in the sentences, but rather from the order of the expression for negation ('not' or 'It is not the case that') relative to the other expressions. In the first, the 'not' governs, or takes as its scope, just 'happy'; in the second, it governs, or takes as its scope, the whole sentence. If we introduce a sign for negation into a sentence '*A*', we say that the result is the negation of '*A*' only if the sign for negation includes the whole of '*A*' in its scope.

In terms of this distinction, 'The present King of France is not bald' is, Russell says, ambiguous. We most naturally read the 'not' as having relatively narrow scope, including 'bald' but not other parts of the sentence. Thus understood, the sentence is not the negation of 'The present King of France is bald', so no issue arises for the law of excluded middle.

Alternatively, one can hear the 'not' as governing the whole sentence, less

---

[15] For those familiar with formal logic, the scope of a connective is the shortest well-formed formula in which it occurs. The idea is extended to English by analogy.

ambiguously expressed as: 'It is not the case that the present King of France is bald'. This is indeed the negation of the other sentence; but, according to Russell's theory, it is true (for it says truly that there is nothing which is uniquely King of France at present and is bald). So the disjunction 'The present King of France is bald or it is not the case that the present King of France is bald' is true, and once again there is no problem for the law of excluded middle.

In my opinion, Russell's reasoning here is impeccable, and the scope distinction is important in the description of the workings of English.[16]

2.3.3. Existence

> How can a non-entity be the subject of a proposition?
>
> (Russell 1905: 48)

If there is no difference between *A* and *B*, then 'The difference between *A* and *B* does not exist' ought to be true; yet it seems to predicate something (non-existence) of what is, by hypothesis, a non-entity. But a non-entity cannot be the subject of a proposition.

The solution is to regard 'The difference between *A* and *B*' not as referring to something non-existent, but as a quantifier phrase, as recommended by the theory of descriptions. The analysis is: 'There is no unique difference between *A* and *B*'; and this no longer appears to have a non-entity as subject.

Russell's theory does indeed solve a problem. We will consider in Section 3 whether there are any alternative solutions.

2.4. Objections

Donnellan (1966); Neale (1992); Peacocke (1973); Sainsbury (1979); Strawson (1950*a*)

The main flow of thought against Russell's theory is that, in at least some uses, definite descriptions are referring expressions. This general thought surfaces in various detailed ways.

---

[16] I sometimes try to persuade beginning students that they need to be sensitive to scope distinctions in order to make the most of their love lives. Suppose you say 'Would you like to go to the cinema tonight?' and she says 'No'. I believe her reply manifests a scope ambiguity. On one reading it is equivalent to 'It is not the case that I want to go to the cinema'; on the other it is equivalent to 'I want not to go to the cinema'. Experience suggests that if the second reading is the right one, it is better to start another subject, whereas if the first reading is right, it may well be worth trying to arouse in her a desire to go to the cinema, perhaps by describing the excellence of the movie.

2.4.1. *Failure of Uniqueness*

Suppose there are two doors in a room and you close one, which squeaks. I say: 'The door squeaks'. If we take Russell's analysis seriously, this is true only if there is exactly one door; but not only are there millions of doors in the world, there are two even in the very room in which I speak. So on Russell's analysis, it would seem that I have said something false, whereas intuitively I have said something true.

Any account of quantifiers needs to allow for the fact that their domains can be modified by context. If during a lecture I exclaim 'There's no more chalk', I say something true if there's no more chalk in the room, even if there is plenty of chalk on the cliffs of Dover. Russell needs to say that the sort of case described in the last paragraph is no more exotic than this. The domain of the quantifier in 'There is exactly one door and it squeaks' must be understood to be restricted by the context.

But what is the relevant restriction? Not, by hypothesis, to doors in the room in which I speak. Perhaps we have to say that the restriction is to doors which are relevant to, or conspicuous in, the conversation. But there might be more than one of these. For example, I might have been talking to you about the problems associated with having a room with two doors, thus making both relevant to, and conspicuous in, the conversation. What makes the door in question specially relevant is no doubt your closing of it; but it seems rather hard to capture this feature in a general way. Perhaps we should say: the restriction is to doors than which no others are more relevant to the conversation and the related activities of those involved.

The suspicion remains that we sometimes say 'The door . . .' when we could as well or better have said 'That door . . .'. And the latter phrase, bar the fact that it is semantically complex, resembles Russell's paradigms of referring expressions, the logically proper names 'this' and 'that'. The question then remains whether in using 'the' in this way, when 'that' would have been as good or better, we use language correctly. One must also stress that this kind of case is of limited application: we certainly could not use 'that' in place of 'the' in a description like 'the greatest prime number'.

2.4.2. *Failure of Existence*

Strawson (1950a) has pointed out that if someone comes up to you and says 'The present King of France is bald' you are unlikely to reply 'That's false'. Yet on Russell's analysis, what is said is in fact false. Strawson believes we explain the phenomena better by saying that, in such a case, the speaker does not succeed in making a statement, in saying anything true or saying anything false. He utters a meaningful sentence; but in the circumstances it suffers from a defect (no reference for the definite description) which prevents its being usable to say anything, true or false. This is why we are not inclined to respond with 'That's false'.

Once again, we see at work the idea that definite descriptions are referring expressions. For if it is the job of a definite description to refer, then if it fails in this job it does not contribute to the determination of a truth-condition for the utterance in which it occurs. It is only an utterance with a *condition* for being true, or false, that can *be* true, or false.

The first comment is that such an account could apply only to some cases. We do not want 'The greatest prime number does not exist' to come out as other than true on the grounds that 'the greatest prime number' fails to refer.

The second comment is that Strawson's conclusion is certainly not established by the phenomenon to which he draws attention. It may be that we don't respond to an utterance of 'The present King of France is bald' with 'That's false' because to do so would mislead our audience into supposing that it is false in the usual way: for usually a sentence of the form 'The so-and-so is *F*' is false because, though there is exactly one so-and-so, it is not *F*.

This second comment can be developed by adapting a suggestion made by Kripke (1977). Even if people were explicitly to use Russell's analysis, and so utter things like 'There is exactly one King of France at present and he is bald', there might well still be a reluctance to respond with 'That's false', for the reasons given in the preceding paragraph. So the phenomenon does not tell seriously against Russell's analysis.

2.4.3. *Attributive and Referential*

Donnellan (1966) has suggested that there are two uses of descriptions: the attributive and the referential. He claims that Russell's analysis is adequate to the attributive use but not to the referential, and that Strawson's account is adequate to the referential but not to the attributive.

The distinction is illustrated as follows. If at the sight of Smith's mangled corpse you say 'The murderer of Smith is insane', you use the description attributively. You don't know who murdered Smith, but you wish to say that whoever did is insane. By contrast, if Jones has been arrested for Smith's murder and you are in court and utter the very same sentence, you will naturally be taken to have referred to Jones. What you say, according to Donnellan, is true iff Jones is insane, whether or not he really murdered Smith.

There is certainly an interesting phenomenon at work here, but it is doubtful if it connects with truth in the way that Donnellan needs if he is to use it against Russell. Consider this example which Donnellan gives of a referential use. At a party, I say 'The man drinking Martini is drunk'. I have in mind someone who is drinking water out of a Martini glass, at a party where no one is drinking Martini; misled by the shape of the glass, I wrongly think it contains Martini. On Donnellan's view, what I say is true just on condition that that man is drunk. But to say this appears to leave no room to register the fact that I have made some kind of mistake.

One who would defend Russell's story would make a sharp distinction between what someone strictly and literally says, and what they mean. No doubt I meant to speak of the man drinking water from a Martini glass; but it is not clear that I fulfilled this intention. A Russellian would say that I did not: what I strictly and literally said is false, since no one is drinking Martini, although I meant to speak of the man drinking water from a Martini glass, and meant what I said to be true iff that man was drunk.

This contrast has been explored by Grice (1961). One example he uses which makes the contrast very plain is as follows. A colleague asks what I think of someone as a philosopher. We both know that I am well placed to make an informed judgement. I say 'He has beautiful handwriting'. I presumably mean that he is no good at philosophy, but I certainly do not strictly and literally say this.

Russell can locate the referential use of definite descriptions at the 'pragmatic' level, the level at which one describes how language is used, rather than at the semantic level, the level at which one describes the truth-conditions of utterances. Since the theory of descriptions is a semantic theory, it can adjust to the pragmatic differences Donnellan describes.

It is not clear that Donnellan is right to say that Russell's account is correct for attributive uses. Sometimes Donnellan seems to identify an attributive use with any non-referential one. But sometimes he seeks to give a more positive characterization of an attributive use, and in doing so he suggests (though he is not entirely explicit) truth-conditions for such uses which are non-Russellian. Thus he says 'A speaker who uses a definite description attributively in an assertion states something about whoever or whatever is the so-and-so' (1966: 285). This suggests that a description used attributively has as its job to refer, which Russell would deny. Moreover, Donnellan suggests that if nothing is F, then nothing has been said to be G by an utterance of 'The F is G' (1966: 287); and, indeed, that nothing at all has been said (1966: 288). On Russell's account, no such suggestion is correct. An utterance of 'The F is G' says just the same whether there is an F or not, and if there is no F it says something false.

2.4.4. Entity-Invoking Uses?

What lies behind most of these suggestions is the idea that definite descriptions function, at least sometimes, as referring expressions: there is an object which it is their job to introduce. Peacocke (1973) invites us to call any such uses of descriptions 'entity-invoking'. The question before us is whether he is right to claim that there are such entity-invoking uses.

The phenomena associated with failures of uniqueness and failures of existence might be taken to suggest an affirmative answer; so might Donnellan's notion of referential use. We have seen that suggestions coming from these sources are not decisive against Russell. However, Peacocke (1973: 117) suggests that there are independent reasons for recognizing entity-invoking uses.

One test for entity-invoking use is the possibility of switching between 'the' and 'that', that is, 'if, in an utterance of "the *F* is *G*", what is strictly and literally said would equally appropriately be said by an utterance of *"that F is G"'* (Peacocke 1973: 117). The idea is that complex demonstratives of the form 'that *F*' are certainly entity-invoking (which we can accept for the present purpose), so an equivalence would make the descriptive phrase also entity-invoking.

Peacocke gives the following example:

If you and I visited the Casino at Monte Carlo yesterday, and saw a man break the bank, and on the same day saw a man break the bank at Nice, and it is common knowledge between us that this is so, then the description 'The man who broke the bank at Monte Carlo yesterday' as it occurs in a particular utterance *today* of 'the man who broke the bank at Monte Carlo yesterday had holes in his shoes' . . . is here entity-invoking both intuitively and by our criterion. (Peacocke 1973: 117)

However, it is unclear that we have a decisive case. First, the criterion, a willingness to say 'that' instead of 'the', may not establish equivalence. I might be as willing to say 'He died of a coronary' as I am to say 'He died of heart failure', but these claims are not equivalent. Second, it would seem that someone who overhears the utterance, but who lacks the common knowledge upon which, according to Peacocke, the claim of entity-invokingness depends, can, intuitively, understand what is said just as well as the participants.

I believe that there is no decisive case for any treatment of definite descriptions other than Russell's. This view has been elaborated and defended in great detail by Neale (1992).

FURTHER READING: Neale (1992).

3. EXISTENCE

3.1. Russell's View

> Russell (1918–19, lecture 5 and pp. 248–51)

The classic problem about existence is how grammatically singular negative existential sentences can be true. Examples are 'Vulcan does not exist' or 'The golden mountain does not exist'. The problem is that it seems that for such sentences to be meaningful, the grammatically singular expression ('Vulcan'[17] or 'The golden mountain') ought to refer; but if the expression does refer, it presumably refers to something which exists, and so the sentence is false.

One response to the difficulty is to allow that there are things which do not exist. Then we can say that 'Vulcan' and 'The golden mountain' refer to such non-existents, and the sentences say truly of them that they do not exist. This response is associated with Meinong (1904).

Russell had two arguments against it. One is that it offends against 'a robust sense of reality' which is 'very necessary in framing a correct analysis of propositions about unicorns, golden mountains, round squares, and other such pseudo-objects' (1919: 170). This appears to be nothing other than the affirmation of a prejudice.

The other argument looks as if it has more bite, since it claims that Meinong's view involves contradictions. The view seems forced to allow that the round square is both round and not round, and that the existent present King of France both exists and does not exist. A general principle invoked by the argument is that it must be true to affirm of the so-and-so that it is a so-and-so.

It would be agreed on all hands that existent objects cannot be contradictory, but it is unclear why one has to suppose that this goes also for non-existent ones. The very contradictoriness of the round square could be taken as a proof of its non-existence.

Russell says that if a theory can be found which does not involve these contradictions, it is to be preferred (1905: 45). We certainly need to decide whether any logical considerations force us into Meinong's position. Russell shows that there is an alternative.

In the case where the grammatically singular expression in the negative existential sentence is a description (e.g. 'The golden mountain does not exist'), we have already seen how Russell handles the situation. He denies that the expression is really a singular one, or that its job is to refer, treating it instead as an existential quantifier. The analysis (to recall) is: It is not the case that there is exactly one thing which is both golden and a mountain. In the analysis, there is no question of referring to the non-existent, and it is no harder to understand how a sentence like this can be true than it is to understand how a sentence like 'There are no unicorns' can be true.

When the grammatically singular expression is a name (e.g. 'Vulcan'), the standard interpretation of Russell sees him as regarding it as synonymous with some one definite description, and thus reducing this case to the one just considered. This does not fit with my interpretation of Russell. Russell as I read him is forced to allow that there may be no public meaning of 'Vulcan does not

---

[17] I am thinking not of the god of Greek mythology but of a planet postulated to explain the orbit of Mercury: it turned out that there was no such planet.

exist', and so no general analysis. Each individual will be able to use these words to make a judgement, but there is no guarantee that there is a single judgement which each will make. Thus one person might use the words to judge that there is no unique planet lying between Mercury and the sun; but if there is a prevalent theory that rays from Vulcan cause cancer, another might use the words 'Vulcan does not exist' to deny that rays from any one planet cause cancer.

In the case of some names without bearers, there is a description one must know in order to understand it. For example, one does not understand 'Santa Claus' unless one knows that he is the bearded sledge-driving Laplander who brings Christmas presents. Russell's analysis can reduce these cases to ones in which the grammatically singular expression is a definite description.

Russell expresses part of his position on this issue by saying that existence is not a predicate of individuals. By this he means that we cannot affirm or deny the concept of existence of any particular thing. His reason is that, if we did, the result would be tautology (in the case of affirmation) or contradiction (in the case of denial: it is contradictory to refer to something and go on to deny its existence). He puts the point as follows: 'To say that they [the actual things that there are in the world] do not exist is strictly nonsense, but to say that they do exist is also strictly nonsense' (Russell 1918–19: 233). 'Exists' is not a predicate of individuals, but rather of propositional functions. By a propositional function Russell means something like 'x is a unicorn'. To say that unicorns exist is to say that this propositional function is true of at least one object; to say that they do not exist is to say that it is not true of anything. Russell's analysis of sentences like 'The golden mountain does not exist' can be similarly expressed: 'x is golden and a mountain and anything which is golden and a mountain is identical to x' is not true of anything.

However, there is some evidence that we do allow that 'exists' can be affirmed and denied of individuals. This will be reviewed in Section 3.2.

3.2. Is 'Exists' Ever a Predicate of Individuals?

If we set aside Meinong's view, then if 'exists' is a predicate of individuals, it is a predicate true of all of them. There is nothing intrinsically wrong with this idea: it makes 'exists' like such predicates as 'is self-identical'.

An expression apt to express the existence of individuals is available in Russell's preferred formal language. To say that x exists is equivalent to saying that there is something it is, and this could be formalized:

$$\exists y(y = x).$$

This is true of everything (and the formula is a theorem); its denial is true of nothing. But the expression is perfectly well-formed. So Russell should not have said that the attempt to affirm or deny existence of an individual results in nonsense. The situation, rather, is that affirmations will be inevitably successful, and denials failures. There is no reason in logic why there should not be such a predicate of individuals.

It is easy to qualify 'exists' in such a way that the result is a predicate not true of everything. Thus one can use 'currently exists' for just those things which exist at the time of utterance, so that the predicate is false of things which no longer exist or which do not yet exist. This ought to be accepted on all hands; the real issue is whether there is a completely unqualified notion of existence applicable to individuals. In favour of such an unqualified notion, one could adduce the obvious explanation of the semantics of, for example, 'currently exists': 'currently' serves to restrict the *predicate* 'exists', taking us to a subset of all existents, rather as 'happy' restricts 'man' in 'happy man', taking us to a subset of all men.

One might be tempted to suppose that an unqualified 'exists', as a predicate of individuals, would not have much role in our language, since it would never allow us to say anything interesting. This may be too swift, as recognition of existence as a predicate of individuals may be required in understanding more complex constructions. One putative example is given at the end of the preceding paragraph. Another is given by Moore (1936: 143–4), who claimed, correctly, that 'This might not have existed' is both intelligible, and potentially debatable. (If 'this' is used to refer to a person, then presumably what is said is true; if to a number, presumably false; and there may be unclear cases as well.) The most straightforward account of 'This might not have existed' is on the following lines:

It might have been that: this does not exist.

What follows the colon can hardly be seen as other than a denial of a predication of existence of an individual.

The other main reason for exploring the idea that 'exists' is a predicate of individuals is that otherwise we have to say something unsatisfactory about negative existential sentences using names. We must either say, with the mythical Russell, that these are synonymous with descriptions, whereas we may be hard put to find any descriptions common to all users of the language; or we must say, with the real Russell, that there is no guarantee that such sentences have any meaning in the public language. Neither option is entirely happy (though the second is hard decisively to refute); so it is worth seeing if there is an alternative.

3.3. Evans's View

Evans (1982, ch. 10)

One alternative is the metalinguistic view. It analyses sentences like 'Vulcan does not exist' as saying that the name has no bearer. The problem with this view is that it imposes no conditions on understanding such sentences. Intuitively, you do not understand the sentence 'Vulcan does not exist' unless you know some astronomical facts (briefly outlined in note 17 above). On the metalinguistic view, it would be impossible to account for this condition, for understanding only requires knowing which name is being referred to (and is being said to be without a bearer).

As far as I am aware, the only serious way to implement the idea that 'exists' is a predicate of individuals is that proposed by Gareth Evans. The kernel of his idea is that singular negative existential truths exploit fiction in order to expose it as fiction. Someone who uses a sentence in this way

is not like someone who tries to prevent a theatre audience from being too carried away by jumping up on the stage and saying: 'Look, these men are only actors, and there is no scaffold or building here—there are only props.' Rather, he is like someone who jumps up on the stage and says: 'Look, Suzanne and the thief over there are only characters in a play, and this scaffold and this building are just props.' The audience must be engaged, or be prepared to engage, in the make-believe, in order to understand what he is saying. (Evans 1982: 369)

The contrast is that, in the case Evans is interested in, we exploit the conventions of the fiction, we treat the persons on the stage as characters, not as actors, and the backcloths as houses, not as mere drops, and thus to some extent stand inside the fiction, in the very act of exposing it as mere fiction.

In order to apply the idea to the linguistic case, Evans believes we must recognize, perhaps as implicit, an operator, 'really', for which he gives precise truth-conditions. When we say, falsely, 'Hamlet exists', we should understand this as having the logical form 'Hamlet *really* exists'. Likewise 'Vulcan does not exist' is said to have the logical form 'Vulcan does not really exist'.

To explain the truth-conditions for 'really', we must first introduce the idea of merely fictional truth-conditions. Thus we can assess 'Hamlet was decisive' as true or false in the fiction, *true* or *false* as Evans puts it, because the fiction imparts fictional truth-conditions (i.e. *truth-conditions*) to the sentence. Roughly, 'Hamlet was decisive' is *true* iff the fiction has it that he was decisive and *false* iff the fiction has it that he was not decisive.

'Really *A*' (for arbitrary sentence '*A*') is true iff:

(1) '*A*' has *truth-conditions*.
(2) '*A*' has truth-conditions.
(3) '*A*' is true (and not merely *true*).

The first condition requires that '*A*' has a use within some kind of fiction. The second condition requires that the sentence also has a proper non-fictional use. It is rare for both these conditions to be met. The only cases, for sentences involving names, are those in which a fiction has been woven around a real person. Thus the story of El Cid was supposedly based on a real person, and so a sentence like 'El Cid was brave' has both *truth-conditions*, those invested by the story, and truth-conditions, in virtue of its ordinary non-fictional use. Thus 'El Cid was really brave' is true iff the component 'El Cid was brave' has both *truth-conditions* and truth-conditions and is true; so it is (I believe) true.

'Hamlet really exists' (more idiomatically, 'existed') is true only if 'Hamlet exists' has truth-conditions. But it does not. The sentence has no use outside the fiction. Hence 'Hamlet really exists' is false, and 'Hamlet does not really exist' is true. This is all as it should be.

There are truths of the form '*x* really exists'. Evans suggests that if you are seeing a little green man but take yourself to be hallucinating, and I know all this, I can truly say 'That little green man really exists'. 'That little green man exists' has *truth-conditions*, generated by your hallucination; and it has truth-conditions, thanks to the fact that there is a little green man to be the referent of 'that little green man'; and it is true. So 'That little green man really exists' is true. Similar remarks apply to 'El Cid really existed'. These results again are as they intuitively should be.

This is an appealing theory for dealing with fictional cases, but it is not obvious how we should apply it to cases like 'Vulcan does not exist', where there is no explicit fiction. The astronomers who introduced the name were in earnest; they were not spinning a yarn. Perhaps we could concoct a notion of 'unwitting fiction': it occurs only when people's linguistic activities are out of line with reality, and resembles fiction except that there is no intention to produce fiction. Then we could allow that the astronomers who introduced the name 'Vulcan' engaged in unwitting fiction, so that the sentence 'Vulcan exists' has *truth-conditions*; however, the sentence has no truth-conditions, since it has no genuine use (that is, no use in which something gets referred to), but only a use within the unwitting fiction. This is enough to ensure that 'Vulcan really exists' is false, and so 'Vulcan does not really exist' is true.

FURTHER READING: Strawson (1967).

4. IDENTITY

Identity raises various questions. We have already seen one major one, in the discussion of Frege's puzzle above: how can we account for the apparent difference between a truth of the form $a = a$ and a truth of the form $a = b$? In this section, we discuss another question: is identity necessary or contingent? Or, more exactly, are any identities contingent?

A proposition is contingent, or contingently true, if it is true, but might not have been. It is merely contingently true that there are two pens on my desk at the moment; things could well have been otherwise. A proposition is necessary, or necessarily true, if it is true and could not have been false. Standard examples are mathematical truths: it could not have been otherwise than that $5 + 7 = 12$.

Following Kripke (1972), we need to distinguish between a proposition being necessary and its being knowable a priori. A proposition can be known a priori if it can be known without appeal to experience, for example by pure reason. It is an open question whether everything knowable a priori is necessary, and also whether everything necessary is knowable a priori. Kripke himself has argued against both suggestions. In particular, he claims that identities are necessary, but that not all are knowable a priori. For example, it is necessary that Hesperus is Phosphorus; things could not have been otherwise. But this is not knowable a priori, or else no doubt the ancient astronomers would have come to know it.

In considering whether it is necessary that Hesperus is Phosphorus, we could try to imagine a situation in which the identity fails. We can imagine a situation in which one planet is the first to appear in the evening, and another the last to fade in the morning; but this is not as such to imagine Hesperus being distinct from Phosphorus. It is consistent with what is imagined that the situation is one in which Hesperus (= Phosphorus) has a different orbit, so that it does not appear in the morning; or with Hesperus (= Phosphorus) having a yet different orbit, so that it does not appear in the evening. To say that one can imagine Hesperus being distinct from Phosphorus now looks like a bare assertion; the opposition will claim that whatever has been imagined cannot properly be thus described.

The view that identity is necessary can be supported by a formal argument, as follows:

(1) Leibniz's law: if x is identical to y, whatever holds of x holds of y.
(2) Necessity of self-identity: everything is necessarily identical to itself.
(3) Application of Leibniz's law to the property of being necessarily identical to x to yield: being necessarily identical to x holds of x (by (2)), so if x is identical to y, being necessarily identical to x holds of y (by (1)). In other words, if x is identical to y, x is necessarily identical to y.

The same argument can also be expressed in a more symbolic form:

(1) $\forall x \forall y (x = y \rightarrow (Fx \leftrightarrow Fy))$.
(2) $\forall x \, \Box \, (x = x)$.
(3) $\forall x \forall y \, (x = y \rightarrow (\Box(x = x) \leftrightarrow \Box(x = y))$.
So: $\forall x \forall y (x = y \rightarrow \Box(x = y))$.

Line (3) of the formal version follows from (1) by replacing 'F . . .' in (1) by '$\Box (x = \ldots)$'; the conclusion is derived from (2) and (3). It is that a true identity is necessarily true.[18]

The most doubtful part of this argument is the claim that '$\Box (x = \ldots)$' is a proper substitute for 'F . . .' in Leibniz's law; or, putting the point less formally, the doubt is whether being necessarily identical to x can properly be said to *hold of* anything. There are those who say, as we shall see, that there are no such properties as being necessarily identical to something, and hence nothing for Leibniz's law to apply to. Why should anyone be moved to make such a claim?

One reason is the feeling that there are independent arguments for the claim that some identities are contingent. Let us first get some uninteresting cases out of the way. It is no doubt contingent that the first Postmaster-General of the US was the inventor of bifocal lenses (see Kripke 1972). Moreover, the sentence might well be classified intuitively as an identity sentence. However, it is obvious that the source of the contingency lies merely in the fact that the definite descriptions might, consistently with meaning just what they do, have referred to other things; in Kripke's terms, they are non-rigid designators. So the case does nothing to suggest that the identity relation itself is contingent.

One must distinguish between the claim that identity sentences are contingent and the claim that the identity relation itself is contingent. For the relation to be contingent, there need to be things between which it holds merely contingently. For it to be necessary, it has to be that if the relation obtains between things, it obtains between those very things of necessity.[19] This is made explicit in the formal version of the conclusion of the argument recently displayed ((1)–(3) above). One can consistently say that there are contingent identity sentences, though the relation itself is necessary. Thus one could say that 'The first Postmaster-General of the US was the inventor of bifocal lenses' is contingent and is an identity sentence, but that if we consider the object, x, which is in fact referred to by 'the first Postmaster-General of the US' and the object, y, which is in fact referred to by 'the inventor of bifocal lenses', it is necessary that x is identical to y. (Would Russell allow that 'The first Postmaster-General of the US was the inventor of bifocal lenses' is an identity sentence?)

Now for a serious challenge to the necessity of the identity relation (see Gibbard 1975). Consider statues which are made out of lumps of clay. Normally, the lump comes into existence before the statue it forms: it is moulded into a statue. Quite often, the lump goes out of existence before the statue: if the statue is chipped, we have a different lump but the same statue. So, normally,

---

[18] The formal version of the argument is generally attributed to Barcan Marcus (1947). The argument is offered by, for example, Kripke (1971); and Wiggins (1980*a*: 109–10).

[19] It is awkward that in English the plural ('things') appears to be grammatically required, though, as only one entity is at stake, the singular would be logically more correct.

statues are distinct from the lumps of clay of which they are made, since they have different life histories.

Now consider a case in which a statue is formed at the very moment that a certain lump of clay comes into existence. For example, two moulded statue-halves are pressed together, thus simultaneously forming a new lump and a statue. Call the lump 'Lump1' and the statue 'Goliath'. Suppose that Goliath's life is ended by being smashed to smithereens, an event which at the same time destroys Lump1. Goliath and Lump1 thus come into existence at exactly the same time, and go out of existence at exactly the same time. Gibbard suggests that we should affirm:

(A) Goliath is identical to Lump1.

If we say that Goliath and Lump1 are distinct, we are faced with puzzles. How could two things occupy exactly the same place at exactly the same times? If Goliath weighs 2 pounds and so does Lump1, and they are distinct, why do not the two together weigh 4 pounds? If they are distinct, then there appears to be no sound inference from the premiss that you have dusted Goliath to the conclusion that you have dusted Lump1.

However, we also know that things could well have been otherwise. Lump1 might have been destroyed while Goliath survived. So although we must affirm (A), we must also affirm:

(B) Goliath might not have been identical with Lump1.

(A) and (B) together, if both are true, constitute a case of contingent identity.

If we were convinced of this, we would have a reason to deny that individuals possess modal properties, properties like being necessarily identical with x. This is what Gibbard denies, and he gives a quite elaborate reconstruction of apparent modal properties of individuals in other terms.

However, I believe that the case for affirming (A) has not been made out. Unless we have already done some monkey business with Leibniz's law, we can prove that (A) is false: Goliath has a property which Lump1 lacks, namely that it can survive the loss of some of its matter; and Leibniz's law tells us that if x has a property which y lacks, x is distinct from y.

Moreover, the puzzles are matters which have to be dealt with whether we affirm or deny (A), so they give us no reason for affirming it. Consider a case in which, as Gibbard would acknowledge, a statue and a lump are distinct, for example because the lump comes into existence before the statue. None the less, there is a period of time during which two things occupy exactly the same places at the same time; and during which each has a weight and the weight of the two together is the same as the weight of each; and during which there is no purely logical inference from having dusted one thing to having dusted the other.

In my view the necessity of the identity relation is not refuted by Gibbard's arguments.

5. NECESSITY

5.1. Boxes and Diamonds

Lewis (1986); Sainsbury (1991, ch. 5)

We have already made use of the notion of necessity. The question to be addressed in this section is: how should one give the logical form of modal sentences of English? A modal sentence of English is one which contains some expression for modality (possibility, contingency, or necessity). Examples are:

(A) Necessarily, $5 + 7 = 12$.
(B) Hesperus is necessarily identical to Phosphorus.
(C) You have to make adequate financial provision for your children.
(D) You must leave now or you'll miss your plane.
(E) If you press down on one end of a rigid rod, freely balanced at its centre, the other end has to go up.
(F) This just has to be a mistake.

In these various examples, no doubt different standards or criteria of necessity are invoked. Perhaps (A) invokes logical necessity, (B) metaphysical necessity, (C) moral necessity, (D) prudential necessity, (E) natural necessity, and (F) epistemic necessity. In this section we will be concerned with necessity in a relatively demanding sense, to include at most examples (A) and (B).

In asking what the logical form of modal sentences is, we are in effect asking how these sentences function, and what their logic is. The suggestion to be considered in this section is that modality is properly expressed by a unary sentence-operator: an expression which, like 'not', takes a sentence to form a sentence. The operator for necessity is written $\Box$ and called 'box'. The operator for possibility is written $\Diamond$ and called 'diamond'. Thus 'Necessarily A' is written '$\Box A$' and 'Possibly A' is written '$\Diamond A$'. We could take just one of box and diamond as primitive, and introduce the other by means of a definition, e.g.:

'$\Diamond A$' is defined as 'not $\Box$ not A'.

In other words, we can define what it is for something to be possible in terms of its being not impossible, that is, not necessarily not the case.

There are interesting distinctions of scope. For example, we need to distinguish the following:

(G) $\Box$ any mathematician is a mathematician.

(H) Any mathematician is □ a mathematician.

(G) says truly that it is necessary that mathematicians are mathematicians. (H) says falsely, of each mathematician, that he or she has to be a mathematician. This is false, for people have career choices.

Another pair to be distinguished is the following:

(I) □ something is human.
(J) Something is □ human.

The first is false: just small disturbances in the values of some of the parameters relevant to the Big Bang would have ensured that no planet would support life. The second is arguably true, for, arguably, anything which is in fact human has to be human.

What is the appropriate logic? We certainly want:

(K) □A entails A,

which says that everything which is necessarily so is so. We also want the rule of inference:

(L) From □A and □(if A then B) infer □B.

Arguably, we should also require

(M) □A entails □ □A.

This is the characteristic axiom of a logic called S4, after C. I. Lewis (Lewis and Langford 1932). It says that it is no accident what is necessary: what is necessary has to be necessary. There could be philosophical arguments against this thesis. For example, perhaps what is necessary is not an objective feature of the world, but is determined by our capacities and interests. If these might have been other than they are, then what is in fact necessary doesn't have to be so.

The thesis characteristic of the logical system called S5 is:

(N) A entails □ ◊A.

This says that what is actually so is, of necessity, possibly so. A consequence is that if something is possibly necessary, it is so. This has a surprising consequence for one version of the ontological argument. The argument could be represented:

(O) The notion of God, as a necessary being, is conceivable.
(P) Whatever exists of necessity exists.
(Q) So God exists.

Treating (P) as so much padding, we might interpret (O) as saying that possibly necessarily God exists: ◊ □God exists. In S5, this entails that God exists (without the need of any further premiss). One possible moral is that we should not be too swift to formalize (O) in terms of boxes and diamonds; another is that the S5 logic is stronger than the one we actually use in reasoning.

How should a semantic theory be given for a language of boxes and diamonds? There are two possibilities. One is that one should proceed 'homophonically', reusing the notion of necessity, expressed by a sentence-operator, in giving the truth-conditions. An analogy here is with negation. We are used to being told that 'not *A*' is true iff '*A*' is not true. Analogously, the relevant semantic axiom for box might be: '□*A*' is true (in some specified language) iff '*A*' is necessarily true (in that language).

A widely canvassed alternative is to give the semantics in terms of possible worlds. Intuitively, to say that it is necessary that *A* is to say that *A* holds in every possible situation or world. So we could offer the axiom: '□*A*' is true iff for every possible world, *w*, *A* is true at *w*. We might then ask whether this commits us to the existence of these entities, possible worlds. Graeme Forbes (1985) has argued that it does not, but I am unpersuaded (see Sainsbury (1991: 284–5)). If using possible worlds semantics for the box and diamond language does involve the ontology of worlds, then one might just as well give logical forms in explicitly possible worlds language, as we explore in the subsequent three sections (5.2–5.4).

5.2. Quantifiers (1): An Extra Argument-Place

Sainsbury (1991: 254–7)

The basic idea behind the approaches discussed in this and the subsequent two sections is that modality should be represented in logical form as quantification over possible worlds. Necessity is represented by universal quantification (truth at all possible worlds), possibility as existential quantification (truth at some possible worlds).

Merely replacing box by 'In every possible world' is not guaranteed to preserve sense. Thus 'At every possible world, *A*' is dubiously intelligible. If it is an abbreviation for ' "*A*" is true at every possible world', it forces a metalinguistic account on us, which is undesirable. (As in the case of other metalinguistic theories, we could not explain why understanding the original claim, 'Necessarily *A*' should require an understanding of '*A*'.)

One way to mend matters is to regard every predicate as having one more argument place than at first appears. Thus 'Necessarily, Socrates is human' would be formalized:

For every possible world, *w*, Socrates is human-at-*w*.

Normally we think of 'is human' as a one-place predicate: by inserting just one name you can make a sentence. The present suggestion, however, sees it as a two-place predicate: you need two names or other singular terms (e.g. a variable) to make a sentence. 'Human' turns out to be as we ordinarily regard 'loves'; and 'loves' itself is not really two-place but three-place, having, in addition to the two slots for lovers, an extra slot for a name of a world, or for a variable ranging over worlds.

David Lewis (1986) has suggested that this is unsatisfactory, since it does not do justice to accidental intrinsic properties. A property is intrinsic to an object if its holding of that object involves no other object. A property is accidental if it is contingent: it holds of something, but might not have done so. For such a property, we need to relativize to different worlds. On the proposal being considered, the logical form of 'This page is white but might not be' is

This page is white-at-w^* but not white-at-w,

where 'w^*' stands for the actual world, and 'w' for some distinct world. *White* is intuitively an intrinsic property: its holding of an object should not depend on any other object. Yet the logical form represents *white* not as an intrinsic property but as a relational property holding between an object and a world. This runs counter to what we regard as the nature of such properties; so if there is an alternative way of giving the logical forms, it is to be preferred.

5.3. Quantifiers (2): 'At w'

Lewis (1986)

David Lewis (1986) has suggested an alternative way of using quantifiers over worlds to give the logical form of modal sentences. (This section details one aspect of Lewis's theory; a further aspect, the notion of counterparts, is detailed in the subsequent section, 5.4.)

In a sentence like

In Australia, all beer is good

the phrase 'In Australia' works by restricting the quantifiers in what follows. In the context, not all beer is relevant to the truth of the sentence; only the beer in Australia. Lewis suggests that we can use this as a model for formalizing modal sentences. The crucial expressions have the form 'at w', where 'w' is a name for a possible world, or a variable ranging over possible worlds. Such an expression serves to restrict the quantifiers in what follows to the world in question. Thus

For some world w, at w (all politicians are honest)

is true iff there is a world all of whose politicians are honest. It would be offered as the logical form of 'It might be that all politicians are honest'.

How should one choose between this kind of approach and, for example, boxes and diamonds? There are two critical considerations. First, Lewis has suggested that there are things we want to say which cannot be expressed in a language of boxes and diamonds, but can be expressed in a language which quantifies over possible worlds. If he is right, this certainly constitutes a very important point in favour of the quantifier approach.

Second, many regard the metaphysics of possible worlds as intolerable. The issue is this: to regard possible worlds as genuinely existing entities has struck some as mad. Accordingly, many have tried to simulate possible worlds in terms of actual entities. For example, perhaps possible worlds can be regarded as set-theoretic constructions out of actual entities. Theories of this kind have been called by Lewis 'ersatzism'. The problem is that ersatzism may fail, in which case one is faced with the outlandish claim that there really are possible worlds other than our own. Just about everyone, including Lewis, regards this as a drawback; the question is whether it is compensated by other advantages, notably, by the greater expressive power of a language which quantifies over possible worlds.

We defer the metaphysical issues just raised until 5.5 below. Here we give two examples of the allegedly superior expressive power of a quantifier approach as opposed to boxes and diamonds.

If we suppose that the quantifier approach has a name, say 'w^*', for the actual world, then it certainly enables us to say things which cannot be said in the language of boxes and diamonds. Consider the English sentence

Everything red could have been shiny,

which I understand as equivalent to: It is possible that everything that is actually red should also have been shiny. (See Davies 1981: 220–1.) This is easily formalized in the 'At w' quantifier language on the following lines:

For some world, w, and for all x, if at w^* (x is red) then at w (x is shiny),

with 'w^*' serving as a name for our actual world. However, it appears impossible to give an adequate formalization in the language of boxes and diamonds.

For all x, if x is red then $\Diamond x$ is shiny

will not do, since it requires only that each red thing might have been shiny, whereas the original calls for a possibility in which all the red things are shiny together.

$\Diamond$ for all x, if x is red then x is shiny

will not do, since it would be true if all the red things in some possible world were shiny, whereas the original speaks of the red things in the actual world.

However, the language of boxes and diamonds can be augmented to overcome this defect. We need to add an expression for actuality, matching 'w^*', but keeping to an operator approach. The English word 'actually', or an abbreviation for it, will do fine. Then we can formalize the problematic sentence correctly, as follows:

◊ for all x, if x is actually red then x is shiny.

(How could you use 'actually' to convert non-rigid definite descriptions into rigid ones?)

The other problem of expressive adequacy I shall consider has been used by Lewis to favour quantifiers over boxes and diamonds in formalizing modality. He discusses the thesis of the supervenience of the mental on the physical:

> there could be no mental difference between two people without there being some physical difference . . . Reading the 'could' as a diamond, the thesis becomes this: there is no world . . . wherein two people differ mentally without there being some physical difference . . . between them. That is not quite right. We have gratuitously limited our attention to physical differences between two people in the same world, and that means ignoring those extrinsic differences that only ever arise between people in different worlds. (Lewis 1986: 16)

On Lewis's theory, the general structural properties of space-time are uniform throughout a world, so a person whose space-time is Reimannian must be in a different world from a person whose space-time is Lobachevskian. Yet if they differ mentally, why should not these differences in the nature of their space-times count as a physical difference which does justice to supervenience?

There is something dialectically unsatisfactory about this argument. We want a language of logical forms which will enable us to express anything we can express in ordinary English. But the thought Lewis wants us to express, that people might differ in merely extrinsic physical respects if they occupy different possible worlds, is one formulated not in ordinary English but in the language special to Lewis's theory. So it is not clear that this is genuinely a counter-example to the expressive adequacy of boxes and diamonds with respect to ordinary English.

What is needed is a statement in ordinary English of what has been left out by a boxes and diamonds formalization of the supervenience thesis. The formalization might be developed on the following lines:

□ for all x, □ for all y, □ (if x and y differ in some mental respect, then they differ in some physical respect).

I find it hard to see how this fails adequately to express the supervenience claim under discussion.

There are many delicate issues involved in trying to compare the expressive resources of boxes and diamonds on the one hand and quantifiers over worlds on the other. The aim of this section has been merely to give the flavour of how the debate might go.

FURTHER READING: Sainsbury (1991, ch. 5.8), and references given there to Lewis (1986) and Hazen (1976).

5.4. Quantifiers (3): Counterpart Theory

Lewis (1986); Sainsbury (1991, ch. 5.9)

Lewis's quantifier treatment of modality is combined with another distinctive, but theoretically separable, view. He holds that nothing exists at more than one world. In considering whether, for example,

> Socrates is necessarily human

is true, we must not ask whether 'Socrates is human' is true with respect to every possible world in which he exists, for he exists only at the actual world. What we have to ask is whether every counterpart of Socrates is human; and just this will be the logical form of the displayed sentence. A counterpart of Socrates at a world is an object such that nothing else in that world is more like Socrates than it is; as we can say, an object 'maximally similar' to Socrates. So the displayed sentence is true iff, in every world, whatever is maximally similar in that world to Socrates in ours is human.

Lewis's motivation for counterpart theory is that he believes that transworld identity is 'inconsistent' (1986: 199; the relevant discussion is at pp. 198–209). His reason is that it is contradictory to suppose that something exists at two worlds, with inconsistent properties in each. Hubert Humphrey has five fingers on his left hand but he might have had six. If we represent the fact that he might have had six fingers on his left hand as his belonging to some alternative world, at which he has six fingers, we have:

> Hubert Humphrey has five fingers on his left hand (at this world) and Hubert Humphrey has six fingers on his left hand (at some other world).

Evidently the parenthetical matter is meant to avoid the looming contradiction, but Lewis argues that it does not succeed, since none of the standard ways in which modifiers can remove contradictions apply in this case.

A tower can be round on the third floor and square on the fourth. However, the inconsistent predicates apply to different parts of the tower, whereas what is being said is that the whole of Humphrey belongs both to this world and to another one.

Humphrey can stand in different relations to different individuals, being the father of one, the son of another. But this also does not model the relevant case, for we are not talking of his relational properties but of his intrinsic ones. Five-fingeredness belongs to someone, or fails to belong to someone, as he is in himself; it is not a matter of his relation to anything else. So we cannot dissolve the contradiction by saying that the predicates are *standing in the five fingered relation to this world* and *standing in the six fingered relation to another world*.

The spatial example of the tower can usefully be compared with a temporal case, for example:

The shop is open (on weekdays) and not open (on weekends).

Lewis believes that the only way to understand the mechanism which explains the consistency is to regard persisting things as made up of temporal parts. Consistency is achieved because we see the first clause of the sentence as saying of some of these parts (weekday ones) that they are open, and the second as saying of other parts (weekend ones) that they are closed. But this mechanism cannot explain the consistency of the Humphrey example, if we suppose that the whole of Humphrey is present at each of two worlds.

As Lewis says, this problem will not arise on every theory. It will not arise on the operator approach, for this theorist must just take for granted the consistency of

A and $\Diamond$ not-A.

Even within possible worlds theory, it will not arise for the ersatzist, who must allow that of two representations, one may represent that A and another that not-A. It arises for Lewis because of his realism about possible worlds. This requires him to understand the problematic sentence as on a par with the spatial and temporal cases. Most people would accept that consistency in the spatial cases (like the tower) is explained in terms of spatial parts; but the analogous claim for the temporal cases (like the shop) is more controversial. If one could provide a good explanation of the consistency of these cases without appealing to temporal parts, it might carry over to the modal case, and sever the link between modal realism and the inconsistency of the supposition that some individuals occupy, and have different intrinsic properties in, different possible worlds.[20]

Whether or not counterpart theory is adequately motivated by problems about transworld identity, we need to ask whether it gives adequate logical forms. Here is a bad argument to the effect that it does not (cf. Kripke 1972: 344; Plantinga 1974: 115–16). When we say, for example, that Socrates might have been foolish, we mean to ascribe a property, that of being possibly foolish, to Socrates himself, and not to some counterpart, however similar. Lewis replies, entirely justly, that the objection misses the point, for in counterpart theory the claim about Socrates remains a claim about Socrates: it is the claim that he has a foolish counterpart (Lewis 1986).

Here is a more interesting objection, which serves to reveal some features of

---

[20] Suggestions for such an understanding of temporal modifications are found in Lowe (1987).

counterpart theory. Plantinga (1974: 109–10) objects that, intuitively, Socrates could have been very much like Xenophon actually is, and Xenophon could have been very much like Socrates actually is. In Lewis's terms, this means that there should be a world in which a counterpart of Socrates is just like the actual Xenophon and a counterpart of Xenophon is just like the actual Socrates. But this appears impossible, for to be a counterpart of Socrates you have to be more like the actual Socrates than anything else, whereas in the supposed world it is Xenophon's counterpart who most closely resembles the actual Socrates.

Lewis's reply depends upon the idea that there are many different respects of similarity, and context will often incline one to focus on one rather than another. In the present case, qualitative features are not relevant to determining the counterpart relation, precisely because a switch of qualitative features is what is being envisaged. So in this case, counterparthood will be determined by such things as origin (who the parents were). A counterpart of Socrates, judged by this standard of similarity, will be someone with the same parents as the actual Socrates; and this leaves plenty of room for the counterpart to diverge from the actual Socrates in endless qualitative respects, like being or not being bearded, being or not being wise, and so on; and so leaves room for a counterpart of Socrates to be qualitatively (though not parentally) similar to Xenophon.

Lewis is explicit that counterpart theory does not validate the necessity of identity, as understood in Section 4 above. This is because something can have more than one counterpart at a world. Suppose x has at w two counterparts, x_1 and x_2. Suppose further that x is identical to y at the actual world, so that y too has two counterparts at w. If the condition for x and y being possibly distinct is that there be a world such that some counterpart of x is distinct from some counterpart of y, the condition is fulfilled by the fact that x_1 is distinct from x_2. Lewis (1986, ch. 4.5) also offers an argument designed to show that this is a not unintuitive result.

The main obstacle to the acceptance of counterpart theory is its metaphysics: in Lewis's hands, it requires believing in the genuine existence of a large number of causally isolated possible worlds. The next section (5.5) provides a framework within which some of the metaphysical issues can be discussed.

5.5. Some Metaphysics

Lewis (1986); Sainsbury (1991, ch. 5.11)

The aim of this section is to trace connections between questions of logical form and metaphysical questions.

Common sense, I believe, holds the following theses about modality. (I do not suggest that this is a reason for thinking the theses true.)

   (A) Realism: some modal sentences, e.g. 'necessarily anything which is round is round', are objectively true; they are true in virtue of how things are independently of our minds and cognitive capacities.

   (B) Actualism: everything is actual; there are no non-actual things.

Common sense also expresses modality without explicit quantification over worlds. The surface forms are quite similar to the boxes and diamonds approach. On the face of it, this fits well with thesis (B): for, on the face of it, all possible worlds other than the actual world are non-actual objects, so if you are an actualist it would seem a bad thing to quantify over all possible worlds. Likewise, if as an actualist you avoid possible worlds at the level of logical forms, by using boxes and diamonds, it would seem a bad thing to introduce them for your semantics, by using an axiom for □ couched in terms of all possible worlds.

However, this connection is good only in so far as one takes possible worlds at face value, as, for the most part, existing but non-actual entities. We saw that there is an alternative, ersatzism. This theory holds that what we call a non-actual possible world is an actual object, but one which somehow represents a non-actual state of affairs. A possible world is like a picture: the picture actually exists, even though it may not depict things as they actually are.

So if one is an ersatzist, one can combine thesis (B) with logical forms for modality which quantify over possible worlds. There is no straightforward link between the question of logical form and the question of metaphysics. However, there may be less straightforward links. For example, Lewis has argued that ersatzism cannot do justice to modality, for reasons some of which are purely logical.

Lewis himself is what he calls a 'modal realist': he denies actualism, and affirms that his possible worlds are (with the exception of the actual world) non-actual objects with non-actual inhabitants. He regards this as a position one should adopt only if forced to, because he realizes that it is out of tune with common sense. One kind of reason for being forced to this non-actualism concerns matters of detail: for example, we cannot make do with boxes and diamonds because they are expressively inadequate, and we cannot accept ersatzism because it doesn't do justice to our modal intuitions. But there is another kind of reason.

People often say that to give an account of 'necessarily' in terms of 'all possible worlds' is footling, since the account exploits the notion of possibility, and we already knew that possibility and necessity are interdefinable. As it stands, the point rests on a misunderstanding. An account of necessity in terms of possible worlds need not be intended as any kind of analysis. Rather, it may be just a suggestion about which kinds of logical form do best justice to our modal idioms.

However, an analysis of modality is something devoutly to be desired, and the feature of Lewis's theory to which I wish to draw attention is that it provides almost the only extant analysis of modality.[21] This is because he can define what it is for something to be a possible world in non-modal terms. Roughly, the idea is that a possible world consists in spatio-temporally related objects, where any object standing in any spatio-temporal relation to any object in a world is also in that world, and in no other. No mention of modality here. If one can give a reductive analysis of *possible world*, and can give the logical forms of English modal sentences in terms of quantifications over possible worlds, one can provide a complete reductive account of modality.

6. TRUTH

6.1. Tarski's Schema and the Liar Paradox

Sainsbury (1995); Martin (1984); Tarski (1969)

A sentence is true if, and only if, things are as it says they are; and false if, and only if, things are not as it says they are. This thought would appear to be basic to our understanding of truth. Since work by Tarski, it has been customary to suggest that the thought, or something close to it, can be captured in the following schema:

'*p*' is true iff *p*.

The schema is supposed to represent the 'disquotational' character of truth: to say of a sentence that it is true (for this we need to refer to the sentence, for example by quoting it) is equivalent to saying the sentence itself (here we use it without quotation marks).

We can structure our discussion of truth by asking two questions about Tarski's schema: (1) is it correct? (2) does it say all that need be said about truth?

In this section, I indicate two defeasible (I suggest defeated) reasons for thinking that the schema is incorrect. In subsequent sections, I consider what, if anything, need be added to the schema in order to develop an adequate theory of truth.

The principle of bivalence holds that, for everything of the kind to which truth and falsehood significantly apply, either it is true or else it is false. Vagueness might give a reason for rejecting the principle of bivalence. Consider the sentence 'This is red'. For some objects the sentence is true and for some it is false, so it is the sort of thing to which truth and falsehood significantly apply.

---

[21] There are other accounts of modality, but many (e.g. projectivism, see Blackburn 1986) eschew analysis. A rival analysis is offered by Armstrong (1989).

But there are some objects, the borderline cases, for which we are unhappy to say that the sentence is true and unhappy to say that it is false. One might explain this unhappiness in terms of the sentence being neither true nor false. (Can you think of an alternative explanation?) In this case, one would be rejecting the principle of bivalence.

This rejection would be inconsistent with accepting Tarski's schema (as that has been understood up to this point). For if 'σ' is a sentence which is neither true nor false, then

'σ' is true

is false, whereas (by hypothesis) σ itself is not. So the instance of Tarski's schema

'σ' is true iff σ

has one false component and one which is neither true nor false; and such a biconditional can hardly count as true. Hence it is an exception to Tarski's schema.

One response would be to resist the rejection of bivalence. (One would have to consider all the various possible reasons for rejecting it, one by one.) For our present discussion, however, we could adopt a different kind of response: we could stipulate that all that accepting the schema amounts to is believing that it has no false instance, where this is understood as an instance in which one component of the biconditional is true and the other false.

Another reason for thinking that Tarski's schema is incorrect is that it is implicated in a paradoxical argument relating to the Liar paradox. Consider the following sentence, L ('the Liar'):

L is not true.

L purports to say of itself that it is not true.

In Tarski's schema, we are supposed to be allowed to replace the schematic letter '*p*' by any sentence of the kind to which we can significantly apply the notion of truth (looking at the left side of the schema), or which can significantly appear as a component in a biconditional (looking at the right side of the schema). We would thus not expect Tarski's schema to hold if '*p*' were replaced by an imperative sentence (e.g. 'Shoot!') or by a meaningless string of words. However, L does appear to be the kind of sentence of which one could meaningfully predicate truth, and the kind of sentence which could properly be a component in a biconditional. So it seems we should be allowed to replace '*p*' in the schema by L, getting:

'L is not true' is true iff L is not true.

Given the way L was introduced, we know that

L = 'L is not true'.

By Leibniz's law (the law that says that identicals may be substituted without loss of truth) we can replace the first occurrence of 'L is not true' in the schema by 'L' yielding:

L is true iff L is not true.

This is tantamount to a contradiction.

One response is to deny the correctness, or at least the universal applicability, of Tarski's schema. On this response, one accepts that L is the kind of sentence to which truth is significantly applicable, or which can appear as a component of a biconditional, but denies that the schema applies to every sentence meeting these conditions. Thus the Liar paradox gives one a reason for rejecting Tarski's schema.

However, there are other responses to the paradox, ones which enable one to accept Tarski's schema. One relatively unpopular one is to deny that Leibniz's law ought to hold in such contexts (see Skyrms 1982). Much more popular is the idea that, for one reason or another, L lies outside the range of expressions to which the schema applies. This response involves explaining how it is that, despite appearances, L is a sentence to which the notion of truth does not significantly apply, and also a sentence which cannot properly appear as a component of a biconditional. (Why must both these features of L be explained? Why would it not be enough merely to explain one?) One suggestion along these lines is that there is something wrong with the sort of self-reference involved in L. One might feel that it ought to be possible to specify all the features of a sentence that are necessary for understanding it without having to presuppose the sentence itself. Yet it would appear that we cannot do this for L. In saying which sentence L is, we have, in the very first word of L, already to refer to the sentence, the very one we are engaged in specifying. This kind of suggestion was pioneered by Russell (1908), in his 'vicious circle principle', and there are a number of recent attempts to make the vague idea more precise. (For example, Kripke 1975; Martin 1984, introduction.)

Tarski's own response is not well classified within the framework so far presented. He thought that the paradox showed that our ordinary notion of truth is inherently paradoxical. The philosophical (and mathematical) task is to construct the closest non-paradoxical substitute. Tarski thought that the basic problem was the supposition that there could be a notion of truth which was legitimately applicable to a sentence involving that very notion. To prevent this, Tarski proposed that languages should be arranged in a hierarchy. The basic language, say $\mathfrak{L}_0$, would not contain the notion of truth at all. The next language, $\mathfrak{L}_1$, would contain every sentence of $\mathfrak{L}_0$ together with a truth-predicate, call it 'true$_1$', defined just for sentences of $\mathfrak{L}_0$. It is crucial that 'true$_1$' cannot apply to a sentence containing that predicate; that is, it cannot apply to any sentence of $\mathfrak{L}_1$, unless the sentence belongs to $\mathfrak{L}_0$. The hierarchy goes on upwards. Truth for sentences of $\mathfrak{L}_1$ is expressible by means of a predicate 'true$_2$', which belongs to $\mathfrak{L}_2$; and so on.

We cannot express L in any language in Tarski's hierarchy. Suppose L (for reductio) belongs to some language $\mathfrak{L}_n$. Then the truth-predicate it contains, if it is to be applicable to L itself, must be in some language higher in the hierarchy, minimally in $\mathfrak{L}_{n+1}$. So, fully expressed, L would read:

L is not true$_{n+1}$.

But then L cannot belong to $\mathfrak{L}_n$; QED.

Tarski's view was that every *coherent* occurrence of the word 'true' could be replaced by an indexed truth-predicate: 'true$_1$', 'true$_2$', or whatever. To the extent that Tarski's schema is intelligible, it is also, for Tarski, correct. If it seems to lead to paradox, it is because we have failed to respect the hierarchy; but in that case it was not properly intelligible at all. In Tarski's hands, his schema is not intended as a claim about our ordinary conception of truth, but rather as a criterion for the coherence of a notion of truth.

Tarski thought that to attain consistency we must abandon our ordinary language, with its inherently paradoxical truth-predicate. Is there a less radical variant of this theory? Could we maintain that something like Tarski's hierarchy is already implicitly present in our language, saving it from inconsistency? It seems hopeless to suppose that there are the kind of fixed-in-advance levels which Tarski's hierarchy requires. But it is worth exploring whether some hierarchy is indexically triggered by our language: triggered, that is, in different kinds of ways, as a function of context. (See Burge 1979.)

For present purposes, the main conclusions we need to draw are two: that the notion of truth is implicated in deep paradoxes, and a full account of the notion would need to do justice to that fact; and that, arguably, a response to these paradoxes need not involve abandoning Tarski's schema. Section 6.2 presupposes that any account of truth will retain the schema.

6.2. Enriching Tarski's Schema

Horwich (1990); Wright (1992)

Once we have Tarski's schema, what *else* needs to be said about truth? One possible answer is: nothing (or almost nothing). The first two subsections give variants of this answer. The remaining two subsections propose different purported additions.

6.2.1. Minimalism

Could we use Tarski's schema to *define* truth? The idea, which we may loosely call 'minimalism' about truth, is that the schema tells you all you need to know: 'true' means whatever an expression must mean in order properly to fill the blank in the following schema:

'*p*' is ——— iff *p*.

An initial worry with the idea is its apparent circularity, since 'properly filling the blank' in the above is filling it in such a way that, whatever sentence (of the appropriate kind) one puts for '*p*', the result is *true*. We can somewhat ease this worry by reverting to a less formal implementation of the minimalist idea. Suppose someone speaks a language which does not contain the predicate 'true', or any equivalent. We could introduce him to the predicate in the following way: whenever he utters something assertively, for example '*p*', we could say: you could just as well have said ' "*p*" *is true*'. Here we use the notion of equivalence; but this does not, at least explicitly, make use of the notion of truth. We could be seen as using instances of the schema to explain truth, without taking truth itself for granted.

I shall consider three more substantial worries: (1) whether anything else could fit the blank; (2) the problem of saying which sentences are apt for truth; and (3) whether enough has been said to explain the notion of truth, as opposed merely to specifying its extension.

1. Here is a list of possible rivals: expressions which, it may be claimed, can properly be inserted in the blank instead of 'true', but which differ from it in meaning:

> is knowable,
> corresponds to the facts,
> is useful to believe,
> will be accepted by all impartial inquirers in the long run.

Minimalists need to consider the rivals one by one. They have two strategies: one is to deny the difference in meaning, the other is to deny that the rival can be properly inserted in the schema in the place of 'true'. The first strategy might be appropriate in the case of 'corresponds to the facts'. The second might be appropriate in the case of 'will be accepted by all impartial inquirers in the long run', perhaps on the grounds that we can envisage sentences which we understand and which are true, but whose truth no amount of inquiry will in fact uncover.

2. The first question could not be pursued in much detail without coming up against the second, that is, how one should specify the appropriate substitutes for '*p*' in the schema. We have seen that nonsense sentences, and sentences

in the imperative mood, are not fit substitutes. However, in the history of philosophy it has been claimed, for various kinds of sentences, that although truth may appear to be significantly applicable to them, it is not so really. A famous example is moral discourse. Sentences like 'Torturing the innocent is wrong' have been claimed not to be the sort of sentence to which truth or falsehood can be significantly applied.[22] In the so-called 'emotivist' school of ethics, they have been likened to expressions of feeling, like 'Ugh!' or 'Boo!' (for torture) and 'Wow!' or 'Hooray' (for expressions of approval). (See e.g. Ayer 1936, ch. 6.)

On the positive side, it might be held that a sentence is a fit substitute for '*p*' in the schema only if it is a representation of an independent reality to which it may or may not succeed in corresponding. It will then be a substantive metaphysical question whether a sentence is apt for truth, not one to be settled by such superficial features as its syntax and our pre-philosophical willingness to use the words 'true' or 'false' of it.

If this view were correct, minimalism about truth would be undermined. For even if one could explain, via Tarski's schema, what it is for a truth-apt sentence to be true, some heavy philosophy would be involved in determining what it is for a sentence to be truth-apt. We cannot use the schema without demarcating explicitly the sentences to which it should apply, and doing this may involve us in some contentious metaphysics. (See Wright 1992.)

3. Has the minimalist said enough to show anyone the role of truth in our lives and language? Here are two reasons for a negative answer.

(*a*) It would seem that the most the minimalist account could achieve is a specification, for each sentence, of what it is for that sentence to be true. Yet the significance of a sentence being true, what that entails with respect to belief, or assertion, or inference, has not been stated. Arguably, we could not see, simply on the basis of Tarski's schema, that the following are platitudes: that one should aim to believe what is true, that one who speaks truly tells things as they are, that to assert is to present as true, that truths cannot conflict, and so on. Unless one has grasped the role of truth in believing, speaking, and asserting, one has not fully understood it.

(*b*) Since distinct properties might apply to the same things (e.g. the property of having a heart and the property of having kidneys), we might know how to apply 'true' (apply it to just those sentences one is disposed to assert with sincerity) without thereby knowing what property the word expresses, and thus without having fully understood it.

In response to the second objection, a minimalist might introduce the notion

---

[22] Supposedly, for example, by David Hume (1738, bk. 3). A version of a broadly Humean position might use the following premisses: (1) a sentence can express a belief iff it is the sort of thing to which the notion of truth significantly applies; (2) every action's motivation must include something which is not a belief (a desire); (3) a moral view, together with beliefs, is enough to motivate an action. From these it follows that a moral view is not a belief, and hence that an expression of it is not the sort of thing to which truth or falsehood significantly applies.

of the *least* meaning: 'true' has the least meaning that it can, consistently with verifying Tarski's schema. Even if this met the second objection, the first would remain to be answered. We need to see how we might enrich Tarski's schema to obtain a fuller understanding of truth (6.2.3 and 6.2.4 below). First, however, I consider a view which is designed to take us in the other direction.

6.2.2. *Redundancy*

Ramsey (1927); Horwich (1990)

Reflection on Tarski's schema might suggest that 'true' is a needless predicate, and that we could eliminate it without loss: instead of predicating truth of a sentence, we could simply assert the sentence itself. This is a version of the so-called 'redundancy theory' of truth.

This theory is demonstrably incorrect as stated, since we can predicate truth even in situations in which we are in no position to assert the sentences of which we predicate it. For example, knowing that you are invariably honest and well-informed, but not knowing what you said when you spoke on the radio, I might say 'Everything he said on the radio is true'. Since I don't know what you said, I cannot use your sentences instead; I need the predicate 'true'.

The standard response by redundancy theorists is that I don't need to use 'true', because I could have expressed myself as follows:

For all p, if he uttered p during his radio talk, then p.

How is the quantification to be understood? Perhaps 'p' ranges over sentences; that is to say, it occupies the kind of position that could be occupied by a *name* of a sentence. (Compare: In 'for all x, if x is a man, x is mortal', the variable ranges over objects. That is, it could be replaced by a name of an object, e.g. by 'Socrates'.) This will make sense of the occurrence of 'p' in 'He uttered p', for here we do state (in a general way) a relationship between the utterer and a sentence we refer to. But it will not make sense of its last occurrence. This marks a position which needs to be occupied by a sentence, and not by a name of a sentence. (Could matters be improved if we replaced 'uttered p' by 'said that p', and construed the quantification as over propositions—the things which sentences state?)

The redundancy theory will ask us to construe the quantifier as *substitutional*.[23] We explain this by saying that the displayed formula is equivalent to the claim that, whatever sentence you put for 'p' in the following,

if he uttered p during his radio talk, then p,

---

[23] See Sainsbury (1991, ch. 4.18).

the result is true. This may serve to make sense of the quantification (though even this is debatable), but it clearly does not serve the purposes of the redundancy theory of truth: for the quantification is explained in terms which make essential use of the supposedly redundant predicate 'true'.

6.2.3. Correspondence
Austin (1950); Strawson (1950b); Horwich (1990, ch. 7)

A sentence is true just if it corresponds to the facts. At first sight, it would seem that no one could dispute this claim. The question would remain, however, whether it tells one anything substantial about truth; whether it serves as a good enrichment to what is provided by Tarski's schema. According to the 'correspondence theory' of truth, it does.

This claim was famously debated by Austin and Strawson. Strawson denied that the correspondence theory succeeded in explaining truth as a relation between a sentence and something else, namely, facts. Success would involve giving an account of facts which was independent of the notion of truth; but 'facts are what statements (when true) state. . . . If you prise the statements off the world you prise the facts off it too; but the world would be none the poorer' (1950b: 38–9).

In developing the details of his theory of truth, Austin (1950) gave a quite theoretical account of how the correspondence was supposed to work.[24] He argued that a sentence is linked to two kinds of thing in the world, by two different sets of conventions. The descriptive conventions link it to a state of affairs, something which may or may not obtain. The demonstrative conventions link it to a particular situation. Thus (to use Austin's example) an utterance of the sentence 'The cat is on the mat' is linked by the descriptive conventions to the state of affairs of the cat being on the mat, and by the demonstrative conventions to some particular situation in some region of the world. (Austin is rather unclear about just what particular situation is involved, as Strawson stresses.) The utterance of the sentence is true just if the particular situation is of a kind with (that is, instantiates) the state of affairs. For many years after this theory was advanced, it was widely thought to have been refuted by Strawson. (Strawson objected that Austin had made truth purely conventional, but this seems to have been a misunderstanding.) Recently, however, Austin's theory has received a new lease of life in the hands of Barwise and Etchemendy (1987), who claim that it can provide an account of truth for which the Liar paradox does not arise.

We have so far taken for granted that the problem for seeing truth as correspondence is triviality. We must now relax this assumption: to think of truth as

---

[24] So perhaps it was unfair of Strawson to claim that Austin had given no truth-free specification of the nature of facts: see Austin (1961). Austin makes much of the difference between a sentence and a statement (cf. above pp. 83–4), but I have abstracted from this here.

correspondence has been taken as the mark of all kinds of villainy, for example empiricism, realism, and atomism. If there is anything to be said for such a perception, we should stop thinking of the doctrine of correspondence as a platitude. Its correctness would be hostage to the correctness of empiricism, realism, and atomism.

If correspondence theorists affirm that to know is to be the passive recipient of the effects of an external reality—the facts—then they are committed to (a somewhat comic-strip version of) empiricism. But this view of knowledge is an optional extra, not something entailed by the correspondence theory of truth. A correspondence theorist could lean towards a rationalist epistemology.

If correspondence theorists affirm a realist view of facts—they obtain mind-independently, and might well outrun our capacity to know them—then they would be committed to realism. But this is an optional extra, not something entailed by the correspondence theory. Even if one thought of facts as somehow conditioned by human capacities, truth might still be a matter of correspondence to them.

If correspondence theorists take the correspondence as a kind of isomorphism, with a chunk of world corresponding to each significant part of a true sentence, then they would be committed to a form of atomism (e.g. Russell 1918–19). But correspondence as such does not require this more detailed kind of mapping.

It is true that those who find the picture of correspondence attractive and revealing may well be tempted towards some or all of empiricism, realism, and atomism. History bears out this tendency. However, the strict content of the correspondence theory as here stated (a sentence is true just if it corresponds to the facts) does not entail these additional views. Hence the correspondence theory is not in jeopardy from arguments designed to refute these views.

We can, after all, regard it as a platitude. If we affirm it as well as Tarski's schema, we do not thereby significantly enrich our account of truth.

6.2.4. Convergence

It would be hubristic to maintain that, for every aspect of reality, we have or could attain the conceptual resources required adequately to describe it. Hence it would be hubristic to maintain that every aspect of reality is one we could come to know about. However, it is much less hubristic, and some hold correct, to suppose that we could in principle come to know all the aspects of reality which we can conceptualize. This would mean that every intelligible sentence is one whose truth or falsehood we could in principle come to know.

This line of thought, now generally referred to as 'semantic anti-realism', has been developed by Dummett (in many writings: I like his (1973c), and the preface to his (1978)). The opposing view, (semantic) realism, is that we could formulate meaningful sentences which are true or false but whose truth or falsehood we could never come to know. On this view, as it is sometimes put, truth is 'evidence transcendent'.

A full account of truth would devote some space to this issue,[25] but I shall move to other, though related, questions: Is there a tendency for best opinion to converge upon the truth? Might we even define truth as that upon which best opinion tends to converge? An affirmative answer at least to the first question would be appealing to the semantic anti-realist. If a sentence is true, it is knowable, so the application of the proper methods of inquiry should ultimately lead to its discovery; hence, convergence.

There is another thought present in the notion of convergence. Truth is closely linked with objectivity. If we are realists, the objectivity of truth is secured by the objectivity of the subject-matter, something existing independently of anything to do with us, and in particular of our methods of inquiry. But if we are not realists, we cannot look to this source of objectivity. What could we say to ensure that, none the less, we are dealing in genuine facts, and not mere play of the fancy? Convergence is one possible source of an answer.

It is too simplistic to suppose that there is a tendency to converge come what may. The relevant thought is that the same evidence as input will tend to lead us to the same views as outputs. We would not expect convergence among people who are exposed to quite different evidence. So a refinement might be that failure of convergence requires an explanation in terms of different inputs, or defects in cognitive mechanism. Thus refined, we have a view which could be accepted by realists as well. But, thus refined, convergence hardly seems a suitable basis for *defining* truth (a question raised two paragraphs back), even for the semantic anti-realist. The account makes essential use of the notion of a *cognitive* mechanism. Without this restriction, we certainly would not have a notion apt to define truth, since divergences even in matters for which truth does not arise, like affective responses, must also be explicable in terms of difference of input or difference of mechanism. But with the restriction in place, we have an obligation to explain what a distinctively *cognitive* mechanism is, and it is hard to see how this obligation could be discharged without using the concept of truth. A cognitive mechanism is just a mechanism which delivers the kinds of output to which the notion of truth applies (and therefore also the notions of belief, justification, and so on).

Perhaps the attempt to *define* truth is in any case misguided. We should be content with an account which, backed by Tarski's schema, specifies truth's proper relation to assertion, belief, warrant, interpretation, and objectivity.

FURTHER READING: Haack (1978), Wiggins (1980*b*)

---

[25] It relates to another germane topic. The realist has a reason to affirm bivalence; Dummett has taken it as a mark of the anti-realist that he has no reason to affirm it (see e.g. Dummett 1973*c* and 1978, preface).

FURTHER TOPICS

This chapter has sampled only a small part of the subject area. Here are some further topics.

Various topics under the heading of necessity have not been discussed (and some not even mentioned), for example:

1. The distinction between necessity *de re* and necessity *de dicto*. One question is 'Is the distinction adequately explained merely in terms of scope?' Sainsbury (1991, ch. 5.4) will get you started.

2. Objections to the very idea of necessity; in particular, to the very idea of necessity *de re*. Here I think of Quine's arguments, and of an argument derived from Frege. Sainsbury (1991, ch. 5.5 and 5.6) will get you started.

3. Counterfactual conditionals. There are famous analyses in terms of possible worlds. Reading these would give you a feel for the utility of possible worlds theories. Sainsbury (1991, ch. 5.2) will serve as a start, but be sure to read the beautiful Lewis (1973).

4. Linguistic analyses of necessity. An old, but unsurpassed, account of this theory (now generally out of favour) is by Pap (1958).

There is a group of topics essentially concerned with the domain of logic.

5. What is a logical constant? The question here is: what makes an expression ('and', 'not', 'all') count as a logical word, or logical constant? Should □ also count as a logical constant? And how about the symbol (∈) for set-theoretic membership? There is a close connection with questions about what makes a truth a truth of logic. Sainsbury (1991, ch. 6.5) provides an introductory survey of some of the main positions.

The central concepts of logic are themselves subject to philosophical scrutiny:

6. Validity and entailment. Can one give a more refined notion of validity than that in terms of truth-preservation? The question is motivated by the fact that arguments with inconsistent premises are valid by the ordinary standard of truth-preservation, yet these have little cognitive value. Analogous issues affect entailment. The issue is famously addressed in articles by Geach (1958, 1970).

The epistemology of logic, notably:

7. The justification of deduction. How can one justify what one takes to be logical laws? See Dummett (1973b, 1991); for the latter, use index entry 'justification of logical laws'.

BIBLIOGRAPHY

I have marked my nap selections with an asterisk.

ARMSTRONG, D. (1989), *A Combinatorial Theory of Possibility* (New York). Not central to this subject area. Armstrong argues that one can give an account of possibility in terms of recombinations of actual things. Mentioned in the text as almost the only rival to Lewis's reductive account of modality.

AUSTIN, J. L. (1950), 'Truth', *Proceedings of the Aristotelian Society*, supp. vol. 24: 111–28; repr. in G. Pitcher (ed.), *Truth* (Englewood Cliffs, NJ, 1964). Classic statement of a correspondence theory of truth. Criticized by Strawson (1950*b*).

—— (1961), 'Unfair to Facts', in *Philosophical Papers* (Oxford). Response to Strawson (1950*b*).

AYER, A. J. (1936), *Language, Truth and Logic* (London). Famous book, mentioned here for its statement of the emotivist theory of ethics (upon which ethical sentences are not apt for truth or falsehood).

BARCAN MARCUS, R. (1947), 'The Identity of Individuals in a Strict Functional Calculus of Second Order', *Journal of Symbolic Logic*, 12: 12–15. Mentioned as the official source of the formal proof, via Leibniz's law, of the necessity of identity. No point reading it.

BARWISE, J., and ETCHEMENDY, J. (1987), *The Liar: An Essay in Truth and Circularity* (New York). Recent theory of truth designed to deal with the Liar paradox. First chapter gives clear review of the issues; the rest strictly for enthusiasts only.

BLACKBURN, S. (1986), 'Morals and Modals', in G. Macdonald and C. Wright (eds.), *Fact, Science and Morality* (Oxford). Mentioned as an example of a projectivist metaphysical view of modality. Necessity is not something out there, but is a projection of our cognitive powers and interests. Peripheral to this subject area, but well worth studying in connection with study of metaphysics or ethics.

BURGE, T. (1979), 'Semantical Paradox', *Journal of Philosophy*, 76: 169–98; repr. in Martin (1984). Gives a response to the Liar paradox in terms of levels of truth, but, unlike Tarski's levels, Burge's levels are fixed indexically: not by the meaning of the sentence, but by the context in which it is used. This makes it a more appealing theory than Tarski's.

CHELLAS, B. (1980), *Modal Logic: An Introduction* (Cambridge). A good, though pretty detailed, introduction to propositional modal logic.

DAVIES, M. (1981), *Meaning, Quantification, Necessity: Themes in Philosophical Logic* (London). Excellent book, but most students find it tough going. Probably best used at most selectively for this subject area, e.g. for the discussion of Donnellan (1966). It is essential for a study of philosophy of language.

DONNELLAN, K. (1966), *'Reference and Definite Descriptions', *Philosophical Review*, 77: 203–15. Classic paper, essential reading, not hard to come to grips with.

DUMMETT, M. (1973*a*), *Frege: Philosophy of Language* (London). Lengthy discussions of Frege's notion of sense, including a direct discussion of Kripke's attack on Frege. First-rate stuff; challenging.

—— (1973*b*), 'The Justification of Deduction', *Proceedings of the British Academy*, 59 (1975), 201–32; repr. in *Truth and Other Enigmas* (London, 1978).

—— (1973c), 'The Philosophical Basis of Intuitionistic Logic' (originally entitled 'Philosophical Foundations of Intuitionistic Logic'), Colloquium '73, Bristol; repr. in Dummett (1978). Despite the off-putting title, this is in my view the clearest full-length exposition of Dummett's anti-realist position.

—— (1978), *Truth and Other Enigmas* (London). Collection of papers by one of the most fertile of contemporary philosophers. Mentioned here for (1) his account of the connection between realism and bivalence in the preface and (2) reprints of his (1973b, c).

—— (1991), *The Logical Basis of Metaphysics* (London). State of the art. Marvellous book, well beyond the range of the syllabus. Useful for the material on justification of logical laws (q.v. in the index).

Evans, G. (1982), *The Varieties of Reference* (Oxford). Brilliant book. Essential for his theory of existence (ch. 10), and also very useful for a wide range of topics about reference, including thumbnail sketches of Frege's and Russell's views in chapters 1 and 2, and an account of proper names in chapter 11. Quite hard; Sainsbury (1985) might be useful as an introduction.

Forbes, G. (1985), *The Metaphysics of Modality* (Oxford). Good book, clear, comprehensive. Goes well beyond what a beginner needs, but a good reading-project for someone who gets really interested in necessity. Lewis (1986) might be more suitable, and less formal.

Frege, Gottlob (1879), *Begriffsschrift, eine der arithmetischen nachgebildete Formelsprache des reinen Denkens*, trans. T. W. Bynum as *Conceptual Notation and Related Articles* (Oxford, 1972). This work is generally regarded as the first presentation of modern logic. Mentioned here as the source of the account of identity which Frege later rejects (1892a).

—— (1891), 'Function and Concept'; repr. in B. McGuinness (ed.), *Collected Papers on Mathematics, Logic and Philosophy* (Oxford, 1984). Important background reading. Describes Frege's notion of a concept whose value is always a truth-value (and thus explains why people use the phrase 'has the truth-value true' rather than simply saying 'is true').

—— (1892a). *'On Sense and Meaning'; repr. in B. McGuinness (ed.), *Collected Papers on Mathematics, Logic and Philosophy* (Oxford, 1984). This is 'Über Sinn und Bedeutung', also translated as 'On Sense and Reference'. Essential reading. The later part consists in Frege's attempt to defend his compositionality principles in the face of various problematic idioms. (The principles are that the sense of a complex expression is determined by the sense of its parts, and the reference of a complex expression by the reference of its parts.) You can pay rather less attention to these issues than to the first few pages, in which the distinction between sense and reference is introduced.

—— (1892b), 'On Concept and Object', *Vierteljahrsschrift für wissenschaftliche Philosophie*, 16: 192–205; repr. in B. McGuinness (ed.), *Collected Papers on Mathematics, Logic and Philosophy* (Oxford, 1984). Elaboration of Frege (1891). In particular, discusses the problematic 'The concept *horse* is not a concept'.

—— (1918), 'Der Gedanke: Eine logische Untersuchung' (usually translated as 'The Thought'), *Beiträge zur Philosophie des deutschen Idealismus*, 1: 58–77; repr. in *Logical Investigations: Gottlob Frege*, ed. P. T. Geach (Oxford, 1977). A later work of Frege's, quite accessible. Notable for the seriousness with which he takes the problem of the different descriptions different people are likely to associate with a proper name.

GEACH, PETER (1958), 'Entailment', *Proceedings of the Aristotelian Society*, supp. vol. 32: 157–72; repr. in Peter Geach (ed.), *Logic Matters* (Oxford, 1972). This and Geach (1970) make a classic contribution to this topic.

—— (1970), 'Entailment Again', *Philosophical Review*, 79: 237–9; repr. in *Logic Matters* (Oxford, 1972).

GIBBARD, A. (1975), **'Contingent Identity', *Journal of Philosophical Logic*, 4: 187–221. Essential reading for identity: classic statement of the view that some identities are contingent.

GRICE, H. P. (1961), 'The Causal Theory of Perception', *Proceedings of the Aristotelian Society*, supp. vol. 35: 121–54; repr. in G. Warnock (ed.), *The Philosophy of Perception* (Oxford, 1967). Buried in this article, whose official topic is perception (and in particular the use of the notion of sense-data in a theory of perception), is a very important distinction between what is said and what is conveyed. Grice developed this in various subsequent writings (e.g. Grice 1975), and one application highly relevant to topics covered in this subject area is his defence of the truth-functional character of English connectives like 'and', 'but', and 'if'. See Sainsbury (1991: 77–87).

—— (1975), 'Logic and Conversation', in P. Cole and J. L. Morgan (eds.), *Syntax and Semantics*, iii: *Speech Acts* (New York). See note under Grice (1961).

GUTTENPLAN, S. D. (1988), *The Languages of Logic* (Oxford). Recommended as an introduction to formal logic; thus, preliminary reading. Alternatives are Lemmon (1964) and Hodges (1978).

HAACK, S. (1978), **Philosophy of Logics* (Cambridge). Useful introduction to a large number of issues.

HAZEN, A. (1976), 'Expressive Incompleteness in Modal Logic', *Journal of Philosophical Logic*, 76: 25–46. Original source of some things which, allegedly, cannot be expressed in the language of boxes and diamonds. To be read by those taking a special interest in this issue.

HODGES, W. (1978), *Logic* (London). Introduction to formal logic. You need to choose either this, Guttenplan (1988), or Lemmon (1964), if you want to get some formal logic under your belt.

HORWICH, P. (1990), **Truth*, (Oxford). Very clear book. Covers a good deal of ground.

HUME, D. (1738), *A Treatise of Human Nature* (London). Mentioned very peripherally as far as this subject area goes. The issue relevant here is his 'non-cognitivism': his view on truth, belief, and morality sketched in note 22 above. There are many inexpensive paperback editions.

KRIPKE, S. (1971), 'Identity and Necessity', in M. K. Munitz (ed.), *Identity and Individuation* (New York). Classic defence of the necessity of identity statements not knowable a priori.

—— (1972), **'Naming and Necessity', in D. Davidson and G. Harman (eds.), *Semantics of Natural Language* (Dordrecht); repr. as a book (Oxford, rev. edn. 1980). Classic text, essential reading. Lightly edited transcripts of lectures, so pleasingly informal style, which makes for easy reading. A joy.

—— (1975), 'Outline of a Theory of Truth', *Journal of Philosophy*, 72: 690–716; repr. in

R. L. Martin (ed.), *Recent Essays on Truth and the Liar Paradox* (Oxford, 1984). Not likely that many beginning students will read this: it's long, hard, and technical.

—— (1977), 'Speaker's Reference and Semantic Reference', in P. A. French, T. E. Uehling, and H. K. Wettstein (eds.), *Midwest Studies in Philosophy*, 2: *Studies in the Philosophy of Language*, rev. edn. 1979: *Contemporary Perspectives in Philosophy of Language* (Minneapolis). Makes a distinction which is important in discussing Donnellan.

—— (1979), 'A Puzzle about Belief', in A. Margalit (ed.), *Meaning and Use* (Dordrecht). Raises a detailed question. Probably too detailed for a beginner in this subject area, though important for studies in philosophy of language.

LEMMON, E. J. (1964), *Beginning Logic* (London). Well-tried introduction to formal logic; thus, preliminary reading. Alternatives are Guttenplan (1988) and Hodges (1978).

LEWIS, C. I., and LANGFORD, C. H. (1932), *Symbolic Logic* (New York). Mentioned as source of the classification of modal logics which includes S4, S5. Not recommended. If you are interested in these matters, it would be much better to read Chellas (1980).

LEWIS, D. (1973), *Counterfactuals* (Oxford). Beautiful, elegant book. Gives a possible worlds semantics for counterfactual conditionals. Along the way, has famous argument for possible worlds: 'things could have been different in countless ways. But what does this mean? Ordinary language permits the paraphrase: there are many ways things could have been besides the way they actually are. . . . I therefore believe in the existence of entities that might be called "ways things could have been". I prefer to call them "possible worlds" ' (p. 84).

—— (1986), *On the Plurality of Worlds* (Oxford). Essential reading for studies on necessity. Heavyweight defence of modal realism, and one learns a good deal of general philosophy on the way.

LOWE, E. J. (1987), 'Lewis on Perdurance versus Endurance', *Analysis*, 47: 152–4. Somewhat peripheral to this subject area, but relevant to studies in epistemology and metaphysics. Considers various ways in which change can be accounted for without inconsistency and without regarding persisting things as composed of temporal parts. Proposes a view which Lewis arguably overlooked in his argument for not allowing individuals to occupy more than one world.

McCULLOCH, G. (1989), *The Game of the Name*: *Introducing Logic, Language and Mind* (Oxford). Useful introduction to a range of topics in this subject area. Easily available paperback.

McDOWELL, J. (1977), *'On the Sense and Reference of a Proper Name'*, *Mind*, 86: 159–85; repr. in Moore (1993). Valuable for an account of the Fregean sense of names which is not given by descriptions. This is a hard article: if you feel you understand it, you are really on top of quite a range of issues concerning names. Worth reading several times.

MARTIN, R. L. (ed.) (1984), *Recent Essays on Truth and the Liar Paradox* (Oxford). Mentioned here as a source for essays on truth and the Liar. These are on the whole too detailed for beginners, but you ought to know where to find them.

MEINONG, A. (1904), 'The Theory of Objects', in *Untersuchungen zur Gegenstandtheorie und Psychologie* (Leipzig); repr. in English in Roderick M. Chisholm (ed.), *Realism and the Background of Phenomenology* (New York, 1960). I don't really suggest you read this, but this is the proper source of Meinong's view, should you wish to go back to it.

MILL, J. S. (1843), *A System of Logic*. Various reprints, e.g. (London, 1973). Just a few pages give this classic account of names. Not essential to read in the original.

—— (1859), *On Liberty*. One of Mill's political works; has probably been more influential than his work in logic. Nothing to do with this subject area (it got mentioned in my thumbnail biography of Mill).

—— (1861), *Considerations on Representative Government*. See comment under Mill (1859).

—— (1863), *Utilitarianism*. See comment under Mill (1859).

MOORE, A. W. (ed.) (1993), *Meaning and Reference*, Oxford Readings in Philosophy (Oxford). Good buy. Contains: Frege (1892a), extract from Russell (1919, ch. 16), Strawson (1950a), McDowell (1977), Kripke (1971), and other useful articles. Good editor's introduction. Cheap and easily available.

MOORE, G. E. (1936), 'Is Existence a Predicate?', *Proceedings of the Aristotelian Society*, supp. vol. 15: 157–88; repr. in T. Baldwin (ed.), *G. E. Moore: Selected Writings* (London, 1993). Classic paper on the topic. Mentioned here primarily for the example 'This might not have existed'; but see also his discussion of the contrast between 'Most tame tigers growl' and 'Most tame tigers exist'. The discussion is taken up in Strawson (1967).

NEALE, S. (1990), *Descriptions* (Cambridge, Mass.). Excellent recent book on the topic. Argues for a more or less Russellian position.

PAKULUK, M. (1993), 'The Interpretation of Russell's Gray's *Elegy* Argument', in A. Irvine and G. Wedekind (eds.), *Russell and Analytic Philosophy* (Vancouver). There are a couple of pages in Russell (1905) which purport to show that Frege's distinction between sense and reference is untenable. The pages are obscure; this article offers the best interpretation of them with which I am acquainted.

PAP, A. (1958), *Semantics and Necessary Truth* (New Haven, Conn.). This contains the best statement of the linguistic theory of necessity.

PEACOCKE, C. A. B. (1973), *'Proper Names, Reference and Rigid Designation', in S. Blackburn (ed.), *Meaning, Reference, Necessity: New Studies in Semantics* (Cambridge). Useful for the claim that in some uses descriptions are referring expressions (are 'entity-invoking'). Clarifies the notion of rigid designation, and also makes clear what Strawson (1950a) was driving at.

PITCHER, G. (ed.) (1964), *Truth* (Englewood Cliffs, NJ). Contains the most important articles for the state of the debate in 1964: Austin (1950), Ramsey (1927), Strawson (1950b); but unfortunately not Austin's 'Unfair to Facts' (1961).

PLANTINGA, A. (1974), *The Nature of Necessity* (Oxford). Now rather dated book on necessity. Has a useful appendix discussing Quine (pp. 220–51). Mentioned here as a source of one bad and one interesting objection to counterpart theory.

RAMSEY, F. P. (1927), 'Facts and Propositions', in Pitcher (1964). Lightning sketch of what is now called the redundancy theory of truth. The full version of the paper is in Ramsey's *Philosophical Papers*, ed. D. H. Mellor (Cambridge, 1990).

RUSSELL, B. (1905), *'On Denoting', *Mind*, 14: 479–93; repr. in R. C. Marsh (ed.), *Logic and Knowledge* (London, 1956). Classic statement of Russell's theory of descriptions.

It is not terribly easy to follow, because it is combined with a general account of quantification in rather unfamiliar terminology. Essential reading, but for the theory of descriptions see also the clearer Russell (1919).

—— (1908), 'Mathematical Logic as Based on the Theory of Types', *American Journal of Mathematics*, 30: 222–62; repr. in R. C. Marsh (ed.), *Logic and Knowledge* (London, 1956). Historically important as the first statement of Russell's mature logicism (containing all the fundamental ideas that were developed in his *Principia Mathematica*, with A. N. Whitehead). Not recommended for this subject area.

—— (1911), *'Knowledge by Acquaintance and Knowledge by Description', *Proceedings of the Aristotelian Society*, 11: 108–28; repr. in *Mysticism and Logic* (London, 1910, 1917, 1963). (Page reference in text is to this reprint.) Essential reading to complete an understanding of Russell's theory of descriptions, and for his theory of ordinary proper names. Most of the article reappears as chapter 5 of Russell (1912), but the 1912 version omits a couple of pretty useful pages at the end.

—— (1912), *The Problems of Philosophy* (London). Nice general introduction to philosophy. The essential chapter for this subject area is 5. See comment under Russell (1910).

—— (1918–19), 'Lectures on the Philosophy of Logical Atomism', *Monist*, 28: 29; repr. in R. C. Marsh (ed.), *Logic and Knowledge* (London, 1956). Wonderful statement of Russell's logical atomism, a position involving epistemology, metaphysics, and philosophical logic. See especially lecture 5 ('General Propositions and Existence') and lecture 6 ('Descriptions and Incomplete Symbols').

—— (1919), *Introduction to Mathematical Philosophy* (London). Chapter 16 is Russell's clearest statement of the theory of descriptions. The rest is not needed for this subject area.

—— (1956), *Logic and Knowledge*, ed. R. C. Marsh (London). Good collection of Russell articles, notably his (1905) and (1918–19).

—— and WHITEHEAD, ALFRED NORTH (1910–13), *Principia Mathematica* (Cambridge). The introduction to the first edition could be read with profit. There are statements of his theory of quantification and of descriptions. But one could not call it essential reading for this subject area.

SAINSBURY, R. M. (1979), *Russell* (London). Useful for an account of Russell's theory of names (ch. 3) and descriptions (ch. 4).

—— (1985), 'Gareth Evans: *The Varieties of Reference*', *Mind*, 94: 120–42. Might be useful as a preliminary to reading Evans (1982).

—— (1991), *Logical Forms: An Introduction to Philosophical Logic* (Oxford). Rather idiosyncratic introduction to a number of topics on the subject area. Probably most useful for the discussion of necessity (ch. 5).

—— (1993), 'Russell on Names and Communication', in A. Irvine and G. Wedekind (eds.), *Russell and Analytic Philosophy* (Vancouver). Attempts to spell out the interpretation of Russell's theory of names sketched here, and examine some objections.

—— (1995), *Paradoxes*, 2nd edn. (Cambridge). Can be used for some more detail on the Liar paradox.

SALMON, N. (1986), *Frege's Puzzle* (Cambridge, Mass.). Excellent discussion of Frege's argument for sense based on the difference in cognitive value between truths of the form $a = a$ and truths of the form $a = b$. Generally hostile to Frege, so it's especially important to read this if you feel persuaded by Frege.

SKYRMS, B. (1982), 'Intensional Aspects of Semantical Self-Reference', in Martin (1984). Mentioned for the development of the idea that the Liar paradox can be blocked by denying that substitution of identicals is valid in the relevant contexts. Probably will be followed up only by enthusiasts.

STRAWSON, P. F. (1950a), *'On Referring', *Mind*, 59: 269–86; repr. in *Logico-Linguistic Papers* (London, 1971). Essential reading. Famous attack on Russell's theory of descriptions. Important for distinctions between sentences, uses of sentences, and statements.

—— (1950b), 'Truth', *Proceedings of the Aristotelian Society*, supp. vol. 24: 129–56; repr. in Pitcher (1964). Classic paper on the correspondence theory; part of a symposium with Austin (1950).

—— (1965), 'Truth: A Reconsideration of Austin's Views', *Philosophical Quarterly*, 15: 289–301; repr. in *Logico-Linguistic Papers* (London, 1971). This concludes the story which begins with Austin (1950) and Strawson (1950).

—— (1967), 'Is Existence Never a Predicate?', *Critica*, 1: 5–15; repr. in *Freedom and Resentment and Other Essays* (London, 1974). Defends a Meinongian position, according to which there are some things, in particular fictional characters, which do not exist. Shows that in ordinary talk we are quite happy with the idea that there are things which do not exist.

TARSKI, A. (1937), 'The Concept of Truth in Formalized Languages'; repr. in *Logic, Semantics, Metamathematics* (Oxford, 1956). The canonical exposition of his definition of truth. Most of the article is extremely technical, but the early pages are informal and worth looking at.

—— (1969), 'Truth and Proof', *Scientific American*, 194: 63–77. Informal exposition of some of his main views. If you want to read some Tarski, this is the first piece to choose.

WIGGINS, D. (1976), 'Frege's Problem of the Morning Star and the Evening Star', in M. Schirn (ed.), *Studies on Frege* (Stuttgart). Useful detailed discussion of Frege's notion of sense. Argues that even expressions with the same sense (by intuitive standards) cannot be substituted *salve veritate* in every context in which they are used.

—— (1980a), *Sameness and Substance* (Oxford). Not really suitable for this subject area (though excellent for epistemology and metaphysics). Mentioned here for the use of the Barcan Marcus proof of the necessity of identity.

—— (1980b), 'What would be a Substantial Theory of Truth?', in Z. van Straaten (ed.), *Philosophical Subjects: Essays Presented to P. F. Strawson* (Oxford). Useful attempt to connect the notion of truth with other notions: assertion, convergence, etc.

WRIGHT, C. (1992), *Truth and Objectivity* (Cambridge, Mass.). Impressive recent book, arguing for a version of minimalism about truth. It's too detailed to be what the average beginner needs. But if you want to make a serious study of the realism–anti-realism debate, this book is for you.

3

METHODOLOGY: THE ELEMENTS OF THE PHILOSOPHY OF SCIENCE

David Papineau

INTRODUCTION

The subject-matter of *methodology* is best defined in opposition to that of *logic*. Logic is the study of deductively valid reasoning: in a deductively valid argument, the premisses provide conclusive reasons for the conclusion; it is quite impossible for the premisses to be true and the conclusion false. However, most of the reasoning that we actually engage in falls far short of this ideal. In both everyday life and in science the arguments we use do not provide conclusive reasons for their conclusions. They may in some sense give us good reason to believe their conclusions, but they do not compel us in the same absolute way as deductive arguments.

This discussion of methodology will be concerned with this kind of non-conclusive reasoning and with various philosophical issues that arise in trying to understand it. There will be five sections: (1) Induction and its Problems; (2) Laws of Nature; (3) Realism, Instrumentalism, and Underdetermination; (4) Confirmation and Probability; (5) Explanation.

1. INDUCTION AND ITS PROBLEMS

1.1. The Problem of Induction

Generally speaking, 'induction' refers to any form of inference in which we move from a finite set of observations or experimental results to a conclusion about how things generally behave. There are various forms of inductive inference, but we shall concentrate on simple *enumerative inductions*, which start from the premiss that one phenomenon has always followed another so far, and conclude that those phenomena will always occur together. So, for example, you might note that, every time you have seen red sky in the evening, there has been fine weather the next day, and conclude on that basis that red sky in the evening is *always* followed by fine weather. Or you might note that all the samples of sodium you have heated on a Bunsen burner have glowed bright orange, and conclude on this basis that in general *all* heated sodium glows bright orange. Schematically, the premiss to an enumerative induction is that '*n As* have all been observed to be *Bs*', and the conclusion is that 'All *As* are *Bs*'.

Note that these inductive inferences start with particular premisses about a *finite* number of past observations, yet end up with a general conclusion about how nature will *always* behave. This is the source of the notorious *problem of induction*. For it is unclear how any finite amount of information about what has happened in the past can guarantee that a natural pattern will continue for all time.

After all, what rules out the possibility that the course of nature might change, and that the patterns we have observed so far turn out to be a poor guide to the future? Even if all red-skyed evenings have been followed by fine weather so far, who is to say that they won't start being followed by rain in the next century? Even if all heated sodium has glowed orange up till now, who is to say it won't start glowing blue at some future date?

In this respect induction contrasts with deduction. In deductive inferences the premisses really do guarantee the conclusion. For example, if you know that 'Either this substance is sodium or it is potassium', and then learn further that 'It is not sodium', you can conclude with certainty that 'It is potassium'. The truth of the premisses leaves no room for the conclusion to be anything but true. But in an inductive inference this does not hold. If you are told that 'Each of the As observed so far has been B', this does not guarantee that 'All As, including future ones, are Bs'. It is perfectly possible that the former claim may be true, but the latter false.

I have illustrated the problem of induction with respect to enumerative inductions. There are other forms of induction apart from enumerative induction, as we shall see later. But the problem of induction is quite general. For what the different forms of induction have in common is that they take us from information about a finite number of instances to some general conclusion about a wider class of cases. Since nothing in logic seems to guarantee that the wider class will display the same behaviour as the finite instances, any such inference is for this reason equally problematic.

The problem of induction threatens both everyday and scientific knowledge. Most of the everyday knowledge we rely on consists of general principles like '*Whenever* you cut yourself, you bleed', or '*Whenever* the brakes are applied, cars stop'. Similarly, all scientific discoveries worth the name are in the form of general principles: Galileo's law of free fall says that '*All* bodies fall with constant acceleration'; Newton's law of gravitation says that '*All* bodies attract each other in proportion to their masses and in inverse proportion to the square of the distance between them'; Avogadro's law says that '*All* gases at the same temperature and pressure contain the same number of molecules per unit volume'; and so on. The problem of induction calls in question the authority of all these general claims. For if our evidence is simply that these generalizations have worked so far, then how can we be sure that they will not be disproved by future occurrences?

1.2. Initial Responses to the Problem

1.2.1. A Principle of Induction

One possible response to the problem of induction would be to appeal to some 'principle of induction' which asserts that, for some number N,

(P) For any α and β, whenever N αs are observed to be βs, then all αs are βs.

If such a principle were available, then we could add it to the original premiss of any enumerative induction—namely, that N (or more) As have been observed to be Bs—to conclude deductively that 'All As are Bs'. For once we add (P) as a premiss, then there is no longer any room for the premisses of the induction to be true and the conclusion to be false.

However, even if we leave to one side the question how big N needs to be to make (P) plausible, there is an obvious difficulty about the status of the proposed principle. Clearly (P) is not an analytic claim whose truth is guaranteed by its meaning: you could understand all the terms in it, yet not believe it. So it must be a synthetic claim, in need of support by empirical evidence. But since (P) is a generalization, this support would have to be some kind of inductive argument, taking as its premisses some finite body of instances where inductive inferences have worked in the past, and seeking to move to (P) as a conclusion. So in the present context of argument this would beg the question at issue, which is to defend inductive arguments against the challenge raised by the problem of induction.

1.2.2. Inductive Arguments for Induction

Suppose we abandon any principle of induction, and thereby accept that we cannot make inductive arguments deductive. Still, cannot we simply argue that inductive arguments are nevertheless acceptable because they *work*? Even if the premisses don't logically *guarantee* the conclusions, don't the conclusions normally turn out to be true anyway? After all, hasn't our experience shown us that patterns like red-sky–good-weather or sodium-heated–orange-flame continue to hold good in the future, once they have displayed themselves in the past?

But this suggestion runs into the same difficulty as the last one. We are arguing that inductions are generally acceptable because our experience has shown them to work so far. But this is itself an inductive argument. After all, even if observed patterns have tended to hold good so far, what guarantees that they will continue to do so? As Bertrand Russell once said, it is no help to observe that *past* futures have conformed to *past* pasts; what we want to know is whether *future* futures will conform to *future* pasts. Given that we are trying to vindicate induction against objections, an inductive argument for induction once more begs the question.

1.2.3. Introducing Probability

Another possible response to the problem of induction is to regard inductive inferences as merely generating *probable* conclusions, rather than certain ones.

Even if past evidence doesn't allow us to be sure about future patterns, might it not at least support conclusions about *probable* patterns?

Later on we shall see that the idea of probability is indeed important for our understanding of inductive arguments. But it is not difficult to show that on its own it is not enough to solve the problem of induction.

In fact, as we shall see later, there are really two notions of probability. Roughly, we need to distinguish probability in the sense of rational *degree of belief* from probability in the sense of *objective tendency*. When we say that it is 50 per cent probable that it will snow today, we might mean one of two things. First, we might be expressing a degree of belief: saying that we have an equal expectation both for its snowing and for its not snowing today. Alternatively, we might be making a claim about an objective tendency: saying that in general it snows on 50 per cent of days like today. Later on we shall look at these 'subjective' and 'objective' interpretations of probability in more detail. Here I merely want to show that neither helps with the problem of induction.

Suppose first that the conclusion of an inductive inference is a statement of *objective* probability, stating that in 90 per cent of cases, say, As turn out to be Bs (for example, that on 90 per cent of days following red-skyed evenings there is fine weather). The evidence for this claim will still be a finite body of observations, namely, that in our experience *so far* more or less 90 per cent of As have been Bs. So the problem of induction is still with us, for we still need to explain how a finite body of evidence can establish a general conclusion. For note that the probabilistic conclusion is still a claim, requiring not just that 90 per cent of As have been Bs in the *past*, but also that this will continue in the *future*. Even if the pattern we are now interested in is probabilistic, rather than exceptionless, we still face the same difficulty in explaining how past patterns can tell us about future ones.

Alternatively, we might take the conclusion of an inductive inference to be a statement of *subjective* probability, asserting that 'We should attach a high degree of belief to the proposition that all As are Bs'. (Note that we could also have a statement of subjective probability about a proposition of objective probability: for example, 'We should attach a high degree of belief to the proposition that 90 per cent of As are Bs'. The point which follows would apply just the same.) The difficulty once more is that our evidence for such a conclusion about subjective probability is simply that As have been observed to go with Bs *so far*. Yet the conclusion says that we should have a high expectation that As will go with Bs in the future as well as the past. So we still face the problem of explaining how facts about the past can tell us what to think about the future.

1.3. Popper's Alternative to Induction

A rather different line of response to the problem of induction is due to Karl Popper. Popper looks to the practice of science to show us how to deal with the problem. In Popper's view, science does not rest on induction in the first place. He denies that scientists start with observations and then infer a general theory. Rather, they first put forward a theory, as an initially uncorroborated conjecture, and then compare its predictions with observations to see whether it stands up to test. If such tests prove negative, then the theory is experimentally falsified and the scientists will seek some new alternative. If, on the other hand, the tests fit the theory, then scientists will continue to uphold it—not as proven truth, admittedly, but nevertheless as an undefeated conjecture.

If we look at science in this way, argues Popper, then we see that it does not need induction. According to Popper, the inferences which matter to science are *refutations*, which take some failed prediction as the premiss and conclude that the theory behind that prediction is false. These inferences are not inductive, but deductive. We see that some *A* is not-*B*, and conclude that it is not the case that all *As* are *Bs*. There is no room here for the premiss to be true and the conclusion false. If we discover that some piece of sodium does not glow orange when heated, then we know for sure that it is not the case that all heated sodium glows orange. The point here is that it is much easier to disprove theories than to prove them. A single contrary example suffices for a conclusive disproof, but no number of supporting examples will constitute a conclusive proof.

So, according to Popper, science is a sequence of conjectures. Scientific theories are put forward as hypotheses, and they are replaced by new hypotheses when they are falsified. However, this view of science raises an obvious question: if scientific theories are always conjectural, then what makes science better than astrology, or spirit-worship, or any other form of unwarranted superstition? A non-Popperian would answer this question by saying that real science *proves* its claims on the basis of observational evidence, whereas superstition is nothing but guesswork. But, on Popper's account, even scientific theories are guesswork—for they cannot be proved by the observations, but are themselves merely undefeated conjectures.

Popper calls this the 'problem of demarcation'—what is the difference between science and other forms of belief? His answer is that science, unlike superstition, is at least *falsifiable*, even if it is not provable. Scientific theories are framed in precise terms, and so issue in definite predictions. For example, Newton's laws tell us exactly where certain planets will appear at certain times. And this means that if such predictions fail, we can be sure that the theory behind them is false. By contrast, belief systems like astrology are irredeemably vague, in a way which prevents their ever being shown definitely wrong. Astrology may predict that Scorpios will prosper in their personal relationships on Thursdays, but when faced with a Scorpio whose spouse walks out on a Thursday, defenders of astrology are likely to respond that the end of the marriage was probably for the best, all things considered. Because of this, nothing will ever force astrologers to admit their theory is wrong. The theory is phrased in such imprecise terms that no actual observations can possibly falsify it.

Popper himself uses this criterion of *falsifiability* to distinguish genuine science, not just from traditional belief systems like astrology and spirit-worship, but also from Marxism, psychoanalysis, and various other modern disciplines he denigrates as 'pseudo-sciences'. According to Popper, the central claims of these theories are as unfalsifiable as those of astrology. Marxists predict that proletarian revolutions will be successful whenever capitalist regimes have been sufficiently weakened by their internal contradictions. But when faced with unsuccessful proletarian revolutions, they simply respond that the contradictions in those particular capitalist regimes have not yet weakened them sufficiently. Similarly, psychoanalytic theorists will claim that all adult neuroses are due to childhood traumas, but when faced by troubled adults with apparently undisturbed childhoods, they will say that those adults must nevertheless have undergone private psychological traumas when young. For Popper, such ploys are the antithesis of scientific seriousness. Genuine scientists will say beforehand what observational discoveries would make them change their minds, and will abandon their theories if these discoveries are made. But Marxists and psychoanalytic theorists frame their theories in such a way, argues Popper, that no possible observations need ever make them adjust their thinking.

1.4. The Failings of Falsificationism

At first sight Popper seems to offer an attractive way of dealing with the problem of induction. However, there is reason to doubt whether he really offers a solution.

The central objection to his account is that it only accounts for *negative* scientific knowledge, as opposed to *positive* knowledge. Popper points out that a single counter-example can show us that a scientific theory is wrong. But he says nothing about what can show us that a scientific theory is right. Yet it is positive knowledge of this latter kind that is supposed to follow from inductive inferences. What is more, it is this kind of positive knowledge that makes induction so important. We can cure diseases and send people to the moon because we know that certain causes *do* always have certain results, not because we know that they *don't*. If Popper cannot explain how we sometimes know that 'All *As* are *Bs*', rather than just 'It's false that all *As* are *Bs*', then he has surely failed to deal properly with the problem of induction.

Popper's usual answer to this objection is that he is concerned with the logic of pure scientific research, not with practical questions about technological applications. Scientific research requires only that we formulate falsifiable conjectures and reject them if we discover counter-examples. The further question whether we should *believe* those conjectures, and *rely* on their predictions when, say, we prescribe some drug or build a dam, Popper regards as an essentially practical issue, and as such not part of the analysis of rational scientific practice.

But this will not do, if Popper is supposed to be offering a solution to the problem of induction. The problem of induction is essentially the problem of how we can base judgements about the future on evidence about the past. In insisting that scientific theories are just conjectures, and that therefore we have no rational basis for *believing* their predictions, Popper is simply denying that we can make rational judgements about the future.

Consider these two predictions:

(A) When I jump from this tenth-floor window, I shall crash painfully into the ground.
(B) When I jump from the window, I will float like a feather to a gentle landing.

Intuitively, it is more rational to believe (A), which assumes that the future will be like the past, than (B), which does not. But Popper, since he rejects induction, is committed to the view that past evidence does not make any beliefs about the future more rational than any others, and therefore to the view that believing (B) is no less rational than believing (A).

Something has gone wrong. *Of course* believing (A) is more rational than believing (B). In saying this, I do not want to deny that there is a *problem* of induction. Indeed it is precisely *because* believing (A) is more rational than believing (B) that induction is problematic. Everybody, Popper aside, can see *that* believing (A) is more rational than believing (B). The problem is then to explain *why* believing (A) is more rational than believing (B), in the face of the fact that induction is not logically compelling. So Popper's denial of the rational superiority of (A) over (B) is not so much a *solution* to the problem of induction, but simply a refusal to recognize the problem in the first place. As a reviewer of one of Popper's books once said, Popper's attitude to induction is like that of someone who stands on the starting-line of a race and shouts, 'I've won, I've won'.

Even if it fails to deal with induction, it should be recognized that Popper's philosophy of science does have some strengths as a description of pure scientific research. For it is certainly true that many scientific theories start life as conjectures, in just the way Popper describes. When Einstein's general theory of relativity was first proposed, for example, very few scientists actually believed it. Instead they regarded it as an interesting hypothesis, and were curious to see whether it was true. At this initial stage of a theory's life, Popper's recommendations make eminent sense. Obviously, if you are curious to see whether a theory is true, the next step is to put it to the observational test. And for this purpose it is important that the theory is framed in precise enough terms for scientists to work out what it implies about the observable world—that is, in

David Papineau

precise enough terms for it to be falsifiable. And of course if the new theory does get falsified, then scientists will reject it and seek some alternative, whereas if its predictions are borne out, then scientists will continue to investigate it.

Where Popper's philosophy of science goes wrong, however, is in holding that scientific theories never progress beyond the level of conjecture. As I have just agreed, theories are often mere conjectures when they are first put forward, and they may remain conjectures as the initial evidence first comes in. But in many cases the accumulation of evidence in favour of a theory will move it beyond the status of conjecture to that of established truth. The general theory of relativity started life as a conjecture, and many scientists still regarded it as hypothetical even after Sir Arthur Eddington's famous initial observations in 1919 of light apparently bending near the sun. But by now this initial evidence has been supplemented with evidence in the form of gravitational red-shifts, time-dilation, and black holes, and it would be an eccentric scientist who nowadays regarded the general theory as less than firmly established.

This example can be multiplied. The heliocentric theory of the solar system, the theory of evolution by natural selection, and the theory of continental drift all started life as intriguing conjectures, with little evidence to favour them over their competitors. But in the period since they were first proposed these theories have all accumulated a great wealth of supporting evidence, and nearly everybody who is acquainted with this evidence has no doubt that these theories are well-established truths.

1.5. Induction is Rational by Definition

I have just insisted, against Popper, that it is often rational to believe the conclusions of inductive inferences. However, as I said, this observation is by no means a solution to the problem of induction. For we still need to explain how inductive inferences can be rational, give that their conclusions are not logically guaranteed by their premises.

Some philosophers have argued that we can solve the problem by focusing on the everyday meaning of the term 'rational'.[1] After all, they point out, in normal usage this term is by no means restricted to deductive reasoning. True, everybody recognizes that deductive reasoning is *one* species of rational argument. But at the same time nearly everybody also applies the term 'rational' to other kinds of reasoning, and in particular to inductive reasoning.

By way of illustration, consider three different ways of forecasting the weather. The first type of forecaster does not pay any attention to past weather patterns, but simply guesses at random at tomorrow's weather. A second type of forecaster does attend to past patterns, but predicts future weather on the

[1] See Paul Edwards, 'Russell's Doubts about Induction', *Mind*, 68 (1949), 141–63; and section 9 in P. F. Strawson, *Introduction to Logical Theory* (London, 1952).

basis of the assumption that future weather patterns are going to be different from past patterns: so, for example, on seeing red sky in the evening, this forecaster reasons that, since red sky has presaged fine weather in the past, tomorrow's weather will not be fine. The third forecaster works on the assumption that past weather patterns are indeed a guide to future patterns, and so, on the basis of past experience, takes red sky in the evening to be a sign that there will be fine weather tomorrow.

Now, if we ask people who understand the meaning of the word 'rational' which of these three weather forecasters is rational, there is no doubt that they will reply that the third forecaster is rational, and the other two are not. And there is no doubt that they would also say that in general people who anticipate the future on the basis of the past are rational, and those who merely guess, or expect the future to be unlike the past, are irrational.

Doesn't this now show that induction is rational? For what more could be needed to show this than that people who understand the meaning of the term 'rational' all agree that this term is applicable to inductive reasoning?

This form of argument is known as the 'paradigm case argument', and was very popular among British 'ordinary language philosophers' in the 1950s and 1960s. It was applied to other philosophical problems apart from the problem of induction. So, for example, in response to the thesis that human beings do not really have free will, ordinary language philosophers pointed out that anybody who understands the phrase 'acting of their own free will' will have no hesitation in applying it to a wide range of human actions. After all, the ordinary language philosophers argued, aren't such actions as drinking a cup of coffee or buying a new car paradigm cases of free actions, as we ordinarily use the term? And what more could be needed to show that free will exists than that people who understand the meaning of the term 'free will' all agree that it applies to this kind of human action?

However, this example also serves to bring out the weakness of paradigm case arguments. The only reason some philosophers doubt the existence of free will is because they think there is an underlying requirement for an action to be free, namely, that it not be determined by past causes, and because, moreover, they doubt that any human actions are not so determined. Any such philosopher will reply to the paradigm case argument for free will as follows: 'Maybe ordinary people are happy to apply the term "free will" to such actions as drinking a cup of coffee or buying a new car. But this is only because they are implicitly assuming that these actions are not determined by past causes. But in fact they are wrong in this assumption. All human actions are determined by past causes. So there is really no free will, and everyday people are just making a mistake when they apply the term "free will" as they do.'

The same point applies to the attempt to establish the rationality of induction by appeal to ordinary usage. For ordinary usage leaves it open that there may be some underlying requirement for a form of inference to count as rational. And inductive inferences may in fact fail to satisfy this requirement, despite the inclination of ordinary people to apply the term 'rational' to induction.

1.6. A Reliabilist Defence of Induction

Let us ask, then, whether there is some underlying requirement which a form of inference must satisfy if it is to qualify as rational. Well, a minimum requirement is surely that the conclusions of these inferences must generally be true, if the premisses are. The whole point of inferences is to increase our stock of knowledge. Inferences make new knowledge out of old: they take old knowledge as input, and generate new knowledge as output. But a form of inference will fail in this task if it issues in false conclusions even when provided with true premisses. For in such cases the inference will not be increasing our stock of knowledge, but rather leading us into error.

It is important to recognize that this requirement—that the conclusions of a form of inference should generally be true if its premisses are—does not necessarily amount to the requirement that the form of inference should be *deductively valid*. A form of inference is deductively valid if it is logically quite *impossible* for the conclusions to be false if the premisses are true. This is far stronger than the requirement that *as a matter of fact* the conclusions are never false when the premisses are true. By way of illustration, consider this form of inference.

X is a human

X is less than 200 years old

This is not deductively valid. It is logically *possible* for someone to be a human and to live for 200 years. But, as it happens, there are no such human beings, and so this form of inference will never in fact take us from a true premiss to a false conclusion. (Of course, this form of inference can be made deductive by adding the premiss that 'All humans are less than 200 years old'. But my point is that, even if we don't add this premiss, and so stop the inference being deductive, it still satisfies the requirement of never going from true premisses to false conclusions.)

Let us use the term 'reliable' for the requirement that true premisses should always yield true conclusions. Then deductively valid inferences can be thought of as inferences that are *necessarily* reliable. In the terminology of possible worlds, a deductively valid inference will generate true conclusions out of true premisses in *every* possible world. A reliable but non-deductive inference, by contrast, always generates true conclusions out of true premisses in the actual world, but would go astray in other possible worlds (such as worlds, say, in which humans live for more than 200 years).

Given this distinction, it seems clear that reliability is a minimal requirement for a form of inference to be acceptable. However, to ask in addition for deductive validity seems like overkill. If we have a form of inference which works in the actual world, why require in addition that it should also work in every other possible world, however unlikely or outlandish?

These points support the ordinary language philosophers in their insistence that deductively valid inferences do not exhaust the category of rational inferences. But they suggest a different kind of reason for recognizing some non-deductive forms of inference as rational. The ordinary language philosophers were prepared to count as rational any form of inference that normal speakers of English call 'rational'. The points made in this section, however, argue that a form of inference should only count as rational if it satisfies the underlying requirement of reliably transmitting truth from premises to conclusion.

It should be said that it is a matter of active controversy whether reliability is sufficient for rationality. This issue is part of a widespread contemporary debate which involves not only the notion of rationality, but also such related notions as *knowledge* and *justification*. Few contemporary philosophers, I think, would still want to say that a belief is rational (knowledge, justified) only if it is arrived at in ways that are necessarily reliable (such as by deductive inference). But among the remainder there is a split, between those (let us call them 'reliabilists' henceforth) who think that a reliable source on its own suffices for a belief to be rational (knowledge, justified) and those who think that some further requirement, such as intuitive persuasiveness, also needs to be satisfied.

However, there is no question of resolving this wider dispute here. So in the remainder of this section I shall discuss the following conditional thesis: *if* you think the reliability of a form of inference is sufficient for its rationality, *then* you will have an answer to the problem of induction.

Note first that, if we do adopt the reliabilist point of view, the original argument against induction ceases to present a substantial problem. For the original argument was simply that the premises of an inductive argument do not deductively imply its conclusion. But since we are no longer demanding that inductive arguments should be logically infallible, but only that they in fact reliably transmit truth, this is no argument against induction at all. For, as I have emphasized, a form of inference can be reliable without being deductively valid.

This is only part of a reliabilist defence of induction. For, even if the traditional argument fails to show that induction is not reliable, the reliabilist still needs to provide grounds for thinking that induction is reliable. Unlike the ordinary language philosopher, the reliabilist cannot simply defend induction on the grounds that most people regard it 'rational'. For, according to reliabilism, a form of inference is only rational if it satisfies the underlying requirement of reliably transmitting truth from premises to conclusion.

But perhaps the reliabilist can answer this challenge. The issue is whether inductive inferences generally yield true conclusions if given true premises. The reliabilist can point out that there is plenty of evidence that they do. When people have made inductions from true premises in the past, the reliabilist can argue, their conclusions have turned out true. So we can infer, from this evidence, that inductive inferences are in general reliable transmitters of truth.

Of course this last step is itself an inductive inference, from the past success of inductions to their general reliability, and so this argument is simply a version of the inductive defence of induction I accused of begging the question in Section 1.2.2. However, at that stage we were assuming that the traditional argument raises a genuine problem for induction, and that therefore it would be illegitimate to use induction in further philosophical analysis. But the first point made by the reliabilist defence of induction was that the traditional argument, which merely points out that induction is not deduction, does nothing at all to discredit induction. So why shouldn't we use our normal inductive methods to ascertain whether induction is reliable? How else, the reliabilist can reasonably ask, are we expected to address the question?

Of course this kind of inductive defence of induction is not going to persuade somebody who does not already make inductions to start making them, for such a person will be disinclined to conclude, from the premiss that inductions have worked in the past, that they will do so in the future. But the reliabilist can respond that the inductive argument for induction is not supposed to cure any eccentrics who might reject induction. Rather, it is simply supposed to explain, to normal people like ourselves, how we are entitled to the view that induction is reliable, and hence rational.

Not all philosophers would agree that this reliabilist defence of induction avoids begging the question. But at this stage I propose to leave this issue and turn instead to a more direct objection. This defence assumes that inductions with true premises have at least generated true conclusions so far, as the premiss to the inductive argument for induction. But is even this true? Aren't there plenty of cases where people have made inductions, and yet have arrived at false rather than true conclusions?

Clearly this is a challenge reliabilists need to answer. For even if we grant them the legitimacy of inductive arguments for induction, reliabilists aren't going to get anywhere if the past evidence indicates that induction is not reliable.

I shall examine two sorts of reason for thinking that induction is downright unreliable. One sort appeals to the history of science and notes that many inductively supported scientific theories, from Ptolemaic astronomy to Newtonian physics, have been shown by later evidence to be false. However, I shall postpone discussion of this sort of historical argument against induction until Section 3. First I want to examine a more abstract reason for thinking that induction, or at least enumerative induction, cannot possibly be generally reliable.

1.7. Goodman's New Problem of Induction

Suppose we define 'grue' as a term which applies to all and only those objects which are *first examined before* AD *2000 and found to be green* OR *which are not first examined before 2000 and are blue*.

Now imagine that we want to ascertain, by inductive means, which properties, if any, are possessed by all emeralds. Well, we can note that all the emeralds that we have observed so far have been green, and conclude on this basis, by an enumerative induction, that all emeralds are green. But we could also note that all the emeralds we have observed so far have been grue (since they have all been first examined before AD 2000 and found to be green) and so infer, by a quite analogous enumerative induction, that all emeralds are grue.

But now note that these two conclusions, that all emeralds are green and that all emeralds are grue, cannot both be true, given that some emeralds will only be first examined after AD 2000. For the first conclusion implies that these emeralds will be green, and the second conclusion implies that they will be blue, and so one of them must be wrong. Intuitively, of course, we are convinced that it is the 'grue hypothesis' that is wrong, and that emeralds will still be green after AD 2000. But this intuitive assumption is not needed to make Goodman's initial point, which is that both conclusions were reached by enumerative inductions of the form: 'A large number n of As have all been seen to be Bs', so 'All As are Bs'; yet at most one of these conclusions is true; so enumerative inductions cannot all reliably generate true conclusions.

Of course, grue is rather a funny property, and I'll come back to that in a moment. But the central moral of Goodman's argument is simply that, unless we put some restrictions on what As and Bs are allowed to enter into enumerative inductions, there are going to be far too many enumerative inductions for them all to have true conclusions. This is because, given any 'normal' predicate like 'green', we can easily cook up an infinity of funny grue-like predicates that will give rise to inductive conclusions that must be false, if 'normal' inductive conclusions are true.

The 'new problem' raised by Goodman is thus to distinguish, among all the complicated predicates that can be defined, that subclass which should be allowed to enter into inductive inferences. Goodman called this the problem of distinguishing 'projectible' from 'non-projectible' predicates.

Some philosophers have suggested that the problem can be dealt with fairly quickly, by simply banning any predicates whose definition makes reference to some particular time, in the way that the definition of 'grue' refers to AD 2000. But Goodman shows that the problem cannot be dealt with this easily. For suppose we define 'bleen' as 'first examined before AD 2000 and found to be blue OR not first examined before 2000 and green'. Then it is true that if we start with the predicates 'green' and 'blue', and define 'grue' and 'bleen' in terms of them, as above, then the definitions make mention of particular times. But suppose we instead started with 'grue' and 'bleen' as our primitive terms. Then we could define 'green' as 'first examined before AD 2000 and found to be grue OR not first examined before 2000 and bleen'; and we could define 'blue' as 'first examined before AD 2000 and found to be bleen OR not first examined before 2000 and grue'; and from this perspective it is then the definitions of 'green' and 'blue' that make mention of time. So in effect the appeal to time begs the question. For it is only because we start with the assumption that 'green' and 'blue' are respectable predicates, in terms of which 'grue' and 'bleen' need defining, rather than vice versa, that we deem 'grue' and 'bleen' not to be respectable.

Goodman's own solution is that the 'projectible' predicates are simply those which happen to be 'entrenched' in our inductive practices, in the sense that they are the ones which our community has used to make inductive inferences in the past. Other philosophers, however, have tried to devise less arbitrary ways of drawing the line, appealing to ideas of simplicity or of importance to science. It would be fair to say, I think, that there is no universally agreed solution to this question.

In any case, simply drawing a line between projectible predicates and the rest is arguably only half the problem. We would also like some explanation of why it is rational to make inductions with projectible predicates but not others. From the reliabilist perspective outlined in the last section, such an explanation would need to establish that inductions made using projectible predicates reliably produce true conclusions given true premisses.

There is the possibility of simply arguing once more that past inductions provide inductive evidence for induction's reliability, as was done at the end of the last section. But it can no longer be taken for granted that this move is available. For when we made this move in the last section, it was via an enumerative (meta-)induction. But we now know that enumerative induction is not always a satisfactory means of reasoning, and that at best some restricted category of such inductions is acceptable, namely, those that deal specifically with 'projectible' features of the world. Until we have some more detailed theory of 'projectibility', we cannot take it for granted that the success of past inductions is itself the kind of projectible pattern that provides inductive evidence for its own continuation.

At this stage, however, I propose to leave this topic. I shall return and consider it from a somewhat different perspective at the end of Section 3.6.

2. LAWS OF NATURE

2.1. Hume, Laws, and Accidents

In this section I want to consider a different puzzle raised by the existence of general truths about nature. Here the puzzle is not to do with our knowledge of such truths, but with the nature of the reality they describe: it is a problem in metaphysics, rather than epistemology. This problem is normally called the problem of distinguishing 'laws of nature' from 'accidental generalizations'.

A helpful way to approach this problem is to go back to David Hume's analysis of causation. Prior to Hume, philosophers assumed that when one thing caused another, this was because the cause possessed some kind of power which necessitated the occurrence of the effect. Moreover, they took it that we can know about these necessitating links a priori, in the sense that we can infer a priori that the effect will necessarily follow the cause, even if we have never had previous experience of their co-occurrence.

Hume argued against this account of causation. He pointed out that when we observe one event causing another (for example, the impact of one billiard-ball causing another to move), we never see any necessitating link. All we see is the initial event (the first ball's impact), and then the subsequent event (the second ball's motion), but never any third thing which might link them together. In addition, Hume argued that there is no a priori knowledge of the kind which such necessitating links would provide. People who have never observed billiard-balls cannot possibly tell, on the first occasion they see a moving ball approaching a stationary one, that the impact will make the stationary one move, rather than explode, or turn into a leprechaun.

Hume's own account of the link between a cause and its effect is simply that events like the cause are always followed by events like the effect. In Hume's view, there is nothing in a particular cause–effect sequence, other than that the first event occurs, and the second occurs after it. The link is simply that this sequence is an instance of a general pattern in which, to use Hume's terminology, events like the cause are 'constantly conjoined' with events like the effect.

One consequence of Hume's analysis of causation is the problem of induction discussed in the last section. Prior to Hume, it was assumed that we could know a priori that certain results would always follow certain causes. According to Hume, however, knowledge of causation is simply knowledge of constant conjunctions which are not the upshot of any a priori link between the cause and the effect. So our knowledge of causation can only derive from our experience of the cause being constantly conjoined with the effect. The problem of induction then emerges as the problem that our experience, which is always of a finite number of past cause–effect instances, is insufficient to guarantee what we need for causal knowledge, namely, knowledge that the cause will be constantly conjoined with the effect, not just in the past, but in the future too.

The problem of induction is a problem about our knowledge of general truths, a problem in epistemology. But Hume's analysis of causation also generates a problem about the nature of general truths, a problem in metaphysics. The problem is that Hume's analysis of causation makes it difficult to distinguish genuine laws of nature which state causal truths from accidental generalizations whose truth is a matter of mere happenstance.

According to Hume, a causal law is simply a statement of the form 'Whenever *A*, then *B*'. However, there are truths of this form which do not seem to express laws. Whenever I go to watch Arsenal play, the score is 0–0. That is a true statement of the form 'Whenever *A*, then *B*'. And it's going to stay true, because I'm not going to watch Arsenal any more. But it clearly isn't a causal law. Even though my attendance is in fact always followed by zero goals, my being at Highbury doesn't stop the players scoring.

But why not? If all that is required for a law is that *A*s are always followed by *B*s, then why isn't it a law that there are no goals when I watch Arsenal? After all, there is, by hypothesis, a perfect correlation between my being at Highbury and nobody scoring.

This is the problem of distinguishing laws from accidents. The Humean account of causation threatens to admit accidentally true generalizations into the category of laws. We need to find some way of keeping them out.

There are two general lines of response to this problem, which I shall call 'Humean' and 'non-Humean'. The Humeans stick to the basic Humean idea that causal laws state constant conjunctions, not necessary connections, and then try to explain why some constant conjunctions (the laws) are better than others (the accidents). Non-Humeans, by contrast, question this basic idea, and argue for a return to the pre-Humean view that the difference between laws and accidents is simply that laws, but not accidents, state necessary connections.

2.2. Counterfactual Conditionals

However, before exploring these two types of response, it will be useful to deal with a connected issue. One often-noted difference between laws and accidents is that laws but not accidents support *counterfactual conditionals*. A counterfactual conditional is an 'if . . . then . . .' statement with a false antecedent clause. So, for example, the claim 'If the temperature had fallen below 0°C, then there would have been ice on the road', made on an occasion where the temperature did not in fact fall below 0°C and the water did not freeze, is a counterfactual conditional. Indeed it is a counterfactual conditional that we intuitively accept as true, in virtue of the law that water always freezes at 0°C. But now consider the counterfactual conditional 'If I had gone to Arsenal, the score would have been 0–0', made about a match to which I did not go and which was not a scoreless draw. Even though it is in fact true that on all occasions when I am present there are no goals, we do not accept this second counterfactual conditional as true on that account. Intuitively we feel that my presence would not have made any difference. Even if I had been there, the goals would still have been scored.

This is the sense in which laws but not accidents support counterfactuals. We intuitively project laws, but not accidents, into counterfactual situations. However, while this is certainly a good symptom of the difference between laws and accidents, it does not amount to an explanation of the difference.

The reason is that the meaning of counterfactuals is itself a matter that calls for philosophical explanation. We might start such an explanation by saying that counterfactuals state what happens in non-actual situations. But in what sense do non-actual situations exist? And if they don't exist, what makes counterfactual claims true?

One possible philosophical theory of counterfactuals is to say that counterfactuals are true just in case there is a law linking up the antecedent and consequent. But if we take this line on counterfactuals, then we obviously cannot turn round and use counterfactuals to explain the law–accident difference. For this theory of counterfactuals presupposes this difference.

As it happens, there are in any case well-known difficulties facing an explanation of counterfactuals in terms of laws. To mention just one, consider counterfactuals in which the antecedent is itself the denial of a law, such as 'If the force of gravity were inversely proportional to r, rather than r^2, then the universe would already be contracting'. This seems a perfectly cogent counterfactual assertion, but the notion of some further law linking antecedent and consequent does not seem to apply.

Because of this, contemporary philosophers have developed various other theories of counterfactual. One popular such theory, due to David Lewis,[2] appeals to the metaphysics of 'possible worlds', and says that the counterfactual 'If A, then B' is true if and only if the 'nearest' possible world in which A is true is also one in which B is true. This is an attractive theory of counterfactuals. But if we adopt this, or any other similar theory of counterfactuals, then we still cannot explain the law–accident difference in terms of counterfactuals. For, since we are now explaining counterfactuals in terms of possible worlds, rather than laws, we will need some further explanation of why laws, but not accidents, 'project' into nearby possible worlds. After all, on the Humean view, both laws and accidents simply state that As are always followed by Bs in the actual world. So why do laws, but not accidents, also tell us about other non-actual worlds?

A complete philosophy of these matters would combine an account of the law–accident distinction with an account of counterfactuals in order to yield an

---

[2] *Counterfactuals* (Oxford, 1973).

explanation why laws and not accidents support counterfactuals. But, until we have such a complete account, the counterfactual-supporting power of laws is part of the problem of explaining the difference between laws and accidents, not a solution.

2.3. Laws as Wide-Ranging Generalizations

The Humean strategy, remember, is to explain why some constant conjunctions (laws) are better than others (accidents). An obvious initial thought is that laws tend to be more general than accidents. The truth that water freezes at $0°C$ covers an indefinite, and perhaps infinite, number of instances. By contrast, the truth that there are never any goals when I am at Arsenal only applies to an odd half-dozen or so cases.

But this isn't in fact an invariable difference. There can well be laws with only a few instances. 'In any expanding universe, the rate of expansion decreases' presumably only has one instance, but it isn't any less a law for that. And it is even arguable that there are laws with no instances, such as 'A body subject to no forces will have zero acceleration'.

A related thought is that accidents are disqualified from lawlike status because they tend to be framed using terms which refer to particular spatio-temporal individuals, like 'David Papineau', and 'Arsenal football ground', rather than in purely qualitative terms like 'water', '$0°C$', and 'freezes'. Terms of the latter kind apply to any objects anywhere which have the right general properties, whereas non-qualitative terms like 'David Papineau' are restricted to specific individuals.

But this does not get to the heart of the matter either. Suppose we start with a true accidental generalization framed in non-qualitative terms, such as 'Whenever David Papineau goes to Arsenal, the score is 0–0', and simply replace the non-qualitative terms by qualitative descriptions detailed enough to pick out just the same individuals. That is, suppose we replaced 'David Papineau' by 'anybody with such-and-such an appearance' and 'Arsenal football ground' by 'any football ground with such-and-such-shaped stands', where the 'such-and-suches' were long descriptions which uniquely identified me and Arsenal football ground. Then 'Whenever somebody with such-and-such an appearance goes to a football ground with such-and-such-shaped stands' would be a true generalization framed in purely qualitative terms. But it would still be an accident.

2.4. Laws are Inductively Supported by their Instances

But still, despite the arguments of the last section, isn't there some sense in which accidents are too specific, too local, to function as general guides to the workings of the universe? J. L. Mackie has argued for a different way of capturing this intuition. The trouble with accidents, according to Mackie, is not that they have too few instances, as such, but rather that they aren't *inductively supported* by their instances. When we observe a number of cases of water freezing at 0°C, then this gives us good reason to suppose that all water freezes at 0°C. By contrast, that the teams failed to score on the first three or four occasions when I went to Arsenal seems a bad reason for supposing that my presence would preclude them from scoring the next time I went.

In effect, Mackie is suggesting that we explain the difference between laws and accidents in terms of the difference between projectible and non-projectible predicates.[3] Recall the discussion of Goodman's 'new problem of induction' in Section 1. Goodman shows that we need to recognize a distinction between patterns involving predicates like green, which can rationally be projected on to further unobserved cases, and patterns involving predicates like grue, which it is irrational to expect to continue. Mackie's suggestion, then, is simply that laws are those true generalizations that contain projectible predicates.

Note how this suggestion yields a natural explanation of why examples of accidents tend to be framed in non-qualitative terms and to have finite numbers of instances. According to Mackie, while laws can be asserted on the basis of subsets of their instances, accidents, which aren't inductively supported by their instances, can only be accepted as true when we know we have exhaustively checked through all the instances. (For example, we only knew the Arsenal generalization was true because I could promise you I wasn't going there any more.)

So it is a condition of an accident's being known to be true that it have a finite number of instances, for otherwise exhaustive examination would be impossible. And one natural way to ensure such finiteness is to frame examples of accidents in non-qualitative terms. (Which is not necessarily to rule out true accidents with an infinite number of instances. The point is only that such accidents cannot be known to be true, and so won't be available as examples for philosophical discussion.)

We can now see exactly why accidents are useless as guides to the workings of the universe. It's not that accidents are less true than laws, nor even that they are necessarily less general. It is just that we are never in a position to *use* them as guides, for we are never in a position to trust an accidentally true generalization, until we have already ascertained everything it might tell us by independent means.

---

[3] J. L. Mackie, *Truth, Probability and Paradox* (Oxford, 1973).

2.5. Laws and Systematization

I now want to look at a different Humean account of the law–accident difference. At the end of this section I shall compare it with Mackie's account. The
central idea is that laws, but not accidents, are part of a scientific account of the
ways the world works: the difference between 'Water freezes at 0°C' and
'There are no goals when David Papineau goes to Highbury' is that the former,
but not the latter, is explainable in terms of basic scientific principles.

Of course, this suggestion needs to give some independent account of 'basic
scientific principles', apart from their being basic *laws*. This is done by appealing to the idea of the *simplest systematization* of general truths. Imagine that
from a God's-eye point of view, so to speak, there is a class of objectively true
generalizations which includes both all the laws and all the accidents. Now
think of the various ways these truths might be organized into a deductive system, based on a set of axioms. Some of these systematizations would have a
greater degree of simplicity than others. (We can take it that the fewer the
axioms, the simpler the system.) But simplicity will be bought at the cost of
leaving some generalizations out of the systematization. (We could include *all*
general truths in the system by simply taking them all as axioms. But this systematization would completely lack simplicity.) Arguably, there will be one systematization that optimally combines strength and simplicity, in that it has a
small number of axioms, for simplicity, but nevertheless manages to include
nearly all the original class of general truths as theorems which follow from
these axioms. We can then distinguish laws from accidents by saying that the
axioms and theorems in this optimal systematization are laws, while the general
truths left dangling are the accidents.

In short, we say that laws are those general truths which follow from the
axioms of science, and then use the simplicity-plus-strength argument to identify those axioms.

How does this idea, which was first put forward by F. P. Ramsey early this
century, and later revived by David Lewis, relate to Mackie's suggestion? Let us
assume, for the sake of this comparison, that the class of projectible predicates
coincides with those which appear in the simplest-plus-strongest systematization. Even if we make this assumption, Mackie's theory differs from Ramsey's
and Lewis's. For Mackie says that *any* true generalization framed in projectible
predicates is a law; whereas Ramsey and Lewis require in addition that the generalization be deducible from the axioms of science.[4] So to decide between
these two theories of lawhood, we need to consider the status of some generalization which is framed in projectible terms, but is not in fact deducible from
the axioms of science.

---

[4] F. P. Ramsey, 'Universals of Law and Universals of Fact' (1928); repr. in *Foundations*, ed. D. H. Mellor
(London, 1978); David Lewis, *Counterfactuals* (Oxford, 1973).

For example, imagine you are doing some research with some complicated electronic equipment, and you notice that, whenever the equipment and your radio are both on, your radio makes a funny noise. Suppose also that this is the only time this kind of complicated equipment will ever be constructed, because you dismantle it at the end of the experiment. Given that the properties of electronic equipment and radios are presumably projectible, if anything is, you infer that, whenever equipment of that kind is on, radios like yours make a funny noise. But suppose that in fact there is no real connection, and that your radio is making funny noises for some quite different reason. Then the generalization 'Whenever equipment of that kind is on, radios like yours make a funny noise' will be exceptionlessly true, and will contain projectible predicates. Yet it clearly isn't a law. This shows that Ramsey and Lewis are right about laws and Mackie is wrong, since the Ramsey–Lewis theory does not count this generalization as a law, while the Mackie theory does. (If you were the experimenter in the example, you would no doubt think that the pattern is a law, for you would no doubt think that it has some explanation in terms of basic science. But still, you will be wrong in thinking this, since it does not have such an explanation.)

2.6. The Non-Humean Alternative

One objection to the Ramsey–Lewis theory of laws is that its dependence on the notions 'strength' and 'simplicity' makes it vague and subjective. But even if we let that pass, and allow that the theory yields a reasonably precise way of distinguishing those true generalizations that qualify as laws, there is another objection, indeed an objection that can be levelled at all Humean theories. Namely, that the whole Humean approach to lawhood is highly counter-intuitive.

Consider these two sequences: (1) The temperature falls below 0°C, and then the water freezes; (2) I go to Highbury, and then there are no goals. Humeans say that the only distinction between them is that, while they are both instances of true universal generalizations, the generalization covering (1) is somehow more significant than that covering (2). But this is surely counter to intuition. For it seems to leave out the idea that in (1) the first event made the second one happen, that it was because of the first event that the second event happened; whereas in (2) there is no such link between the two events. To say that this difference is a difference in the covering generalizations seems to put the difference in the wrong place, to make it a linguistic matter rather than an aspect of nature. Intuitively, the issue is whether there is a link in nature between the particular events, not whether the covering generalizations are sufficiently general, or inductively supported by their instances, or even part of the optimal systematization.

Of course, to side with intuition here is simply to reject Hume's analysis of causation. But a number of recent philosophers have argued that we should do just that. In the last two decades David Armstrong, Fred Dretske, and Michael Tooley[5] have all argued that causal laws are not simply statements of constant conjunction, but rather state *necessitating relationships* between the properties involved. They say that the way to represent the content of a causal law is not simply as 'All As are (as it happens) followed by Bs', but rather 'Nec(A, B)', where 'Nec' stands for the relationship of necessitation between the properties A and B. So, in the contrasting pair above, the low temperature necessitates the freezing, but my being at Highbury does not necessitate the absence of goals.

On the Armstrong–Dretske–Tooley view, a necessitating relationship between A and B certainly implies that all As are Bs. But the converse implication does not hold: there can be cases where all As are Bs even though it is not true that Nec(A, B)—namely, when it is an accident that all As are Bs.

So this non-Humean view offers an entirely straightforward explanation of the law–accident difference. The difference is simply that laws state something that accidentally true generalizations do not, namely, the existence of a necessitating relationship between properties.

Given the possibility of this simple solution, the obvious question to ask is why most philosophers in the 250 years since Hume have not availed themselves of it.

Hume had two arguments against the idea that causal laws involve necessitating links. First, we never see such links. Second, we cannot know laws of nature a priori, as would be possible if they stated necessities.

We need not dwell too long on Hume's first argument. The assumption that we cannot meaningfully talk about things we cannot observe has had few supporters in this century, even if it was generally accepted in Hume's time. The example of modern science, with its talk of atoms, electrons, and radio waves, has shown that meaningful reference is not restricted to observable phenomena. So the fact that we cannot see necessitating links does not automatically mean we cannot talk about them.

Hume's second argument deserves more attention. This argument assumes that if laws state necessities, then they must be knowable a priori (and so concludes that, since laws clearly cannot be known a priori, they cannot state necessities). The assumption that necessity implies aprioricity went unchallenged until very recently in the Western philosophical tradition. At the beginning of the 1970s, however, the American philosopher Saul Kripke argued that the *metaphysical* notion of necessity needs to be sharply separated from the *epistemological* notion of aprioricity. In particular Kripke argued that many statements of identity (for example, 'The Evening Star = the Morning Star') are necessary (for

[5] David Armstrong, *What is a Law of Nature?* (Cambridge, 1983); Fred Dretske, 'Laws of Nature', *Philosophy of Science*, 44 (1977), 248–68; Michael Tooley, 'The Nature of Laws', *Canadian Journal of Philosophy*, 7 (1977), 667–98.

how *could* that planet not be itself?), even though it is only after a posteriori empirical discoveries that they can be *known* to be true.

It is striking that Armstrong, Dretske, and Tooley all put forward their non-Humean view of laws within five years of the publication of Kripke's ideas. This suggests that the key which allowed them to reject Hume's view of laws was the separation of necessity from aprioricity. For when they say that laws of nature state that *A* necessitates *B*, they certainly do not mean to imply that these laws can be known a priori. To this extent the kind of necessary connection they uphold is different from the kind Hume rejected. (It also means that their view of laws makes no difference to the problem of induction: since laws have to be derived from a posteriori evidence, we still need to explain how past evidence can tell us something that implies future patterns.)

While it seems highly plausible that Kripke's views about necessity prompted the re-emergence of non-Humean views of laws of nature, there are important differences between these two developments. Most centrally, the non-Humean necessitating connections are not in fact *necessary* in Kripke's sense. Kripkean necessities are supposed to obtain in all possible worlds. It is simply impossible that a planet should exist yet not be itself. But the modern non-Humeans do not require their laws of nature to be necessary in this sense. They allow that it is possible that the force of gravity might have been weaker than it is, that water might have frozen at a different temperature, and so on. Their idea of a necessitating connection is that of one property making another happen, not the Kripkean idea of a claim that *could not possibly* be false.

This difference points to a difficulty facing the non-Humean views of laws of nature. The non-Humeans say that necessitation involves something more than constant conjunction: if two events are related by necessitation, then it follows that they are constantly conjoined; but two events can be constantly conjoined without being related by necessitation, as when the constant conjunction is just a matter of accident. So necessitation is a stronger relationship than constant conjunction. However, the non-Humeans say very little about what the extra strength amounts to. We are told that it is not necessity in the Kripkean sense of truth in all possible worlds. But we are not given any positive characterization of this extra strength, except that it distinguishes laws from accidents. Critics of the non-Humean view argue that a satisfactory account of laws ought to cast more light than this on the nature of laws. They complain that the notion of necessitation simply restates the problem, rather than solving it.

So we can sum up our overall discussion of laws of nature with a choice. If you like explanations, and don't mind too much about intuitions, then you can go for a Humean strategy, with the Ramsey–Lewis theory the most promising version. But if you want an account of laws of nature that fits our pre-theoretical intuitions, and don't mind the complaint that it simply reifies the law–accident difference without explaining it, then you can take the modern non-Humean option.

3. REALISM, INSTRUMENTALISM, AND UNDERDETERMINATION

3.1. Instrumentalism versus Realism

In the first section I discussed the problem of induction. In this section I want to consider a different difficulty facing our knowledge of the natural world and scientific knowledge in particular. Much of science consists of claims about unobservable entities like viruses, radio waves, electrons, and quarks. But if these entities are unobservable, how are scientists supposed to have found out about them? If they cannot see or touch them, doesn't it follow that their claims about them are at best speculative guesses, rather than firm knowledge?

It is worth distinguishing this problem of unobservability from the problem of induction. Both problems can be viewed as difficulties facing theoretical knowledge in science. But where the problem of induction arises because scientific theories make general claims, the problem of unobservability is due to our lack of sensory access to the subject-matter of many scientific theories. (So the problem of induction arises for general claims even if they are not about unobservables, such as 'All sodium burns bright orange'. Conversely, the problem of unobservability arises for claims about unobservables even if they are not general, such as, 'One free electron is attached to this oil drop'. In this section and the next, however, it will be convenient to use the term 'theory' specifically for claims about unobservables, rather than for general claims of any kind.)

There are two schools of thought about the problem of unobservability. On the one hand are *realists*, who think that the problem can be solved. Realists argue that the observable facts provide good indirect evidence for the existence of unobservable entities, and so conclude that scientific theories can be regarded as accurate descriptions of the unobservable world. On the other hand are *instrumentalists*, who hold that we are in no position to make firm judgements about imperceptible mechanisms. Instrumentalists allow that theories about such mechanisms may be useful 'instruments' for simplifying our calculations and generating predictions. But they argue that these theories are no more true descriptions of the world than the 'theory' that all the matter in a stone is concentrated at its centre of mass (which is also an extremely useful assumption for doing certain calculations, but clearly false).

Earlier this century instrumentalists used to argue that we should not even interpret theoretical claims literally, on the grounds that we cannot so much as meaningfully talk about entities we have never directly observed. But as I said in the last section, the development of modern science, with its talk of atoms, electrons, and so on, has made this restriction on meaningful talk difficult to defend. So nowadays this kind of *semantic* instrumentalism is out of favour.

Contemporary instrumentalists allow that scientists can meaningfully postulate, say, that matter is made of tiny atoms containing nuclei orbited by electrons. But they then take a sceptical attitude to such postulates, saying that we have no entitlement to believe them (as opposed to using them as an instrument for calculations.)

3.2. Initial Arguments for Realism

An initial line of argument open to realism is to identify some feature of scientific practice and then argue that instrumentalism is unable to account for it. So, for example, realists have pointed to the fact that scientists characteristically seek to unify different kinds of scientific theory in pursuit of a single 'theory of everything'. In the nineteenth century, for instance, physicists working in thermodynamics developed the kinetic theory of gases, which explained variations in the temperature, pressure, and volume of gases by postulating that gases are made of swarms of tiny particles; at the same time chemists were developing the atomic theory of matter, which explained chemical combinations on the assumption that matter was made of atoms, one kind of atom for each element. An obvious question was to investigate the relation between the two theories: were the particles of the physicists combinations of atoms, and if so what kinds of combination? The resolution of this issue was not always easy, but in time a satisfactory conclusion was arrived at.

However, this whole procedure, the realist points out, only makes sense on the assumption that scientific theories are *true* descriptions of reality. After all, says the realist, if theories are simply convenient calculating-devices, then why expect different theories to be unifiable into one consistent story? Unification is clearly desirable if our theories all aim to contribute to the overall truth, but there seems to be no parallel reason why a bunch of instruments should be unifiable into one big 'instrument of everything'.

Other features of science appealed to by realists as arguments against instrumentalism include the use of theories to explain observable phenomena, and the reliance on theories to make novel predictions. I shall take these in turn. The topic of explanation will be discussed in detail in Section 5 below. But for the moment we need only note that scientists often explain the behaviour of observable phenomena in terms of unobservable mechanisms. Thus, to use one of the above examples, scientists explain why the pressure of an enclosed gas increases when its temperature does by referring to the behaviour of the tiny particles making up the gas. But surely, the realist urges, this only makes sense if these tiny particles really exist and the theory describing them is not just an instrument for making calculations. We surely cannot say that the pressure goes up because the tiny particles are moving faster if we don't believe in the existence of those particles.

Then there is the argument from prediction. Scientists often predict surprising and hitherto quite unknown observable phenomena on the basis of their theories. For example, Einstein predicted, on the basis of the general theory of relativity, that light would bend in the vicinity of the sun. Apart from his theory, there was no reason whatsoever to expect this. Yet this prediction was triumphantly confirmed by Sir Arthur Eddington's famous observations in West Africa during an eclipse of the sun in 1919. This provides another argument for realism. For the realist can insist that there would be no reason why such predictions should ever work if the theories behind them were not true.

These three arguments, from unification, explanation, and prediction, all give some support to realism. But none of them are conclusive. In each case, there are two possible lines of response open to instrumentalists. They can offer an instrumentalist account of the relevant feature of scientific practice. Alternatively, they can deny that this feature really is part of scientific practice in the first place. I shall go through the three cases in turn.

3.3. Initial Instrumentalist Responses

3.3.1. Unification

First, the argument from unification. The first possibility is for instrumentalists to offer an instrumentalist account of the scientific practice of unifying theories. They can do this by arguing that the unification of science is motivated, not by the pursuit of one underlying truth, but simply by the desirability of a single, all-purpose calculating instrument instead of a rag-bag of different instruments for different problems. If the aim of theories is convenience, rather than veracity, is it not more convenient to have one device that will deal with all problems, rather than having to worry which tool will be most effective for the problem at hand?

The second possibility for an instrumentalist faced by the argument from unification is to deny that unification is essential to science to start with. Thus Nancy Cartwright argues, in *How the Laws of Physics Lie*,[6] that science really *is* a rag-bag of different instruments. She maintains that scientists faced with a given kind of problem will standardly deploy simplifying techniques and rules of thumb which owe nothing to general theory, but have shown themselves to deliver the right answer to the kind of problem at hand. So, in Cartwright's view, unification is not central to science in the first place, and so not something instrumentalists need to account for.

---

[6] (Oxford, 1983).

3.3.2. Explanation

The same two lines of response can be made to the realist argument from explanation. Here the more normal line of response is the second, namely, to deny that explanation really is an essential feature of scientific practice. Instrumentalists can argue that the essential aim of science is to describe, not to explain. What we want of science, they will say, is an accurate account of how the observable world behaves. The further issue of why it behaves like that is a far more difficult question, which takes us beyond science, if it can be answered at all. (After all, the instrumentalist can observe, even realists have to stop explaining at some point. Maybe they can explain observables in terms of unobservables, and some unobservables in terms of others. But even realists will have to admit that at some point, perhaps with quarks or other fundamental particles, they run out of explanations, and can only describe the behaviour of the fundamental particles, without explaining it in terms of further mechanisms.)

As I said, this kind of denial that explanation is essential to scientific theorizing is the normal instrumentalist response to the argument from explanation. But a minority of instrumentalists try the opposite tack, and argue that there is nothing in scientific explanation that instrumentalism cannot account for. According to instrumentalists of this stripe, it is a mistake to think of scientific explanation as a matter of identifying genuine hidden causes for observable phenomena, as opposed to simply showing how these phenomena are part of some wider pattern. The scientist who 'explains' variations in the pressure of gases by the kinetic theory is not, from this perspective, specifying the true unobservable causes of those variations, but simply showing how they conform to the same underlying equations as other kinds of observable gas behaviour. (Perhaps this second response to the argument from explanation does little more than invent a new meaning for 'explanation'. But if this makes you uneasy, there is always the first response to fall back on.)

3.3.3. Prediction

There remains the realist argument from prediction. Here the two lines of instrumentalist response are again open. The more radical, and perhaps less plausible, would be to deny that the ability to make such predictions is a genuine feature of scientific practice. Instrumentalists who take this line will of course allow that scientists make 'predictions' in the sense that they draw observable consequences from their theories. But they can deny that this practice generates any more *true* predictions than random guessing would. After all, they can point out, the only predictions that we remember are those that succeed, like Einstein's prediction of light bending. But for every such successful prediction there are thousands of scientific experiments that do not produce the results that are expected. So what real reason do we have for thinking that theories about unobservables enable us to anticipate new observable phenomena? Maybe this is just an impression created by selective memory. If this is right, and science is not really predictively successful, then there is obviously no need for an instrumentalist explanation of this success.

However, as I said, this response is not entirely plausible. It seems unlikely that the ability of theories about unobservables sometimes to anticipate new observable phenomena is just a chance matter. However, even if we accept that science is predictively successful, there remains room for an instrumentalist account of this. The realist account, remember, was that theories about unobservables are themselves characteristically true, so it is no surprise that they issue in true predictions. Instrumentalists, who deny the truth of theories about unobservables, cannot say this. But they can say something else. They can accept that there is a well-established pattern, displayed in the history of science, of novel observable predictions suggested by theories about unobservables turning out to be true. And then they can simply insist, in line with their general instrumentalism, that there is no need to give any further explanation of this pattern, in terms of such hidden facts as the truth of the theories concerned. After all, instrumentalism is precisely the view that we do not need to explain manifest patterns in terms of hidden causes (or at most that we should 'explain' them by fitting them into larger manifest patterns). Given that instrumentalists start off by denying the need for unobservable explanations, it begs the question against them to insist that they should produce such an explanation for the predictive success of science.

3.4. The Underdetermination of Theory by Data

In the last section I argued that various arguments against instrumentalism can be resisted. I shall now allow instrumentalism to go on the offensive, and consider some positive arguments against realism. There are two strong lines of argument that instrumentalists can use to cast doubt on realism. In this section and the next I shall discuss 'the underdetermination of theory by evidence' and some related issues. In Section 3.6 I shall consider 'the pessimistic meta-induction from past falsity'. As it happens, I do not think that either of these arguments succeeds in discrediting realism. But they are both arguments which merit careful consideration.

The argument from underdetermination asserts that, given any theory about unobservables which fits the observable facts, there will be other incompatible theories which fit the same facts. And so, the argument concludes, we are never in a position to know that any one of these theories is the truth.

Why should we accept that there is always more than one theory which fits any set of observable facts? There are two routes to this conclusion. One stems from the Duhem–Quine thesis, originally formulated by the French philosopher and historian Pierre Duhem at the turn of the century and later revived by the American logician W. V. O. Quine.[7] Duhem and Quine point out that a scientific theory T (such as the Newtonian theory of gravitation) does not normally imply predictions P on its own (about the motions of planets, say), but only in conjunction with auxiliary hypotheses H (concerning such things as the number of other planets, their masses, the mass of the sun, and so on).

$$T \& H \to P$$

Because of this, T can always be defended in the face of contrary observations (such as the well-known anomaly for Newtonian theory presented by the orbit of Mercury) by adjusting the auxiliary hypotheses H (by postulating a hitherto unobserved planet, say, or an inhomogeneous mass distribution in the sun). The point is that the observational refutation of P does not disprove T, but only the conjunction $T \& H$.

$$\text{Not-}P \to \text{not-}(T \& H)$$

So T can be retained, and indeed still explain not-P, provided we replace H by some alternative, H', such that

$$T \& H' \to \text{not-}P.$$

This yields the Duhem–Quine thesis: Any theoretical claim T can consistently be retained in the face of contrary evidence by making adjustments elsewhere in our system of beliefs. The underdetermination of theory by evidences (UDTE) follows quickly. For the Duhem–Quine thesis seems to imply that the adherents of competing theories will always be able to maintain their respective positions in the face of any actual observational data. Imagine two competing theories T_1 and T_2. Whatever evidence accumulates, versions of T_1 and T_2, conjoined with greatly revised auxiliary hypotheses if necessary, will both survive, consistent with that evidence, but incompatible with each other.

The other route to UDTE, first put forward by physicists such as Henri Poincaré at the turn of the century, has a different starting-point.[8] It begins, not with two competing theories, but with some given theory, all of whose observational predictions are supposed to be accurate. Imagine that T_1 is the complete truth about physical reality, that it implies observational truths O. Then we can always construct some 'de-Occamized' T_2 which postulates some more complicated unobservable mechanism, but which nevertheless has precisely the same observational consequences.

For example, suppose we start with standard assumptions about the location

[7] P. Duhem, *The Aim and Structure of Physical Theory*, Eng. edn. (London, 1962); W. V. O. Quine, 'Two Dogmas of Empiricism', in *From a Logical Point of View* (Cambridge, Mass., 1953).

[8] H. Poincaré, *Science and Hypothesis*, Eng. edn. (New York, 1952).

of bodies in space-time and about the forces acting on them. A de-Occamized theory might then postulate that all bodies, including all measuring instruments, are accelerating by 1 ft/sec^2 in a given direction, and then add just the extra forces required to explain this. This theory would clearly have exactly the same observational consequences as the original one, even though it contradicted it at the unobservable level.

To bring out the difference between the two arguments for UDTE, note that the Duhem–Quine argument does not specify exactly which overall theories we will end up with, since it leaves open how T_1 and T_2's auxiliary hypotheses may need to be revised; the de-Occamization argument, by contrast, actually specifies T_1 and T_2 in full detail, including auxiliary hypotheses. In compensation, the Duhem–Quine argument promises us alternative theories whatever observational evidence may turn up in the future; whereas the de-Occamization argument assumes that all future observations are as T_1 predicts.

3.5. Simplicity and Elimination

My view is that the arguments of the last section give us good reason to accept UDTE, the thesis that there will always be incompatible theories to explain any given body of observational facts. I do not agree, however, that UDTE yields a good argument against realism. What UDTE shows is that more than one theory about unobservables will always fit any given set of observational data. But it is too quick to conclude, as many philosophers do, that this makes realism about unobservables untenable. For we should recognize that there is nothing in the arguments for alternative underdetermined theories to show that these alternative theories will always be equally well supported by the data. What the arguments show is that different theories will always be consistent with the data. But they do not rule out the possibility that, among these alternative theories, one is vastly more plausible than the others, and for that reason should be believed to be true. After all, 'flat-earthers' can make their view consistent with the evidence from geography, astronomy, and satellite photographs, by constructing far-fetched stories about conspiracies to hide the truth, the effects of empty space on cameras, and so on. But this does not show we need take their flat-earthism seriously. Similarly, even though Newtonian gravitational theory can in principle be made consistent with all the contrary evidence, by bringing in various hidden forces and other *ad hoc* devices, this is no reason not to believe general relativity theory.

Certainly practising scientists do not regard the UDTE as blocking their access to the theoretical truth. They recognize that we can always in principle concoct alternative explanations for any given body of data; but they simply discount as not worth taking seriously those complex alternatives that need to invoke hidden planets, or hidden forces, or other truth-hiding conspiracies. In effect, scientists are taught, in the course of their scientific training, that only certain sorts of theory are possible candidates for the truth; and once they have data that rule out all but one of *these* theories, they quite happily ignore all the other conspiratorial theories that remain consistent with the data. (Perhaps the best way of describing this aspect of scientific practice is to say that scientists ignore all theories that are not sufficiently 'simple'; but if we do so we should not think of 'simplicity' as some innate or intuitive idea; rather, the relevant kind of simplicity is part of what scientists learn when they are trained as meteorologists, embryologists, physicists, or whatever.)

Still, even if scientists don't regard the UDTE as a serious obstacle, many philosophers, as I said, move quickly, from the premiss that different theories are consistent with the observational evidence, to the conclusion that none of them can be regarded as the truth. However, I think that they only make this move because they assume that the only good inferences from data to theories are deductively valid ones: they note that the data cannot deductively imply T, if they leave open the possibility that some inconsistent theory T' is true; and they conclude that this shows we are never entitled to believe such a T.

However, as we saw in our earlier discussion on induction in Section 1, there are good reasons for allowing that other inferences, apart from deductively valid ones, can be rational. In particular, in that discussion I suggested that the important underlying requirement might merely be that inferences should be reliable, not deductively valid.

In fact, the issue we are now addressing is closely related to our earlier discussion of induction. In Section 1 I focused on *enumerative* induction, in which we go from instances of a pattern to the theory that this pattern holds generally. The theory-choices we are now considering can be thought of as *eliminative* inductions, in which we assume that the truth lies among one of a limited number of theories (the reasonably 'simple' theories), and then use our observations to eliminate all but one of those theories.

The essential difference between these two forms of induction is that eliminative inductions consider only a limited number of theories to be candidates for truth. This might make it seem as if enumerative induction is a more general form of inference, since it rests on no such presupposition. But in fact our discussion of Goodman's 'new problem of induction' in Section 1 shows that even enumerative inductions rely on a similar presupposition: since there are so many possible ways of projecting observed patterns into the future, enumerative inductions are forced to restrict the generalizations they regard as candidates for the truth to the limited number which involve projectible predicates. For example, propositions of the sort 'All emeralds are green (yellow/red/etc.)' are reasonably 'simple', and so candidates for truth, but propositions of the sort 'All emeralds are grue (bleen/etc.)' are not. Someone investigating emeralds can then reach the natural conclusion by noting which of the candidates for truth is consistent with the observations made so far.

Given this, we may as well regard all inductions as in essence eliminative, rather than enumerative. Still, the question of the reliability arises in just the same way for eliminative induction as for enumerative induction. The fact that eliminative inductions are not logically valid does not itself mean that they are not reliable. But there remains the question whether they are reliable.

In Section 1 I suggested that it might be acceptable to answer this question for enumerative inductions by providing (enumeratively) meta-inductive evidence for their reliability. Perhaps we can try the same move again. That is, maybe we can take as evidence those occasions where scientists have chosen whichever 'simple' theory is consistent with the evidence, and then argue meta-inductively that the only 'simple' account of the success of these inferences is that such eliminative inductions are in general reliable guides to the truth. This move obviously involves some element of circularity, but, as I noted in Section 1, it is not clear that this kind of circularity is vicious.

It should be said that this is only one possible way in which we might try to defend the rationality of eliminative induction. The main point I want to make in this section is that the rationality of eliminative induction does not require that it be deductively valid. So the UDTE does not show that such inductions are never acceptable, and so does not discredit the realist view that well-attested theories about unobservables can be regarded as true descriptions of nature. How best to go beyond this, and show positively that eliminative inductions *are* rational, is perhaps too difficult a question to resolve here.

3.6. The Pessimistic Meta-induction from Past Falsity

Let me now turn to the other argument against realism mentioned earlier. This argument takes as its premiss that past scientific theories have generally turned out to be false, and then moves inductively to the pessimistic conclusion that our current theories are no doubt false too.

There are plenty of familiar examples to support this argument. Newton's theory of space and time, the phlogiston theory of combustion, and the theory that atoms are indivisible were all at one time widely accepted scientific theories, but have since been recognized to be false. So doesn't it seem likely, the pessimistic induction concludes, that all our current theories are false, and that we should therefore take an instrumentalist rather than a realist attitude to them?

This is an important and powerful argument, but it would be too quick to conclude that it discredits realism completely. It is important that the tendency to falsity is much more common in some areas of science than others. Thus it is relatively normal for theories to be overturned in cosmology, say, or fundamental particle physics, or the study of primate evolution. By contrast, theories of the molecular composition of different chemical compounds (such as that water is made of hydrogen and oxygen), or the causes of infectious diseases (that chicken-pox is due to a herpes virus), or the nature of everyday physical phenomena (that heat is molecular motion), are characteristically retained once they are accepted.

Nor need we regard this differential success-rate of different kinds of theories as some kind of accident. Rather, it is the result of the necessary evidence being more easily available in some areas of science than others. Palaeoanthropologists want to know how many hominid species were present on earth three million years ago. But their evidence consists of a few pieces of teeth and bone. So it is scarcely surprising that discoveries of new fossil sites will often lead them to change their views. The same point applies on a larger scale in cosmology and particle physics. Scientists in these areas want to answer very general questions about the very small and the very distant. But their evidence derives from the limited range of technological instruments they have devised to probe these realms. So, once more, it is scarcely surprising that their theories should remain at the level of tentative hypotheses. By contrast, in those areas where adequate evidence is available, such as chemistry and medicine, there is no corresponding barrier to science's moving beyond tentative hypotheses to firm conclusions.

The moral is that realism is more defensible for some areas of science than others. In some scientific subjects firm evidence is available, and entitles us to view certain theories, like the theory that water is composed of H_2O molecules, as the literal truth about reality. In other areas the evidence is fragmentary and inconclusive, and then we do better to regard the best-supported theories, such as the theory that quarks and leptons are the ultimate building-blocks of matter, as useful instruments which accommodate the existing data, make interesting predictions, and suggest further lines for research.

At first sight this might look like a victory for instrumentalism over realism. For didn't instrumentalists always accept that we should be realists about observable things, and only urge instrumentalism for uncertain theories about unobservable phenomena? But our current position draws the line in a different place. Instrumentalism, as originally defined, takes it for granted that everything unobservable is inaccessible, and that all theories about unobservables are therefore uncertain. By contrast, the position we have arrived at places no special weight on the distinction between what is observable and what is not. In particular, it argues that the pessimistic meta-induction fails to show that falsity is the natural fate of all theories about unobservables, but only that there is a line within the category of theories about unobservables between those theories that can be expected to turn out false and those whose claims to truth are secure. So our current position is not a dogmatic instrumentalism about all unobservables, but merely the uncontentious view that we should be instrumentalists about that subclass of theories which are not supported by adequate evidence.

4. CONFIRMATION AND PROBABILITY

4.1. The Notion of Confirmation

At the end of the last section I argued that the history of science gives us reason to be cautious in our commitment to certain scientific theories. In at least some areas of science the evidence for even the best theories is often fragmentary and inconclusive, with the consequence that we should expect that such theories will turn out to be false.

It would be nice to be able to say more about the degree to which a given body of evidence supports a given theory. That is, it would be nice to have a quantitative account of the relationship between evidence and theory. Philosophers have sought to develop such accounts, under the name of 'confirmation theory'. They seek to understand the extent to which different bodies of evidence 'confirm' different theories. If a theory is highly confirmed by the available evidence, then we can be reasonably confident it is true; but if it has a lower degree of confirmation, then we should moderate our trust in it accordingly.

However, this intuitive notion of confirmation is less straightforward than it seems. I shall introduce some of the difficulties by describing two well-known paradoxes that any theory of confirmation must deal with.

4.2. The Paradox of the Ravens

Let us assume that there is a relationship of confirmation, according to which sometimes *E confirms T*, where *E* is some body of evidence and *T* some theory. Then it certainly seems natural to make the following two assumptions about confirmation:

  (1) If $E = (Fa \ \& \ Ga)$ and $T = $ All *Fs* are *Gs, then E confirms T.*

(This first assumption simply says that generalizations are confirmed by their instances.)

  (2) If *E* confirms *T*, and *T* is logically equivalent to *S, then E confirms S.*

As I said, these two assumptions seem highly uncontentious. But they can easily be shown to generate a puzzle.

Note first that the following two generalizations are logically equivalent:

  (L) All ravens are black.

(M) All non-black things are non-ravens.

Now take as our evidence an observation that:

(I) The white thing over there is a shoe.

Since (I) is an instance of a non-black thing which is a non-raven, then assumption (1) tells us that (I) confirms (M).

But if we now put this together with the fact that (M) is logically equivalent to (L), then assumption (2) tells us that (I) confirms (L).

However, this seems absurd. For (L) is the claim that all ravens are black, and surely we cannot confirm *that* just by observing that some white thing is a shoe.

Something seems to have gone wrong somewhere. But it is difficult to see where. For there can scarcely be anything wrong with assumption (2)—logically equivalent propositions make exactly the same claims about the world, so it is hard to see how some piece of evidence could support one such proposition, without therewith supporting the other proposition. And assumption (1) seems almost as obvious—if anything is ever confirmed by anything, surely generalizations are confirmed by their instances.

(Some of you might think that the flaw in the reasoning lies with assumption (1). For isn't the lesson of Goodman's new problem of induction precisely that *Fa* & *Ga* cannot always confirm $(x) (Fx \rightarrow Gx)$? Goodman shows that, unless we restrict *F* and *G* to 'projectible' predicates, there are far too many *F*s and *G*s for all such generalizations to be confirmable by their instances. However, I do not think this helps with the raven paradox, given that there isn't anything particularly 'gruesome' about the predicates used to formulate it, namely, 'black', 'raven', 'non-black', and 'non-raven'. It is of course true that Goodman's argument shows that (1) is not acceptable as formulated without qualification above. But the paradox will still be generated even if (1) is restricted to apply only to 'projectible' predicates.)

4.3. The Tacking Paradox

Now for the second paradox. Here are two further assumptions that seem pretty obvious:

(3) If *T* entails *E*, then *E confirms T*.

(This is just the idea that a theory is confirmed if its consequences are observed to be true.)

(4) If *E* confirms *T*, and *T* entails *P*, then *E confirms P*.

(This is just the idea that, if some evidence entitles you to believe some theory, then it entitles you to believe what follows from it.)

But now take *any* theory N—Newtonian gravitational theory, say—and *any* consequence M it entails—the planets move in ellipses. And then consider *any* other proposition Q you like—the moon is made of green cheese. Since N (Newtonian theory) entails M (elliptical orbits), by hypothesis, N & Q (Newtonian theory *plus* the moon is made of green cheese) also entails M. So, by (3),

(*a*) M confirms N & Q.

But

(*b*) N & Q entails Q, trivially,

so by (4), applied to (*a*) and (*b*), it follows that M (elliptical orbits) *confirms* Q (the moon is green cheese). But this means that anything that follows from one theory—the planets move in ellipses—confirms any other theory you like—the moon is made of green cheese. And this is surely absurd.

Even so, this absurd conclusion follows from the apparently uncontentious assumptions (3) and (4). Once more, it is difficult to see where the fault in our reasoning lies.

This paradox is called the 'tacking' paradox, because it involves 'tacking' an arbitrary hypothesis (the moon is made of green cheese, in the above example) on to the theory you start with (Newtonian mechanics). A common initial reaction is that assumption (3) is at fault. Do the motions of the planets really confirm Newtonian-theory-and-that-the-moon-is-green-cheese? But I shall argue that this is in fact a perfectly sensible thing to suppose, and that it is assumption (4) that is really responsible for the tacking paradox. However, before I explain how I think the tacking paradox (and the paradox of the ravens) should be dealt with, it will be necessary to digress at some length, and explain some ideas about *probability*.

4.4. Interpretations of Probability

The notion of probability can be understood in a number of different ways. In particular, as I said in Section 1, there are both objective and subjective notions of probability. But there is one thing that ties together all the different notions of probability, namely, that they satisfy the *axioms of the probability calculus*.

These axioms are normally stated as follows:

(1) $0 \leqslant \text{Prob}(p) \leqslant 1$, for any proposition p.
(2) $\text{Prob}(p) = 1$, if p is a necessary truth.
(3) $\text{Prob}(p) = 0$, if p is impossible.
(4) $\text{Prob}(p \text{ or } q) = \text{Prob}(p) + \text{Prob}(q)$, if p and q are mutually exclusive.

Any way of assigning numbers to propositions so as to satisfy these axioms constitutes an interpretation of the probability calculus. We shall concentrate in particular on the contrast between subjective and objective interpretations of probability.

The subjective interpretation takes the probability of *p* to be a measure of the strength with which you believe *p*. More specifically, for any person *X*, the subjective interpretation equates *X*'s probability for *p* with the degree *to which X believes p*.

Some extreme subjectivists argue that this is the only notion of probability we need. But most philosophers who recognize subjective probabilities also recognize objective probabilities. Objective probabilities apply specifically to propositions which claim that a certain kind of result will occur on a certain kind of repeatable trial, such as that a certain kind of coin will come down heads when tossed. And in this kind of context a statement of objective probability specifies how much trials of that kind *tend* to produce the result in question. This kind of tendency is displayed by the frequency with which the result occurs—for example, by how often coins like this come down heads.

It should be clear that these subjective and objective interpretations give us different notions of probability. A degree of subjective belief is one thing, and an objective tendency is another. There is no guarantee that any particular person's subjective expectations should correspond to the objective tendencies; and there would still have been objective probabilities of atoms decaying, even if there had never been any human beings to form degrees of belief. Let us now look more closely at these two notions in turn.

4.5. Subjective Probabilities

The central assumption of the subjective interpretation is that belief comes in *degrees*. Normally we think of belief as something you either have or have not. But consider the attitude of someone who takes both umbrella and sunblock cream on a walk. Does this person believe it will rain or not? The natural answer is that the person has some expectation that this proposition is true, and some that it is not. Or consider the attitude of a company director who gives money to both the Labour Party and the Conservative Party before the election. Again it seems natural to say that the company director has a positive degree of belief that each outcome will happen. (Some people object to the idea of 'degrees of belief' because they think of beliefs as definite attitudes to propositions, for or against. If one preferred, one could think in terms of degrees of expectation rather than belief. This will make no difference to the points which follow.)

It is one thing to argue that beliefs come in degrees. It is another to show that we can attach definite numbers between 0 and 1 to these degrees. But the subjective theory needs to show this, since degrees of belief will have to equal such numbers if they are to have any chance of satisfying the probability axioms.

However, this is not necessarily as far-fetched as it seems at first sight. The obvious way to attach a number to someone's degree of belief is to see what minimum *odds* would induce them to bet on *p*. If you are only prepared to put up £*N* once your opponent offers £*M* or more, with the winner taking all if *p* turns out true, then this arguably shows that your degree of belief in *p* is *N*/(*N* + *M*).

True, some people hate betting *per se*. And in such cases the odds that will induce them to bet will overestimate their degrees of belief. For example, you may be convinced that you are betting on a fair coin, and so attach a 50–50 probability to heads, but may be disinclined to risk your treasured £10 on heads until I am putting up £40 or more. The test suggested in the last paragraph would indicate that your degree of belief in heads is 0.2, rather than 0.5. But perhaps in this kind of case an investigator could still find out your true degree of belief by asking you to choose fair odds for bets on *p*, without telling you which way you are going to bet, or how much the bet is going to be. In this situation, any aversion to betting should cancel out and leave your chosen odds expressing your true degree of belief.

Despite these ingenious suggestions, you may still feel it is unrealistic to suppose that there are precise numerical degrees of belief for all propositions. Surely there is no fact of the matter of whether my degree of belief that *X* will win the next election is 0.3456 rather than 0.3457. But the defender of the subjective interpretation can reasonably respond that the postulation of exact numerical degrees of belief is a useful *idealization*, which facilitates our theorizing, and does no harm when understood as such. By way of comparison, consider the way that physicists suppose that physical objects, like stones and planets, have precise masses and sizes. This is never strictly true, since there are always some molecules dropping off or joining on to such objects. But the fiction of precise quantities is extremely useful in physics, and misleads no one.

Even if we grant the subjective interpretation that degrees of belief can be thought of as precise numbers, it still needs to be shown that these numbers actually conform to the probability axioms. It need of course be nothing more than convention that we assign 0 to the lowest possible degree of belief (namely, disbelief) and 1 to the highest (full belief), and so satisfy axiom (1). But it would not be a matter of convention that degrees of belief should satisfy the other axioms.

The normal way of establishing that degrees of belief conform to the probability axioms is via the 'Dutch book argument', which shows that somebody whose degrees of belief violate axioms (1)–(4) can be induced to make manifestly irrational bets.

Suppose that you attach a probability of 0.8 to 'It will rain today', and a degree of belief of 0.7 to 'It won't rain today'. Then your degrees of belief violate the probability axioms. (This is because the proposition that 'It will or it won't rain' is a necessary truth, and so, to satisfy axiom (2), needs to have degree of belief 1; but it is also the disjunction of the exclusive propositions 'It will rain today' and 'It won't rain today', and so, to satisfy axiom (4), needs to have a degree of belief equal to the sum of these propositions' separate degrees of belief; however, this sum is 1.5, not 1.)

Note also that, because you have these degrees of belief, you will be prepared to wager your £8 to my £2 on the proposition 'It will rain today'; and you will be prepared to wager your £7 to my £3 on 'It will not rain today'. But this is clearly a quite silly pair of bets, since you are guaranteed to lose £5 whatever happens.

It is provable, along the lines of this last example, that people are open to 'Dutch books' if and only if their degrees of belief fail to conform to the probability axioms. Since it seems clearly irrational to have degrees of belief which can lead you to do things which are guaranteed to fail, this shows that everybody's degrees of belief ought rationally to conform to the probability axioms.

Note that the conclusion of this argument is only that a rational person's degrees of belief ought to conform to the probability axioms, not that everybody's degrees of belief will in fact so conform. After all, most people probably have degrees of belief that don't sum to 1 for at least some sets of exclusive and exhaustive propositions. So the most that the subjective interpretation can say is that *rational* degrees of belief are an interpretation of the probability calculus, not that all actual degrees of belief are.

Note also that while the Dutch book argument shows that your degrees of belief ought to conform to the probability calculus, it does not show that you ought to attach any *particular* number to the proposition 'It will rain today'. You can attach 0.7 or 0.1 or 0.435 or whatever number you like to this proposition, provided only that the degree of belief you attach to 'It won't rain today' is 1 minus that number. The Dutch book argument only shows that your degrees of belief must be 'coherent' (that is, must somehow satisfy axioms (1)–(4)); beyond that it is a matter of subjective choice which degrees of belief you have. Different people can attach different 'subjective probabilities' to the same proposition. The requirement is only that for each person the numbers in question satisfy the probability axioms; but these can be quite different numbers for different people.

It is this last point that makes most people think that we need another notion of probability—objective probability—to cover the idea that coins (or dice, or radium atoms) have certain tendencies to land heads (land 'six' up, decay). For these objective tendencies presumably have definite objective values, even if different people have different degrees of belief in the relevant result occurring.

4.6. Objective Probabilities

There are two competing ways of thinking about objective probability, the *frequency* theory and the *propensity* theory. I shall consider them in turn.

4.6.1. *The Frequency Theory*

The traditional way of making sense of objective probabilities is to equate them with the relative frequencies of results. Thus we equate the probability *p* of result *R* (heads, 'six', decay) in situation *S* (coin-toss, throw of a die, radium atom) with:

the number of *R*s/the total number of *S*s.

Note that this only allows us to ascribe probabilities to results that happen in repeatable situations where we have some number of *S*s, and not to all propositions, as on the subjective theory. But this is not a criticism, since it is arguable that the notion of objective probability only applies to such repeatable situations, and not to once-off propositions like 'Prince Edward will get married this year'.

An obvious problem facing the above definition is to know which 'total number' of trials *S* we should consider. It cannot normally be the actual trials of kind *S*, since these will normally be finite in number. The problem here is that we know (since it follows from the probability axioms) that there is always a non-zero probability that the relative frequency after *N* trials will be different from *p*, if *N* is finite. For example, it is entirely possible (indeed highly likely) that 1,000 tosses of coins with a 0.5 objective probability of heads will end up with something other than exactly 500 heads. So there is no guarantee at all that the relative frequency in any finite number of trials will equal the objective probability.

Because of this, the frequency theory standardly defines probabilities, not in terms of frequencies in finite sets of trials, but rather in terms of the proportion of *R*s that would occur *if* trial *S* *were* repeated infinitely many times.

This appeal to infinite sequences of trials raises a technical difficulty. For the notion of a *proportion* of *R*s in an infinite sequence of *S*s does not make sense. If we toss a fair coin an infinite number of times, then there will be an infinite number of heads and an infinite number of tails. So the proportion of heads in the total number of tosses is infinity divided by infinity, which is nonsense. The way round this difficulty is to equate the probability with the *limit* of the *finite* relative frequency of *R*s in the first *n* *S*s, as *n* gets bigger and bigger. More precisely, we can say that the relative frequency of *m* *R*s in the first *n* *S*s *tends* towards such a *limit p* (and then equate the objective probability with this *p*) if

for any *e*, however small, there is an *N*, such that, for all $n > N$,
$-e < m/n - p < +e$.

(This is just the standard mathematical idea of a limit—a number such that, for any tiny region around it, the relative frequency will eventually stay within that region once you have gone far enough along the sequence.)

However, even if the frequency theory can deal with this technical problem raised by infinite sequences, many philosophers still feel unhappy with defining probabilities in terms of hypothetical facts about what *would* happen *if* S happened infinitely often. Since most Ss, like coin-tosses, dice-throws, or indeed atomic-decays, do not actually happen infinitely often, this means that we are trying to define objective probabilities in terms of non-existent, imaginary facts. This has persuaded many philosophers to seek an alternative approach to objective probabilities.

4.6.2. *The Propensity Theory*

The propensity theory of objective probability turns away from the idea of relative frequencies in repeated trials, and argues that we should simply take objective probability as a *primitive* notion which measures the strength of the *propensity* for each particular S to produce R. Propensity theorists normally use the term 'chance' to refer to this quantity. So when they say that the chance is 0.4 that this coin will land heads when I toss it, they simply mean that this particular combination of coin and tosser has a 0.4 tendency to produce heads.

The propensity theory has the disadvantage that it does not define probability, but simply takes it as primitive. On the other hand, it has the advantage that it does not need to appeal to the non-existent infinite sequences of the frequency theory. Which of these two theories you prefer will depend mainly on whether you think the infinite sequences are a price worth paying for an explicit definition.

At first sight it might seem that the propensity theory will find it harder than the frequency theory to explain how we *find out* about objective probabilities. For surely our knowledge of objective probabilities comes from the observation of frequencies. Yet the propensity theory seems to deny any link between objective probabilities and frequencies.

However, propensity theorists can retort that they do recognize a perfectly good link between objective probabilities and frequencies, even if not a link that defines the former in terms of the latter. For they can point out that it is a theorem of the probability calculus that

> in a sequence of n trials each with probability p of result R, the *probability* that the relative frequency of Rs will be close to p can be made as high as you like, by making n big enough.

This does not yield a definition of probability in terms of frequency, since it *uses* the notion of probability in explaining the link between probability and frequency (note the emphasized 'probability' in the statement of the theorem). But it is still a link that entitles us to take frequencies as evidence for probabilities.

True, they don't provide sure-fire evidence, since even for large n it is only *probable* that the frequency will be close to the probability, not certain. But this problem ('the problem of statistical inference') is not a problem for the propensity theory alone. After all, even frequency theorists have to find out about objective probabilities on the basis of *finite* frequencies (since we never observe infinite sequences). So they also face the problem that it is at most probable, not certain, that the objective probability (that is, for frequency theories, the frequency in the infinite limit) will be close to the observed frequency.

This problem of statistical inference is just one aspect of the philosophy of probability that we cannot deal with any further here. Our treatment of both objective and subjective probability has done little more than scratch the surface of these topics. But we now have enough to continue our discussion of confirmation theory.

Let me just make one further point before returning to the main line of argument. So far I have said nothing about the connection between subjective and objective probability. There is no question but that these are distinct notions, as I pointed out earlier. But this does not mean that they are unconnected. More specifically, the following principle seems to encapsulate an important connection:

> If you know that the objective probability of R at time t is p, then at t your degree of belief in R ought to equal p.

This idea seems almost too obvious to be worth saying. Of course, if I know that this coin now has an objective probability of 0.5 for heads, I will make my degree of expectation for this outcome equal 50 per cent. However, it is worth observing, before we leave this topic of probability, that none of the theories of objective and subjective probability outlined above offers any obvious explanation of why this principle is true. Once more, there is more to probability than we have been able to deal with here.

4.7. Bayesian Confirmation Theory

I now return to the topic of confirmation theory. In the rest of this section I shall concentrate on Bayesian confirmation theory. Bayesians are philosophers who think that we can use the notion of subjective probability to explicate the relation of confirmation. This is not necessarily the only way of thinking about confirmation. But Bayesianism offers a powerful and uniform way of thinking about issues of confirmation. In particular, as we shall see, it yields natural solutions to the two paradoxes of confirmation described earlier.

The initial assumption made by Bayesian confirmation theory is that our attitudes towards theories are measured by the subjective probabilities we attach to them. So if I fully believe a theory, I give it a subjective probability of 1;

whereas if I regard it as a hazardous speculation, I give it a subjective probability close to 0.

Bayesians then say that a piece of evidence *E confirms a theory T* if learning *E* should make people *increase* their probability for *T*. (In the rest of this section I shall tend to omit the qualification 'subjective'; unless I say otherwise, 'probability' will mean 'subjective probability'.)

In order to develop the Bayesian theory further, we need the notion of conditional probability. The *conditional probability of A given B* (written 'Prob(*A*/*B*)') is defined as the quotient Prob(*A* and *B*)/Prob(*B*), and can be thought of as the probability-of-*A*-on-the-assumption-that-*B*-is-true. To see why, note that Prob(*B*) is a measure of the likelihood of *B* happening, while Prob(*A* and *B*) is a measure of the likelihood of *A* *also* happening when *B* happens. So if we divide Prob(*A* and *B*) by Prob(*B*) we get a measure of the likelihood of *A* happening *given* that *B* has happened.

Now consider the case where *E* is some possible evidence and *T* is some theory. Prob(*T*/*E*) is then the probability of *T*, on the assumption that *E* is true. Bayesians therefore argue that when you learn *E*, you should increase your probability for *T* to equal this number. So for Bayesians *E will confirm T*, in the sense that discovering *E* will increase the probability we attach to *T*, if and only if *Prob(T/E) is greater than Prob(T)*. (In fact this claim is rather less straightforward than it may seem at first sight. But I shall assume it henceforth. For further discussion see the further reading.)

We can say more about *when E* will confirm *T* if we take note of *Bayes's theorem*, originally discovered by the English clergyman Thomas Bayes in the eighteenth century. This theorem follows quickly from the definition of conditional probability. According to this definition Prob(*T*/*E*) = Prob(*T* and *E*)/Prob(*E*), while Prob(*E*/*T*) = Prob(*T* and *E*)/Prob(*T*). Putting these two together, we can derive

$$\text{Prob}(T/E) = \text{Prob}(T) \times \text{Prob}(E/T)/\text{Prob}(E).$$

This is Bayes's theorem. Its significance is that it tells us that Prob(*T*/*E*) is greater than Prob(*T*)—that is, *E* confirms *T*—if and only if *Prob(E/T) is bigger than Prob(E)*. This is pre-theoretically just what we would expect. For it says that *E* confirms *T* to the extent that *E* is likely given *T*, but unlikely otherwise. In other words, if *E* is in itself very surprising (like light bending in the vicinity of the sun) but at the same time just what you would expect given your theory *T* (the general theory of relativity) then *E* should make you increase your degree of belief in *T* a great deal. On the other hand, if *E* is no more likely given *T* than it would be on any other theory, then observing *E* provides no extra support for *T*. The movement of the tides, for example, is no great argument for general relativity theory, even though it is predicted by it, since it is also predicted by the alternative Newtonian theory of gravitation.

4.8. The Paradoxes Resolved

Let us now consider how this Bayesian approach to confirmation deals with the paradoxes of confirmation.

4.8.1. *The Raven Paradox*

First, the paradox of the ravens. The assumptions generating this paradox, remember, are (1) that generalizations are confirmed by their instances, and (2) that confirmation bears equally on logically equivalent propositions. The standard Bayesian response to this paradox is to accept both these assumptions, and therewith the apparently absurd conclusion that a white shoe does confirm that all ravens are black. But Bayesians then explain this appearance of absurdity by saying that a white shoe only confirms this hypothesis a *tiny bit*, by comparison with the confirmation it gets from a black raven.

Let me use some simple figures to illustrate the point. Suppose that you initially think that about $\frac{1}{5}$ of physical objects are black, and that about $\frac{1}{10}$ are ravens. (This isn't very realistic, but let's keep the figures simple.) Then, in the absence of any special views about the colours of ravens, your probability for the next object you see being a black raven will be $\frac{1}{50}$, and for its being a non-black non-raven will be $\frac{36}{50}$ (and similarly for its being a non-black raven $\frac{9}{50}$ and a black non-raven $\frac{4}{50}$).

Now consider the conditional probability of a black raven, and a non-black non-raven, on the assumption (T) that all ravens are black. This assumption will tend to increase your probability for both these observations, simply because it decreases the probability that you will see a non-black raven from $\frac{9}{50}$ to zero. Suppose this conditional probability for a black raven is $\frac{2}{50}$, for a non-black non-raven $\frac{38}{50}$ (and for a black non-raven $\frac{10}{50}$).

Now we can apply Bayes's theorem. The initial probability of a black raven is $\frac{1}{50}$, while the conditional probability given T is $\frac{2}{50}$. So, whatever your initial probability for the hypothesis that all ravens are black (equivalently, for all non-blacks are non-ravens), Bayes's theorem tells us that an observation of a black raven will double it. By contrast, where the initial probability of a non-black non-raven is $\frac{36}{50}$, the probability conditional on T is only $\frac{38}{50}$. So the observation of a white shoe will only increase our degree of belief in the hypothesis by $\frac{2}{36}$ths. The point is that the hypothesis that all ravens are black makes the observation of a black raven significantly less surprising than it would otherwise be; whereas the observation of a non-black non-raven, never very surprising to start with, becomes only marginally less so on the hypothesis that all ravens are black. So black ravens confirm the hypothesis a lot; white shoes confirm it scarcely at all.

It is perhaps surprising to learn that white shoes give *any* support to the hypothesis that all ravens are black, even if only a small amount. But we can see that, with any realistic figures, this support would be so minuscule that it would be very odd indeed to say, in an everyday context, that a white shoe gives us any reason to believe that all ravens are black. So this is how Bayesians deal with the raven paradox: they do not deny that white shoes confirm that all ravens are black; they just point out that they confirm it so little as to make no difference in an everyday context.

4.8.2. The Tacking Paradox

Now for the 'tacking' paradox. Recall that the assumptions here were (1) that theories are confirmed by the observation of anything they entail, and (2) that any evidence that confirms a theory also confirms its consequences. Many people, as I said earlier, think that there must be something wrong with (1), since it allows that a theory-plus-a-'tacked-on'-part (Newtonian-theory-plus-the-moon-is-green-cheese, say) is confirmed by the predictions of the original theory (the planets move in ellipses), which seems odd.

However, Bayesians are committed to (1). For if some T entails E, then $\mathrm{Prob}(E/T) = 1$. So, as long as E is not itself necessarily true, with an unconditional probability of 1, E must confirm T, by Bayes's theorem.

But Bayesians point out that this is consistent with E only confirming T in the sense that it increases the probability of some part of T, while leaving the probability of the rest of T untouched. So, for example, Bayesians would say the motion of the planets only confirms Newtonian-theory-plus-the-moon-is-green-cheese in the sense that it increases the probability of Newtonian theory itself, while being irrelevant to the green-cheese part of the joint hypothesis.

In line with this, Bayesians will deny (2). For, when some evidence confirms some theory only in the sense that it increases the probability of part of it, while leaving the rest untouched, then we would expect that evidence to confirm the consequences only of that part, and not of the other part. So while the motion of the planets confirms the joint thesis Newtonian-theory-plus-the-moon-is-green-cheese, it does not confirm the consequence that the moon is made of green cheese, or anything that follows from this.

Not only does this Bayesian line offer a natural solution to the tacking paradox, it is also helpful in thinking about the relation between theory and observation generally. Much recent philosophy of science has inferred, from the Duhem–Quine observation that specific theoretical assumptions only generate predictions with the help of auxiliary hypotheses, that the relation between theory and evidence is irredeemably *holistic*, in that it is always the totality of our beliefs about the world that is confirmed or refuted by evidence. But the Bayesian approach shows that even if predictions are generated by a *conjunction* of assumptions, that evidence can support different elements of that conjunction to different degrees.

4.9. Problems for Bayesianism

It should not be forgotten that Bayesianism confirmation theory is derived from the notion of *subjective* probability. As I pointed out earlier, there is nothing in the idea of subjective probability to ensure that different people will attach the same subjective probabilities and conditional probabilities to any set of assumptions, provided they each arrange their own probabilities 'internally' in such a way as to satisfy the probability calculus. Can such a subjective notion really provide a satisfactory basis for the apparently objective notion of how much theories are confirmed by the existing evidence? Surely we do not want to allow that I can be right to hold that the evidence shows relativity theory to have probability 0.8, while you can be equally right to think it has probability 0.2.

Different Bayesians make different responses to this challenge. Some simply say that Bayesianism is only a theory of how to change your probabilities, and not of which probabilities you ought to start or finish with. On this view, Bayes's theorem shows us how to update our subjective probabilities, given that we start with certain initial conditional and unconditional probabilities; but it says nothing about what those initial probabilities ought to be, and therefore nothing about which final probabilities we ought to end up with. There isn't anything wrong with my ending up thinking relativity theory has probability 0.8, while you think it has 0.2, provided we both reached this end-point by updating our initial probabilities in response to the evidence in the way required by Bayes's theorem.

Many Bayesians, however, find the possibility of such divergence worrying, and so offer a more ambitious answer. They say that, whatever your initial degrees of belief, Bayes's theorem will ensure convergence of opinion. The idea is that, given enough evidence, everybody will eventually end up with the same probabilities, even if they have different starting-points. There are a number of theorems of probability theory showing that, within limits, differences in initial probabilities will be 'washed out', in the sense that sufficient evidence and Bayesian updating will lead to effectively identical final degrees of belief. So in the end, argue Bayesians, it does not matter if you start with a high or low degree of belief in relativity theory—for, after a number of observations of light bending, gravitational red-shifts, and so on, you will end up believing it to a degree close to one anyway.

However, interesting as these results are, they do not satisfactorily answer the fundamental philosophical worry. For they do not work for *all* possible initial degrees of belief. Rather they assume that the people in question, while differing among themselves, all draw their initial degrees of belief from a certain range. While this range includes most initial degrees of belief that seem at all plausible, there are nevertheless other possible initial degrees of belief which are consistent with the axioms of probability, but which will not lead to eventual convergence. So, for example, the Bayesians do not in fact explain what is wrong with people who never end up believing relativity theory because they always think it is probable that the course of nature is going to change tomorrow.

This seems to me to show that Bayesianism provides at best a partial account of confirmation. Bayesianism shows us how our initial degrees of belief constrain the way we should respond to new evidence. But it needs to be supplemented by some further account of why some initial degrees of belief are objectively superior to others. Perhaps one way to fill this gap would be to appeal to the kind of 'simplicity' mentioned in Section 3.6 above. But it would take us too far afield to pursue this issue here.

5. EXPLANATION

5.1. The Covering-Law Model

Our main concern so far has been our knowledge of general truths. In this section I shall focus on the use to which this knowledge is put in *explanation*. Both in science and in everyday life the aim of investigation is often to find an explanation for some puzzling phenomenon. But what exactly is an explanation? And how does our knowledge of general truths contribute to our ability to explain?

Most modern discussion of explanation starts with Carl Hempel's 'covering-law model'. Let me first illustrate this model for the case where the item to be explained is some particular event, such as that the ice in your water-pipes froze last Tuesday, or that it rained this morning. According to Hempel, the explanation of any such event conforms to the following schema:

Initial conditions: $I_1, I_2, ..., I_n$
Laws: L
_____
Explained event: E.

So, for example, we might explain the fact E that it rained this morning by citing the initial conditions I_1, I_2 that there was a certain level of humidity and that the atmospheric pressure fell to a certain level and the law L that such a fall of pressure in such humidity is always followed by a precipitation of rain.

The law in such an explanation 'covers' the initial conditions and consequent event, in the sense that it shows that the sequence of events behind a particular occurrence is simply an instance of a general pattern. The fact that gets explained, E, is sometimes referred to as the 'explanandum', and the facts that do the explaining, the Is and L, as the 'explanans'. Note that while I have represented the law involved in the explanans as a single proposition, L, in most cases we will need a conjunction of simpler laws to see why *E* follows the relevant *I*s. For example, we would need both Newton's second law and the law of gravitation to explain why a meteor moves in the way it does.

Note also that, on this model of an explanation, explaining an event is the same thing as *deducing* it from initial conditions and laws. Given the initial conditions and a law which says that in general such initial conditions are followed by an *E*, then logic alone allows us to infer that the explanandum occurs. Because they involve *deduction* via a *law* in this way, such explanations are often called 'deductive-nomological' explanations, or 'D-N' explanations for short. (There is a variant of the covering-law model which allows probabilistic rather than deterministic laws, and in which this requirement of deducibility is therefore relaxed. So 'covering-law' is strictly a wider term than 'deductive-nomological'. But for the moment let us stick to deductive cases, and leave probabilistic explanations to one side.)

It is worth being clear that the idea of a 'deductive' explanation does not assume that the law *L* can somehow be 'deduced' from first principles in an a priori way. Such laws still have to be established by *induction* from past observations of results. The idea is simply that, if we have established such a law, then it will deductively imply, together with suitable initial conditions, certain further results.

The covering-law model implies a certain symmetry between explanation and prediction. The structure of explanations, in which we deduce that *E* had to occur from initial conditions and laws, exactly parallels the structure of predictions, in which we deduce that *E* is *going* to occur from the same initial conditions and laws. For example, if we can explain its raining this morning by the prior conditions and the relevant law, then we could presumably have predicted its raining beforehand on the basis of the same information. So for the covering-law model the difference between explanation and prediction depends only on whether you know the explanandum before you deduce it from the explanans. If you already know *E*, then deducing it from initial conditions and laws will serve to explain it. If you do not already know *E*, then the same deduction will serve to predict it. A prediction tells you what to expect. An explanation shows you that what you already know was only to be expected.

5.2. Theoretical Explanation

In the last section I considered explanations of particular events, such as its raining this morning, or a particular meteor taking a certain path. However, the covering-law model is also designed to accommodate explanations of laws as well as explanations of particular events. For example, suppose you are puzzled about some general law, such as, say, that there is always a rainbow when you look towards rain with the sun at a given angle behind you. I can explain this by showing that it follows from the laws that (1) sunlight involves a mixture of all wavelengths of light, (2) these different wavelengths refract differently on moving from light to water, and (3) raindrops are of a shape which will lead to internal reflection off the back of the raindrop. Here I have explained one law by reference to other laws. Schematically:

Explanans: $L_1, L_2, ..., L_n$
Explanandum: L.

Because the explanandum here is a general truth, and not a particular event occurring at some specific place and time, it is not necessary that initial conditions be involved in the explanation. But despite this difference, it is still a *deductive* explanation from *laws*, and so still a species of 'deductive-nomological' explanation. Explanations of this kind are often called 'theoretical explanations', to distinguish them from 'particular explanations'.

The possibility of theoretical explanations shows how the covering-law model can respond to a common initial objection. Consider once more the particular explanation of this morning's rain offered in the last section. Somebody might say that it is all very well to attribute this morning's rain to the drop in pressure and the humidity, but object that this is no kind of explanation until you have shown why drops in pressure at high humidity are in general followed by rain.

The covering-law model can respond by insisting that the explanation of a particular rainfall this morning is one thing, and the explanation of the law that falls in pressure at high humidity are followed by rain is another. If you want explanations of both, you can have them. But it does not follow that you have not explained the first, the particular rainfall, until you have also explained the second, the law which accounts for the particular rainfall.

Indeed, it would be obviously self-defeating to require that all explanations should contain explanations of the facts adduced in the explanans. We would be forced into infinite regress. As soon as we explained the laws which originally appeared in the explanans by other laws, we would then have to explain those other laws by further laws, and so on. And, in the case of particular explanations, there would be an additional regress, for we would need to explain the initial conditions mentioned in the explanans (why did the pressure drop? why was the humidity high?), and this would require mention of yet prior initial conditions, which would themselves need to be explained, and so on again.

So it does not make any sense to demand that in an explanation the explanatory facts should always be explained too. This is not because there is anything wrong with asking for further such explanations in specific cases. It is just that we cannot give the answer to an infinite number of questions in a finite time.

Exactly which explanatory questions have to be answered in order to yield explanatory satisfaction is an interesting question. But it probably is not one that admits of any general answer. Whether an explanation is satisfying depends on the practicalities of what is being explained to whom. Any given person has a rough overall picture of the world, in which earlier events lead on to later ones according to familiar patterns. But some phenomena do not fit into these pictures. The role of an explanation is to show how such puzzling phenomena can be fitted in. However, different people can be puzzled by different aspects of a given situation, in that the situation will fail to fit into their respective pictures in different ways. And then different explanations will be needed to satisfy them.

5.3. Do All Explanations Fit the Covering-Law Model, and Vice Versa?

In this section I want to start raising some questions about the adequacy of the covering-law model. The covering-law model was originally proposed by Hempel as an analysis of the intuitive pre-analytic notion of a scientific explanation. So it is possible to ask whether this analysis is adequate. This question has two parts. (A) Is it true that every scientific explanation is an instance of the covering-law pattern? (B) Conversely, does every instance of the covering-law pattern amount to a scientific explanation?

5.3.1. Do All Explanations Fit the Covering-Law Model?

Let me start with (A). Consider this example. Little Katy contracts chicken-pox. You want to know why. You are told that she played with Miranda, who had it. This seems a perfectly cogent explanation. However, it does not seem to conform to the covering-law model. Suppose we think of playing with another child with chicken-pox as an initial condition in a covering-law deduction of Katy getting chicken-pox. Then we need as the law something like 'Whenever a child who has not had chicken-pox plays with another child who has it, the first child gets it too'. But there isn't any such law. There are plenty of cases where children do not come down with chicken-pox after playing with another child with it, even if they have not had it before.

So this is a prima-facie counter-example: an intuitively satisfactory explanation that does not fit the covering-law model.

5.3.2. Are All Instances of the Covering-Law Model really Explanations?

Question (B) raised the converse issue: is every instance of the covering-law pattern really an explanation? Here is one case which is not.

I_1, I_2: The barometer fell this morning; and the humidity was high.

   L: Whenever the barometer falls in high humidity, it rains.

   E: It rained this morning.

This deduction conforms perfectly to the requirements of the covering-law model of a particular explanation. But intuitively it just is not a satisfactory explanation. The barometer falling might account for how you know it is going to rain. But its actually raining is a different fact from your knowing it will rain. And intuitively it seems quite wrong to say that the barometer's fall was responsible for the rain itself.

Here are some similar cases.

I_1, I_2: The shadow of a pole P is n feet long; and the sun is at angle a.

   L: Whenever a pole casts a shadow of n feet with the sun at angle a, the pole itself is m feet high.

   E: Pole P is m feet high.

   I: Star S emits red-shifted light.

   L: All stars with red-shifted light are rapidly receding.

   E: Star S is rapidly receding.

Both of these seem impeccable cases of covering-law deductions. But, again, it seems quite wrong to say that the pole is m feet high because its shadow is n feet long, or that the star is rapidly receding because its light is red-shifted.

5.3.3. Explanations that are not Predictions, and Vice Versa

Let me make a general point about the two kinds of counter-example to the covering-law model raised in this section. The covering-law model is committed, as I pointed out earlier, to the view that every explanation is a potential prediction, and vice versa. So if we can find explanations that are not potential predictions, then we will have examples of explanations that do not fit the covering-law model. The example of Katy and the chicken-pox was of this sort. You cannot immediately predict that she will get it just from knowing she played with another infected child. Because it insists that all explanations should be potential predictions, the covering-law model has trouble admitting these prima-facie plausible explanations.

Then we looked at the converse kind of example, predictions that are not in fact explanations, and which therefore get counted as explanations by the covering-law model when they should not be. You can predict the rain from the barometer's fall, or the pole's height from the length of its shadow, or the star's recession from its red-shift. And so, because it accepts that all potential predictions are explanations, the covering-law model has trouble ruling out these prima-facie non-explanations.

5.4. Probabilistic Explanation

Defenders of the covering-law model can make various responses to these counter-examples. Let me first consider counter-examples of type (A), namely, intuitively satisfactory explanations, like that of Katy's chicken-pox, which do not fit the covering-law model.

One possible response here would be to argue that, if Katy's chicken-pox isn't predictable for lack of any law that says she was sure to get it in the circumstances, then, despite first appearances, her playing with Miranda does not explain it. (After all, other children in contact with the infection sometimes do not get chicken-pox. So why suppose that Katy's contact with Miranda is in itself enough to explain her getting the disease?) This line would save the covering-law model of explanation by denying that the apparent counter-example was really a genuine example of an explanation.

However, this move seems unattractive. It would be very odd to deny that Katy got chicken-pox because she played with Miranda. So most covering-law theorists of explanation, from Hempel onwards, have weakened the requirements of the covering-law model to allow that there can be explanations that appeal to *probabilistic* laws, rather than exceptionless ones. After all, in our example it is presumably true that most children in contact with chicken-pox get it themselves, and this means that we can at least anticipate that Katy would get it from Miranda with high probability, if not with certainty. Accordingly Hempel put forward the following model of 'inductive-statistical explanations' as another species of covering-law explanations alongside 'deductive-nomological explanations'.

Initial conditions: $I_1, I_2, ..., I_n$
Probabilistic laws: L, to the effect that *most* $I_1, ..., I_n$s are Es
Explained event: E.

Explanations fitting this schema are 'inductive' because the premises do not deductively imply the conclusion, but only indicate it has a high probability; and they are 'statistical' because they appeal to probabilistic laws rather than exceptionless ones.

Note that Hempel's 'inductive-statistical' model requires that the explanans should give the explanandum a high probability. It is not clear that this is quite the right requirement for probabilistic explanation. Suppose that John Smith gets lung cancer. In explanation we are told that he has smoked fifty cigarettes a day for forty years. Intuitively this seems like a good explanation. But note that the explanans here does not give the explanandum a *high* probability. Even people who smoke fifty a day for a long period still have a low probability of getting lung cancer in absolute terms. What is true, though, is that they have a much *higher* probability of getting lung cancer than if they did not smoke. Because of this, a number of theorists have suggested that Hempel's requirement of *high* probability be replaced by the different requirement that the initial conditions merely increase the probability of the explanandum, compared to the probability if those initial conditions were absent. (Wesley Salmon has dubbed this the 'statistical-relevance' model, as opposed to the 'inductive-statistical' model, because the requirement is in effect that the initial conditions should be probabilistically relevant to the explanandum.[9])

This issue of probabilistic explanation raises a number of further questions which cannot be resolved here. Most obviously, you might have been wondering whether the probabilistic laws appealed to in such explanations are supposed to be reflections of genuine indeterminism or whether they simply reflect our ignorance of the full set of initial conditions which do determine Katy's chicken-pox, John Smith's cancer, etc. Different answers to this question will lead to different views of probabilistic explanation. But there is little agreement among philosophers on how it should be answered.

5.5. Causation and Explanation

Let me now consider the other kind of counter-example, instances of the covering-law model which are not in fact explanations, such as the deduction of the rain from the barometer's fall, or the pole's height from its shadow's length, or the star's recession from its red-shift.

The obvious reason why these deductions are not in fact explanations is that the initial conditions do not specify the *cause* of the explanandum event. Instead they deduce the explanandum event from a *symptom* (like the barometer's fall) or an *effect* (like the shadow's length, or the red-shift).

The obvious remedy is to add to the covering-law account the further requirement that in explaining particular events the initial conditions should always include the cause of the explanandum event. I think this is the right move. But it calls for a number of comments.

5.5.1. The Direction of Causation

In a sense this move simply shifts the original problem into the analysis of causation. The barometer/pole/red-shift counter-examples arose because the

---

[9] See W. Salmon, *Statistical Explanation and Statistical Relevance* (Pittsburgh, 1971).

original requirements of the covering-law model failed to ensure that the 'causal arrow', so to speak, pointed from the initial conditions to the explanandum. We can remedy the defect by appealing to the existence of such a directed arrow between causally related events, and requiring that genuine explanations proceed in the same direction as this arrow.

But that causation does have such a direction is itself a problematic assumption. Consider Hume's equation of causation with constant conjunction. This in itself does not tell us, given two constantly conjoined events, which lies at the tail of the arrow, and is therefore the cause, and which lies at the point, and is therefore the effect.

So something needs to be added to Hume's constant conjunction analysis to put the direction into causation. How to do this is a matter of active controversy. Hume himself argued that, given two constantly conjoined events, it is always the *earlier* which is the cause and the *later* the effect. But this appeal to temporal precedence is not entirely satisfactory. (After all, the barometer's fall precedes the rain, but still does not cause it. And cannot some causes be simultaneous with their effects?)

I do not propose to pursue this issue any further here. Even if it is unclear how to *account* for causal direction, it is intuitively clear that causation *has* a direction, and that requiring that explanations follow this direction is the way to rule out the barometer/pole/red-shift counter-examples.

5.5.2. *Are All Explanations of Particular Events Causal?*

It is not clear that it is appropriate to impose the requirement that the explanans should mention a cause on *all* explanations of particular events. Suppose we explain why some frozen substance is water by citing the fact it is H_2O; or suppose we explain why something has a temperature t by citing the fact that the mean kinetic energy of its molecules is k. These are arguably reasonable explanations. But being made of H_2O does not cause something to be water, so much as constitute its being water. Similarly, having a mean molecular kinetic energy of k does not cause the temperature of t, but again constitutes it.

Perhaps these are not really explanations in the same sense as most explanations. They do seem slightly peculiar, at least to my ear.

Still, even if we do count them as mainstream explanations, it is of no great importance in the present context. To rule out the barometer/pole/red-shift counter-examples we need to require *some* stronger link between explanans and explanandum than demanded by the original covering-law model. Maybe requiring a specifically causal link is too strong, because we will then rule out the H_2O/mean kinetic energy explanations too. If so, then the solution is simply to say that we need a *metaphysical* link of one sort or the other, in which the explanans either causes *or* constitutes the explanandum.

5.5.3. Teleological Explanations

Perhaps one reason why Hempel and other early proponents of the covering-law model were unwilling to impose this kind of metaphysical link was that there is one important class of explanations in which the explanans neither causes nor constitutes the explanandum. These are the *functional*, or *teleological*, explanations which play such a central role in biology, such as 'Plants contain chlorophyll so that they can photosynthesize' or 'Polar bears are white so that they cannot be seen'. Indeed these explanations are striking precisely because the item that gets explained (chlorophyll, whiteness) is the *cause*, not the effect, of the item that does the explaining (photosynthesis, camouflage).

If we take these explanations at face value, then it is not open to us to require that (non-constitutive) explanations always go from cause to effect. For these explanations seem to go in just the other direction.

Until fairly recently most philosophers of science did take such explanations at face value. Thus Hempel himself regarded teleological explanations as simply another way, alongside normal causal explanations, of exemplifying the covering-law model: the only difference is that in causal explanations the explaining fact (lower temperature) temporally precedes the explained fact (freezing), whereas in functional explanations it is the explained fact (white fur) that comes temporally before the consequence (camouflage) which explains it.

Most contemporary philosophers of science, however, take a different view, and argue that functional explanations, despite appearances, are really a sub-species of causal explanations. On this view, the reference to future effects in functional explanations is merely apparent, and such explanations really refer to past causes. In the biological case, these past causes will be the evolutionary histories which led to the natural selection of the biological trait in question. Thus the functional explanation of the polar bears' colour should be understood as referring us to the fact that their *past* camouflaging led to the natural selection of their whiteness, and not to the fact that they may be camouflaged in the future.

If we take this line on functional explanations, then we can continue to uphold the requirement that all (non-constitutive) explanations should flow from cause to effect, and so deal with the barometer/pole/red-shift difficulty in the way suggested.

BIBLIOGRAPHY

A classic introduction to the problem of induction is section 6 of Bertrand Russell, *The Problems of Philosophy* (Oxford, 1967). For the Popperian response to the problem of induction, see section 1 of Karl Popper, *The Logic of Scientific Discovery*, 1st Eng. edn. (London, 1959). A critical discussion of Popper's views can be found in sections 2 and 3 of Anthony O'Hear, *An Introduction to the Philosophy of Science* (Oxford, 1989). A reliabilist approach to induction is defended in section 4 of David Papineau, *Philosophical Naturalism* (Oxford, 1993). For Goodman's 'new problem of induction', see section 3 of Nelson Goodman, *Fact, Fiction and Forecast* (London, 1954) and the paper by S. Barker and P. Achinstein, 'On the New Riddle of Induction', and the reply by Goodman, 'Positionality and Pictures', in P. H. Nidditch (ed.), *The Philosophy of Science* (Oxford, 1968).

A good general introduction to the problem of distinguishing laws from accidents, as well as a defence of his own non-Humean view, is given by David Armstrong in his *What is a Law of Nature?* (Cambridge, 1983).

Much of the contemporary debate between realists and instrumentalists focuses on the arguments in Bas van Fraassen, *The Scientific Image* (Oxford, 1980). These arguments are discussed further in P. Churchland and C. Hooker (eds.), *Images of Science* (Chicago, 1985).

There are two excellent books on Bayesianism, both of which also provide a general introduction to confirmation theory and concepts of probability: Paul Horwich, *Probability and Evidence* (Cambridge, 1982), and Colin Howson and Peter Urbach, *Scientific Reasoning* (La Salle, Ill., 1989).

The starting-point for all modern discussions of explanation is section 4 of Carl Hempel's *Aspects of Scientific Explanation* (New York, 1965). For more recent debates, see David Ruben, *Explaining Explanation* (London, 1990) and the essays in David Ruben (ed.), *Explanation* (Oxford, 1993).

4

METAPHYSICS

Tim Crane and David Wiggins

INTRODUCTION
A. C. Grayling

Metaphysics is the branch of philosophy which is concerned with the ultimate nature of reality. Its primary questions are 'What is there?'—that is, what exists?—and 'What is it like?'

The question 'What is there?' is not intended to invite as answer an inventory of things in the universe—my left shoe, my right shoe, my pen, this paper, and so forth—but rather a general account of the fundamental character of reality. In Aristotle's words the enterprise is 'the study of being *qua* being'.

The primary questions quickly invite others. Being able to say what exists involves being able to say something about the nature of existence. What is it for something to exist? How are we to understand assertions and denials of existence—'Quarks exist', 'Unicorns do not exist'? And as soon as candidates are proposed in answer to the 'What is there?' question—for example, material objects occupying space and time; minds; God or gods; abstract entities like numbers, properties, and meanings—further questions immediately press—for example, whether only one or some of these things or kinds of thing is truly ultimate; what true ultimacy means; which if any among these things exist only at our conceptual convenience; what the connections are between the things that exist, if there is more than one and especially if there is more than one kind; and so on.

Metaphysical questions are indeed so numerous and important that discussions of some of them constitute branches of philosophy in their own right, for example the philosophy of mind and philosophical theology. But metaphysical questions about the existence and nature of given kinds of thing arise in almost all philosophical debates. They arise in ethics, in connection with the nature of value. They arise in the philosophy of mathematics, in connection with the nature of mathematical entities like numbers and sets. And they arise in epistemology, where questions about the nature of knowledge cannot proceed independently of questions about the objects of knowledge.

With the pressure of the more specific questions a range of typical metaphysical problems present themselves. What is time? Are particulars more basic than events? Do human beings have free will? Is there a distinction between appearance and reality, and if so, what are their relations? What is causality? In what if any sense do universals exist? Does the world exist independently of our knowledge of it? What is substance? And so on. In the pages to follow just some of these debates are taken up, the idea being that discussion of a few metaphysical topics selected for their centrality and importance will prime study of the rest.

The topics considered are causation, time, universals, and substance. In the course of discussion of them much philosophy, and its history, becomes salient.

CAUSATION
Tim Crane

1.1. Introduction

The hurricane caused the famine; HIV causes AIDS; smoking causes cancer; signing that last cheque caused my financial ruin. Judgements about causation—about what causes what—are so common in our lives that we hardly notice them. But what is it for something to cause something else? What makes something a cause of another thing?

We should distinguish first between understanding what the relation of causation is and understanding what causation relates. Suppose smoking causes cancer. What is the relation, causation, that links smoking and cancer? That is the first question. But we can also ask, what kinds of entity must smoking and cancer be, so that they can stand in this relation? Smoking is the cause, and cancer is the effect. But what are causes and effects? This is the second question.

Most of this discussion of causation is concerned with the first question. Section 1.5 will be explicitly concerned with the second, but Section 1.3 will also have a bearing on it.

1.2. Causation and Regularity

Modern discussions of causation begin with David Hume's views on the question. Hume saw that there is more to our idea of causation than just the idea of one thing following another. Our concept of causation involves the idea of something following something else with a kind of necessity—in some sense, the cause 'necessitates' its effects. But Hume thought that this was an illusion: in reality there is no such necessity. The appearance of necessity is a product of the fact that our minds expect similar causes to have similar effects. This feeling of expectation we 'project' on to the world, and confuse it with necessitation.

So what does Hume think causation is, in reality? He gave the following definition of causation: 'a cause is an object, followed by another, such that all objects similar to the first are followed by objects similar to the second. Or in other words, where the first object had not been, the second never had existed.' So Hume defined causation in terms of temporal succession—the cause preceding its effects in time—and constant conjunction—like causes being constantly accompanied by like effects.

Two aspects of Hume's theory have retained the interest of contemporary philosophers. The first is the idea that causation does not consist in a necessary connection between cause and effect, and nor can causal relations be known a priori. The second idea is that regularity is involved in causation in some way: to say that A caused B commits us to the claim that things sufficiently like A will cause things sufficiently like B. I shall take these points in turn.

1.2.1. *Causation, Necessity, and the A Priori*

What does it mean to deny that causation is a necessary relation? When philosophers say that something is necessarily true, they normally mean that it could not be otherwise: it must be true. For example, truths of mathematics, like 2 + 2 = 4, are necessarily true. This just could not be false, given what the symbols '2', '4', '=', and '+' mean. The opposite of necessity is contingency: something is contingently true if it could have been otherwise: it might have been false. For example, Hume died in Edinburgh, but he might not have. It is possible that he could have died in Glasgow, or even in Spain. There is no necessity about where Hume died.

A further important distinction is between a priori and a posteriori knowledge. Something is knowable a priori when it is justifiable independently of any further experience. Mathematical knowledge is generally thought to be a priori because there are no further experiences someone needs to have in order to know that 2 + 2 = 4. Most of our knowledge of the world, however, is a posteriori (or 'empirical'): we need experience to justify our belief that, for example, water boils at 100 °C.

Hume thought both that causal relations cannot be known a priori, and that they are not necessary. In his day these two ideas were not clearly distinguished, but philosophers these days try to keep them apart. To say that causation cannot be known a priori is to say this: in order to know whether a causal relation holds between A and B, we need experience or evidence of some other kind (e.g. testimony). We cannot know by reasoning alone whether A caused B, as we can with mathematical truths. To say that causation is not a necessary relation is to say that even if A caused B, it might not have done so. Suppose our billiard-ball A collided with billiard-ball B, and B moved. There is no impossibility in supposing that B simply stood still and did not move.

(One might wonder why we need to distinguish necessity and the a priori in this way. One reason, as we shall see, is that on certain theories of causation, judgements about cause and effect can be known a priori—yet they are still contingent. The other reason is that many philosophers have been persuaded by Saul Kripke's arguments that there are necessary truths which can only be known a posteriori.)

1.2.2. Regularity and Constant Conjunction

The other influential element of Hume's theory of causation is the idea that causation involves regularity, or 'constant conjunction'. As we saw, Hume thought that a cause is an 'object, followed by another, such that all objects similar to the first are followed by objects similar to the second'. So if this short circuit caused this fire, then all events similar to this short circuit will cause events similar to this fire. Maybe no two events are ever exactly similar; but all the claim requires is that two events similar in some specific respect will cause events similar in some specific respect.

Hume thought that regularity was essential to causation because he did not think there could be anything else involved in causation. For Hume, causation could not have a 'hidden' essence, because of his empiricism: his theory of ideas requires that every idea is formed from a prior impression, and since we have no impression (i.e. experience) of the essence or nature of causation, we can have no real idea of it. All we have impressions of are constant conjunctions of events: objects colliding followed by objects moving, matches striking followed by fires, and so on. These constant conjunctions, plus the other connotations mentioned above, are all the idea of causation amounts to.

In effect, Hume held that a constant conjunction between As and Bs is both necessary and sufficient for a causal relation between any particular A and B. That is, if As and Bs are constantly conjoined, then there is a causal relation between A and B (sufficent condition); and if there is a causal relation between A and B, then As and Bs are constantly conjoined (necessary condition). (We need to be careful to distinguish the idea of a necessary condition from the idea of a necessary truth. To say that Q is a necessary condition for P is to say that if P is true, then Q is true; this does not mean that Q is necessarily true. Example: being in England is a necessary condition for being in London, since if I am in London, then I am in England. But this does not mean that it is a necessary truth that I am in England.)

The claim that constant conjunction or regularity is sufficient for causation is a very strong claim. For it seems that there are many regularities in nature which are not causal. Take a famous example of the Scottish philosopher Thomas Reid (1710–96): day regularly follows night, and night regularly follows day. There is therefore a constant conjunction between night and day. But day does not cause night, nor does night cause day. So it seems that constant conjunction between A and B is not sufficient for the existence of a causal relation between A and B.

But is constant conjunction necessary for causation? To hold this would be to hold that if there is a causal link between A and B, then As and Bs are constantly conjoined. If striking the match caused the match to light, then similar strikings will produce similar lightings. Regularity is essential to causation, even though it may not be all there is to it, as Hume thought it was. Is this plausible?

We certainly believe in such regularities, and many of our everyday actions seem to rely on them. We expect similar causes to have similar effects: when we strike a match, we rely on the fact that struck matches have lit in the past, and we expect this struck match to light. When we throw a ball in the air, we expect it to return to the ground, since balls thrown in the past have returned to the ground. And if the match had not lit, or the ball had not fallen to the ground, we would normally think that this is because something (or someone) else intervened, in which case this cause was not sufficiently similar to the other causes to produce the same effect. Of course, some events are so unusual that they may never happen again. But what the regularity thesis says is not that causes imply actual regularities, but only that if a similar cause had happened, a similar effect would have happened.

So our everyday beliefs about the world seem to commit us to the idea that regularity is a necessary condition of causation. But can we say any more than this? Can we justify our everyday belief? To justify this belief would require at least two things: first, we would need to show that there could not be a case of causation that did not imply a regularity—there could not be what we might call 'single-case' causation. Second, we would need an explanation of why it is that causation implies regularity.

Some philosophers have argued that there are no good reasons for thinking that there could not be single-case causation. For example, G. E. M. Anscombe has argued that it is a mere philosophical dogma to think that regularity is essential to causation. For Anscombe, what is essential is the idea of derivativeness: effects are derived from their causes, and there is no contradiction in saying that something might produce an effect even if something very similar to it did not. Some of the examples philosophers use in these cases are of indeterministic or probabilistic causes, such as those postulated in modern physics. But on close consideration, it is not so obvious that these cases are incompatible with the regularity thesis, because there can be indeterministic regularities (see Bibliography).

1.3. Causation and Conditionals

The idea that regularity is a necessary condition of causation is only the beginning of an analysis of causation. Since regularity is not sufficient, it obviously can't be the whole story. And one generally unsatisfactory aspect of the regularity thesis is that it explains why this *A* caused this *B* in terms of facts about things other than this *A* and this *B*: that is, in terms of all the other (actual or merely possible) *A*s and *B*s in the universe. But what we want to know is: what is it about this *A* and this *B* that makes one the cause of the other? What is it about this short circuit and this fire that makes the former the cause of the latter?

1.3.1. Causes and Causal Circumstances

The trouble is that, while we think of the short circuit as the cause of the fire, there are many other elements which contribute to the occurrence of the fire. The presence of oxygen and inflammable material certainly contribute to the fire, as does the fact that there is not a sprinkler system designed to extinguish the fire. And we can go further: the fact that no one intervened to put the fire out, and even the fact that the whole world did not come to an end before the fire happened, certainly made the fire possible. Sometimes people draw the conclusion from reflections like this that, while only the short circuit was the cause of the fire, the other things were just the causal circumstances. But this seems to label the problem rather than solve it—for what we wanted to know was why we are justified in calling the short circuit, rather than any of the other circumstances, 'the cause'.

John Stuart Mill thought that the 'whole' cause of an effect like our fire was the entire state of the universe before the fire. One problem with saying this is that we never really know what the whole cause of something is, since we never know the whole state of the universe before a given effect. But we do think that we know at least some of the causes of some effects; so Mill's account misrepresents what we ordinarily take ourselves to know. To this it may be responded that we only know 'partial' causes, not 'whole' causes. But now we are back with the distinction between causes and causal circumstances, expressed in different terms.

What we need is to find a way of picking out the cause from all the conditions prior to an effect. We need a principled way of 'homing in' on the class of conditions that constitute the entire state of the universe before the effect which will yield those conditions which constitute the cause.

1.3.2. Causes and Necessary and Sufficient Conditions

The beginning of an answer is found in this talk of 'conditions'. Perhaps causes are necessary and/or sufficient conditions for their effects? To say that a cause A is a necessary condition of an effect B is to say that if it is not the case that A, then it is not the case that B. (If there is no short circuit, then there is no fire.) To say that A is a sufficient condition of B is to say that if it is the case that A, then it is the case that B. (If there is a short circuit, then there is a fire.) Let us call any theory which analyses causation in terms of such conditions a 'conditional theory' of causation. The simplest kind of conditional theory says that A causes B just when A is necessary and sufficient for B.

Put like this, the idea is obviously inadequate. The short circuit cannot be a straightforward necessary condition of the fire, since it could be true that there is a fire without it being true that there is a short circuit. And nor can it be sufficient for the fire, since it could be true that there is a short circuit without there being a fire: as we saw, if there is no oxygen, then the short circuit will not cause the fire.

But perhaps we can modify the simple conditional theory to account for these problems. This was proposed in a famous paper by J. L. Mackie. Mackie's idea was that while *A* is itself not necessary for *B*, it is a necessary part of a wider condition. And while *A* is not sufficient for *B*, this wider condition is sufficient for *B*. So according to Mackie, the cause, *A*, is an insufficient but necessary part of a set of conditions which is sufficient (though not necessary) for *B*. He called this complex condition an INUS condition, after the initial letters of the words used in the definition: the cause is an Insufficient but Necessary part of a condition that is itself Unnecessary but Sufficient. This looks very complex; it can be best explained through an example.

The short circuit is not itself sufficient for the fire, since without oxygen and inflammable material the fire would not have happened. But there is a wider set of conditions, including the presence of oxygen and inflammable material, which is sufficient. This is the 'S' part of the INUS condition. But this wider set of conditions is unnecessary for the fire, since there could be a fire without all these conditions holding. This is the 'U' part of the INUS condition. But the short circuit is a necessary part of this wider sufficient condition, since, without the short circuit, this condition would not have brought about the fire. This is the 'N' part of the INUS condition. However, the short circuit will not do it on its own: it is an insufficient part of the wider condition. This is the 'I' part of the INUS condition.

1.3.3. *Causation and Counterfactuals*

The details of Mackie's analysis are complex, but the general idea is fairly intuitive: the cause is a part of a wider set of conditions which suffices for its effect. This seems to allow us to simplify Mackie's analysis, and say that *A* is the cause of *B* when, given certain other conditions, *A* is sufficient for *B*. That is, in the circumstances, *A* is sufficient for *B*. But what about the necessary condition? Can we say that in the circumstances, *A* is necessary for *B*?

Mackie denies this: the short circuit is not necessary for the fire, since fires can occur (even given these or very similar circumstances) without short circuits. And of course, it would be wrong to say that fires cannot occur in such circumstances without short circuits. As an extreme example, God could intervene with a thunderbolt and start the fire. But this is not the only way to understand the claim that causes are, in the circumstances, necessary for their effects.

We might want to say not that the fire *could* not occur without a short circuit, but that this fire *would* not have occurred without this short circuit. This would be to understand the necessary condition as a 'counterfactual' condition: if *A* caused *B*, then (given the circumstances) if *A* had not occurred, *B* would not have occurred. This does not say that *B could* not have occurred if *A* had not occurred: compare the difference between 'I would not have made such a fool of myself if I had not been so drunk' and 'I could not have made such a fool of myself if I had not been so drunk'.

The idea that causation involves this counterfactual element was anticipated by Hume in the second part of his famous definition of cause: 'where the first object had not been, the second never had existed'. Many philosophers today, notably David Lewis, think that the notion of a counterfactual is the key to causation. Before outlining their view, we need to say a little about counterfactual conditionals.

Philosophers of language typically make a distinction between two kinds of conditional statement in natural language, normally called 'indicative' and 'subjunctive' conditionals. Compare 'If Oswald did not kill Kennedy, someone else did' (indicative) with 'If Oswald had not killed Kennedy, someone else would have' (subjunctive). Since Kennedy was killed, the first is obviously true; but accepting the truth of the second depends on accepting some conspiracy theory about Kennedy's assassination. Subjunctive conditionals have the form 'If it were the case that *A*, then it would be the case that *B*'. Counterfactual conditionals belong to the class of subjunctive conditionals: they are called 'counterfactual' because the statement after the 'if' (called the 'antecedent') is contrary to fact—as in our Kennedy example.

Events seem to stand in relations of counterfactual dependence to one another. To say that if there had not been a short circuit, there would not have been a fire is to say that the fire is counterfactually dependent on the short circuit. Lewis's idea is to define causation in terms of a relation of counterfactual dependence. Roughly, *A* caused *B* when there is a chain of counterfactually dependent events linking *A* and *B*.

To state this theory fully, we need more details. For one thing, there are many relations of counterfactual dependence which are not causal relations. If I drive through a red light, I break the law. So in the circumstances, if I had not driven through the red light, I would not have broken the law. But intuitively, my driving through the red light does not cause me to break the law—rather, it constitutes my breaking the law in this specific case.

To answer this, the counterfactual theory can appeal to another idea of Hume's: that causes and effects must be 'distinct existences'. My breaking the law (on this occasion) cannot exist independently from my driving through the red light: these are not 'separable' entities. So one cannot cause the other. (This is really another way of putting Hume's point that causation is not a necessary relation.)

It should be remembered that one can hold that causation involves counter-factual dependence without holding that it can be entirely analysed in terms of counterfactuals.

1.4. The Relata of Causation

So far we have looked at the relation of causation: when two phenomena are related as cause and effect, what makes this relation the relation of causation? But this leaves the outstanding question: what sorts of entity are the phenomena related in this way (the 'relata' of causation)? What sorts of thing are causes and effects? Hume calls causes and effects 'objects': are they ordinary material objects like sticks and stones?

We need to distinguish between two sorts of causal claim. One is where we say that a certain general kind of thing causes another general kind of thing—as when we say that smoking causes cancer. The other is when we say some specific thing causes another specific thing—as when we say that this short circuit causes this fire. Let us call the first kind of claim a general causal claim and the second a singular causal claim. (Note that I am not assuming that these are two different kinds of causation.) In this section I shall only be considering the relata of singular causation.

At first sight, it seems odd to say that objects like sticks and stones are singular causes—in themselves, objects seem, so to speak, too inert to do any causing. Of course, we do say things like 'The stone broke the window'—but surely what we mean here is that the motion of the stone, and its impact on the window, broke it. Considered in itself, the stone is not doing anything.

1.4.1. *Causes and Effects as Events*

The idea that causes are things like stones moving or being thrown is the idea that causes are events. An influential account of causes and effects as events has been proposed by Donald Davidson. Davidson, like most philosophers, takes events to be particulars: that is, unrepeatable, dated happenings. An event such as the death of Caesar is unrepeatable, since it can never happen again—even if, like a cat, Caesar had nine lives, each of his nine deaths would be unrepeatable. Events are dated in the sense that they occur at a particular period of time. While two events can occupy the same period of time, one event cannot occupy two distinct periods of time. This is part of what it means to say that events are particulars (in some respects like material objects, for example) rather than universals (like properties and relations: see the discussion of universals below for more on this distinction).

Like material objects, events can be described and redescribed in many ways. Just as I can describe Julius Caesar as 'the famous Roman conqueror of Gaul' or as 'the husband of Calpurnia' or as 'the historical figure who most interests me', I can describe Caesar's death as 'the death of the famous Roman conqueror of Gaul' or as 'the death of Calpurnia's husband' or as 'the death of the historical figure who most interests me'. I could also describe it as 'the event caused by the stabbing of the assassins' knives' or as 'the murder described on page 100 of my copy of Shakespeare'. But these are all descriptions of the same event: Caesar's death.

Davidson saw that if events are particulars that can be truly described in many ways, then we must distinguish between statements of causation and causal explanations. If Caesar's death caused Brutus' remorse, then the following statements are all true statements of causation:

> The death of the famous Roman conqueror of Gaul caused Brutus' remorse.
> The killing of Caesar by Brutus caused Brutus' remorse.
> The murder described on page 100 of my copy of Shakespeare caused Brutus' remorse.

So much for statements of causation. But there is a link between the concept of causation and the concept of explanation. An explanation is an answer to a 'why?' question. If you ask a physicist why unsupported things fall to the ground, he or she should give an explanation of this phenomenon in terms of gravity. Many explanations—like this one—are causal explanations: they explain why an effect happened by telling you about its causes. (Bear in mind, though, that not all explanations are causal.)

To return to our example: suppose you ask me 'Why did Brutus feel remorse?' and I reply 'Because the murder described on page 100 of my copy of Shakespeare occurred', I am not being very helpful. I am not giving you an explanation of why Brutus felt what he did—for the fact that he felt remorse has, obviously, nothing to do with my copy of Shakespeare! But if events are particulars, then this is a description of the cause of Brutus' remorse.

Davidson concludes that only some statements of causation are causal explanations: those statements that describe the cause in a certain way. Which ways of describing the cause count as causal explanations is a matter for the theory of explanation. One possibility would be that only descriptions which show the cause to be an instance of a law of nature are to be counted as explanations; but there are other options.

One curious consequence of Davidson's view of causation and causal explanation is that some causal truths can be known a priori (see Section 1.2.1 above). Consider the causal claim:

> The death of Caesar caused Brutus' remorse.

If this is true, then the death of Caesar can be truly redescribed as 'the cause of Brutus' remorse'. But then if it is true that Brutus' remorse had a cause, it follows by logic alone that

> The cause of Brutus' remorse caused Brutus' remorse

is true. But we knew this already, so long as we knew that Brutus' remorse had a cause at all.

1.4.2. *Causes and Effects as Facts*

The alternative to thinking of causation as a relation between events (understood as particulars) is to think of it as a relation between what philosophers call facts. How do facts differ from events? A useful linguistic distinction is that events are picked out using descriptions ('The death of Caesar'), facts are picked out using whole sentences ('Caesar died'). We say 'It is a fact that Caesar died' but not 'It is a fact that the death of Caesar'.

(Some philosophers use the term 'event' for what I am calling 'fact'. They call their view the 'property instance' theory of events. This is an entirely terminological issue, though it can be confusing to those approaching the subject for the first time. See Kim's articles cited in the Bibliography.)

One reason there is a dispute between fact and event theories of causal relata is because there is a dispute about which of two kinds of causal claim is more fundamental. On the one hand we have claims of the form '*A* caused *B*'; for example,

(1) The death of Caesar caused Brutus' remorse.

On the other hand, we have claims of the form '*B* because *A*', where the 'because' is meant to indicate causation (as opposed to the 'because' in 'I broke the law because I drove through a red light'). For example,

(2) Brutus felt remorse because Caesar died.

Both fact and event theories agree that we make these claims, and that they are often true. The dispute between the theories is over whether (1) is more basic to causation than (2), or vice versa. Davidson takes (1) as more basic, while D. H. Mellor takes (2) as more basic (see Bibliography).

Metaphysically, what seems to distinguish facts from particulars is that facts involve features or properties of things. If it is a fact that a certain brick weighs 2 kilos, then this fact involves the brick, and a property of the brick, the property of weighing 2 kilos. This may seem to help in accounting for causal relata, because when we try to explain something causally, we invariably look for properties of the items involved. The brick broke the window because it was travelling at a certain velocity, and it had a certain mass, etc. This is what some philosophers mean when they say that a cause has its effects in virtue of its properties.

It follows that, on the fact theory, there is not the sharp distinction between causation and causal explanation which the event theory uses. A statement of causation will be an adequate causal explanation when it correctly describes the property which is incorporated in the fact.

TIME

Tim Crane

2.1. Introduction

Time seems to be both one of the most obvious and one of the most puzzling aspects of reality. Our lives take place in time, we think about time constantly—what we are doing at the present time, when we are going to do something in the future, what we have done in the past, and how little time we have left. Yet when we try and think about what time is, we find it very perplexing. Time seems so different from other aspects of our world. As St Augustine wrote in his *Confessions*: 'What then is time? If no one asks me, I know: if I wish to explain it to one that asketh, I know not.'

This discussion will address the three issues that dominate most contemporary philosophy of time: the 'passage' of time; 'absolute' versus 'relational' theories of time; and the 'direction' of time. Some of the issues here are very complicated, and some require a certain amount of knowledge of logic, philosophy of language, and the basic ideas of modern physics. But it is worth persevering: in each of the topics there are fascinating questions which can be understood without too much technical knowledge.

2.2. The Passage of Time

2.2.1. The Distinction between Dates and Tenses

The first issue I will discuss is what has been called the 'passage of time' (or the 'flow of time'). We think about time in two very different ways. One way is in terms of the ideas of past, present, and future. My birth is in the past, my writing this is in the present, and my death is in the future. It is natural to think of the apparent 'motion' of time in these terms: events 'move' or 'pass' from the past, through the present, and into the future. Or to put it another way, events that were once future become present, and then retreat into the past: the First World War, for example, was once in the future, became present, and is now past.

The other way in which we think about time is in terms of the ideas of earlier, later, and simultaneous. My birth was earlier than my writing this, but later than the First World War; my writing this is later than my birth, but earlier than my death; my birth was also simultaneous (roughly) with the beginning of the

Second Vatican Council. On this way of thinking about time, things and events in time may be ordered by their dates—their places in the sequence of events making up the history of the world.

Philosophers use a number of technical terms to distinguish these two ways of thinking about time. I will call the first way of ordering events in time the 'dynamic time series', and the second way the 'static time series', because these terms are a little more vivid than most of the terms used. J. M. E. McTaggart (1866–1925) called them the 'A' and 'B' series respectively, while many philosophers call the first series the 'tensed' series, and the second the 'dated' series: points in these series are called 'tenses' and 'dates' respectively.

These two ways of thinking are very different. The obvious difference is that, while an event can only have one position in the static time series, it must have every position on the dynamic series. The First World War occupied the period 1914–18 (its 'date'), and this is its unique position: it can't occupy another period in the static series. But the First World War can occupy all the positions in the dynamic series, since it was once future, was then present, and is now past.

The difference can be illustrated by a puzzle invented by Lewis Carroll in 1849. Suppose you are offered the choice between a clock that is right twice a day and a clock that is never right. We naturally choose the clock that is right twice a day, and are given a stopped clock! The stopped clock does register the right position in the static time series: after all, twice a day it is 6 o'clock, for example, and the clock registers this. But it gives us no idea when this moment is in the dynamic time series: it does not tell us when it is 6 o'clock now.

Some philosophers think that not only are these two ways of thinking very different, they also seem to be incompatible, and combining them leads to a contradiction. This contradiction was first explicitly developed by McTaggart as part of an argument for the conclusion that time is unreal.

2.2.2. McTaggart's Argument for the Unreality of Time

McTaggart's argument can be stated quite simply, though spelling it out soon introduces more complexities. Consider an event, such as the beginning of the First World War in August 1914. This event has a location in the static time series which we label as 'August 1914'. But what is its location in the dynamic time series? Since every event is constantly changing its position in this series, every event has every position in the series: past, present, and future. So the following three claims all can be true:

(1) The beginning of the First World War is in the future.
(2) The beginning of the First World War is in the present.
(3) The beginning of the First World War is in the past.

But now it looks as if the beginning of the First World War is in the past, in the present, and in the future. But being past, being present, and being future are jointly incompatible: nothing can be past, present, and future. And nothing with incompatible features can exist—for example, nothing can be red and not red. But if an event has one location in the dynamic time series, it has all the other incompatible ones too. Therefore being past, being present, and being future cannot exist: so there is no dynamic time series.

Why did McTaggart think that this shows that time itself is unreal? Because he thought that the dynamic time series is essential to time. It is essential to time for two reasons:

(a) Change is essential to time; time is impossible without change.
(b) The dynamic time series is essential for change; change is impossible without the dynamic time series.

If the dynamic time series does not exist, then (a) and (b) together imply that time itself does not exist. For if there is no time without change, and no change without the dynamic time series, then there is no time without the dynamic time series.

Let us leave this conclusion of McTaggart's for a while. For there is an obvious response to McTaggart's argument, which will probably have occurred to you. For brevity, let us abbreviate 'the beginning of the First World War' to 'the assassination'. The response is that while the assassination does have all these positions (past, present, and future) in the dynamic series, it does not have them all at the same time. So the assassination is not past, present, and future all at once—rather, it was future, was present, and is past. For there to be a contradiction, the event would have to have all these incompatible locations at the same time, which it doesn't. But there is nothing wrong with something having incompatible properties at different times: something can be red at one time, but not red at another time—if in between it was painted green, for example.

Defenders of McTaggart will not be impressed by this, however. They will respond that this just attributes to the assassination another set of dynamic locations: it was future, it was present, and it is past. The assassination has all these. But since all events have all locations in the dynamic series, the assassination also has the locations: was past, will be past, is future, will be future, is present and will be present. And while some of these (e.g. was present, is past) are incompatible, others will not be (e.g. was present, will be future). So, they argue, appealing to these complex dynamic locations will not avoid the contradiction.

2.2.3. Responses to McTaggart

McTaggart's argument has inspired a vast amount of debate, and there are many different responses to it (see Bibliography). Here I mention a few issues worth pursuing.

Suppose McTaggart's argument is successful. What conclusion should we draw from it? One conclusion is McTaggart's own: that time itself is unreal. But, as we saw, this conclusion relies on the ideas that change is essential to time, and that change is impossible without the dynamic series. And as we shall see, these ideas can be questioned.

A more popular conclusion is that developed by D. H. Mellor. Mellor argues that McTaggart's argument shows only that the dynamic time series is unreal; but the static time series is none the less real. (Mellor puts this by saying that while time is real, tense is not.) Reality, on this view, contains dated events and facts. But there is no past, present, or future in reality. This is known as the 'tenseless' theory of time.

In order to be a defensible theory of time, the tenseless theory has to explain at least two things. The first is change: change seems to be of the essence of time, so unless we can explain change, we cannot explain time. The dynamic, or tensed, view of time builds change into the very nature of the time series: facts or events are constantly changing since they are 'moving' from the past, through the present, into the future. (Alternatively, we could say that all events are first future, then become present, then become past.) In effect, the dynamic view explains the fact of change by appealing to changing facts. But events and facts in the static series do not change: if some event happened at a certain time (or at a certain 'date'), then it cannot change its position in the static time series.

So the tenseless view needs an account of change. The account it offers is Bertrand Russell's: a change in an object, *O*, is either a matter of *O* having a property or feature at one time and failing to have that property at a later time; or a matter of *O* not having a property or feature at one time and having the property at a later time. For example, a poker might be hot at one time and cold at a later time; or it might be cold at one time and hot at a later time. In both cases it has changed. Notice that this definition of change does not allow that facts (such as the poker being hot at a certain time) or events (such as the poker heating up) change. Change is rather a matter of a temporal succession of events or facts.

One question this account of change raises is whether it can adequately distinguish between time and space. A poker can be hot at one time and cold at another; but similarly, a poker can be hot at one end and cold at the other. This is not change—but it does look very similar to the definition of change offered by the static theory. The issue is whether the tenseless theory can adequately account for the difference between time and space. I shall discuss the difference between time and space in Section 2.4 below.

The other thing that the static theory needs to explain is how time seems to us. How can past, present, and future be unreal, since they are surely crucial to our experience of the world? Consider a famous example of A. N. Prior's. You have to go to the dentist tomorrow, and you have been dreading it for weeks.

After it happens, you think to yourself with relief, 'Thank goodness that's over!' What were you relieved about? Not the fact, surely, that the visit to the dentist occurs on a certain day (say, Tuesday 5 August)—for you already knew this, and could have had the thought 'My visit to the dentist occurs on Tuesday 5 August' weeks before the visit. But these sorts of 'dated' facts are the only facts the tenseless view allows. So how can the tenseless view account for the sense of relief that you feel after you have been to the dentist? Prior says that it cannot: only the dynamic fact that the visit to the dentist moves from the present into the past adequately explains your relief.

The standard static response to this is rather complex, and relies on certain theories in the philosophy of mind and language. Briefly, the view is that these apparent dynamic facts are not features of reality, but consequences of some of our ways of thinking or speaking about reality. When we say 'That's now over' the 'now' does not refer to a special 'now' in reality—rather, an utterance of 'now' refers to the time of that particular utterance. 'Now', like 'I' and 'here', is known in the philosophy of language as an indexical expression—that is, an expression whose reference (the item in the world it refers to) depends on when, where, or by whom it is uttered. (I use 'I' to refer to me, you use 'I' to refer to you, etc.) To say that 'now' is an indexical does not entail that there is a special feature of 'nowness' picked out by 'now'. For consider 'here': no one would say that an utterance of 'here' picks out a special feature, 'hereness'!

The opponents of the tenseless view (e.g. Prior) will emphasize the radical difference between 'here' and 'now' in this respect—just as they emphasize the radical difference between time and space. But Mellor and others use the fact that 'now' is an indexical to explain Prior's puzzle: 'Thank goodness that's now over' therefore means something like 'Thank goodness that is not occurring at the time of this utterance'.

2.3. Absolute and Relational Conceptions of Time

As McTaggart observed, time and change are intimately related. Things change in time, and change is impossible without time. On the 'static' view of time, as we saw, a change in an object is defined in terms of an object's having properties at one time and not having them at another time. On the 'dynamic' view, a change is a matter of an event's changing its location in the dynamic time series: 'moving' through from being future, into being present, and becoming past. However one analyses time, change cannot be understood except in terms of time.

2.3.1. *Time and Relations between Events*

But can time be understood independently of change? Many philosophers have thought not—the most famous of these being Aristotle, who thought that time simply is the measure of change. But other philosophers have thought that time is not reducible to change, but rather the 'container' in which changes occur. This was Isaac Newton's view. The issue here is often described as whether time is 'absolute' or 'relational'.

The question is whether time has any sort of existence independently of the events that occupy it. Relational theories of time say that it has not: time can be reduced to the temporal relations between events or changes. So to say that the First World War happened at a certain time is just to say that it stands in certain temporal relations to other events—e.g. it was later than the Wars of the Roses, and earlier than the Second World War. And what makes these events occur at the times they did is just the fact that they stand in certain temporal relations to other events.

Leibniz held a relational view of time as well as a relational view of space (i.e. space does not have an existence over and above the things which occupy it). Leibniz engaged in a debate with Newton's follower Samuel Clarke (1675–1729) over these two issues. Clarke defended Newton's view that time and space are absolute: both space and time are entities which are in a sense independent of their inhabitants. (The word 'absolute' is used simply to indicate that temporal items (moments, years, etc.) do not exist relative to the events that go on in them). On the absolute view of time, to say that the First World War happened at a certain time is not just to say that it stands in certain relations to other events, but that it literally occupies a region of time which would have existed even if the First World War and all the events around it had not existed.

(Notice that certain other terms are sometimes used for these views. The absolute view of time is sometimes called 'substantivalism' because it holds that time is a substance—in the sense that it is something that can exist independently of other things. This is one sense in which many philosophers (e.g. Descartes, Hume) use the term 'substance'. And the relational view is sometimes called 'reductionism' because it aims to 'reduce' time to temporal relations between events.)

To appreciate the difference between absolute and relational conceptions of time, we should look at their consequences. Leibniz thought that it is a consequence of absolute time that God could have created the world an hour earlier than he did; and he thought this supposition was absurd. But the relational view seems to have the equally odd consequence that there cannot be time without change. That is, there cannot be a period of 'empty' time, or a 'temporal vacuum': a period of time in which nothing is going on.

2.3.2. *Time without Change*

Relational theories of time will be happy to accept this consequence: they will say that the notion of time without change is incoherent. One reason they might give for this is Aristotle's: there cannot be time without change because nothing could count as evidence for it. How could we possibly know that there had been a period of time without change? We could not perceive anything going on during this period, and form the belief that a temporal vacuum was occurring, since that would require us to change during this period, which would mean that the period is not a temporal vacuum. But neither could we know that a temporal vacuum had occurred after it occurred. For suppose that things 'froze' in time for a period of, say, a year. When the year ended, things would seem exactly the same as they had a year ago: our experience would seem the same as it would if there had not been such a 'freeze'. Therefore we could never have reason to believe that a temporal vacuum could occur. (Compare the hypothesis that the world might have doubled in volume and mass overnight.)

Of course, the relational theory can accept that periods of time can pass in which we do not, as a matter of fact, notice change. This happens to all of us when we are asleep. But the fact that we do not notice change when we are asleep does not make us believe things are not changing. For not only do we notice that the world has changed when we wake up, but we also believe that, if we wished, we could go and observe the world changing instead of sleeping. What the argument claims is not that actual observation of change is essential to time, but that possible observation is: it must be possible for us to notice change in order for us to have a reason for believing that a period of time has passed.

One response to this is to say that reality is one thing, but our observation of it another. There are many things which many people believe to exist, or believe could exist, but which are unobservable—for example, the tiny particles postulated by modern physics, black holes, gravitational fields, the past, God, and so on. Perhaps time without change is just an extreme example of a possible, unobservable existent thing—extreme, because we cannot say that we know it through its effects. On this view, Aristotle's argument smacks of 'verificationism', the view that, for a claim to be meaningful, it must be verifiable by us.

However, the difference between temporal vacua and the other cases of non-observables is that, in the other cases, we do have an idea of what it would take to verify their existence. We build machines to detect microparticles, and we debate about whether the existence of evil is compatible with a loving omnipotent god. But in the case of temporal vacua, we have no idea what it would take to find out that one had occurred. And the hypothesis that there can be something which transcends all possible ways of finding out about it is, to say the least, rather worrying.

A subtler response was advanced in a famous paper by the American philosopher Sydney Shoemaker. Shoemaker argues against the Aristotelian position by describing a possible situation (what philosophers call a 'possible world') in which we would have reason to believe that a temporal vacuum had occurred. I shall conclude this section by briefly describing Shoemaker's argument.

Suppose that there is a universe consisting of three regions, which we shall call '*A*', '*B*', and '*C*', and suppose that we inhabit *A*. This universe has a curious feature: we in *A* observe that every third year in *B* things 'freeze'—nothing happens there at all for a whole year. After the year is up, the inhabitants of *B* carry on with their lives as before. To them it does not seem as if a year has passed.

Suppose that we also observe that region *C* undergoes a similar freeze every fourth year. Nothing happens for a whole year, and, after the year is up, the inhabitants of *C* get on with their lives as before. We must also suppose that we are unable to interact with *B* or *C* during the periods of their 'freezes'.

The local freezes we observe in *B* and *C* do not constitute time without change, since we are observing them and we are changing during these freezes. But now suppose that, during one unfrozen year, the inhabitants of all regions meet to figure out what is going on. We tell the inhabitants of *B* and *C* that we observe their freezes. And the inhabitants of *B* and *C* tell us in *A* that we undergo a local freeze every five years. Of course, all the inhabitants of the universe will be unwilling to accept that their region is subject to freezes, since none of them can notice it. But they reluctantly accept that freezes have occurred, since it explains why every so often the other regions seem to undergo a 'jump' or discontinuous change: this is when one's own region has just emerged from a freeze.

It does not take long for the inhabitants to realize that if the freezes keep occurring in the regular way they have, all regions will freeze every sixty years. Between year 1 and year 60, say, *C* will have undergone fifteen freezes, *B* will have undergone twenty, and *A* will have undergone twelve. So in year 60, it seems reasonable to suppose that all regions will freeze. This total freeze would be a period of time without change. What is more, the inhabitants of the universe would have some reason to believe that such a freeze had occurred, but they would have no means of directly detecting it.

It is important to realize what this ingenious thought experiment is trying to show. Shoemaker is not arguing that our world is like this. Nor is he claiming that his thought experiment shows or entails that time without change is possible. What he is doing is rebutting the argument to the conclusion that time without change is impossible from the premise that we could never have reason to believe it occurs. He does this by describing a world in which we would have reason to believe that time without change occurs—that is, a world in which the hypothesis that there has been time without change is the best explanation of certain phenomena.

The argument therefore poses a challenge to the relational theorists of time. To defend their theory, they must provide another explanation of the phenomena in the world Shoemaker describes, an explanation which does not postulate a total freeze. Or they must show that Shoemaker's world is, contrary to appearances, impossible.

2.4. The Direction of Time

Modern physics takes time to be one of the four dimensions of space-time, the other three being the three dimensions: up–down, left–right, forward–back. Accepting this view does not require us to take a stand on the debate about absolute and relational theories of time. We could hold an absolutist view of time, and think that the four dimensions could be empty; or we could hold a relational view of time, and hold that time is the dimension constructed out of relations between events, just as the spatial dimensions are constructed out of the spatial relations between objects and events.

2.4.1. *Time as a Dimension*

How should we understand this talk of dimensions? At first it seems rather puzzling how time could be a dimension like the spatial dimensions; for example, we see things laid out in space, but we do not see events laid out in time. We can't see into the future, or into the past. D. H. Mellor has suggested a useful way of answering this question: Think of dimensions as ways things fail to coincide. I can fail to coincide with the chair I am sitting on by failing to occupy the same space as it. But I can none the less occupy some of this space: if I move the chair, I can occupy the space it previously occupied. What I cannot do is occupy the same space as the chair at the same time.

This approach treats time as being, in some sense, the same sort of thing as space. But if time is a dimension of space-time, how does it differ from the spatial dimensions? One obvious way in which time is different from space is that time seems to have a 'direction'. While an object can travel in any of the spatial dimensions, up, to the left, or backwards, objects can only 'travel' in one direction in time: from the past, through the present, into the future.

2.4.2. *Time travel*

But why can we only move in one direction through time? And why are we compelled to move at the same 'rate' as everything else? These questions are about the possibility of time travel, which is of interest to philosophers as well as to writers of science fiction. They are of interest to philosophers because if it is possible to travel backwards in time, then the direction of time which we experience is not a necessary feature of time—i.e. a feature which all possible temporal worlds must have—but merely a contingent feature of our world.

What is time travel? We can imagine it by imagining something that is not time travel, but might appear like it. Suppose I wake up in the morning and feel the same age as I did when I last went to bed. But when I go outside, the world has changed, and I discover that it is now the year 2093. I discover that I have been given a drug which puts me to sleep for a hundred years and slows down my physiological processes.

Is this time travel? It seems not: I am actually 130 years old, though I feel as if I am 30, and have many years to live. This disparity between how old one is and how old one feels is a well-known phenomenon. Time travel, on the other hand, is not.

What we need for time travel, as the name suggests, is a journey. This is how David Lewis characterizes time travel. The traveller sets off at a certain time (the 'departure time') and arrives at a certain time (the 'arrival time'), and the journey takes a certain time (the 'journey time'). On normal journeys, the length of time between the time of departure and the time of arrival is the same as the journey time. But in forwards time travel, for example, the time elapsed from departure to arrival does not equal the time of the journey. In a case of forwards time travel, the time traveller sets off at 1 o'clock, travels for an hour, and returns at, say, 8 o'clock.

Backwards time travel appears even less plausible or coherent than this. In backwards time travel, the time of arrival is earlier than the time of departure. Many people think that if backwards time travel is possible, then it is possible for you to return to the past and (say) kill your parents before you were born, or even kill yourself as a child. Think of the number of science fiction stories and films that exploit this possibility.

Some philosophers rule out backwards time travel, because it involves back-wards causation—an effect preceding its cause. They then supply independent arguments against backwards causation. David Lewis, however, argues that backwards time travel is possible, but that this does not entail that you could kill your parents. (See the Bibliography for further reading.)

2.4.3. *Theories of the Direction of Time*

Finally, I shall briefly mention two common ways of accounting for the direction of time. The first is that it is derived from the direction of causation—the fact that a cause must necessarily precede its effects. Time is therefore the causal dimension of space-time. If this theory is not to be circular, then it must explain the direction of causation in non-temporal terms. It is no good, for example, to appeal to the idea of a cause preceding its effects in time. (See the discussion of causation above.)

The other popular way of accounting for the direction of time is to appeal to the irreversible nature of certain physical processes: in particular, the increase of entropy (roughly, disorder) in this world. This is supposed to be a 'scientific reduction' of the direction of time, rather in the way that some think causation can be 'scientifically' reduced to the flow of energy. One apparent consequence of this view is that if it is possible to reverse these physical processes, then it is possible for time to go backwards.

UNIVERSALS
Tim Crane

3.1. Introduction

3.1.1. *The Distinction between Universals and Particulars*

One of the most basic concepts of metaphysics is the concept of identity or sameness. The question when are two things the same can have a number of answers, each of which distinguishes various uses of the concept of identity. One obvious answer is that two things are never the same, since if they were they would then be one thing! The notion of identity used in this answer is what philosophers call numerical identity, for obvious reasons. But someone might intend the question to have a more informative answer, as when they might wonder whether this person they saw today is the same person as that person they saw yesterday. Asking the question is now asking for the conditions of one object's identity over time (sometimes called 'diachronic identity').

But there is a sense in which two things can be the same, which is the concern of this discussion of universals. Two chairs can be the same colour, or the same shape, or be made of the same material. When we say that this chair is the same as that one, we do not seem to be talking about numerical identity: no two chairs can be literally the same chair. So what do we mean when we say that two chairs have the same colour? Philosophers say that the chairs are of the same kind, or the same type. But what is this 'sameness of type'?

This question has led some philosophers to postulate two distinct kinds of entity: particulars and universals. The essential distinction goes back to Plato. In the *Republic*, Socrates asks 'What is justice?', and makes it clear that what he wants to know is not which action or person is just, but what actions and people have in common that makes them all just. Plato's answer is that there is an eternal, unchanging realm of 'Forms' (the Form of justice, the Form of wisdom, etc.) which is distinct from the imperfect empirical world. Just actions and people are just because they participate in the Form of justice. The actions and people are what philosophers these days would call 'particulars'; and the Forms are one kind of thing that philosophers have called 'universals'. (For more on Plato's theory of Forms, see Section 3.4.1 below.)

3.1.2. Varieties of Particular

This distinction between universals and particulars may seem a little obscure at first. Before examining a number of theoretical ways in which we can spell out the distinction, it will help to consider the various kinds of thing which philosophers have typically classified as particulars and those they have typically classified as universals.

First, particulars. The obvious cases of particulars are ordinary material objects, like tables, chairs, aeroplanes, restaurants, and so on. Some philosophers think that as well as material objects, events, like the First World War or my tenth birthday, are material particulars too. They hold that the First World War is not identical with all the objects it involves, but must be recognized as a particular in its own right. Events and material objects are both, on this understanding, material particulars. But a particular need not be a material (or physical) particular: some philosophers think that there are immaterial particulars. Descartes, for example, thought human minds were immaterial—but they are still particulars.

A further distinction we must make is between abstract and concrete particulars. Let us say that an entity is concrete when it exists in space and/or time, and abstract when it does not. (This is only one way of understanding the distinction between abstract and concrete: see Bibliography.) So my table is a concrete object since it exists in space and time; and, according to Descartes, my mind is a concrete object because it exists in time, though not in space. But some philosophers have thought that there are abstract particulars too—particulars which do not exist in space and time. For these philosophers, numbers are the paradigm examples of such abstract particulars: the number three, for example, is not the same thing as all the inscriptions or utterances of 'three'. For all these inscriptions of 'three' could be destroyed, and one would not thereby have destroyed the number three. To hold that numbers are abstract objects is to hold that numbers do not exist in space—they are not located at any place—nor in time—they do not exist at some times and not at others.

(We need to be careful to distinguish this use of the term 'abstract particular' from another, older use. Some philosophers, notably G. F. Stout (1860–1944), thought that the world consists fundamentally not of particulars and universals, but of entities like the brownness of this chair, or the squareness of this table. These are like particulars in that they are unrepeatable, but they are not ordinary material objects. Stout called these entities 'abstract particulars'—but they are abstract not in the sense above, but in the sense that they are less 'substantial' than particulars like tables and chairs. Other philosophers have called them 'particularized qualities' or, rather oddly, 'tropes'. See the Bibliography.)

So the main examples of entities philosophers call 'particulars' are: material objects (the table), material events (the First World War), immaterial objects (minds, according to Descartes), abstract objects (the number three). As we shall see, many philosophers dispute that there are all these kinds of particular—most contemporary philosophers think that minds are material particulars, for example—but before deciding whether these things exist, we have to be clear about what we are denying.

3.1.3. Varieties of Universals

What about universals? Traditionally, universals are divided into two broad categories: qualities (or 'one-place properties') and relations (or 'relational properties'). Sometimes the term 'attribute' is used instead of 'quality'. Some modern writers use the term 'property' for qualities or attributes, and 'relational property' for relations. On this terminology, there are two kinds of property—relational and non-relational.

However, it is not the words which matter, but the concepts. In what follows I shall use the term 'property' for non-relational properties, or qualities, or attributes, and 'relation' for relational properties.

The distinction between properties and relations is easy to understand in an intuitive sense, but more difficult to make precise. The intuitive understanding is as follows. A property is something which is 'attached to' or is 'instantiated in' one object. An object's mass, for example, is a property of the object—roughly, it attaches to it regardless of how things are with other objects (though, of course, other objects can have this property). But a relation 'holds between', or is instantiated by, more than one object. The relation *longer than*, for example, must hold between at least two objects (e.g. my car is longer than your car); the relation *between* must hold between at least three objects (e.g. York is between Edinburgh and London). And so on. An obvious exception here is the philosophically puzzling relation of identity—an object can only be (numerically) identical with itself.

It might be helpful to mention some terminology which you will come across in your reading on this topic. First, in order to understand the definitions in the last paragraph, we need to understand the idea of a property or relation 'attaching' to an object, or an object 'instantiating' a property or relation. For the moment, these terms are just being used for whatever it is that 'connects' a universal to a particular—but the idea will be examined in more detail in Sections 3.3–3.4 below. Second, some philosophers talk about properties and relations having a number of 'places'. What they mean by this is the number of objects that are required to instantiate the property. Properties, for the most part, are 'one-place' universals: they only need one object to instantiate them (e.g. mass, wisdom). One-place universals are sometimes called 'monadic'. Relations can have many places: *longer than* is a two-place (or 'dyadic') relation, but relations can be three-place, four-place, and so on. In general, a universal is *n*-place (or is '*n*-adic'), for some number, *n*, when it needs *n* objects to instantiate it. (Identity, again, is one obvious exception to this rule.) Sometimes, in describing universals, the letters '*x*' and '*y*'—called 'variables' in logic—are used to fill in the places the universal has (e.g. '*x* is taller than *y*').

3.1.4. Universals and Language

None of these examples of particulars and universals are supposed to be unproblematic. Indeed, part of the philosophical difficulty about universals and particulars is finding a way of clearly spelling out the distinction between them. But now that we have in mind some typical examples of what universals and particulars are supposed to be, we can return to the distinction and see whether we can make it more precise.

Some philosophers define the distinction between universals and particulars in terms of the linguistic distinction between a predicate and a singular term. A singular term is a term whose role in a language is to pick out, or stand for, a particular thing. So, for example, the proper name 'Julius Caesar' stands for the particular man, as does the description 'the Roman conqueror of Gaul'. A predicate has a different role. It does not make sense to say that the predicate 'is tall' stands for a particular object—which object could it possibly stand for? Rather, predicates are said to 'apply to' or be 'true of' objects: the predicate 'is tall' applies to, or is true of, all tall things. An intuitive way of getting a grip on the notion of a predicate is to think of a predicate as what you get when you extract a name from a simple sentence like 'Julius Caesar is tall'. (Notice that singular terms are sometimes called 'subject terms' or 'referring expressions'. For more on singular terms and predicates, see the Bibliography and Chapters 2 and 3. Notice too that the logical distinction between singular terms and predicates is not the same as the grammatical distinction between nouns and verbs.)

The idea now is that we understand the distinction between universals and particulars fundamentally in terms of the linguistic distinction between singular terms and predicates. The idea of a particular is the idea of what is referred to by a singular term; the idea of a universal is the idea of what is referred to by a predicate. Predicates refer to universals, and are true of or apply to particulars. We understand the metaphysical structure of our world through understanding the logical structure of our language.

Frank Ramsey (1903–30) showed that matters cannot be as simple as this: 'in "Socrates is wise", Socrates is the subject, wisdom the predicate. But suppose we turn the proposition round and say "wisdom is a characteristic of Socrates", then wisdom, formerly the predicate, is now the subject . . . Hence there is no essential distinction between the subject of a proposition and its predicate, and no fundamental classification of objects can be based upon such a distinction.'[1]

---

[1] 'On Universals', in *F. P. Ramsey: Philosophical Papers*, ed. D. H. Mellor (Cambridge, 1990), 12.

There are a number of ways of responding to Ramsey's objection. One is to point out that universals and particulars can be distinguished by the fact that, while there can be incompatible universals (fat and thin, for example), there are no incompatible particulars: there is no such particular as not-Julius Caesar, for example.

Another response is to reject the attempt to characterize the distinction in linguistic terms. The fundamental difference between universals and particulars is a metaphysical one: while a universal can be instantiated by, or apply to, many things, it makes no sense to say that a particular can be instantiated by many things. Many things can be tall, but only one thing can be Julius Caesar. This idea is sometimes expressed by saying that universals are 'multiply exemplifiable entities'. To assess this idea, we need to look at some of the theories of universals which philosophers have proposed.

So far we have considered various ways of distinguishing between universals and particulars, and various examples of particulars and universals. The question now is whether there are any universals, or whether the world consists solely of particulars. This is the question posed by the problem of universals.

3.2. The Problem of Universals

There are two traditional ways of posing the problem of universals. One is traditionally called the problem of 'one over many': how can many things be, in some sense, the same? Many things are red, or wise, or square, or good—so, in some sense, they share a nature. But how can this be? How can things which are distinct also be the same?

To distinguish, as in Section 3.1, between numerical (or 'quantitative') sameness and sameness of type (or 'qualitative' sameness) does not solve the problem, but postpones it. For what we want to know is—what is sameness of type? What does it consist in? Is it a kind of genuine identity (i.e. identity of universals), or is the use of the terms 'same' and 'identical' for qualitative and quantitative identity a kind of pun? The question is not idle, since we constantly use sameness and difference of type to explain features of our world: 'it is because this peg is a different shape from that one that it will not fit in this hole—you need one of the same shape'; 'it is because I am just like my father that I did that—it is exactly the same as what he would have done'. And so on.

The other way of posing the problem is linguistic: how is it possible to apply general terms or predicates to more than one object? It seems, on the face of it, that there is something 'simpler' about the way names and other singular terms apply to objects than there is about the way predicates apply to objects. Here is the desk; here is the term I use to refer to it: 'my desk'. I can see the desk and apply the word to it on the basis of seeing it. But what about the 'brownness' of the desk? I can see that too, but how is that different from seeing the desk?

Where is this brownness, and how can I use the word 'brown' to talk about it? As Locke puts it, 'since all things that exist are only particulars how come we by general terms?' (*Essay Concerning Human Understanding*, II. iii. 10).

This second way of posing the problem interacts with issues in the philosophy of language and the philosophy of mind: specifically, how do predicates come to mean what they do, and how does the mind form general ideas of things? In the rest of this discussion I will not consider these issues, but will concentrate on the metaphysical issue: how can we explain sameness of type?

Possible answers to this question fall into four kinds. First, there are nominalist answers, which deny that we need to postulate universals in order to account for sameness of type. Nominalists hold, with Locke, that 'all things which exist are only particulars': there are no universals. Second, there are realist answers, which hold that both universals and particulars exist, and that they are fundamentally different kinds of entity. Third, there is the answer given by trope theories (see Section 3.1.2 above), which hold that neither (ordinary) particulars nor universals are fundamental, but both are constructed out of more basic entities called 'tropes' or 'particularized qualities'. Finally, and most unusually, it is possible to hold that only universals exist: there are no particulars. In the next two sections, I shall only consider the first two of these responses to the problem of universals, since these are the most commonly held views.

3.3. Nominalism

A very natural reaction, among philosophers and those approaching this issue for the first time, is the nominalist reaction: in reality there are no universals, but only particulars. The entities which we encounter in experience are all particular things: particular people, particular houses, particular restaurants, and so on. One main reason for being a nominalist is the thought that universals are mysterious, obscure entities. We know pretty well what an object is, the nominalist says, but no one has yet been able to tell us, in a philosophically satisfactory way, what a universal is. So we should do without them in our metaphysics.

(Another word about potentially confusing terminology: I am using the term 'nominalism' in the most widespread contemporary sense, to mean the view that only particulars exist. These particulars may be abstract or concrete, mental or physical. But the term has been used for the denial of all abstract objects, including those entities we classified earlier as abstract particulars—e.g. numbers. Quine, for example, uses 'nominalism' in this latter sense, and rejects it since he believes in abstract objects. But in my sense Quine is a nominalist. See the Bibliography for more details.)

But although nominalists deny that there are universals, they cannot deny the fact that objects can be of the same type: that more than one object can be red, wise, etc. What they must do is accept the apparent facts of sameness of type, but give an account of these facts in terms which do not mention universals. There are many ways a nominalist can do this. Here I shall outline the three most common ways: sameness of type is analysed in terms of (1) the idea of resemblance; (2) the idea of belonging to a class; and (3) dependence on the classifications of the mind.

3.3.1. Resemblance

The first account is that what makes (for example) all red things be of the same type, red, is the fact that they resemble a suitable exemplar or paradigm of a red thing. Suppose our paradigm is a British post-box. We can then say that red shoes, red shirts, and red sunsets are all red because they resemble (to a greater or lesser extent) the post-box. Here we have only appealed to particulars—the post-box and the shoes, shirts, etc.—so appeal to universals is not needed.

But there are certain difficulties with this approach. For example, the theory seems to get things the wrong way round. Surely red objects resemble the paradigm because they are all red; so how can they be red because they resemble the paradigm? Also, the theory has difficulty coping with certain remote logical possibilities. Suppose there is only one red object in the universe. What makes it red? Not, surely, the fact that it resembles itself—for everything resembles itself.

A more subtle objection was advanced by Russell. If a red shoe is red because it resembles the paradigm of red, and the red sunset is red because it resembles the paradigm of red, then it seems that both the shoe and the sunset stand in a certain relation to the paradigm: the relation of resembling. So there are further cases of sameness of type—sameness of the resemblance relation—which have to be explained. The resemblance theory can try and argue that all these resemblances are of the same type because they all resemble a suitable paradigm of the resemblance relation. But there will be many such resemblances which resemble a suitable paradigm of the resemblance relation—what do all these resemblances have in common? To appeal to a further 'higher order' resemblance to a paradigm of resembling a suitable paradigm of the resemblance relation is not just hard to read—it also shows that the resemblance theory is on the verge of an infinite regress. Russell concludes that resemblance must be a universal, and that once you have admitted one universal, you might as well admit them all.

Russell's argument is a version of an argument that Armstrong calls the 'relation regress'. The general idea of the relation regress is that nominalism must appeal, at some point in its theory, to a relation (in this case x resembles y). Accounting for this relation in nominalist terms leads to an infinite regress; and realists argue that the only way to account for the regress is to suppose that the relation is in fact a universal. As we shall see, an argument of this form not only threatens every form of nominalism—it threatens realism too.

3.3.2. Classes

The second nominalist view is the view that what makes red things red is that they all belong to the class of red things. The term 'class' here is meant in the technical sense employed in logic and the branch of mathematics known as set theory, or the calculus of classes. (For the purposes of this topic, 'set' and 'class' mean the same thing.) A class is just a collection of objects. Ordinary objects of any kind can be members of classes: as well as the class of red things, there is the class consisting of everything larger than me, or the class of my left toe and China. In logic, classes are represented using curly brackets, with their members separated by commas, namely: {My left toe, China}. The relation of being a member of a class is expressed by the symbol $\in$. So 'My left toe is a member of the class consisting of my left toe and China' is written: My left toe $\in$ {My left toe, China}.

Since, for class nominalism, only particulars are members of classes, and a class is a particular—classes cannot be instantiated by anything—it claims that it can account for sameness of type purely in terms of membership of a class. Among contemporary philosophers, this approach has been favoured by philosophers whose background is in logic or mathematics. Quine, for example, takes this view; as does David Lewis. (One question to ask is whether they are attempting to solve the problem of one over many—and perhaps others besides.)

Armstrong has argued that class nominalism is a victim of the relation regress. The red shoe and the red shirt are red because they are members of the class of red things. But being a member of a class is, on the face of it, a relation, the relation symbolized by '$\in$'. So there is an apparent sameness of type to be explained: the red shoe and the red shirt stand in the relation 'is a member of' to the class of red things. How do we explain this sameness without appealing to a universal, membership? There is not space here to spell out the nominalist · response. But the intuitive objection should be fairly clear, since the structure of the argument is the same as the argument which applies to the resemblance theory.

3.3.3. Mind-Dependence

The third nominalist account which I shall consider is the claim that what makes red things red is the fact that we classify them as red. This view is sometimes known as 'conceptualism'. Red shoes, red shirts, and red sunsets are red

because we apply the predicate or concept '*x* is red' to them. Individual applications of predicates or concepts are particulars—in fact, they are events. So it
seems as if we can do without universals.

But are concepts themselves—aside from their applications—particulars?
When you and I share a concept—say, red—what do we share? We do not share
the particular item in my mind, any more than you share my hair when we have
the same hair colour. Could it be that we share a concept because we apply the
same concept—i.e. the concept *concept*—to our particular concepts? But even if
it were true that we apply the concept *concept* to our concepts of red, we now
need to know what makes these applications of the concept the same. Because
we apply the concept *application of a concept* to them both? But obviously the
question arises again, and a regress threatens. (Notice that this is not the same
regress as the 'relation regress'.)

A deeper worry about the mind-dependence theory is that it makes the
nature of reality too dependent on the nature of human thought. In one sense
of the term, it is committed to a certain sort of idealism. What kinds of thing
there are in the world is deeply dependent on our minds (and, in some cases, on
our language). This claim is often made, but it is very hard to spell out, and
raises important issues elsewhere in metaphysics.

3.4. Realism about Universals

Persuaded, perhaps, of the difficulties with nominalism, we might be tempted
to reconsider the less commonsensical alternative, realism. Realism says that
there are universals as well as particulars. What makes all red things red is that
they all share a property, redness. This property is exactly the same thing in all
red particulars. Therefore, realism takes sameness of type to be, essentially,
numerical identity—except that it is numerical identity of universals that makes
all red things red. Nominalists, by contrast, say that sameness of type is
analysable into something other than numerical identity: resemblance, class
membership, or whatever.

3.4.1. *Plato's Theory of Forms*

As we have seen, Plato, the first philosopher to tackle these issues, was a realist.
He thought that red objects were all red because they all stood in a certain relation to an eternal, unchanging entity, the Form of redness. (In the past some
people called this the 'idea' of redness, the term 'idea' being phonetically closer
to the original Greek. But 'Form' is better because it does not have the psychological connotations of 'idea': Plato's Forms are not in people's minds.)

Plato thought that particulars 'participate' in the Forms: good actions participate in the Form of the good, wise people participate in the Form of wisdom.

Unfortunately he never adequately explains what 'participation' is. Let us assume it is meant to be the same sort of thing as what contemporary philosophers call 'instantiation'. But what is instantiation supposed to be?

The natural answer is that instantiation is a relation between the particular that has the property (e.g. the red shirt) and the Form (e.g. redness). But if this relation is a universal, as it ought to be on Plato's theory, the theory is in trouble, for the relation regress looms again. If the instantiation relation (call it I) holds between the red shirt and the Form of redness, then I is instantiated. But if I is instantiated, then it must be related, by a further instantiation relation, I*, to the Form of I. But I* too is instantiated; so this must be related, by a yet further instantiation relation, I**, to the Form of I*. And so on with I**. Arguments like this may appear at first as if they are mere word-play; but what they show is that nothing is really explained by appealing to instantiation or participation, since they presuppose the very notions they are intended to explain.

3.4.2. Contemporary Realism

The relation regress is very similar to a famous argument which Plato himself discussed, known as the 'third man' argument. It is also similar to an argument of the English philosopher F. H. Bradley (1846–1924). Among contemporary philosophers, D. M. Armstrong takes the regress to show that instantiation cannot be a relation of any kind, since, wherever you have a relation, you have the possibility of the relation regress. But he none the less thinks that there are universals, and that they are instantiated in particulars. But they are not related to those particulars.

This is a little obscure. If instantiation is not a relation, what is it? It is not a particular, obviously, and it is not a (monadic) property. What else could it be? Armstrong says that 'different particulars may be (wholly or partially) identical in nature. Such identity in nature is literally inexplicable, in the sense that it cannot be further explained. But that does not make it incoherent.'[2] He offers us an analogy with the size and shape of an object. The size and shape of an object are inseparable—nothing can have size without shape and vice versa—but they are not related to one another. Analogously, particulars may be bound together with universals, without being related to them.

But if realists can help themselves to primitive, indefinable identities in nature explaining the 'link' between particulars and universals, why can't nominalists do a similar thing? Why can't the class nominalist, for example, say that being a member of a class is a primitive notion, ultimately indefinable, which 'links' a class's members to the class? Class nominalists might support this position by saying that, while the realist's rejection of an instantiation relation between

---

[2] D. M. Armstrong, *Universals and Scientific Realism*, i: *Nominalism and Realism* (Cambridge, 1978), 109.

universals and particulars is somewhat *ad hoc*—designed only for this special purpose—the notion of being a member of a class does have uses elsewhere, in logic and mathematics.

SUBSTANCE
David Wiggins

4.1. Introduction

4.1.1. The notion of a substance—of a persisting and somehow basic object of reference that is there to be discovered in perception and thought, an object whose claim to be recognized as a real entity is a claim on our aspirations to understand the world—has been host at various times to countless internecine battles, not all of them very well understood by the protagonists of the warring doctrinal persuasions. That is often the fate of technical notions. For philosophy to aspire to the state where it might avoid wars about words like those that 'substance' has occasioned (contrast just wars about the identity or nature of that which is denoted by a word with an established use), it would be necessary to give an explicit definition for every term of art, using only language that had an established everyday life outside philosophy. The effort of making definitions would identify the presuppositions of the author—which he could then avow. In cases of doubt, technical terms would be defined over and over again by each author who was prepared to use them.

Unluckily 'substance' (variously *ousia, on, hupokeimenon, substantia, ens*) was never introduced in this way. It is true that Aristotle began with the Greek word for being, which had an established life outside philosophy; and it is true that he offered definitions of substance. We shall look at one of his definitions in a moment. But the non-philosophical life of the verb to be was already a complex matter; nor did Aristotle define being/a being in such a way that anyone could readily have said what his topic of discussion was and *then* said what his thesis was about that topic. Indeed Aristotle was never in a position to fix his topic of discussion once and for all, because his conception of what ought to be achieved by a discussion of *ousia* constantly outgrew his definitions. Things did not improve when Aristotle's successors decided to treat it as more or less clear what topic it was that he had introduced—as if the only problem were to improve or complete or correct or supersede his investigation of it or to add to the list of ancillary notions that Aristotle had already introduced for its further elucidation, such as form, essence, entelechy, actuality, potentiality. (How many of his successors even paused to ask whether the notion they were concerned with was *substance* or *a substance*, for instance?) When Aristotelians or rationalists insisted upon the notion of a substance and empiricists like Hume or Russell

claimed to reject it, were they really talking about the same thing? It is hard here
to disentangle topic from thesis.

4.2. An Objection and a Preliminary Defence

4.2.1. Shortly we must try to disentangle some of these things. But there is a
real point in facing immediately the empiricist rejection of substance—if only
because it will promote the effort to attend to what Aristotle and the rationalists meant by substance (or a substance).

Among representative statements of the empiricist rejection, it may be best
to consider Hume, *A Treatise of Human Nature*, I. i. 16:

We have no idea of substance distinct from that of a collection of particular qualities.
. . . The idea of a substance as well as that of a mode is nothing but a collection of simple ideas that are united by the imagination and have a particular name assigned them,
by which we are able to recall . . . either to ourselves or others that collection.

Compare *Treatise*, I. iv. 4:

The imagination is apt to feign something unknown and invisible which it supposes to
continue the same under all these variations: and this intelligible something it calls a
substance, or original and first matter.

Compare also I. iv. 5:

If any one should [say] that the definition of a substance is *something which may exist by
itself* . . . I should observe that this definition agrees to everything that can possibly be
conceived.

These are hostile characterizations by one who deliberately made no use of the
idea of a substance. Inheriting the situation we now inherit—anxious not to be
mesmerized by the history of the subject yet unable to turn our back on it lest
we repeat old errors or neglect old insights—we can only gain a fresh or authen-
tic grasp upon the ideas that Hume was rejecting by referring back to the questions that prompted Aristotle to introduce them and his inheritors to take their
stand upon them. Grasping the sense of 'substance' from these philosophical
uses, we must look for a unitary or central idea of substance: but we have to be
ready for the possibility that the idea is sustained by a diversity of theoretical
interests, some of them enjoying better philosophical prospects than others.
Unless, of course, we now want to abandon it. But to abandon it is less easy than
Hume has made it appear.

Look back at Hume's characterizations. How else can a set of qualities
cohere together than by being properties of one and the same subject? Or, abandoning that line of defence as question-begging, let us ask what sort of a collection it was that Hume had in mind. How is it to be specified? Either the kind of

collection Hume speaks of is specified by reference to some subject of the properties, or else it is specified enumeratively by reference to the properties that are members of the collection. In the first case, Hume does not escape the questions that come with the idea of the subject of the properties. In the second case, every new property and every old property deleted must result in a new collection of the kind Hume proposes. But then there will be no question of doing justice to the thought, which we do not know how to do without, that we can gradually amass and correct a larger and larger amount of information about one and the same thing, the same subject, and can come to understand better and better in this way how these properties intelligibly cohere or why they arise together. Nor is there any question of doing justice to the thought that this last is what we *have* to do if we are to make sense of the world at all. Salient among things that we have to recognize, if we are to make sense of the world, are the substances. Or that will be the claim of those who lie within the sphere of influence of Aristotle.

4.3. Aristotle's First Account of Substance

4.3.1. The idea of a substance (henceforth, till further notice, *a* substance) begins its serious philosophical life in Aristotle's *Categories* (treated in Chapter 7, Section 1.2. following). A substance—or, in the terms of that work of Aristotle's, a primary substance—is something that is neither in anything else nor predicable of anything else. That is a definition of a sort. It is Aristotle's earliest definition of a substance. Point and sense need clarification, but the intuitive idea that Aristotle appears to be seeking to explicate in these terms may prove to be as good a thread as any by which to find our way.

Begin with the idea of a subject of discourse, or anything at all that you can talk about. Then we arrive at substances by disentangling them from other subjects of discourse.

Among the different subjects you can talk about, some are and some are not in others in the way in which colours and their determinate shades are in things. Some are and some are not in things in the way in which knowledge in general or some specific and particular knowledge (e.g. that 'Socrates' is spelled with the letter sigma in Greek) is in things. (Henceforth let us italicize this special *in*.) To the extent that anything is not *in* other things in this way, it enjoys a certain autonomy. Something that has this autonomy may be causally dependent on other things in the way in which the infant depends on the mother; but, ontologically speaking, it is still independent—at least to the extent so far explained. Note also that according to this conception, before it is made radically stricter in the way in which it was at the hands of Leibniz, ontological autonomy of the kind we are concerned with is prima facie consistent with one substance's being a part of another substance.

On Aristotle's view of matters, when items are excluded that are *in* other items, the items that are left over to be ontologically more fundamental are genera like animal, species like horse or man, and particular concrete things like Arkle or Victor or Socrates. But now, if we stipulate that a primary substance should be not only ontologically autonomous (not *in* anything in the manner previously explained) but also not predicable of anything else, then animal, horse, or man—secondary substances, as Aristotle calls these—can be set aside as less fundamental than particular concrete things. A particular concrete thing, Socrates or Arkle, is the sort of thing that *is* other things (e.g. is a man, is an animal, is a horse) and can be *qualified* by other things (e.g. colour or knowledge). But it is not itself true of other things. Nor does it qualify other things. Rather, a concrete substance, a this such-and-such, is the sort of thing to support and to make possible all other kinds of subjects of discourse.

Suppose that is all right so far. Then, if the question is asked, 'What makes up the world?', one kind of answer can be found in the claim that the primary substances are the basic constituents of the world and that everything else that is is by virtue of being either one *kind* of primary substance (that is, by virtue of being some secondary substance), or by virtue of being some *qualification* of primary substance, or . . .

4.3.2. Entering into philosophy on these terms—furnishing an answer to displace or improve upon certain sorts of Pre-Socratic answer to the question of what there is, the Milesian or Eleatic answers, for instance—the notion of a substance is of course attuned from the outset to an ontology of things that are salient and privileged within the world-view of a human inquirer, the inquirer who reasons, argues, draws conclusions, asks questions about the world, and inquires there for an answer to these questions. Such a one thinks of primary substances as *continuants*, and he thinks of himself as one continuant among many, etc. Such an inquirer has from the nature of the case to be ready or eager to make new discoveries about these or those substances, to conclude that certain primary substances that he has recognized as a kind are composed thus or so, or behave thus and so, or whatever. He is ill prepared for the suggestion that the world of primary substances is a mere by-product of his natural and epistemological situation; that the one and only real world is a world of flux, or a world of atoms or electrons or packets of energy, or a world where the persistence of a particular through time is problematic. He might be better prepared for the opposite suggestion, that these other entities were abstractions from the familiar world of primary substances.

There are real issues here. But if we postpone them and we prescind from the issue of the ultimacy or privilege of the human viewpoint that descries the Aristotelian primary substances or singles them out, then it will be best to accept that there are such things as the primary substances Aristotle delimits. Unless and until we are prepared to take it as a brute fact that substances such as Aristotle recognizes are presented to us as things that are *there anyway*, ready to be picked out as this man, that horse, etc., the philosophical issue of substance will be more or less unintelligible to us. (The reader will now find that a provisional conviction is forming in his mind that the interest in substances as the locus or concern of systematic inquiry in its first stages is a more durable interest than the interest in substances as the fundamental things that make up the world. See Section 4.13.1 following. See also 4.6.1.)

4.3.3. What else is there to say about substances ordinarily so conceived, in advance of any particular study of particular kinds of them? Well, working freely from the suggestions that Aristotle furnishes in chapter 5 of *Categories* and exploiting the connections between primary and secondary substances, one may take off from the point that, given any object that is putatively a primary substance, one can ask the question 'What is this thing?' and expect there to be a certain sort of answer to the question. This will neither presuppose another answer in the way in which 'runs' or 'white' do (these are answers in the Aristotelian predication-kinds *what it is doing* and *what it is like*, which presuppose the first predication-kind, namely *what it is*) nor presuppose another answer in the way in which 'tinker', 'tailor', 'soldier', 'sailor' do. (A soldier is a man who is engaged to fight for a given army, a sailor is a man in some way engaged in navigation, etc.) Rather, the answer must bring us to a certain sort of conclusion, as 'man', 'horse', or 'daisy' do. Unless some such conclusory answer is provided to the question 'What is it?', it is indeterminate what we are thinking about. (If it is indeterminate what we are thinking about, the situation is not to be redescribed as there being something indeterminate that we are thinking about. It is not yet a situation in which there is *anything* we are thinking about.)

It is true of course that conclusory answers to the question 'What is it?' will be required for any object of reference whatever, in whatever ontological category, *quality, quantity, relative, place, time*, etc. It should also be remarked that there are objects of reference in the non-Aristotelian category of *event*, and further objects in any further ontological categories there may be, of *state, process*, etc. Where substances are at issue, however, conclusory answers will identify primary substances by determining which secondary substance a given object falls under (horse, animal, plant, etc.). By inviting us to see the object in question as *this such-and-such* or *that so-and-so*, these answers will not say what complete account is to be given of the nature of continuants like the one in question, but they will positively commit the identifier in certain ways about the empirical nature of things of its sort. Such answers identify the object as one of a class of continuants whose stereotype will be that members of the class *survive* certain sorts of change, *come into being* in a certain specifiable way, *tend to be qualified* in certain specifiable ways, *tend to behave* in certain specifiable ways, and *tend to cease to be* in certain specifiable ways.

We need an example. One might identify the thing one finds under a tree-stump by saying 'See that maggot!' Identifying it as a maggot commits the identifier to think of it as a creature with specifiable tendencies of movement and behaviour (e.g. flight from light or interference) of which a great deal more might be discovered, as a creature with a certain life-cycle of which much more might be discovered, as a creature with a certain way of appearing, and so on. If that is right, then to pick something out as a maggot is to take a certain epistemological risk (which is how it should be) and to subsume it under a conception that the entomologist's conception supplements, sorts out, and situates in a larger explanatory framework. This is the place to remark that the entomologist's work will reveal that the maggot is the larva of the fly commonly called the bluebottle and that 'maggot' is not the unproblematically conclusory answer that it seemed to the question 'What is it?' An entomologist will study in depth the actual nature of this species of insect. By these efforts, he will focus the question—make it clearer what the issue turns on—and he will also reveal the further facts by which the question whether an arbitrary *w* is or is not the same thing (the same insect) as that maggot might be determined.

4.4. Kinds and Activity

4.4.1. Consolidating all this, we may say that primary substances belong to kinds (or secondary substances) whose members (instances) will receive different and opposite qualifications at different times: they persist through change—not just any and every change but changes that can be specified on the basis of an explanatory true account of the way of being and acting of members of the kind, or on the basis of their mode of activity, as one might say. This last, the principle of activity, will be founded in their shared nature, which Aristotle characterized at a later moment in his philosophical development (but compatibly enough with *Categories* in respect of the point we are concerned with here) as follows:

The primary and proper sense of nature/*phusis* is the *ousia* [being, way of being] of those things which contain in themselves as such a source of change [or principle of activity]. Matter is called nature/*phusis* in so far as it is capable of receiving this nature/*phusis*, and the processes of generation and growth are called nature/*phusis* because they are processes derived from this nature/*phusis*. Nature/*phusis* in this sense is the source of change in natural objects [that is substances], which is somehow inherent in them, either potentially or actually. (*Metaphysics*, book 5, 1015ª11)

Substances are things that have a source of change or principle of activity within them. He who has the conception of a particular kind of substance *k* endowed with the corresponding particular nature and, by means of that conception, grasps the concept of horse or plant or man or bluebottle, or whatever *k* it is, is one who can single out *k* things. He can tell them apart from other things, or draw boundaries around them. He knows what it is synchronically to tell one from another and, understanding the principle of activity of things of the kind *k*, he knows what it is diachronically to trace a particular one of them through space and time. More picturesquely, substances are what the world is articulated into when the segmentation of kinds corresponds to the real divisions in reality. (In Aristotle's picture, the world will be articulated into substances without distinct substance-concepts ever cross-classifying anything, that is without one and the same entity's turning up in the extension of any two of them.)

4.5. Further Developments of the Aristotelian Idea

4.5.1. Substances are what the world is articulated into when the segmentation of kinds corresponds to the real divisions in reality—or so the philosopher of substance will say. Can we lend any serious, better than pictorial, content to this reality claim? Here are two ways in which we might do so.

First, when the world is divided into the kinds or sorts *f, g, h, j, k*, ... that divide it into true primary substances, there will be, for each such *f*, indefinitely many true generalizations in the form

for every *x* such that *x* belongs to *f*, *x* is ϕ,

where being ϕ is a property well chosen for *f*. That is to say that an Aristotelian secondary substance *f* that articulates genuine primary substances will make possible the extrapolation across all *f* things of a host of manifest or discoverable properties. In further development of this, one notices that this is the place to accommodate an insight that originates with Bertrand Russell. Suppose we go down to the beach and for the first time in our life we encounter a seal; and suppose that we hear the seal bark. Then, if we venture the guess that all seals bark, nature will reward our daring. Barking (unlike being wounded or ill, say) is a property that is well made for extrapolation across the whole class of seals. When we divide the world into the kinds that divide it into true substances, we find indefinitely many kind–property pairs $\langle f, \phi \rangle$ that are well made for scientific generalization and the other purposes of description and explanation. What is more, we know what it is for this condition to fail. If we were to treat the complement of each secondary substance or substance-kind as itself a secondary substance or substance-kind—something that Aristotle cautions us against at *Categories* 3^{b}26—we should find no such kind–property pairs. (The complement of a kind would comprise absolutely everything that did not belong to that kind.) If, despite our not falling into this absurd error, the kinds we divide the world into nevertheless fail to determine genuine substances, then there will be rather few kind–property pairs that are well made for scientific and explanatory generalization. Or that is the picture.

There is a second, more complex way in which content might be attached to the claim that a system of secondary substances that subsumes the genuine substances will segment kinds in a manner conformable to the real divisions in reality. We begin with the point that, if we have an entity x that belongs to the genuine secondary substance or substance-kind of *f*s, then x is not more or less of an *f* than other things that belong to that kind . . . (Nor, incidentally, is it more or less of a substance than some object y that falls under a distinct substance-sort or secondary substance k.) The Aristotelian claim is that, given a true secondary substance g, either the object x is a g and fully a g or x is not a g at all. ('Substance, it seems, does not admit of a more or a less . . . any given substance is not called more or less that which it is' (*Categories* 3^{b}34–6).)

That is one point. The next point we need, if we are to find the further content that we seek for the reality claim, relates to the logic of identity. Suppose that an entity a is the same as an entity b. If so, then whatever is true of a is also true of b and vice versa. (This principle is often called Leibniz's law, because it is entailed or presupposed by Leibniz's stronger two-way claim, *eadem sunt quorum unum alteri substitui potest salva veritate*: 'the same are those things that can be substituted the one for the other without detriment to truth'.) But every object is entirely determinately the object it is. So, manifestly, the object a is entirely determinately the same as the object a. But then, by Leibniz's law, if a is indeed b, b is entirely determinately the same as the object a.

The result has been found controversial by some writers. But in truth the deduction is simple and elementary and depends only upon two things: (1) the weakest and most modest of logical principles and (2) that which is utterly distinctive of the concept of identity (Leibniz's law). The real doubt it ought to leave us with is not the question of validity but the question of how to sustain the application to the world of so strict and unrelenting a conception as the deduction shows our conception of the concept of identity to be. How shall we answer that question and relate it to the logic of primary and secondary substances?

Here let us attend once more to what it takes for an object of reference to be singled out. We have stressed that what is singled out is never a bare this or that, but this or that *something or other*. We expect the sortal or secondary substance identification of an object to commit the identifier to provide whatever is needed to put himself or another into a position to specify what it turns on whether or not an arbitrary object w, referred to in whatever way (whether or not synchronically with our reference to the object we have in mind), is or is not the same as the object singled out. (How else could we count as making it clear which object is at issue?) But in that case we should not assume that just any grammatically suitable filling can count as the adequate or explicitly conclusory value for the 'something or other' that says what the thing singled out is. Not just any substantive stands for a genuine secondary substance. An example may assist. We can pick out someone as a poet. But, alerted by Aristotle, one will note that one person *can* be more or less of a poet than another. This confirms the fact that 'poet' is not a conclusory answer to the question 'What is it that is singled out here?' 'Poet' rides on the back of the answer 'human being'. (Let us fill out the example a little. Byron was born in 1788. But the baby who was born in 1788 was not the same poet as the poet who published *Childe Harold* I–II in 1812. For the baby was not a poet. The baby was, however, a human being and the same human being as Byron, the poet. It is in the light of what a human being is and does that the identity of baby and the author of *Childe Harold* has to be judged. It is in the light of the corresponding principle of activity that the biography of the human being who became the poet is to be understood.) What then do we expect of 'human being' if that is to be the properly conclusory answer to the *what is it?* question. Well, if it is satisfactory, it must underwrite the definiteness both of the question 'Is *w* the same as the thing singled out?' and of all satisfactory answers to that question.

That is what reference and singling out require. What follows? It follows that any system of secondary substances with a claim to separate reality into its genuine primary substances must arise from an understanding of some set of principles of activity on the basis of which identity questions can be glossed as questions about the holding or non-holding of a completely determinate relation. This is not to say that everything that is needed can be written down or said in a finite space—only that the system of real secondary substances must be such that there can be an open-ended understanding of the system that is good enough for it to be capable of being filled out *ad libitum* to the point where any identity question that actually arises can be glossed or elucidated as a question about the all-or-nothing relation that we have seen identity to be.

4.6. Legacy of the Aristotelian Conception

4.6.1. These are exigent requirements that the philosopher of substance is making: and it will now be manifest that, because of the close coherence that is coming to light between the formal logic of identity, Aristotelian metaphysics, and Aristotelian philosophy of nature, the philosophy of substance is in danger of committing us to positions that the progress of science since Aristotle makes it harder and harder to sustain. It no longer seems right to look for philosophical support for the scientific ultimacy of a biological and physical science pitched at the particular level of insight that Aristotle himself found so compelling and at which he expected to be able to describe the operation of an explanatory set of final causes. (See *Physics*, book 2.) Plainly, we must come back to this, only remarking here that the theory of substance becomes yet more complex in Aristotle's writings subsequent to the *Categories*. It also becomes more confusing, in ways to which we shall recur. (See Section 4.11.2 below.) In the interim, however, let us mine the conceptual riches that come to us with the simple neo-Aristotelian conception.

The idea we now have of a primary substance is not the idea of a 'we know not what'. Nor is it the idea of substance that we find in Kant, when, under the influence of Hume, he writes: 'People have long since observed that in all substances, the real subject, that which remains after the abstraction of all accidents (as predicates), remains unknown' (*Prolegomenon to Any Future Metaphysics*, sect. 46). The real subject Socrates or Arkle is one and the same as the palpable, perceptible substance Socrates or Arkle. This is nothing inherently unknown. It is something we know much about, albeit imperfectly. And, however difficult the empiricists were destined to find the Aristotelian idea of a substance—we have already seen Hume's hostile account of these things—this is the notion of substance we find has been communicated by the Scholastics to modern philosophy as it was before Kant or Hume—or at least to the rationalists—when Descartes claims that a substance is something that exists in and through itself and can exist without dependence on anything else (*Fourth Replies*, 226) or when Spinoza stipulates:

By a substance I mean that which is in itself and is conceived through itself: that whose concept makes no essential reference to anything else. (*Ethics*, first part, definition III)

It was this same notion that Leibniz was drawing out further when he wrote in his correspondence with De Volder, the Dutch physicist,

Nothing is permanent in a substance except the law itself which determines the continuous succession of its states and accords within the individual substance with the laws of nature that govern the whole world.

Simple partless substances are nothing more than sources and subjects of the whole unfolding series of perceptions. These series of perceptions all express with the greatest and most fitting variety the same world of phenomena. By these means the supreme substance communicates its own perfection so far as it is possible to many substances which depend upon it. Each of these many substances must be conceived as a microcosm or concentration of the whole world and (some less so, some more so) as, so to speak, an assemblage of the attributes of divinity. Nor do I think that any other rationale for the way of things can be understood. Everything had to be this way if it was to be at all.

Aristotle had not said in *Categories* that substances were partless or the sources and subjects of the whole unfolding series of perceptions. The world-view of the rationalists was no longer that of Aristotelian science. It was anti-Aristotelian. But the rationalists continued to conceive of intelligible ultimate reality in terms of the substances that make up the world. They conceived of substances both formally and in respect of their explanatory role much as Aristotle had. Leibniz's search for that which underlies all the rest of reality had begun with the Aristotelian conception of a subject of predications (*hupokeimenon*) conceived as that which is self-sufficient and in no need of other things. Then he was led to doubt that any true substance could stand in a part–whole relation to any other substance, or be other than causally autonomous. His disagreement with Aristotle issued in a disagreement about the extension of the notion. But (even at the furthest point, where Leibniz concluded that only souls or soul-like things could be substances) this was still a reinterpretation of the original idea of substance in Aristotle, whose influence we can see directly at work in such passages as this:

Aristotle has called nature the principle of motion and of rest. . . . [The] divine law once established has truly conferred upon substances some created impression which endures within them or . . . an internal law from which their actions and passions follow . . . there is a certain efficacy residing in things, a form or force such as we usually designate by the name of nature, from which the series of phenomena follows. (*On Nature itself or on the Inherent Force and Actions of Created Things*, Gerhardt, IV. 505)

4.7. The Collision of Rationalist and Empiricist Claims

4.7.1. Prescinding from the various farther determinations of the idea of a substance that are proprietary to the rationalists and postponing further difficulties (already mentioned but not yet expounded) with which Aristotle embarrassed the idea in his later writings, the time has come to ask why the idea of a subject that is an individual substance represented such a difficulty for the empiricists.

Perhaps the best place in which to witness the clash between empiricism and the philosophy of substance is Leibniz's *New Essays*. This work represents a conversation between Locke, whose part Leibniz compiles from Locke's *Essay* and assigns to a character he calls Philalethes, and Leibniz himself, whom he calls for these purposes Theophilus. The most important exchange on this matter is at II. 23. In Bennett and Remnant's translation of chapter 23 ('Of our Complex Ideas of Substances') we have:

PHILALETHES. §1. The mind takes notice that a certain number of 'simple ideas go constantly together: which being presumed to belong to one thing . . . are called so united in one subject by one name; which [through heedlessness] we are apt afterward to talk of . . . as one simple idea, which indeed is a complication of many ideas together'.

THEOPHILUS. I see nothing in the ordinary ways of talking which deserves to be accused of 'heedlessness'. We do take it that there is one subject, and one idea, but not that there is one simple idea.

What gloss have we committed ourselves to make (see Section 4.2 above) on this exchange? The idea of the sun cannot be a conjunction of properties, we have said, because that would mean that, whenever we learned a new property of the sun, we should have got ourselves a new 'complication' and a new idea of the sun. Every enrichment or impoverishment would have to determine a new complication. Surely the idea of the sun needs rather to be the idea of that which *has* this and the other properties. Locke recognizes this, but it seems that he recognizes it in his own way. He continues:

PHIL. Not imagining how these simple ideas can subsist by themselves, we accustom ourselves to suppose some substratum [something which supports them] wherein they do subsist, and from which they do result, which therefore we call substance.

THEO. I believe that this way of thinking is correct. And we have no need to 'accustom' ourselves to it, or to 'suppose' it; for from the beginning we conceive several predicates in a single subject, and that is all there is to these metaphorical words 'support' and 'substratum'. So I do not see why it is made out to involve a problem. On the contrary, what comes into our mind is the concretum conceived as wise, warm, shining, rather than abstractions or qualities such as wisdom, warmth, light etc., which are much harder to grasp. (I say qualities, not ideas.) It can even be doubted whether these accidents are genuine entities at all, and indeed many of them are only relations. We know, too, that it is abstractions which cause the most problems when one tries to get to the bottom of them. Anyone knows this who is conversant with the intricacies of scholastic thought: their thorniest brambles disappear in a flash if one is willing to banish abstract entities, to resolve that in speaking one will ordinarily use only concrete terms and will allow no terms into learned demonstrations except ones which stand for substantial subjects. So to treat qualities or other abstract terms as though they were the least problematic, and concrete ones as very troublesome, is to 'look for a knot in a bullrush' [Plautus], if you will allow me the phrase, and to put things back to front.

The way in which Locke really needed to see the complication of ideas (or qualities) that make up our idea of the sun was as follows: we conceive of the sun by conceiving of it as a substance / substratum (something he says we do not know) which shines on us *and* warms us *and* rises *and* sets *and* . . . Perhaps that is how Locke himself did see the relevant complication, even at the point when he decided to describe our ignorance of the nature of the sun as an ignorance of that which the ideas or qualities *shine, warm,* . . . inhere or subsist in. Indeed, if I understand him aright, this is how Michael Ayers reads Locke in his 'Ideas of Power and Substance' (see Bibliography). Ayers argues in a way sympathetic to Locke that our ignorance of the substratum is not distinct from our ignorance of the real essence or nature of a given kind of thing: it is our ignorance of the second of these things that shapes Locke's whole treatment.

Yet this ('the idea of the sun is the idea of a substance / substratum which shines on us *and* warms us *and* rises *and* . . .') was not the way in which Leibniz read Locke; and it seems that even Ayers is prepared to allow the other and traditional reading the measure of support that is restored to it when he states his own reading as follows: 'In order to mark the presumption of such a natural unity among [the powers, dispositions, properties that] we include under one complex idea on the basis of their observed coexistence [in a given kind of thing], we add the idea of "some substratum wherein they do subsist and from which they do result". Substance is a dummy concept. Locke's derision is directed against those who suppose it is something more.' The reason why this exposition supports the traditional reading, even as it seeks to subvert it, is that, on the sympathetic reading ('the idea of the sun is the idea of a substance/substratum which shines on us *and* warms us *and* rises . . .'), there cannot be any possibility to *add* the idea of substratum—if only because, in its absence, we could never have *embarked* upon giving the conception that the sympathetic interpretation claims Locke says we have of the sun. The substratum is required by the very grammar of the more sympathetic reading. (By the '. . . which – – – and . . .' construction, that is.) It is not optional. Hence the charm of the reading by which it *can* be added in just the way in which Locke seems to add it.

For this kind of reason or for other reasons, few if any of Locke's philosophical successors were able to understand Lockean 'complications' of ideas otherwise than as follows: the idea of the sun is a complication of the idea of shining and/with the idea of warming and/with the idea of rising and/with the idea of setting and/with the idea of substance, which is the idea of we know not what support or substratum. (Note the entirely different role of 'and' in this reading and the sympathetic reading, as I began by stating that. In that statement 'and' conjoined sentential clauses. In this traditional reading of Locke it means, more or less, 'conjoined with'.) The complication in question amounts then to a series of items that Leibniz calls abstractions.

Leibniz is only the first of many to read Locke in this way. It seems obvious that Hume read Locke very similarly. If Hume had read Locke in the other way, he would have had much more difficulty in taking substance to be as superfluous as it was (according to Locke) inscrutable.

4.8. Subject and Properties

4.8.1. Here let us continue the exchange between Philalethes and Theophilus.

PHIL. §2. A person's only notion of pure substance in general is that of I know not what subject of which he knows nothing at all but which he supposes to be the support of qualities. We talk like children; who, being questioned, what such a thing is, which they know not, readily give this [to them] satisfactory answer, that is something; which in truth signifies . . . when so used . . . that they know not what it is.

THEO. If you distinguish two things in a substance—the attributes or predicates, and their common subject—it is no wonder that you cannot conceive anything special in this subject. That is inevitable, because you have already set aside all the attributes through which details could be conceived. Thus, to require of this 'pure subject in general' anything beyond what is needed for the conception of 'the same thing'—e.g. it is the same thing which understands and wills, which imagines and reasons—is to demand the impossible; and it also contravenes the assumption which was made in performing the abstraction and separating the subject from all its qualities or accidents.

At risk of painting the lily, let us distinguish within Theophilus' diagnosis two distinct objections.

First objection. The Lockean idea of an *I know not what*, the bare idea of a substratum, which Hume later dispensed with but Locke added to the other ideas that Leibniz thinks Locke thinks of as jointly constituting such-and-such a substance, is only the product of the separation of the subject from all its properties.

How was such a separation possible? Well, obviously no substance is any property or quality. It does not follow from this, however, that a subject can be conceived of as *lacking* just any or every arbitrary set of properties. It would have been helpful, and it would have discouraged Philalethes from giving his thesis about the limitation of human understanding of material objects and our ignorance of their real essence a most implausible formulation, if at this point Theophilus had mentioned Aristotle's distinction between answers to the question '*What is* this thing?' and answers to the question 'What is this thing *like*?' Perhaps the empiricist knows as well as anybody else that the process of abstracting all the properties from a subject and amassing them as a conjunction of qualities will in the end cause the subject itself to disappear. But the real palpable subject becomes invisible even more quickly than the empiricist realizes. It becomes invisible so soon as one seeks to abstract from the subject, a dog, a horse, a man, a tree or whatever, the property of being a dog or a horse or a man or a tree. What is an individual tree taken in abstraction from its being a tree? What is a dog when one prescinds from its being a dog? How are these things even to be conceived under this abstraction? If the subject is that which has the qualities, why suppose that we can reach this subject by not thinking of it as having any qualities, not even the qualities that are essential to its being singled out as that very subject? (Or even worse by thinking of it as *not having* any qualities.) The *bare idea* of a subject is one thing. To have such an idea is to conceive of an ordinary subject while leaving it entirely *open* what the subject is. (One can only approximate to that sort of conceiving. For when we seek to imagine how things might have been for a certain thing x, we have to hold constant what x is, what palpable substance it is, and only then can we explore all the variations in how it might otherwise have been that are consistent with what x is.) The idea of a *bare subject* is an altogether different thing; no reader of Aristotle's *Categories* will ever agree to make sense of it. By subject (*hupokeimenon*) Aristotle had meant the visible, palpable subject that has qualities—not a substratum that is in itself quality-less, or has no qualities.

In short, every empiricist about substance must measure how far he stands from the seductively inviting but utterly absurd claim that, because the subject is what *has* the qualities, it has itself *no qualities*. The fact that 'substratum' began as a Latin translation of Aristotle's ordinary word for 'subject', namely 'hupokeimenon', but then came to be understood as denoting something hidden, then as denoting an absurdity, only signals how old and how persistent the temptations are to commit the confusions with which Theophilus here charges Philalethes, never mind whether justly or unjustly. (For Aristotle's own albeit modest contribution to this confusion, see below, Section 4.11.2.)

That is one objection. Here is another just distinguishable objection. Locke insisted that, in speaking of substance as we know not what, he in no way intended to deny the existence of substances, i.e. the kinds of things that answer to what he calls in the heading for II. 23 'our complex ideas of substances'. (Cf. Locke's Letter to Stillingfleet, pp. 32–3.) But, from the nature of the case, Locke's doctrine leaves us wondering how there can be different kinds of *substratum*, or different determinations of the determinable 'pure subject in general'. It leaves us still inquiring for the better understanding that is needed to overcome the division Locke so recklessly insists upon—and that any Aristotelian must reject—when he writes that 'all the idea of substance of anything is is an obscure idea of what it *does* and not any idea of what it *is*'. (Cf. *Essay*, II. xiii. 19–20.)

4.9. Clear Ideas and Ignorance

4.9.1. Just once more let us revert to Philalethes' and Theophilus' conversation:

PHIL. §4. We have 'no clear idea of substance in general' . . .

THEO. My own view is that this opinion about what we don't know springs from a demand for a way of knowing which the object does not admit of. The true signs of a clear and distinct notion is one's having means or giving a priori proofs of many truths about it. I showed this in a paper 'Meditations on Knowledge, Truth and Ideas' [Gerhardt, IV. 422–6]

The point becomes clearer in the light of the paper of Leibniz's that Theophilus cites. Clear and distinct knowledge—knowledge that not only supports recognition (clearness) but also represents the analysis and exhaustive enumeration of the marks of a kind (distinctness)—is too much to ask in an area where (from the nature of the case) there is no question (for finite minds such as ours) of a priori proofs. No readily imaginable extension of our scientific understanding could give those. But there is something else that is a possibility for us, namely clear *indistinct* knowledge, and this is knowledge too. (Leibniz sometimes calls this clear confused knowledge.) That is to say that, where understanding is based on ideas that suffice for the recognition of kinds of things, even if it falls far short of the enumeration of all the marks of the kind, such understanding can count as knowledge. Such is the ordinary knowledge that we have of what a man or a horse is; and such is the knowledge we have of Socrates or Arkle. It is on this possibility that we depend, moreover, for our grasp upon the sense of ordinary substantives like 'horse', 'man', etc. That grasp becomes philosophically intelligible when we reconstruct it, however artificially, as follows. Suppose we do not know what 'horse' means. Then someone can say to us, pointing to a horse:

That is a horse. A horse is anything that resembles that thing in the right sort of way. If you want to know what the right sort of way is, well, simply on the basis of how much you need to know, study that thing, study what it does, study how it behaves and how it interacts with other things. When you have studied it well enough to have a reliable recognitional capacity of the kind—and this will come very swiftly indeed—then, even if you stop there, you will know, however minimally, what a horse is. You will know enough to understand 'horse'.

In our own times, the principal champion of one version of this Leibnizian conception of the semantics of natural kind substantives has been the American philosopher Hilary Putnam. (See his 'Is Semantics Possible?', in *Collected Papers*, ii.) We must note, however, that the reconstruction just offered cannot *guarantee* that speakers will always grasp the sense of names of new kinds of substance. Nor does it guarantee that all substantives that people try to introduce in the manner described will have senses that are well founded. Nothing ought to guarantee either of these things. The reconstruction explains the one thing that needs explaining, namely how, where a substantive does have a well-founded sense, a grasp of the sense is possible. The reconstruction builds upon a natural and convincing account of how ordinary knowledge of such things as ordinary substances is possible.

One word more to those who persist in a preference for Locke's attribution to us of ignorance over Leibniz's attribution to us of clear indistinct knowledge. What kind of ignorance is Locke attributing to us? This ignorance, is it a privation of *knowing of*, or is it a privation of *knowing which*, or is it a privation of *acquaintance*? Or what is it a privation of? If, as it seems, knowing of, knowing which, and acquaintance are all different kinds of knowledge, surely the lack of one of these may be different from the lack of any other. Even if we are indeed ignorant in that way, why should we not count as having clear indistinct knowledge of substances—of substances themselves?

4.9.2. The combination of ideas that we have drawn from Aristotle and Leibniz is a powerful prescription against most of the vexations with which empiricists from Hume onwards—J. S. Mill, Ernst Mach, Bertrand Russell, and A. J. Ayer, for instance—have attempted to undermine the concept of substance (or in

Mill's case, to reduce it to that of mere body). What now stands in the way of the proper reinstatement of the concept? Three things perhaps. First there are certain unintended effects of the symbolism of modern logic. (See Section 4.10.1 following.) In the second place, there are the further accretions to the doctrine of substance for which Aristotle himself and his admirers have been responsible. (See Section 4.11.2 following.) Thirdly, there is some continuing obscurity about the need, if any, for an idea of substance that is more than an idea of body. (See Section 4.13.1.) We shall conclude by attending to these points.[3]

4.10. Recent Further Misunderstandings of Substance and Property

4.10.1. In any account of substance like the Aristotelian one, we have seen how important it is to mark the distinction between predications that answer the question *what is x?* (sortal predications, as they are often called in present-day philosophy) and predications that answer questions like *what is x like?*, *how big is x?*, etc. The symbolism of modern first-order logic, employing the notation 'ϕx', 'ϕx' for all such answers, does not mark this distinction. Indeed it has discouraged many twentieth-century philosophers from attending to it. (Not all. See the references to Strawson and Quine in the Bibliography.) In truth, however, modern logic neither forbids nor obstructs the distinction. Nor, it must be added, does it direct us to see the distinction as a mere distinction in idiom rather than as what it is, namely, a distinction in thought.

Something similar needs to be said about a difficulty that has recently been urged against the very idea of continuants that endure through time (all in one piece, so to say) by philosophers who have wanted to replace the ontology of enduring, changing substances with a supposedly more basic ontology of things-at-moments or things-in-phases (or of shorter-lived objects, not changing in their

---

[3] Before going on, the reader may wish to test his or her degree of acceptance of the contentions so far advanced by considering what answer to offer to three questions: *Question 1*: 'This table is the same and not the same as the table I bought four years ago from the furniture store in Westbourne Grove. It is one and the same table: but it is not in the same condition.' Is Aristotle's distinction between the categories of substance and quality helpful in explicating the difference here signalled between numerical identity and qualitative identity? (This author would say 'yes'.) *Question 2*: 'My table is now brightly, now dimly lighted. Its temperature varies. It may receive an ink stain. One of its legs may be broken. It may be repaired, polished and replaced part by part. But, for me, it remains the table at which I daily write ... A body is one and unchanged only so long as it is unnecessary to consider its details' (Ernst Mach). Is it all right to assume, as Mach apparently does here, that what it involves for table T_i, with no ink stain and all its original legs, to be *strictly* one and the same table as table T_j, with an ink stain and two legs of recent provenance, is for T_i and T_j to figure in the history of a table that *has not changed*? What would Aristotle have said about that? Can Mach really restore plausibility to his conception of these things by saying that it may be 'unnecessary to consider' the changes that have actually taken place; that *for me* the table is the same? (Your author would say 'no'.) What further comment, if any, do you want to make on the last sentence quoted? *Question 3*: Noam Chomsky has written: 'If we abstract from the perspective provided by natural language ... then intuitions collapse: Nixon would have been a different entity, I suppose, if his hair were combed differently.' What are you moved to say about this claim?

intrinsic properties, see below), which they suppose to be scientifically or metaphysically less problematic and from which they expect to be able to see enduring, changing continuants as composed. These philosophers are constructionalists, one might say, with respect to substances. They expect to be able to treat questions like whether x is the same man as y by deploying some equivalence of the following general kind: x is the same man as y if and only if the thing-at-a-moment x (thing-in-a-phase x) bears to the thing-at-a-moment y (thing-in-a-phase y) the ancestral of that relation R (whatever R may be) which holds between arbitrarily nearly simultaneously existing men-at-a-moment or arbitrarily temporarily close men-in-a-phase. (Explanation of 'ancestral': x bears to y the ancestral of the relation R just if either x bears R to y or x bears R to some w that bears R to y, or x bears R to some w that bears R to some z that bears R to y or . . .)

Before we go any further, let us note that it is one question whether such treatments of identity can ever be made intelligible independently of the scheme that they are supposed to supplant. (Can one really characterize the relation R independently of one's diachronic understanding of what a man is, independently, that is, of one's understanding of the relevant principle of activity and so on? It seems perfectly extraordinary that so many philosophers should be happy simply to *assume* this.) It is another question whether such a treatment is mandatory and that is the question we are now concerned with.

David Lewis, the most distinguished among active champions of the constructionalist view, writes:

> The principal and decisive objection against endurance as an account of the persistence of ordinary things such as people . . . is the problem of intrinsic [properties].

Explanation: metaphysicians such as Lewis wish to distinguish intrinsic properties, which things have in virtue of the way they themselves are, from extrinsic properties, which things have in virtue of their relations or lack of relations to other things. (It is far from certain whether this distinction can be satisfyingly made out. But the question does not need to be disputed here.)

> Persisting things change their intrinsic properties, for instance shape: when I sit, I have a bent shape; when I stand, I have a straightened shape. Both shapes are intrinsic properties: I have them only some of the time. How is such change possible? First solution: contrary to what we might think, shapes are not genuine properties. They are disguised relations which an enduring thing may bear to times. One and the same enduring thing may bear the bent-shape relation to some times and the straight-shape relation to others. And likewise for all other temporary intrinsic [properties]; all of them must be reinterpreted as relations that something with an absolutely unchanging intrinsic nature bears to different times . . . This is simply incredible if we are speaking of the persistence of ordinary things . . . If we know what shape is, we know that it is a property, not a relation.

The conclusion to which Lewis himself comes on the basis of this difficulty is a striking one, namely the solution that people and other continuants do not endure but 'perdure': they are made up of temporal parts, which parts can have intrinsic properties such as a bent shape or a straight shape but do not last through changes in intrinsic properties. The question of identity through change is transformed into the question whether distinct but putatively related items belong to a unitary but more complex thing, a certain complex or sum of temporal parts.

Lewis takes the problem of temporary intrinsic properties exceedingly seriously then. What would Aristotle have said about it? He might have said (cf. *De Interpretatione* 16ᵃ14–18) that it was all very well to represent these supposedly troublesome claims in the fashion of modern logicians as

> Bent, t_1 (David).
> Straight, t_2 (David).
> Sit, t_1 (David).
> Stand, t_2 (David).

Such renderings are perfectly neutral between all accounts of the matter, he might have said: but, if we use these renderings, we must ask what makes these strings into sentences. As Aristotle said

Names and verbs just by themselves—for instance [*bent, straight, stands, sits, David*] when nothing further is added—are like the thoughts that are without combination or separation. For, just by themselves, such strings are neither true nor false . . . unless 'is' or 'is not', either simply or with reference to some time, is added [or unless a finite verb-ending is supplied, as in 'David sits' or 'David stands'].

In other words, the renderings of sentences that are given by first-order logic will assign to bare concatenation the work of natural language devices like the copula 'is' or verb-endings ('stand' + 's' etc.). There is nothing wrong with that, so long as we remember that the copula was the locus of time indication, modality, negation, etc. Once we remember that in the sentence 'Bent, t_1 (David)', the 't_1' goes with an 'is' that has been suppressed, we can see that being bent is indeed a property a person *has* at a time. Being bent then is not a relation between a person and a time. Nor need symbolic logic set any store by insisting that it is a relation. (On these and related matters, the reader may wish to read the paper by Mark Johnston cited in the Bibliography. Aristotle's position anticipates Johnston's.)

4.11. Aristotle's Further Thoughts

4.11.1. In *Categories*, Aristotle provided most or all of what we really need in order not to misunderstand our own thoughts about change and to escape the

idea that change stands in need of philosophical reconstruction. But in his subsequent writings he aspired to do more than this. He wanted to give a positive
answer to Parmenides' doubts about change and to build upon this answer a
more ambitious philosophical account of substances, the so-called hylomorphic
account, which is presented in the *Metaphysics*. Within this account, the ordinary substances of *Categories* come to be seen as compounds of matter and form
and there is a settled tendency for the title of true substance to be taken from
ordinary things such as Socrates, seen now as a compound of matter and a
form, and transferred to forms actualized in matter (entelechies), where the
form of Socrates either is or is correlative with the *essence*. (In Aristotle's technical language, the essence of Socrates is 'what being is for Socrates'.) The form
is that which makes Socrates the this something that he is. Or in another
remarkable turn of Aristotelian philosophical speech, it is *the substance* of
Socrates (see *Metaphysics* 1017^{a}22, 1038^{b}10) and that which remains constant
throughout all the changes which Socrates undergoes. (It may help to keep in
mind the question whether in 'the substance *of* Socrates' one is to take the 'of'
as like the of in 'the body of Socrates' or 'the hand of Socrates' or as like the
appositive 'of' in 'the city of Paris'. In the latter case, the substance of Socrates
would be just Socrates, the *real* Socrates.)

These developments have given endless trouble. If we had aimed at a more
complete or fair account of all the philosophical problems that critics have
found in the idea of substance, then we could not have waited so long to do
what must now be attempted, however briefly. This is to paint into the picture
so far presented some of these later Aristotelian details, to note their effect, and
then, for purposes of the final, updated defence of the idea of substance, to consider in each case whether or not to retain the new detail.

The reader should be warned that, on the view to be submitted here for consideration, few if any of Aristotle's emendations or additions (even the most
interestingly reasoned) will count as straightforward improvements.

4.11.2. Advancing into the philosophy of nature from what he called dialectic
(and we might call the philosophy of logic or language), that is from the philosophical pursuits of the *Categories* and other logical writings, Aristotle had confronted the Eleatic denial of change. He had summed up their attack upon
change in the question 'How can what is come to be from what is not?' His
response in book 1 of the *Physics* had come down to this: in the course of a normal or non-substantial change, a change like the becoming sunburnt of a white
man, for instance, or the becoming educated of an ignorant one, we do not have
the coming to be of something from nothing. We have the coming to be sunburnt of something that is there throughout, namely that which was first white
and then sunburnt. Aristotle claimed that all change (all non-substantial

change, rather) involved a change between two contrary attributes and involved a subject, the subject being that which first has the one attribute and then has the other. This is not something's coming from nothing.

So far so good. The *hupokeimenon*, or underlying thing, in this case is simply the subject or substance itself. There is no need to talk of matter—except in so far as we are already impressed by the materiality and mutual displacing tendencies of ordinary substances (which are not points specifically requiring hylomorphism for their statement). But what about the other case of change, substantial change, the kind of change where something new comes into existence, as happens with the generation of an animal or a plant? Here too Aristotle had wanted to insist that this is not a case of something's coming to be from nothing, but a case of something's coming to be from something that is always underlying, namely matter, the matter first lacking and then acquiring a certain structure or form. 'By matter I mean the first *hupokeimenon* (subject/substratum) of each thing, that from whose presence something arises non-accidentally' (192^a30–3).

Aristotle's only pretext for using the word 'hupokeimenon' in such a place—hitherto meaning 'subject', not anything covertly underlying, but now suggesting something possibly covertly underlying—was the analogy between non-substantial and substantial change that Parmenides' denial of change had forced him to postulate. That analogy is surely both strained and troublesome, however. It is not just that the matter from which a thing is generated may be lost and need supplementation in the process. It is not just that the way in which Socrates pre-exists and persists through sunburning is very unlike the way in which a seed plus that which the germinating of that seed sucks up from the environment pre-exists and persists (in so far as it does) through generation. The whole argumentative strategy is completely misguided.   •

All that Aristotle needs to say to Parmenides (as Aristotle reads him) is this: you deny change by asking how anything can come to be from nothing. Most change, where something comes to be ϕ, having previously been not ϕ, carries no semblance at all of involving this. But even in the case where a change is a coming into being of something that previously did not exist, the only thing that could pose any philosophical or dialectical difficulty would be such a thing's coming to pass inexplicably or without any reason—lawlessly, that is. There is simply no ground to think that the coming into being of a new thing is inherently inexplicable or lawless, however. As things are, the availability of matter helps to render intelligible the generation of substances. But intelligibility is the only issue and one might wonder whether there is anything *incoherent* in the idea as such of the creation of new matter or the destruction of old. (When early physicists postulated the conservation of matter, what they had got hold of was surely a place-holder for a much more abstract kind of conservation law. Why should the creation or destruction of matter offend against that more abstract law or be *inherently* lawless?) Even at the level of its ultimate constituents, what is the incoherence in the idea that the world could be made anew every day?

These questions are not easy to debate against the background of Aristotle's conception of matter, which permits any kind of matter to become any other kind of matter. Letting them pass, we should note a more straightforward point. However things may stand with the question of the generation or destruction of the ultimate constituents of the world, there seems to be no incoherence in the idea that at that level and/or higher levels, everything could be in a steady state of incessant flux. In so far as there appears to be any difficulty in this, the appearance of difficulty arises from confusing flux with chaos. Consider the river in Heraclitus' fragments 12 and 91: 'Upon those who step into the same rivers different and again different waters flow. The waters scatter and gather, come together and flow away, approach and depart.' The river is in constant flux. The waters are constantly renewed. We may even suppose that, consequentially upon this changing of constituents, the river changes in any and every property range, in depth, strength, speed, temperature, colour, noise-level, etc. These changes, however extreme, need not be lawless. Nor, incidentally, do they prevent us from singling out one and the same river. To say that the river is changing constantly in every respect is not to say that it is changing in respect of being a river. Rather, that is precisely *not* a respect in which the constantly changing river changes, even under condition of total flux. (The only thing we need in order to make sense of this last point is to see it as an application of the familiar distinction between what a thing is like and what the thing is.) But in that case there is no sound analogy between the way in which an enduring subject undergoes qualitative change and the way in which matter underlies substantial change.

4.11.3. So much for Aristotle's introduction of matter, an introduction grounded in an unwise and unnecessary concession to the Eleatics. The next speculative leap is briefly recorded in Aristotle's philosophical lexicon, namely *Metaphysics*, book 5 (Δ), where he anticipates the conclusions of books 7 (Z) and 8 H about what a substance is by saying that substance, *ousia*, can mean 'either [as in *Categories*] (1) the final subject/substratum which is not predicated of other things or else (2) that which is a "this" and separable: of this nature is the shape [*morphē*] of anything or the form [*eidos*, the same word as Plato had used for Platonic Form and Aristotle himself had used for species]' (1017^{b}23–5). As we have said already in Section 4.11.1, the second understanding of *ousia* that Aristotle mentions here scarcely differentiates the substance of a thing from the essence of a thing. 'The essence, the formula of which is a definition, is also called the substance of each thing' (1017^{b}21; cf. 1028^{b}15–18). But this is a conclusion that gives notorious trouble to Aristotle and then to his interpreters. (See Z, chapter 13.) Such an essence seems too much akin to a universal, too much akin to something multiply instantiable, that is, for it to be a true substance.

Has not something gone badly wrong—the same thing that has gone astray when a philosopher is visited by the temptation to add into English the absurd expression 'thisness'? Perhaps one should reflect at this point that there can hardly be a general answer to the question 'What is the substance of *x*?', because the answer must be different in each case. If the answer is different in each case, should Aristotle even be asking the question? Or, rather, should he be interpreting the question what a substance is in such a way that an answer to it must confront that question?

Well, perhaps it is all right for him to allow his inquiry to generate such a question if there is some prospect of finding a universal schema that generates or otherwise informs the varying answers that apply in each particular case. If there is such a schema to be found, then Aristotle will surely insist that it relates to the hylomorphic paradigm of matter and form. The strange thing about Aristotle's use of that paradigm, however, is that he should have been led by it to promote form not only over matter, but also over the compound of which the form is 'the substance'.

4.11.4. Let us focus on the first moves by which Aristotle advances in the direction of his conclusion that substance is form and his idea that there is something that is the substance of *x*, which is its 'shape' or its form or 'the plan of the form'.

In Z. 3, having enumerated as candidates to be substance (1) the essence, (2) the universal, (3) the genus, (4) the subject/substrate or ultimate subject, Aristotle then subdivides (4) in accordance with the matter–form scheme brought forward from *Physics* 1, saying that subject/substrate or ultimate subject is that of which other things are predicated, while it is not itself predicated of anything else.

Hence we must first determine its nature, for the first subject/substrate is considered to be in the truest sense substance. [Cf. *Categories*.] Now in one sense we call the matter the substrate/subject, in another the shape, and in a third sense the compound of these. By the matter I mean, for instance, the bronze, by the shape the plan of the form, and by the compound of these (the concrete thing), the statue. *Therefore if the form is prior to matter and more real, it will be prior to the compound also for the same reason.* (1029ª1 f.)

In the sentence italicized, we see one part of the supposed rationale for shifting attention away from what counted as a primary substance in the *Categories* and towards form. On the supposition that being not itself predicated but having other things predicated of it is the mark of substancehood, the candidacy of matter leads us to something that cannot even be a this, or separable, or individual. If matter were substance, then we should expect that there would be an answer *f* to the question what such-and-such matter was, and we should expect that, holding *f* constant, we could treat everything besides being *f* as inessential to that particular substance. (Here see our comments at Section 4.8.1 upon Leibniz, *New Essays*, II. xxiii. 2.) But, measured by this test, matter fails completely to furnish anything that is a 'this' or separable. (What does matter have to be in order to count as matter, or as that matter?) One misconceives matter by thinking of it even as a candidate to furnish anything to play the role of a substance.

From this Aristotle concludes that, since matter cannot be substance, it is form that must be substance. For as regards the other candidate, namely the 'substance compounded of both matter and form, [it] must be dismissed. For it is posterior and its nature is obvious . . . We must inquire into the third kind of substance [namely form]: for this is most difficult.' It is from here that the path leads on to essence and the troublesome conclusions already mentioned. At this crucial point we need more detail, however, in order to appraise what is going on.

4.11.5. Let it be clear that Aristotle has not simply abandoned the items that were called in *Categories* primary substances. They will have their proper place in the full theory, if the full theory does what it is meant to do: but the introduction of the new scheme of matter and form has had the effect of depriving the primary substances of *Categories* when seen as compounds of their previously undisputed title to being regarded as the substances *par excellence*.

The text of the argument I have reported in the paragraph before last against the claims of matter to be a substance reads as follows (with interpretative intercalations in square brackets):

Substance is not that which is predicated but that of which other things are predicated. But it is not enough to make this ruling [which we proposed in *Categories*]. For it is unclear and one of its apparent effects is to make matter into substance. [For matter, once we introduce it into our ontology, becomes the final subject/substrate.] If matter is not [by the terms of this ruling] substance then we cannot say what other substance there is.

Suppose we take away from matter [considered as candidate to be substance] everything else [everything else but its supposed substance *qua* matter, this what-the-matter-is being held constant while we imagine everything else being varied]. Then nothing at all remains. [For in the case of matter there is no what-it-is to hold constant.] What is removed in this thought-experiment will comprise all the affections, the products and the capacities of matter. The [remaining] length, breadth and depth of matter are simply the quantities or dimensions of matter. Mere quantity or dimension does not give us the substance of matter [or what the matter is]. The substance [if matter were substance] would have to be that to which the quantity or dimension belonged. When we take away [from matter] length, breadth, depth etc., we find nothing left over except that which is bounded by them, in which case matter [in the sense of what *has* the length, breadth, and depth] will appear to be the only substance.

This is a conclusion Aristotle is going to say that he finds absurd and impossible, on the grounds (1029ª27–9) that matter so conceived cannot be singled out as 'this' and 'it is accepted that separability and being a "this" belong especially to substance'. It is this absurdity that opens the way, as we have said, to the candidature of form; it is from this point on that Aristotle sees form as offering better prospects for separability and being a this, and treats separability and being 'this' as better indicators of substancehood than not being predicable. But in the *Metaphysics* as we have it (not a finished work but lecture notes, interspersed perhaps with other notes and memoranda), before he gives his grounds for finding the candidature of matter absurd, a passage intervenes that has given endless trouble over the ages:

By matter I mean that which *in itself* is neither some particular thing nor a quantity nor anything else that belongs in one of the other categories of being. For there is something of which each of these [including primary substances such as Socrates or Arkle] is predicated. Its being is different from that of the things predicated of it. For all the other things are predicated of a substance, but substance itself is predicated of this. So that ultimate [substance/substrate] is in itself neither some thing nor some quantity nor anything else. Nor indeed is it the negative of any of these things. For these too would apply to it only as accidents.

Coming where it does in Aristotle's discussion, this passage will probably remind the reader of Locke's something-we-know-not-what account of substance and lead him to question the stand that has been taken here to distance Aristotelian substance from the Lockean we-know-not-what. But, even if something almost equally lamentable is in train, what is going on here is importantly different.

Note first that what we find in this passage is precisely not Aristotle's account of substance. It is an account of matter. But nor is matter here matter as Aristotle normally thinks of matter. (Examples of that would be wine, bronze, earth.) Nor yet is matter in this passage matter as Aristotle defined it in the *Physics*. ('By matter I mean the first subject/substrate from whose presence something arises non-accidentally', already quoted. Nothing at all could answer to this description if it had no properties that made it the right matter for that which arose from it.)

If the Z. 3 conception of matter is special in these ways, why is it special? It is special because it arises from three suppositions that are local to the dialectical context—namely, the assumption (1) (to be tested here, supposedly to destruction) that substancehood is equivalent to ultimate non-predicability; the supposition (2) that only what is predicated of a substance substantially is really a property of it—a supposition that can be relied upon to give amazing results where the subject is something like matter and matter is thought not to admit any real (or what-it-is-type) predications; the supposition (3), which hylomorphism seems to import, that if the man Socrates is a compound (a compound of flesh and bones and the form of man), then Socrates and/or man are predicated of the flesh and bones.

This explains why the Z. 3 account of matter is so strange. But what is one to think of the steps by which Aristotle reaches his conclusion? Well, there is no point in denying that (2) may have arisen from a trend of thought similar to that which leads into the seductive but absurd proposition mentioned at the beginning of the penultimate paragraph of Section 4.8.1 above. But far more important than that mistake—a dead end leading to no Aristotelian conclusion not otherwise available—is the fact that supposition (3) is false. To see why it is false, consider ordinary predication. If Socrates is a man, then there is a man whom Socrates is identical with and with whom he shares all properties. This is an entirely general point about predication, not to be confused with the silly aspiration to reduce all predications to identities. (To test it, try another kind of predication. If Socrates is white, then Socrates is identical with some white thing and he shares all his properties with that.) Now suppose we try saying that the flesh and bones is Socrates. On a proper understanding of what is being said, that does not mean that Socrates shares all properties with the flesh and bones. The flesh and bones does not sit or talk. And Socrates predeceases the flesh and bones. 'This flesh and bones is Socrates' is misleading. What it really means is that this flesh and bones *makes up* or *constitutes* Socrates. What is predicated of the flesh and bones is not Socrates or man but the property of constituting Socrates or constituting a man. If hylomorphism entails (3), then so much the worse for hylomorphism.

4.12. Complaints about Aristotle's Further Thoughts

4.12.1. What follows? It follows that there was never any real danger of matter's counting as the ultimate subject. More importantly, the whole case against the *Categories* criterion of substancehood and against Aristotle's election in that work of Socrates, Arkle, Victor, etc. to be the first substances simply collapses. (It also means that there is no connection between ultimate subjecthood and the kind of ultimacy with which physics is concerned.) In so far as hylomorphism rests on a denial of the *Categories* doctrine (rather than hylomorphism's being an idea to be worked out in the progressive reconciliation with Aristotle's earlier views that I believe some readers want to find in the succeeding books of the *Metaphysics*), well, hylomorphism was simply a mistake.

But what mistake? Does it have to be a mistake? Let us go back now to the very idea, presumably definitive of hylomorphism, that a substance such as Socrates is a compound of matter and form. Socrates is 'this in that', Aristotle says—this sort of thing, namely man, in that sort of matter, namely flesh and bones. To understand such claims it is important to see that making them is utterly unlike saying that bronze is copper mixed with lead, and very unlike saying that a hammer is a stick of wood (the handle) attached to a piece of iron (the head). To say that Aristotelian form and matter are utterly different sorts of thing is not simply to say that they are very different *components*. The form is not a component at all. It is that which corresponds in the thing to a true statement of 'the shape' or 'the plan of the form'.

These points are philosophical reminders for ourselves. They are not yet criticisms of Aristotle, who attained to a state of incomparably subtle awareness of these and kindred matters—not least the difficulty of characterizing the form of a perceptible substance independently of the requirements upon its realization in matter (how to say what a man is without reference to his embodiment?) and the difficulty of characterizing a substance's matter in a manner independent of all reference to the form that it is to realize. (How to say how matter must be for it to realize man? Flesh and bones presuppose animal. What is more, not any old flesh and bones will suffice. We need the right sort of flesh and bones for a man in particular.) The question is how to follow these insights through into a simple or soundly based philosophy of substance that might still serve as a part of a sane philosophy.

At 1029ᵃ1 f., already quoted, Aristotle says 'If form is prior to matter and more real it will be prior to the compound also, for the same reason.' We have more or less allowed Aristotle, if not his exact argument, then at least the conclusion that matter is a poor candidate to furnish a substance or a this. Maybe we could also allow him the claim that, if the issue is how to arrive at a 'this', form is a better candidate than matter. But can we allow it to him that the form is prior to the compound of form and matter and therefore a better candidate than the compound for being a substance? The sense of priority that is to be understood here is a matter of debate among scholars. But it seems certain that, whatever its intended sense, it is a necessary condition of such a contention's being correct, and of Aristotle's being right to transpose his search for substance to the level of form, that hylomorphism should progress to the point where the form of Socrates should be specifiable and specifiable independently of the identification of Socrates himself (and of things that are like Socrates in being men).

Can Aristotle meet this requirement? Can Aristotle advance beyond this claim:

Socrates = the form of man in such-and-such matter?

By a pseudo-algebraic conversion, it might be suggested we can progress from this to the form of man = Socrates without (or in abstraction from) such-and-such matter.

But, even if this be held to make sense, Aristotle cannot 'solve' the equation for *form* until a value is supplied for 'such-and-such matter'. Indeed Aristotle's heightened awareness of the points mooted in the paragraph before last would have forewarned him of the extraordinary difficulty of solving it (as well as of making sense of it). To recognize the materiality of the things that he had designated primary substances in *Categories* and to think of matter as he does at *Physics* 192^{b}30–3 (already quoted) will not yet supply the equation with an independent fix upon 'such-and-such matter'. So where the specification of form is concerned, the would-be equation does not advance him beyond what he knew about the secondary substances that he spoke of in *Categories* or beyond the species (the *eidos* as Aristotle had first conceived of it). But this was something universal, multiply instantiable, and all the rest. Meanwhile, before the equation is solved for 'form', the matter of a thing can only be conceived of by abstraction from that thing. That is perfectly satisfactory for many purposes, but not for the purposes of metaphysical hylomorphism.

4.12.2. It is possible that, in defiance of Aristotle's teleological or final cause approach to biological questions, a molecular biologist might seek to supply the extra information that would be required to solve (if not to explicate) the 'equation' recently considered.

Faced with such a specification of the matter, a philosopher of substance might seek to revive and renew hylomorphism, no longer as metaphysics or metaphysical chemistry and biology—a funny business at the best of times—but as a scientific programme. He would then have to seek to adjudicate in an open-minded way the collision between biology as Aristotle conceived it in top-down fashion and the pretensions (perhaps inflated) of molecular biology to solve questions of organic development and the rest. It is unclear, however, that, transposing Aristotelian hylomorphism to this new key, a philosopher of substance ought to imitate Aristotle further in demoting 'compounds' such as Socrates or Arkle in favour of (what we might tendentiously call 'their own'!) forms or principles of biological organization. For these forms or principles are surely in principle multiply instantiable—as they are in the real-life case of twins, unless we distinguish the form of one twin from the form of the other twin by reference to the difference in the histories of the two twins. But then the primary substances or 'compounds', one twin and the other, play an indispensable part in the individuation of their forms, contrary to the claim that the forms are prior to the 'compounds'.

The questions that still remain here are at least as obscure as the question that we have postponed so often, namely that of the philosophical significance of the idea of a substance. What point is there in having a notion of substance that is more than the notion of a material body—or more than the notion of matter at a moment?

4.13. What is at Issue when we Ask whether Something is a Substance?

4.13.1. Let us find our way back to questions of this sort by considering things that have often been treated as (at best) marginal candidates for the full status of substances (have even been treated as marginal by philosophers like Aristotle who made constant use of them as examples), namely artefacts. Why should one doubt the proper substantiality of artefacts?

The grounds for doubt would run as follows: We claimed in Section 4.4.1, Section 4.5.1 (the last paragraph but one), and Section 4.10.1 that the singling-out of a thing at a time *t* reaches backwards and forwards to points arbitrarily much earlier or later than *t* at which that same thing exists. If so, then the way in which we have to conceive of kinds of artefact in singling them out will force us to think of artefacts of a given kind both *diachronically* and *by reference to the function that defines their kind*. How that function is to be conceived does not depend on something out there in nature that could further saturate our thoughts about clocks or chisels or houses or bicycles or fishing-rods. It is up to us (us collectively) how to conceive of it. Nor again is it sensible to expect there to be any such thing as the natural development of a clock by which the question of identity and persistence might be judged. In the third place, even though artefacts are themselves things out there in nature and in no way exempt from the laws of nature (indeed artefacts represent the exploitation and application of those laws), it will be silly to expect the sorts *house*, *bicycle*, or *clock* to figure in rich open-ended sets of sort–property pairs that are well-made for inductive extrapolation across the whole kinds that they determine. Contrast what was said in Section 4.5.1 about genuine substances. Indeed, being variously constructed out of various materials and working by various different mechanisms, clocks need have little in common with one another, over and above being things designed to tell the time. Even if we subdivide clocks into subvarieties, it may be hard to see that the activity of any particular clock need amount to much more than its doing what it must do to tell the time. Little else can flow from the fact that it is this or that device, deliberately designed to tell the time. Finally, if artefacts are natural substances as well as being artefacts, then artefact kinds and natural kinds will have to cross-classify substances, contrary to Aristotle's desiderata. (See the last two sentences of Section 4.4.1.)

Such might be the grounds for the doubt. The doubt rests on an undeniable difference between artefacts and the cases that we began with, where the sense of the sortal term under which we pick out an individual expands into the scientific account of things of that kind (see Section 4.9.1), where that account first clarifies what is at issue in questions of the sameness and difference of specimens of that kind and then assists in their resolution. (See Sections 4.3.3, 4.4.1 (end), 4.5.1 (end).)

It follows that there is a temptation to maintain the purity of the original conception of substance. This temptation is only strengthened by the intractability of some of the other questions in which artefacts involve us (especially questions of identity and difference). Yet the solidity, durability, and internal cohesiveness of a vast preponderance of our artefacts, some of them outlasting their makers (who certainly were substances) by millennia, would be a standing reproach to any would-be puristic ruling to the effect that artefacts stand at too great a distance from the natural continuants that furnished us with our original paradigm of substance. Indeed such a ruling would represent in at least one way an affront to the spirit of the original conception. For not only do artefacts submit to predication without being predicated, not only can they furnish us with a 'this' and furnish (in so far as we know what this means) something 'separable'. Their usefulness and effectiveness in the performance of their functions signals and celebrates the very same evolving understanding of the way ordinary perceptible things behave that made the notions of substance, of nature, and of substances with their natures so interesting and important to us in the first place.

At the outset it was suggested that the notion of a substance is the notion of something persisting, basic, endowed with a nature, something possessing claims to be recognized for a real thing which are claims on our aspiration to make practical and theoretical sense of the world. Hence the indispensability of the notion of substance to the rationalists, who expected nothing to hold true but that there be a reason for its holding true and who expected the world to conform in every particular to transparent reason as they thought they understood that. But hence too the sense of dislocation that would result from our withholding the status of substance from all artefacts. For artefacts are contrived to exploit, often by interaction with substances, that low-level, dependable, indispensable understanding in whose name we engage in the individuation and articulation of the natural substances that are Aristotle's original exemplars.

4.13.2. But do we know what we are arguing about here? It will relax the intellectual cramp that threatens if, instead of trying to decide the question whether artefacts as a class are or are not substances, we resolve to reinterpret the question and see it as a question about the *distance* at which this or that particular artefact (or this or that group of artefacts) lies from the central case, in respect of durability, internal cohesiveness, having a relatively self-contained principle of activity, and exemplifying some simple law of change.

The reader will now try asking why we do not go the whole way and allow the title of substance to any and every material body, however short-lived or gerrymandered. It is not as if some bodies exemplify better than others the fundamental physical laws of nature. All bodies are equally subject to those laws.

The question is fundamental to the philosophy of substance. And here is the place where we have to acknowledge the wide chasm that lies between our outlook and the outlook of a philosopher like Aristotle, for whom the best insight into the nature of reality was that afforded by the final causality exemplified by living things, or the outlook of a philosopher like Leibniz, for whom the ultimate reality was a mental reality of simple partless soul-like substances on which the whole physical world depended or supervened (see Leibniz's letter to De Volder, quoted in Section 4.6.1 above). One with our outlook will tend, however mindlessly, to assume an opposite dependence or a dependence of the macroscopic on the microscopic. For us, the importance of the category of substance, if it has any importance, is not so much ontological as relative to our epistemological circumstances and the conditions under which we have to undertake inquiry. These circumstances and conditions determine where we have to begin in order to find our way about, in order to designate spatial and temporal landmarks, and in order to find workable, dependable, low-grade generalizations about how identifiable classes of things come into being, persist, and behave. Objects of these kinds are special and important and important by virtue of things about the human condition that will not change. But the considerations that make them important in this way cannot help but pull apart from the question of the ultimate physical reality that is to be revealed by the forward advance of the sciences of matter. (See Sections 4.3.1 (end), 4.3.2 (beginning), 4.3.2 (end), 4.11.5 (end), 4.12.1 (beginning).)

For us then the question that is at stake when we ask what counts as a substance cannot be momentous in the way in which it is momentous for Leibniz or Aristotle. Yet in so far as we take ourselves to be substances (and continue to find a Humean idea of the self unsustainable in practice, as Hume himself did in his ethical writing), the question is not one that simply disappears. It will never disappear, even though it can only regain its full or earlier significance if we are carried by the conviction of our own substancehood to the point of reasserting *something* of the autonomy of substance. (Such a declaration, however welcome it might be to the present author, would signal rather more than a mere change in intellectual fashion.)

4.13.3. Artefacts are not the only objects that challenge reflection. In the chapter of *New Essays* succeeding the one from which we have quoted already, we find in Bennett and Remnant's translation of II. xxiv. 1:

PHILALETHES. After simple substance, let us look at collective ideas. Is not the idea of such a collection of men as make an army as much one idea as the idea of a man?

THEOPHILUS. It is right to say that this aggregate makes up a single idea, although strictly speaking such a collection of substance does not really constitute a true substance. It is something resultant, which is given its final touch of unity by the soul's thought and perception. However it can be said to be something substantial, in a way, namely as containing substances.

There are substances, we have said, that we have no choice but to recognize. Their claim is a claim on our practical and theoretical reason. Everything conspires to force them upon us if we have the slightest concern to find our way about the world or understand anything at all about how it works. We can concur with Leibniz in his conclusion (if not in his special route to that conclusion) that human beings, animals, and other continuants rank high among such things. But these are not all of the things that we can identify or single out or that enter into the ways in which we make sense of what happens in the world.

Suppose a large body of men is moving across the countryside, billeting itself upon the inhabitants and commandeering their goods and services, advancing slowly but manifestly enough in some common direction. The best way of making sense of their activities may seem to be to see these men not just as individuals pursuing their own largely rapacious concerns but as men acting in ways answerable to the centralized authority of a commander. If the army the men belong to is an impressively cohesive and disciplined instrument of political will, then it may seem almost mandatory to one who observes the soldiers to 'give the final touch to the unity' of the aggregate entity that they collectively constitute. The observer may find it almost impossible not to see in the presence of the soldiers the presence of that to which they belong—at least until such time as indiscipline or the tendencies of individual soldiers to defect or disregard authority shatter (if they do) all sense of the presence of a larger thing with its own dependable principle of activity and its own way of conducting itself. Is an army then a substance?

Similar questions will arise with the ontological and explanatory claims of other corporate entities such as states, civic associations, clubs, companies, trusts, banks, and other 'legal persons', or with cabinets, committees, boards of management, and the rest, or with clans or nations or families. There are so many things that we want to say that seem to make ineliminable reference to such things. (Another quite different set of questions arises if someone asks whether God is a substance.)

Let us distinguish here two questions. (1) Can we adequately describe reality without making mention of these things? (Can we find a recipe to translate every apparent indispensable truth about armies or nations or states into another truth that lacks such existential commitments? This will normally involve us in finding predicates coextensive with the predicates that occur in the sentences to be reduced and in other potentially troublesome tasks not to be lightly undertaken.) (2) Are the entities in question sufficiently like our paradigms of substances to count as having any claim to substantiality? Do they tend to extrude one another from a given place or can two of them be in the same place at the same time? How important is that? Are there low-grade laws about how they behave? A negative answer under (2) will not commit the answerer to any particular answer to (1). But then, pending our retreat to some of the assumptions of earlier philosophical epochs, it will not be sensible to feel that we have to find conclusive arguments here. Nor do we need to cling to those assumptions in order to hold on to Aristotle's cleverly commonsensical understanding of the relation between a subject and its various properties or qualities.

BIBLIOGRAPHY

CAUSATION

The best collection of readings on causation is: Ernest Sosa and Michael Tooley (eds.), *Causation* (Oxford, 1993), referred to below as 'Sosa and Tooley'. There is no decent introductory full-length book on causation, though David Owens, *Causes and Coincidences* (Cambridge, 1992) presents a novel theory of causation in a very readable, clear way, and contains interesting discussions of some of the theories mentioned in this chapter.

Hume's view of causation, see *A Treatise of Human Nature*, I. iv, and *An Enquiry Concerning Human Understanding*, ch. 7. A good introductory book on Hume is David Pears, *Hume's System* (Oxford, 1990). Recently, a number of writers have argued, against the standard interpretation of Hume, that Hume did think that there is a causal relation in nature: see Galen Strawson, *The Secret Connexion* (Oxford, 1989).

For arguments that regularity is not necessary for causation, see G. E. M. Anscombe, 'Causality and Determination', in Sosa and Tooley. See also C. J. Ducasse, 'On the Nature and Observability of the Causal Relation', in Sosa and Tooley.

For conditionals and the counterfactual theory see J. L. Mackie's paper 'Causes and Conditions', in Sosa and Tooley, which expounds the INUS condition view of causation. See also his paper 'A Conditional Analysis of the Concept of Causation', in Ted Honderich and Myles Burnyeat (eds.), *Philosophy as it Is* (Harmondsworth, 1979). Mackie's views are criticized by Jaegwon Kim, 'Causes and Events: Mackie on Causation', in Sosa and Tooley. The counterfactual theory is presented by David Lewis, 'Causation', in Sosa and Tooley. For the general idea of a counterfactual conditional see Lewis, *Counterfactuals* (Oxford, 1973). Lewis presents his theory of causal explanation in 'Causal Explanation', in *Philosophical Papers*, i (Oxford, 1986). Lewis's views are discussed by Jaegwon Kim, 'Causes and Counterfactuals', in Sosa and Tooley. More difficult is Jonathan Bennett, 'Event Causation: The Counterfactual Analysis', in Sosa and Tooley.

Concerning the relata of causation, Davidson's theory that causes and effects are events is outlined and defended in a classic paper: Donald Davidson, 'Causal Relations', in Sosa and Tooley. The alternative view, that causation relates facts, is argued for by D. H. Mellor, 'The Singularly Affecting Facts of Causation', in *Matters of Metaphysics* (Cambridge, 1991). Mellor's collection also contains a number of other important papers on causation, notably 'On Raising the Chances of Effects'. These are both quite difficult, but well worth the effort. For another perspective, see Jaegwon Kim, 'Causation, Nomic Subsumption and the Concept of Event', *Journal of Philosophy*, 70 (1973), 217–36, and Jonathan Bennett, *Events and their Names* (Cambridge, 1988).

TIME

An excellent collection of readings on the philosophy of time is Robin Lé Poidevin and Murray MacBeath (eds.), *The Philosophy of Time* (Oxford, 1993), referred to below as 'Le Poidevin and MacBeath'. This is well worth buying; it contains some of the essential readings on the topics dealt with in this section. Another collection, of more variable quality, which includes articles by physicists and mathematicians, is Raymond Flood and Michael Lockwood (eds.), *The Nature of Time* (Oxford, 1986). Two excellent general books on time are D. H. Mellor, *Real Time* (Cambridge, 1980) (this also contains a good bibliography); and W. Newton-Smith, *The Structure of Time* (London, 1980).

For the passage of time, the essential reading is from Le Poidevin and MacBeath. McTaggart's argument is in J. M. E. McTaggart, 'The Unreality of Time', in Le Poidevin and MacBeath. This is responded to by A. N. Prior, 'Changes in Events and Changes in Things', in Le Poidevin and MacBeath, and D. H. Mellor, *Real Time* (Cambridge, 1980), ch. 6; repr. as 'The Unreality of Tense', in Le Poidevin and MacBeath. See also Michael Dummett, 'McTaggart's Argument for the Unreality of Time', in *Truth and Other Enigmas* (London, 1978), and Robin Le Poidevin, *Change, Cause and Contradiction* (Basingstoke, 1991).

On absolute and relational conceptions of time a very readable introduction is W. Newton-Smith, 'Space, Time and Space-Time: A Philosopher's View', in Raymond Flood and Michael Lockwood (eds.), *The Nature of Time* (Oxford, 1986). Newton-Smith's book *The Structure of Time* (London, 1980) is an excellent, clear investigation of these topics. Shoemaker's argument is from Sydney Shoemaker, 'Time without Change', in Le Poidevin and MacBeath. Lawrence Sklar, *Space, Time and Spacetime* (Berkeley, Calif., 1974) is a difficult but extremely interesting account of this issue, employing many of the concepts of contemporary physics.

On the direction of time, David Lewis's argument that time travel is possible is in 'The Paradoxes of Time Travel', in Le Poidevin and MacBeath. Other essential reading is D. H. Mellor, *Real Time* (Cambridge, 1980), chs. 9 and 10, and Michael Dummett, 'Bringing about the Past', in *Truth and Other Enigmas* (London, 1978).

UNIVERSALS

Unfortunately, there is very little good introductory material on this topic, and much of the best advanced reading is buried in obscure journals. A very good introduction, from the point of view of a committed realist, is D. M. Armstrong, *Universals: An Opinionated Introduction* (Boulder, Colo., 1990). This summarizes some of the main lines of argument of Armstrong's two-volume study *Universals and Scientific Realism* (Cambridge, 1978); i: *Nominalism and Realism* is a critique of nominalism, and of the other theories which Armstrong rejects; ii: *A Theory of Universals* presents his positive account. Armstrong always writes clearly, though some of the arguments can be a little technical. A good collection of readings is M. J. Loux, *Universals and Particulars* (South Bend, Ind., 1976).

On the distinction between universals and particulars, the argument of Ramsey's mentioned in the text is in his difficult but rewarding paper 'On Universals', in *F. P. Ramsey: Philosophical Papers*, ed. D. H. Mellor (Cambridge, 1990). An excellent discussion of the nature of properties and their relation to causation is Sydney Shoemaker, 'Properties and Causality', in *Identity, Cause and Mind* (Cambridge, 1984). The relation between properties and predicates is discussed in D. H. Mellor, 'Properties and Predicates', in *Matters of Metaphysics* (Cambridge, 1991).

For the view that events are particulars, see Donald Davidson, 'Events as Particulars', in *Essays on Actions and Events* (Oxford, 1980). For the view that numbers are abstract objects, see Bob Hale, *Abstract Objects* (Oxford, 1988). For a good discussion of what 'abstract' means, see David Lewis, *The Plurality of Worlds* (Oxford, 1986), ch. 1.5. For the view that tropes, or so-called 'abstract particulars', should be considered as metaphysically fundamental, see Keith Campbell, *Abstract Particulars* (Oxford, 1986). These last three items are quite difficult reading.

Concerning nominalism, Locke's views on universals and particulars can be found in John Locke, *An Essay Concerning Human Understanding* (1690; Oxford, 1975). Various forms of nominalism are examined by Armstrong in *Nominalism and Realism* (details above). A prominent modern nominalist is Quine. See 'On What There Is', in *From a Logical Point of View* (Cambridge, Mass., 1953). See also Nelson Goodman, 'A World of Individuals', in *Problems and Projects* (Indianapolis, Ind., 1972) and David Lewis, *On the Plurality of Worlds* (Oxford, 1986), ch. 1.5.

Russell's argument against resemblance theories can be found in Bertrand Russell, *The Problems of Philosophy* (Oxford, 1912), ch. 9.

A good introduction to set theory is John Pollock, *Technical Methods in Philosophy* (Boulder, Colo., 1990).

Concerning realism, for Plato's theory of Forms, see his dialogues *Republic* and *Phaedo* in *The Collected Dialogues of Plato*, ed. E. Hamilton and H. Cairns (Princeton, NJ, 1961). Armstrong defends his realism in detail in *A Theory of Universals* (see above). Unfortunately, most of the criticisms of Armstrong are in academic journals.

SUBSTANCE

A general introduction to the idea of substance will be found in M. Ayers, *Locke*, 2 vols. (London, 1991), ii.

More Aristotelian general treatments will be found in: David Wiggins, *Sameness and Substance* (Oxford, 1980), 2nd edn. (Cambridge, 1996); G. E. L. Owen, 'Particular and General', in his *Logic, Science and Dialectic*, ed. M. Nussbaum (New York, 1985);

M. Frede, 'Substance in Aristotle's Metaphysics', in his *Essays in Ancient Philosophy* (Oxford, 1987):

These works presuppose some readiness to turn to the texts of Aristotle, especially to the first five chapters of Aristotle, *Categories*, trans. and ed. J. L. Ackrill (Oxford, 1974), and, much harder and far less indispensable, to all the chapters that are cited in 4.11.5 ff. from Aristotle's *Metaphysics*, book Z. The best and most helpful translation and commentary is in David Bostock, *Aristotle: Metaphysics Z and H: A Commentary and Translation* (Oxford, 1994).

An important Aristotelian point (alluded to in 4.10.1) about the substantives or sortal terms that stand for kinds of substance is transposed into modern idiom by P. F. Strawson, *Individuals* (London, 1959), part 2, and W. V. Quine, *Word and Object* (Cambridge, Mass., 1960), sect. 15.

The full reference to Leibniz's *New Essays* referred to and quoted in 4.7 (and elsewhere) is G. W. Leibniz, *New Essays Concerning Human Understanding*, trans. Jonathan Bennett and Peter Remnant (Cambridge, 1981).

Leibniz's 'Meditations on Knowledge, Truth and Ideas' will be found in G. W. Leibniz, *Die philosophischen Schriften*, ed. C. I. Gerhardt (Berlin, 1875–90), iv. 422–6. His essay 'On Nature itself or on the Inherent Force and Actions of Created Things' mentioned in 4.6.1 is at p. 505 of the same volume. The quotations (in 4.6.1) from Leibniz's letters to De Volder are drawn from the same text, ii. 263 and 278.

The citation from *Fourth Replies* of Descartes given in 4.6.1 will be discovered in *Œuvres de Descartes*, ed. C. Adam and P. Tannery (Paris, 1964), vii. 226.

Another text that fills out the history of the idea of substance is the first dialogue in N. Malebranche, *Dialogues on Metaphysics and on Religion*, trans. Morris Ginsberg (London, 1923).

An important article on John Locke's conception of substance is M. Ayers, 'Ideas of Power and Substance', *Philosophical Quarterly*, 25 (1975); revised for I. C. Tipton (ed.), *Locke on Human Understanding* (Oxford, 1977).

An important further article on Aristotle's theory of substance in his *Metaphysics* is by John Driscoll in Dominic O'Meara (ed.), *Studies in Aristotle* (Studies in Philosophy and in History of Philosophy, 9; Ann Arbor, Mich., 1981).

Hilary Putnam's article, mentioned in 4.9.1, 'Is Semantics Possible?', is in *Collected Papers* (Cambridge, 1975), ii.

In further pursuit of the outlook expressed by David Hume quoted in 4.2.1, the reader may wish to look at the remarks in B. A. W. Russell, *Outline of Philosophy* (London, 1927), 254–5, or to look up 'substance' in the index in B. A. W. Russell, *History of Western Philosophy* (London, 1961).

The paper by Mark Johnston cited in 4.10.1, is 'Is there a Problem about Persistence?', *Proceedings of the Aristotelian Society*, supp. vol. 61 (1987), 107–55.

5

THE PHILOSOPHY OF MIND

Martin Davies

INTRODUCTION

Philosophy of mind is, simply and roughly, the area of philosophy that deals with questions about the mind. Many of these are metaphysical and epistemological questions. Metaphysical questions about the mind include whether minds are immaterial substances, and how mental phenomena fit into the causal order. Probably the most fundamental metaphysical questions in the philosophy of mind concern the relationship between mental phenomena and physical phenomena—the mind–body problem. Epistemological questions about the mind include how we can come to have knowledge about minds other than our own, and whether we have an especially authoritative way of gaining knowledge about our own minds.

It is not very accurate to describe philosophy of mind, simply, as addressing philosophical questions about the mind, because the same could be said about philosophy of psychology. Different philosophers will vary in their views about these two parts of the subject. But we can achieve a working distinction if we say that philosophy of mind is concerned with our ordinary, everyday conception of mental phenomena, while philosophy of psychology addresses questions that arise out of the scientific study of mental phenomena (of the kind that takes place in university departments of experimental psychology). The distinction is somewhat artificial, of course, since scientific psychology imports a good deal of our everyday way of thinking about the mind, while that ordinary conception is doubtless influenced, in turn, by what psychologists discover. Nevertheless, the distinction will suffice.

Our ordinary conception of mental matters makes use of notions of thought—and more specifically of belief, desire, intention, inference, and planning—and of acting for a reason. The everyday scheme also includes ideas of experience, and more specifically of perception, sensation, emotion, and consciousness. This conceptual scheme is known as 'folk psychology'. Philosophy of mind sets out to analyse, elucidate, and interconnect folk psychological concepts, and to help us understand better our everyday ways of describing and explaining the thoughts, experiences, and actions of others and ourselves.

We have said that philosophy of mind overlaps with epistemology and metaphysics, and lies adjacent to philosophy of psychology. It also has close connections to many other areas of philosophy, including philosophy of language, ethics, and aesthetics. In contemporary work, the links with philosophy of language are particularly salient. During the 1960s and 1970s, philosophy of language occupied centre stage, and was seen as a way of approaching a wide range of traditional philosophical issues. But investigation of the key concept in philosophy of language—the concept of linguistic meaning—leads inevitably to questions about the thoughts that language is used to express, and in recent decades philosophy of mind has come to take over the dominant position in philosophical research.

Most students of philosophy find philosophy of mind more readily accessible than philosophy of language, and—unlike philosophy of language—philosophy of mind is well provided with introductory-level textbooks. A few of these books are listed at the beginning of the Bibliography. There has also been tremendous growth in the publication of anthologies in recent years, and it is now possible to have easy and cheap access to very large numbers of key articles. Some of these excellent anthologies are also listed in the Bibliography.

Philosophy of mind textbooks usually begin with the mind–body problem, and this chapter follows that same pattern. Section 1 is about the relationship between mind and body, and particularly between mind and brain. The questions addressed in that section are primarily metaphysical. Modern metaphysics of mind is mainly materialist, and for this very reason it presents us with a challenge. For it is not easy to understand how, in a wholly material world, mental states can have their characteristic properties.

Paradigm examples of mental states are beliefs and sensations. Each of these two kinds of mental state presents a problem. In the case of beliefs, our problem is to understand how beliefs can be about things. In the case of sensations, the difficulty attaches to their phenomenology.

Descartes's world-view included two different kinds of substance: space-occupying substance (matter) and thinking substance (mind). When Descartes sat in front of his fire, engaged in his meditations, his body filled some of the space in front of the fire, and his mind entertained thoughts ('I am here, sitting by the fire, wearing a winter cloak . . .'). Given that world-view, the question how it can be that minds have beliefs that are about things could seem as pointless as the question how it can be that bodies are extended in space. Thinking about things is just what minds do, as being extended in space is just what bodies do.

But, once we move to the view that minds are somehow part of the material fabric of the world, we face the question how it can be that space-occupying substance can also be the seat of thought. How does it come about that some (but not all) material goings-on in some (but not all) physical things are about other things in the world—about a fire, or a cloak? This is the question for Section 2.

The question how it is that some of the goings-on in a physical thing—namely, sensations—can have a subjective phenomenal character is, if anything, even more acute. We may accept that the physical brain is, in some way, responsible for consciousness. But how neural whirrings and grindings can give rise to phenomenology is apt to strike us as utterly mysterious. Section 3 explores this apparent mystery.

Certain neural happenings are—or, at least, compose, or constitute—beliefs and sensations. So, certain occurrences in our brains have properties such as the property of being a belief about a fire, or the property of being a sensation of warmth, as well as having neurophysiological, chemical, and ultimately physical properties. We are at home with the idea that these latter properties—material properties that are studied in the physical and biological sciences—play a role in the causal order. They make a difference to the way things turn out. It is also part of our ordinary, everyday, folk psychological scheme that mental properties make a difference. It is because I have a particular belief about something, or have a specific sensation, that I act in a certain way, a human body moves in a certain way, and the course of events is affected. But there are philosophical arguments that seem to undermine the idea that the mental aspects of a material world play a causal role in determining how the course of history continues. This is a very difficult area, and one that is the focus of much research. Section 4 provides an introduction to some of the issues.

These four sections are reasonably representative of what is standard and what is central in philosophy of mind. But there is still a great deal that is left out, and not even hinted at. A list of all that is not here would be too long; but three important further topics can be mentioned.

There is very little in this chapter about epistemological questions concerning the mind. These come in two groups. On the one hand, there are questions about the ways in which mental processes—perception, memory, learning—enable us to gain knowledge. On the other hand, there are questions about our knowledge of mental states and processes themselves. This second group divides further into questions about our knowledge of other people's minds, and questions about our—apparently special—way of knowing our own mind.

There is not much here about the nature of folk psychology. We have an ability to describe, explain, and predict what people experience, and think, and do. We engage in a practice that draws upon our folk psychological conceptions. But, when we reflect upon our folk psychological practice, it is not immediately obvious what kind of thing the basis of the ability is. Many philosophers argue that our ability is grounded in knowledge of a common-sense empirical theory about experiences, beliefs, and actions—about how they come about, and what their typical consequences are. But the issue is controversial, and there is a good deal of support for an alternative view that says that our understanding of other people depends fundamentally upon a capacity to identify with them in imagination.

This philosophical debate about the nature of folk psychology is paralleled by a debate in developmental psychology about the way in which children come to understand the mental lives of others. In both philosophy and psychology, a good deal of the work has taken off from research into the emotions. That is a third area about which this guide is silent. Yet, no account of our mental lives could be complete so long as it ignored our emotions. And the topic is vital when we come to link philosophy of mind to questions in ethics and aesthetics.

Introductory reading on these three further topics is included at the end of the Bibliography. Otherwise, the Bibliography is arranged into sections and subsections corresponding to those in the body of the chapter. For each subsection, a handful of pieces of core reading are suggested, along with a longer list of further reading. The division into core reading and further reading does not correspond to any deep distinction in reality. The core readings are generally heavily cited in the body of the guide, but many alternative routes through the territory, relying on different readings, are possible.

1. MIND AND BRAIN

What place do minds have in the real world? At one extreme is the answer that minds are real things of a fundamentally different kind from material objects, and that mental properties and mental states are, properly speaking, properties and states of these immaterial things. On this view (called *dualism*), some material bodies, such as human beings, are—to say the least—closely associated with minds, and a person is a kind of composite of a material thing and an immaterial thing. At the other extreme is the answer that there are no such things as minds, and that talk of distinctively mental properties and mental states cannot figure in a fully serious account (sometimes equated with a scientific account) of the natural world. On this view (called *eliminativism*), the world is made up of material things that have physical properties—such as the property of having a mass of five kilograms—and are in physical states—such as the state of being at a temperature of 15°C; and all that is really real can be explained in these terms. Mental properties and states are eliminated from the category of what is really real because, and to the extent that, they cannot be identified with physical properties and physical states.

Between these two extremes are views that say that talk of mental properties and mental states is in good standing, but that it is material things, such as human beings, that are the bearers of these mental properties and states. Such intermediate views disagree with the first extreme answer, because they deny the need for persons to be partly composed of immaterial things. And they disagree with the second extreme answer, because they allow talk of mental properties and states to be taken at face value. In fact, there are two different ways in which an intermediate view might disagree with that second extreme view. It might agree with eliminativism that only physical properties and states are really real, but hold that mental states and properties can be identified with physical counterparts. Intermediate views of this first kind are called *reductionist* views of the mental domain. (We consider some of the ways in which a view can be reductionist in Section 1.5.) Alternatively, it might reject altogether the insistence that mental properties and mental states should be identified with physical properties and physical states. Intermediate views of this second kind are called *anti-reductionist* views.

These various views about the metaphysical status of minds and mental properties and states are the subject-matter for this section. Recent and contemporary work in the philosophy of mind is, for the most part, broadly materialist in its background assumptions; so it rejects dualism. But it does not—again, for the most part—go as far as eliminativism. (For an introduction, see Churchland 1988, ch. 2; Fodor 1981.)

1.1. Dualism

Dualism is primarily associated with Descartes: hence *Cartesian dualism*. In his *Second Meditation*, Descartes finds the 'fixed and immovable point' that his method of doubt has led him to seek—the point at which sceptical doubt must cease. The proposition about which he can be certain is 'I am' or 'I exist': since 'whenever I utter it or conceive it in my mind, it is necessarily true'.

This statement of necessity should not be misunderstood. Descartes is not saying that this *I* enjoys necessary existence in the way that, perhaps, abstract objects like numbers do, or in the way that God does. Descartes's point is, rather, that even the mental act of doubting the proposition 'I exist' already guarantees its truth. Indeed, any kind of thinking—whether it be doubting, or wondering, or affirming—guarantees the truth of this proposition; and this realization is summarized in Descartes's famous statement in the *Discourse on the Method*: *cogito ergo sum*—'I am thinking, therefore I exist'. (For a detailed discussion of this statement, addressing the questions whether it is really an inference—as the word 'therefore' certainly suggests—and whether Descartes is entitled to the claim 'I am thinking' rather than the apparently weaker claim 'There is thinking going on', see Williams 1978, ch. 3.)

Descartes then inquires about the nature of this *I*, of whose existence he can be certain. The *I* is not to be identified with a body. Rather, he says, ' "I am" precisely taken refers only to a conscious being.' 'What then am I? A thing that thinks.' Descartes thus distinguishes two kinds of thing in the world. There are bodies, or material things, whose essence is to be extended in space. And there are minds, which are immaterial things, whose essence is thinking. (Here again, we are setting aside many issues of exegesis and evaluation, including the fact that a fuller account of the 'real distinction' between mind and body occurs in the *Sixth Meditation*.)

The question that arises for Descartes is this: What is the relation between the mind and the body that jointly make up what we ordinarily regard as a person? There is one dualist view about the relation of mind and body which is very familiar: it might be called *popular dualism*. According to this view, the body is a kind of container, and the mind, or soul, is located inside this container; somewhat as a piece of priceless jewellery may be located inside a box made of cardboard and velvet. This popular dualism is different from Descartes's dualism (see Churchland 1988: 8–9 for this distinction). Descartes explicitly rejected, for example, the idea that the mind is present in the body 'as a pilot is present in a ship'.

According to Cartesian dualism, it cannot be literally correct to say that the mind is within the body, because minds do not have spatial properties. The properties of spatial position, shape, and size belong to matter, and not to mind. But when he is talking about the phenomenology of embodiment—the way we experience the states of our body—Descartes sometimes speaks of the mind being 'mixed up with' the body. (For detailed examination of Descartes's account of the relationship between mind and body, see Williams 1978, ch. 10; Coady 1983.)

For Descartes, talk about minds is not just talk about the mental aspects of material things. Minds are things in their own right; things that can be counted: there is a difference, for example, between one mind and two qualitatively similar minds. Cartesian dualism is, thus, a kind of *substance dualism*. (There is a distinction between substance (or substantial) dualism and property (or attributive) dualism. The property dualist accepts that there is no immaterial substance, but maintains that mental properties are still importantly different from, and cannot be fully explained in terms of, physical properties. See Churchland 1988: 10; Williams 1978: 293.)

In his paper 'Self, Mind and Body' (1974a), Strawson describes Cartesian dualism as giving 'a persuasive and lastingly influential form to one of those fundamental misconceptions to which the human intellect is prone when it concerns itself with the ultimate categories of thought' (p. 169). Strawson does not rehearse the kinds of arguments against dualism that we find, for example, in Churchland's book (1988, ch. 2). His argument is, perhaps, more purely philosophical or more theoretical.

In the early part of the article, Strawson sketches a first objection. This objection is that a Cartesian is committed to saying that a predication of a person—say, 'Susan is writing a letter'—can (in principle) be analysed into two parts. One part would be a statement about a body and its occupancy of space; the other part would be a statement about a mind and its thinking processes. This is an objection because it is so implausible that the analysis can actually be carried out. But, it is an objection that a Cartesian might resist, since it is possible to claim that there are good reasons why our actual language does not have the resources that the analysis would need.

The objection that Strawson thinks is more telling shifts the focus from predicate to subject: it concerns the concept of an individual mind. To say that minds are countable objects is to say that, where minds are concerned, there is a difference between numerical and merely qualitative identity (between one mind and two qualitatively similar minds, between the same mind again and another one just like it). The Cartesian must give an account of the concept of *a* mind—of the difference between one mind and two—without resting the account upon the difference between one person and two, since according to the Cartesian it is the concept of a mind that is more fundamental than the concept of a person (rather than, as Strawson would urge, the other way around). This is an objection because, Strawson says, 'there is not the slightest reason for thinking that this can be done' (p. 175).

In Strawson's terms, Cartesian dualism says that a person is really composed of two one-sided things, whereas his own view is that a person is one two-sided thing. According to Strawson, our concept of a person is primitively the concept of a thing that has properties of two kinds: physical, or material, properties and mental, or psychological, properties. (For more details, see Strawson 1959, ch. 3; and for a general introduction to his anti-reductionist approach, see Strawson 1992.)

Although there are philosophers who defend substance dualism (e.g. Foster 1991), it is certainly very far from being the dominant view in recent and contemporary philosophy of mind. Set against Cartesian dualism there are the broadly materialist alternatives. There are those who retain a measure of property dualism and say, with Strawson, that a person is one two-sided thing. And there are those with more reductionist aspirations who maintain that a person is really just one one-sided thing.

1.2. Behaviourism

The first of these materialist alternatives to Cartesian dualism is *analytical behaviourism*. This is a doctrine about the meaning of our mental discourse. The behaviourist aims to avoid a commitment to two kinds of substance by analysing or translating talk about emotions, sensations, beliefs, desires, hopes, wishes, and the rest into complex talk about patterns of behaviour. The basic idea is that any mental predication—such as 'x is in pain', or 'x is in love', or 'x wants a CD player', or 'x believes that the ice is thin'—is to be analysed as a bundle of hypothetical or conditional ('if . . . then . . .') statements about how x would behave in various circumstances.

To the extent that the project is to analyse all mental talk in behavioural terms, the conditional statements about behaviour should not themselves make any ineliminable use of the mental terms that are being analysed. If those mental terms were used in the conditional statements, then the putative analysis would be straightforwardly circular. Indeed, if the aim is to analyse mental talk in other terms—to provide a reduction of mental properties—then mental notions should not intrude at all into the conditional statements. Both the description of the circumstances ('if . . .') and the description of the behaviour ('then . . .') should be couched in terms of physical properties (size, shape, mass, velocity, and so on) of material objects. In particular, the behaviour should be described in terms of the trajectory carved out by a person's body.

Now, analytical behaviourism is usually associated with Ryle (1949), but as Hornsby (1986: 99) points out, Ryle does not impose a stringent reductionist standard upon himself. He says, for example:

> to believe that the ice is dangerously thin is to be unhesitant in telling oneself and others that it is thin, in acquiescing in other people's assertions to that effect, in objecting to statements to the contrary, in drawing consequences from the original proposition, and so forth. But it is also to be prone to skate warily, to shudder, to dwell in imagination on possible disasters and to warn other skaters. (Ryle 1949: 129)

Terms like 'acquiesce in other people's assertions' and 'dwell in imagination on possible disasters' are, on the face of it, mental terms much like 'wants' or 'thinks'; they are terms that an analytical behaviourist should not use in an analysis of 'believes that the ice is dangerously thin'. Perhaps we can suppose that these mental terms could be replaced by behavioural terms in further steps of analysis. But, even so, it is still clear that Ryle does not attempt to characterize the behaviour of someone who believes that the ice is thin in terms of specific bodily movements or trajectories. Skating warily is, we may suppose, an observable and recognizable kind of behaviour, but it is not one that can be defined trajectorially.

Talk about being in pain, or in love, wanting a CD player, or believing that the ice is thin might initially be regarded as talk about mental states that lie hidden behind observable bodily behaviour. Ryle analyses this talk as being about the observable behaviour instead. The kind of analysis that Ryle proposes would be enough to show that mental talk does not have to be construed as being about states of an immaterial mind. But it does not show that we could do without mental terms altogether, in our descriptions of behaviour. We can say that Ryle's view is a form of analytical behaviourism. But it is not a fully reductionist view in the way that a proposal to analyse mental talk in trajectorial terms would be.

In any case, there are several problems with analytical behaviourism, whether or not it is of the boldly reductionist variety. One objection is that behaviourism does not give an adequate account of the causal roles of mental properties and mental states. Behaviourism can (at least partially) reconstruct the idea of a mental state being operative in the production of a piece of behaviour. This can be done by following the lines of an account of a disposition—fragility, say—being operative in a vase's breaking in certain circumstances. So, suppose that the presence of a particular belief is analysed in terms of a conditional statement saying that if certain circumstances obtain then such-and-such behaviour is produced. Then we might say that the belief is operative if the specified circumstances do indeed obtain and the behaviour is forthcoming. But it is not so clear how analytical behaviourism can allow for the idea of one mental state causing, or causally interacting with, another one.

However, the most important objection to analytical behaviourism is that there is a reason of principle why we cannot avoid having to reintroduce terms for mental states into the analysis. Behaviour is explained in terms of beliefs and desires. People act on the basis of what they want and what they believe. Bruce walked across the room, for example, because he wanted a cookie and he believed that there were cookies on the other side of the room. So, if we were to attempt an analysis of the mental predication 'x believes that there are cookies on the other side of the room' in terms of behaviour, it would not be a surprise to find that we had to reintroduce mental terms—something about what x desires—into the analysis.

We might even elevate this insight into why analytical behaviourism must be wrong into a general requirement on the description of any creature or system as having beliefs. We might say that attributions of beliefs cannot be correct if they merely summarize the creature's or system's dispositions to behave in various ways in various circumstances.

1.3. Central State Materialism

The second materialist proposal to be considered is *central state materialism* (sometimes known as the *identity theory*). Central state materialism focuses upon inner states that produce behaviour, rather than just upon the behaviour itself. It aims to identify mental states and processes with physical states and processes of the brain and central nervous system.

In an early presentation of this theory, Place (1956) accepts the idea of an analysis of talk about beliefs, desires, and the like (the *propositional attitudes*; see below, Section 2.1.1) in terms of dispositions to behaviour, but rejects behaviourism for sensations and other conscious experiences: 'there would seem to be an intractable residue of concepts clustering around the notions of consciousness, experience, sensation, and mental imagery, where some sort of inner process story is unavoidable' (1956/1990: 30).

Analytical behaviourism is a semantic thesis—a thesis about the meaning of mental discourse. So, Place anticipates an objection to his proposal; namely, the objection that talk about consciousness and sensations is not equivalent in meaning to talk about brain processes. In response to this anticipated objection, Place says that his thesis is not a semantic one. Consciousness is to be identified with a brain process in the same way that a cloud is identified with a mass of tiny particles in suspension, or lightning is identified with a certain kind of electrical discharge, or temperature with the mean kinetic energy of molecules.

The central state materialist theory is further developed and defended by

Smart (1959), who criticizes Ryle for seeming to hold that hypothetical ('if . . . then . . .') statements can 'float in free air'. Rather, says Smart (1994: 19): 'They need a categorical, or relatively more categorical, basis.' The idea here is that, if it is true of some system that *if* it is in certain circumstances *then* it behaves in such-and-such a way, then there should be something about the inner constitution of the system in virtue of which this is true of it. This motivation for dissatisfaction with behaviourism extends beyond talk of sensations to talk of beliefs and desires too. Smart would identify beliefs and desires, as well as sensations and experiences, with brain states or processes. As a result, Smart would be in a better position than the analytical behaviourist to give an account of the causal roles of mental states, including their causal interactions with each other.

Advocates of central state materialism have good replies to many of the objections that have been launched against their theory. (See Churchland 1988: 29–34 for a review.) But there is an objection that remains problematic. In order to consider this objection, we first need to note the distinction between *type–type identity theories* and *token–token identity theories*.

Central state materialism is sometimes called the type–type identity theory because a type of mental state (say, pain, whether it be in you or in me, now or tomorrow) is identified with a type of physical state (in this well-worn example, with the firing of c-fibres). Type–type identity theories are contrasted with token–token identity theories. Suppose that my pain right now (a token of the type pain) is identified with a particular physical occurrence in me (a token of some physical type), and that your pain tomorrow is identified with a particular physical occurrence in you. My pain today and your pain tomorrow are two tokens of the same mental type: they are both instances of pain. But the physical occurrence in me today and the physical occurrence in you tomorrow might be tokens of the same physical type (for example, c-fibre-firing) or of quite different physical types. If it turns out that the physical occurrences are of different types, then we still have a case of token–token identity (since each token of a mental type is identified with a token of some physical type or other). But we do not have a case of type–type identity (since different tokens of the same mental type are identified with tokens of different physical types).

The objection against central state materialism is that it seems to be guilty of a kind of chauvinism. If—to continue with the well-worn example—being in pain is simply identified with having one's c-fibres firing, then any being that lacks c-fibres is automatically classified as a being that does not experience pain. Similarly, any creature or machine whose material constitution is sufficiently different from that of a human being is automatically classified as a system that does not have beliefs, desires, or any other mental states. The third materialist proposal that we shall consider—functionalism—is less open to this charge of chauvinism.

Before we move on, however, it will be useful to note a response that an analytical behaviourist might make to central state materialism. By doing so, we can prepare a little for the topic of Section 2.2, below. The analytical behaviourist could say that, even if we accept the idea that dispositions require a categorical basis, the identification of belief states—such as the state of believing that the ice is thin—with brain states or processes goes beyond what is strictly required by that idea. According to analytical behaviourism, a belief attribution ('*x* believes that . . .') is to be analysed into a bundle of hypothetical statements about behaviour in various circumstances. If many belief attributions are true of a person, then very many hypothetical statements are likewise true of that person. Now, suppose it is agreed that it must be in virtue of the inner constitution of the person that those hypothetical statements are all true. Their truth is supported—it is plausible to suppose—by the processes going on in the person's brain. Still, the analytical behaviourist may say, it is far from obvious that those brain processes must be able to be segmented, or partitioned, in a way that maps neatly on to the description of the person in terms of beliefs. The idea about categorical bases for dispositions does not guarantee that there should be a single brain state or process that underpins precisely the dispositions that are in the bundle associated with a single belief attribution.

From this point of view, the central state materialist's claim has the status of a bold hypothesis, going significantly beyond what is strictly required. The analytical behaviourist could offer a less committed alternative by saying that belief attributions are analysed in terms of behavioural dispositions, and that these dispositions depend—taken together—upon the overall state of the person's brain.

The analytical behaviourist's proposal is more cautious than central state materialism, but it is open to serious objections of its own, since it retains the unattainable commitment to an analysis of belief attributions in behavioural terms. But there is an even more modest alternative to central state materialism that is still broadly behaviouristic, but abandons any analytical ambitions. This alternative would say, merely, that belief attributions are answerable to the facts about a person's behaviour in various circumstances, in such a way that different belief attributions require differences in the person's actual behaviour or dispositions to behaviour in other, non-actual, circumstances. Furthermore, these behavioural dispositions depend upon the person's brain processes, and talk about the causal roles of mental states is ultimately to be cashed out in terms of the causal powers of brain states and processes. This alternative moves us in the direction of an account of belief attributions given by Dennett (e.g. 1987), which we shall discuss in Section 2.2.

1.4. Functionalism

According to *functionalism*, a type of mental state is defined by a causal role. This causal role has three components: it involves causal relations between the state and inputs from the environment, causal relations between the state and behavioural outputs, and causal relations between the state and other mental states. (It is in this third component of the causal role that functionalism differs sharply from behaviourism.)

The basic idea, then, is that what is crucial if a state is to be a pain state, for example, is not the particular physical nature of the state, but rather the role that the state plays. This is how functionalism avoids the charge of chauvinism that is made against central state materialism. Firing of c-fibres plays a certain causal role in you; but a quite different physical state might play that same role in another creature (a Martian, say). You are in pain because you are in a state (c-fibres firing, as it happens) which plays a certain kind of role in you, and in other creatures of your type. The Martian is in pain because she, too, is in a state which plays that same role in her and in other creatures of her type. In you and in the Martian, the same *role* is being played by different *realizers*. (Strictly speaking, functionalism need not be regarded as a materialist alternative to dualism, since, in principle, causal roles might be realized by non-physical states of an immaterial system. However, we shall restrict attention to the physical case here.)

Functionalism does not say, merely, that it is an important fact about mental states that they have causal roles—that they are causally related to inputs, to outputs, and to other mental states. Functionalism makes the much stronger claim that mental states can be defined, or specified, or individuated, by way of their causal roles. This is explained formally and very precisely by Lewis (1970, 1972; for helpful exposition and background, see Block 1980).

Suppose that we have a theory, *T*, that talks about various mental states—pain, seeing red, believing that the ice is thin, wanting a CD player—and about their causal relations to each other and to inputs and outputs. This theory can be thought of as one very lengthy statement, containing a large number of mental terms, along with terms describing sensory inputs and behavioural outputs, and terms describing causal relations. The theory will also contain plenty of logical words and phrases like 'and', 'not', 'if . . . then . . .', and 'for all'.

For present purposes, we can regard the mental terms used in the theory as names of mental states; and we can suppose that the theory makes use of some number *n* of these mental terms. If we remove those specific terms and replace them with *n* place-holders—$X_1, ..., X_n$—then we arrive at an expression—$T(X_1, ..., X_n)$—that still contains logical words, plus terms for inputs and outputs, and causal relations. But $T(X_1, ..., X_n)$ no longer contains any mental terms. If 'pain' was the first mental term on the list, then where T said that a blow on the thumb from a hammer causes pain, $T(X_1, ..., X_n)$ says that a blow on the thumb from a hammer causes X_1. This is the beginning of a specification of a causal role (the pain role), with 'X_1' marking the place for the name of a realizer of the role. $T(X_1, ..., X_n)$, taken as a whole, simultaneously specifies n interlocking causal roles. For any person, creature, or other physical system of which the theory T is true, there will be n physical states that realize those n causal roles. That is to say that the statement:

$$(\exists x_1) ... (\exists x_n)\ T(x_1, ..., x_n)$$

will be true. (The change from upper case 'X' to lower case 'x' signals a change from place-holders to quantified variables, but is not important for the present exposition. This existentially quantified statement is called the *Ramsey sentence* of the theory T.) If we consider a human being, then it will be c-fibre-firing that realizes the first causal role (corresponding to the position marked by X_1).

If the theory T says relatively little about the causal relations in which mental states are involved, then correspondingly few constraints will be placed upon the causal roles that are specified. So, it will be relatively easy for a state to fill each of those roles. In that case, it will be likely that a state could fill the first causal role, say, without really being pain. And so, it will be implausible to hold that pain can be defined, or individuated, in terms of that causal role.

On the other hand, if T is a rich theory that says a lot about the ways in which mental states are related to each other and to inputs and outputs, then it may be reasonable to suppose that—for any person, creature, or other system to which the theory applies—there will be only one sequence $\langle R_1, ..., R_n \rangle$ of states that realize the n causal roles that T specifies.

The claim of functionalism is that there is a rich enough mental theory, T, so that if any person or other physical system is in a state that realizes, say, the first causal role, then that is sufficient for the person or system to be in pain—and so on, for the other $(n-1)$ mental terms.

Recall that analytical behaviourism is a semantic doctrine; it is a thesis about the meaning of mental discourse. Central state materialism, in contrast, is not a thesis about meaning. It is not part of the meaning of the word 'pain' that pain is c-fibre-firing, any more than it is part of the meaning of the word 'lightning' that lightning is a kind of electrical discharge. Now, functionalism does not tell us what the realizers of the mental state roles are. It does not tell us that c-fibre-firing realizes the pain role. It simply tells us that a state's realizing the pain role is enough for the state to be a pain state for the system in question. So, it may not be immediately obvious whether or not functionalism is intended as a doctrine about the meanings of mental terms.

In fact, there is a distinction to be drawn between two kinds of functionalism, depending upon the kind of theory from which we begin. Lewis invites us to begin from a common-sense theory:

Collect all the platitudes you can think of regarding the causal relations of mental states, sensory stimuli, and motor responses. . . . Include only platitudes which are common knowledge among us . . . For the meanings of our words are common knowledge, and I am going to claim that names of mental states derive their meaning from these platitudes. (1972/1991: 207–8)

So, Lewis's version of functionalism is a doctrine about the meaning of mental terms. To that extent (and only to that extent) Lewis's functionalism resembles analytical behaviourism. Alternatively, a functionalist could begin from a more scientific theory about mental states and their causal relations. Such a theory would not be a matter of common knowledge, and the functionalist analyses of mental terms generated from this starting-point would have the status of 'substantive scientific hypotheses' (Block 1978/1991: 213).

According to functionalism—whether of the more analytic, or the more scientific, variety—what all pains inevitably have in common is not something physical, but something specified by a role—something functional. To the extent that a mental state type is not identified with a physical state type, functionalism is not a type–type identity theory. On the other hand, to the extent that the realizers of mental state roles are always physical, functionalism is committed to token–token identity (between mental and physical occurrences). But—at least according to some functionalists—it under-describes functionalism to say simply that functionalism is a token–token, rather than a type–type, identity theory.

The idea here is that functionalism does envisage that there is something physical in common between my pain today and my pain yesterday, and between my pain and your pain, even though it is allowed that you and I might not share this physical commonality with all other creatures who experience pain. So, there is a kind of type–type claim in the offing, though it is a relativized one. Pain (the type) is c-fibre-firing (the type) in humans. The state (type) that realizes in humans the pain role specified by theory *T* is c-fibre-firing.

But the realizer state, even considered as a type, must be distinguished from the role state or functional state (Jackson and Pettit 1988). Pain, in humans, is c-fibre-firing. But *being in pain* is a property that can, in principle, apply to humans, and to other creatures and systems that lack c-fibres. So, being in pain is not the property of having one's c-fibres firing:

$$\lambda y(y \text{ has c-fibres firing}).$$

(The 'λy' notation is used to form a description of a property. Here, it is the property that any object *y* has when *y* has its c-fibres firing.) Rather, being in pain is the more complex property of being in whatever physical state it is that realizes the first of the n causal roles that are simultaneously specified by $T(X_1, ..., X_n)$. It is the property formally represented:

$$\lambda y[(\exists x_1) ... (\exists x_n)\,(T(x_1, ..., x_n)\ \&\ y\text{ has }x_1)].$$

(Here the 'λy' notation is used to form a description of the property that any object y has when there are n realizer states that play the n causal roles that are specified by $T(X_1, ..., X_n)$, and y is in the first of those states.)

This property is specified without any use of mental terms. All the mental terms originally occurring in the theory T have been replaced by quantified variables. In this way, functionalism is reductionist. But, functionalism does not equate the mental property of being in pain with any physical (neurophysiological) property like having c-fibres firing. Rather, the mental property is equated with a property that is specified by way of quantification over physical (neurophysiological) properties or states. For this reason, functionalism is sometimes said to offer a *second-order reduction* of mental terms.

Whereas central state materialism seems to be guilty of a kind of chauvinism, functionalism faces the opposite problem. It is too liberal. It seems to be possible to make up examples in which the causal roles that are supposed to be characteristic of mental states are being played, yet where, intuitively, we would say that there is no mental life. Theories about mental states and their causal relations—whether the theories be scientific or platitudinous—do not seem to say enough to afford an implicit definition of those mental states (Block 1978; McDowell 1985; Pettit 1986).

If functionalism, with its relatively modest reductive ambitions, falls short of capturing the mental aspects of reality, then that would encourage the thought that an explicitly non-reductive theory should be considered. We turn to such a theory next. But before moving on, we should note that there is an importantly different kind of functionalist theory in the literature.

Putnam (1967) advances the hypothesis that mental states are functional states, where the example of a functional state is one of the states specified in the machine table of a Turing machine. For present purposes the details do not matter. It is enough that a Turing machine is abstractly defined by a table that specifies, for each state of the machine and each permissible input, an output and a state (the next state of the machine). So, a typical entry in a machine table will say: If the machine is in state S and receives input I, it gives output O, and goes into state S' (see again Block 1980).

Strictly speaking, a machine table says nothing about causation. It does not say that the input plus the machine state causes the output, nor that the input causes the change in the machine state from S to S'. But, even if the idea is interpreted causally, still Putnam's version of functionalism offers a poorer account of the causal relations amongst mental states than Lewis's version provides. A Turing machine is in only one state at any given time; so a state of a Turing machine is not analogous to a mental state such as being in pain or believing that the ice is thin. Rather, a machine state would have to be analogous to a person's total mental 'set' at a given time. So, this version of functionalism can allow for causal relations between earlier and later mental 'sets', but it cannot offer an account of causal relations amongst the mental states that a person has at a given time (Block and Fodor 1972).

1.5. Interlude: Reductionist and Non-reductionist Materialism

The broadly materialist views of the mind that we have considered so far have all been reductionist views, though in varying ways. Analytical behaviourism is reductionist, in that it seeks to analyse mental talk in other terms. Mental properties are to be identified with (dispositional) behavioural properties. We noted, however, that behaviourists vary in the kinds of descriptions of behaviour that they regard as admissible. The most boldly reductionist behaviourists would insist that behaviour should, in principle, be described in trajectorial terms. Central state materialism does not make an analytical claim (a claim about meaning), but it is reductionist in that it proposes simply to identify mental states and processes with physical (specifically, neurophysiological) states and processes. Functionalism is reductionist, though here again we need to distinguish varieties. Lewis's functionalism is a kind of analytical reductionism, since mental talk is to be analysed in other terms. Mental properties are to be identified with second-order physical properties (role properties), and relative to a given species a mental property will be realized by a physical property. Block's functionalism does not make an analytical claim, but it proposes similar property identifications. (Putnam's (1967) functionalism is also reductionist to the extent that it proposes to identify mental states with states of computing-machines whose overall organization is specified by a machine table.)

But a broadly materialist view of the mind might not postulate any correspondences at all between types of mental occurrence and types of physical occurrence (see Charles and Lennon 1992). It might not even postulate correspondences between mental types and functional types (types that have a second-order definition in physical terms). It could claim that every particular mental occurrence is to be identified with a particular physical occurrence, without making any claim about what the physical occurrences identified with occurrences of a certain mental type may have in common. In short, a broadly materialist view of the mind might make token–token identity claims, but not type–type identity claims.

Any view that includes the (token–token identity) claim that every mental occurrence, or event, is also a physical occurrence (event) is a *monist* view about events. In contrast, any view that includes the claim that mental events are distinct from physical events is a dualist view about events. (Event dualism is not the same as Cartesian dualism, since both mental and physical events might involve only material substances.)

1.6. Anomalous Monism

The fourth materialist alternative to Cartesian dualism is a particular kind of monist view about events. *Anomalous monism* (Davidson 1970, 1974a, 1993) says that, while every mental event is also a physical event (monism), still there are no strict laws connecting the mental and physical domains (no strict *psychophysical* laws).

One component of this position is the claim that 'there are no strict deterministic laws on the basis of which mental events can be predicted and explained' (Davidson 1970/1991: 248; Davidson calls this 'the anomalism of the mental'). This claim is intended to apply to beliefs, desires, and intentions, and in general to the class of mental states called propositional attitudes (see Section 2.1.1 below). It is not meant to apply to sensations, such as pains. It has the consequence that there are no strict correlations between mental types of event (specifically, propositional attitude types) and physical types of event. In order to draw out this consequence, we need to make use of the assumption that there are strict laws governing physical events, on the basis of which physical events could, in principle, be predicted and explained.

Suppose, then, that there were strict correlations between mental types of event and physical types of event. They might be either strict laws linking mental events and physical events, or else reductive analyses of mental occurrences in physical terms. In either case, it would appear that these correlations could be put together with strict physical laws and would yield equally strict derived laws about mental events. But that would contradict the claim about the anomalism of the mental. So, we can conclude that, if the anomalism claim is correct, then there are no psychophysical laws, and there is no prospect of a physicalist reduction of mental terms.

Since Davidson's position is materialist, but does not aim at any identification of mental properties with physical properties, nor any analysis of mental talk in other terms, it is a form of non-reductionist materialism. But our brief exposition so far has actually reversed the order of Davidson's own argument in favour of the position. Davidson (1970) moves from the claim that there are no psychophysical laws to the claim that every mental event is also a physical event.

The first step in Davidson's argument is to substantiate the claim that there are no psychophysical laws. While it is very difficult to give a fully accurate account and evaluation of this first step, the key idea is clear enough. It is that the two domains—the mental and the physical—are subject to such different overarching constraints that there cannot be strict connections between them.

In the case of the physical domain, Davidson gives the principle of transitivity for length, as an example of an overarching constraint (a 'constitutive element' in a physical theory). Any assignment of lengths to physical objects is subject to this principle (which says that if x is longer than y and y is longer than z then x is longer than z); the principle is part of what keeps the concept of length in place. In the case of the mental domain—the domain of beliefs, desires, intentions, and other propositional attitudes—the crucial overarching constraint is 'the constitutive ideal of rationality' (1970/1991: 254). Any assignment of propositional attitudes to a thinking subject must make the subject out to be fairly coherent, consistent, and cogent: 'To the extent that we fail to discover a coherent and plausible pattern in the attitudes and actions of others we simply forgo the chance of treating them as persons' (p. 253). The difference between the kinds of constitutive principle that are operative in the two domains is at the heart of Davidson's argument against there being any strict psychophysical laws.

Suppose that we accept the first step in Davidson's argument, and that we consider a particular mental event that stands in a causal relation to a particular physical event. The mental event e_m might be the cause or the effect of the physical event e_p; let us suppose that it is the cause. So, e_m caused e_p. Now, Davidson invokes a principle ('the principle of the nomological character of causation') which says that every instance of a causal relation—such as that between e_m and e_p—must be subsumed by a strict law.

Given that principle, there must be some property, G, of e_m and some property, H, of e_p such that there is a strict law connecting G-events with H-events. If G were to be a mental property of the mental event e_m, then this would be a psychophysical law. But, by the first step in the argument, there are no psychophysical laws; and, in fact, it is widely agreed that it is only in physics that strict laws are to be found. Thus, the strict law must be a physical law, and the properties G and H must both be physical properties. So e_m, since it has physical properties, turns out to be a physical event. Since there was nothing special about e_m, save that it was assumed to stand in some causal relation to a physical event, every mental event meeting that condition is also a physical event. And, since it is implausible that any mental event is completely causally isolated from all physical events, it is plausible that every mental event is a physical event.

This, in outline, is how Davidson argues from there being no psychophysical laws to event monism. In order to complete the picture, we need to see where the anomalism of the mental fits in. The argument for the anomalism claim is this. If there were strict laws allowing the explanation and prediction of mental events, then they could either be psychophysical laws or else purely psychological laws. But, there are no strict psychophysical laws. And purely physical goings-on intrude upon the mental domain to such an extent that it is extremely implausible that there are any strict purely psychological laws. If there are any psychological laws at all, then they will not be strict; they will contain *ceteris paribus* ('all else being equal') clauses. Similarly, if there are any psychophysical laws, then they will be *ceteris paribus* laws (that is, laws containing *ceteris paribus* clauses).

(The introduction of the notion of non-strict laws leads to important and difficult questions that we must leave aside here. Davidson (1970) contrasted strict laws with 'rules of thumb', but more recently (1993) he explicitly allows for laws that are not strict. It is then interesting to ask whether the differences between the ideal of rationality and such principles as the transitivity of 'longer than' would license the stronger conclusion that there are no psychophysical laws at all—whether strict or otherwise—or only the weaker conclusion that there are no strict psychophysical laws. Davidson (1993) only claims the weaker conclusion, but this leaves a question whether the resulting position is properly described as non-reductionist. It is fairly widely agreed that the laws in special sciences (that is, in sciences other than the presumably fundamental science of physics) are always *ceteris paribus* laws. The commonly cited examples of intertheoretic reduction involve pairs of theories that do not both fall within the boundaries of fundamental physics. So, in these examples there will be no strict interlevel laws. But if the standard examples of reductionism do not involve strict laws, then the absence of strict laws connecting the mental and physical domains does not so obviously conflict with psychophysical reductionism (see Kim 1993).)

Given our sketch of the argument for anomalous monism, we can consider two kinds of query that could be raised. On the one hand, queries might be raised about the first step of the argument, leading to the interim conclusion that there are no psychophysical laws. On the other hand, queries might be raised about the continuation of the argument, leading to the final conclusion that mental events are physical events.

So far as the first step goes, we have already said that it is difficult to provide an accurate account and evaluation. We would need to explore the constitutive ideal of rationality in great detail, and also to examine the similarities and differences between that ideal and the constitutive elements in physical theories. But perhaps it is enough, for present purposes, to say that, since it is plausible that special science laws are *ceteris paribus* laws, it is likewise plausible that there are no strict psychophysical laws.

Given the interim conclusion that, if there are any psychophysical laws, they are not strict, the remainder of the argument for event monism depends crucially upon the principle of the nomological character of causation, which says that every causal relation between events is backed by a strict law. Davidson quite explicitly offers no argument for this principle (1970/1991: 248; 1993: 3). So, it is natural that queries should be raised about it. In particular, the intuition that causal relations are always backed by causal laws might be satisfied, in the case of psychophysical causal relations, by the existence of (non-strict) psychophysical laws (McLaughlin 1989, 1993). Furthermore, there may be something question-begging about Davidson's use of the idea that, in the case of physical theory, laws are strict.

To see why there is a risk of begging the question, we need to note that Davidson (1970) makes a connection between whether the laws about a certain domain can be strict and whether theories of the domain can be closed and complete. Thus, there is a connection between the claim that psychological laws are not strict and the claim that psychological theories are not closed and complete. The reason given for the latter claim is that the causes and effects of mental events are often physical (and not mental) events. There is likewise a connection between the claim that physical laws can be strict and the claim that physical theories can be closed and complete. But, the causes and effects of physical events are often mental events, and, pending an argument for monism, we cannot assume that these mental events are also physical events. So, pending an argument for monism, we cannot really assume that physical theories can be closed and complete; and so we cannot assume that physical laws can be strict. But, to the extent that even physical laws might not be strict, doubt is cast upon the principle of the nomological character of causation (on pain of there being no causal relations at all). So, pending an argument for monism, doubt is cast upon that principle; and so, there is something question-begging about relying upon the principle in an argument for monism (McLaughlin 1989).

If monism is, in the end, denied, this need not mean that the mental description of what is going on in the world floats entirely free from the physical description of what is happening. For another part of Davidson's overall position is a claim about *supervenience*. The position he describes 'is consistent with the view that mental characteristics are in some sense dependent, or supervenient, on physical characteristics. Such supervenience might be taken to mean that there cannot be two events alike in all physical respects but differing in some mental respect, or that an object cannot alter in some mental respect without altering in some physical respect' (1970/1991: 250). This claim does not merely say that there happens not to be any pair of events that are mentally different though physically the same. It does not just say that objects do not, as a matter of fact, alter mentally without altering physically. It says that these things *cannot* happen. So, it is a *modal* claim (a claim about necessity, possibility, or impossibility).

We can gloss the supervenience claim (like any other modal claim) in terms of possible situations or *possible worlds*. What the supervenience claim says is that, in any possible situation, if two events differ mentally, then they also differ physically. Because the two events are imagined to occur within the same possible situation, or possible world, we can call this a 'within a world' supervenience claim. This is to be contrasted with an 'across worlds' supervenience claim saying that if an event (in some possible world) has certain mental and physical properties, then that event could not have (in any other possible world) those same physical properties but different mental properties. Davidson does not make this 'across worlds' supervenience claim, and that fact is important for a number of discussions of his work (e.g. Kim 1984*a*, *b*, 1993; see also Section 4.2 below).

However, our present point is just that, if supervenience claims are in the offing, then a non-reductionist materialist could hope to keep mental goings-on firmly anchored in happenings in the physical world without actually identifying mental events with physical events. A ('within a world') supervenience claim about the mental and physical properties of whole thinking subjects might say, for example, that there cannot be two subjects who are physically alike in all respects yet who differ in some mental respect. By way of some such claim as this, one further materialist alternative to Cartesian dualism might emerge.

This view could share the non-reductionism of anomalous monism. It could say that the role of an overarching ideal of rationality in the attribution of beliefs, desires, and intentions to thinking subjects stands in the way of any identification of mental properties with physical, or even functional, properties. But it would go a step further in that non-reductionist direction, and deny that there need be any physical event that is identical with a particular subject's desiring (or coming to desire) a CD player, or believing (or coming to believe) that the ice is thin. According to the supervenience claim, if a subject changes from not believing that the ice is thin to believing it, then there must be some physical changes in the subject—plausibly including some changes in the subject's brain. But, it does not follow that there must be some neural event (or some physical event) with which precisely that change of belief is to be identified. This rejection of even a token–token identity claim may seem particularly plausible where some discovery, say, results in many simultaneous changes in beliefs and desires. The subject's total mental 'set' changes, and this requires unspecified changes at the subvening (neural, ultimately physical) level. But it is far from obvious why we should assume that components of the overall neural change can be paired up with components of the overall mental change.

This view would be a kind of anomalous event dualism (cf. Davidson 1970/1991: 250). But it would still be far from Cartesian dualism, since it would allow that the thinking subject is wholly composed of material stuff. Indeed, the talk of composition might even be extended to events. It might be said that mental events—taken as an aggregate—are composed of physical events, but that the boundaries between the composed (mental) events do not line up with any boundaries between composing (physical) events. (For this kind of event dualism, see Hornsby 1981, 1985; McDowell 1985. For a challenge to all non-reductive versions of materialism, see Kim 1989.)

1.7. Eliminativism

The final materialist proposal, *eliminativism* (or eliminative materialism), is the
view that there are no such things as beliefs, desires, and intentions—no one
really believes that the ice is thin, or wants a CD player, or intends to become a
professional philosopher—and that mental talk should be eliminated from any
serious discourse about the way the world works. Thus, Churchland says:
'Eliminative materialism is the thesis that our common-sense conception of
psychological phenomena constitutes a radically false theory, a theory so fundamentally defective that both the principles and the ontology of that theory
will eventually be displaced, rather than smoothly reduced, by completed neuroscience' (1981/1990: 206). Implicit in this eliminativist view is the idea that
'our common-sense conception' (often called *folk psychology*) is a theory that
aspires after the sort of vindication that could only, ultimately, be provided by a
'smooth reduction' to neuroscience (and presumably, thence, to physics).
Against the background of this idea, the argument in favour of eliminativism is
this: 'the most central things about us remain almost entirely mysterious from
within folk psychology. And the defects noted cannot be blamed on inadequate
time allowed for their correction, for folk psychology has enjoyed no significant
changes or advances in well over 2,000 years, despite its manifest failures'
(Churchland 1988: 46). In short, folk psychology, considered as a theoretical
research programme, is going nowhere. Developing neuroscience will reveal
that our common-sense framework of psychological notions provides a false
and radically misleading picture of cognition and the causes of behaviour.

If this is the argumentative strategy that the eliminativist adopts, then there
are clearly a number of points at which someone might resist. Someone might
object, at the very outset, to the idea that our common-sense conception
amounts to a theory. This is a difficult objection to assess since—for one
thing—an assessment would require prior agreement about what constitutes a
theory. In any case, we shall not pursue that initial objection now.

For now, let us say that a theory is a body of generalizations, and let us grant
that our everyday conception of the mental domain has some theoretical components. Churchland offers some examples of generalizations, including
(1981/1990: 209):

$(\forall x)(\forall p)$ (if x fears that p then x desires that not-p),

$(\forall x)(\forall p)$ [if (x hopes that p and x discovers that p) then x is pleased that p],

which seem to be part of our common-sense conception. But even so, there are
objections that might be entered against the eliminativist's argument.

Whether the falsity of a theory licenses the elimination of the things that the
theory appears to talk about is not a straightforward question. People once

accepted theories that talked about witches and theories that talked about phlogiston. These theories turned out to be badly wrong, and we now agree that there are no such people as witches and no such stuff as phlogiston. On the other hand, many ordinary people hold badly false theories about what philosophers are and what they do. But this does not begin to show that there are really no such people as philosophers. So, some extra premiss is needed to get from the discovery that a theory is false to the elimination of the theory's ontology.

In fact, the situation is even a little more complicated. For generalizations like the ones that we have quoted quantify over people ('$\forall x$') and over propositions ('$\forall p$'), and talk about people fearing, and desiring, and hoping things. But they do not talk (or do not talk explicitly) about fears, desires, and hopes as individual internal states. Ontologically, these generalizations are rather bland; they do not wear upon their sleeve any commitment to one view about the metaphysical status of minds and mental properties and states rather than another. So, if they were discovered to be radically false, and if this were to license the elimination of their characteristic ontology, it would still not be entirely clear what should be eliminated. Furthermore, read in this ontologically bland way, these generalizations do not seem to be very likely candidates for radical falsehood. So, the eliminativist argument needs some extra metaphysical premisses.

The eliminativist argument depends upon a reading of statements about people and their propositional attitudes on which those statements invoke internal states and events that enter into causal relationships. Furthermore, it depends upon the idea that, on such a reading, statements about propositional attitudes will only be true if 'the concepts of folk psychology [find] vindicating match-ups in a matured neuroscience' (Churchland 1988: 47). Given those two premisses, the argument for eliminativism begins from the plausibility of the claim that there will not turn out to be 'vindicating match-ups' between folk psychological properties and neuroscientific properties.

But those two premisses are quite substantive and controversial. The first premiss rules out not only analytical behaviourism, but also the more cautious view that we sketched at the end of Section 1.3—a view that we said is similar to Dennett's (1987) account of belief attributions, to be discussed in Section 2.2. The second premiss rules out the non-reductionist materialist views, such as Davidson's (1970) anomalous monism (cf. Horgan and Woodward 1985 / 1990: 403; see also Jackson and Pettit 1990*a*; Churchland 1991).

The general pattern exemplified by Churchland's eliminativist argument is this. Substantive pieces of philosophical theory postulate or reveal commitments within our common-sense conception of folk psychological phenomena—commitments that might not be obvious without considerable philosophical reflection. Developments in the scientific investigation of the mind—whether in cognitive psychology or in neuroscience—may show that those commitments are not met in the world as it really is. Supposing that the philosophical theory is correct, it would then follow that nothing in the real world corresponds to our current conception of the folk psychological phenomena. (See Ramsey *et al.* 1990 and Davies 1991 for arguments that are very clearly of this form.)

If we were to find ourselves in that situation, then we would have a number of options. One option would be to conclude that the substantive pieces of philosophical theory are wrong; that they do not provide a good elaboration and precisification of our current conception. In that case, our actual folk psychological practice could continue just as before; it would only be the philosophical commentary on it that would need to change. Another option—the opposite extreme—would be to abandon wholesale our folk psychological practice of describing, interpreting, and explaining people's behaviour as made up of actions performed for reasons that are based upon beliefs, wants, hopes, fears, and the rest. (At least, this is a formal option. Whether it is a real option for us is doubtful. For an analogy, see Strawson 1974*b* on the formal option of abandoning our 'personal reactive attitudes' towards each other.)

In between these two extremes lies the possibility of negotiation. Suppose that the philosophical theory does correctly elaborate our current conception and its commitments, but that those commitments are not met in the real world. Then we may be able to sustain the greater part of our folk psychological practice if we negotiate our way to a new, revised conception. Whether this would amount to the adoption of an eliminativist position would itself be a matter for philosophical judgement. It might be a matter of saying that no one really believes or desires anything, as those psychological phenomena are currently conceived, but that people do believe* things and desire* things (where *belief** and *desire** are new concepts, descended from our current concepts of belief and desire). Or, it might be a matter of saying that people do indeed believe and desire things—just as we have always said—but that we need to revise some of our deeply held opinions about believing and desiring. In either case, the details of the negotiations would depend upon the particular discoveries that might be made in cognitive psychology and neuroscience—and also, of course, upon the philosophical theories that connect those discoveries with our current conception of folk psychological phenomena.

1.8. Preview: Intentionality and Consciousness

We have been considering the place of minds, and mental properties and states, in the real world. Between Cartesian dualism (Section 1.1) and eliminative materialism (Section 1.7), we have arrayed analytical behaviourism (Section 1.2), central state materialism (Section 1.3), several versions of functionalism (Section 1.4), and anomalous monism (Section 1.6). Along the way we have also noted the possibility of a broadly behaviourist view that is shorn of any aim in the direction of analytical reduction (at the end of Section 1.3), and the prospect of a form of anomalous event dualism (at the end of Section 1.7). With so much by way of an overview of possible views of the metaphysics of mind, it is now time to turn in more detail to two characteristic features of our mental lives.

Some of our mental states—principally beliefs and desires—have intentionality, or content, or aboutness. Our beliefs and desires are about objects and properties in the world—about ice and thinness, and CD players. And some of our mental states—principally sensations and perceptual experiences—have a phenomenal aspect to them. They are conscious states in the sense that there is something that is like to be in those states.

Nagel (1994: 63) says:

Much discussion in the philosophy of mind is concerned with the problem of intentionality: what it means to attribute content to mental states like belief, desire, thought, perception, and so forth. This topic also links discussion of the relation between the mind and the brain with discussion of the relation between natural and artificial intelligence, and of the possibility of ascribing mental states to computers, in some distant stage of their development. However, I believe that the most fundamental problem in the area is that of consciousness. While consciousness in the form of pure sensation does not in itself guarantee intentionality, I believe true intentionality cannot occur in a being incapable of consciousness. The nature of this relation is very unclear to me, but its truth seems evident.

In the next section, we shall review some contemporary theories of intentionality. How is it that mental states—conceived as states of material things—can be about other things in the world? And then, in Section 3, we shall turn to the difficult topic of consciousness. At the end of that section, we shall take a look at the kind of dependence that there might be between intentionality and consciousness. Finally, Section 4 will provide a very brief introduction to questions about the causal and explanatory roles of mental states.

2. INTENTIONALITY

Our topic for this section is the problem of intentionality, or 'aboutness'. It is usual to begin with the point that there is an idea, going back to Brentano, that intentionality is what distinguishes the mental domain from the physical domain. A consequence of that idea would be that mental phenomena cannot be a species of physical phenomena.

This idea is no longer widely accepted. It has been replaced by the contemporary view that mental phenomena are, somehow, to be located amongst physical phenomena. The problem of intentionality then takes the form: How can one part of the physical world have significance, or meaning, or content—how can it be *about* another part? (For an introductory account, see Dennett and Haugeland 1987.)

2.1. Varieties of Aboutness

On the face of it, there are many different kinds of thing that have aboutness.

2.1.1. *Attitude Aboutness*

Our belief states have aboutness. Suppose that Fiona believes that Venus is a planet. Her belief is about an object, Venus, and a property, being a planet: it is the belief that the former exemplifies the latter. More generally, beliefs, desires, hopes, fears, wishes, and intentions have aboutness. These mental states are known as propositional attitude states, since they involve an attitude—believing, hoping, fearing—towards a proposition—I believe, hope, or fear that the ice is thin, for example. Since we shall be distinguishing several other species of aboutness, we shall call this first kind—the aboutness of the propositional attitudes—*attitude aboutness*. Some philosophers would reserve the term 'intentionality' for this kind of aboutness. This is no bad thing, since there is certainly something special about attitude aboutness.

One striking feature of attitude aboutness is that it is very fine-grained. Beliefs are about objects and properties; but two beliefs can be different in content, even though they concern the same object and the same property. This fine-grained character of belief content is reflected in the logical properties of sentences that report beliefs. Thus, to take a familiar example, from

> Fiona believes that Hesperus appears in the evening sky

and

> Hesperus = Phosphorus

we cannot validly infer

> Fiona believes that Phosphorus appears in the evening sky.

Rather similarly, from

> Fiona believes that triangle *ABC* has three equal angles

and

> For any triangle *XYZ*, *XYZ* has three equal angles if and only if *XYZ* has three equal sides

we cannot validly infer

> Fiona believes that triangle *ABC* has three equal sides.

These logical properties are aspects of the *intensionality* of belief reports. Beliefs have intentionality, or aboutness; belief reports exhibit the logical characteristics of intensionality.

Intensionality contrasts with extensionality. For any predicate, the set of objects of which the predicate is true is called the extension of the predicate. Two predicates that are true of just the same objects are said to be coextensive. A sentence containing a predicate is said to constitute an extensional context for the predicate if replacing the predicate by another predicate that is coextensive with it leaves the truth-value of the whole sentence unchanged. (We say that the substitution can be made *salva veritate*—preserving the truth-value.) If we are talking about triangles, then the predicates 'has three equal angles' and 'has three equal sides' are coextensive. The sentence

Triangle *ABC* has three equal angles

constitutes an extensional context for the predicate 'has three equal angles' since, for example, replacing that predicate with the coextensive predicate 'has three equal sides' is bound to leave the truth-value of the sentence the same. But the sentence

Fiona believes that triangle *ABC* has three equal angles

does not constitute an extensional context for that predicate. Replacing 'has three equal angles' with the coextensive predicate 'has three equal sides' might well change the truth-value of the whole sentence. A context that is not extensional is said to be intensional.

In the formal language of first-order predicate calculus, all contexts for predicates are extensional, and the language itself is said to be extensional. When a language is extensional, there are two other important kinds of substitution that can also be made *salva veritate*. If, in a sentence, one name for an object is substituted for another name of the same object, then the truth-value of the sentence remains unchanged. And, if in a complex sentence (say, a conjunction), a constituent sentence (say, one of the conjuncts) is replaced by another sentence having the same truth-value, then the truth-value of the whole complex sentence is preserved. (This is just to say that an extensional language is truth-functional.) However, when a language contains intensional contexts—as the language of belief reports does—these two kinds of substitution are no longer guaranteed to preserve truth-value. In the case of names, replacing the name 'Hesperus' with another name of the same object, 'Phosphorus', in the sentence

Fiona believes that Hesperus appears in the evening sky

might result in a change of truth-value. Similarly, in the case of sentences, 'Hesperus appears in the evening sky' and 'Phosphorus appears in the evening sky' have the same truth-value; but replacing one with the other in a belief report may turn a true report into a false one.

2.1.2. Linguistic Aboutness

Propositional attitude states are not the only things that have aboutness. A second clear example is provided by sentences of a public language. The English sentence 'Venus is a planet', like Fiona's belief, is about Venus and the property of being a planet. Also, like Fiona's belief, the sentence is true—or correct—if and only if Venus is indeed a planet.

Belief states and public language sentences both have aboutness. But it would be wrong to assume that a philosophical account of the aboutness—or meaning—of sentences in a public language will take just the same form as an account of the aboutness—or content—of beliefs. It is plausible that the meaning of public language sentences has something to do with the way that utterances of those sentences are conventionally used to communicate particular messages. Indeed, in the philosophy of language, there is a major programme aimed at giving an analysis of the notion of public language meaning for sentences in terms of such notions as convention, intention, and belief (see Grice 1989). That kind of analysis speaks of agents perpetrating utterances of those sentences with various intentions, often including the intention to get the person hearing the utterance to form certain beliefs. So what it offers is a way of analysing the notion of linguistic meaning for sentences by taking the contents of intentions and beliefs for granted.

Furthermore, the Gricean analytical programme cannot be applied a second time over to the states of intending and believing themselves. For propositional attitude states are not utterances performed by agents with communicative intentions. Even if we think of believing or intending as involving the occurrence of an event that is a token of a neural or physical type, and even if we think of these types as analogous to linguistic types and of the tokens as analogous to tokens of linguistic expressions, still we cannot give a Gricean account of the aboutness of those mental events. For a Gricean account would require not only neural analogues of linguistic expressions, but also neural analogues of agents producing those linguistic expressions—agents with communicative intentions. This would involve peopling the brain of every thinking subject with a host of further intending and believing subjects, whose propositional attitudes would have to be taken for granted by the second-time-around Gricean analysis. In short, it would involve an utterly unhelpful regress.

This is not to say that it is a mistake to think of mental events as involving analogues of linguistic expressions. On the contrary, the proposal that occurrences of propositional attitudes involve tokens of symbols that have structural properties like those of linguistic expressions (the *language of thought* hypothesis: Fodor 1975, 1987) has very considerable plausibility. The mistake would be to suppose that a Gricean account of linguistic aboutness could be transformed, via the language of thought hypothesis, into an account of attitude aboutness.

Thus, as well as the attitude aboutness of beliefs and desires, we have the *linguistic aboutness* of sentences and utterances. To the extent that conventional signs, and perhaps also maps and pictures, inherit their aboutness from the intentionality of beliefs in a similar way, we might also call this *conventional aboutness*. But, whatever we call it, we should keep in mind the plausibility of the idea that the aboutness of language is derived from the aboutness of propositional attitudes.

We should now notice at least three other kinds of intentionality.

2.1.3. Indicator Aboutness

Some phenomena have meaning in the sense that they *indicate* something about the world. Thus, we say, 'Those spots mean—or indicate—measles', 'Those clouds mean—or indicate—rain', 'The position of the fuel gauge means—or indicates—that the tank is almost empty', and even, 'The existence of thirty rings in that tree trunk means—or indicates—that the tree was thirty years old when it was cut down'.

This *indicator aboutness* is clearly distinct from the other two kinds that we have listed so far. We can consistently say, 'The content of Fiona's belief is that it will rain; but in fact it will not rain'. And we can say, 'The meaning of that sentence is that it will rain—that was the message that was communicated; but in fact it will not rain'. But we cannot consistently say, 'Those clouds mean—or indicate—that it will rain; but in fact it will not rain'. Indicator aboutness, at least in its simplest form, does not allow for the possibility of misrepresentation.

There are broadly two views that we might have towards indicator aboutness. On the one hand, we could treat indicator aboutness as another instance of aboutness that is derived from the aboutness of propositional attitudes. The idea would be that the aboutness of the clouds—the clouds' meaning that it will rain—is inherited from the attitude aboutness of the belief that someone could form on the basis of observing the clouds. On the other hand, we could regard indicator aboutness as a feature of the world that is not dependent upon the propositional attitudes of observers. On this second view, the fact that clouds in general, and those clouds in particular, mean that it will rain is something that we can discover, and can then rely upon in forming our beliefs. But the clouds' aboutness is a fact, whether it is discovered or not.

There are reasons for holding that the second of these two views is the more plausible. As Dretske says (1986: 18): 'Naturally occurring signs mean something, and they do so without any assistance from us.' To the extent that indicator aboutness is independent of our discovery, it appears to be a matter of a reliable *causal covariation* between events of two types. In the example of the clouds, the two types would be occurrences of a certain kind of cloud formation and occurrences of rain shortly afterwards. We shall return to this kind of account of aboutness in Section 2.3.

The remaining two kinds of intentionality are like attitude aboutness in that they concern mental—or, more broadly, psychological—states.

2.1.4. *Experiential Aboutness*

Perceptual experiences present the world as being one way or another. They present objects as having certain properties. Thus, we may hear a sound as coming from the left; or we may see a box as being cubic and about four feet in front of us. This *experiential aboutness* is closely related to attitude aboutness; for we can form beliefs on the basis of experiences such as these. Thus we may have an auditory experience and come to believe that the sound is coming from the left; or we can have a visual experience and come to believe that the box is cubic and about four feet in front of us.

But still, it is worth distinguishing the content of experiences from the content of the beliefs that we form on the basis of those experiences. For, it is an important point about belief content that, in order to believe that a box is cubic, one has to possess the concept of a cube. But, it is arguable that merely having a box presented in experience as cubic does not, in the same way, require possession of that concept. This is to say that, while attitude aboutness is a kind of *conceptualized content*, experiential aboutness is (or includes) *non-conceptual content* (Evans 1982; Peacocke 1992a, ch. 3; Crane 1992; Davies 1995a). So experiential aboutness is different from attitude aboutness. It is also different from linguistic aboutness, since it is not derived from attitude aboutness, and is not a matter of convention. And it is different from indicator aboutness, since it allows for the possibility of misrepresentation: perceptual experiences can present the world as being different from the way that it really is.

2.1.5. *Subdoxastic Aboutness*

Finally, there are unconscious psychological states that have aboutness. Our concern here is with the unconscious processes that lead up to experience—and ultimately to belief. The very idea of information-processing psychology is committed to there being information in, for example, a creature's visual system or auditory system: information about other states of the creature and also about states of the external world. The internal states that carry this information are often said to be *mental representations*.

We shall call this unconscious psychological aboutness *subdoxastic aboutness*, in line with Stich's (1978: 499) labelling of states which 'play a role in the proxi-mate causal history of beliefs, though they are not beliefs themselves', as sub-doxastic states. (The Greek word *doxa* means 'opinion' or 'belief'.) Subdoxastic aboutness seems to be distinct from attitude aboutness, since the creature does not need to possess the concepts that would be used to specify the information that is being processed. (It is non-conceptual content: Davies 1989.) It is clearly distinct from linguistic aboutness, since mental representations are not pro-duced by internal agents participating in a convention. It is also distinct from indicator aboutness, since it allows for the possibility of misrepresentation: we can say, for example, that a state of the auditory processing system represents the presence of a sound coming from the left even though there is not in fact any sound coming from the left. Finally, subdoxastic aboutness seems quite unlike experiential aboutness, since it is not tied to consciousness.

2.1.6. Review

For expository purposes, we have distinguished, and labelled, five notions of aboutness:

attitude aboutness—the aboutness, or intentionality, of propositional atti-tudes, such as beliefs, desires, intentions, hopes, fears;

linguistic aboutness—the aboutness, or meaning, of public language sen-tences, and of conventional signs and signals;

indicator aboutness—the aboutness of natural signs, such as spots, clouds, and tree rings;

experiential aboutness—the aboutness of perceptual experiences, such as an auditory experience that presents a sound as coming from the left;

subdoxastic aboutness—the aboutness of unconscious information-processing states that lead up to experience and belief.

But it is important to recognize that philosophical disputes surround these dis-tinctions. We have suggested that linguistic aboutness is to be explained in terms of attitude aboutness; but there are philosophers who argue that the real explanatory order is just the reverse (Dummett 1991)—and yet further philoso-phers who claim that both notions need to be explained simultaneously (Davidson 1974*b*). We have distinguished experiential aboutness from attitude aboutness; but there are philosophers who reckon that the idea of content that does not require concepts is a spurious idea (e.g. Hamlyn 1994; see also 1990). And we have included subdoxastic aboutness on our list; but (as the quotation from Nagel at the end of Section 1 would suggest) there are philosophers who are suspicious of the idea that there can be genuine intentionality that is not tied to consciousness (Searle 1990).

Furthermore, although we have distinguished these five notions, it might turn out, in the end, that one of them is just a variant of another. For example, to the extent that subdoxastic aboutness is a legitimate notion, it might be seen as a variant of indicator aboutness—a variant that somehow allows for the possibility of misrepresentation. In any case, the focus for our attention now is attitude aboutness: the intentionality of beliefs and other propositional attitudes.

2.2. The Intentional Stance

Our philosophical project is to give some kind of analysis or elucidation of attitude aboutness (or intentionality). The first division we can make amongst potential accounts is between those that take the believer—the whole person or whole system—as fundamental and those that take the belief state—an internal state of the system—as fundamental. The former accounts fit the format

For any thinking subject x, x believes that . . . if and only if ———,

while the latter accounts take the form

For any internal state s, s is a belief that . . . if and only if ———.

Any account in the second format can, of course, be made to yield an account in the first format. We just say:

For any thinking subject x, x believes that . . . if and only if there is an internal state s of x such that ———.

But the converse is not true. Analytical behaviourism, for example, fits the first format, but says nothing at all about internal states.

One bold suggestion that would fit the second format (a suggestion that we shall consider in Section 2.3) would be that attitude aboutness is some kind of construct out of indicator aboutness. The starting-point for that suggestion would be something like

For any internal state s, s is a belief that there is a predator nearby if and only if the occurrence of s *indicates* that there is a predator nearby.

The account of attitude aboutness that we shall consider in this section fits the first format. Like analytical behaviourism, it focuses on the whole person or whole system.

Dennett introduces the idea of an *intentional system*: 'a system whose behaviour can be—at least sometimes—explained and predicted by relying on ascriptions to the system of beliefs and desires . . .' (1971/1981: 3). The methodology for this kind of explanation and prediction of the behaviour of a system involves two assumptions. First, we assume that the machine will function as it was designed to do; and second, we assume that the design is optimal. Then: 'One predicts behaviour in such a case by ascribing to the system the possession of certain information and supposing it to be directed by certain goals, and then by working out the most reasonable and appropriate action on the basis of these ascriptions and suppositions' (1971/1981: 6). This explanatory strategy is what Dennett calls adopting the *intentional stance*, and the intentional stance is distinguished from the *physical stance* and the *design stance*.

Adopting the physical stance, we make predictions that 'are based on the actual physical state of the particular object, and are worked out by applying whatever knowledge we have about the laws of nature' (1971/1981: 4). This does not involve making either of the assumptions mentioned in the previous paragraph.

Adopting the design stance, we make predictions 'solely from knowledge or assumptions about the system's functional design, irrespective of the physical constitution' (p. 4). This involves making just the first of the two assumptions, namely, that the system will function as it was designed to do. If you have the manual for the word-processing program that your computer is running, then—if you assume that the system will do what it is designed to do—you can predict what the computer will do when you press a particular combination of keys. But the design stance cannot be used to predict or explain malfunctions. In order to predict or explain what the computer will do after you have poured a carton of yoghurt into it, you need to descend to the physical stance.

Adopting the design stance allows us to abstract away from the details of the physical realization of a designed system. Adopting the intentional stance allows us to make a further abstraction. We abstract away from the details of the design, and just assume that it is sensible or rational. If you do not have the manual for the program that your friend's computer is running, you may still be able to make predictions about what the computer will do if you press particular keys. You just rely on the assumption that the design of the system is sensible.

Here is a later description of how the intentional stance strategy works:

. . . first you decide to treat the object whose behaviour is to be predicted as a rational agent; then you figure out what beliefs that agent ought to have, given its place in the world and its purpose. Then you figure out what desires it ought to have, on the same considerations, and finally you predict that this rational agent will act to further its goals in the light of its beliefs. (Dennett 1987: 17)

The account of belief that this yields is very simple. Thus, for example,

For any thinking subject (or other system) x, x believes that snow is white if and only if x can be predictively attributed the belief that snow is white.

That is, x believes that snow is white if ascribing that belief to the system figures in the predictively successful adoption of the intentional stance towards the system. Similarly,

x believes that Venus is a planet if and only if x can be predictively attributed the belief that Venus is a planet.

And, quite generally,

all there is to really and truly believing that *p* (for any proposition *p*) is being an intentional system for which *p* occurs as a belief in the best (most predictive) interpretation. (Dennett 1987: 29)

There are two related points that we should notice about this account of belief. The first is simply that the account is completely non-reductionist: it makes no attempt to analyse or define the notion of belief in more basic terms, nor to identify the property of believing that snow is white with a behavioural, functional, or neural property. On the contrary, the notion of believing that snow is white occurs within the statement of necessary and sufficient conditions for *x* to believe that snow is white. The second point is that, as a consequence, the account does not say anything distinctive about any particular belief. What the account says about the belief that Venus is a planet is just that a subject *x* has that belief if and only if that belief figures in the best interpretation of the subject. But this, of course, is also what the account says about the belief that snow is white, or about any other belief.

Adopting the intentional stance towards a system is a strategy for explaining and predicting that system's behaviour. But, Dennett's account of belief is not a form of analytical behaviourism, since having a particular belief—say the belief that Venus is a planet—is not analysed in terms of a disposition to behave in some particular way. As we saw (in Section 1.2), there is a reason of principle why analytical behaviourism cannot work. Behaviour is explained in terms of both beliefs and desires; given a particular belief, what behaviour is forthcoming depends upon what desires are present. So having a belief cannot itself be equated with a disposition to behave in a certain way.

Nevertheless, there is something behaviouristic about Dennett's account of belief. For, on that account, what makes the attribution to a subject of beliefs and other attitudes *true* is just the presence of patterns in that subject's behaviour. As a matter of philosophical analysis, nothing more than suitably patterned behaviour is required if propositional attitude attributions are to be true. One aspect of this behaviourism is that, if two systems show exactly the same dispositions to behaviour, then the intentional stance licenses just the same descriptions of the two systems in terms of beliefs and desires: no mental difference without a behavioural difference. So, we might call it *supervenient behaviourism*. This is the kind of view that we sketched at the end of Section 1.3.

It is, however, a controversial matter whether this degree of behaviourism is consistent with our ordinary conception of mental states. Challenges to Dennett's position can be mounted by considering (science-fictional) examples in which a system's behaviour is produced by way of an automatic look-up procedure operating extremely rapidly upon a massive library of sequences of behavioural routines (Block 1981; Peacocke 1983, ch. 8). Roughly, the idea of these examples is this. What are stored in the library are sequences of behavioural routines—say, $\langle B_1, B_2, B_3, ... \rangle$—interleaved with codes for patterns of sensory stimulation. So, an interleaved sequence might be $\langle S_1, B_1, S_2, B_2, S_3, B_3, ... \rangle$. These strings meet the condition, for example, that B_3 is a sensible continuation of behaviour in the situation that would produce stimulation S_3, for a system that has already done B_1 in the situation corresponding to S_1, and then B_2 in the situation corresponding to S_2. Given this stored library, the system generates behaviour in the following way. Given sensory stimulation S, the look-up procedure locates a sequence that begins with $\langle S, ... \rangle$ and then finds the next member of the sequence, say behavioural routine B. As that routine is executed and further sensory stimulation, T, is provided, the look-up procedure locates a sequence that begins with $\langle S, B, T, ... \rangle$ and then finds the next member of that sequence, say behavioural routine C. And so on.

These examples are set up in such a way that the behaviour produced by the system is just as susceptible to prediction using the intentional stance as is the behaviour of a real person. But, intuitively, it is far from clear that the attributions of beliefs and other propositional attitudes that would be made in accordance with the intentional stance would be true of such a system. Block remarks of an example of this kind—in which a machine is programmed so that the sensible continuations match the behavioural dispositions of his Aunt Bubbles—that the machine 'has the intelligence of a jukebox' (1990a: 252).

Those who find these challenges to the intentional stance to be persuasive draw the conclusion that supervenient behaviourism is inadequate as a philosophical theory. They argue in favour of theories saying that attributions of propositional attitudes do, after all, impose some conditions upon the structure and processing inside the system whose behaviour is in question. As a result, they create more of an opening for an eliminativist argument. (See again, Section 1.7.) In contrast, no discovery about what happens inside our brains could license an eliminativist conclusion according to supervenient behaviourism.

However, a defender of supervenient behaviourism may seek to account for some of the intuitions that seem to support more committed philosophical theories. For it might be that the supervenient behaviourist requirement that appropriately patterned behaviour should be consistently forthcoming (and in real time) does impose some conditions upon the internal architecture of the system. It might turn out (though as a matter of empirical fact, rather than as a matter of philosophical theory) that only a particular class of internal architectures can sustain the patterns in behaviour that make the attributions of propositional attitudes true. To the extent that the existence of such *de facto* requirements is intuitively plausible, that might have an effect upon our intuitions concerning the science-fictional examples.

For example, Dennett (1987) considers the possibility that Fodor's (1975, 1987) language of thought hypothesis (see above, Section 2.1.2) might afford the best explanation of the consistently patterned behaviour of human beings. But entertaining this as a serious possibility is very different, of course, from arguing for a philosophical theory that makes the truth of the language of thought hypothesis a necessary requirement for the presence of propositional attitudes.

The language of thought hypothesis says that the internal cognitive architecture of human beings involves symbol manipulation, in the style of a digital computer. Other processing architectures are possible, and are being actively investigated. In particular, in contemporary psychology and neuroscience, there is a massive amount of research into *connectionist* architectures. Connectionist networks are made up of simple units linked together by connections that can have various strengths or weights. Units can be activated, and the activation is passed to other units along the weighted connections. Instead of using symbols, connectionist networks code information by using patterns of activation over groups of units. A particular pattern of activation over a group of input units will lead to a pattern of activation over a group of output units. Because units and connections are somewhat analogous to neurons and synapses, connectionist networks are sometimes called *artificial neural networks*. (For an introductory account, see Churchland 1988: 156–65.)

The details of the comparison between language of thought architectures and connectionist architectures do not matter here. All that we need to note is that the discovery that human beings have a connectionist cognitive architecture and not a language of thought architecture would have very different significance for Dennett, on the one hand, and for the advocate of a more heavily committed philosophical theory, on the other. For Dennett, this imagined discovery would simply show that the patterns in human behaviour can, after all, be generated in real time without being underpinned by a language of thought. For the philosophical theorist who sees the language of thought hypothesis as one of the commitments of our common-sense conception, in contrast, the imagined discovery would trigger an eliminativist argument.

Overall, then, the dialectical situation concerning supervenient behaviourism is this. If we had a general argument to show that no philosophical theory should create the opportunity for an eliminativist argument to get started, then that would count very much in favour of supervenient behaviourism. On the other hand, if we had a philosophical argument showing that some particular cognitive architecture is a necessary condition of beliefs and other propositional attitudes, then that would count decisively against supervenient behaviourism. As it is, what we have are some science-fictional examples in which the right behaviour is forthcoming but where—according to the intuitions of many —there is no real mental activity. That surely counts against supervenient behaviourism to some extent. But a more definite judgement would require a detailed assessment of the possible responses to those examples (see again Block 1981).

2.3. Covariation and Teleology

Whereas the interpretational approach to belief exemplified by Dennett adopts the format

For any thinking subject x, x believes that . . . if and only if ———,

the approaches to be considered in this subsection and the next take the alternative form

For any internal state s, s is a belief that . . . if and only if ———.

The starting-point for these approaches is the idea of giving an account of the content of an internal state in terms of lawful *covariation* between that state and some state of the world. In essence, then, these approaches begin from the notion of indicator aboutness (Section 2.1.3). We have already noted that indicator aboutness differs importantly from attitude aboutness, in that it does not allow for the possibility of falsehood—or misrepresentation. So, the first challenge that faces these covariation approaches is to move away from their starting-point in such a way as to permit misrepresentation.

Cummins provides a clear example of the covariation approach to intentionality in terms of a simple mechanical device, LOCKE:

LOCKE is equipped with a TV camera hooked up to some input modules . . . which in turn are hooked up to a card punch. When the TV camera is pointed at something, a punch card called a . . . *percept* is produced. Percepts are fed into a sorter, which compares them with a stack of master cards called . . . *concepts*. When a percept matches a concept . . . LOCKE displays the term written on the back of the concept. Any word can be written on the back of any concept; that is a matter of convention. But once the words are printed on the concepts, everything else is a matter of physics. (1989: 37)

This device establishes lawful covariation between particular punch card patterns in LOCKE and particular states of the world that lie in front of LOCKE's TV camera. We can then make use of this covariation in a definition of aboutness. (Cummins uses the notion of *representation*.)

x represents y in LOCKE if and only if x is a punch pattern that occurs in a percept when, only when, and because LOCKE is confronted by y.

Thus, for example,

a punch card pattern, C, in LOCKE represents the presence of a cat if and only if that pattern, C, occurs in LOCKE when, only when, and because LOCKE is confronted by a cat.

And we can see immediately that this definition of aboutness renders misrepresentation logically impossible.

Misrepresentation should be able to occur either when the device is in a state that means *cat* although there is no cat present, or when the device is confronted by a cat but fails to be in a state that means *cat*. Certainly, this is possible for belief states and for visual experiences. In the case of beliefs, for example, you may be in a belief state with the content that there is a cat in front of you, although there is really no cat present (you mistake a dog for a cat). Or you may fail to be in a belief state with the content that there is a cat in front of you, even though you really are confronted by a cat (you mistake the cat for a dog). But, this is not possible for the kind of intentionality defined by the simple covariation approach. For, if the pattern *C* occurs although LOCKE is not confronted by a cat, or if the pattern *C* fails to occur although LOCKE is confronted by a cat, then according to the definition that just shows that the pattern *C* does not mean *cat*.

There are several ways that we might try to improve upon the simple covariation approach. We might, for example, say that

> *x* represents *y* in LOCKE if and only if *x* is a punch pattern that occurs in a percept when, only when, and because LOCKE is confronted by *y* *unless there is a malfunction in LOCKE*.

or

> *x* represents *y* in LOCKE if and only if *x* is a punch pattern that occurs in a percept when, only when, and because LOCKE is confronted by *y* *under ideal circumstances*.

or

> *x* represents *y* in LOCKE if and only if *x* is a punch pattern that *would* occur in a percept when, only when, and because LOCKE is confronted by *y* *but for performance limitations*.

But there are objections that can be raised against each of these attempts at improvement (Cummins 1989: 40–55). The first attempt, for example, has the unwanted consequence that misrepresentation only occurs when a system malfunctions. But, there can be misrepresentation in visual experience (visual illusions, for example) even though the visual system is working properly.

In response to problems such as these, Dretske (1986) introduces a teleological element into his theory of representation. The core idea is contained in this definition of the notion of *meaning_f*:

> *d*'s being *G* means_f that *w* is *F* if and only if *d*'s *function* is to *indicate* the condition of *w* and the way *d* performs this *function* is, in part, by *indicating* that *w* is *F* by *d*'s being *G*. (1986/1990: 133)

By putting together indicator aboutness (analysed in terms of causal covariation) and the notion of *teleological function*—what a system is supposed to do or what it was selected to do—Dretske hopes to move closer to the notion of attitude aboutness (see also Fodor 1990*a*).

We can see how this core idea is supposed to work if we consider the example that Dretske uses:

Some marine bacteria have internal magnets (called magnetosomes) that function like compass needles, aligning themselves (and, as a result, the bacteria) parallel to the earth's magnetic field. . . . The survival value of magnetotaxis (as this sensory mechanism is called) is not obvious, but it is reasonable to suppose that it functions so as to enable the bacteria to avoid surface water. Since these organisms are capable of living only in the absence of oxygen, movement towards geomagnetic north will take the bacteria away from oxygen-rich surface water and towards the comparatively oxygen-free sediment at the bottom. (1986/1990: 135–6)

In this example, it is plausible that it is the function of the magnetosome to indicate the direction of oxygen-free water. The way that the magnetosome performs this function is to indicate that the oxygen-free water is in such-and-such a direction (towards the bottom of the sea) by having its own orientation in that same direction (thanks to the fact that the lines in the earth's magnetic field point downwards in the northern hemisphere). So, the notion of meaning$_f$ that Dretske has defined can be applied to the state of the magnetosome's being oriented in a certain direction. Furthermore, we can demonstrate the possibility of misrepresentation (meaning$_f$ something that is false) by introducing a bar magnet into the magnetosome's environment. For now the magnetosome may orient itself in a direction that is not the direction of the oxygen-free water. And, a notion of aboutness that allows for the possibility of misrepresentation—in particular, the notion of meaning$_f$—is, to that extent, more like attitude aboutness. We can well imagine, for example, that a thinking subject might have a false belief about the direction of oxygen-free water.

But there are at least two problems with this. One problem is that the analysis in terms of teleological function might not generalize. The definition of meaning$_f$ may work well for magnetosomes that represent the direction of oxygen-free water, where oxygen-free water is something that the bacteria housing the magnetosomes need. For, in that case, the magnetosome has a teleological function or purpose relative to that need. But many of our beliefs represent states of affairs that have nothing to do with our needs. So, we may wonder how a theory based on the notion of meaning$_f$ is going to apply to those beliefs.

A second problem is that it is not even clear that the magnetosome example really does allow us to give a clear case of misrepresentation. It is certainly plausible to say that the function of the magnetosome is to indicate the direction of oxygen-free water. But, in the bacteria's normal environment, north in the local magnetic field is reliably the direction of oxygen-free water. So, it might be just as correct to say that the function of the magnetosome is to indicate the direction of magnetic north. If that is the function of the magnetosome, and we apply the definition of meaning$_f$, then we get the result that the magnetosome's pointing in a certain direction means$_f$ that that is the direction of north in the local magnetic field. But then, there is no misrepresentation in the case where a bar magnet is introduced into the bacteria's environment, and we are no closer to the notion of attitude aboutness after all.

There are several ways that someone might respond to these two problems. In the case of the first problem, Dretske (1986/1990: 137) suggests that instances of representation that apparently have nothing to do with needs might, nevertheless, be regarded as built up out of building-blocks that are associated with need, and to which the definition of meaning$_f$ could, therefore, be applied. In the case of the second problem, one strategy would be to defend the definite assignment of one function rather than the other to the magnetosome, by relying upon some developed theory of what it is for something to have a particular teleological function. Such a theory is likely to begin from the idea that doing a particular thing, X, is the function of some component of an organism if natural selection has favoured organisms with that component just because the component does X. (See Millikan 1989 for an example of this strategy within a teleological theory of aboutness.)

Dretske's own response to the second problem is to say that we need to move to more complicated systems, and, in particular, to systems that have several ways of indicating the same state of the world and—most crucially—systems that learn. Thus, he says, 'A system at this level of complexity, having not only multiple channels of access to what it needs to know about, but the resources for expanding its information-gathering resources, possesses, I submit, a genuine power of misrepresentation' (1986/1990: 142).

There are further questions that can be raised here, and there are many other variations on the themes of covariation and teleology to be considered. (Fodor's (1987, 1990*a*, *b*) theory, which is based on lawful covariation but does not make use of teleological notions, is of particular importance.)

But perhaps we can focus upon the fact that, on the face of it, causal covariation and teleology will not distinguish, for example, between meaning that Hesperus is thus-and-so and meaning that Phosphorus is thus-and-so, or between meaning that water is thus-and-so and meaning that H_2O is thus-and-so. Indicating the state of Hesperus is just the same as indicating the state of Phosphorus, and a need for water is just the same as a need for H_2O. In short, covariation-plus-teleology theories seem to cut content too coarsely to yield an adequate account of attitude aboutness. The account of content to be considered in the next subsection certainly does not have that problem.

2.4. Functional Role and Holism

The theory of content known as *functional role semantics* results from applying the basic idea of functionalism (Section 1.4), not to a type of mental state—pain versus pleasure, belief versus desire—but specifically to the contents of propositional attitude states—the belief *that p* versus the belief *that q*. Very roughly, the basic idea is that a belief state has a particular content—it is, say, the belief that the ice is thin—in virtue of its causal role, where this includes input-side causal relations, output-side causal relations, and causal relations to other mental states. (We should pause to note two terminological points here. First, the term 'semantics' is usually applied to the study of the meanings of expressions in a language. But here it applies to a theory about the aboutness of mental states. Second, the term 'functional' as it occurs in 'functional role semantics'—or in 'functionalism'—is not intended to introduce a teleological element.)

There are important variations upon the basic theme of functional role semantics. There are, for example, distinctions between different kinds of functional role—between causal, computational, and inferential roles (see Cummins 1989, ch. 9). There is also a distinction between what are sometimes called *short-armed* and *long-armed* functional roles (Block 1986/1994: 101). A short-armed functional role is defined in terms of short-range causal relations—usually, causal relations between states within the person, creature, or system under discussion. A long-armed functional role, in contrast, includes long-range causal relations between the belief states and states of distal items, such as the objects and properties that the belief is about. While it is long-armed functional roles that figure in accounts of aboutness as we ordinarily conceive of it, short-armed functional roles are adverted to in accounts of so-called *narrow* content. This is supposed to be a kind of content that is guaranteed to be preserved between systems that are internally the same, even if they are embedded in quite different environments.

But, in all these cases, the main problem that has been posed for functional role theories is that they are virtually certain to have the result that there is no *intersubjective synonymy*. (The term 'synonymy', like 'semantics', is more commonly used in discussions of linguistic meaning. Here, the term is being used to talk about different mental states' having the same content. We have a case of intersubjective synonymy when mental states of different subjects have the same content.) The reason is that it is a virtual certainty that no belief state in one person's head stands in exactly the same causal relations as any belief state in another person's head. Thus Fodor and LePore:

[Functional role semantics] appears to be intractably holistic. This is because, once you start identifying the content of a belief with its inferential role in a system of beliefs

. . . it's hard to avoid proceeding to identify the content of a belief with its *whole* inferential role in the system of beliefs. And, having gone that far, it's hard to avoid the conclusion that if belief systems differ at all with respect to the propositions they endorse,
then they differ completely with respect to the propositions they endorse. (1991: 331)

We shall consider possible responses to this problem shortly; but first we need
to say a little more about some of the ideas that figure in discussions of functional role semantics.

As a number of authors point out, functional role semantics is a kind of *use
theory* of content. In the case of a public language, a use theory of meaning says
that the meaning of an expression is a matter of the use—principally, the communicative use—to which the expression is put; or better, a matter of the communicative use to which sentences containing the expression are put. In the
case of mental states, a use theory of content or aboutness says that the content
of an internal state is a matter of the use—or role—of that state in the overall
cognitive economy of the thinking subject.

In some of the literature on functional role semantics, there is a background
assumption that propositional attitude states involve symbols in an inner code:
the language of thought (Fodor 1975, 1987). In that case, a use theory of content for mental states may—rather like a use theory of meaning for a public language—speak of the use of linguistic expressions. But, as we noted in Section
2.1.2, there is still an important difference between the two cases. For, even if
the language of thought hypothesis is correct, we should not conceive of the
expressions of the language of thought as having their content in virtue of the
intentions with which they are used by little communicating agents inside our
brains.

Thus, Harman says:

Conceptual role [functional role] semantics may be seen as a version of the theory that
meaning is use, where the basic use of symbols is taken to be in calculation, not in communication, and where concepts are treated as symbols in a 'language of thought'.
Clearly, the relevant use of such symbols—the use which determines their content—is
their use in thought and calculation rather than in communication. (1982: 243)

And Block says:

According to functional role semantics, for me to have a thought is for something (a
representation) to have a certain functional role in me, that is, for it to be inferrable in
certain contexts from certain other representations with their own functional roles, and
for other representations with their own functional roles to be inferrable from it. But to
be able to have these other representations with their own functional roles is to be able
to have other thoughts corresponding to these other representations. Thus, having one
thought involves being able to have others. (1987: 164)

Now, the idea that having one thought involves being able to have others is very
plausible; it is not an idea that is especially characteristic of functional role

semantics. It is difficult, for example, to imagine circumstances in which we would credit a system or person with thoughts about the colour red, but with no thoughts about any other colours, and with no thoughts about colour in general. Surely, if someone is to have thoughts about red at all—is to have the concept of red—then he or she needs to know such things as that whatever is red is coloured, and that whatever is red is not also green. But, functional role semantics is not merely committed to the plausible-sounding idea that having one thought involves being able to have others.

Suppose that, from the thought that the vase is red, you infer that Granny will like the vase, while I do not draw that inference, since I have no views about Granny's colour preferences. Then your thought that the vase is red does not have the same functional role in you as my thought that the vase is red has in me—even though we are thinking of the same vase, and would identify just the same surfaces as being red. According to functional role semantics, strictly speaking, your thought does not have the same (fine-grained) content as my thought. This is how functional role semantics has the consequence that there is no intersubjective synonymy.

However, you and I are both described as believing that the vase is red. One and the same belief ascription is true of both of us. So, according to functional role semantics, public language ascriptions of belief cannot be fully specifying the contents of belief states. The natural thing for functional role semantics to say at this point is that the ascription 'x believes that the vase is red' only specifies which object and property x's belief is about.

More generally, it is natural to distinguish between the extremely fine-grained kind of content to which functional role semantics applies and a very coarse-grained kind of content, which could be called *referential content*. The idea here would be that, just as the words 'Hesperus' and 'Phosphorus' have the same reference, even though they differ in meaning (or sense: Frege 1892), so two belief states could be about the very same objects and properties, even though they differ in their functional roles. Given this distinction between functional role content and referential content, the claim would be that the public language belief ascription only specifies the referential content of x's belief.

This distinction between functional role content and referential content might be combined with the idea of narrow content to yield a certain kind of *two-factor* account of content (Block 1986/1994: 101). This two-factor theory would say that content has an internal (narrow) factor that depends upon short-armed functional role, and is indeed holistic, and an external factor that depends upon the way that the subject is embedded in the environment. The external factor of content (referential content) specifies which objects and properties the subject's mental states are about, and it can be shared across individuals even though their overall cognitive economies are very different. Narrow content is usually contrasted with *wide* or *broad* content. In the context of a two-factor theory, wide content could be identified with just the external factor (Block 1986/1994: 85), or it could be regarded as a composite of the two factors (so that it would depend upon long-armed functional role).

We are now in a position to consider two possible responses to the problem about intersubjective synonymy. The first response is to admit that no two subjects have beliefs with quite the same fine-grained contents, but to point to the fact that the beliefs of two subjects might, nevertheless, have the same referential content. So, referential content does offer a kind of (coarse-grained) intersubjective synonymy.

This strategy for responding to the problem does not, however, quite measure up to our intuitions about belief contents. For, intuitively, we suppose that two people can both believe that Hesperus is a planet (that they can have beliefs with the same content). And we suppose that believing that Hesperus is a planet is not the same as believing that Phosphorus is a planet (that those beliefs have different contents). That is, we take it that two subjects may have beliefs with the same content, where this is not as coarse-grained as referential content.

An alternative response to the problem of intersubjective synonymy would be to demarcate some sub-part of the total functional role of a belief state as essential to its content—the remainder being inessential. In fact, the most natural way to implement this strategy would be to consider the inferential role of the belief state, rather than its total causal role, and to mark out some designated subclass of the belief's inferential liaisons.

If we consider the analogous distinction in the case of sentences of a public language, it would be the distinction between those inferential liaisons that are necessary, given what the terms in a sentence mean, and those that are not. (A standard example of an inferential link that is necessary given what the words mean would be the inference from 'Bruce is a bachelor' to 'Bruce is unmarried'.) In short, the distinction that we would need to draw would be a version of the *analytic versus synthetic* distinction. Quine (1951) has famously argued that this distinction cannot be drawn clearly; so, from a Quinean perspective, the prospects for this kind of revision to functional role semantics do not look good. For the most part, both advocates (e.g. Block 1986, 1987, 1993) and opponents (e.g. Fodor and LePore 1991, 1992, 1993) of functional role semantics operate on the assumption that Quine is right about the analytic–synthetic distinction.

2.5. Concepts and Possession Conditions

The final approach to attitude aboutness that we shall consider rests upon the assumption that we can reject at least some aspects of Quine's critique of the analytic–synthetic distinction. A key notion in this approach is that of a *possession condition* for a concept.

Believing that the ice is thin is taking a certain attitude towards a certain proposition. The proposition specifies the content of the belief, and we have noted that belief contents are fine-grained. These fine-grained propositions or contents are sometimes called *thoughts* (Frege 1918). In this use of the term, thoughts are structured, abstract entities. A thought is built up out of concepts as constituents, somewhat as a sentence is built up out of words. The thought that the ice is thin involves the concept of ice and the concept of being thin, and these concepts are combined in a particular way. In order to frame the thought, a thinker needs to have the constituent concepts. Drawing this analogy between structured thoughts (as abstract entities) and structured sentences is not the same as supposing that the language of thought hypothesis is true. The language of thought hypothesis concerns states or events of thinking, and says that they involve not just structured contents, but structured vehicles of content.

A concept can be regarded as a way of thinking of an object or property. Having or possessing a concept is having a cognitive ability—the ability to think of an object or property in a certain way. Making a judgement, or forming a belief, involves the exercise of several of these abilities. So, we can approach questions about attitude aboutness—the content of beliefs and other attitudes—via questions about possession of concepts. Questions about having a belief with the content that the ice is thin can be approached by way of questions about possession of the concepts of ice and of being thin. Likewise, but the other way about, we might approach questions about possession of concepts via questions about attitude aboutness. Questions about possession of the concept of ice or the concept of being thin might be approached by way of questions about beliefs in whose contents those concepts figure, such as the belief that the ice is thin.

One project for any theory about having concepts is to spell out conditions for possessing various concepts. The general form of such a condition is:

For any thinking subject x, x possesses the concept . . . if and only if———.

Because of the close connection between having beliefs and possessing concepts, we can derive a theory of concept possession from a given account of attitude aboutness. Thus, for example, we can reconfigure the characteristic statements of the intentional stance approach into statements of possession conditions for concepts:

For any thinking subject x, x possesses the concept of being white if and only if x can be predictively attributed some beliefs in whose content the concept of being white is involved (such as the belief that snow is white).

This surely tells us something true about the concept of being white, and we can highlight just exactly what it tells us about that concept if we reformulate the statement of possession conditions in two stages. First, we italicize the points at which the statement explicitly mentions the concept of being white:

> For any thinking subject x, x possesses *the concept of being white* if and only if x can be predictively attributed some beliefs in whose content *the concept of being white* is involved (such as the belief that snow is white).

Then, second, we move the explicit mention of the concept of being white to the front of the statement, and link it with what is said later by introducing a variable 'C' and some use of 'such that' terminology, where what follows the 'such that' is just what the original statement tells us about the concept of being white:

> *The concept of being white* is a concept C such that: for any thinking subject x, x possesses the concept C if and only if x can be predictively attributed some beliefs in whose content the concept C is involved.

This makes plain how little the original statement of possession conditions tells us about the concept of being white, since what this tells us about that concept does not distinguish it from any other concept. It is just as true to say of the concept of being green, for example, that:

> *The concept of being green* is a concept C such that: for any thinking subject x, x possesses the concept C if and only if x can be predictively attributed some beliefs in whose content the concept C is involved.

or of the concept of the number two that:

> *The concept of the number two* is a concept C such that: for any thinking subject x, x possesses the concept C if and only if x can be predictively attributed some beliefs in whose content the concept C is involved.

In all three cases, what follows the 'such that' is exactly the same.

Since the intentional stance approach yields a possession condition for the concept of being white that does not say anything distinctive about that concept, it would be quite false to say:

> The concept of being white is *the* concept C such that: for any thinking subject x, x possesses the concept C if and only if x can be predictively attributed some beliefs in whose content the concept C is involved.

We can summarize this by saying that the possession condition for the concept of being white does not *individuate* that concept.

To see how a different kind of possession condition might individuate a concept, imagine for a moment that the simple covariation account of attitude aboutness were correct. (This is just to illustrate a formal point. In fact, we already found reasons to reject the simple covariation account in Section 2.3.) Then, we could say:

> For any thinking subject *x*, *x* possesses the concept of being white if and only if there is an internal state of *x* that occurs in *x* when, only when, and because *x* is confronted by something white.

This differs from the intentional stance approach because it explicitly invokes internal states of the subject. But there is another difference that is more important for our present purposes.

In the possession condition based on the intentional stance, the concept of being white—considered as a constituent of the contents of beliefs—had to be mentioned after the 'if and only if'. In essence, this was because the notion of having (or being predictively attributed with) beliefs about things being white—such as the belief that snow is white—crucially makes use of the idea of a subject having the concept of being white. In contrast, the notion of having an internal state that covaries with the presence of things that are white does not reimport the idea of a subject having the concept of being white. This has important consequences when we take the two steps to switch to a 'such that' formulation of the covariation based possession condition. First, we italicize the points at which the statement explicitly mentions the concept of being white. But this time, there is only one such point:

> For any thinking subject *x*, *x* possesses *the concept of being white* if and only if there is an internal state of *x* that occurs in *x* when, only when, and because *x* is confronted by something white.

Then, second, we move the explicit mention of the concept of being white to the front of the statement:

> *The concept of being white* is a concept *C* such that: for any thinking subject *x*, *x* possesses the concept *C* if and only if there is an internal state of *x* that occurs in *x* when, only when, and because *x* is confronted by something white.

Now, this is clearly not a correct possession condition for the concept of being white. Since it is based on the idea of covariation, it does not allow for the deployment of the concept of being white in a false belief about a presented object. Furthermore, it does not allow for the use of the concept of being white in beliefs about absent objects, or in imagination, for example. But, if we overlook those flaws for a moment, we can see that what follows the 'such that' here does say something quite distinctive about the concept of being white. What it says about the concept of being white could not be said equally correctly about the concept of being green, for example:

> *The concept of being green* is a concept *C* such that: for any thinking subject *x*, *x* possesses the concept *C* if and only if there is an internal state of *x* that occurs in *x* when, only when, and because *x* is confronted by something white.

Indeed, if we were overlooking the general difficulties with the covariation approach, then it would be quite plausible to move to the idea that what this possession condition tells us about the concept of being white picks out that concept uniquely:

> The concept of being white is *the* concept *C* such that: for any thinking subject *x*, *x* possesses the concept *C* if and only if there is an internal state *s* of *x* that occurs in *x* when, only when, and because *x* is confronted by something white.

It would be quite plausible to suppose, that is, that the condition for possession of the concept actually individuates the concept.

Since we already have grounds for thinking that the covariation approach to attitude aboutness is not adequate (Section 2.3), this example can only serve as an illustration of the way in which a possession condition might be individuative. The possession condition approach that is being developed by Peacocke (1989, 1992*a*, *b*) is not any kind of covariation-plus-teleology theory. Rather, Peacocke puts together the idea of a possession condition that also individuates a concept, and the claim that certain inferential liaisons figure crucially in a subject's possession of a given concept. Roughly, we can say that certain inferential liaisons amongst the belief states of a subject are necessary to the subject's possessing the concepts involved in the contents of those states. (The reason why this would only be rough is that Peacocke actually formulates his account in terms of thinking subjects rather than in terms of internal states.)

A typical formulation of a possession condition offered as an individuation condition for a concept is:

> ... the logical concept *and* is individuated by this condition: it is the unique concept *C* to possess which a thinker has to find these forms of inference compelling, without basing them on any further inference or information: from any two premises *A* and *B*, *ACB* can be inferred; and from any premise *ACB*, each of *A* and *B* can be inferred. (Peacocke 1992*b*: 74–5)

The simpler statement of a possession condition from which this individuation condition would be developed would be:

> For any thinking subject *x*, *x* possesses the concept of logical conjunction, *and*, if and only if *x* finds these forms of inference compelling [etc.]: from any two premises *A* and *B*, *A and B* can be inferred; and from any premiss *A and B*, each of *A* and *B* can be inferred.

Here we speak of a subject finding inferences compelling, and so we speak of a subject thinking thoughts whose contents involve the proposition that *A and B* and so involve the concept *and*. The concept of logical conjunction—considered as a constituent of the contents of beliefs—is mentioned after the 'if and only if'. So, the next stage would be the 'such that' formulation, with each mention of the concept *and* replaced by the variable *C*:

> The concept *and* is a concept *C* such that: for any thinking subject *x*, *x* possesses the concept *C* if and only if *x* finds these forms of inference compelling [etc.]: from any two premisses *A* and *B*, *ACB* can be inferred; and from any premiss *ACB*, each of *A* and *B* can be inferred.

In this formulation, the word 'and' still occurs after the 'if and only if'. The concept of logical conjunction is used in this statement of a possession condition for that very concept (just as the concept of being white was used after the 'if and only if' in the covariation-based possession condition, above). But what we do not find—once the variable *C* has been introduced *en route* to an individuation condition—is any mention of the concept *and*—considered as a constituent of the contents of beliefs.

Formulating a possession condition—and, thence, an individuation condition—for the concept of logical conjunction involves us in assigning a privileged status to certain patterns of inference involving that concept. The two patterns of inference corresponding to the natural deduction rules of conjunction introduction (from *A* and *B* infer *A* & *B*) and conjunction elimination (from *A* & *B* infer *A*, and from *A* & *B* infer *B*) are privileged over other patterns that also involve the concept of conjunction. A subject who possesses the concept of logical conjunction will doubtless find many patterns of inference compelling. But these are the patterns that must be found compelling if a subject is to count as possessing the concept. Similarly, in the case of a public language, we might say that a subject cannot count as using a symbol to mean logical conjunction unless the subject regards as compelling certain inferential transitions involving that symbol.

When the possession conditions approach to individuating concepts is extended beyond logical concepts—like the concept *and*—the same general structure is exhibited. First, a possession condition for the concept is formulated. This possession privileges certain inferential transitions (or other transitions, such as that from having a certain kind of experience to making a certain judgement). It is here that the approach rests upon the assumption that we can reject at least some aspects of Quine's critique of the analytic–synthetic distinction. Second, wherever the concept is mentioned in the possession condition, we replace that mention of the concept with a variable, and we convert the possession condition into the 'such that' form. Third, the 'such that' form of the possession condition is elevated to the role of an individuation condition. Needless to say, the success of the approach would depend upon there being, for any given concept, liaisons that could plausibly be privileged.

Although this approach differs from the intentional stance approach in aiming at individuative accounts of concepts, it is like the intentional stance approach in two important ways. First, it is cast in terms of thinking subjects and not in terms of internal states. Second, it is non-reductionist: the account makes use of mental notions like that of finding an inference compelling.

However, it is plausible to argue that this approach does carry with it some quite heavy commitments about the internal states and internal processing that underpin a subject's conceptual abilities. Indeed, it may even be possible to argue that this approach requires those abilities to be underpinned by a language of thought architecture (Davies 1991). If that is right, then the possession conditions that are stated at the level of the thinking subject can be seen as imposing conditions upon the cognitive processing within the subject. These would be conditions upon the causal role of sentences and words in the subject's language of thought. So, in the end, the possession conditions approach may indirectly impose conditions that can be stated in the terms favoured by functional role semantics. These conditions would say, for example, that if a symbol in a subject's language of thought is to be the vehicle of the subject's possession of the concept *and*, then the functional role of that symbol must include a special or canonical sub-part. This sub-part of the functional role would involve causal relations between tokens of sentences containing the putative conjunction symbol and tokens of the putative conjuncts. These causal relations would underpin the subject's finding inferences of the *and*-introduction and *and*-elimination patterns to be compelling.

So, we might say that the possession conditions approach has a certain affinity with a kind of functional role semantics—a kind that appeals to canonical, rather than holistic, functional roles. But, it is important to notice, once again, that the approach is non-reductionist. It provides no reason to think that a set of conditions upon internal states, couched in the terms favoured by functional role semantics, will necessarily add up to possession of concepts.

2.6. Theories of Intentionality

The term 'intentionality', we noted (Section 2.1.1), might well be reserved for attitude aboutness. In this section, we have distinguished intentionality from other varieties of aboutness (Section 2.1), and then considered various theories of intentionality. It would be wrong to base any firm judgement upon this brief survey, but there may be some grounds for the thought that no reductionist theory of intentionality—cast in terms of covariation, or teleological function, or functional role—is ultimately satisfactory.

To the extent that this first thought is right, there may also be some grounds for a second thought; namely, that these unsatisfactory theories of intentionality might be more satisfactory as theories of some other variety of aboutness. Indeed, in the case of covariation theories, this thought is quite trivial. A simple covariation theory is obviously correct when taken as a theory of indicator aboutness. But, not so trivially, it might also be that the less simple theories—designed to allow for the possibility of misrepresentation—are better regarded as theories of subdoxastic aboutness than as theories of intentionality. If any of this is correct, then we may have to regard intentionality as a mental phenomenon characterized by resistance to reduction. And, if we do so regard it, then we shall be bound to ask why intentionality resists reduction. One possible answer to that question is that intentionality (unlike subdoxastic aboutness) enjoys a special relationship with consciousness, and that it is consciousness that is the primary locus of this resistance. In the next section, we shall turn our attention to consciousness.

3. CONSCIOUSNESS

In Section 1 we considered a range of broadly materialist alternatives to Cartesian dualism, without raising what might seem to be the most obvious objection to them: the objection, namely, that they fail to account for consciousness. In Section 2 we examined theories of intentionality, while still holding questions about consciousness to one side. It is now time to confront what Nagel (1994: 63) describes as 'the most fundamental problem in the area' (see above, Section 1.8).

3.1. An Argument for Elusiveness

Back in Section 1.3 we noted that Place introduced central state materialism in response to the thought that, even if analytical behaviourism were acceptable for the propositional attitudes, still 'there would seem to be an intractable residue of concepts clustering around the notions of consciousness, experience, sensation, and mental imagery, where some sort of inner process story is unavoidable' (Place 1956/1990: 30). However, the idea that types of conscious experience are to be identified with types of brain process seems to leave an important question unanswered. We can make the question vivid, by using the idea of there being *something that it is like* to be in a certain state—and, more generally, the idea of there being something that it is like to be a certain creature or system. Nagel introduces the idea this way: 'no matter how the form [of conscious experience] may vary, the fact that an organism has conscious experience *at all* means, basically, that there is something that it is like to *be* that organism. . . . fundamentally, an organism has conscious mental states if and only if there is something that it is like to *be* that organism—something it is like *for* the organism' (1974/1979: 166). The intuition is that, since a brick does not have conscious experiences, there is nothing that it is like to be a brick. Likewise, there is nothing that it is like to be a laser printer. On the other hand, supposing that bats and dolphins do have conscious experiences, there is something that it is like to be a bat, or a dolphin. Certainly, there is something that it is like to be a human being.

If there is something that it is like to be a certain creature, then there may also be something that it is like, for that creature, to be in some specific state. In our own mental lives, perceptual and sensational states provide clear examples. There is something that it is like to see a bottle of red wine on a white table-cloth, to hear a piano playing somewhere off to the left, to feel an itch, a pain, or a tickle. These experiences—conscious experiences—have a subjective, phenomenal character.

We can now pose the question that central state materialism seems to leave unanswered. Why should there be something that it is like for certain processes to be occurring in our brains? Nagel's view is that this question is one that we do not even know how to begin to answer. Thus, 'If mental processes are indeed physical processes, then there is something that it is like, intrinsically, to undergo certain physical processes. What it is for such a thing to be the case remains a mystery' (1974/1979: 175). Indeed, Nagel argues that the subjective phenomenal properties of experience fall outside the compass of a physicalist view of the world: 'If physicalism is to be defended, the phenomenological features must themselves be given a physical account. But when we examine their subjective character it seems that such a result is impossible. The reason is that every subjective phenomenon is essentially connected with a single point of view, and it seems inevitable that an objective, physical theory will abandon that point of view' (1974/1979: 176). Clearly, the notion of a *point of view* is crucial to Nagel's argument.

Someone might take a point of view to be something that is private to an individual; but this is not the notion that Nagel uses. He is concerned with a type: something that is shared by many individuals in virtue of their having similar perceptual systems. A point of view—determined by a collection of perceptual systems—constitutes a kind of limitation upon what is conceivable for an individual. Since experience furnishes the raw materials for imagination, there may be some aspects of the world that are beyond the imaginative reach of creatures with one point of view, but within the imaginative reach of creatures with a different point of view.

Nagel offers an example that has become '[t]he most widely cited and influential thought experiment about consciousness' (Dennett 1991: 441). It concerns the 'specific subjective character' of a bat's experience, which, Nagel suggests, might be 'beyond our ability to conceive' (1974/1979: 170). The point here is not just that we might not be able to conceive how the bat's brain gives rise to the bat's consciousness. The point is more dramatic. We might not be able to form a conception of the subjective character of a bat's conscious experience. We might not be able to imagine what it is like to be a bat. In contrast, because human beings share a point of view, we can conceive of, think about, and talk about, the character of our own, and each other's, experience.

The facts about the subjective character of a bat's experience might be inaccessible to us. This would not be, fundamentally, because we could frame the relevant hypotheses but could not gather the evidence to confirm them. Rather, the problem is that we may lack the conceptual resources even to frame the correct hypotheses. In contrast, we have the resources to frame hypotheses about the subjective character of the experience of another human being. The examples of a bat and of a human being illustrate that the accessibility or inaccessibility of facts about the subjective character of another creature's experience is quite sensitive to our point of view.

This basic point is not diminished by the suggestion that some human beings may have more flexible imaginations, and so may be better placed than others to achieve an adequate conception of bat phenomenology. What matters is that, where the subjective character of experience is concerned, accessibility of the facts is sensitive to our point of view, at least to some considerable extent. The contrast that is crucial for Nagel's argument is the contrast between these facts about the subjective character of experience, on the one hand, and facts about physics or neurophysiology, on the other hand.

Our grasp of subjective facts depends very much upon our point of view, and so upon our particular perceptual systems. But, in order to grasp the concepts deployed in physical or neurophysiological theory, a creature does not need to have the same perceptual systems that we have: 'intelligent bats or Martians might learn more about the human brain than we ever will' (Nagel 1974/1979: 172). So, in contrast to the accessibility of subjective facts, the accessibility of physical or neurophysiological facts is not especially sensitive to our point of view. This is the difference between phenomenological facts and physical or neurophysiological facts upon which Nagel's argument turns. The difference may be one of degree; and, of course, we are able to grasp both phenomenological and physical facts about ourselves and other human beings. But, in the one case (the phenomenological) and not in the other (the physical), that ability depends upon the nature of our perceptual systems and the character of the experiences that they furnish.

Phenomenological facts seem to have a property that physical facts lack. If that is right, then it follows by logic alone that phenomenological facts are not physical facts. The subjective character of experience eludes a physicalist theory of the world.

Nagel's conclusion about the elusiveness of phenomenal consciousness is thus arrived at by an argument that turns upon a distinction between two kinds of fact. In order to be clear about just what is established by this argument, we have to pay attention to a potential ambiguity in the idea of a fact.

Consider again the fine-grained nature of attitude aboutness (Section 2.1.1). The thought that Hesperus is a planet is arguably a different thought from the thought that Phosphorus is a planet. The two contents involve different concepts, different ways of thinking of the planet Venus. The first content involves a concept, possession of which is grounded in the ability to recognize the planet Venus in the evening sky. The second content involves a concept whose possession is similarly grounded in the ability to recognize Venus in the morning sky. We might even say that the first thought is inaccessible for someone who goes to bed sufficiently early, while the second thought is inaccessible for someone who sleeps in sufficiently late.

But, now, should we say that the fact that Hesperus is a planet is a different fact from the fact that Phosphorus is a planet? The answer depends upon how fine-grained facts are. We might take facts to be correct thoughts, in which case facts will be just as fine-grained as attitude aboutness. On the other hand, we might take facts to be states of affairs, built from the objects and properties that the correct thoughts are about. In that case, facts will be as coarse-grained as referential content (cf. Section 2.3). In Fregean (1892) terminology, we could say that, on the first construal, facts belong at the level of sense; on the second construal they belong at the level of reference.

If facts belong at the level of sense and are equated with correct thoughts, then the fact that Hesperus is a planet is different from the fact that Phosphorus is a planet. But if facts belong at the level of reference and are equated with states of affairs, then we have just one fact. For what in the world makes the first thought correct is just the same as what in the world makes the second thought correct; namely, the object Venus exemplifying the property of being a planet. One and the same state of affairs can be thought about in two different ways, because one and the same object can be thought about in two different ways.

We said that, for a late sleeper, Phosphorus thoughts are inaccessible, while Hesperus thoughts are, of course, accessible. The late sleeper is not able to apprehend the thought that Phosphorus is a planet, since he lacks a certain conceptual ability. The late sleeper does not possess the way of thinking of Venus that is grounded in an ability to recognize that planet in the morning sky. But the late sleeper might build up a body of knowledge—a theory—about the planet Venus. He might come to know that Hesperus is a planet, that Hesperus appears in the evening, that Hesperus also appears in the morning, that Hesperus is called 'Hesperus', that Hesperus is also called 'Phosphorus', and so on. In thinking these thoughts—including the thought that Hesperus is called 'Phosphorus'—the late sleeper would deploy the way of thinking of Venus that is grounded in the ability to recognize it in the evening sky.

Now, are there facts about the planet Hesperus (that is, Phosphorus; that is, Venus) that elude the late sleeper's theory? There are certainly thoughts about Venus that are inaccessible to the late sleeper; namely, Phosphorus thoughts. But it does not follow that the late sleeper's theory provides an incomplete account of the planet Hesperus (that is, of Phosphorus; that is, of Venus). It would certainly be wrong to infer that reality includes items that are different in kind from the items that the late sleeper's theory speaks of. For the inaccessible thoughts are thoughts about the very same item that the accessible thoughts are about.

Just as it would be wrong to draw this inference about reality, so also someone might object to Nagel's argument leading up to the conclusion about the elusiveness of consciousness. It is open to someone to say that Nagel's argument does not show that physicalism provides an incomplete account of the world. What it shows is only that certain physical states can be thought about in very different ways; rather as the planet Venus can be thought about in different ways. A Fregean might put the point by saying that Nagel demonstrates a difference between the physical and the phenomenal at the level of sense, but does not demonstrate a difference at the level of reference.

Anticipating this line of response to his argument, Nagel suggests that the case of conscious experience is different from typical cases where we can separate the level of reference from the level of sense. In the case of a planet, there is a clear separation between the object that is thought about and the *mode of presentation* (Frege 1892) of that object—between the object as it is and the way that the object appears. In such a case, two different modes of presentation can make possible two different ways of thinking about one and the same object. But, in the case of an experience, there is no separation between the way that the experience is and the way that it appears. So, Nagel claims (1974/1979: 173–4), his argument for the metaphysical elusiveness of consciousness is not open to the objection based on the ambiguity in the idea of a fact.

3.2. An Announcement of Mystery

There are further turns that this dispute can take. For now, it is enough to note that there is a fair measure of consensus that Nagel's argument cannot establish the metaphysical conclusion that conscious experiences are not identical with physical processes in the brain (e.g. Levine 1993). But, even if we allow that conscious experiences are to be identified with physical events or processes, the unanswered question still remains:

If we acknowledge that a physical theory of mind must account for the subjective character of experience, we must admit that no presently available conception gives us a clue how this could be done. The problem is unique. If mental processes are indeed physical processes, then there is something that it is like, intrinsically, to undergo certain physical processes. What it is for such a thing to be the case remains a mystery. (Nagel 1974/1979: 175)

This announcement of mystery is echoed by several other philosophers, including Block (1978) and Jackson (1982, 1986), and it is given a particularly strong formulation by McGinn (1989).

Jackson (1982), Nagel (1986), and McGinn (1989) claim that it should be intelligible to us that there may be much about the way that the world works that lies beyond our human understanding. McGinn (1989) develops this idea (building on work of Chomsky (1975) and Fodor (1983)) and advances an argument for the proposition that understanding how physical processes give rise to consciousness—how it is that 'there is something that it is like, intrinsically, to undergo certain physical processes'—is beyond us.

McGinn argues that, although the brain is the seat of consciousness in virtue of certain of its properties, what those properties are, and how they give rise to phenomenal consciousness, is beyond our cognitive grasp. Metaphysically, consciousness has a material basis; but epistemologically, we are doomed to be without an explanation of this. McGinn's argument for this prospect proceeds by considering in turn the ways in which we might hope to achieve a grasp of what it is about the brain that gives rise to consciousness.

There are two putative routes to a grasp of the neural basis of consciousness. On the one hand, we might rely upon consciousness itself, and hope for an introspective fix upon the explanatory basis of phenomenal consciousness. On the other hand, we might turn to the scientific study of the brain. Of the two, the first seems utterly hopeless, since 'Introspection does not present conscious states *as* depending upon the brain in some intelligible way' (McGinn 1989/1991: 8). So, the argument focuses for the most part upon the prospects for a neuroscientific explanation of consciousness. Can we attain any conception of a neuroscientific property of the brain adequate to explain consciousness?

McGinn's argument for a negative answer to this question proceeds in two steps. The first step says that ordinary perception of the brain does not bring us up against any such property. The second step says that no such property is going to be introduced by inference to the best explanation from perceptible properties of the brain.

The first step of the argument seems right. When we casually observe a human brain we do not come upon any property that makes it intelligible that the brain is the seat of phenomenal consciousness. The colour, texture, and mass of the brain—being properties that the brain shares with other organic and inorganic chunks of matter—do not carry any hint of the subjective character of conscious experience.

These gross observable properties of the brain—and other, smaller-scale properties, too—have to be explained. But, according to the second step of the argument, whatever explanation of these observable properties may be offered, it will not introduce any property of the brain that could explain consciousness: 'To explain the observed physical data we need only such theoretical properties as bear upon those data, not the property that explains consciousness, which does not occur in the data. Since we do not need consciousness to explain those data, we do not need the property that explains consciousness' (McGinn 1989/1991: 13). Putting the two steps together, we arrive at the conclusion that neither experience nor theory yields us any grasp upon a natural property of the brain that can explain consciousness. Consciousness has a material basis, but what that basis is we cannot grasp.

This argument is controversial, and is far from being universally accepted. Flanagan (1992, ch. 6), for example, offers a detailed critique. One aspect of the argument that is striking is that the treatments of the two putative routes to a grasp of the neural basis of consciousness are structurally different. The assessment of the second route involves two steps, one concerning perception and one concerning inference to the best explanation. But the assessment of the first route involves only one step. Introspection does not reveal to us the neural basis of consciousness. We might have expected that here, too, there would be a second step, considering whether a property that could explain consciousness might be introduced by way of inference to the best explanation. So long as that possibility is not closed off, the argument seems to be incomplete.

If the treatments of the two routes were to have the same structure—so that the argument could be seen to be complete—then the crucial question would concern inference to the best explanation of the phenomena that are revealed to introspection. Could this afford us a grasp upon the material basis of conscious experience? But the problem with this question is that it is too close to the question that the argument as a whole is supposed to answer: Can we understand how a property of the brain could give rise to the subjective character of experience—the character that is revealed to introspection? So, on the face of it, there is something question-begging about the argument as a whole. (Cf. Flanagan 1992: 113: 'McGinn's misstep comes from forgetting that consciousness has already been introduced.')

Nagel announced a mystery, and McGinn went a step further by arguing that mystery is inevitable here. Even if there are queries that can be raised about McGinn's argument for inevitability, still the actual mystery seems to remain.

3.3. Higher-Order Thoughts

One possible strategy for demystifying the notion of consciousness—the 'what it is like' aspect of experience—is to claim that consciousness is a matter of thought about mental states.

One philosopher who favours this strategy is Rosenthal (1986, 1993; see also Nelkin, 1986, 1989, 1993a). He begins (1986/1991: 463) from the idea that mental states have either intentional properties or phenomenal (or sensory) properties. Furthermore, it is plausible that mental states are the only things that have these properties non-derivatively. (Sentences of a public language have meanings, but their aboutness is plausibly derived from the mental states of language users. See Section 2.1.2.) Consequently, Rosenthal proposes, we can use the disjunction of phenomenal and (non-derived) intentional properties to mark out the class of mental states, and then use some further criterion to distinguish conscious states as a subclass of mental states.

The aim of the exercise is to provide a non-circular account of consciousness in terms that do not appear to be so mysterious. So, it is important that the notions of phenomenal property and intentional property should not already involve the idea of consciousness.

If we allow this starting-point, then the basic idea in Rosenthal's construction of the notion of consciousness is fairly straightforward: 'Conscious states are simply mental states we are conscious of being in. And, in general, our being conscious of something is just a matter of our having a thought of some sort about it. Accordingly, it is natural to identify a mental state's being conscious with one's having a roughly contemporaneous thought that one is in that mental state' (1986/1991: 465). In this construction, consciousness *of* something is analysed in terms of having a thought about that thing. And consciousness— considered as a property of mental states—is analysed in terms of consciousness *of* that mental state. For a mental state to be a conscious mental state is for the subject of the state to have a thought about it. Since the item being thought about is a mental state—perhaps itself a thought—the thought about it is said to be a *higher-order thought*, and the resulting account of consciousness is said to be a higher-order thought theory of consciousness.

If such a theory were to be correct, then the occurrence of consciousness in the natural order need not be especially mysterious: 'Since a mental state is conscious if it is accompanied by a suitable higher-order thought, we can explain a mental state's being conscious by hypothesizing that the mental state itself causes that higher-order thought to occur' (Rosenthal 1986/1991: 465). But, in fact, there are some quite serious problems for higher-order thought theories.

We shall consider, first, an objection that does not constitute a serious problem. Someone might say that, while she certainly enjoys conscious mental states, she is largely unaware of the higher-order thoughts that Rosenthal's account of conscious mental states requires. This is not a serious problem for the account, since to say that the subject is unaware of (or is not conscious of) the higher-order thoughts is—according to the account—to say that those higher-order thoughts are not themselves conscious mental states. But the analysis does not say that for a mental state to be conscious the subject must have a *conscious* thought about it—just that the subject must have a thought about it (Rosenthal 1986/1991: 465).

Another challenge arises from the fact that the account appears to allow for the coherence of the idea of unconscious sensations. A mental state with phenomenal properties might occur without being accompanied by a thought about that state. And, at least initially, this may seem quite counter-intuitive.

But it is not obvious that there is a really serious problem for the account here. The role of unconscious sensations might, for example, be underwritten by everyday experience—the persistent headache from which one is nevertheless distracted, or which one forgets about for a while. And, in any case, we might be willing to overcome the initial impression of counter-intuitiveness if the higher-order thought theory had other highly attractive features (Nelkin 1989, 1993a).

The challenge that Rosenthal reckons to be '[p]erhaps the strongest objection' (1986/1991: 472) to the higher-order thought account of consciousness is that we intuitively ascribe consciousness to the states of creatures that we would not credit with the power of thought. His response comes in two stages.

The first stage of the response is to stress that the thought that is required if a phenomenal (rather than intentional) mental state is to be conscious is not a very sophisticated thought—so the potential for such thoughts imposes relatively modest demands upon a creature. The second stage is to suggest that, where a creature does not even measure up to those modest demands, an intuition that the creature is nevertheless conscious can still be salvaged. For, in one sense of the term, 'For an organism to be conscious means only that it is awake, and mentally responsive to sensory stimuli' (1986/1991: 473).

This second stage of the response is not wholly satisfying. From the point of view of someone who starts with any sympathy at all for Nagel's position, it will seem that what is being offered here is not really consciousness without thought. Being 'awake, and mentally responsive to sensory stimuli' is not clearly sufficient for the 'what it is like' notion of consciousness. Indeed, unless so much weight is laid on the term 'mental' as to rob the second stage of its dialectical point, it is unclear that 'awake, and mentally responsive' requires anything more than a functioning stimulus–response system. The real issue turns upon the first stage of the response.

But the first stage of the response invites the worry that the higher-order thought theory faces a dilemma. If the notion of thought that is employed is a demanding one, then, it seems, there could be something that it is like for a creature to be in certain states even though the creature did not have (perhaps, even, could not have) any thoughts about those states. Higher-order thought is not necessary for consciousness. But, if the notion of thought that is employed is a thin and undemanding one, then higher-order thought is not sufficient for consciousness. Suppose, for example, that thought is said to require no more than having discriminative capacities. Then it seems clear that a creature, or other system, could be in a certain type of mental state, and could have a capacity to detect whether or not it was in a state of that type, even though there was nothing that it was like to be that creature or system.

In fact, the situation is a little more complex than this dilemma reveals. According to the dilemma, there is a query about the necessity of the account, given a rich notion of thought, and a query about its sufficiency, given a thin notion of thought. But, by considering conscious beliefs as well as conscious sensations, we can see that there is also a worry about the sufficiency of the account, even given a rich notion of thought. It is possible to imagine cases in which a subject has a belief, and also judges himself to have that belief, but where both the first-order belief and the second-order belief would intuitively be counted as unconscious beliefs. One kind of example would involve unconscious guilt about having an unconscious belief, since the guilt would plausibly be based upon recognition (also unconscious) that one has the belief. This recognition would amount to a higher-order thought about the first-order belief; but it would not be enough to make the belief conscious (cf. Peacocke 1992*a*: 154).

3.4. Interlude: Explaining Consciousness

In Section 3.1 we gave a rather critical assessment of Nagel's argument aimed at showing that conscious experiences elude a physicalist account of reality. But, even if conscious experiences are physical happenings, still we need some explanation of how it is that there is something that it is like to have certain physical happenings going on in one's brain.

In Section 3.2 we also took a rather critical view of McGinn's argument towards the conclusion that there is something inevitable about our inability to find a satisfying explanation of consciousness in terms of neural goings-on. But, even if that argument is flawed, still the need for an explanation is obvious, and our current inability to give a fully satisfying explanation is also clear. Indeed, for all that we have said, McGinn may be right in thinking that no such explanation is conceptually available to us.

In Section 3.3 we examined one proposal for demystifying consciousness, and discovered some serious problems with it. There is a great deal more that should be said about work towards demystification. Such work has a negative and a positive aspect. The negative aspect consists in seeking to reveal unclarities and paradoxes in the notion of the subjective phenomenal character of experience (e.g. Dennett 1988, 1991; Dennett and Kinsbourne 1992). The importance of this work is that it raises the possibility that the sense of mystery surrounding consciousness is not the result of a clear insight about an explanatory gap (Levine 1983), but is rather the product of deeply tempting fallacies and confusions.

The positive aspect of work towards demystification consists in offering putative explanations of one or another property of conscious experience in neural terms. Churchland (1988: 148) provides a clear example of a way of explaining some features of our experiences of colour (see also Land 1977; Campbell 1982). Intuitively, we say that an experience of orange is more like an experience of red than it is like an experience of blue. And we say that the experience of orange is somehow intermediate between an experience of red and an experience of yellow. The neural coding of colour involves triples of activation values $\langle x, y, z \rangle$, corresponding to the illumination reaching three families of cones (photoreceptors in the retina), which are, in turn, sensitive to three ranges of wavelengths. These triples of values can be plotted as points in a three-dimensional space. In that space, the neural correlate of an experience of orange is closer to the neural correlate of an experience of red than to the correlate of an experience of blue. And the neural code for orange is between the code for red and the code for yellow.

This does seem to provide a satisfying explanation of those particular properties—phenomenal similarity and 'betweenness'—of our colour experience. We might call these *structural* properties of experience, and surmise that we have here a vindication of a remark of Nagel's (1974/1979: 179): 'structural features of perception might be more accessible to objective description . . . Aspects of subjective experience that admitted this kind of objective description might be better candidates for objective explanation of a more familiar sort.' But Nagel actually says a little more: 'structural features of perception might be more accessible to objective description, even though something would be left out'. Experiences have properties other than their structural properties, and these, Nagel is saying, still resist explanation in objective (physical) terms. Perhaps we can capture this idea by saying that the triples of activation values, and the structural properties of the three-dimensional space in which they are plotted, provide an explanation why what it is like to see red is similar to what it is like to see orange, and so on. But they do not provide an explanation why it is like anything at all to see red. Why there are experiential correlates of these neural codes is left as a brute unexplained fact.

In response to the idea that explanations of consciousness can go a long way but still a kernel of mystery remains, an advocate of demystification is liable to say that the appearance of mystery is an artefact of an overly severe standard for explanations. Flanagan, for example, says that McGinn imposes an 'impossibly high standard on intelligibility' (1992: 115). The demystifier says that Nagel and others are asking for an explanation that presents an a priori logical connection between the explaining facts (facts about neural activations and the like) and the facts to be explained (facts about what it is like to have this or that experience). This is a standard that we do not impose in the natural sciences. But the defender of Nagel's position may retort that the demystifier is pitching the standards of explanation too low. Statements of brute correlation are not to be mistaken for genuine explanations. So, it seems that further progress here may depend upon a better understanding of the nature of explanation itself.

3.5. Consciousness and Intentionality

In Section 2.6, we noted that there may be grounds for thinking that no reductionist theory of intentionality—cast in terms of covariation, or teleological function, or functional role—is ultimately satisfactory. The difficulties that we found in providing any kind of reductive analysis of attitude aboutness are bound to suggest that we are leaving something essential out of the equation. According to Searle (1989, 1990, 1992), the crucial ingredient that is missing from the reductionist accounts that we considered in Section 2 is consciousness. (See also McGinn 1988; and, for a contrasting view, Nelkin 1993*b*.)

Searle notes a lack of serious work on consciousness in cognitive science—a lack which is perhaps less apparent now than it was when Searle was writing—and he says: 'I believe that it is a profound mistake to try to describe and explain mental phenomena without reference to consciousness. . . . any intentional state is either actually or potentially a conscious intentional state' (1989: 194). The bold conclusion for which Searle argues is: 'Roughly speaking, all genuinely *mental* activity is either conscious or potentially so. All the other activities of the brain are non-mental, physiological processes' (1989: 208).

In the slightly later treatment (Searle 1990; see also 1992), the corresponding argument is directed towards what he calls the connection principle: 'The ascription of an unconscious intentional phenomenon to a system implies that the phenomenon is in principle accessible to consciousness' (1990: 586). There is a weaker and a stronger way of construing this claim about the connection between intentionality and consciousness.

On the weaker construal, Searle would merely be saying that psychological states that are inaccessible to consciousness have an importantly different kind of aboutness, or have aboutness in a different way, from conscious—or potentially conscious—mental states. On the stronger construal, he would be saying that the only genuine aboutness belongs to conscious (or at least potentially conscious) mental states; so that supposedly psychological states that are inaccessible to consciousness do not really have aboutness at all—and do not deserve the label 'mental'.

If Searle were only trying to establish the weaker claim, then his argument would fit in neatly with the distinctions that we drew, in Section 2.1, between five different species of aboutness. The unconscious states that are cited in cognitive science and information-processing psychology would be allowed to have subdoxastic aboutness (Section 2.1.5), which is perhaps some kind of variation on the theme of indicator aboutness (Section 2.1.3). But there would still be an important difference between subdoxastic aboutness and attitude aboutness; namely, the difference between a kind of non-conceptual content, on the one hand, and conceptualized content, on the other.

But, in fact, Searle intends the stronger construal of his conclusion: all non-trivial aboutness requires accessibility to consciousness (unless, as in the case of linguistic aboutness, it is derived aboutness). Consequently, his argument appears to threaten the very legitimacy of the greater part of information-processing psychology and also theoretical linguistics. (Thus, the argument has connections with another argument of Searle's, not discussed here: the Chinese room argument. See Searle 1980; and for a brief discussion, see Block 1990*a*: 282–6.)

In the argument that Searle advances for the connection principle, the pivotal notion is that of *aspectual shape*:

Whenever we perceive anything or think about anything, it is always under some aspects and not others that we perceive or think about that thing. . . . Aspectual shape is most obvious in the case of conscious perceptions . . . And what is true of conscious perceptions is true of intentional states generally. A man may believe, for example, that the star in the sky is the Morning Star without believing that it is the Evening Star. A man may, for example, want to drink a glass of water without wanting to drink a glass of H_2O. (1990: 587)

Intentionality requires aspectual shape; and—by way of several further steps of argument—aspectual shape requires consciousness.

Searle's explanation, and the examples that he provides, both suggest that his notion of aspectual shape is much the same as the Fregean notion of a mode of presentation. So, the claim that intentionality involves aspectual shape is similar to a claim that we are bound to find plausible; namely, the claim that attitude aboutness is fine-grained because it involves concepts (ways of thinking of objects and properties, belonging at the level of sense rather than at the level of reference). The question that then remains is whether there is a close link between conceptualization and consciousness.

Searle's argument for the connection principle—from its pivotal point to its conclusion—makes good sense if it is interpreted as being directed towards a positive answer to this question. For example, when Searle says: 'The aspectual feature cannot be exhaustively or completely characterized solely in terms of third person, behavioral, or even neurophysiological predicates. None of these is sufficient to give an exhaustive account of aspectual shape' (1990: 587), it is impossible not to be reminded of what Nagel says about the subjective character of conscious experience: 'If physicalism is to be defended, the phenomenological features must themselves be given a physical account. But when we examine their subjective character it seems that such a result is impossible. The reason is that every subjective phenomenon is essentially connected with a single point of view, and it seems inevitable that an objective, physical theory will abandon that point of view' (1974/1979: 167). But, this is not to say that the argument is compelling.

In fact, the argument faces a dilemma. As we have noted, the argument pivots on the claim that 'Intrinsic intentional states . . . always have aspectual shapes' (Searle 1990: 587). If a requirement of consciousness is built into the notion of aspectual shape, then the argument onwards from the pivotal point is plausible, but the claim itself becomes controversial. For it is not obvious that the fine-grainedness of attitude aboutness essentially requires there to be something that it is like to believe something. But, if a requirement of consciousness is not built into the notion of aspectual shape, then, although the pivotal claim itself becomes less controversial, the onward argument is unconvincing.

Indeed, Searle himself accepts that the argument for the connection principle is not absolutely compelling (1990: 634). But still, it is very plausible that there is a deep connection between the intentionality of propositional attitude states and conscious experience. The issues here are, however, far from being well understood.

Suppose that we grant that there is an important link between intentionality (attitude aboutness) and consciousness. Then we should ask whether Searle's argument rules out the possibility of other kinds of aboutness that are not so closely tied to consciousness. If it does, then the legitimacy of cognitive science is threatened.

But, it seems fairly clear that the argument for the connection principle does not itself cast any doubt upon a notion like subdoxastic aboutness (Davies 1995b). A challenge to the legitimacy of that notion would have to be mounted from another direction.

4. MENTAL CAUSATION

Mental events stand in causal relations. They may be causes of other events, both mental and physical. But, in the production of these effects, are the mental properties of mental events causally potent, or are they *epiphenomenal?*

We can ask this question about the phenomenal properties of experiences, or about the intentional properties of propositional attitude states. Back in Section 3.2, we mentioned that Jackson (1982) echoes Nagel's announcement of mystery concerning consciousness. In fact, Jackson maintains that the phenomenal properties of experiences elude any physicalist theory of the world, and that they are epiphenomenal, in the sense that 'their possession or absence makes no difference to the physical world' (1982/1990: 473). Our concern in this section, however, will not be with phenomenal properties of experience, but with the causal potency or relevance of the intentional properties of mental events.

4.1. Causal Relevance

One way in which a worry arises about the causal potency of mental properties is this. On many materialist views, events that have mental properties also have more fundamental properties—physical properties—and these more fundamental properties figure in causal laws. According to those views, then, the real causal action seems to be taking place at that more fundamental level, and the mental properties appear to be a causally inert and irrelevant overlay. But this seems to go against our intuitive conviction that the mental properties of mental events are relevant—indeed, crucial—to the causal relations that those events stand in. Intuitively, we reckon that it is because my mental state is of a particular mental type—it is a belief, say—and has a particular content—it is a belief that I am being attacked by a bear, say—that it has the specific effects that it does.

Towards the end of Section 1.6, we noted the possibility of a kind of anomalous event dualism that would say that mental events are composed out of physical events but are not individually identical with physical events. A problem about causal potency could be raised for this kind of view too. It would not be true, on this view, that mental events themselves have physical properties. But it might still be tempting to suppose that the real causal action is taking place at the composing (physical) level rather than at the composed (mental) level. We shall not, however, pursue this version of the worry here (see Pietroski 1994).

While the worry about mental causation is not specific to any one materialist view of the mind, a good deal of the recent work on this topic begins from Davidson's (1970) anomalous monism. One way to bring the worry more sharply into focus is to set out four of the propositions that are associated with Davidson's position (Section 1.6).

The *first proposition* is just a reminder about a basic background assumption concerning the nature of causation; namely, that causation is a relation between particular events. Thus, a typical statement about causation will say that event c caused event e.

The *second proposition* is that every particular mental event is identical with some physical event. (This is event monism.) A consequence of this proposition is that every mental event has both mental and physical properties.

The *third proposition* is that wherever there is causation there are causal laws. Roughly, this is Davidson's principle of the nomological character of causation, though we are not stressing the idea that the causal law must be strict. The proposition is just that if c causes e then there is some property F of c and some property G of e, such that there is a causal law linking F-events and G-events.

Following on from this, the *fourth proposition* is the more specific claim that if both the cause event c and the effect event e are physical events then there are physical properties *F* and *G* of *c* and *e* respectively, such that there is a causal law linking *F*-events and *G*-events.

Against the background of these propositions, we can set out an argument that certainly seems to suggest that the mental properties of mental events are epiphenomenal. Let *c* be, for example, the event of your deciding to raise your arm; and let *e* be the event of your arm rising. And suppose that *c* causes *e*. Then, since *c*—as well as *e*—is a physical event (by the second proposition), there are physical properties of *c* and *e* in virtue of which *c* and *e* are subsumed by some causal law (by the fourth proposition). But, this seems to say that there is a physical property of *c* that is already sufficient to determine that *c* causes *e*. So, apparently, the mental property of *c*—that it is a decision with a particular content—is excess to requirements; it is epiphenomenal in the production of the movement of your arm.

We shall need to be more precise about this argument (see Section 4.2). But, for now, it is enough to notice that the conclusion certainly goes against our intuition that the event *c* causes *e* in virtue of being a mental event of a particular type with a particular content. Intuitively, we would say that it was because you decided to raise your arm that your arm rose. If you had decided something else, or had reached no decision at all, then, all else equal, your arm would not have risen. Intuitively, we would say that the mental property of the mental event is causally relevant.

The question about epiphenomenalism is not whether mental events have effects. It is agreed that they do. The question is, rather, whether the mental properties of mental events are relevant to the causal relations that those events stand in. Is it, we might ask, in virtue of their specifically mental properties that mental events have the effects that they do? The problem arises because, on an anomalous monist view (and on many other views too), it seems tempting to say that mental events cause their effects in virtue of their physical properties—rather than their mental properties (e.g. Sosa 1984; Antony 1989, 1991).

Davidson himself (1993) rejects this way of posing the problem. His objection begins from the fact that causation is just a two-place relation between events. For any pair of events, either the causal relation holds between them, or else it does not. Talking of an event causing another event in virtue of its physical properties, or in virtue of its mental properties, Davidson says, goes against the simple relational character of causation. For it suggests that it would make sense to say that *c as physical* caused *e*, but that *c as mental* did not cause *e*. Thus, Davidson says of his own position:

given my concept of events and of causality, it makes no sense to speak of an event as being a cause 'as' anything at all. . . . On the view of events and causality assumed here, it makes no more sense to say event *c* caused event *e* as instantiating law *l* than it makes to say *a* weighs less than *b* as belonging to sort *s*. If causality is a relation between events, it holds between them no matter how they are described. (1993: 6)

On the face of it, then, Davidson is saying that there is no question of a distinction between those properties of an event that are causally relevant and those that are not.

However, Davidson's objection is not compelling. In general, if two objects stand in a relation, it may make sense to ask in virtue of which of their properties those objects are related in that way. Some of their properties may be relevant to their standing in the relation, while other properties may be irrelevant. For example, being longer than is a two-place relation between objects. Suppose that an object *a* is longer than an object *b*. Then it certainly makes sense to say that it is in virtue of the length of *a* and the length of *b*, and not in virtue of, say, the colour of *a*, or the smell of *b*, that they stand in the being-longer-than relation. Similarly, it is surely in virtue of their weight properties, rather than their colours, smells, or lengths, that objects stand in the weighing-less-than relation (Kim 1993; McLaughlin 1993).

What applies in the case of the being-longer-than relation or the weighing-less-than relation applied also to the causation relation. Consistently with acknowledging that we are dealing with a simple two-place relation, it makes sense to ask about the properties of objects in virtue of which they stand in that relation. So, it is legitimate to distinguish between causally relevant properties of events and epiphenomenal properties; and the problem posed by the argument we set out does need to be faced.

As we said at the outset, the basic idea of the argument is this. Events that have mental properties also have more fundamental properties that figure in causal laws. So, it seems that the real causal action is taking place at that more fundamental level, and that the mental properties are excess to requirements.

One response to this general style of argument is to note that it does not apply only to mental properties. Suppose that *c* and *e* are chemical, or biological, or geological, or aerodynamic events that are related as cause and effect. It is more or less plausible that every such event is identical to some physical event. So, there are physical properties *F* and *G* of *c* and *e* respectively such that there is a causal law linking *F*-events and *G*-events. Then, by following the same reasoning as in the original argument, we reach the conclusion that all chemical, biological, geological, or aerodynamic properties of events are epiphenomenal. Indeed, the argument could be adapted to show that all properties that are different from the fundamental properties cited in physical theory are epiphenomenal. But, it seems quite wrong to say that chemical properties, for example, make no difference to what happens in the physical world. So, there must be something wrong with the argument.

We could allow, perhaps, that there is some very special sense of causal relevance according to which only fundamental physical properties are causally relevant. But that special sense would have to be set against some more everyday sense of causal relevance that applies to non-fundamental properties such as chemical, biological, geological, and aerodynamic properties. For all that the argument shows, this everyday sense of causal relevance applies equally to mental properties.

This is the kind of response to the threat of epiphenomenalism about mental properties that is recommended by Fodor (1989). Fodor suggests that a property, P, of events is a causally responsible property just in case it is a property in virtue of which individual events are subsumed by a causal law (1989/1990: 143). So, consider again the two events c and e. We suppose that there are physical properties F and G of c and e respectively, and a causal law linking F-events and G-events. But that is quite consistent with there also being a mental property P of c and a property Q of e, such that there is also a causal law linking P-events and Q-events. So, on Fodor's account of causal responsibility, there is no problem about the causal responsibility of the property of being a decision to raise one's arm, provided only that there are causal laws that speak of decisions with such contents—what Fodor calls intentional causal laws. Such laws will not be strict; they will contain *ceteris paribus* clauses. But the same goes for chemical, biological, geological, or aerodynamic laws.

Chemistry, biology, geology, aerodynamics, and psychology are special sciences, while fundamental physics is, we suppose, basic science (Fodor 1974). There are important differences between the laws of special sciences and the laws of basic science. We have already noted that it is widely accepted that special science laws are *ceteris paribus* laws, while basic science contains strict laws. But there is another difference that we should notice here. If there is a basic science law linking F-events and G-events, then there is no answer to the question *how* do F-events cause G-events: they just do—that is the way the world works. In contrast, if there is a special science law that says that P-events cause Q-events, then there is always a further story to be told about the mechanism by which P-events cause Q-events (Fodor 1989). The need for an underlying causal mechanism applies equally to the cases of chemical, biological, geological, aerodynamic, and intentional laws. In the case of intentional laws, Fodor's own preferred story about the causal mechanism is that it is computational—that it involves manipulation of symbols in a language of thought (Section 2.2). But the general strategy for responding to the problem about mental causation and epiphenomenalism does not depend upon the correctness of this particular view about the nature of the underlying mechanism.

4.2. Causation and Supervenience

It is time to be a little more precise about the argument that we have been considering. It begins from four propositions. (1) Causation is a relation between events. (2) Every particular mental event is identical with some physical event. (3) Wherever there is causation there are causal laws. And (4) causal relations between physical events are always subsumed by physical laws. Let us pay a little more attention to that third proposition. Davidson's principle of the nomological character of causation (1980) actually requires rather more than merely that wherever there is causation there are laws. It says that wherever there is causation there are *strict* causal laws. So, we should ask whether this principle creates a more specific threat of epiphenomenalism for anomalous monism.

Davidson does not draw a distinction between causally relevant properties of events and epiphenomenal properties. But, in the Davidsonian (1970) framework, it might be natural to attempt to draw the distinction by saying that the causally relevant properties of events are those properties that are mentioned in the strict laws that subsume particular causal relations between events. If we do draw the distinction in that way, then it is clear that only physical properties can be causally relevant (since only physical laws are strict). So, if we impose the distinction upon Davidson's framework, then we quite naturally end up with the idea that anomalous monism counts the mental properties of events as epiphenomenal.

There are at least two ways of responding to this worry about anomalous monism. The first way makes use of the idea of *non-strict laws*; the second way employs the notion of *supervenience*. We shall consider them in turn. The first line of response is to say that properties that are mentioned in either strict laws or non-strict laws can be causally relevant. In essence, this is to employ Fodor's notion of causally responsible properties.

This first line of response on behalf of anomalous monism then faces a challenge. It is a challenge that is quite general, in that it applies to any theory of causal relevance that allows several different properties of one event to be causally relevant. If a physical property of a cause event is relevant to the production of the effect, and a mental property is relevant as well, then what is the relation between the two causal contributions? We do not want our account to say that the effect event is caused twice over. To be sure, there are cases of causation where we might describe the effect event as being doubly caused (or overdetermined). The case of an unfortunate victim who is simultaneously struck by bullets from two assassins would provide an example. But ordinary cases of mental causation seem quite different from this.

(In fact, there is also a second challenge that the first line of response (in terms of non-strict laws) faces. This second challenge is specific to Davidson's anomalous monism and it concerns the principle of the nomological character of causation. The problem is that once the notion of non-strict special science laws is in play, some of the motivation for this principle is removed. For (as we noted in Section 1.6), the intuition that causal relations are always backed by causal laws might be satisfied by the existence of non-strict causal laws (McLaughlin 1989, 1993). So, although a defender of anomalous monism can respond to the threat of epiphenomenalism by appealing to non-strict laws, this may, in turn, undermine the position.)

Despite the challenge, the first line of response to the threat of epiphenomenalism might still be defended. Certainly there are further replies that can be made on behalf of anomalous monism. But for now, we shall turn to the second line of response. We can see how this line of response goes if we consider the way that Fodor (1989) presents the threat of epiphenomenalism, for his presentation invites a response using the notion of supervenience.

Fodor's presentation begins with premises saying that 'the causal powers of an event are entirely determined by its physical properties', and that 'no intentional property is identical to any physical property' (1989/1990: 138). Then we are invited to consider a mental event m—your desiring to lift your arm—and a behavioural event b—your lifting your arm. Given the premises, 'it appears that m's being the cause of your lifting your arm doesn't depend on its being a desire to lift your arm; m would have caused your lifting of your arm even if it hadn't had its intentional properties, so long as its physical properties were preserved. So, it appears that m's intentional properties don't affect its causal powers' (p. 138). The crucial hypothesis here is that an event could have had different intentional properties while preserving its physical properties. For this hypothesis is incompatible with a supervenience thesis.

We are asked to consider an actual mental event, and to imagine a counterfactual situation in which that event has different intentional properties, without any difference in its physical properties. But, according to an 'across worlds' supervenience claim (see Section 1.6), there cannot be two possible worlds between which an event differs in its mental properties but not in its physical properties. If the event that is actually your desiring to raise your arm were to have had different intentional properties, then it would also have had different physical properties. This does not quite, by itself, guarantee that it would have differed physically in a way that would have made a difference to its producing an arm-rising event as effect. But we can see, at least in outline, how an 'across worlds' supervenience claim provides a response to the threat of epiphenomenalism.

Davidson's overall position (1970) does include a supervenience claim, and he says: 'a change in mental properties is always accompanied by a change in physical properties' (1993: 7). But (as we noted in Section 1.6), Davidson makes only a 'within a world' supervenience claim. This kind of claim says that, within any possible situation, if two events differ mentally, then they also differ physically. (For the distinction between 'within a world' and 'across worlds' supervenience claims, see Kim 1984a; McFetridge 1985.) Within any possible situation, if two events differ in their intentional properties, then they also differ in their physical properties. And, within any possible situation, a change in intentional properties over time is always accompanied by a change in physical properties.

This says nothing about what happens when an event that has certain intentional properties in the actual situation has different intentional properties in some counterfactual situation. Strictly speaking, for all that the 'within a world' supervenience claim says, events that actually have intentional properties might, in some counterfactual situation, lack intentional properties altogether, while yet preserving all their actual physical properties (Kim 1993; McLaughlin 1993). In particular, in that counterfactual situation, the event that is your desiring to raise your arm would have just the same physical properties that it actually has, and so it would cause your arm to rise; but it would have no intentional properties.

It is for this reason that critics of Davidson's position claim that it does not provide an adequate response to the threat of epiphenomenalism. A supervenience claim does offer the prospect of a line of response to that threat. But, anomalous monism needs to be augmented with an 'across worlds' supervenience claim, and not just a 'within a world' claim.

We have been considering the specific threat of epiphenomenalism that is posed by Davidson's principle of the nomological character of causation. The dialectical situation that we have sketched is this. If we focus upon strict laws, and draw the distinction between causally relevant properties and epiphenomenal properties in a fairly natural way, then we are led to the idea that anomalous monism counts the mental properties of events as epiphenomenal. One line of response to the threat of epiphenomenalism uses the idea of non-strict laws, and it faces two challenges. One challenge is general—posing a problem for a wide variety of theories of mental causation—while the other challenge is specific to anomalous monism. A second line of response employs the notion of supervenience, and does not make any direct use of the notion of a non-strict law. This line of response requires an 'across worlds' supervenience claim, and not merely a 'within a world' claim. Clearly, more work would be required in order to decide how best to elaborate or modify Davidson's overall position.

4.3. Explanatoriness and Efficacy

Fodor (1989) offers what we might call the nomological theory of causal responsibility. A property of an event is causally responsible if it is a property in virtue of which the event is subsumed under a causal law. Intentional properties—and mental properties more generally—count as causally responsible to the extent that there are intentional (mental) causal laws; and Fodor's view is that there are such laws, even though they are not strict laws.

Whether Fodor's account of the causal relevance of mental properties is fully satisfying depends upon the real source of the apparent threat of epiphenomenalism. Certainly, to the extent that the threat flows from the fact that intentional properties do not figure in basic science, it is helpful to have it pointed out that, in this respect, intentional properties are no worse off than chemical, biological, geological, or aerodynamic properties. But we also need to consider whether there might be something especially problematic about the causal relevance of intentional properties.

We can investigate this proposal a little further if we draw a distinction between *causally explanatory* properties and *causally efficacious* properties. As Jackson and Pettit say: 'Features which causally explain need not cause' (1988: 392). That is, a causally explanatory property need not be a causally efficacious property. To the extent that causal explanation is linked to causal laws, Fodor's proposal seems to concern the notion of a causally explanatory property. But that leaves it open whether intentional properties of mental events are efficacious properties, and, in fact, Jackson and Pettit argue that intentional properties are not causally efficacious.

The background assumption for their argument is some kind of functional role semantics (see Section 2.4). Thus, they say:

What makes a state my belief that that cup contains water is, in part, its causal connection with that cup and with water. . . . Now these causal connections will be quite invisible to the other states of mine which link my belief to behaviour. For example, if my belief is my having B-fibres firing, then the effect of my belief on other states of mine along the causal path to behaviour will simply be the effect of B-fibres' firing. The fact that the B-fibres' firing was caused in a certain way will be quite invisible to the other states. (Jackson and Pettit 1978: 392)

This argument, as Jackson and Pettit go on to say:

turns on the highly relational nature of . . . content. . . . For the effect that one neurophysiological state has on another . . . is a function of the states' relatively intrinsic properties, not of their highly relational ones. (p. 392)

It is the fact that intentional properties are relational properties of mental states and events that unfits them for causal efficacy. If this is right, then the consequences extend far beyond functional role semantics. For all the theories of content that we considered in Section 2, if the theory focuses upon internal states at all, then it treats intentional properties of those internal states as relational properties. Thus, to consider just one of those theories, the covariation theory defines content for an internal state in terms of a relation of covariation between that state and states of the external world. And it is plausible that, on that account, content properties are not causally efficacious. In the case of the mechanical device LOCKE (Cummins 1989: 37), for example, the effect of having a particular punch card pattern occur will be determined by the arrangement of holes in the card. The fact that this pattern occurs when, only when, and because LOCKE is confronted by a cat, say, will be quite invisible to the states that lie along the chain of causal consequences of the occurrence of that punch card pattern.

This suggests that there is something problematic about the causal relevance of intentional properties—something that goes beyond the fact that intentional properties do not figure in basic science. For, even at the level of a special science, we can distinguish between properties that are 'relatively intrinsic' and properties that are 'highly relational'. Indeed, Jackson and Pettit draw the distinction at the level of neurophysiology, which is certainly not basic science. Relatively intrinsic properties are candidates for being causally efficacious, while highly relational properties—including intentional properties—can only be causally explanatory.

However, some of Jackson and Pettit's examples of explanatory properties that are not efficacious seem to suggest that, whenever a higher-level property can have variable realizations at a lower level, the higher-level property is not itself causally efficacious. The clearest example is provided by functional role properties. They certainly exhibit variable realization since, at least in principle, a role can be played by many different realizers (Section 1.4). And it is relatively plausible that functional role properties—explicitly defined by a formula along the lines of

$$\lambda y[(\exists x_1) \dots (\exists x_n)\,(T(x_1, \dots, x_n)\ \&\ y \text{ has } x_1)]$$

—are not themselves causally efficacious. It is not so obvious that all higher-level (non-fundamental) properties that allow variable realization are functional role properties. Nor is it obvious that, if there are higher-level properties that allow variable realization but are not functional role properties, then they are inevitably not efficacious. But, if what Jackson and Pettit's examples seem to suggest is right, then causal efficacy will be absent from the higher levels of the special sciences, and will be squeezed down to the level of the most fundamental physical properties.

This would be an unpromising development of the distinction between causal efficacy and causal explanatoriness. For if there should turn out not to be a most fundamental level, then there would be no causally efficacious properties at all. And even if there is a most fundamental level of physical properties, still it is very unclear that our ordinary intuitive notions of causation and of causal efficacy have any role to play there. In short, this development threatens to rob us of causal efficacy altogether.

Furthermore, if causal efficacy is absent altogether from the special sciences, then we have scarcely moved beyond the nomological theory of causal relevance. Intentional (and other mental) properties are classified as not being causally efficacious, but this is something that they share with all other properties except, perhaps, fundamental physical properties. Certainly they share the property of being inefficacious with chemical, biological, geological, and aerodynamic properties. In that case, the claim that intentional properties are not causally efficacious is lacking in theoretical interest. We need a notion of causal relevance that can apply to chemical, biological, geological, and aerodynamic properties. And, for all that has been shown, this notion—which can only be causal explanatoriness—applies equally to intentional properties. (See further, Block 1990*b*; Burge 1989; Jackson and Pettit 1990*b*; Blackburn 1991.)

The original introduction of the distinction between efficacy and explanatoriness promised much more than this. It promised a way of making sense of the idea that there might be a problem about the causal relevance of intentional properties, going beyond the fact that intentional properties are not fundamental physical properties. If we are to recover that promise, then we need a way of drawing a distinction between efficacious and explanatory properties, while also meeting a pair of conditions. The distinction must allow that some non-fundamental properties can be efficacious, while also revealing a prima-facie problem in the idea that intentional properties are efficacious.

Here, as at many points in contemporary philosophy of mind, there is an urgent need for new insights that will allow theoretical progress to be made.

BIBLIOGRAPHY

The Bibliography is arranged into sections and subsections corresponding to those in the text. For each of the four main sections, anthologies and other items that are particularly appropriate to the topic are listed. Thereafter, the lists for the subsections are generally divided into core reading and further reading. The core reading is usually made up of two or three items that are mentioned frequently in the text. The further reading includes all other items referred to in the text. Cross-references are given for books found in other sections except books listed under 'General Books'.

GENERAL BOOKS

The philosophy of mind is well provided with introductory-level textbooks. The three listed here are all excellent. Churchland's book is the one that is referred to most often in this chapter. Of the four general anthologies listed, the two edited by Lycan and Rosenthal would be particularly useful for readers of this chapter.

INTRODUCTORY TEXTS
CHURCHLAND, P. M. (1988), *Matter and Consciousness*, rev. edn. (Cambridge, Mass.).
McGINN, C. (1982), *The Character of Mind* (Oxford).
SMITH, P., and JONES, O. R. (1986), *The Philosophy of Mind: An Introduction* (Cambridge).

ANTHOLOGIES
BEAKLEY, B., and LUDLOW, P. (eds.) (1992), *The Philosophy of Mind: Classical Problems/Contemporary Issues* (Cambridge, Mass.).
BLOCK, N. (ed.) (1980), *Readings in Philosophy of Psychology*, i and ii (Cambridge, Mass.).
LYCAN, W. G. (ed.) (1990), *Mind and Cognition: A Reader* (Oxford).
ROSENTHAL, D. M. (ed.) (1991), *The Nature of Mind* (New York).

1. MIND AND BRAIN

ANTHOLOGY
WARNER, R., and SZUBKA, T. (eds.) (1994), *The Mind–Body Problem: A Guide to the Current Debate* (Oxford).

TEXTBOOK
MACDONALD, C. (1989), *Mind–Body Identity Theories* (London).

SURVEY CHAPTERS
CHURCHLAND, P. M. (1988), *Matter and Consciousness*, rev. edn. (Cambridge, Mass.), ch. 2: 'The Ontological Problem (The Mind–Body Problem)'.
FODOR, J. A. (1981), 'The Mind–Body Problem', *Scientific American*, 244 / 1: 114–23; repr. in Warner and Szubka (1994).

1.1. Dualism

Core Reading
DESCARTES, R. (1641), *Meditations on First Philosophy*, in *Descartes: Philosophical Writings*, trans. E. Anscombe and P. T. Geach (London, 1964); and in *Descartes: Selected Philosophical Writings*, ed. J. Cottingham, trans. J. Cottingham, R. Stoothoff, and D. Murdoch (Cambridge, 1988).
STRAWSON, P. F. (1974*a*), 'Self, Mind and Body', in *Freedom and Resentment and Other Essays* (London).
WILLIAMS, B. (1978), *Descartes: The Project of Pure Enquiry* (Harmondsworth).

Further Reading
COADY, C. A. J. (1983), 'Descartes' Other Myth', *Proceedings of the Aristotelian Society*, 83: 121–41.
DESCARTES, R. (1637), *Discourse on the Method*, in *Descartes: Philosophical Writings*, trans. E. Anscombe and P. T. Geach (London, 1964); and in *Descartes: Selected Philosophical Writings*, ed. J. Cottingham, trans. J. Cottingham, R. Stoothoff, and D. Murdoch (Cambridge, 1988).
FOSTER, J. (1991), *The Immaterial Self: A Defence of the Cartesian Dualist Conception of the Mind* (London).
STRAWSON, P. F. (1959), *Individuals: An Essay in Descriptive Metaphysics* (London), ch. 3: 'Persons'.
—— (1992), *Analysis and Metaphysics: An Introduction to Philosophy* (Oxford).

1.2. Behaviourism

Core Reading
RYLE, G. (1949), *The Concept of Mind* (Harmondsworth), ch. 1: 'Descartes' Myth'.

Further Reading
HORNSBY, J. (1986), 'Physicalist Thinking and Conceptions of Behaviour', in P. Pettit and J. McDowell (eds.), *Subject, Thought, and Context* (Oxford).

1.3. Central State Materialism

Core Reading

PLACE, U. T. (1956), 'Is Consciousness a Brain Process?', *British Journal of Psychology*, 47: 44–50; repr. in Lycan (1990); and in Beakley and Ludlow (1992).

SMART, J. C. C. (1959), 'Sensations and Brain Processes', *Philosophical Review*, 68: 141–56; repr. in Rosenthal (1991).

Further Reading

DENNETT, D. C. (1987), 'True Believers: The Intentional Strategy and why it Works', in *The Intentional Stance* (Cambridge, Mass.); repr. in Lycan (1990); in Rosenthal (1991); and in Stich and Warfield (1994) (see Section 2).

SMART, J. C. C. (1994), 'Mind and Brain', in Warner and Szubka (1994) (see Section 1).

1.4. Functionalism

Core Reading

BLOCK, N. (1980), 'Introduction: What is Functionalism?', in N. Block (ed.), *Readings in Philosophy of Psychology*, i (Cambridge, Mass.).

LEWIS, D. (1972), 'Psychophysical and Theoretical Identifications', *Australasian Journal of Philosophy*, 50: 249–58; repr. in Block (1980), i; and in Rosenthal (1991).

Further Reading

BLOCK, N. (1978), 'Troubles with Functionalism', in C. Wade Savage (ed.), *Minnesota Studies in the Philosophy of Science*, ix (Minneapolis); repr. in Block (1980), i; excerpts repr. in Lycan (1990); in Rosenthal (1991); and in Beakley and Ludlow (1992).

—— and FODOR, J. (1972), 'What Psychological States Are Not', *Philosophical Review*, 81: 159–81; repr. in Block (1980), i.

JACKSON, F., and PETTIT, P. (1988), 'Functionalism and Broad Content', *Mind*, 97: 381–400.

LEWIS, D. (1970), 'How to Define Theoretical Terms', *Journal of Philosophy*, 67: 427–46; repr. in *Philosophical Papers*, i (Oxford, 1983).

MCDOWELL, J. (1985), 'Functionalism and Anomalous Monism', in E. LePore and B. P. McLaughlin (eds.), *Actions and Events: Perspectives on the Philosophy of Donald Davidson* (Oxford).

PETTIT, P. (1986), 'Broad-Minded Explanation and Psychology', in P. Pettit and J. McDowell (eds.), *Subject, Thought, and Context* (Oxford).

PUTNAM, H. (1967), 'The Nature of Mental States'; originally titled 'Psychological Predicates', in W. H. Capitan and D. D. Merrill (eds.), *Art, Mind, and Religion* (Pittsburgh); repr. in Block (1980), i; in Lycan (1990); in Rosenthal (1991); and in Beakley and Ludlow (1992).

1.5. Interlude: Reductionist and Non-reductionist Materialism

CHARLES, D., and LENNON, K. (eds.) (1992), *Reduction, Explanation, and Realism* (Oxford).

PUTNAM, H. (1967). See Section 1.4.

1.6. Anomalous Monism

Core Reading

DAVIDSON, D. (1970), 'Mental Events', in L. Foster and J. W. Swanson (eds.), *Experience and Theory* (Amherst, Mass.); repr. in D. Davidson, *Essays on Actions and Events* (Oxford, 1980); in Block (1980), i; in Rosenthal (1991); and in Beakley and Ludlow (1992).

—— (1974*a*), 'Psychology as Philosophy', in S. C. Brown (ed.), *Philosophy of Psychology* (London); repr. in J. Glover (ed.), *The Philosophy of Mind* (Oxford, 1976); and in D. Davidson, *Essays on Actions and Events* (Oxford, 1980).

—— (1993), 'Thinking Causes', in J. Heil and A. Mele (eds.), *Mental Causation* (Oxford).

Further Reading

HORNSBY, J. (1981), 'Which Physical Events are Mental Events?', *Proceedings of the Aristotelian Society*, 81: 73–92.

—— (1985), 'Physicalism, Events and Part–Whole Relations', in E. LePore and B. P. McLaughlin (eds.), *Actions and Events: Perspectives on the Philosophy of Donald Davidson* (Oxford).

KIM, J. (1984*a*), 'Concepts of Supervenience', *Philosophy and Phenomenological Research*, 65: 153–76; repr. in *Supervenience and Mind: Selected Philosophical Essays* (Cambridge, 1993).

—— (1984*b*), 'Epiphenomenal and Supervenient Causation', in P. A. French, T. E. Uehling, and H. K. Wettstein (eds.), *Midwest Studies in Philosophy*, ix: *Causation and Causal Theories* (Minneapolis); repr. in Rosenthal (1991); and in Kim, *Supervenience and Mind: Selected Philosophical Essays* (Cambridge, 1993).

—— (1989), 'The Myth of Nonreductive Materialism', *Proceedings of the American Philosophical Association*, 63: 31–47; repr. in Warner and Szubka (1994) (see Section 1); and in Kim, *Supervenience and Mind: Selected Philosophical Essays* (Cambridge, 1993).

—— (1993), 'Can Supervenience Save Anomalous Monism?', in J. Heil and A. Mele (eds.), *Mental Causation* (Oxford).

McDOWELL, J. (1985). See Section 1.4.

McLAUGHLIN, B. P. (1989), 'Token Epiphenomenalism, Type Dualism, and the Causal Priority of the Physical', in J. E. Tomberlin (ed.), *Philosophical Perspectives*, iii: *Philosophy of Mind and Action Theory* (Atascadero, Calif.).

—— (1993), 'Davidson's Response to Epiphenomenalism', in J. Heil and A. Mele (eds.), *Mental Causation* (Oxford).

1.7. Eliminativism

Core Reading

CHURCHLAND, P. M. (1981), 'Eliminative Materialism and Propositional Attitudes', *Journal of Philosophy*, 78: 67–90; repr. in Lycan (1990); and in Rosenthal (1991).

—— (1988), *Matter and Consciousness*, rev. edn. (Cambridge, Mass.), 43–9.

Further Reading

CHURCHLAND, P. M. (1991), 'Folk Psychology and the Explanation of Human Behavior', in J. D. Greenwood (ed.), *The Future of Folk Psychology* (Cambridge).

CHURCHLAND, P. M. (1993), 'Evaluating Our Self Conception', *Mind and Language*, 8: 211–22.

DAVIDSON, D. (1970). See Section 1.6.

DAVIES, M. (1991), 'Concepts, Connectionism, and the Language of Thought', in W. Ramsey, S. Stich, and D. Rumelhart (eds.), *Philosophy and Connectionist Theory* (Hillsdale, NJ).

DENNETT, D. (1987). See Section 1.3.

HORGAN, T., and WOODWARD, J. (1985), 'Folk Psychology is here to Stay', *Philosophical Review*, 94: 197–225; repr. in Lycan (1990); and in J. D. Greenwood (ed.), *The Future of Folk Psychology* (Cambridge, 1991).

JACKSON, F., and PETTIT, P. (1990a), 'In Defence of Folk Psychology', *Philosophical Studies*, 59: 31–54.

RAMSEY, W., STICH, S., and GARON, J. (1990), 'Connectionism, Eliminativism and the Future of Folk Psychology', in J. E. Tomberlin (ed.), *Philosophical Perspectives*, iv: *Action Theory and Philosophy of Mind* (Atascadero, Calif.); repr. in J. D. Greenwood (ed.), *The Future of Folk Psychology* (Cambridge, 1991).

STRAWSON, P. F. (1974b), 'Freedom and Resentment', in *Freedom and Resentment and Other Essays* (London).

1.8. Preview: Intentionality and Consciousness

NAGEL, T. (1994), 'Consciousness and Objective Reality', in Warner and Szubka (1994).

2. INTENTIONALITY

ANTHOLOGY
STICH, S. P., and WARFIELD, T. A. (1994), *Mental Representation: A Reader* (Oxford).

2.1. Varieties of Aboutness

Core Reading
CRANE, T. (1992), Introduction, in T. Crane (ed.), *The Contents of Experience* (Cambridge).

DAVIDSON, D. (1974b), 'Belief and the Basis of Meaning', *Synthese*, 27: 309–23; repr. in *Inquiries into Truth and Interpretation* (Oxford, 1984).

DENNETT, D. C., and HAUGELAND, J. C. (1987), 'Intentionality', in R. L. Gregory (ed.), *The Oxford Companion to the Mind* (Oxford).

DRETSKE, F. (1986), 'Misrepresentation', in R. J. Bogdan (ed.), *Belief: Form, Content and Function* (Oxford); repr. in Lycan (1990); and in Stich and Warfield (1994).

DUMMETT, M. (1991), *The Logical Basis of Metaphysics* (Cambridge, Mass.), ch. 4: 'Meaning, Knowledge, and Understanding'.

GRICE, H. P. (1989), *Studies in the Way of Words* (Cambridge, Mass.).

HAMLYN, D. W. (1990), *In and Out of the Black Box: On the Philosophy of Cognition* (Oxford).

—— (1994), 'Perception, Sensation and Non-conceptual Content', *Philosophical Quarterly*, 44: 139–53.

SEARLE, J. R. (1990), 'Consciousness, Explanatory Inversion, and Cognitive Science', *Behavioral and Brain Sciences*, 13: 585–96.

STICH, S. P. (1978), 'Beliefs and Subdoxastic States', *Philosophy of Science*, 45: 499–518.

Further Reading

DAVIES, M. (1989), 'Tacit Knowledge and Subdoxastic States', in A. George (ed.), *Reflections on Chomsky* (Oxford).

—— (1995*a*), 'Externalism and Experience', in A. Clark, J. Ezquerro, and J. M. Larrazabal (eds.), *Categories, Consciousness and Reasoning* (Dordrecht); repr. in N. Block, O. Flanagan, and G. Güzeldere (eds.), *The Nature of Consciousness: Philosophical Debates* (Cambridge, Mass.).

EVANS, G. (1982), *The Varieties of Reference* (Oxford).

FODOR, J. A. (1975), *The Language of Thought* (New York).

—— (1987), *Psychosemantics* (Cambridge, Mass.), app.: 'Why there still has to be a Language of Thought'.

PEACOCKE, C. (1992*a*), *A Study of Concepts* (Cambridge, Mass.).

2.2. The Intentional Stance

Core Reading

DENNETT, D. C. (1971), 'Intentional Systems', *Journal of Philsophy*, 68: 87–106; repr. in *Brainstorms* (Brighton, 1981).

—— (1987), 'True Believers: The Intentional Strategy and why it works', in *The Intentional Stance* (Cambridge, Mass.); repr. in Lycan (1990); in Rosenthal (1991); and in Stich and Warfield (1994).

Further Reading

BLOCK, N. (1981), 'Psychologism and Behaviorism', *Philosophical Review*, 90: 5–43.

—— (1990*a*), 'The Computer Model of the Mind', in D. N. Osherson and E. E. Smith (eds.), *An Invitation to Cognitive Science,* iii: *Thinking* (Cambridge, Mass.).

DENNETT, D. C. (1991), 'Real Patterns', *Journal of Philosophy*, 88: 27–51.

FODOR, J. A. (1975). See Section 2.1.

—— (1987). See Section 2.1.

PEACOCKE, C. (1983), *Sense and Content* (Oxford), ch. 8: 'Between Instrumentalism and Brain Writing'.

2.3. Covariation and Teleology

Core Reading

CUMMINS, R. (1989), *Meaning and Mental Representation* (Cambridge, Mass.), ch. 4, 'Covariance I: Locke'.

DRETSKE, F. (1986), 'Misrepresentation', in R. J. Bogdan (ed.), *Belief: Form, Content and Function* (Oxford); repr. in Lycan (1990); and in Stich and Warfield (1994).

Further Reading

CUMMINS, R. (1989), *Meaning and Mental Representation* (Cambridge, Mass.), ch. 7: 'Adaptational Role'.

DRETSKE, F. (1983), 'Précis of *Knowledge and the Flow of Information*', *Behavioral and Brain Sciences*, 6: 55–63.

FODOR, J. A. (1987), *Psychosemantics* (Cambridge, Mass.), ch. 4: 'Meaning and the World Order'.

—— (1990a), 'Psychosemantics, or; Where do Truth Conditions Come From?', in Lycan (1990).

—— (1990b), 'A Theory of Content, I: The Problem', and 'A Theory of Content, II: The Theory', in *A Theory of Content and Other Essays* (Cambridge, Mass.); 'A Theory of Content II: The Theory' is repr. in Stich and Warfield (1994).

McGINN, C. (1989), *Mental Content* (Oxford), ch. 2: 'The Utility of Content'.

MILLIKAN, R. G. (1989), 'Biosemantics', *Journal of Philosophy*, 86: 281–97; repr. in *White Queen Psychology and Other Essays for Alice* (Cambridge, Mass., 1993); and in Stich and Warfield (1994).

PAPINEAU, D. (1987), *Reality and Representation* (Oxford), ch. 4: 'The Teleological Theory of Representation'.

2.4. Functional Role and Holism

Core Reading

BLOCK, N. (1986), 'Advertisement for a Semantics for Psychology', in P. A. French, T. E. Uehling, and H. K. Wettstein (eds.), *Midwest Studies in Philosophy*, x: *Studies in the Philosophy of Mind* (Minneapolis); repr. in Stich and Warfield (1994).

FODOR, J. A., and LePORE, E. (1991), 'Why Meaning (Probably) isn't Conceptual Role', *Mind and Language*, 6: 328–43; repr. in Stich and Warfield (1994).

Further Reading

BLOCK, N. (1987), 'Functional Role and Truth Conditions', *Proceedings of the Aristotelian Society*, supp. vol. 61: 157–81.

—— (1993), 'Holism, Hyper-analyticity and Hyper-compositionality', *Mind and Language*, 8: 1–26.

BOGHOSSIAN, P. A. (1993), 'Does an Inferential Role Semantics Rest upon a Mistake?', *Mind and Language*, 8: 27–40.

CUMMINS, R. (1989), *Meaning and Mental Representation* (Cambridge, Mass.), ch. 9: 'Functional Roles'.

FIELD, H. (1977), 'Logic, Meaning and Conceptual Role', *Journal of Philosophy*, 74: 379–409.

FODOR, J. A. (1975). See Section 2.1.

—— (1987), *Psychosemantics* (Cambridge, Mass.), ch. 3: 'Meaning Holism'.

—— and LePORE, E. (1992), *Holism: A Shopper's Guide* (Oxford).

—— —— (1993), 'Reply to Block and Boghossian', *Mind and Language*, 8: 41–8.

FREGE, G. (1892), 'On Sense and Reference', in *Translations from the Philosophical Writings of Gottlob Frege*, ed. P. T. Geach and M. Black (Oxford, 1970); repr. in A. W. Moore (ed.), *Meaning and Reference* (Oxford, 1993).

HARMAN, G. (1982), 'Conceptual Role Semantics', *Notre Dame Journal of Formal Logic*, 23: 242–56.

QUINE, W. V. O. (1951), 'Two Dogmas of Empiricism', *Philosophical Review*, 60: 20–43; repr. in *From a Logical Point of View* (New York, 1953).

2.5. Concepts and Possession Conditions

Core Reading
PEACOCKE, C. (1989), 'Possession Conditions: A Focal Point for Theories of Concepts', *Mind and Language*, 4: 51–6.
—— (1992*a*). See Section 2.1.

Further Reading
DAVIES, M. (1991). See Section 1.7.
FREGE, G. (1918), 'The Thought: A Logical Inquiry', in P. F. Strawson (ed.), *Philosophical Logic* (Oxford, 1967).
PEACOCKE, C. (1992*b*), 'Concepts', in J. Dancy and E. Sosa (eds.), *A Companion to Epistemology* (Oxford).

3. CONSCIOUSNESS

ANTHOLOGIES
BLOCK, N., FLANAGAN, O., and GÜZELDERE, G. (eds.) (1995), *The Nature of Consciousness: Philosophical Debates* (Cambridge, Mass.).
DAVIES, M., and HUMPHREYS, G. W. (eds.) (1993), *Consciousness: Psychological and Philosophical Essays* (Oxford).
NAGEL, T. (1994). See Section 1.8.

MONOGRAPHS
DENNETT, D. C. (1991), *Consciousness Explained* (Boston, Mass.).
FLANAGAN, O. (1992), *Consciousness Reconsidered* (Cambridge, Mass.).

3.1. An Argument for Elusiveness

Core Reading
NAGEL, T. (1974), 'What is it Like to be a Bat?', *Philosophical Review*, 83: 435–50; repr. in *Mortal Questions* (Cambridge, 1979); and in Rosenthal (1991).

Further Reading
FREGE, G. (1892). See Section 2.4.
PLACE, U. T. (1956/1990). See Section 1.3.

3.2. An Announcement of Mystery

Core Reading
BLOCK, N. (1978), 'Troubles with Functionalism', in C. Wade Savage (ed.)., *Minnesota Studies in the Philosophy of Science,* ix (Minneapolis); excerpts repr. in Lycan (1990); in Rosenthal (1991); and in Beakley and Ludlow (1992).

McGinn, C. (1989), 'Can We Solve the Mind–Body Problem?', *Mind*, 98: 349–66; repr. in *The Problem of Consciousness* (Oxford, 1991); and in Warner and Szubka (1994).

Further Reading
Chomsky, N. (1975), *Reflections on Language* (London).
Flanagan, O. (1992), *Consciousness Reconsidered* (Cambridge, Mass.), ch. 6: 'The Mystery of Consciousness'.
Fodor, J. A. (1983), *The Modularity of Mind* (Cambridge, Mass.).
Jackson, F. (1982), 'Epiphenomenal Qualia', *Philosophical Quarterly*, 32: 127–36; repr. in Lycan (1990).
—— (1986), 'What Mary didn't Know', *Journal of Philosophy*, 83: 291–5; repr. in Rosenthal (1991).
Levine, J. (1993), 'On Leaving Out what it's Like', in Davies and Humphreys (1993).
Nagel, T. (1986), *The View from Nowhere* (Oxford).

3.3. Higher-Order Thoughts

Core Reading
Rosenthal, D. M. (1986), 'Two Concepts of Consciousness', *Philosophical Studies*, 94: 329–59; repr. in Rosenthal (1991).

Further Reading
Nelkin, N. (1986), 'Pains and Pain Sensations', *Journal of Philosophy*, 83: 129–48.
—— (1989), 'Unconscious Sensations', *Philosophical Psychology*, 2: 129–41.
—— (1993a), 'What is Consciousness?', *Philosophy of Science*, 60: 419–34.
Peacocke, C. (1992a), *A Study of Concepts* (Cambridge, Mass.).
Rosenthal, D. M. (ed.) (1991), *The Nature of Mind* (New York).
—— (1993), 'Thinking that One Thinks', in Davies and Humphreys (1993).

3.4. Interlude: Explaining Consciousness

Core Reading
Churchland, P. M. (1988), *Matter and Consciousness*, rev. edn. (Cambridge, Mass.), ch. 7: 'Neuroscience'.
Dennett, D. C. (1988), 'Quining Qualia', in A. Marcel and E. Bisiach (eds.), *Consciousness in Contemporary Science* (Oxford); repr. in Lycan (1990).

Further Reading
Campbell, K. (1982), 'The Implications of Land's Theory of Color Vision', in *Logic, Methodology and Philosophy of Science*, vi (Amsterdam); repr. in Lycan (1990).
Dennett, D. C., and Kinsbourne, M. (1992), 'Time and the Observer: The Where and When of Consciousness in the Brain (with Open Peer Commentary and Authors' Response)', *Behavioral and Brain Sciences*, 15: 183–247.
Flanagan, O. (1992). See Section 3.2.
Land, E. (1977), 'The Retinex Theory of Color Vision', *Scientific American*, 237/6: 108–28.

LEVINE, J. (1983), 'Materialism and Qualia: The Explanatory Gap', *Pacific Philosophical Quarterly*, 64: 354–61.

3.5. Consciousness and Intentionality

Core Reading

SEARLE, J. (1989), 'Consciousness, Unconsciousness, and Intentionality', *Philosophical Topics*, 17: 193–209.

—— (1990), 'Consciousness, Explanatory Inversion, and Cognitive Science (with Open Peer Commentary and Author's Response)', *Behavioral and Brain Sciences*, 13: 585–642.

Further Reading

BLOCK, N. (1990a), 'The Computer Model of the Mind', in D. N. Osherson and E. E. Smith (eds.), *An Invitation to Cognitive Science*, iii: *Thinking* (Cambridge, Mass.).

DAVIES, M. (1995b), 'Consciousness and the Varieties of Aboutness', in C. Macdonald and G. Macdonald (eds.), *Philosophy of Psychology: Debates on Psychological Explanation*, i (Oxford).

McGINN, C. (1988), 'Consciousness and Content', *Proceedings of the British Academy*, 74: 219–39; repr. in *The Problem of Consciousness* (Oxford, 1991).

NELKIN, N. (1993b), 'Intentionality and Consciousness', in Davies and Humphreys (1993).

SEARLE, J. R. (1980), 'Minds, Brains, and Programs', *Behavioral and Brain Sciences*, 3: 417–24.

—— (1992), *The Rediscovery of Mind* (Cambridge, Mass.).

4. MENTAL CAUSATION

ANTHOLOGY

HEIL, J., and MELE, A. (eds.) (1993), *Mental Causation* (Oxford).

FURTHER READING

JACKSON, F. (1982/1990). See Section 3.2.

4.1. Causal Relevance

Core Reading

DAVIDSON, D. (1970), 'Mental Events', in L. Foster and J. W. Swanson (eds.), *Experience and Theory* (Amherst); repr. in D. Davidson, *Essays on Actions and Events* (Oxford, 1980); in Rosenthal (1991); and in Beakley and Ludlow (1992).

—— (1993), 'Thinking Causes', in Heil and Mele (1993).

FODOR, J. A. (1989), 'Making Mind Matter More', *Philosophical Topics*, 17: 59–79; repr. in *A Theory of Content and Other Essays* (Cambridge, Mass., 1990); and in Beakley and Ludlow (1992).

Further Reading

ANTONY, L. (1989), 'Anomalous Monism and the Problem of Explanatory Force', *Philosophical Review*, 98: 153–87.

—— (1991), 'The Causal Relevance of the Mental', *Mind and Language*, 6: 295–327.

FODOR, J. A. (1974), 'Special Sciences', *Synthese*, 28: 77–115; repr. in Block (1980), i; and in J. A. Fodor, *Representations* (Brighton, 1981).

KIM, J. (1993), 'Can Supervenience Save Anomalous Monism?', in Heil and Mele (1993).

MCLAUGHLIN, B. P. (1993), 'Davidson's Response to Epiphenomenalism', in Heil and Mele (1993).

PIETROSKI, P. (1994), 'Mental Causation for Dualists', *Mind and Language*, 9: 336–66.

SOSA, E. (1984), 'Mind–Body Interaction and Supervenient Causation', in P. A. French, T. E. Uehling, and H. K. Wettstein (eds.), *Midwest Studies in Philosophy*, ix: *Causation and Causal Theories* (Minneapolis).

4.2. Causation and Supervenience

Core Reading

KIM, J. (1984*a*), 'Concepts of Supervenience', *Philosophy and Phenomenological Research*, 65: 153–76; repr. in *Supervenience and Mind: Selected Philosophical Essays* (Cambridge, 1993).

Further Reading

DAVIDSON, D. (1970). See Section 1.6.

—— (1993). See Section 4.1.

FODOR, J. A. (1989/1990). See Section 4.1.

KIM, J. (1993). See Section 4.1.

MCFETRIDGE, I. G. (1985), 'Supervenience, Realism, Necessity', *Philosophical Quarterly*, 35: 246–58; repr. in *Logical Necessity* (London, 1990).

MCLAUGHLIN, B. P. (1989), 'Token Epiphenomenalism, Type Dualism, and the Causal Priority of the Physical', in J. E. Tomberlin (ed.), *Philosophical Perspectives*, iii: *Philosophy of Mind and Action Theory* (Atascadero, Calif.).

—— (1993). See Section 4.1.

4.3. Explanatoriness and Efficacy

Core Reading

JACKSON, F., and PETTIT, P. (1978), 'Functionalism and Broad Content', *Mind*, 97: 381–400.

Further Reading

BLACKBURN, S. (1991), 'Losing your Mind: Physics, Identity, and Folk Burglar Prevention', in J. D. Greenwood (ed.), *The Future of Folk Psychology* (Cambridge).

BLOCK, N. (1990*b*), 'Can the Mind Change the World?', in G. Boolos (ed.), *Meaning and Method: Essays in Honor of Hilary Putnam* (Cambridge).

BURGE, T. (1989), 'Individuation and Causation in Psychology', *Pacific Philosophical Quarterly*, 70: 303–22.

CUMMINS, R. (1989). See Section 2.3.

FODOR, J. A. (1989). See Section 4.1.

JACKSON, F., and PETTIT, P. (1990b), 'Causation in the Philosophy of Mind', *Philosophy and Phenomenological Research*, 50 (supp.), 195–214.

FURTHER TOPICS

Epistemological Questions

AYER, A. J. (1956), *The Problem of Knowledge* (Harmondsworth), ch. 5: 'Myself and Others'.

CASSAM, Q. (ed.) (1994), *Self-Knowledge* (Oxford).

CHURCHLAND, P. M. (1988), *Matter and Consciousness*, rev. edn. (Cambridge, Mass.), ch. 4: 'The Epistemological Problem'.

HAMLYN, D. W. (1983), *Perception, Learning and the Self* (London).

MALCOLM, N. (1958), 'Knowledge of Other Minds', *Journal of Philosophy*, 55: 969–78; repr. in Rosenthal (1991).

STRAWSON, P. F. (1959), *Individuals: An Essay in Descriptive Metaphysics* (London), ch. 3: 'Persons'.

The Nature of Folk Psychology

CHURCHLAND, P. M. (1991), 'Folk Psychology and the Explanation of Human Behavior', in J. D. Greenwood (ed.), *The Future of Folk Psychology* (Cambridge).

DAVIES, M. (1994), 'The Mental Simulation Debate', in C. Peacocke (ed.), *Objectivity, Simulation and the Unity of Consciousness: Current Issues in the Philosophy of Mind* (*Proceedings of the British Academy*, 83) (Oxford).

GOLDMAN, A. I. (1989), 'Interpretation Psychologized', *Mind and Language*, 4: 161–85.

GORDON, R. M. (1986), 'Folk Psychology as Simulation', *Mind and Language*, 1: 158–71.

HEAL, J. (1986), 'Replication and Functionalism', in J. Butterfield (ed.), *Language, Mind and Logic* (Cambridge).

STICH, S., and NICHOLS, S. (1992), 'Folk Psychology: Simulation or Tacit Theory?', *Mind and Language*, 7: 35–71.

Emotions

DE SOUSA, R. (1987), *The Rationality of Emotion* (Cambridge, Mass.).

GORDON, R. M. (1969), 'Emotions and Knowledge', *Journal of Philosophy*, 66: 408–13; repr. in Rosenthal (1991).

—— (1987), *The Structure of Emotions: Investigations in Cognitive Philosophy* (Cambridge).

HURSTHOUSE, R. (1991), 'Arational Actions', *Journal of Philosophy*, 88: 57–68.

LYONS, W. (1980), *Emotion* (Cambridge).

RORTY, A. O. (ed.) (1980), *Explaining Emotions* (Berkeley and Los Angeles).

6

ANCIENT GREEK PHILOSOPHY I: THE PRE-SOCRATICS AND PLATO

Christopher Janaway

INTRODUCTION

I.1. Why Study Greek Philosophy?

The period of Western thought known as ancient philosophy stretches for roughly 1,000 years, from about 600 BC into the early Middle Ages. We shall concentrate on the two giant figures, Plato and Aristotle, and their forerunners, known as the Pre-Socratics. All these thinkers wrote in the Greek language between 600 and 300 BC.

Why do we study the philosophy of this ancient culture? It was in the Greek world that the whole of philosophy as understood by the Western tradition took shape. As Bernard Williams has written:

The legacy of Greece to Western philosophy is Western philosophy. . . . the Greeks initiated almost all its major fields—metaphysics, logic, the philosophy of language, the theory of knowledge, ethics, political philosophy, and . . . the philosophy of art. Not only did they start these areas of enquiry, but they progressively distinguished what would still be recognised as many of the most basic questions in those areas. In addition, among those who brought about these developments were two, Plato and Aristotle, who have always, where philosophy has been known and studied in the Western world, been counted as supreme in philosophical genius and breadth of achievement.[1]

In studying these early thinkers, then, we discover where philosophy came from; but we also discover in a more rounded way what philosophy is for us today. The Greek thinkers were inventing our subject, and confronting its most profound problems for the first time. Their writing has a directness and a freshness which later philosophy never quite recaptured. It is exciting to retrace these steps and discover that we can converse with the ancient philosophers—we are still doing the same subject.

Nevertheless, some ancient Greek ways of thinking can appear remote. What seems obvious to us may not even have been thinkable in their day, and what is obvious to them may be obscure to us. Before we can work with their philosophy, we must try to construct a picture of what their concepts and arguments meant to them. There is a balance to be struck between testing one of Plato's arguments for its cogency and trying to explain why he wrote as he did: we are called upon to think philosophically, but also to take a historical perspective. Students of ancient philosophy sometimes find that balance hard to achieve. Yet the very blend of historical remoteness and philosophical brilliance found in the ancient thinkers makes them a uniquely rewarding object of study.

What follows aims to introduce some of the central themes in Greek

---

[1] Bernard Williams, 'Greek Philosophy', in M. I. Finley (ed.), *The Legacy of Greece* (Oxford, 1984). The book as a whole attempts a summary of many aspects of the ancient Greek world and its influence.

thought, concentrating on metaphysics, theory of knowledge, and philosophy of mind (but saying comparatively little about ethics, political philosophy, or the philosophy of art), and showing how they can be studied in a philosophically sensitive way.

I.2. Plan

The first part of this discussion deals with some of the Pre-Socratic philosophers, the second with Plato, and the third (Chapter 7) with Aristotle. These sections are best read in order, for Aristotle especially will be more easily understood in the light of his predecessors, and the discussion becomes more advanced as it proceeds.

On the other hand, the *writings* dealt with do not divide into less and more advanced. The Pre-Socratics are in many ways more difficult to study than Plato; and Section 2.5 deals with material in Plato which might prove more rewarding for more advanced readers. The best advice is that everything *referred to* can profitably be studied by a philosopher of whatever degree of experience.

It is essential to read the texts of the Greek philosophers directly in translation. The point is to understand and argue with Plato or Aristotle or Parmenides. Other reading should be regarded only as an aid towards this goal.

What follows is selective and intended only as a preliminary to an understanding of ancient Greek thought. A survey that aspired to be comprehensive would be unmanageably long.

References in the text are explained in the Bibliography.

1. THE PRE-SOCRATIC PHILOSOPHERS

1.1. Introduction

'Pre-Socratic' means 'before Socrates'. Although some of the philosophers under this heading lived during Socrates' lifetime (469–399 BC), we can regard them all as belonging to a chapter in the history of thought distinct from that initiated by Socrates and continued by Plato. The dominant concern of the Pre-Socratics is with explaining the world-order (*kosmos*) or nature (*phusis*) of things in a unified way. Their thinking is the beginning of science as well as philosophy, and marks a shift away from earlier mythical ways of understanding the world. Each of them attempts an improved account of the world, rather than relying on the authority of traditional beliefs. Their concern with innovation and their need to challenge and justify their positions eventually gave birth to the sophistications of philosophical argument.

What we know of the Pre-Socratics is contained in fragments, which are sometimes only a handful of words, and often hard to interpret. They are found in remarks and quotations by later authors, who are sometimes hundreds, or even a thousand, years distant. Generations of modern scholars have sifted this evidence and put together a picture of Pre-Socratic philosophy.[2] Although the reader must take this scholarly construction for granted, it might help to bear in mind that our knowledge here is both slight and controversial. That does not diminish the challenge of trying to understand these remarkable minds.

I shall not give equal weight to all the Pre-Socratics, but give predominance to two who stand out as especially important in the history of philosophy: Heraclitus (see Section 1.3 below) and Parmenides (Section 1.4), both of whom influenced Plato. Another school of thought which impressed Plato was Pythagoreanism (Section 1.6). The remaining sections sketch the immediate predecessors of Heraclitus (Section 1.2) and the effect on philosophy of Parmenides and his followers (Section 1.5). There are other paths through Pre-Socratic philosophy than that taken in this discussion; see the Bibliography.

1.2. Ionian Cosmology

Thales, Anaximander, and Anaximenes came from the city of Miletus on the coast of Ionia (in present-day Turkey); they are sometimes referred to as the Milesians. Anaximander is reported as the pupil of Thales, and Anaximenes as the pupil of Anaximander. They had different doctrines, though what unites them is the aspiration to give a single, rational account of the natural order. Such accounts are given the name *cosmology*. (Another term used in discussing the Pre-Socratics is *cosmogony*: an account of the origin or birth of the world.)

1.2.1. Thales

Thales is traditionally regarded as the founder of philosophy, and also accredited with achievements in geometry, astronomy, and engineering. But our knowledge of him is hazy, and in the evidence we have from antiquity it is hard to disentangle fact from legend and misinformation.[3]

The most famous doctrines of Thales concern water. At this time the common belief was that the earth was flat and stationary, and the Milesians were all concerned with the question how the earth was 'held up'. Thales appears to have believed that the earth was supported by floating on water.

Thales also, apparently, had the view that water was the fundamental stuff in

---

[2] Jonathan Barnes, *Early Greek Philosophy* (Harmondsworth, 1987), 24–31 and 295–301, gives helpful information on this process.

[3] Barnes, *Early Greek Philosophy*, 65–70 gives a good example of such material, which illustrates the more general problem of interpreting the evidence about the Pre-Socratics.

the universe. Aristotle, writing around 250 years later, reports that for Thales water was 'the element and first principle of the things that exist . . . that from which they all are and from which they first come into being and into which they are finally destroyed'.[4] This does not necessarily mean that everything in the world consists of water—although we may wonder how everything could otherwise arise out of water and eventually return to it. If Thales had any answer to that, we can only guess what it might have been.

It is perhaps more fruitful to ask why Thales would have believed that everything arose out of water. Aristotle says it was because of water's observed role in nourishment and generation. It is plausible that Thales was seeking a single hypothesis about all natural processes, starting from one commonly observed substance and its behaviour.

Another interesting view ascribed to Thales is that magnets have a soul. Again, this seems an attempt to unify different phenomena under a single account, the magnet being assimilated to other things (living creatures) with the power to move objects.

1.2.2. Anaximander

Anaximander is a more exciting subject for the historian of philosophy: we know more about his views, and possess a small fragment of his actual words. Moreover, he is a thinker of great imagination.

Anaximander believed that the earth was a flat cylinder, stationary at the centre of the universe, surrounded by vast revolving hoops of fire covered by air. In each hoop was a hole, through which the fire was visible—thus accounting for the appearance of the heavenly bodies.

His explanation of how the earth retains its position is especially significant. Thales had said that the earth floats on water, but, as Aristotle comments, that is a short-sighted explanation, since we have to ask what supports the water. Anaximander's view evades this problem (though it may encounter others): for him the earth is held in place not by any physical thing, but by *its being at the centre*: 'not supported by anything but resting where it is because of its equal distance from everything', as a later writer put it.[5] This is a subtle idea, which cannot be arrived at by empirical observation, and does not involve generalization from familiar stuffs and processes such as water and floating. Behind Anaximander's idea seems to be some purely a priori reasoning—that is, reasoning which does not require confirmation by experience.

We do not know how Anaximander reasoned here. But Aristotle offers us a plausible reconstruction: 'there is no reason why what is situated in the middle and is similarly related to the edges should move upwards rather than

---

[4] Ibid. 63.   [5] Ibid. 72.

downwards or sideways. But it cannot move in opposite directions at the same time. So it necessarily rests where it is.'[6] (The principle that nothing happens without a reason is now known as the principle of sufficient reason.)

Anaximander also shows originality in his account of the principle from which things originate. In place of Thales' water, he hypothesizes something which he calls *apeiron*—'the infinite', or 'the unlimited'. This notion is intriguing, though difficult for us to interpret. Anaximander (along with other Ionian thinkers) believed that the elements of the universe changed into one another— they were in a state of conflict, each striving to dominate by changing its opposite into itself: wet, for example, continually tended to destroy dry, and the other way around. The only surviving fragment of Anaximander's actual words refers to this mutual destruction of opposites: 'they give justice and reparation to one another for their injustice in accordance with the arrangement of time'.[7]

But he found it necessary to assume that the originating principle behind the whole universe was no one definite thing, but 'the infinite'. Why? One reason is probably that if the original stuff of the universe was any one definite thing, no opposing force would have achieved a foothold, and no change would have been possible. However, the reader is advised to consider carefully what reasons Anaximander might have had for his belief in the *apeiron*, beginning perhaps with those suggested by Aristotle.[8]

1.2.3. Anaximenes

Anaximenes is reported to have been a younger contemporary of Anaximander. At first sight, his cosmological views seem something of a disappointment by comparison with those of his predecessor. On the question what supports the earth he gave the answer: air. On the question of the originating principle of the universe he also answered: air.

Although this air was like Anaximander's principle in being infinite, Anaximenes' system seems decidedly more prosaic. Yet clarity and intelligibility are always virtues in philosophy, and, on the slight evidence we have, Anaximenes is to be admired on this count.

Anaximenes takes the important step of explaining by what process the original air is changed so as to become other things. (How things came to be out of Anaximander's *apeiron* is not at all obvious—how could it even change into the basic definite forces of wet, dry, hot, and cold, or the stuffs such as air, fire, or water?) Anaximenes held that there were two fundamental processes to which air was subject: condensation and rarefaction. Air in its pure state was originally invisible. As it progressively became denser, it became fire, and then wind; when denser still it became cloud, then water, then earth, then stone.

---

[6] Barnes, *Early Greek Philosophy*, 74.   [7] Ibid. 74–5.   [8] Ibid. 75–6.

This cosmology has a clear mechanism for explaining change. The constant generation and destruction in the world can be plotted on a single dimension: some things change out of air and others back into air by a simple reversal. And the single underlying principle of the world-order can remain the same throughout all change.

1.3. Heraclitus

Heraclitus was also an Ionian, from Ephesus, and lived later than the Milesians. His philosophy shows their influence, but makes new and profound departures. He stands out as one of the most important Pre-Socratics.

The fragments of Heraclitus repay careful reading and reflection—they are potentially an inexhaustible subject of philosophical study. A problem is that they are not arguments, but bare pronouncements which offer wide scope for speculative interpretation. Commentators disagree profoundly over Heraclitus.

1.3.1. *The* Logos

The Greek word *logos* can be translated as 'account', 'word', and 'reason'. Heraclitus pronounces that there is a single *logos* to which everyone ought to listen—though he thinks human beings are not usually able to comprehend it. The *logos* is an account of reality, and may also be—as some recent commentators have suggested—*that which is revealed by* the account: the reason for things' being as they are, the fundamental principle of the world.

Fragment B 50 of Heraclitus says: 'Listening not to me but to the account (*logos*), it is wise to agree that all things are one.' This is best taken to mean that there are many things, stuffs, and processes, but that they all together make up one whole. There is a single world-order, or *kosmos*, which is 'the same for all' (B 30).

Heraclitus says: 'Of this account which holds forever men prove uncomprehending' (B 1). Why? So far the *logos* does not seem very difficult to understand. But he tells us more: 'They do not comprehend how, in differing, it agrees with itself—a backward-turning connection, like that of a bow and a lyre' (B 51).

One interpretation is that in a musical instrument such as the lyre, the strings and the frame are exerting opposing forces on one another, but the tension between them, far from being destructive, is actually what makes the instrument. Opposition between things is what makes them cohere into a single system. The point is difficult to comprehend because we usually see opposing forces as destructive of order, rather than as constituting it. (The connection is 'unapparent'—see B 54.)

In a related passage, Heraclitus replies to Anaximander, who said that opposing forces do an 'injustice' to one another which is paid back in the course of time. Heraclitus says: 'One should know that war is common, justice is strife, that all things come about in accordance with strife and with what must be' (B 80). To say that strife or conflict *is* justice is to put provocatively an idea similar to that of B 51: an opposition may be a form of agreement or connectedness, when properly understood.

1.3.2. Flux and Opposites

Two doctrines traditionally attributed to Heraclitus are 'Everything is always changing', and the view that there is a unity among opposites. Both, however, are controversial. One is advised to proceed with caution here.

'Flux' means flowing. Plato attributed to Heraclitus the view that 'everything moves and nothing rests' (Plato, *Cratylus* 402a). Later writers stated the same idea as 'Everything flows' or 'Everything is in a state of flux'. The problem is whether Heraclitus himself really thought that everything is always changing.

Discussion has centred on his famous river example: 'On those who enter the same rivers, ever different waters flow' (B 12), or 'it is not possible to step into the same river twice' (B 91: though some think this second statement does not come from Heraclitus himself). The point is that what we call one thing—a river—is constantly changing over time. In one sense you can step into the same *river* twice, but the *water* which made up the river will meanwhile have been replaced by different water.

But did Heraclitus believe that every supposedly constant thing is in some way changing all the time? Guthrie[9] is one commentator who accepts this view, the view reported by Plato. Kirk[10] puts an opposing case, saying that Plato's report is not borne out by evidence in the Heraclitean fragments.

We should ask *why* Heraclitus might have thought that everything was always changing at least in some way. Fragment B 125 uses a Greek concoction as an example: 'the barley-drink separates if it is not moving'. This drink was made of wine, grated cheese, and barley: if you did not stir it, the ingredients broke up. This suggests the idea that things are held together by motion or change: if change ceased, the order of things would be lost. If Heraclitus believed that change is necessary for the preservation of stable order, it is possible that he would think every part of the world-order must always be changing, given the view that 'all things are one'.

What then is Heraclitus' doctrine of the unity of opposites? Did he have any such doctrine? Opposites are related to one another in the fragments in a number of different ways. For example: (1) opposites change into opposites, and (2)

---

[9] W. K. C. Guthrie, *A History of Greek Philosophy*, i (Cambridge, 1962), 449 ff.; repr. as 'Flux and *Logos* in Heraclitus', in A. P. D. Mourelatos (ed.), *The Pre-Socratics* (New York, 1974).

[10] G. S. Kirk, 'Natural Change in Heraclitus', in Mourelatos (ed.), *The Pre-Socratics*.

opposites depend upon one another for their existence. A third possibility quite distinct from these is the bizarre idea that (3) opposites are really identical: being alive and being dead are the same; day and night are the same. Heraclitus' words sometimes seem to suggest that he holds this idea. See B 57, 'day and night . . . are one'; also B 88. But can his real point be translated into a case of (1) or (2) above—i.e. 'Day always changes into night' and 'There would not be night if there were not day'? Or, again, did he think the constant succession of day and night must mean that some one thing was both day and night?[11] Kahn thinks Heraclitus' point is that 'day and night are complementary aspects of the same unit'[12]—and possibly the 'unity of opposites' amounts to little more than this.

However, there is another idea about opposites in the fragments: (4) a single thing can have two opposite properties. There are some famous instances of this kind: 'The sea is most pure and most polluted water: for fish, drinkable and life-preserving; for men, undrinkable and death-dealing' (B 61); and 'The path up and down is one and the same' (B 60).

Here, one unchanging thing can be described in contrary ways. Heraclitus thinks that, because there is a way in which sea-water is pure and a way in which it is polluted, then it is both pure and polluted. Probably he has a similar view of change over time: if a thing is alive at one time and dead at another, then it is both alive and dead. Barnes[13] suggests that something like (4) is at the heart of Heraclitus' theory of the unity of opposites, and that Heraclitus was led to it both by examples of change over time and by examples like the sea-water.

1.3.3. Fire

'The world (*kosmos*), the same for all, neither any god nor any man made; but it was always and is and will be, fire ever-living, kindling in measures and being extinguished in measures' (B 30). This raises many questions. Is Heraclitus continuing the tradition of the Milesians? Does this fire have a role similar to that of Anaximenes' air? Secondly, what does 'kindling in measures and being extinguished in measures' mean? And thirdly, what is the significance of calling this fire 'ever-living'?

Consider the last question first. There are perhaps two central points here. The fire is everlasting: that presumably means that the world-order never had a beginning and will never cease. If so, Heraclitus will be different from the Milesians in one way: he will not have to say how the universe *came into being*. Most commentators have accepted that Heraclitus has no cosmogony. (But Kahn[14] is one who disagrees.)

---

[11] See J. Barnes, *The Presocratic Philosophers* (London, 1989).

[12] C. H. Kahn, *The Art and Thought of Heraclitus* (Cambridge, 1979).

[13] J. Barnes, *The Presocratic Philosophers*, 69–75.   [14] *The Art and Thought of Heraclitus*.

The other point is that the fire is ever-*living*. The *kosmos* is alive. Heraclitus thinks of the world-order as a kind of immortal, divine being. He speaks of a divine wisdom and 'purpose', and of the universe being 'steered' (B 41, B 78): 'the thunderbolt steers all things' (B 64). The thunderbolt is fire, but is also the traditional weapon of the Greek god Zeus. Heraclitus thus implies that the cosmic fire controls everything in the universe, and that it is to be regarded as the supreme deity. In another, highly paradoxical fragment, he shows that his deity has both continuity and discontinuity with traditional religious ideas: 'One alone is the wise, unwilling and willing to be called by the name of Zeus' (B 32).

In other places Heraclitus suggests that the human soul is also a manifestation of fire: 'for souls it is death to become water' (B 36), just as elsewhere he says that fire turns into sea (B 31a). B 117 and B 118 also seem to link soul with fire.

Fire transforms itself in an ordered fashion ('in measures') into material parts of the universe. This aspect of Heraclitus' thought may bear some comparison with Anaximenes' view of air, although whether Heraclitus saw everything as always composed of fire as an underlying substratum is a much disputed question. Illumination may be sought from B 90, which says: 'all things are an exchange for fire and fire for all things, as goods are for gold and gold for goods'. If fire is a kind of currency, does this suggest that it is not (like Anaximenes' air) a stuff which all things are made of?

It is clear that, in some way, as things change, an overall quantity in the universe remains constant, and this is measured in terms of fire. So, in a sense, fire is the *kosmos*, i.e. the order in the world—it is the divine measure which remains constant throughout continual change.

1.3.4. *Human Life*

Heraclitus' message that all things are one and that opposites are in unity can tell us what our own values should be. The idea that justice is strife (and that 'war is father of all', B 53) also has a direct application to human affairs. Conflict is what holds human communities together, for Heraclitus.

His examples of the opposites are often taken from human life: being asleep and being awake, being young and being old, being dead and being alive. Heraclitus says 'the latter change and are the former, and again the former change and are the latter' (B 88).

Finally, to want only what we think of as a positive good is an error, according to him: 'It is not good for men to get all they want. Sickness makes health sweet and good, hunger plenty, weariness rest' (B 110, B 111). We must embrace both opposites, because only in their opposition to one another do they have any significance for us.

It has been suggested that Heraclitus' picture of the *kosmos* is primarily intended to change attitudes to our own life and death.[15] It would, however, be typical of Heraclitus to leave his reader uncomfortably in the balance, not knowing whether it is really the universe or ourselves, or both, that he is talking about. Enigma and ambiguity are central to his method.

1.4. Parmenides and the Eleatics

Elea was a Greek-speaking town in southern Italy, to the west of the Greek world, geographically distant from the Ionian east. Elea's best-known inhabitants are the philosophers Parmenides and Zeno. Parmenides was the instigator of a new chapter in the history of philosophy, and of all the Pre-Socratics he is the single most important figure. The term 'Eleatic' came to apply to philosophy done in the tradition inaugurated by Parmenides, whose effect on later philosophy was profound.

Eleatic philosophy is distant from Heraclitus in more than geography. It says that the world contains no real diversity, plurality, change, or motion. The world is homogeneous, complete, and static: nothing flows, and there cannot be genuine opposites. Sometimes people wonder whether Parmenides was deliberately disagreeing with Heraclitus (the two were contemporaries). But experts tend to be sceptical about this: there are at best only a few hints to go on, and no hard evidence that Parmenides could have been thinking about Heraclitus. It is better to try to understand the two independently.

Another marked difference is that Eleatic philosophy consists of *argument*. Heraclitus makes pronouncements which induce perplexity and challenge us to make sense of them. Parmenides and his followers argue: their works typically show the following sorts of pattern: '*A* must be, because *B*'; 'if *A*, then *B* or *C*, but how could *C* be the case?' 'Only *A* is possible, so *B* is impossible.' Stretched out sometimes to great length, these patterns give evidence that philosophical argument as we know it today has come into being. This alone should lead us to rate the historical importance of the Eleatics very highly. But it also tells us how we must study the Eleatic fragments. We must try to work out for ourselves a linear structure into which their argument falls.

1.4.1. Parmenides' Poem

All the passages from Parmenides fit into one work, which is in verse form, and seems consciously modelled on the Homeric *Odyssey* with its tale of a single man's heroic voyage. We do not have a complete picture of Parmenides' work, but its overall shape is fairly generally agreed.

Stage 1. There is an introductory section (often called the 'proem') in which Parmenides comes closest to writing genuine poetry. The narrator describes the progress of his chariot, which meets with the daughters of the sun, who convey him to the house of Night, where a goddess addresses him. One may speculate about the symbolism of all this. It seems that Parmenides wishes to compare his philosophical argument to a heroic quest and to give his utterances authority. The house of Night is traditionally a place where there is no distinction between the opposites of Night and Day. That may be significant for what he goes on to say.

Stage 2. The goddess announces that one must choose between two ways: the way of 'It is' and the way of 'It is not'. But the latter is impossible to follow: it is not possible to think of something that 'is not'—so the only way possible is 'It is'. This part of the argument is extremely important, but difficult. What does Parmenides mean by 'It is' and 'It is not'? And why is it not possible to think of 'what is not'?

Stage 3. Another seeming possibility is a confused route which is a mixture of 'It is' and 'It is not'—this is the way of most ordinary mortals, says the goddess. But, like the way of 'It is not', the mixed way is also not a true possibility.

Stage 4. The Way of Truth. Assuming that one may think only 'It is', how can reality be described? The answer is contained in the so-called 'Way of Truth', which is in the long, continuous fragment B 8. If you cannot think 'is not', then you will have to describe reality as containing no change, no generation or destruction, no differences, no imperfections. Why? Because 'it is all full of what is' as Parmenides says (B 8, line 24). This long, ambitious argument will bear a good deal of study.

Stage 5. The Way of Opinion. Finally the goddess tells of something other than the truth, which it is necessary also to hear: the 'deceitful arrangement of words' (B 8, line 52), which sets out opinions 'in which there is no true trust' (B 1, line 30). This is very puzzling. If these opinions are not true, why must we hear them? Many different interpretations have been suggested. The Way of Opinion appears to be a traditional cosmogony, in which the opposites fire and night play the central role. It seems most likely that the Way of Opinion is an illustration of how not to proceed, or an immunization against accounts of the world which call on notions of plurality and change that have been ruled out in the Way of Truth.

It is most useful to concentrate first and foremost on Stages 2 and 4. Stage 2, the argument that one cannot think 'It is not', is contained in fragments B 2, B 3, B 6, and B 7. Stage 4, the Way of Truth, in B 8, uses as its premiss the claim that one cannot think 'It is not', and deduces a complete account of reality.

1.4.2. 'It Is' and 'It Is Not'

Parmenides is talking about the being ('is') and not-being ('is not') of something. It is not immediately obvious what the 'it' is here. But many interpreters believe he means an indefinite 'anything one is thinking about'. Then the goddess is in effect saying: 'Take anything you are thinking about: either it is or it is not.'

What is meant by 'is' (or 'be')? In English we distinguish several uses of these words, which the Greeks at this time did not have enough theory to distinguish clearly. (This will be an issue when we discuss Plato later.) The most popular view is that 'is' here means 'exists'.[16]

Let us continue on the assumption that 'is' means 'exists'. Then the conclusion that Parmenides first reaches (end of Stage 2) is that anything one can think about must exist.

Next we shall want to know by what argument he reaches that conclusion. The place to look is in fragments B 2, B 3, and B 6. These lines are extremely difficult to comprehend at first sight, but it is essential to read them.[17]

The best approach to these difficult words is to make from them an argument with clear steps, leading to the conclusion 'you cannot think "it is not" '. A crucial premiss appears to be that anything you can think of (or speak of) is always something that *can* exist (see B 3). Another premiss is that something that 'is not' (or something that is 'nothing', as in B 6, line 2) *cannot* exist. If one cannot think about something that cannot exist, then one cannot think about something that 'is not', because that cannot exist.

Does the conclusion follow from the premisses? Do we believe the conclusion? If the answer to both these questions is Yes, then there is no problem (apart from a certain obscurity, perhaps). But do we really believe that you cannot think of anything that does not exist? If the conclusion is false, something must have gone wrong earlier in the argument.

A problem lies in Parmenides' idea that what does not exist ('what is not', or 'nothing') *cannot* exist. This can mean two quite different things: either (1) 'It is impossible that something both exists and does not exist', or (2) 'If something does not exist, it is impossible that it should exist'. One of these is trivially true, the other a wild claim which is probably false. Which is which—and which one does Parmenides' argument require?

Parmenides believed he had refuted the idea that you can think 'is not' about anything. He calls his reasoning a 'battle-hardened proof' (B 7), and says that

---

[16] See G. E. C. Owen, 'Eleatic Questions', in *Logic, Science and Dialectic* (London, 1986), and Barnes, *The Presocratic Philosophers*, 160–1. Some interpreters of Parmenides have taken different views about his 'is', one example being M. Furth, 'Elements of Eleatic Ontology', in Mourelatos (ed.), *The Pre-Socratics*. Barnes discusses others in *The Presocratic Philosophers*.

[17] See Barnes, *Early Greek Philosophy*. (In the first line of B 6, 'being' is wrongly printed instead of 'saying'.)

one should trust this proof rather than what one's senses seem to tell one about the world. This is an important point about his method. Empirical observation is no guide to truth for Parmenides. Instead, the correct description of the world can be reached solely from the deduction that you cannot think 'It is not', once all its consequences are worked out. The world, therefore, is very different from the way it appears to the senses.

1.4.3. The Way of Truth

B 8, containing the Way of Truth, elaborates the consequences of the earlier argument that you cannot think 'It is not'. The first four lines state a prospectus for the Way of Truth:

> Only one story, one road, now
> is left: that it is. And on this there are signs
> in plenty that, being, it is ungenerated and indestructible,
> whole, of one kind and unwavering, and complete.

The rest of the fragment falls into sections. Lines 5–21 argue that 'it' is ungenerated and indestructible: nothing in reality can ever come into existence or go out of existence. Lines 22–5 argue that 'it' is whole, undivided, or continuous: there is no time or place in reality which lacks being, either absolutely or in terms of degree. Lines 26–33 argue that reality is 'unmoving' or 'unwavering' and 'remains fixed there': there cannot be any change or motion.

Lines 34–41 seem to be a kind of résumé of the whole of Parmenides' argument. Lines 42–52 deal with the idea that reality is 'complete' (though note that already lines 32–3 talked about its being complete or 'not lacking'), and say that it is 'like the bulk of a well-rounded ball'. This probably does not mean that the universe is a finite sphere. For what would be beyond the limit of such a universe? Parmenides is not allowed to reply 'Nothing'!

In B 8 we reach Parmenides' extraordinary world-view: there is no change or motion, no generation or destruction, no imperfection, no division. Reality is simply 'full of what is'.

1.4.4. Arguments of Melissus

Melissus is known to us as a follower of Parmenides, rather than as a thinker of independent standing. His arguments are, however, clearer than those of Parmenides and he makes some additions to the latter's deductions about the world.

Because of their clarity, the fragments of Melissus are quite easy to read if one has some knowledge of Parmenides' arguments. The following arguments are especially noteworthy: (1) that what exists must have everlasting existence, since otherwise it would have to be 'nothing' at some time (see B 1); (2) that reality is one single thing, which he says follows from its being infinite (B 6); (3) that there can be no alteration in anything (B 7); (4) that there can be no motion (B 7).

The argument against motion assumes that something could only move if there was emptiness for it to go into. But if emptiness is *nothing*, then emptiness cannot exist—so motion is impossible. The argument against change assumes that if a thing alters by becoming hot when it was cold (for example), then something goes out of existence and something comes into existence (i.e. the cold and the hot respectively).

The argument that everything is just one thing results in the view known as 'Eleatic monism'. This has always been regarded as one of the chief Eleatic doctrines, but it is Melissus who establishes it rather than Parmenides. Hence it has been commented that 'When Plato and Aristotle represent monism as the principal thesis of the Eleatics, they must be reading Parmenides through Melissan spectacles.'[18]

1.4.5. Zeno's Paradoxes

Zeno was from Elea, and is treated as some kind of disciple of Parmenides. His chief contribution was to advance the skilful manipulation of argument to an unprecedented degree. He produced a number of arguments whose conclusion is that there is no motion, and others whose conclusion is that there is no plurality. Hence his themes are central to Eleatic philosophy.

However, his arguments are rather self-consciously paradoxical. The arguments against motion provide well-known examples. An arrow cannot move, Zeno argues, because it is always in a place equal to itself and, if it is in a place equal to itself, then it is at rest—so it is always at rest.[19] In another argument Achilles, the fastest runner, cannot catch up with the tortoise, the slowest, because their proportionate speeds mean that the tortoise is always ahead by a proportion of the distance Achilles covers in any given time. These paradoxes, and those concerning plurality, which are perhaps less well known, are often studied in a self-contained way, apart from the mainstream of Greek philosophical thought. To examine them properly is a fairly taxing exercise in logic.[20]

---

[18] G. S. Kirk, J. E. Raven, and M. Schofield, *The Presocratic Philosophers*, 2nd edn. (Cambridge, 1983), 395.

[19] See Barnes, *Early Greek Philosophy*, 155–7.

[20] R. M. Sainsbury, *Paradoxes* (Cambridge, 1988), ch. 1, presents the paradoxes from the contemporary logician's point of view. A succinct analysis of the arguments can also be found in G. Vlastos, 'Zeno of Elea', in P. Edwards (ed.), *Encyclopaedia of Philosophy* (London, 1967).

1.5. Cosmology after the Eleatics

The next chapter in Greek philosophy is a reaction to the powerful Eleatic arguments against plurality and change. The main figures here are Empedocles, Anaxagoras, and the Atomists (chiefly Democritus).

1.5.1. *The Problem*

All these philosophers wished to continue the earlier Ionian tradition of cosmology. They wished to explain the order of the world by accounting for change, growth, and motion, and by drawing on the diversity of things or elements that make up the world.

But the Eleatics' arguments purported to show that there *could not be* change, growth, motion, or diversity, because of the supposed impossibility of thinking of nothing, or of 'what is not'. The Eleatic arguments exerted such a powerful hold that cosmology either had to avoid mentioning 'what is not'—or it had to challenge the Eleatics head on and declare that 'what is not' can be thought of after all. The Atomists adopted the latter strategy, as we shall see. Empedocles and Anaxagoras in their different ways attempt complex cosmological accounts which allow for plurality and change.

1.5.2. *Empedocles*

The cosmological idea that Empedocles relies on is that of mixture. He says 'there is only mixing and interchange of what is mixed' (B 8). The basic constituents of mixtures never begin or cease existing, but can continually recombine. So, he says (in B 17): 'to that extent they come into being and have no lasting life; but in so far as they never cease their continual change, to that extent they exist forever, unmoving in a circle'. Thus on one level the constituents of reality are everlasting and immutable; on another level their mixture makes change possible. Often in Empedocles' fragments, such as with the long cosmological fragment B 17 with its 'twofold story' about the one and the many, he is partially agreeing with the Eleatics, while at the same time finding ways of avoiding their criticisms.[21]

The elements of the world for Empedocles are earth, air, fire, and water, though he sometimes gives them other names.[22] Aristotle tells us that Empedocles was the first to make the elements four.[23] This is worth remembering: there is no need to assume that any of the earlier cosmologists must have recognized four elements.

[21] See e.g. B 8, B 11, B 15, B 12, B 13, B 14, in Barnes, *Early Greek Philosophy*, 171–3.
[22] See B 22, B 98, B 6, B 38.
[23] *Metaphysics* A, 985ª31–3; see Kirk *et al.*, *The Presocratic Philosophers*, 286.

Another central notion to grasp in Empedocles is the pair of forces Love and Strife, which are responsible for drawing the elements together or keeping them apart.[24]

The cyclical description of the universe, where at the lowest level nothing really goes out of existence or comes into existence, also applies to human life, according to Empedocles:

> . . . there is no birth for any
> mortal thing, nor any cursed end in death.
> But there is only mixing and interchange of what is mixed—
> but men name these things birth. (B 8)

So far we have discussed extracts from a work called *On Nature*. Empedocles also wrote one called *Purifications*, although the relation of the two works is a matter of some doubt.[25] A central doctrine in Empedocles' *Purifications* is the transmigration of souls (metempsychosis): the same soul (*psychē* or *psukhē*) can be present successively in different bodies. He even claims himself to have been a boy, a girl, a bush, a bird, and a fish (B 117)—though it is unclear how the same soul can be in all these diverse things, or how it can have been *Empedocles* when it was in a bush, for example, if that is what he means. The idea of metempsychosis is found also in Pythagoreanism (see Section 1.6 below), which is usually regarded as an influence on Empedocles. As we shall see, the idea also influenced Plato.

1.5.3. Anaxagoras

The thought of Anaxagoras is regarded by many as particularly difficult. Probably the simplest idea to begin with is contained in his fragment B 17.[26] Here he says that the Greeks 'do not have a correct notion of generation and destruction; for no things are generated or destroyed, but they are commingled and dissociated from things that exist. And for this reason they would be correct to call generation commingling and destruction dissociation.' Anaxagoras is complying with the Eleatic prohibition against saying that anything begins to exist or ceases to exist—there is, for him, no absolute generation or destruction. But there can be mixing together and separating out. A cup of coffee is 'made' where none was before, but clearly only by mixing water, milk, and coffee which already existed. Anaxagoras thinks that all change can be accounted for by the processes of mixing and separation, without saying 'is not' about anything that is.

---

[24] See Barnes, *Early Greek Philosophy*, 174–6, for initial material on this.

[25] See Charles H. Kahn, 'Religion and Natural Philosophy in Empedocles' Doctrine of the Soul', in Mourelatos (ed.), *The Pre-Socratics*.

[26] See Barnes, *Early Greek Philosophy*, 232–3.

He maintains that in the original state 'all things were together' in a massive mixture, in which everything that ever could exist already did exist. Provided that one allows motion to occur—Anaxagoras uses rotation, producing a whirl, or vortex—then different stuffs can separate off.

However, Anaxagoras believes that everything still continues to be mixed now, and it is this part of his thought which is at once the most ingenious and the most difficult to grasp.

Anaxagoras holds that everything (every stuff) at any time contains a portion of every other stuff. Containment seems to be required to explain the possibility of change. For example, bread can be changed into flesh, or blood, or hair by biological processes. Anaxagoras apparently believes that this is possible only if these substances are already present in the bread. From this it is a bold generalization to claim that *every* substance must contain a portion of *every* other—but that is indeed what he claims. Everything remains always a mixture, then, though local areas of the world can be composed of different stuffs because the proportions of the mixture become varied by motion over time. Gold is different from bread because, even though both gold and bread contain a portion of every stuff, one contains greatly more gold than anything else, and the other greatly more bread (if that is an appropriate stuff).

Another claim Anaxagoras makes rejoices in the name of 'homoeomerity', the principle that the composition of a thing's parts is exactly the same as the composition of the whole. If gold is a homoeomerous stuff then, whatever part of a lump of gold you take, that part will be made up of exactly the same as the whole lump.

It has sometimes been thought that the principle of homoeomerity conflicts with the principle that everything contains a portion of everything else. This is, however, not true. If gold is made up of every stuff in a unique set of proportions, then the homoeomerity principle says that any part of a lump of gold will be made up of every stuff in exactly the same unique way as the whole lump itself.[27]

A further complication to Anaxagoras' theory is his view that stuffs are infinitely divisible. The Atomists, as we shall see, thought that everything must ultimately be made up of indivisible units (atoms). Anaxagoras thought just the opposite: you can never reach a smallest portion, however much you divide something up ('there is no smallest, but there is always a smaller' (B 3)).[28] It is often said that Anaxagoras has a more subtle understanding of infinity than any earlier thinker.

Another much-discussed aspect of Anaxagoras' thought are his views about mind (*nous*). Mind 'arranged everything', he says (see the long fragment B 12).[29]

---

[27] Cf. G. B. Kerferd, 'Anaxagoras and the Concept of Matter before Aristotle', in Mourelatos (ed.), *The Pre-Socratics*, and/or Barnes, *The Presocratic Philosophers*, 325–6.

[28] Barnes, *Early Greek Philosophy*, 229.   [29] Ibid. 227–8.

Mind is the finest and the purest of things, and it is not mixed with anything else; it has understanding of the whole of reality and is the motive force which brought about the separation of everything out of the original mixture. In his *Phaedo* Plato makes Socrates say that he read this theory and was excited by the idea that everything was brought about by an intelligence for a purpose—but that he could not see how this fitted in with the physicalistic explanations Anaxagoras gave of natural processes.[30]

1.5.4. Democritus and Atomism

The most powerful theory to respond to the Eleatics was atomism. It is common to talk of 'the Atomists', Leucippus and Democritus. Leucippus is said to have been Democritus' teacher, but little else is known of him.[31] The study of Pre-Socratic atomism is thus chiefly the study of the prolific writer Democritus, whose thought we largely reconstruct from later writers whom he influenced. It has been said that the atomist theory 'began a line of thought whose influence upon philosophy and upon science was of unparalleled consequence'.[32] Plato does not mention Democritus, but the reader of Chapter 7 will find him of great significance to Aristotle.

In Eleatic theory, with its ban on 'It is not', it is difficult to understand how there can be change or motion, and also how there can be many distinct things. Atomism solves both difficulties by the bold stroke of accepting that 'what is not' exists: part of 'what there is' is void or emptiness.

Motion, therefore, is possible: 'something which is' can come to occupy what was previously void. And there can be genuinely distinct portions of 'what is', separated by 'non-being'.

For Democritus, the parts of reality that can be called 'being' are atoms. 'Atom' means 'uncuttable' or 'indivisible'. Each atom is a unitary thing, incapable of becoming more than one; and each is solid, containing absolutely no 'non-being'. We may be reminded of Parmenides' requirement that 'it is all full of what is'. Each atom satisfies not only this requirement, but the requirement that there be no generation and destruction, and no change. Atoms themselves exist eternally and are unchanging in their properties. What they can do is move, because of the inclusion of void in reality.

Democritus believed that there were infinitely many atoms, moving around in an infinite void. They each had a permanent shape, and because there were many different shapes, atoms could become entangled in many different ways. In this way, Democritus sought to explain the coming into being (and the destruction) of the things of which we usually consider the world to be composed. Given atoms, which were full only of 'being', plus the 'non-being' of

---

[30] Ibid. 235.   [31] Ibid. 242–3.   [32] Barnes, *The Presocratic Philosophers*, 377.

void, Democritus was able to hypothesize infinite possibilities of movement and combination among atoms, hence offering a powerful explanation for the observed change, generation, and destruction in the world.

An important further feature of atomism is that the atoms are too small to be seen by the human observer. So the observer's picture of the world is not a good guide to the way things really are. Perhaps the most famous saying of Democritus is that 'in reality [or "in truth"] there are atoms and void' (B 125).[33] The full quotation is 'By convention colour, by convention sweet, by convention bitter: in reality atoms and void.' Although one may debate precisely what philosophical position this enunciates, it seems safe to say the following: that things are sweet, bitter, and coloured *to us*, but that such qualities will not be present at the level of atoms. (This is reminiscent of the distinction between primary and secondary qualities in modern philosophy.) The idea that true reality does not contain many of the qualities, or indeed the ordinary objects, which human observers take it to contain is conducive to a form of scepticism, and was taken thus by later thinkers in antiquity.

1.6. Pythagoreanism

1.6.1. Pythagoras and the Pythagoreans

Although Pythagoras is among the more famous names in ancient thought, very little is known about him. He lived before Heraclitus and Parmenides, and there are many legends about him—of his performing various miracles, for example. He was possibly a kind of shaman who claimed supernatural wisdom. The 'Pythagorean' doctrines which became influential in the history of philosophy were developed by much later thinkers belonging to sects which traced their origins to Pythagoras, but many of whose doctrines were not his.[34]

1.6.2. The Soul

It seems likely that the Pythagorean belief in metempsychosis, the migration of the soul from one kind of animal body to another, may date back to Pythagoras himself. Reports about him say that he claimed to have lived before as somebody else and to be reincarnated. If so, then the attribution to him of at least the view that 'soul is immortal'[35] is plausible. This is a view which runs right through the later Pythagorean tradition, and which Plato makes use of, especially in his *Phaedo* (see Section 2.4.1 below).

[33] See Barnes, *Early Greek Philosophy*, 252–5.
[34] See C. H. Kahn, 'Pythagorean Philosophy before Plato', in Mourelatos (ed.), *The Pre-Socratics*, 182–5, for suggestions about cosmological doctrines which may just possibly originate with Pythagoras.
[35] See Barnes, *Early Greek Philosophy*, 86.

1.6.3. Numbers and Harmony

The Pythagoreans studied music, and discovered that musical intervals such as the fourth, the fifth, and the octave could be represented as numerical ratios. They also appear to have thought that the whole of the universe could be understood in similar terms—see Aristotle's report that 'they supposed that the elements of numbers were the elements of all the things that exist, and that the whole heaven was harmony and number'.[36] Aristotle connects this interest in numbers with advances in mathematics, though it is unclear how much of a contribution the Pythagoreans really made in this area. The evidence suggests that their interest in numbers may have been chiefly a combination of the metaphysical and the mystical.

Pythagorean metaphysical beliefs concern the opposed principles, odd and even, the limit and the infinite (or unlimited), one and many. They were concerned with generating the series of numbers from these principles, and then seem to have wanted to understand the whole of reality in terms of the patterns to which these principles gave rise. Some of their views about numbers are purely symbolic and others quite fanciful.

Part of the interest of Pythagoreanism is that it influenced Plato, who was stimulated by its ideas about the immortal soul, the fundamental nature of numbers, and the general idea of harmony. In his *Phaedo*, probably written after a trip to Sicily where he was in contact with Pythagoreans, Plato goes out of his way to allude to Pythagorean philosophers and doctrines.[37]

2. PLATO AND SOCRATES

2.1. Introduction to Plato

Few would contradict the statement that Plato is one of the greatest philosophers. He is also one of the world's great writers. He has left us more than twenty-five works which touch every area that philosophy has subsequently investigated, and display an unequalled blend of argument and creativity. One can find one's way around Plato's works with greater ease than any other ancient philosopher. For these reasons, studying them is a joy.

Plato wrote in the form of dialogues. Why he did this is an interesting question. But one thing it enables him to do is clear: he can put forward opposing views, and make his characters seem to understand less than the attentive reader about where the argument is leading. This draws the reader in, to

---

[36] Ibid. 208–9.

[37] For an assessment of this influence, see D. Bostock, *Plato's* Phaedo (Oxford, 1986), 11–14.

continue the debate for himself or herself. It can, however, also make it difficult to settle exactly what is 'Plato's own view'.[38]

2.1.1. *Early, Middle, and Late Plato*

Plato's works belong to different periods within a long life. He changed his mind about many issues and certain ways of doing philosophy. So it is a mistake to assume that everything he wrote makes up a uniform system of doctrines. The most customary division is between 'early', 'middle', and 'late' parts of his career. The early period is dominated by Plato's examination of the philosophy of his teacher, Socrates. The middle period, to which the *Republic* belongs, is where our attention will be most concentrated; this period contains the original doctrines for which Plato is best known, and some works written after the *Republic*—*Phaedrus, Parmenides, Theaetetus*—in which he expands his range and subjects his own views to rigorous argumentative scrutiny. These works are harder to read, but philosophers often admire them most.

Questions about the order in which Plato wrote his works are hotly disputed among scholars. The following list of Plato's works relies on the most generally agreed groupings by period:

Early (in alphabetical order):
  Apology of Socrates, Charmides, Crito, Euthydemus, Euthyphro, Gorgias, Hippias Major, Hippias Minor, Ion, Laches, Lysis, Menexenus, Protagoras, Republic, book 1 (possibly earlier than rest of the *Republic*); *Meno* (end of early period, transitional to middle period).

Middle:
  Cratylus, Phaedo, Symposium, Republic, Phaedrus, Parmenides, Theaetetus (the last three are later than *Republic* and have been described as late, or 'late middle').

Late:
  Sophist, Statesman, Timaeus, Critias, Philebus, Laws.

2.1.2. *Influences on Plato*

It was earlier remarked that Plato was influenced by Heraclitus, Parmenides, and Pythagoreanism. This becomes apparent as one reads works in the middle and late periods. From the Pythagoreans Plato adopts the notion that numbers and other mathematical entities are an eternal reality underlying the changing world of appearance, and the idea that the human soul is immortal and can be reincarnated. From Heraclitus he takes a concern with change and unity of opposites in the world of appearance; from Parmenides he inherits the idea that

---

[38] See Richard Kraut (ed.), *The Cambridge Companion to Plato* (Cambridge, 1992), 25–30 on this.

what truly *is* cannot in any way *not be*. His central epistemological and meta-physical doctrines—that there is a realm of appearance and change, and also one of eternal, unchanging being inhabited by Forms, that knowledge requires contact with Forms, and that the human soul which knows Forms is itself eter-nal—constitute a new departure in the history of philosophy, but can also be seen as attempts to come to terms with the ideas of these earlier thinkers.

But at the beginning of his career there is little clue that any of these thinkers is of concern to Plato. The early dialogues all portray the philosopher Socrates in conversation with contemporaries from different walks of life. The topic of conversation is ethical: What is a good life? How, if at all, do we learn to be excellent human beings? What is excellence, or fineness, or justice, or courage? We can judge from this that the overwhelming influence on the early Plato is Socrates' ethics.

Plato also gives Socrates opponents, prominent among whom are the thinkers known as the Sophists (examples are Protagoras, Hippias, Gorgias, and Thrasymachus in *Republic*, book 1).

2.2. Plato, Socrates, and the Sophists

The Socrates portrayed in the early dialogues is the antithesis of the Sophists. They are professional teachers who charge often substantial fees; Socrates pur-sues knowledge for its own sake and never accepts payment. The Sophists claim to have knowledge and to transmit it to others; Socrates claims only to seek knowledge, not to have it. The Sophists (in Plato's portrayal) frequently aim at winning arguments by various forms of intellectual trickery (see the dialogue *Euthydemus* for extreme examples); Socrates aims not to win, but to discover the truth. Plato recognizes the Sophists as an important intellectual movement, but consistently contrasts their methods with those of philosophy. The English derogatory terms 'sophistry' and 'sophistic' originate in the critical stance Plato takes to these thinkers. A proper assessment of their importance should not therefore rely solely on the evidence Plato provides.[39]

2.2.1. The Sophists

The Sophists belonged to a movement in fifth-century Greece which shifted emphasis away from the study of nature, and gave philosophy what might be called a 'humanistic' tendency. A distinction made at this time is that between nature (*phusis*) and convention (*nomos*). Many things exist not 'by nature', but because of human custom, institution, or convention: examples are laws, lan-guages, ethical codes, political constitutions. The Sophists advanced the study

---

[39] Cf. G. B. Kerferd, *The Sophistic Movement* (Cambridge, 1981) and possibly W. K. C. Guthrie, *The Sophists* (Cambridge, 1971), and E. Hussey, *The Presocratics* (London, 1972), ch. 6.

of (for example) the nature of language, the techniques of public speaking and persuasion, human history and society, and the nature of right and wrong. It is plausible to say that they provided the context without which the philosophy of Socrates, which neglects cosmology and metaphysics in favour of defining the virtues, would not have been possible.

It is worth noting two aspects of the Sophists' work, both of which troubled Plato. One was relativism. Protagoras was famous for his doctrine that 'a man [person] is the measure of all things, of those that are, that they are, and of those that are not, that they are not'. This may be taken to mean that anything is true only *for me* or *for you*, or at least *for someone*; i.e. that nothing is simply or absolutely true or false. Although Protagoras is portrayed in the early dialogue named after him (which contains lively portraits of a number of Sophists), his relativism is most fully dealt with by Plato in the comparatively late *Theaetetus*, in which he sets out to refute it.

Another preoccupation of some of the Sophists was with rhetorical persuasion. A central figure here is Gorgias, who was a renowned orator, but also a theorist about language and its ability to sway opinion. He believed that language could not pursue truth, but was powerful at persuading or deceiving. A good speech could 'bewitch' its hearers and change their minds. (Not all scholars class Gorgias as a Sophist, but see Kerferd, *The Sophistic Movement*, 44–5.) Plato accuses the Sophists in general of training the young to speak cleverly and to appear to have knowledge and virtue when really they have none. Philosophy, a disinterested pursuit of knowledge of the truth by rational argument, must be established as a superior discipline in order to drive out the errors of the Sophists.

2.2.2. Socrates

In most of his dialogues Plato uses the character of Socrates as the archetypal exponent of philosophy. But Socrates is also a historical figure, and there has been much discussion of whether the dialogues report the activities of the real Socrates. This question (usually referred to as 'the Socratic question') has no simple answer. It is neither true that everything uttered by the character Socrates must be taken as a view of the historical Socrates, nor that the character Socrates is a mere fictional invention.

It is fairly certain that Socrates wrote nothing, that he practised philosophy by conversation in which he repeatedly cross-examined and refuted answers given to questions, and that he was concerned with questions of ethics, in particular with defining the virtues (justice, wisdom, courage, piety, temperance). This is how Socrates is portrayed by Plato in the early dialogues, and is how he makes Socrates describe himself in the *Apology*.[40] The *Apology* is a record of

---

[40] See esp. 21a–23b, 37d–38a.

Socrates' defence speech at his trial in 399 BC, which is likely to be accurate in substance since it was a well-known public occasion and Plato tells us plainly that he was there himself.

In the early dialogues, however, Plato does not report Socrates in purely journalistic fashion; he creates a literary portrait, and gives to Socrates arguments which he thinks he would or should have used, because they make philosophical sense. Nevertheless, it is likely that Plato begins by portraying a figure recognizable as the historical Socrates.[41]

But in dialogues of the middle period, especially *Phaedo* and *Republic*, philosophical views are put into Socrates' mouth which certainly are not those of the historical Socrates—so that we may even talk about an 'early Socrates' and a 'middle Socrates' as two distinct figures in the dialogues.[42] In the middle period Socrates is still the archetypal philosopher pursuing truth by rational argument—but now he is Plato's mouthpiece. The epistemological and metaphysical doctrines of this period (for which see Section 2.4 below) are Plato's own.

2.3. Socrates' Philosophy in the Early Dialogues

2.3.1. The Elenchus

Socrates' most characteristic method is called in Greek *elenkhos* (more usually written *elenchus*) meaning 'refutation'. It can be seen most clearly in the short dialogues *Laches*, *Euthyphro*, and *Charmides*. But it is also used in *Republic*, book 1, *Protagoras*, *Gorgias*, and in the first part of *Meno*. A sense of how the method works can only be gained by reading the works themselves. The following is merely a sketch of the bare bones of Socrates' most usual procedure.

Socrates claims to seek a definition of some moral quality, such as courage, justice, or virtue. He claims not to have knowledge of his own that would enable him to define these qualities, and also that to lack a definition is to lack any knowledge at all about them. So his philosophical argument is dominated by the pursuit of a single central question of the form 'What is F?' where F stands for some moral quality.

Socrates induces his interlocutors to put forward their own definition of courage or justice.[43] What he requires is the one single characteristic which is shared by all things we call courageous or just, and which makes those things courageous or just. By contrast, he rejects mere examples, or lists of examples.[44]

---

[41] Gregory Vlastos argues powerfully for this view, in *Socrates: Ironist and Moral Philosopher* (Cambridge, 1991), chs. 2 and 3, drawing also on evidence from other ancient writers.

[42] This is also Vlastos's idea, ibid., ch. 2, which is excellent on the differences between them.

[43] See *Laches* and *Republic*, book 1, for these examples.

[44] See *Laches* 191d–192b, *Meno* 71d–77b.

It is important that the definition tested is something to which the interlocutor is committed: the test is of the soundness of the person as much as of the truth of the proposition being examined. However, Socrates next convinces his interlocutors that they hold other beliefs which conflict with the definition. Of many examples, *Laches* 192b–193d is one of the clearest: Laches' definition of courage as endurance is shown to conflict with other propositions which Laches accepts when Socrates offers them.

The *elenchus* is a good method for revealing contradictions in people's thinking. The result is to replace the semblance of knowledge with the awareness of ignorance. Socrates presents this as progress.[45] Yet the failure of the method to reach knowledge of a definition is seen as an embarrassment. The state induced by the *elenchus* is perplexity (*aporia*).

There are many questions to ask about the method of *elenchus*. First, is Socrates' apparent faith that the method will lead to knowledge unfounded? His questioning unmasks a great many false answers, but it is unclear how interrogating people with false and confused beliefs will lead to knowledge.

Secondly, why are Socrates' suggestions, when they contradict a given definition, always treated as more reliable than the definition itself? This is strange because Socrates claims not to have knowledge himself.

Thirdly, is Socrates sincere in his claims (1) not to have any knowledge, and (2) to be seeking knowledge? If we were to answer no to both questions, the *elenchus* would take on the worst possible complexion: Socrates would be seeking only to reveal his interlocutors' ignorance, and dishonestly using knowledge of his own to ensure that their ignorance is revealed most clearly.

Vlastos has recently argued for a greatly more optimistic reading of Plato's Socrates. Socrates may be more reliable than others because he has subjected his own beliefs to the same process of refutation which he uses on others: his beliefs are all consistent. He can then assert his moral beliefs with confidence, while falling short of what he would call knowledge on moral matters. He also appears to be sincere—if perhaps over-optimistic—in his faith that we can eventually reach knowledge of the truth by this method. He may at times allow his interlocutors to lead themselves astray in argument, but this is different from deceiving them.[46]

There are more general philosophical worries about the Socratic *elenchus*. Is Socrates asking a kind of question to which there is no proper answer? Why assume that when many things are called 'just' or 'excellent', there must be one single characteristic they all share? (A modern attack on this assumption is made by Wittgenstein with his notion of 'family resemblance' between things to which the same word applies.[47]) And finally, why insist, as Socrates does, that

---

[45] See *Apology* 21a–23c and *Meno* 84a–c, with 79e–80d for explicit reflection on this.

[46] See Vlastos, *Socrates: Ironist and Moral Philosopher*, chs. 1 and 5.

[47] *Philosophical Investigations*, sect. 66.

you cannot know anything about justice unless you can know what it is, in the sense of defining it?

2.3.2. Inductive Arguments

Writing about Socrates' contribution to Philosophy, Aristotle said that his innovations were to seek general definitions of the virtues, and to use 'inductive arguments' (or 'arguments from particular to general').[48]

An 'inductive argument' of the Socratic type is one which reaches a general conclusion by collecting together a small number of particular instances. From the general conclusion it may then move on to conclude a further particular instance. The form of argument might be exemplified thus:

> Particular instances:
> In England March is colder than July.
> In Germany March is colder than July.
> In Canada March is colder than July.
> General conclusion:
> In all countries March is colder than July.
> Further instance drawn from general conclusion:
> In Australia March is colder than July.

The example reveals how questionable this form of argument can be.

In the Socratic dialogues this form of argument is sometimes used very informally, without stating the general conclusion. It then becomes the same as arguing by analogy: such-and-such applies in cases *A* and *B*, so it will apply in *C* also: not a very strong form of argument. Alternatively, Socrates merely moves from some instances to a general conclusion and is satisfied with that.

One use to which these inductive and analogical forms of argument are put is to reach conclusions about ethics by comparison with cases of successful performance or expertise in other walks of life (see Section 2.3.4 below).

2.3.3. Virtue and Knowledge

Discussions of Socrates often revolve around 'virtue'. This is a translation of the Greek word *aretē*, which may also be translated as 'excellence'. The healthy condition of the body is its *aretē*. An artefact which is well made and serves its proper function would also have *aretē*. Socrates is concerned with what it is to be an excellent human being, or with *aretē* as such. 'Virtue' is also an appropriate translation in this context, because Socrates is concerned that human

---

[48] *Metaphysics* (M), 1078[b]28. For some reading on inductive arguments in the early Socratic dialogues, see R. Robinson, *Plato's Earlier Dialectic* (Oxford, 1953), ch. 4, and Gerasimos Xenophon Santos, *Socrates: Philosophy in Plato's Early Dialogues* (London, 1979), ch. 5.

excellence be conceived as *moral* excellence. *Aretē* for Socrates consists of the virtues courage, wisdom, justice, piety (holiness), and temperance (moderation).

Central propositions in Socrates' ethics are: virtue is knowledge; all the virtues are one; virtue is happiness.

He believes that until one has knowledge of what is good and evil one cannot possess virtue, and that having such knowledge is sufficient for possessing virtue. Two consequences drawn from this are (1) that no one knowingly does wrong—if you knew the right thing to do, that knowledge would be enough to ensure that you did it, and (2) that weakness of will (Greek *akrasia*) is impossible. This would mean that no one could do one thing while wanting to do something else that they think better. (Socrates argues for the impossibility of *akrasia* in *Protagoras*, from 352b.)

Socrates also believes that no one who has knowledge of good and bad can lack any of the virtues—with such knowledge one must also be courageous, holy, temperate, and just. Finally, he thinks that the perfectly virtuous person is bound to be happier—to have greater well-being in fact—than someone who lacks virtue. There can be no higher good than possessing virtue. Many of these beliefs run counter to everyday views (both then and now).

But given these beliefs, the prime task is to attain knowledge of what is good and evil. If one has it, one is morally excellent (and without it one's success in life is only hit-and-miss). If one has this knowledge, there is no form of moral excellence that one will lack. One will be incapable of acting wrongly or in a weak-willed manner. And one will achieve what is best in human life. This explains why *knowledge* in ethics is the central and distinctive concern of Socratic philosophy—a concern which remains central for Plato too.

2.3.4. Ethics and Craft

Another Greek term worth knowing is *tekhnē*. This is most often translated as 'craft' (occasionally as 'art' or 'skill'); other recent suggestions for it are 'expertise' or 'expert knowledge'. Thinking that virtue is a form of knowledge, Socrates looks at other examples of knowledge in human life, and tends to assume that ethical knowledge will share some of their features. Prominent examples are medicine, arithmetic, and building. These can be passed on by teaching, and they have precisely specifiable subject-matter and general principles that apply reliably to many instances. Socrates believes that knowledge of good and evil will be in some ways analogous to these forms of expertise.[49]

---

[49] Cf. Paul Woodruff, 'Plato's Early Theory of Knowledge', in Stephen Everson (ed.), *Epistemology* (Cambridge, 1990).

2.3.5. Criticisms of Socrates in the Meno

The *Meno* is a crucial dialogue in Plato's career, customarily regarded as transitional between his early and middle periods, and therefore listed sometimes as early, sometimes as middle. The transition is apparent within the dialogue. Up to 81a it appears to be a Socratic dialogue in which a definition of virtue is sought, but perplexity is the only result. After 81a we are told that the soul is immortal, and that it is eternally in possession of truths and able to recollect them during this life; we are treated to mathematical examples, and told that there is an important distinction between knowledge and true belief—all of these being preoccupations of Plato's middle period. They will be dealt with in Section 2.4 below.

But the first part of the *Meno*, up to 81a, is useful when studying Plato's Socrates. For here it is as if Plato marshals the features of Socrates' method of arguing in order to have a critical look at them. Socrates insists emphatically on the priority of his 'What is *F*?' question and on his own ignorance (71a–c, 80c–d). He explains at length what is required of a definition that answers the 'What is *F*?' question (72a–77b). Plato gives to Meno the pointed accusation that the whole process of Socratic argument ends only in a numbing or befuddling *aporia* (79e–80d). Finally (80d–81a), he has Meno raise a paradox (the so-called 'paradox of inquiry') which stems from the insistence that if you do not know 'what *F* is', then cannot know anything at all about *F*. It is useful to read this section of the dialogue thoroughly as a reflection on the nature of Socratic method.

In the second part of the *Meno* there are explicit challenges to Socrates' philosophical method, and to his ethics. The challenge to his method is the introduction of argument by 'hypothesis' or provisional assumption.[50] If we lack a definition of virtue, we are not, after all, debarred from all knowledge of it. We can be confident that *if* virtue is knowledge, *then* it is teachable (and conversely that *if* virtue is not teachable, *then* it is not knowledge). This conditional premiss can be held fixed as an assumption.

However, if we then come to think that virtue is not teachable (as Socrates does on the rather weak grounds that there are no instances of its being taught), we can conclude, using our hypothesis, that virtue is not knowledge. In the second half of the *Meno* (89c–100b) Plato makes his character Socrates argue for this denial of one of the mainstays of Socratic ethics. This, added to the new doctrines concerning knowledge, recollection, and the soul, makes it clear that Plato has now broken out of the Socratic mould, taking with him the search for knowledge of the virtues and the conception of philosophy as the pursuit of truth by rational argument, but on the point of inventing an entirely new way of going about it.

---

[50] See Robinson, *Plato's Earlier Dialectic*, on hypothesis in Plato.

2.4. Plato's Middle Period Philosophy

In the middle period of his career Plato broke away to some extent from the influence of Socrates and developed his own philosophical position in the *Republic* and other works, using the character of Socrates as his mouthpiece. The most characteristic doctrines of the *Republic* period are Plato's conception of the nature of knowledge, his doctrine of Forms, his claim that the soul is immortal, and his description of the human individual as a composite of the reasoning, spirited, and appetitive elements.

2.4.1. *Recollection and Immortality*

One of Plato's most original and ambitious ideas is that learning is recollecting something: either a true proposition which one believes or knows (as in the *Meno*), or knowledge of a Form (as in the *Phaedo*).

Recollection in the Meno   The place to begin is *Meno* 81a–86c. Here Socrates proclaims that coming to know something is possible because the soul 'has learned everything' prior to this life. He claims to 'demonstrate' this by discussing a geometrical example with a slave-boy. The slave-boy starts out not knowing the answer to a specific question about the area of a square. After repeated questioning, he comes to hold a true belief which is the answer to the original question.

The conversation with the slave-boy is in some ways a Socratic dialogue in miniature. We start out in ignorance, acknowledge our ignorance and become perplexed, and then, by continued cross-examination of our answers, arrive at a true belief which can eventually be converted into knowledge by the same method. Meno is supposed to realize from this that the quest for knowledge of the virtues by *elenchus* can succeed.

But Socrates says in particular that true beliefs (or opinions) about the area of squares 'were somewhere in' the boy himself. This allegedly can be explained only by the extravagant idea that his soul existed before he was born, and was then in possession of these truths. But what is meant by the claim that true beliefs are somewhere in a person, when on the surface the person is ignorant of them—and why does Socrates think this correctly describes the slave-boy's case?[51]

An important suggestion is that the slave-boy's beliefs may be 'in him' in the sense that they are implicit in beliefs he already holds: he can then acquire new knowledge by realizing the implications of what he knows already. Mathematics is an instance of what philosophers call a priori knowledge,

---

[51] Cf. Vlastos, Moravcsik, and Nehamas in *Plato's* Meno, ed. J. M. Day (London, 1994).

knowledge which one can have prior to, or independently of, experience. One view, then, is that in the *Meno* Plato is impressed by—perhaps even discovers—the fact that there is a priori knowledge. He can account for this only by thinking that the soul has access to these truths previous to this life.

But that cannot be the whole story. The end of the *Meno* contains a further discussion of knowledge (see 96e–100b). Socrates distinguishes between knowledge and true belief. A person who knows the way to Larissa (a town some way to the north of Athens) and a person who has a correct belief about the way to Larissa will both get you there—and yet knowing seems to be distinct from merely believing truly, and also more secure in some way. The difference between knowledge and true belief is explained figuratively: true beliefs can be converted into knowledge if they are 'tied down'. At 98a Socrates describes this process as 'working out the reason', and equates it with recollection.

This is puzzling. Can knowing the way to Larissa be a priori knowledge, like mathematical knowledge? And how can Plato think *all* knowledge involves recollection?

As to 'working out the reason', many have taken this to mean *justifying* one's belief (Plato's view would then be that knowledge is justified true belief). But it might also mean '*explaining* why one's belief is true'.[52]

Immortality in the Phaedo   The doctrine of recollection requires that the soul has an existence before this life. Plato returns to this subject in the middle period dialogue *Phaedo*, written before the *Republic* but after the *Meno*. The topic of the dialogue is the immortality of the soul, which Socrates is portrayed as discussing in the hours before he dies by drinking hemlock (the penalty prescribed by the Athenian state).

In the *Phaedo*'s Recollection Argument (72e–78b), Plato combines the doctrine of recollection with that of Forms. He lists some examples of Forms at 65d, stating that Justice, Beauty, Goodness, Largeness, Health, and Strength exist, and that they cannot be perceived by the bodily senses, only by the intellect on its own.

The conception of Forms is central to Plato's middle period philosophy. He regards Beauty, Justice, Goodness, and the rest as eternally existing entities which are distinct from ordinary things in the perceptible world, and which the mind (of the philosopher, at least) can grasp by a kind of pure thought. To grasp one of these Forms is, for Plato, to have true knowledge of an absolute value. The Forms thus provide Plato with an answer to the Socratic demand for definitions of the virtues and a reply to the relativism of the Sophists. But they also lead him deep into metaphysics and the theory of knowledge, and compel

---

[52] On the important difference between these two notions, see Myles Burnyeat, 'Plato and the Jury: Paradoxes in Plato's Distinction between Knowledge and True Belief', *Proceedings of the Aristotelian Society*, supp. vol. 54 (1980), 173–91.

him to consider both how the human mind can have a nature which allows it to know the eternal Forms—he thinks of it as having a kinship with them—and how such knowledge can be made to guide a whole community. Some questions about the nature of Forms and their relation to sensible things are dealt with in Section 2.4.5 below.

In the Recollection Argument of the *Phaedo* he uses the further example of Equality or the Equal itself. ('Equality' and 'the Equal itself' are two ways of referring to the Form: compare Beauty/the Beautiful itself, and Largeness/the Large itself.) He argues that Equality is distinct from any set of equal things, such as stones or logs, and then suggests that seeing two equal objects puts one in mind of Equality itself. The issue in this difficult passage is how we are able to think of, and know about, the general property (as we would call it) Equality, when what we perceive with the senses are particular things that are equal to one another. Plato's answer is that seeing equal things prompts us to think of the distinct thing Equality. He then argues that when we perceive one thing and are put in mind of a distinct thing which we do not perceive, that is recollecting or being reminded. Finally, he suggests that this knowledge of Forms must pre-date our birth. If that is so, the intellect which grasps Forms must have existed before we were born.

There are many serious difficulties in this argument. Here one might simply note two ways in which Plato could be begging the question. First, why must our thought of Equality here be a case of recollection at all? At 74c–d Plato says, 'So long as on seeing one thing, one does, from this sight, think of another . . . this must be recollection.' But it will be recollection only if one has *prior* knowledge of the thing thought of—which is the very question at issue.

Secondly, why must our knowledge of the Form pre-date our birth? At 76c Simmias makes the objection that such pieces of knowledge could have been acquired at birth, rather than previously. Socrates replies: 'Then at what other time, may I ask, do we lose them?' But does this not again beg the question?

Two other arguments for immortality in the *Phaedo* make use of Forms: the Affinity Argument (78b–84b) and the Final Argument (102b–107b).

The Affinity Argument sets up some ways in which the soul is *analogous* to the Forms, and suggests it is more likely therefore to be eternal and indestructible in the way Forms are. This passage tells us more about Plato's understanding of Forms. They are eternal and unchanging. Each is one, not composed of parts, and distinct from the many changeable things in the perceptible world.

The *Phaedo*'s Final Argument is an intricate and ambitious piece of philosophy, and the preparatory stages of the argument yield insights into Plato's reasons for believing in Forms.

The Final Argument, in outline, is that soul is incompatible with death. Life is the opposite of death, and soul always brings life with it. So, as Plato puts it, when death approaches, the soul must either get out of the way or perish—it cannot stay and become qualified by death. There are many curiosities in this argument. One question it prompts is: Plato takes himself to have shown that the soul must 'get out of the way' when death approaches—but what has he done to show that it does not simply *perish*? (See 105c–106e, and especially 106b onwards.)

The passages prior to this argument, 95a–105c, are the most difficult in the *Phaedo*. Socrates is made to tell a fictional autobiographical story, in which he deals with different kinds of explanation—different kinds of answer to the question 'Why?' Explanation in terms of cause and effect must be distinguished from explanation in terms of purpose (teleological explanation). Socrates says he was attracted by Anaxagoras' idea that everything could be explained teleologically, as being as it is because an intelligence or mind directed it to be so, but that he found no such explanations had in fact been given. (On Anaxagoras see Section 1.5 above.)

Socrates recommends explanation in terms of Forms. If asked 'Why is this thing beautiful?' he will reply, 'Because of its participating in Beauty itself.' Forms are said to provide the explanations for things' being and becoming as they are.[53]

What is the Soul?   The main arguments in the *Phaedo* all concern the immortality of the soul. Plato assumes that the soul is distinct from the body, and that it can exist separately from the body (see 64c). (One might ask whether he assumes immortality, which is what he is going to argue for: different answers are conceivable here.)

However, a problem commentators have found with the *Phaedo* is that in different parts of the work 'the soul' seems to be something different. For example, in the discussion of the soul's becoming separate from the body at 64c–67e Plato gives a long list of activities which are associated with the body, and contrasts these with *one* activity of the soul, namely reasoning. This raises a number of questions: Is the soul something which has only this one function? Does Plato think that the body, not the soul, has the functions of seeing and hearing, feeling pleasure and pain? How good a view does that seem to be? It is possible that Plato thinks the soul sees, hears, and feels pain, using the body as its means or instrument. Nevertheless, he does say here that the only activity of the soul 'by itself' is pure reasoning. What will survive when the soul splits off from the body, then, is only a pure reasoning intellect. Does this mean that *I* can survive death?

At other times it is as if the soul that may survive separation from the body

---

[53] Cf. Vlastos, 'Reasons and Causes in the *Phaedo*', in *Platonic Studies* (Princeton, NJ, 1981), and Bostock, *Plato's* Phaedo, ch. 7, for contrasting views here.

is the person. Socrates chides his friend Crito for asking how he wants to be buried: 'he imagines I'm that dead body he'll see in a little while, so he goes and asks how he's to bury me!' (115c–d)—but Socrates has been arguing 'that when I drink the poison, I shall no longer remain with you, but shall go off and depart for some happy state of the blessed'. This would suggest that Socrates himself is simply identical with the separable soul.

In the Final Argument, another conception of the soul comes to light. Soul seems to be a life-principle: something that, by entering a body, makes that body alive, or animates it. This prompts a number of questions. Has Plato considered whether a soul could be this animating principle in Socrates' body, and be Socrates' pure intellect, and also be identical with Socrates? Can a coherent picture of the soul be built from these materials?

Yet more questions are prompted by Plato's conception of death in the *Phaedo*. Dying is said to be the separation of the soul from the body. But is it the person that is dead after this separation, or is it the soul? In the so-called Cyclical Argument for immortality (69e–72e) Plato speaks of the soul 'being born' into a body, and argues that if something 'comes to be alive' then it must be from its having been in the opposite state, i.e. dead. So does he think that the soul progresses in a cycle between being alive and being dead? One notable feature here is the assumption that if something is dead then it must exist, in order to come back to life again. When we say 'Socrates is dead', we might take ourselves to be saying that Socrates does not exist (now). But it is not clear whether Plato can look at the matter in this way.

2.4.2. *Parts of the Soul in the* Republic

It is usually reckoned that the *Republic* was written after the *Phaedo*. Some important doctrines are the same—especially those centring around Forms and the philosopher's supposed knowledge of them. However, Plato treats the soul differently in the *Republic*. In book 4 of that work he confronts not the metaphysical question of the soul's relation to the body and its endurance after death, but the question how the human mind or personality is organized in life. In particular, he is concerned with discovering how different desires and motivations may govern the human individual.

In the *Republic* the concern is with justice and the other virtues: Plato is trying to explain what it is for someone to be just, and to have courage, wisdom, and moderation. He argues that to understand this we must see the human soul as divided into three 'parts' or elements. It is in the functioning of the various 'parts' within each individual's soul, and their relation to one another, that the person's virtue will be found.

It is hard to decide exactly what Plato takes these 'parts' of the soul to be. But it can be said that the three 'parts' are the 'reasoning part', the 'spirited part', and the 'appetitive part' (i.e. the part having appetites). At 436a–b he asks, 'Do we learn with one part, get angry with another, and with some third part desire the pleasures of food, drink, sex, and the others that are closely akin to them?'— to which his answer is yes.

Sometimes in English the third, appetitive part is labelled 'desire'. This is misleading in one way, because *all* the parts have desires.[54] The 'third part' desires *to satisfy bodily appetites*. Reason, by contrast, is conceived as that in us with which we pursue truth by rational means. It is not just the capacity for reasoning, but embraces also the desire *to learn the truth* and to regulate one's behaviour accordingly. Similarly, the aggressive, spirited part 'with which we get angry' is thought of as desiring its own characteristic end, namely *to gain honour*.

It can appear that these 'parts' are more like miniature personalities within the person, each with its own aims and ways of understanding the world. How much of a problem Plato encounters if he thinks of the 'parts' in this way is an interesting question, related to recent discussions of personal identity and the nature of the mind.[55]

The argument Plato advances for there being these three elements to the soul is subtle, but full of problems. A single principle dominates it: 'the same thing will not be willing to do or undergo opposites in the same part of itself, in relation to the same thing, at the same time' (436b). Plato discusses a number of examples where the mind has two opposing attitudes to the same object at the same time. The simplest is that of someone both wanting and not wanting a particular drink (439a–d). Plato thinks this shows that the appetitive part of oneself wants the drink while the rational part shuns it.

Two other examples in this discussion are worth noting. At 439e–440a Plato discusses Leontius, who has a desire to satisfy an appetite, but is angry with himself for having this desire. At 441a–c he gives the example of Homer's Odysseus feeling anger towards his rivals, but taking a rational attitude towards his anger, 'arguing with himself' that it is better not to be angry at this moment. Plato thinks that the Leontius and Odysseus examples are evidence of distinctions between different parts of the soul. But how does his general principle about opposites work here? The complication is that Leontius and Odysseus exhibit what philosophers nowadays call second-order attitudes where, in addition to a desire, one has feelings *about that desire* or, in addition to an emotion, one has a desire *not to have that emotion*.

The tripartite division of the soul may be seen as an advance in Plato's views towards a more subtle moral psychology. Compare the earlier *Phaedo* 64c–67e, and *Protagoras* 352b–357e. In the *Phaedo* Plato seems to think that the soul's only proper function is to reason and pursue the truth; in the *Protagoras* the view (put

---

[54] An introductory reading on this point would be Sabina Lovibond, 'Plato's Theory of Mind', in Stephen Everson (ed.), *Psychology* (Cambridge, 1991).

[55] J. Annas, *An Introduction to Plato's* Republic (Oxford, 1981) addresses this issue.

simply) is that the only desires one could ever act on are rational desires. This is the view according to which *akrasia* seems paradoxical. Now, in the *Republic*, Plato has a way of accounting for *akrasia*.

The division of the soul is introduced in book 4 of the *Republic*, but the idea permeates the whole work. Plato draws an analogy throughout between the internal structure of the soul and that of the city he designs. Books 8–9 examine ways in which different parts of souls and cities can assume a governing role. Book 10 also uses an idea of the divided soul (602c–606d)—though there Plato abandons the three parts and talks instead of a 'superior' and an 'inferior' part.

2.4.3. The Argument of the Republic

The *Republic* is a long work by Plato's standards. It is also extraordinarily rich in argument and provocative use of imagination. Plato's ideas about the best organization of a community still have an important place in political philosophy. Yet it is a mistake to think of the work only as an exercise in political philosophy: it is also a contribution to ethics, theory of knowledge, metaphysics, philosophy of education, philosophy of art, philosophy of mind, and other things besides. Plato himself does not make these divisions in his subject-matter.

The theme of the *Republic* is justice. Plato poses the questions 'What is justice?' and 'Is justice beneficial to the person who is just?' At first sight 'justice' suggests something like fairness in relation to others—a just person would be one who neither has nor wants more than he or she is entitled to. But Plato seems to turn the question into one about morality generally: What is the right way to live? (see *Republic* 352d). Some commentators claim that the true topic is 'morality' rather than 'justice'.[56] There are complications in trying to decide whether 'justice' or 'morality' is Plato's true topic. One is that he tries to explain simultaneously what it is for a community to be just and for an individual to be just. The other is that the city Plato invents as the paradigm of justice is also 'completely good' (427e). The just city, and indeed the just soul, have every other kind of virtue as well as justice (see 427e–434d, 441c–445e).

Republic, book 1, is different from the remainder of the work. Some think it is an earlier, Socratic dialogue to which the other nine books were added later in Plato's career. It certainly proceeds in Socratic manner, trying to define justice by asking questions and refuting answers. But the attempt is unsuccessful. From book 2 onwards the *Republic* is Platonic rather than Socratic, putting forward positive doctrines about the soul, philosophy, knowledge, and Forms.

The chief topic of study in book 1 is the position put forward by the character Thrasymachus, a Sophist who confronts Socrates with the idea that justice is not beneficial for the person who has the power to be unjust. He puts forward

---

[56] See Annas, *An Introduction to Plato's* Republic, intro., for an initial discussion. (Aristotle's *Nicomachean Ethics*, ch. 5, is relevant here.)

two seemingly different definitions of justice (at 338c–339a and at 343c–344c): justice as 'the advantage of the stronger' and justice as 'the good of another'.

By the end of book 1 the challenge to Socrates is set: he must explain how it is that justice is beneficial, or why it is better to be just than unjust. Book 2 opens with a clearer statement of Socrates' task. Note especially 357a–358a on kinds of good: things that are good for their own sake, things that are good because of their consequences, and things that are good on both counts. The characters Glaucon and Adeimantus then intensify the challenge by putting forward the popular view that injustice is the course to choose if one can get away with it (358a–367e).

Socrates declares that in order to find the true nature of justice, one must examine it on a large scale. Hence, instead of first asking what justice is in the individual, he proposes to ask about justice in a city (368c–369a). From this point on, the *Republic* is dominated by the dual inquiry into the city and the individual's soul.

In the Greek world a city (*polis*) was commonly a self-governing state. Since the number of citizens in this unit was small—a matter of thousands—there is an assumption that citizens will be closely involved in the running of the city's affairs. Plato was disillusioned with the kinds of government of which he was aware in Greek city-states (democracy, oligarchy, and tyranny), and sets out to invent a model of what the perfectly just city-state would be.[57]

Plato's construction of the model city-state arises from an analysis of the roles which must be carried out within it. In books 2, 3, and 4 he arrives in stages at the idea of three classes in the city: an economic class of producers and traders, a military class, and a ruling class (see 369b–376c, 412b–417b). Plato calls the military class 'guardians', but later, when he creates the class of rulers from out of their ranks, he calls the rulers 'guardians', and the military class 'auxiliaries'.

Plato's main point about his model city is that it is just because each of the three elements in it fulfils its role without usurping those of the others. There is room for much debate of the question in what way Plato's state is 'just'. It is worth noting that he has no conception of individuals' rights, that he prescribes that each citizen shall have only one role from which they are not allowed to deviate (the so-called principle of specialization), and that he proposes a very high degree of intervention by the city in people's education, culture, marriage, and reproduction. His views about the role of women are ambivalent and have often been discussed.[58] Details of the organization of the model community are fairly easily gleaned from reading books 2–5 (up to about 473b).

A large section spanning books 2–3 (376c–403c) is taken up with discussing

---

[57] George Klosko, *The Development of Plato's Political Theory* (New York, 1986), ch. 1, provides a short introduction to Plato and Greek politics.

[58] See Annas, *An Introduction to Plato's Republic*, ch. 7.

story-telling and poetry as they figure in the education of the guardians. These passages show the moral character Plato wishes to instil, and are important for those wishing to ascertain Plato's views on poetry, which are largely critical because he assigns poetry an important role in moral education. The *polis* will have absolute control over the arts in Plato's set-up. He advocates censorship of even the greatest poetic works, thereby raising issues which are very much alive today. Book 10 returns to poetry, and contains Plato's most well-known and most hostile discussion of the arts. Artists, he claims, do not have genuine knowledge and can corrupt the soul by appealing to its 'lower' emotional part, rather than to the rational part. Plato's views about the arts are best appreciated in conjunction with his central ethical, metaphysical, and epistemological argument.

Plato makes a parallel between the city with its three classes and the soul with its three 'parts'. Justice in both cases resides in the way the elements play their roles in the whole (see especially 432b–436b and 441c–445e). But how much is Plato using the city as an analogy or illustration for the soul, and how much is he interested in the city in its own right? There is space to indicate just two of the general questions that might be raised about justice in the city and the soul:

1. What problems arise when, instead of using the city as a parallel to the soul, Plato starts to think of his city as populated with individuals whose souls are tripartite (see 435d–e)? It appears that the different classes are successful in their roles because individuals in these classes are governed by different parts of their souls. But then, since the just soul is only one in which the *reasoning part* governs, Plato will be committed to saying that the majority of his citizens will not be just.

2. We are told that to be just is to be governed by the reasoning part of oneself, which oversees the appetites and has the spirited part acting as its ally (see 441d–442b, 443c ff.). But commentators have sometimes suggested that this is simply to give the name 'justice' to something new. Justice is not concerned with one's external actions, Plato says (443c), but with the internal state of the soul. For the grand scheme to succeed, a connection must be established between being just in this sense and being just in the sense that Thrasymachus used when he proclaimed injustice to be preferable.

Plato continues to use the analogy of soul and city in books 8 and 9, where he considers the different ways in which both may deviate from the ideal of justice. Book 9 contains a vivid psychological portrait of the antithesis of the just person, the totally unjust person who is subject to the tyranny of lawless desires. Book 9 ends with three interesting and complex arguments to the effect that the just, reason-governed, philosophical person is greatly more happy than the most unjust person.

Book 5 (from about 473) and books 6 and 7 of the *Republic* concern issues in epistemology and metaphysics, which may at first sight appear to be a digression from the main subject. Yet these books are not only essential to Plato's argument, but the most intensely studied part of the *Republic*. There he suggests that the only hope for the foundation of the ideally just city is that its ruling class should be philosophers. This leads him to clarify what distinguishes a philosopher from others, to inquire into the nature of knowledge, to consider the different ways in which the mind has cognition, to state certain aspects of the theory of Forms, and finally to devise a programme of education, embracing mathematics and astronomy as well as philosophy, which he thinks will fit his philosopher-rulers for their task.

The most prominent sections of books 6–7 (503e–517c) contain three images or similes in which Plato attempts to convey his thinking. They are the Sun, the Divided Line, and the Cave.

The Sun simile compares the visible, physical world with the realm of Forms (an 'intelligible place' or place of the intellect), saying that the highest Form, the Form of the Good, has a role analogous to that of the sun: being illuminated by the Form of the Good is what makes things knowable. Plato seems to think there is one answer to the question 'When is something good?', and that the answer to that question can be known only by knowing a Form, the Good itself. His further assumptions appear to be that philosophers, by knowing the Form of the Good, can work out the best way for everything in the world to be, and that once they know that they will be able to deduce the nature of everything.

The Divided Line describes four different kinds of cognitive access to reality, in an ascending order which culminates in knowledge of Forms. Note that there is no reason to see this passage as conflicting with the three parts of the soul discussed earlier. Plato's concerns now are different: 'imagination', 'belief', 'thought', and 'understanding' (often differently translated—and note that Plato does not stick precisely to the terminology he introduces here) are stages on the way to full knowledge. The material on mathematics, dialectic (Plato's term for the philosopher's method), and hypothesis should be read in connection with the later passages 532a–535a.

The Cave simile is probably the most famous part of the *Republic*. The picture conveyed is vivid, the interpretation harder: do we take this as a powerful metaphor for any transition from the 'darkness' of misconception to the 'light' of knowledge, from the deception of metaphorical images, shadows, and counterfeits to grasp of something genuine? Or—as many commentators think—does every twist and turn in the Cave narrative have some exact correspondence to Plato's own theory of knowledge and the philosopher's role within the ideal *polis*?

2.4.4. *Knowledge and Belief in the* Republic

One of Plato's perennial interests is in the distinction between knowing something and merely believing it (albeit truly). The *Meno* (see Section 2.4.1 above)
represents an earlier attempt to come to grips with this distinction, and the
Theaetetus (see Section 2.5.3 below) contains a later attempt. In between lies the
discussion in *Republic*, book 5. It is best to enter the argument at 473c where
Socrates makes his famous pronouncement that philosophers should rule as
kings. This raises the question what constitutes a philosopher. Since knowledge
turns out to be distinctive of the philosopher, the argument to establish the
nature of knowledge is of the utmost importance for the *Republic* as a whole.

Plato argues that knowledge is of 'what is', belief of 'what is and is not'. As
with Parmenides, we face the problem of what is meant by 'is'. This time the
view *least likely to be correct* is that 'is' means 'exists'. One must *not* assume Plato
is saying 'Knowledge is of what exists' and 'Belief is of what exists and does not
exist'. One reason for rejecting this view is that something either exists or it
does not: it is not sensible to think existence is a matter of degree.

So what is Plato talking about? Commentators differ over this, but here are
two candidate readings. When Plato says 'knowledge is of what is' (or of 'something that is'—see 476e–477a) he may mean either (1) knowledge is of something that is true (the so-called veridical reading), or (2) knowledge is of
something that is *F* (the so-called predicative reading). *F* here stands in for some
predicate: in other words, on the predicative reading Plato will be saying,
'knowledge is of something that is beautiful, is good, is just, is large, or is something-or-other'. 'Being something-or-other' in this predicative sense is one way
of 'being' in Plato's Greek.[59]

The predicative reading is popular because it allows a link between knowledge and the Forms with which Plato is so preoccupied in the central books of
the *Republic*. This reading fits with a version of the theory of Forms championed
by Owen and Vlastos among others.[60] In this version a Form, for Plato, is something which strictly and truly is *F*, in contrast with other things which are only
imperfectly or variably *F*. For more discussion of this, see Section 2.4.5 below.
Some would say[61] that Plato is not restricting knowledge to Forms in book 5,
and at most he is arguing that without knowing Forms someone cannot know
anything. (If knowledge of the Form Justice itself is to have any practical application, one would hope that the philosopher could also know that a particular
city or person was just, for example.)

---

[59] For a discussion of the different readings, see Gail Fine, 'Knowledge and Belief in *Republic* V–VII', in
Everson (ed.), *Epistemology*, and Annas, *An Introduction to Plato's* Republic, ch. 8.

[60] See Gregory Vlastos, 'Degrees of Reality in Plato', in *Platonic Studies*, and G. E. L. Owen, 'A Proof in the
Peri Ideōn', in R. E. Allen (ed.), *Studies in Plato's Metaphysics* (London, 1965).

[61] Cf. again Fine, 'Knowledge and Belief in *Republic* V–VII'.

Plato contrasts philosophers (lovers of wisdom) with other characters whom he refers to as 'lovers of sights' and 'lovers of sounds'. These people are full of curiosity about the beautiful things to be seen and heard in the cultural sphere. Plato says of them that they recognize 'many beautifuls', but not the one Form: 'the Beautiful itself' (see 475d–476d). He argues to the conclusion that what these people come into contact with is something that 'is and is not'. Since knowledge is of what is, the lovers of sights and lovers of sounds are excluded from knowledge proper, and have only belief or opinion (see 478d–479d).

There are two crucial questions here: (1) What is 'recognizing many beautifuls' (as opposed to the Form of Beauty itself)? (2) How is it that these 'many beautifuls' both are and are not, and 'are rolling about as intermediates between what is not and what purely is' (479d)?

Consider two possible answers to each. Plato may be thinking of objects—a beautiful statue, a beautiful painting, a beautiful melody—and he may think that each of them *is* beautiful in a way, and *is not* beautiful in a way: this answers question 2, understanding 'is' and 'is not' predicatively.

Or he may be thinking of properties—being made of gold, being symmetrical, being in a certain musical key—and he may think that having these properties makes some things beautiful and some not beautiful. In the latter case, the lovers of sights and sounds attempt to answer the question 'What is beauty?' by saying that it is no one thing, because there are many, many properties which count in different circumstances as being beautiful. Question 2 is answered (again adopting the predicative reading) by saying that some things that have these properties *are* beautiful, but some *are not*. (Consider especially 479a–d.)[62]

A final point to note about this argument is that it appears to make the class of things one can know and the class of things one can have beliefs about quite distinct classes. This seems to go against the idea in the *Meno* that a true belief could be converted into knowledge—with that idea, what you believe and what you know would be the same. Yet in the argument of *Republic* 476d–478e Plato thinks he can establish that what is knowable must be distinct from what is believable (or opinable).

2.4.5. *The Theory of Forms*

The theory of Forms has been discussed in English-speaking philosophy probably more than any other topic in Plato over the last forty years. There is much disagreement among scholars in this area, and the debate can become rather abstruse.[63]

[62] T. H. Irwin, 'Plato's Heracliteanism', *Philosophical Quarterly*, 27 (1977), 1–13, and/or his *Plato's Moral Theory* (Oxford, 1977), 144–52, are of help.

[63] A newcomer to the topic is advised to consult some of the introductory literature, such as Harold Cherniss, 'The Philosophical Economy of the Theory of Ideas', in Gregory Vlastos (ed.), *Plato*, i (Garden City,

One point to make is so basic that commentators often take it for granted. Plato's Forms are thought of as part of reality. Each of them eternally exists, regardless of changing human conceptions and of changes in the world of ordinary perceptible objects. In other words, Plato believes that Beauty and Justice exist and always will do, even if no one has a correct conception of them, and even if there are no beautiful or just things around in the perceptible world at any given time. (The older translation 'Ideas' instead of 'Forms' may encourage the error of thinking Forms exist 'only in our minds'. For Plato they are things the mind may grasp, but not mental entities.)

But what are Forms? An initial thought is that they are what today's philosophers call properties: beauty, or being beautiful, largeness or being large. This distinguishes them from things that *have* properties: the statue or person that is beautiful, is large, and so on. This is certainly one part of Plato's theory: each single Form is always distinguished from the many things which 'participate' in it. There are many beautiful things, but they all share in the one Form, Beauty. Properties are what are often called universals, as opposed to particulars. (Some of Plato's Forms are rather what we would call relations—Equality, Likeness, Doubleness—but these would also be classed as universals.) Note, however, that Plato does not use the terminology of 'property', 'universal', or 'particular'.

A way to approach the theory of Forms is to ask two overall questions: (1) How do Forms differ from the 'other' or 'many' things which Plato says have a share in them? (2) How do these 'other' things relate to a Form in each case?

In answer to question 1, the most obvious points are that 'other' things are many, but a Form is always only one; 'other' things can be perceived by the senses (they are perceptible or sensible), while Forms cannot; 'other' things are subject to various kinds of change and variation while Forms are not.

Forms, unlike the sensible things that share in them, suffer no mixture between being and not being. But what does that mean? Think again of the predicative sense of 'being' (introduced in Section 2.4.4). A sensible beautiful thing, Plato claims, *is* beautiful, but—in different ways—it also *is not* beautiful. In this sense it 'is and is not'. Forms, as Plato says, simply *are*, and never are not. They 'truly are'—i.e. whatever they are, they are without any qualification, variation, or imperfection.

NY, 1971) (also in Allen (ed.), *Studies in Plato's Metaphysics*), and the relevant chapters in Bostock, *Plato's Phaedo*, or Annas, *An Introduction to Plato's Republic*, or sections of the general books I. M. Crombie, *An Examination of Plato's Doctrines*, ii (London, 1963), J. C. B. Gosling, *Plato* (London, 1973), and Nicholas P. White, *Plato on Knowledge and Reality* (Indianapolis, 1976); and then the articles Vlastos 'Degrees of Reality in Plato', Irwin, 'Plato's Heracliteanism', and Owen, 'A Proof in the *Peri Ideōn*'. Bostock, *Plato's* Phaedo, 15–31, is also useful. But Plato's own words are best. Here is a list of passages with which one should be reasonably familiar before pursuing more general questions about Plato's Forms: *Phaedo* 65d–e, 72e–76e, 78c–79a, 95e–107b; *Republic* 507a–511e, 514a–518d, 523a–525b, 533b–535a, 596a–b; some short passages in dialogues not yet discussed: *Symposium* 210a–211b, *Cratylus* 389a–d, 439b–440e; *Parmenides* 128e–130a, discussed in Section 2.5.2 below.

Here many have thought that Plato gets into a serious muddle. If beautiful sensible things are and are not beautiful, and the Form, by contrast, simply is, then do we not have to say that the Form, the Beautiful itself, *is beautiful*? This—which is often called the 'self-predication' of Forms—would be a confusion on Plato's part because the property of being beautiful is not itself a beautiful thing, the property of being large is not a large thing, and so on.

Some of the time Plato seems to think of Forms as paradigms. A paradigm of a property is a supreme instance of it which sets a standard for other instances to live up to: something perfectly beautiful would give an absolute standard against which to judge all other beautiful things. Does Plato think of Forms as paradigms, or as properties, or as both? Our answer here (which may not be conclusive) will have repercussions for the general question 2 raised above. If Forms are paradigms, we might expect the relation between them and sensible things to be one of likeness or resemblance; if they are properties, then, whatever the relation is, we would expect it not to be one of resemblance. (Note that Plato is often openly vague about what this relation is: see *Phaedo* 100d, *Parmenides* 130e–133a.)

It is clear that Plato in his 'middle' period wants Forms to be things of absolute value. What Justice or Goodness *is* cannot be relative to different times, people, or places. Justice and Goodness are admirable to contemplate; in the *Symposium*, and also in the *Republic* and *Phaedo*, Plato describes philosophers as passionately loving the Forms. At times he speaks of other things trying or aspiring to be like Forms, but being only an imperfect copy. Plato wants Forms to give an explanation of things' having the characteristics they have—and it may be that he thinks beautiful things can be beautiful only by sharing in something which itself truly *is beautiful*.[64]

So a question which must be considered is whether Plato believes in the self-predication of Forms. If so, the easiest verdict is that he is in a muddle. But there may be an alternative verdict: perhaps when Plato thought of the propositions 'Beauty is beautiful' or 'Largeness is large', he was not confusing properties and paradigms. This would be the case if '. . . is beautiful' or '. . . is large' were being used in two different ways, one way when applied to Forms, another when applied to other things.[65]

What were Plato's reasons for believing in Forms? Did he have arguments for them? Answering these questions is not simple. Unfortunately Plato mostly does not argue for the existence of his Forms, but assumes them. However, Aristotle says (*Metaphysics* M, ch. 4): 'The theory of Forms occurred to the people who stated it because as regards truth they were convinced by the

---

[64] See *Phaedo* 100b–101c, with the interpretation of Bostock, *Plato's* Phaedo, ch. 7 (esp. 146–56).

[65] Such a line is taken, for example, by R. E. Allen, 'Participation and Predication in Plato's Middle Period Dialogues', in Allen (ed.), *Studies in Plato's Metaphysics*, and Constance C. Meinwald, 'Good-bye to the Third Man', in Kraut (ed.), *The Cambridge Companion to Plato*.

Heraclitean arguments that all perceptible things are always in flux, so that if there is to be knowledge of anything, or understanding, there must be some other, permanent kinds of thing over and above perceptible things, because there is no knowledge of things in flux.' A passage where something approaching this sort of argument occurs is *Phaedo* 74a–c—though the existence of Forms is not a *conclusion* of this argument. (Similar trains of thought seem to be at work in *Republic* 523a–525b and *Cratylus* 439b–440d.)

Much hangs on what one takes 'in flux' to mean. Often Plato seems less concerned about change over time, more about the simultaneous presence of opposites in things (also a Heraclitean idea, one may recall—see Section 1.3 above)—a finger may be both large and small, something may be both equal and not equal. The general form of argument seems to be: if we are to know what *F*ness is, the object of our knowledge cannot be both *F* and not-*F*; but sensible things are both *F* and not-*F*, so the object of our knowledge (*F*ness itself) must be other than sensible things. Sometimes Plato may be talking about sensible properties, rather than things (see Section 2.4.4 above).[66]

This discussion leaves us with a great many problems. Two may be mentioned: (1) Does it make sense to say that, while a finger can be large or small, Largeness itself is just large? Presumably the finger is 'variable' because it is larger than some things, smaller than others: does this mean that Largeness is larger than everything else? Or is it supposed to be large 'absolutely'—i.e. not in relation to anything else? How can this make sense if 'large' is essentially a relative term? (2) If this kind of argument from 'being and not being' among sensibles gives Plato his reason for believing in Forms, will there be a Form for every property? Or will there be only a restricted range of Forms? (In the light of *Republic* 523a–e, should there be a Form of Finger, for example?)

The latter question is made difficult by the well-known passage in *Republic*, book 10, where Plato says there are Forms of Bed and Table, and appears to be saying (596a) that whenever we have a collection of particulars to which we 'apply the same name', we may hypothesize a single Form. If there is a Form of Bed, should there not be a Form of Finger?

Interpreting the theory of Forms is thus an enormous challenge. Plato invests great importance in Forms, but does not seem to have a very well worked out theory about them. In the later *Parmenides* he returns to the topic in more analytical mood, seemingly aware that many crucial questions about Forms still need to be answered (see Section 2.5.2 below).

---

[66] Irwin, 'Plato's Heracliteanism', and *Plato's Moral Theory* (Oxford, 1977), 144–52, examines different ways in which Plato may be taking a 'Heraclitean' view of sensible reality.

2.5. Problems in Plato's Epistemology and Metaphysics

2.5.1. *After the* Republic

Many of the dialogues which are normally regarded as later than the *Republic* are philosophically challenging and important. The *Phaedrus* contains more discussion of Forms, recollection, and the parts of the soul, woven into a brilliant treatment of love, and an exploration of the relationships between philosophy and rhetoric. The *Timaeus* gives Plato's cosmology, accounting for the creation of the universe by a divine agency who copies the eternal Forms. The *Sophist* includes an intricate further discussion of Forms, and an attempt to take on Parmenides' claim that you cannot think 'is not'. The *Philebus* has as its central theme pleasure and its relation to the best human life. Each of these works contains far more than could be discussed in the space available here.

I concentrate here on two works which are often studied for their contribution to Plato's epistemology and metaphysics: *Parmenides* and *Theaetetus*.

2.5.2. *Criticisms of the Theory of Forms in Plato's* Parmenides

The *Parmenides* is a strange dialogue, whose interpretation is a difficult and contentious matter. It falls into two clear parts, only the first of which appears to concern the theory of Forms directly. Over the last forty years most discussion of the *Parmenides* in English-speaking philosophy has centred on the first part (126a–136e or thereabouts): anyone wishing to follow the debate should especially attend to it.[67]

The characters in the first part of the dialogue are Parmenides, Zeno, and Socrates in his youth. It is fairly clear that the young Socrates stands in for Plato himself. Plato is here looking back on his own previous views in a critical spirit. One may ask what Plato's attitude is or should be to the various objections against the theory of Forms. Does Plato take these arguments seriously? If they are successful, does he need to abandon his theory of Forms—or will some modifications save it? However, the prior task must be to understand each of the main objections to the theory of Forms. After the introductory section 126a–128e, the first part of the *Parmenides* has the following structure:

(1) Socrates states the theory of Forms (128e–130a).
(2) Parmenides elicits more information from Socrates about Forms (130a–e):
    (*a*) Separation of Forms themselves from 'the other things that share in them'.

---

[67] A recent commentator who regards the mystifying second part as highly important for interpreting the first is Constance C. Meinwald: *Plato's* Parmenides (New York, 1991), and/or 'Good-bye to the Third Man'.

(b) Question: What classes of things have Forms? Socrates' different answers.

(3) Arguments which reveal problems over the nature of 'participation' (130e–133a):

(a) Participation as 'sharing': problems with wholes and parts.

(b) The so-called 'Third Man' argument: an infinite regress of Forms?

(c) Could Forms be thoughts? (Two reasons are given why they could not be.)

(d) Forms as paradigms or patterns in nature: a regress arises again.

(4) Final objection: Forms would be unknowable to us if they were completely separate from the sensible world (133a–134e).

(5) Parmenides' closing remarks to Socrates: Forms are necessary for thought and discourse, but Socrates needs to practise dialectical method (134e–136e).

The Statement of the Theory of Forms (128e–130a and 130a–e)   Parmenides asks Socrates whether he himself has drawn the distinction between Forms and other things—he answers yes, but this cannot be taken as a genuine statement of what the historical Socrates believed. The theory is Plato's own. It is usually thought that as stated here it corresponds to the views on Forms put forward in the earlier *Phaedo* and *Republic*.

What Classes of Things Have Forms? (130a–e)   This is an intriguing section. Note that Parmenides asks about five groups of things that might be thought to have Forms associated with them: (1) likeness, unity, plurality (etc.); (2) rightness (or justice), beauty, goodness (etc.); (3) man; (4) fire, water; (5) mud, hair, or dirt. Socrates gives one answer for (1) and (2), another for (3) and (4), and a third different answer for (5). Why?

Socrates expresses 'puzzlement'—in some cases he does not know whether there are Forms or not. Finally, Parmenides tells him that his difficulties arise because he is still too young: 'philosophy has not taken hold of you so firmly as I believe it will some day. You will not despise any of these objects then' (130e). It is tempting to view this as the more mature Plato telling his former self that the theory of Forms must in the end have a Form for all the things listed. But why then does he make Socrates give the different answers?

If one thinks of the Forms in the *Phaedo*, *Republic*, and *Symposium*, there are a number of considerations that may be relevant to answering this question. Plato wanted his Forms to be objects of admiration because of their absolute value. He used arguments to do with flux and the unity of opposites in the sensible world and to do with relative terms (see Section 2.4.5 above). On the other hand, in one passage he said there was a Form of Bed, that craftsmen could 'look towards' Forms in making artefacts, and that for any group of things which we collect together under the same name there will be a Form. *Parmenides* 130a–e suggests that Plato is calling not only for a much-needed clarification of the extent of Forms, but also for a thorough examination of the reasons there might be for believing in Forms at all.

Participation as Sharing (130e–131e) In this section Parmenides poses a dilemma. The 'other' things participate in Forms—but does each thing have a whole or a part of the Form in it? The image of the sail spread over many people is his attempt to illustrate the problem. Is it well chosen? Socrates makes another suggestion: perhaps a Form is present in many things as a single day is present in many places. Is there a way of following up this suggestion which reveals anything relevant to the problem of participation? Is it right to think of a Form being 'divided up' at all?

An overall question about this section (and those following it) is whether Plato means us to make any specific conclusion about what is wrong with Socrates' thinking, or whether he is simply recording a confusion about Forms.

The 'Third Man' Argument (131e–132b and 132d–133a) This is the most discussed of all the arguments in the *Parmenides*. The argument appears first at 131e–132b, in an extremely short stretch of text.

The argument is called the 'Third Man', though this term does not appear in the text itself. The name arises because Aristotle reports the same argument using the example of 'Man'. The Form Man and any particular man—say, Socrates—appear to have something in common since they are both called 'man'; the theory of Forms (the argument goes) ought therefore to provide for a third 'Man', which both the Form Man and the man Socrates can participate in. Aristotle mentions this as a well-known objection made by his contemporaries to the theory of Forms. It is an objection presumably because the theory wants each Form to be only one. By the 'Third Man' argument we end up with infinite Forms as soon as we have one.

Plato's example is not 'Man', but 'Large' or 'the Large'—by which he means the Form that could otherwise be referred to as 'Largeness'. The conclusion of the argument is that, according to the theory of Forms, each of the Forms will be infinite in number. But where is the argument? In order to reach this conclusion we need some premises, but all we have is one premiss: 'When it seems to you that a number of things is large, there seems to be a certain single character which is the same when you look at them all; hence you think that Largeness is a single thing' (132a).

If the Third Man Argument is to be an objection to the theory of Forms there must be a valid argument which leads to the conclusion: the objection will then be that that conclusion is absurd, so something in the starting-point of the theory is wrong. Analytical philosophers have responded with ingenuity to the challenge of reconstructing the argument. But can we find a valid argument here? One positive answer is to be found in Colin Strang's 'Plato and the Third Man',[68] where he supplies several unstated or unclear premises to produce a neat and valid piece of reasoning. Others have concluded that when we attempt to reconstruct the argument, we find there is no valid way to reach the absurd conclusion of an infinity of Forms—hence Vlastos's famous pronouncement[69] that this stretch of text is 'a record of honest perplexity' in which Plato realizes something is seriously wrong with his theory, but is not clear what.

Whether or not Plato realizes it, there is one assumption which is *needed* to make the Third Man Argument intelligible at all, and which is quite questionable. This is the assumption which has been called 'self-predication': the assumption that a Form has predicated of it the property which it names, e.g. that the Form of Largeness is large. Since many discussions of the argument centre around 'self-predication', the reader would be well advised to devote some effort to understanding what it means and why it may be an odd view, then to discover how the Third Man Argument requires the assumption of self-predication, and finally to ask whether the argument is designed to reveal that self-predication is a mistake.

Some more evidence is provided by the second occurrence of an infinite regress of Forms at 133a. This results from Socrates' new suggestion ('the best he can make' of the theory which appears to be falling apart under Parmenides' questioning) that Forms are 'as it were patterns fixed in the nature of things' and that the other things 'are made in their image and are likenesses'. The Greek word translated as 'patterns' is *paradeigmata*. Here Socrates is trying out the idea of Forms as paradigms (see Section 2.4.5 above).

What one should note here is that the same problem arises as before—a regress of Forms—and that the explicit conclusion is drawn that 'It follows that the other things do not partake of Forms by being like them; we must look for some other means by which they partake.' In other words, the relation between Forms and other things cannot simply be one of resemblance.

The Final Objection: 'Knowledge Itself' (133a–134e)   This objection is somewhat less discussed, although Parmenides calls it the worst difficulty for the theory of Forms (133b). Immediately afterwards Plato gives a subtle hint, however, that he does not think it ultimately holds water: if someone made this 'worst' objection, he says, one could not convince him that he was mistaken 'unless he chanced to be a man of wide experience and natural ability, and were willing to follow one through a long and remote train of argument'. One might wonder whether this sort of remark applies to all the objections to the theory of Forms:

---

[68] In Vlastos (ed.), *Plato*, i.

[69] In 'The Third Man Argument in Plato's *Parmenides*', in Allen (ed.), *Studies in Plato's Metaphysics*.

perhaps they are problems only for someone who understands the theory superficially?[70]

The gist of the final objection is that things in 'our world' are related to one another, while Forms are related to one another in a realm of their own: how can the divide be bridged? In particular, how can *our* knowing reach across to the Forms?

Parmenides' closing remarks (135a–c) do not suggest that the theory of Forms has to be abandoned because of the objections made. But whether the theory needs to be altered (and if so how), or whether it needs to be thought through more clearly so that its proponent can overcome the objections, are questions of interpretation that are much harder to answer.

2.5.3. *The* Theaetetus: *What is Knowledge?*

The *Theaetetus*, one of Plato's richest works in terms of philosophical argument and insight, was probably written after the *Parmenides*. (Something which Socrates says at 183e–184a has led people to see an allusion to the *Parmenides*.) At any rate, the *Theaetetus* belongs to the same period of Plato's life, after the *Republic*, when he seems to become more self-critical and not content to accept his earlier central doctrines without a great deal more analysis.

After the *Parmenides* we may expect the *Theaetetus* to be concerned with Forms. However, despite the fact that the dialogue pursues the question 'What is knowledge?', there is no explicit discussion of Forms. The easiest way to approach the *Theaetetus* is as an investigation of the *nature* of knowledge which holds in abeyance any assumptions about what the *objects* of knowledge are. Some commentators on this dialogue have, however, found that it implicitly supports the earlier theory of Forms. This is a general issue of interpretation to which the reader should be alert. Sooner or later one will want to ask how Forms might relate to some of the arguments in this dialogue.

In its pursuit of the single central question 'What is knowledge?', the *Theaetetus* preserves something of the character of a Socratic dialogue. It is also inconclusive: three attempted definitions of knowledge (knowledge as perception, knowledge as true judgement, knowledge as true judgement with an account (*logos*)) are all refuted. Socrates' methods are also pointed up: he describes himself as like a midwife who can assist others in bringing their philosophical ideas to birth (148e–151d). It is fairly clear that the reader is to be prompted into active philosophical debate by this dialogue: it will reach its completion when something is brought to birth in each of our minds.

---

[70] See Meinwald, 'Good-bye to the Third Man', who suggests that Socrates falls into this category in the first part of the dialogue.

Knowledge   Prior to the three main definitions of knowledge, there is a discussion in which some examples of knowledge arise (145c–148e). Knowledge covers both craft (*tekhnē*) and mathematics. (Theaetetus, portrayed here in his youth, went on to be a mathematician.) One further feature is worth noting. We may tend to think of knowledge as *knowledge that . . .*, where what is known is a proposition. But Plato often talks simply of *knowing a thing*. We can say 'I know London' or 'I know Mary'. This prompts the question whether Plato thinks that all knowing can be described in this way. Writers commonly point to the difference in French between *connaître* and *savoir* (or in German between *kennen* and *wissen*). Does Plato then think that all knowledge can be described as being acquainted with a thing (*connaître, kennen*)? Or does he vacillate between describing knowledge in this way and in other ways?

If the superficial outcome of the *Theaetetus* is that we do not yet know what knowledge is (see 210a–d), writers on the dialogue have often come forward with a more positive 'moral' concerning the nature of knowledge which the dialogue supposedly identifies. But such ideas are often only implicit in the text, which presents itself as a series of problems the reader must work through.

Knowledge as Perception (151d–186e)   Theaetetus offers the definition of knowledge as perception by the senses. This definition is eventually rejected, in the course of a discussion whose structure is as intricate as anything Plato wrote. It is as if Plato is using this definition as a way of demonstrating how to follow up all the ramifications a simple statement may produce. One should be prepared for a very challenging, extended argument. The whole section divides into a larger and a smaller part. The smaller (184b–186e) is a direct refutation of the claim that knowledge is perception. Its crucial idea is that knowledge must involve judging, which is distinct from perceiving. Judgements about a thing's *being* are made by the soul itself, not using any of the particular senses through which it perceives. This powerful objection is a turning-point in the dialogue. One thing that is not questioned from here to the end is that knowledge must at least involve *judgement*.

The much larger part (151d–184b) is difficult to interpret for two main reasons: (1) its structure is so complicated as to be initially baffling, (2) its purpose may be in doubt: at 183c it looks as if 'knowledge is perception' has already been refuted, so do we have two parallel refutations in the two parts of this section? Or is the refutation really only accomplished in 184b–186e?

In barest outline the structure of 151d–184b is as follows. Theaetetus defines knowledge as perception. Socrates says that this definition is equivalent (see 151e–152a, 160d–e) to two other philosophical theses: Protagoras' relativist doctrine that 'a man is the measure of all things', and Heraclitus' doctrine that everything is always changing. After argument and counter-argument have been exchanged, both the Protagorean doctrine and the Heraclitean doctrine are refuted.

A neat way to understand the structure of this section is to say that the Heraclitean doctrine leads to absurdity, the Heraclitean doctrine is required by the Protagorean doctrine, and the Protagorean doctrine is required by 'knowledge is perception'—hence this definition is false because it ultimately leads to absurdity (the form of argument known as *reductio ad absurdum*). But that leaves many questions: Why does Plato spend a long time refuting the Protagorean theory on its own terms? And why does he also need the second chunk of argument to attack 'knowledge is perception'?

There is an alternative reading which sees Plato as on the same ground as he was when he distinguished knowledge from perception in the *Republic* and *Phaedo*. This reading says that Plato thinks perception is correctly accounted for by Protagoras and Heraclitus, and that for that reason perception cannot be knowledge.[71]

Knowledge as True Judgement (187a–c; 200d–201c)   'Judgement' translates *doxa*, which elsewhere has been translated as 'belief'. (Translators who prefer 'judgement' in the *Theaetetus* probably do so because of its link with *doxazein*, which they render as 'judging' or 'making a judgement'.)

Thinking back to the *Meno* and the *Republic*, it would be astounding if Plato were now to say that knowledge is the same as true judgement or belief. The *Theaetetus'* short discussion of this definition does indeed reject it outright. But, having introduced the definition in 187a–c, Plato postpones the refutation until 200d–201c. The intervening pages concern false judgement—see below.

The brief argument against the definition of knowledge as true judgement seems to reveal some surprising underlying assumptions. On the one hand, Plato is surely right to say that someone can be persuaded into making a true judgement (for example, in a law court) without thereby *knowing* the truth. On the other hand, why does he think a jury that had been persuaded in a short time would lack knowledge? Is it because they do not have sufficient understanding of the evidence, or (as he seems to imply at 201b) because they were not present to witness the events they are making a judgement about?[72]

The Problem of False Judgement (187c–200d)   At first sight this section is an island within the dialogue: one can read it on its own as a small masterpiece of argument which sets up a paradox and pursues it with sustained reasoning. However, Plato gives more than a hint that the problems he encounters with false judgement reflect the general inability to understand knowledge (200c–d).

---

[71] See Myles Burnyeat on 'Readings A and B'; his discussion in *The* Theaetetus *of Plato* (Indianapolis, 1990), 7–65 is helpful.

[72] Burnyeat, ibid. 124–7, and 'Plato and the Jury', draws some interesting conclusions from this passage.

The problem is simply how false judgement (or false belief) is possible at all. Plato believes it is possible, but presents a piece of reasoning according to which it is not: hence we have a paradox. The paradox is set up at 187e–188c: this passage should be studied very carefully in its own right before looking at Plato's attempted solutions. Two crucial assumptions are that in order to make a judgement about anything one must know it, and that if one knows something, one cannot make certain kinds of mistake about it. Clearly something must go wrong with the reasoning which sets up the paradox, but it is not entirely straightforward to say what it is. There follow a number of ingenious attempts by Plato to resolve the paradox, including the striking analogies of the wax tablet (or block) and the aviary. No satisfactory resolution is found.

Knowledge as True Judgement with an Account (Logos) *(201c–210a)*   This final section of the dialogue falls into two main parts. The first is a theory which Socrates presents as a 'dream' he has had: the theory says that there are complexes and primary elements, and that an account can be given only of the complexes. This has as a consequence that primary elements are not knowable. It is a theory of considerable abstraction, and has produced much speculation among commentators. (One issue, though perhaps not a central one for the initial reader, is why this theory is put forward as a 'dream' in the first place.) The dream theory is then subjected to two objections: one is based on the idea that a whole is identical with all its parts, another on the idea that elements (such as letters that make up a word or syllable) are knowable.

After the dream theory comes an attempt (206c–210a) to understand what 'knowledge is true judgement plus an account' (*logos*) might actually mean. Plato considers three senses which *logos* might have, and decides that none of them will provide a satisfactory definition of knowledge. The first sense of *logos* is the unpromising 'making one's thought apparent vocally'; the second is the enumeration of the elements of something (seeming to hark back to the concerns of the dream theory); the third, which is perhaps the most promising of the three, is 'telling some mark by which the object you are asked about differs from all other things' (208c): knowledge of X would then be having a true or correct belief about X, while also being able to give an account of what distinguishes X from everything else. However, this definition quickly runs into the problem of circularity. One would have to *know* that one's account of the thing's differentness was correct: so part of the definition of knowledge is that it involves knowing something, which Socrates describes as 'just silly'. However, commentators have attempted to draw a number of different 'morals' from the dialogue's inconclusive ending.[73]

---

[73] Cf. Bostock, *Plato's* Theaetetus, 241–67.

BIBLIOGRAPHY

IRWIN, T. H., *Classical Thought* (Oxford, 1989) is a good, short introduction to the whole of ancient philosophy, covering much wider ground than this chapter.

1. THE PRE-SOCRATIC PHILOSOPHERS

Passages from the Pre-Socratics are quoted in the translation by Jonathan Barnes, *Early Greek Philosophy* (Harmondsworth, 1987). Passages are also referred to by their standard fragment numbers (B 1 and so on), which relate to their ordering in the collection of the Greek texts made by Diels–Kranz (*Die Fragmente der Vorsokratiker*, ed. H. Diels and W. Kranz, 10th edn. (Berlin, 1952)). The Diels–Kranz fragment numbers are used here simply for convenience: all recent commentators use them to identify the fragments. Recommended books may arrange fragments in different orders, but all provide an index or concordance which will assist in finding a fragment if one has its Diels–Kranz (DK) number.

ESSENTIAL READING

BARNES, J., *Early Greek Philosophy* (Harmondsworth, 1987). Barnes's introduction, synopsis, and other information are also valuable.

RECOMMENDED READING

BARNES, J., *The Presocratic Philosophers*, Arguments of the Philosophers (London, 1989). The most stimulating philosophical account. Sometimes hard going for a beginner in philosophy, but worth persevering with.

GUTHRIE, W. K. C., *A History of Greek Philosophy*, i: *The Earlier Presocratics and the Pythagoreans* (Cambridge, 1962); ii: *The Presocratic Tradition from Parmenides to Democritus* (Cambridge, 1965). Guthrie's two volumes provide a thorough and relatively easy-going account of the whole period.

HUSSEY, E., *The Presocratics* (London, 1972). Short and introductory.

KIRK, G. S., RAVEN, J. E., and SCHOFIELD, M., *The Presocratic Philosophers*, 2nd edn. (Cambridge, 1983). Fragments of the Pre-Socratics in translation, with commentary (and Greek text).

ADDITIONAL READING

These items are meant as an additional resource for those engaged in more detailed study of particular topics. Initial reading and further bibliographies are available in each of the books cited under Essential and Recommended Reading. Classic collections of articles often cited (and best used for further work on a specific philosopher) are:

FURLEY, D. J., and ALLEN, R. E., *Studies in Presocratic Philosophy*, i and ii (London, 1970, 1975).

MOURELATOS, A. P. D. (ed.), *The Pre-Socratics: A Collection of Critical Essays* (New York, 1974).

1.2. Ionian Cosmology

KAHN, C. H., *Anaximander and the Origins of Greek Cosmology* (New York, 1960). A major scholarly work. Illuminating about Anaximander and much else, for those who want to specialize in this area. Some parts require Greek.

—— 'Anaximander's Fragment: The Universe Governed by Law', in A. P. D. Mourelatos (ed.), *The Pre-Socratics: A Collection of Critical Essays* (New York, 1974). This is an extract from Kahn, *Anaximander and the Origins of Greek Cosmology*, cited above.

1.3. Heraclitus

KAHN, C. H., *The Art and Thought of Heraclitus* (Cambridge, 1979). The most important recent study of all the fragments. Very readable.

GUTHRIE, W. K. C., 'Flux and *Logos* in Heraclitus', in A. P. D. Mourelatos (ed.), *The Pre-Socratics: A Collection of Critical Essays* (New York, 1974). This is an extract from W. K. C. Guthrie, *A History of Greek Philosophy*, i: *The Earlier Presocratics and the Pythagoreans* (Cambridge, 1962).

KIRK, G. S., 'Natural Change in Heraclitus', in A. P. D. Mourelatos (ed.), *The Pre-Socratics: A Collection of Critical Essays* (New York, 1974).

VLASTOS, G., 'On Heraclitus', in D. J. Furley and R. E. Allen, *Studies in Presocratic Philosophy*, i (London, 1970).

WIGGINS, D., 'Heraclitus' Conceptions of Flux, Fire and Material Persistence', in M. Schofield and M. Nussbaum (eds.), *Language and Logos* (Cambridge, 1982).

1.4. Parmenides and the Eleatics

FURLEY, D., 'Parmenides of Elea', in P. Edwards (ed.), *Encyclopaedia of Philosophy* (London, 1967). This and the next piece cited give a clear insight into Parmenides' arguments.

GALLOP, D., *Parmenides of Elea: Fragments* (Toronto, 1984). Gallop gives the Greek text with a translation. Of greatest use to the beginner is his introduction.

OWEN, G. E. L., 'Eleatic Questions', in *Logic, Science and Dialectic: Collected Papers in Greek Philosophy* (London, 1986) is an influential article, though not very easy to read.

FURTH, M., 'Elements of Eleatic Ontology', in A. P. D. Mourelatos (ed.), *The Pre-Socratics: A Collection of Critical Essays* (New York, 1974).

SAINSBURY, R. M., *Paradoxes* (Cambridge, 1988), ch. 1: 'Zeno's Paradoxes: Space, Time, and Motion'.

VLASTOS, G., 'Zeno of Elea', in P. Edwards (ed.), *Encyclopaedia of Philosophy* (London, 1967).

1.5. Cosmology after the Eleatics

FURLEY, D. J., 'The Atomists' Reply to the Eleatics', in A. P. D. Mourelatos (ed.), *The Pre-Socratics: A Collection of Critical Essays* (New York, 1974).

KERFERD, G. B., 'Anaxagoras and the Concept of Matter before Aristotle', in A. P. D. Mourelatos (ed.), *The Pre-Socratics: A Collection of Critical Essays* (New York, 1974).

VLASTOS, G., 'The Physical Theory of Anaxagoras', in A. P. D. Mourelatos (ed.), *The Pre-Socratics: A Collection of Critical Essays* (New York, 1974).

Books for more detailed study:

BAILEY, C., *The Greek Atomists and Epicurus* (Oxford, 1928).

FURLEY, D. J., *Two Studies in the Greek Atomists* (Princeton, NJ, 1967). Some parts require Greek. Includes D. J. Furley, 'The Atomists' Reply to the Eleatics', cited above.

INWOOD, B., *The Poem of Empedocles* (Toronto, 1992). Has a long introduction and a translation of the fragments.

SCHOFIELD, M., *An Essay on Anaxagoras* (Cambridge, 1980).

1.6. Pythagoreanism

Relevant sections of the works cited under Essential and Recommended Reading, of which W. K. C. Guthrie, *A History of Greek Philosophy*, vol. i, ch. 4, and J. Barnes, *The Presocratic Philosophers*, chs. 6 and 18 may be most useful. Chapters 5, 13, and 15 in Jonathan Barnes, *Early Greek Philosophy*, contain the most relevant sources. In addition:

BURKERT, W., *Lore and Science in Ancient Pythagoreanism*, trans. E. L. Minar (Cambridge, Mass., 1972). A massive work of scholarship, sometimes presupposing Greek. It is not required except for those making a special study of Pythagoreanism (in which case it is indispensable).

KAHN, C. H., 'Pythagorean Philosophy before Plato', in A. P. D. Mourelatos (ed.), *The Pre-Socratics: A Collection of Critical Essays* (New York, 1974).

2. PLATO AND SOCRATES

References to Plato's works follow the current standard procedure, and are in the form *Meno* 80e, *Phaedo* 65d, and so on. Following the title of the work are the page numbers and page subdivisions (a–e) of the Greek edition of Plato by Stephanus (1578). They appear in the margins of most good translations. Sometimes line numbers are added for further precision, e.g. *Meno* 80e1, or *Meno* 80e1–5.

ESSENTIAL READING

Plato: Collected Dialogues, ed. E. Hamilton and H. Cairns (Princeton, NJ, 1961). Contains all Plato's dialogues in one volume and is well worth having. It makes the Tredennick and Guthrie translations cited below redundant by incorporating all the latter and all but one of the former. *Meno* is also translated in *Plato's* Meno, ed. J. M. Day (London, 1994).

Plato: Early Socratic Dialogues, ed. Trevor J. Saunders (Harmondsworth, 1987). Contains translations of *Ion, Laches, Lysis, Charmides, Hippias Major, Hippias Minor, Euthydemus*, and good additional material. Useful to have even in addition to the *Collected Dialogues*, ed. Hamilton and Cairns, cited above.

Plato: The Last Days of Socrates, trans. Hugh Tredennick (Harmondsworth, 1969). Contains the early dialogues *Euthyphro, Apology, Crito* (and the middle period *Phaedo*).

Plato: Protagoras and Meno, trans. W. K. C. Guthrie (Harmondsworth, 1956).

RECOMMENDED READING
Introduction to Plato

GRUBE, G. M. A., *Plato's Thought* (1935; repr. London, 1980). Despite its age, still a good
short introduction to Plato's philosophy as a whole.

KRAUT, RICHARD (ed.), *The Cambridge Companion to Plato* (Cambridge, 1992).
Comprehensive up-to-date collection on many aspects of Plato's thought, clearly
presented for the new reader but also useful at more advanced levels. The bibliography is particularly good.

Socrates and the Socratic Dialogues

ROBINSON, R., *Plato's Earlier Dialectic* (Oxford, 1953). Chapters 1–8 are good on Socratic
method. Three of these chapters are reprinted in Gregory Vlastos (ed.), *Socrates: A
Collection of Critical Essays* (New York, 1971).

VLASTOS, GREGORY, *Socrates: Ironist and Moral Philosopher* (Cambridge, 1991). Masterly
and readable study by the foremost modern scholar on Socrates.

—— *Socratic Studies*, ed. M. Burnyeat (Cambridge, 1994). Collection of articles by Vlastos:
the 'companion volume' to his *Socrates: Ironist and Moral Philosopher*, cited above.

The Sophists

KERFERD, G. B., *The Sophistic Movement* (Cambridge, 1981). A good, clear book on the
Sophists.

ADDITIONAL READING
Socrates and the Sophists

GUTHRIE, W. K. C., *A History of Greek Philosophy*, iii: *The Fifth Century Enlightenment*
(Cambridge, 1969); repr. in two parts as *Socrates* and *The Sophists* (both Cambridge,
1971).

VLASTOS, GREGORY (ed.), *Socrates: A Collection of Critical Essays* (New York, 1971; repr.
Notre Dame, Ind., 1980). A good collection of essays by many scholars.

Socratic Ethics

IRWIN, T. H., *Plato's Moral Theory* (Oxford, 1977). An important if controversial book.
Chapters 1–5 are on Socrates and the early dialogues.

Socratic Method

SANTAS, GERASIMOS XENOPHON, *Socrates: Philosophy in Plato's Early Dialogues*, Arguments
of the Philosophers (London, 1979). Thorough and rather dry analysis of Socratic
arguments.

VLASTOS, GREGORY, 'Socrates' Disavowal of Knowledge', *Philosophical Quarterly*, 35
(1985), 1–31; repr. in Gregory Vlastos, *Socratic Studies*, ed. Myles Burnyeat
(Cambridge, 1994).

—— 'The Socratic *Elenchus*', *Oxford Studies in Ancient Philosophy*, 1 (1983), 27–58; repr. in Gregory Vlastos, *Socratic Studies*, ed. Myles Burnyeat (Cambridge, 1994).

Knowledge and Tekhnē

WOODRUFF, PAUL, 'Plato's Early Theory of Knowledge', in Stephen Everson (ed.), *Epistemology*, Companions to Ancient Thought, i (Cambridge, 1990). A good introduction to Plato's use of the concept *tekhnē*. The Everson volume contains other items on Plato, and a useful bibliography.

Protagoras *and* Gorgias

Plato: Gorgias, trans. with intro. and comm. by T. H. Irwin, Clarendon Plato series (Oxford, 1979).

Plato: Protagoras, trans. with intro. and comm. by C. C. W. Taylor, Clarendon Plato series (Oxford, 1976).

Plato's Middle Period Philosophy

ESSENTIAL READING

PLATO, *Meno*, in the Guthrie translation or Hamilton and Cairns's *Collected Dialogues*, cited under Essential Reading, above; or in *Plato's* Meno, ed. J. M. Day (London, 1994).
—— *Phaedo*, trans. with notes by David Gallop, Clarendon Plato series (Oxford, 1975).
—— *Phaedo*, trans. David Gallop, World's Classics (Oxford, 1993). Revised version of the above, without the commentary.
—— *Republic*, trans. G. M. A. Grube, rev. C. D. C. Reeve (Indianapolis, 1992).
—— *Republic*, trans. Robin Waterfield (Oxford, 1993). Alternative to the Grube translation cited above. These recent translations of *Republic* are to be preferred as combining accessibility and accuracy.

RECOMMENDED READING

In addition to Richard Kraut (ed.), *The Cambridge Companion to Plato*, and G. M. A. Grube, *Plato's Thought*, cited above under Recommended Reading: Introduction to Plato:

CROMBIE, I. M., *An Examination of Plato's Doctrines*, i and ii (London, 1962, 1963).
GOSLING, J. C. B., *Plato*, Arguments of the Philosophers (London, 1973).
WHITE, NICHOLAS P., *Plato on Knowledge and Reality* (Indianapolis, 1976).

ALLEN, R. E. (ed.), *Studies in Plato's Metaphysics* (London, 1965). This and the next two collections cited are very often referred to.
VLASTOS, GREGORY, *Platonic Studies* (Princeton, NJ, 1981). Collected essays by Vlastos, many important; pt. 1 most relevant here.
—— *Plato*, i: *Metaphysics and Epistemology* (Garden City, NY, 1971).

Meno

Plato's Meno, ed. J. M. Day (London, 1994).

Phaedo

BOSTOCK, D., *Plato's* Phaedo (Oxford, 1986). A lively philosophical commentary.

PLATO, *Phaedo*, trans. with notes by David Gallop, Clarendon Plato series (Oxford, 1975), commentary. Sometimes inaccessibly written, but useful on points of detail.

Republic

ANNAS, J., *An Introduction to Plato's* Republic (Oxford, 1981).

CROSS, R. C., and WOOZLEY, A. D., *Plato's* Republic: *A Philosophical Commentary* (London, 1974). A more old-fashioned commentary; quite approachable.

FINE, GAIL, 'Knowledge and Belief in *Republic* V–VII', in Stephen Everson (ed.), *Epistemology*, Companions to Ancient Thought, i (Cambridge, 1990).

REEVE, C. D. C., *Philosopher-Kings: The Argument of Plato's* Republic (Princeton, NJ, 1988).

WHITE, N. P., *A Companion to Plato's* Republic (Oxford, 1979).

The Soul

All items listed so far under Recommended Reading contain something relevant. Further suggestions:

DODDS, E. R., *The Greeks and the Irrational* (Berkeley, Calif., 1956).

LOVIBOND, SABINA, 'Plato's Theory of Mind', in Stephen Everson (ed.), *Psychology*, Companions to Ancient Thought, ii (Cambridge, 1991). Everson's bibliography (pp. 225 ff.) lists more specialized pieces on the soul.

SNELL, BRUNO, *The Discovery of the Mind: The Greek Origins of European Thought* (New York, 1982). This and Dodds's book cited above are two classic books that may be consulted for the wider background on the soul in Greek culture.

The Theory of Forms

All items listed above under Recommended Reading, *Phaedo*, and *Republic* contain sections on the theory of Forms. Bostock, *Plato's* Phaedo, and Annas, *An Introduction to Plato's* Republic, cited above, have chapters at fairly introductory level. Further suggestions:

ALLEN, R. E., 'Participation and Predication in Plato's Middle Period Dialogues', in R. E. Allen (ed.), *Studies in Plato's Metaphysics* (London, 1965); also in Gregory Vlastos (ed.), *Plato*, i: *Metaphysics and Epistemology* (Garden City, NY, 1971).

CHERNISS, HAROLD, 'The Philosophical Economy of the Theory of Ideas', in Gregory Vlastos (ed.), *Plato*, i: *Metaphysics and Epistemology* (Garden City, NY, 1971); also in R. E. Allen (ed.), *Studies in Plato's Metaphysics* (London, 1965).

IRWIN, T. H., 'Plato's Heracliteanism', *Philosophical Quarterly*, 27 (1977), 1–13.

OWEN, G. E. L., 'A Proof in the *Peri Ideōn*', in R. E. Allen (ed.), *Studies in Plato's Metaphysics* (London, 1965); also in G. E. L. Owen, *Logic, Science and Dialectic: Collected Papers in Greek Philosophy*, ed. M. Nussbaum (Ithaca, NY, 1986). This is a classic article, but not very easy to read.

VLASTOS, GREGORY, 'Degrees of Reality in Plato', in *Platonic Studies* (Princeton, NJ, 1981); also in R. Bamborough (ed.), *New Essays on Plato and Aristotle* (London, 1965).

ADDITIONAL READING
Poetry and the Arts

FERRARI, G. R. F., 'Plato and Poetry', in G. A. Kennedy (ed.), *The Cambridge History of Literary Criticism*, i: *Classical Criticism* (Cambridge, 1989).
JANAWAY, CHRISTOPHER, *Images of Excellence: Plato's Critique of the Arts* (Oxford, 1995).
MORAVCSIK, J., and TEMKO, P. (eds.), *Plato on Beauty, Wisdom and the Arts* (Totowa, NJ, 1982).

Love

PRICE, ANTHONY, *Love and Friendship in Plato and Aristotle* (Oxford, 1989).
VLASTOS, GREGORY, 'The Individual as Object of Love in Plato', in *Platonic Studies* (Princeton, NJ, 1981).

Political Philosophy

KLOSKO, GEORGE, *The Development of Plato's Political Theory* (New York, 1986).
POPPER, KARL, *The Open Society and its Enemies,* i: *Plato* (London, 1966).

Moral Philosophy

IRWIN, T., *Plato's Moral Theory* (Oxford, 1977), chs. 6–7.

Problems in Plato's Epistemology and Metaphysics

ESSENTIAL READING
PLATO, *Parmenides* (up to 136e), in *Plato: Collected Dialogues*, ed. E. Hamilton and H. Cairns (Princeton, NJ, 1961).
—— *Theaetetus*, trans. M. J. Levett, in Myles Burnyeat, *The Theaetetus of Plato* (Indianapolis, 1990). This is especially recommended: an excellent translation combined with Burnyeat's long philosophical commentary, which is indispensable for any serious student of this dialogue.
—— *Theaetetus*, trans. with an essay by Robin Waterfield (Harmondsworth, 1987). An alternative to Levett's translation.

RECOMMENDED READING
Parmenides

MEINWALD, CONSTANCE C., 'Good-bye to the Third Man', in Richard Kraut (ed.), *The Cambridge Companion to Plato* (Cambridge, 1992). This condenses her *Plato's Parmenides* into a short article for non-specialists.
—— *Plato's Parmenides* (New York, 1991).
RYLE, GILBERT, 'Plato's *Parmenides*', in R. E. Allen (ed.), *Studies in Plato's Metaphysics* (London, 1965); first pub. in *Mind*, 48 (1939), 129–51, 302–5.
STRANG, COLIN, 'Plato and the Third Man', in Gregory Vlastos (ed.), *Plato*, i: *Metaphysics and Epistemology* (Garden City, NY, 1971); first pub. in *Proceedings of the Aristotelian Society*, supp. vol. 37 (1963), 147–64.

VLASTOS, GREGORY, 'Plato's "Third Man" Argument: Text and Logic', in *Platonic Studies* (Princeton, NJ, 1981).

—— 'The Third Man Argument in Plato's *Parmenides*', in R. E. Allen (ed.), *Studies in Plato's Metaphysics* (London, 1965); first pub. in *Philosophical Review*, 63 (1954), 319–49.

The Theaetetus

The commentaries by Burnyeat and Waterfield, cited above, should be used. In addition:

BOSTOCK, DAVID, *Plato's* Theaetetus (Oxford, 1988). An accessible but thorough philosophical commentary.

PLATO, *Theaetetus*, trans. with notes by John McDowell (Oxford, 1973). Fairly advanced philosophical commentary on particular passages. Translation more literal than Levett's and Waterfield's.

BURNYEAT, MYLES, 'Plato and the Jury: Paradoxes in Plato's Distinction between Knowledge and True Belief', *Proceedings of the Aristotelian Society*, supp. vol. 54 (1980).

ADDITIONAL READING

Items listed above give plentiful additional reading on *Parmenides* and *Theaetetus*. Here are a few suggestions on other dialogues for those who wish to study Plato further.

Phaedrus

PLATO, *Phaedrus*, trans. Walter Hamilton (with *The Seventh and Eighth Letters*) (Harmondsworth, 1973).

Plato's Phaedrus, trans. with an intro. and comm. by R. Hackforth (Cambridge, 1972).

FERRARI, G. R. F., *Listening to the Cicadas: A Study of Plato's* Phaedrus (Cambridge, 1990).

Timaeus

PLATO, *Timaeus*, trans. H. D. P. Lee (Harmondsworth, 1965).

CHERNISS, HAROLD, 'The Relation of the *Timaeus* to Plato's Later Dialogues', in R. E. Allen (ed.), *Studies in Plato's Metaphysics* (London, 1965).

OWEN, G. E. L., 'The Place of the *Timaeus* in Plato's Dialogues', in R. E. Allen (ed.), *Studies in Plato's Metaphysics* (London, 1965); also in G. E. L. Owen, *Logic, Science and Dialectic: Collected Papers in Greek Philosophy*, ed. M. Nussbaum (Ithaca, NY, 1986).

SORABJI, RICHARD, *Time, Creation and the Continuum* (Ithaca, NY, 1983).

Sophist

PLATO, *Sophist*, in *Plato: Collected Dialogues*, ed. E. Hamilton and H. Cairns (Princeton, NJ, 1961).

ACKRILL, J. L., 'Sumplokē eidōn', in Gregory Vlastos (ed.), *Plato, i: Metaphysics and Epistemology* (Garden City, NY, 1971).

BOSTOCK, DAVID, 'Plato on "Is Not" ', *Oxford Studies in Ancient Philosophy*, 2 (1984).

FREDE, MICHAEL, 'Plato's *Sophist* on False Statements', in Richard Kraut (ed.), *The Cambridge Companion to Plato* (Cambridge, 1992).

Owen, G. E. L., 'Plato on Not-Being', in Gregory Vlastos (ed.), *Plato*, i: *Metaphysics and Epistemology* (Garden City, NY, 1971); also in G. E. L. Owen, *Logic, Science and Dialectic: Collected Papers in Greek Philosophy*, ed. M. Nussbaum (Ithaca, NY, 1986).

Philebus

Plato, *Philebus*, trans. with notes and comm. by J. C. B. Gosling (Oxford, 1975).
Plato's Philebus, trans. with intro. and comm. by R. Hackforth (Cambridge, 1972).

Frede, Dorothea, 'Disintegration and Restoration: Pleasure and Pain in Plato's *Philebus*', in Richard Kraut (ed.), *The Cambridge Companion to Plato* (Cambridge, 1992).

7

ANCIENT GREEK PHILOSOPHY II: ARISTOTLE

Hugh Lawson-Tancred

1. ARISTOTLE'S EARLY METAPHYSICS

1.1. Introduction

1.1.1. The Nature of the Texts

The philosophy of Aristotle has been of enormous historical importance. It extends the work of Plato, but emerges with a very different view of reality.

Aristotle is far less easy to approach than Plato. There are two main reasons for this. The first is that, since he lived in a later and more complex age, philosophical discussion had moved on from Plato's time and increased in elaboration and technicality. It is necessary to have some understanding of these changes in order to appreciate what Aristotle is trying to do. The second reason is that the texts that have come down to us under Aristotle's name are quite different in character from the Platonic dialogues.

We know that Aristotle composed accessible, literary works of philosophy which were famous in antiquity for their eloquence, and fragments of these are extant. However, the works that have survived intact and form what is known as the Aristotelian corpus are severe, even crabbed, in style. They are, in effect, lecture notes, intended not for the general public but for members of the school that Aristotle founded, the Lyceum, fully initiated into the way of thinking that they embody. They are therefore almost devoid of literary graces, often elliptical, and heavily laced with technical terms. The term 'esoteric', which means literally 'inwardly directed', was coined for texts of this kind.

1.1.2. Aristotle's Development

Another problem about the corpus is that it contains many apparent contradictions, or at any rate tensions. The traditional approach to this difficulty in the late ancient and medieval periods was to seek, often heroically, to harmonize the text. To some extent, those doctrines that could not be accommodated were rejected as spurious. The assumption throughout was that the corpus embodied a single monolithic system which had to be made sense of as a whole.

In the twentieth century this assumption has been challenged, initially by the pioneering German scholar Werner Jaeger. He proposed that the inconsistencies could best be explained by taking them not as the attempt to produce a single complete system but as the products of various stages of a career that developed and evolved through a variety of philosophical positions. He thus launched the developmental approach to the corpus which has become widespread. It is also diverse. Jaeger himself saw Aristotle's development as being a steady progress away from a Platonistic youth, but others have suggested that Aristotle began his career in rebellion from Plato and then came gradually to sympathize more and more with his former master. There is, of course, scope for many kinds of combination and variation within these two approaches. Recently, there has been a reaction against developmentalism, though few scholars wish to revert to the traditional monolithic picture. One view is that the treatises of the corpus were indeed first composed at different stages of Aristotle's career but that, rather than rejecting them when he changed his mind, he sought to adjust his earlier to his newer views, not always with success. The approach that I will assume here is that suggested by David Graham.[1] He holds that we should divide the corpus into two more or less complete systems. The first comprises the logical treatises known as the *organon*—which literally means 'instrument' (of thinking)—and the *Art of Rhetoric*, and the second, later system comprises all the other texts. We shall examine the first system through the *Categories* and the second through the *Physics* and *Metaphysics*. In my view, the first system is that which Aristotle produced during the time that he was still in Plato's school, the Academy, before the death of Plato in 347 BC. The second system represents his mature philosophy, consolidated after his return to Athens to found the Lyceum in 335 BC. These historical claims are not, however, required by the philosophical interpretation that I will offer.

1.1.3. Aristotle's Philosophical Agenda

The difficulty of Aristotle's works does not derive only from their aloof style and technical terminology, but also from the fact that the philosophical problems that they address are not immediately familiar to modern readers. Aristotle had two main philosophical projects. These were, first, the clarification of the nature, scope, and possible results of the activity which he, following Plato, called *dialectic*[2] and, secondly, the defence of the logical coherence of the notion of change and thus of the possibility of a genuine science of nature, including the science of man. Moreover, these two projects were intimately connected.

  Dialectic was, we may presume, a central preoccupation of the Academy. Plato, in the *Republic* (531d–534e), puts it at the summit of the philosopher's education. It is, however, hard to say what exactly it involved. Its name comes from the ordinary Greek word for conversation (*dialogos*), and it was concerned with the critical scrutiny of those terms which are both of philosophical significance and tend to occur naturally in non-specialist discussions of difficult topics. Its ancestor is the technique of critical examination (*elenchus*) to which Socrates subjected his interlocutors. This usually amounted to the examination of what was entailed in claims to the effect that '*X* (or some *X*) is *Y*'. When the variety of such claims came to be appreciated, it was apparent that the simple

---

[1] D. Graham, *Aristotle's Two Systems* (Oxford, 1987).
[2] See esp. T. H. Irwin, *Aristotle's First Principles* (Oxford, 1988).

verb 'to be' is used in a crucially different range of ways. It began to seem as though the traditional problems of philosophy had all, or at least mostly, derived from failure to grasp the significance of this point. A central task, then, of dialectic is the systematic attempt to get clear about the uses of the verb 'to be', and this is precisely what Aristotle is seeking to do in the first work that we shall examine, the *Categories*.

A paradigm example of the philosophical dangers attendant on the miscomprehension of the verb 'to be' was, in Aristotle's view, that it lent credence to the monistic position adopted by Parmenides and his Eleatic successors. They took the view that, since not-being is an incoherent notion, any idea of change must also be rejected, since it seems to involve the thought that something can combine being with *not-being*. This seems a strange philosophical puzzle to us, since we are the beneficiaries of Aristotle's solution to it, but its force can still to some extent be felt by taking Zeno's paradoxes seriously. Its historical importance, at any rate, can hardly be exaggerated. It is clear that Aristotle felt that it had paralysed Pre-Socratic physics and that it lay behind the radically non-naturalistic philosophy of the theory of Forms. All this he regarded as a disaster, but one that could be remedied by the correct application to the language of change of the careful distinctions between the uses of the verb 'to be' that had been systematically explored in the *Categories*. This is the central task of the first book of the *Physics*.

The analysis of change in the *Physics* solved definitively the Parmenidean problem, so effectively that it is hard for us today even to appreciate the seriousness of the difficulty. However, it created an equally severe problem for Aristotle's ontology, his theory of the metaphysically basic entities of the world. In the *Categories*, he had insisted on the fundamental ontological status of particular individuals (in diametric opposition to the theory of Forms). However, the analysis of the *Physics* seemed to show that these entities are in fact composites of two quite different ingredients, form and matter, and there were strong intuitive grounds for doubt that anything with such a composite nature could be a fundamental item of reality. Aristotle examines inconclusively the dual nature of individual things in his account of scientific method in the second book of the *Physics*, and he finally arrives at a solution to the difficulty about particular entities in the central books of his late masterpiece the *Metaphysics*.

1.2. The *Categories*

1.2.1. The Dialectical Background

For reasons already discussed, the *Categories* is not a work whose point is immediately obvious. A first-time reader is likely to be deterred by the abundance of technical terms and distinctions and the apparent lack of direction. This reflects the fact that the work is succinct even by Aristotle's standards, and that it addresses problems that were so familiar to its contemporary audience as to need no introduction. These problems are connected, as noted, with the development of dialectic in the Academy, evolving out of Socratic techniques of cross-questioning. It is clear that Socrates' technique, apart from its influence on the development of Plato's philosophy, caused a vogue in the Greece of the early fourth century BC, and logical arguments of every kind were the subject of keen study. Some of this study should be considered authentically philosophical, but much of it is better classed as what the Greeks called *eristic*, the practice of raising paradoxical problems purely for the purpose of being vexatious.

The philosophical consequences of dialectical reasoning were, as mentioned earlier, most clearly followed by those who developed the position of Parmenides that the normal concepts of space, time, and plurality are incoherent. This Eleatic position sought to demonstrate the essential unreality of the world of change of which we seem to have experience through the senses. As we shall see, their principal argument turned on just the sort of difficulty that the study of dialectic was intended to clear up. On the other hand, the more eristic or mischievous style of dialectic was pursued by the school that flourished in Megara under the leadership of Antisthenes, which sought in effect to demonstrate the self-defeating futility of all argument. In the Academy there may well have been those sympathetic to both these positions, but Aristotle certainly regarded them as a profound threat to the development of science, and his first task was to clarify the sort of logical difficulties that the dialecticians were bringing to light. Among these difficulties, there was one of pre-eminent philosophical importance, that of the various uses of the verb 'to be' (*einai*) and the associated abstract noun *ousia* (literally 'being').

Now, if a concept is proving philosophically puzzling, it is natural enough to suppose that the solution lies in the provision of a more satisfactory definition of the term in question. This is an approach to which the Academy was sympathetic, and the later phase of Plato's work was much concerned with the development of the technique of definition in terms of genus and differentia. This is first clearly demonstrated in the *Sophist* (eg. 219–21), in which we are shown how types of thing can first be collected together into kinds (genera) and then subdivided (by differentiae, uniquely distinguishing features) in response to simple yes–no questions that apply to each kind. For example, if one wanted a definition of the species man, one would begin with the fact that he belonged to the genus animal and then ask whether he was or was not a feathered animal. Having concluded that he was not, one would ask whether he was an animal with feet. On finding that he was, one would ask whether he had two feet or not. If one then found that he was the only species of animal that was featherless and biped, then one could conclude that 'featherless biped animal' was a definition of man. There are no doubt grave limitations in any such approach, but at least it seemed to offer the prospect of beginning the science of definition, which was seen as playing a crucial part in blocking the eristic consequences of the development of dialectic. Aristotle is in general sympathetic to this approach, though he criticizes it in detail. A major theme in his philosophy is the need to clarify what is involved in the concept of definition.

1.2.2. *Synonymy, Paronymy, and Homonymy (Chapter 1)*

Aristotle was interested in definition as a way of shedding light on the underlying structure of reality. One might pre-theoretically suppose that for every term in the language there is one appropriate definition of its meaning; Aristotle, however, held that this is not the case. There are many cases of different things being picked out by the same term, something that Aristotle describes as different things' being named by the same name (*onoma*). (For us this description is naïve in drawing no distinction between names, which refer to individuals, and general terms, which apply to many things.) Now, in many cases, the sharing of an Aristotelian name by many things will not be problematic, since the definition of the name as applied to each of those things will be the same. For instance, the name 'animal' can be applied both to a man and to a horse, but the definition associated with it in each case is the same. Aristotle says that man and horse (not 'man' and 'horse') are synonymous—with respect, as he omits to add, to the name 'animal'. For Aristotle, synonymy is thus a property of things, not of names; two or more things are synonymous when a name can be applied to them under the same definition. However, there are cases in which the same name is applied without this coincidence of the associated definition. A clear example is the use of the word 'bank' in English, which can be defined in at least two quite different ways. In such cases, Aristotle will say that the river-bank and the financial institution are homonymous with regard to the name 'bank'. Now many homonymous terms are completely harmless—in this example, there is nothing wrong with there not being a general definition that will cover all senses of 'bank'. But Aristotle takes the view that this is not always the case and that many important philosophical terms are homonymous and insusceptible of a general definition. The failure to realize this, moreover, is responsible for many of the problems that have beset dialectic. Above all, it is vital for philosophy to clarify the homonymous ambiguity of the verb 'to be'.

So important did Aristotle consider these points that they are the first to be made at the start of the *Categories*. The first four short chapters of the work introduce the general notion of the categories, and then the remaining ones deal in detail with each particular category. The fifth chapter discusses the fundamental category of substance. In addition to the clarification of the contrast between synonymy and homonymy (1^a1–12), chapter 1 introduces the related notion of paronymy (1ª13–15). Unfortunately, Aristotle does not here make explicit the point that many things are homonymous with respect to the verb 'to be', but this clearly emerges from the first four chapters.

1.2.3. Ontology and Language (Chapter 2)

For Aristotle, the ambiguity of the verb 'to be' reflects not merely a quirk of language but a deep feature of the structure of reality. Things *are* in radically different ways, and it is the primary function of metaphysics to make this perspicuous. This is, he holds, a fact about the ontological diversity of the world, but he shares with many philosophers the view that if we are to achieve a correct ontology we must use the structure of natural language as a guide. The second chapter of the *Categories* thus sets out two very general divisions, first that of 'the things that are said' into two kinds, those said with, and those said without, combination (*sumplokē*), and then that of 'the things that are' into four kinds.

The first division (1ª16–20) is mysterious. It is not clear whether things said with combination are meant to be sentences or merely elements of language more complicated than the most basic units, as seems to be implied by 1ᵇ25 f.[3] It is also unclear what correlation there is supposed to be between the elements of language and the elements of reality. We are later told (1ᵇ25 f.) that the wholly uncombined elements of language signify items within one at most of the categories, but in fact combined expressions can signify items in some of the categories (such as 'in the Lyceum') and uncombined expressions (such as 'bachelor') can signify compounds of items from different categories.

The second division (1ª21–ᵇ6) is a fourfold division of reality. All 'the things that are' are either *said-of* something or not and either *in* something or not. There are thus four types of thing, (1) things said-of something else, but not in something else, (2) things said-of something else and in something else, (3) things in something else, but not said-of something else, and (4) things neither in something else nor said-of something else. This is an entirely formal specification of the relations in which things that are can stand to one another. It is at this stage unclear both what these mysterious relations are and what the entities are that stand in them.[4] We are also told that there is a further distinction between things being in a particular way and things being in a universal way and that the former, while they cannot be said-of anything, can certainly be in something else (1ᵇ6–9).

Historically, there has always been controversy about the precise interpretation that should be given to this formal scheme, intensified by the fact that

---

[3] See the excellent, but difficult, discussion of this in J. M. E. Moravcsik (ed.), *Aristotle* (London, 1968), 125–35, and also *Aristotle's* Categories *and* De Interpretatione, trans. with notes by J. L. Ackrill (Oxford, 1963).

[4] See Graham, *Aristotle's Two Systems*, 20–36.

Aristotle says so little about the relations that he has in mind. He tells us nothing at all about the said-of relation and all he says of the in relation is 'By "*in a subject*" I mean what is in something, not as a part, and cannot exist separately from what it is in.'[5] It is at least clear that neither of these two relations is simply to be identified with any purely linguistic or logical concept of predication. The only way, in fact, in which a coherent interpretation can be given of the two relations is by moving beyond the formal schema to its instantiation. To do this is to introduce the crucial notion of substance (*ousia*). This notion has two uses for Aristotle. Primary substances are individual particular things in the world and it is these that fall into slot 4 of the schema; by contrast, secondary substances are those things that can be said-of the primary ones but which are not in them, and these secondary substances are the classificatory entities, species and genera, into which all particulars must fall. The other two schematic classes cover all the non-substantial things that are, which things are all somehow in substances. Of the two, those that are merely in substances form the class of individual non-substantial entities, and those that are also said-of other entities (i.e. said-of non-substantial individuals) comprise the non-substantial universals. (In fact, the individual–universal distinction is far less intuitively palatable in connection with non-substantial items, and Aristotle has much less to say about it than in the case of substances.)

1.2.4. *The Role of the Categories (Chapters 3 and 4)*

We have seen how the two relations 'said-of' and 'in' effect a fourfold division among the things that are. In the third chapter of the *Categories*, Aristotle, somewhat untidily, gives further information about the said-of relation. The said-of relation is transitive, in that if *A* is said-of *B* and *B* is said-of *C*, then *A* is also said of *C*. Thus if an individual man, Callias, is brought within the species man, and that species is brought within the genus animal, then Callias is, by substance, an animal as well as a man (1^b10–16). As Ackrill points out, in making this sort of point Aristotle is hindered by the lack of an indefinite article in Greek.[6] (The introduction at this point of the classificatory entities leads to a remark about differentiae, to the effect that each is peculiar to its genus, which is perhaps intended to underline the close connection between a differentia and the species that it introduces into one, and only one, genus (1^b17–24).)

In the fourth chapter, we return to the ontological schema. In addition to the two divisions, of things that are said-of and things that are, we are now given a further list of the ten ways in which things said without combination can signify. This famous list of the ten categories is presented as a refinement of the division of things that are said, but it is also intended to effect an elaboration of

---

[5] See *Aristotle's* Categories *and* De Interpretatione, trans. Ackrill.   [6] Ibid.

the ontological schema, the division of things that are. However, since it is never made clear what the things said without combination are, facts about language are not used in the text to point us towards the identification of the entities that fall into the categories.[7] Nor is it made clear how the new tenfold division of reality is to be squared with the fourfold division that we have just examined.

What we can say is that the first category is clearly, on any interpretation, intended to be significantly different from the other nine. The category of substance corresponds, as we have seen, to those entities that are formally specified as never being in anything else. The other nine categories subdivide those entities that are in other things, namely in substances. So what we are really being told is that the things-that-can-be-in divide into nine sorts. As has often been remarked, the categories are a remarkably heterogeneous list and it is very unclear in what sense, if in any, they are meant to be exhaustive.[8] A popular and plausible way of accounting for the list is to take Aristotle as regarding it as corresponding to the nine sorts of non-definitional question that could be asked of any substance.[9]

The philosophical importance of the in relation is that it underlies affirmation, by which Aristotle means the production of a subject–predicate sentence, which involves the combination of items from more than one of the categories (2^a5–10). 'Inherence' is a term invented by later writers for the in relation, and it is by the doctrine of inherence that the various Eleatic and monistic paradoxes are to be refuted. Still greater importance attaches to the said-of relation, which can apply to any of the categories, but is most significant, as we have seen, in that of substance. The importance of the said-of relation, which is sometimes known as 'strong predication', is that it is in terms of the hierarchy that it generates that the crucial notion of definition can be made clear. This is illustrated by the subtle discussion of substance that occupies the whole of the fifth chapter of the *Categories*.

1.2.5. Species, Genera, and Definition (Chapter 5)

The fifth chapter opens with a clear statement that the category of primary substance, that which is neither said-of nor in, comprises ordinary particular individual items in the world of our experience, such as a particular man, Socrates perhaps, or Callias, and a particular horse. Secondary substance, by contrast, embraces both species and genera, which are (ultimately) all said-of particular primary substances (2^a11–18). This ontological arrangement is trenchantly

---

[7] See the discussions in Moravcsik (ed.), *Aristotle*, 125–35, mentioned above, and *Aristotle's* Categories *and* De Interpretatione, ed. Ackrill.

[8] See C. M. Gillespie, 'The Aristotelian Categories', in J. Barnes *et al.*, *Articles on Aristotle*, iii (London, 1975), 1–13.

[9] Moravcsik (ed.), *Aristotle*, 135–45.

anti-Platonic, asserting the fundamental existence of sensible particulars against that of general entities. The species and genera that classify individuals exist, but they are only secondary in the ontological scheme. We might say that individual entities are, in Strawson's phrase, basic particulars and that classificatory entities are dependent upon them for their existence. We are explicitly told later that species and genera could not exist without individuals (2^b6–7).

It is not, perhaps, obvious why when one predicates manhood of Callias one is invoking the said-of relation (strong predication) while when one predicates courage of him one is invoking the in relation (inherence). However, there is a real and important difference. The central idea is that the said-of hierarchy is definitional of the individual. If one asks what something is, which is to ask for its definition, then the only sort of informative answer that can be given is one that refers to its species. And if one asks what that is, then one must refer to the subgenus in which it is most immediately included, and so on up to the highest genus to which it can belong, which is that of the general category of substance. The full definition will involve the tracing of the entire tree, and the reason for this is that, as Aristotle points out, the said-of relation is not only transitive, as we have already seen, but also definitional, in the sense that not only the name of the said-of entity can be applied to that of which it is said but also the definition of it. So the individual man is brought within the general definition of animal. By contrast, in affirming a case of inherence, for instance in uttering 'Socrates is white', one is, according to Aristotle, predicating the name 'white' of Socrates but not its definition. To be Socrates is not, as we might say, to be whiteness (2^a19–33).

In this sense, then, even genera are definitional of individuals, but not as definitional as species. It is clearly more informative to say that some individual is a man or a horse than that it is an animal. Aristotle takes the greater informativeness of this answer to indicate that species are actually more substantial than genera (2^b8–22). (The notion of degree is not supposed to apply within a single level of the category of substance (3^b34–4^a9), but there is no reason why it should not do so between levels.) What is important is that species reveal the nature of the individuals in them, and it is this that makes them secondary substances rather than mere non-substantial qualifications (2^b28–37). Secondary substances also share with primary ones the property of being subjects of inherence. Just as particular non-substances exist by inherence in primary substances, so universal non-substances exist by inherence in secondary substances. There can, however, be no case of the latter that does not involve a case or cases of the former (2^b37–3^a6).

The other points that Aristotle makes about substance in the fifth chapter follow directly from these central considerations. It is evident, for instance, that no substance (not even secondary) can be in anything else, since to be in something is incompatible with being definitional of it (3^a8–21). It is also reasonable, though not strictly consistent, to include differentiae among things said-of, not in. Grammatically, differentiae belong in the category of quality, the first of the non-substantial categories, but the definition of a differentia, unlike that of a mere quality, does apply to the appropriate primary substance, and this is Aristotle's criterion for the said-of relationship (3^a22–7). For a similar reason, Aristotle is able to say that strong predication, when a secondary substance is used to define a primary one, involves synonymy, since individuals are picked out by their species name under the strict definition of the latter (3^a33–$^b9$). It is also intuitively coherent that it should be a distinctive mark of the category of substance that it cannot admit contrariety, though a substance can, of course, be the bearer of contrary properties (3^b24–4^a22). Aristotle spells out the way in which this feature makes substances in one way like sentences but in another way unlike them (4^a23–$^b20$).

The discussion of substance appropriately concentrates on the said-of relation, but Aristotle also makes a clarificatory remark about the in relation. He makes it clear that parts do not inhere in wholes, since they are in them but not *in* them (this is entirely in line with his original introduction of the in relation at 1^a24–5). (We might say that Aristotle is drawing the distinction here between a constituent and a property of something.) This is important in that it blocks the counter-intuitive consequence that parts turn out not to be substances (3^a29–32). There is also a discussion of the different ways in which the notion of thisness applies to primary and secondary substances (3^b10–23). Thisness is an important, but difficult, concept in Aristotle. It is not to be thought of as particularity, since species can also possess it, and it seems to be closer to our concept of determinacy, a property that belongs to anything that can be precisely defined.[10] As Ackrill points out,[11] Aristotle seeks in this passage to emphasize the secondary character of secondary substances but in doing so risks rendering their substantiality obscure.

The exposition in the first five chapters of the *Categories* is not always perspicuous, and there are both terminological and conceptual dissonances. However, they present a powerful, systematic, and comprehensive ontology, which we may suppose Aristotle to have evolved while still in the Academy (467–448 BC). Having thus discharged his first task, that of clarifying the uses of the verb 'to be', he was able to apply his ontological system to his real target, the solution of the Eleatic puzzles that were undermining the progress of natural science.

---

[10] M. L. Gill, *Aristotle on Substance* (Princeton, NJ, 1989), 31–4.
[11] *Aristotle's* Categories *and* De Interpretatione.

2. THE *PHYSICS*

2.1. The Defence of Change (Book 1)

It is in the *Physics* that the distinctions that are drawn in the *Categories* are first put to explanatory use. This work seeks to provide a foundation for the scientific explanation of nature, and the primary need that Aristotle faces is that of refuting the Eleatic claim that the apparent plurality and changeability of the world are an illusion.

The effect of the Eleatic attack on science, which Aristotle held to have been a real obstacle to progress, was to undermine confidence in the conceptual coherence of the notions of plurality and change (191^a24–33). The Eleatics claimed that change was impossible on the logical grounds that either any change involved a process from something to the same thing, in which case it was not really a change, or change from nothing at all to something, which would involve, in effect, creation from nothing, an idea which the Greeks consistently held to be absurd. Aristotle's achievement was to show that change was after all possible and that its explanation involved looking at the subject of change from different perspectives: from one perspective, there was a feature of the apparent change situation that involved a real change, but from the other it was a case rather of continuation. The analysis of change was intended to cover both cases in which the inherent properties of a substance change (alteration) and cases in which new substances come into existence (substantial generation). In the latter case, the analysis led to the treatment of primary substances, the ordinary objects around us in the world, as composites of underlying matter and imposed form. In the second book of the *Physics*, Aristotle considers such composites and the methodology of their scientific explanation. He distinguishes ordinary objects into artefacts and natural things, which he calls simply natures (*phuseis*). He is primarily interested in the latter, and he asks whether they are to be equated with, and explained by reference to, their form or their matter, or both.

In the first book, however, the target is Eleatic monism. The claim that all things are one and unchangeable is, Aristotle tells us, not a claim of physical science (184^b24–5), but it does raise a philosophical question (185^a19), which must be resolved before we proceed to the analysis of change. The resolution is provided in the second and third chapters of the first book.

2.1.1. The Role of Principles in Aristotle's System (1. 1)

Aristotle approaches the refutation of monism, however, by way of his introduction of a crucial notion that has not been present in the purely dialectical

writings. This is the notion of a first principle (*arkhē*) which it is the primary purpose of empirical science to discover. The term was inherited from Pre-Socratic
science, but Aristotle, characteristically, gives it a much wider and more abstract
use. The discovery of *arkhai* is the business of science, and this formulation represents Aristotle's distinctive solution to the 'paradox of inquiry' of the *Meno*.
How, the *Meno* had asked, can we inquire into what we already know (80^d)? The
answer given by Aristotle is that by inquiry we come to grasp the principles
underlying that with which we are already familiar. Thus is mere familiarity
converted into true scientific knowledge. This knowledge will, when it is complete, be susceptible of ordering in the way shown in the *Posterior Analytics*.
Another way to put the point about science's being the pursuit of first principles
is to say that in acquiring scientific knowledge we move from what is clear to us
to what is clear in itself, and this is in fact the formulation with which Aristotle
works in the first chapter of the first book of the *Physics* (184^{a}17–23).[12]

There is, however, an ambiguity in the Aristotelian notion of a principle. On
the one hand, the principles are regarded as being propositions that the mind
can come to grasp, but on the other they are regarded as concrete factors that
underlie the behaviour of natural things. Aristotle never clarifies which of these
two formulations of the concept he has primarily in mind, but he is able to
launch his discussion of the weaknesses of monism by posing the question how
many principles there are in the world. It is important to see that this question
is much more abstract than the traditional Pre-Socratic issue about how many
fundamental stuffs went into the creation of the world.[13] It is also a striking feature of Aristotle's discussion of science that principles are singled out for their
clarity rather than their generality. Indeed, Aristotle says obscurely at the end of
the first chapter of the *Physics*, we actually begin with what is more general and
move to what is more particular. This seems paradoxical until we remember
that the more general is also the more confused.[14]

2.1.2. The Refutation of Monism (1. 2–3)

The monistic thesis is, then, that there is only one principle and that this principle is unchanging in all respects. Aristotle begins by remarking, as we have
seen, that to adopt such a view is, right off, to deny the possibility of a science
of nature, so that monism is not strictly speaking a physical thesis at all. He justifies the claim that monism is not part of physics by appeal to the need for principles to be separate from what they explain (185^{a}3–4) and by the requirement
that the study of nature presuppose the possibility of change and thus, *a fortiori*,
of plurality (185^{a}12–14).

---

[12] Cf. *Metaphysics* 1013^{a}14–15, and Irwin, *Aristotle's First Principles*, 3–4.
[13] Cf. J. L. Ackrill, *Aristotle the Philosopher* (Oxford, 1981).
[14] See *Aristotle's* Physics Books I and II, trans. with notes by W. A. Charlton (Oxford, 1970).

His direct attack on monism consists of two stages. In the first (185ᵃ21–ᵇ26), he adopts the ontological standpoint that he has presented in the *Categories*, but, in the second (186ᵃ4–187ᵃ11), he argues from the sort of premises that would have been acceptable even to Parmenides and the other Eleatics.[15] Of the arguments based on Aristotelian assumptions, both make use of the notion of homonymy. The first argument turns on the homonymy of the verb 'to be' and the second on that of the concept of unity.

The first argument, or rather set of arguments (185ᵃ21–ᵇ5), makes the claim that Parmenides' position collapses once he is forced to make it clear in what way all things are one. If he wishes to assert that all things are some one thing in any non-substantial category, then, in addition to having to make clear to which item within the favoured category he is assimilating all things, he also has to deal with the problem that nothing in a non-substantial category can exist without the existence of something in the category of substance. Nor indeed can a substance exist without any inherent qualifications, so that even the postulation of a single substance will not save the position for the monist. The second set of arguments (185ᵇ5–26) exploits a similar homonymy in the concept of unity. Aristotle considers three ways in which a thing may form a unity. It may do so by being a continuum, but then it can clearly be divided and so is at least not conceptually a unity. More promisingly, it may be indivisible, but it can only be so if it is not extended, and extension is a property that even Parmenides wants to attribute to his unitary world. Thirdly, the unity of something may consist in its having a single essence, in the way, to use Aristotle's illustration, in which the wine and the grape have the same essence (185ᵇ8–9). However, any monistic thesis of this colour will end up in the same position as Heraclitus, with the difficulty that there can, as a result, be no discriminating knowledge of anything, presumably including even knowledge of the monistic thesis itself.

The authentically Aristotelian arguments against monism are bolstered by those based on Eleatic assumptions. The first argument (186ᵃ12–21) is directed against Melissus, whom Aristotle several times characterizes as being a less serious threat. Melissus makes two fallacious assumptions, first that what does not exist necessarily had no beginning in time, and secondly that what comes to exist must do so spatially and gradually come into existence across an area of space. Once these two fallacies are pointed out, his argument collapses. Parmenides, however, is a more serious opponent, and a more elaborate refutation is called for by his thesis (186ᵃ22–187ᵃ11). The first part of the argument (186ᵃ25–ᵇ14) is that even if we accept a unitary account of the verb 'to be', which, as we have seen, Aristotle is not prepared to do, then we can still only establish that being is, as it were, a unitary property, that there is only a single thing that something has to do to be. Even if this is so, then it would not at all

---

[15] See ibid.

follow that there is only a single thing that actually does this, that actually is. Further, the second part of the argument (186^{b}14–35) goes on to show that, for Parmenides to move, as he seeks to, from the singularity of existence to the singularity of existents, a premiss is required which is not only not forthcoming but could not in principle be supplied. This being so, the case for monism collapses.[16]

2.1.3. *Opposites and the Problem of Change (1. 4–6)*

Having refuted the suggestion that the world might have a single unchanging principle, Aristotle turns to consider the other possibilities. These are that the world has a single, but changing, principle and that it has a plurality of principles. The first view was that variously espoused by the Ionian monists, who held that the changes in the underlying substrate explained the diversity of things (187^{a}12–20). Aristotle himself actually holds a more sophisticated version of such a view, so that in reviewing his non-Eleatic predecessors in chapter 4 he concentrates on those thinkers who had postulated a diversity of principles, among whom the most important are Empedocles and Anaxagoras (187^{a}21–188^{a}18).

He then, in the fifth chapter, turns to the preparation of the ground for the posing of the main problem confronting those who are prepared to accept the plurality of the world but are still uncertain about how it is to be made the object of scientific study. This is the problem of the coherence of the concept of change. He begins the approach to this difficulty by establishing the need to postulate opposites among the principles of nature. The first paragraph of the fifth chapter (188^{a}19–32) is devoted to detailing the popularity of the claim that the principles are opposites. The rest gives Aristotle's own argument for accepting it.

He takes the empirical speculations of the monists and converts them into logical or dialectical ones. His key point is that change into any characteristic must not merely be from something other than that characteristic, but from its actual opposite (188^{a}33–^{b}26). This is a logical point. We do not speak of change to the red from the musical, but rather to the red from the not-red. The not-red might be musical as well, but this would be accidental from the point of view of the change in question. This might seem a completely pedantic remark—and Aristotle has often been mocked for making this sort of distinction—but, in fact, he is drawing attention to a crucial, and purely philosophical, point that the coherence and explanatory value of an account of a change is relative to the description of the changing items. (This is a special case of what philosophers of science call the 'intensionality of explanation'. Whether an account of any

---

[16] The argument of these difficult chapters is very fully discussed in *Aristotle's* Physics *Books I and II*, trans. Charlton.

process is to count as an explanation depends on the way in which it describes the aspects of that process.) By the end of the fifth chapter, he has established the ineliminability of opposites from among the principles, so laying the first stage of the foundations for his own resolution of the problem of change. The second stage is laid in the sixth chapter.

In the sixth chapter Aristotle considers the question whether, given that we can neither invoke a monistic interpretation of nature nor eliminate opposition from the principles, we should say, in the case of any particular change, that there are just the two principles of opposition, or also a third, or even some larger number. First, in an obscure paragraph (189ᵃ13–19), he denies the possibility of an indefinite number of principles. Then he argues that there cannot merely be the two principles of opposition—there is a strong case for supposing that something must underlie the exchange of opposites (189ᵃ20–ᵇ17). (Three reasons are given for this conclusion. The first is that otherwise opposites would have to act on one another (189ᵃ22–6), the second that no opposite is the substance of anything (189ᵃ29–32), and the third, closely connected, that no substance seems to have an opposite (189ᵃ32–4). Thus opposites cannot be the only principles, since they are necessarily the sort of things that apply to other items, namely primary substances.) Finally, and again obscurely (189ᵇ18–27), he rejects the supposition that there might just be a plurality of opposing principles.[17]

2.1.4. Aristotle's Solution (1. 7–9)

Aristotle has now shown that there is an intuitive case for supposing that the principles must be opposites and also one for supposing that there must be some third underlying principle. He must now show how, in a way, both these intuitions are correct, and in doing this he must resolve the puzzle posed by the Eleatics, that coming to be is impossible since it must either be from what already is, in which case it is not a coming-to-be, or from nothing, which is absurd. It is important to appreciate that Aristotle is the first thinker clearly to understand that this is a difficulty about our concept of change, to be resolved not by speculation about nature, in the style of the Pre-Socratics, but by philosophical clarification. It is also an original feature of his method that he seeks this clarification by attending to the expressions in ordinary language by which we describe change. He assumes that these reflect the structure of the world and that by scrutinizing them we will render that structure perspicuous.

[17] The structure of these chapters, especially the sixth, is clear, but many details are compressed and difficult. Consultation of *Aristotle's Physics Books I and II*, trans. Charlton, is recommended, and, for an excellent reconstruction of the whole argument, see S. Waterlow, *Nature, Change and Agency in Aristotle's Physics* (Oxford, 1982), ch. 1. Ackrill, *Aristotle the Philosopher*, ch. 3, is also useful.

He thus begins by assembling linguistic observations (189^b32–190^a12). If we take the case of a change by which a previously unmusical man becomes musical, then there are three ways in which this change can be described:

1. the unmusical becomes musical,
2. a man becomes musical,
3. an unmusical man becomes a musical man.

The terms 'unmusical', 'musical', and 'man' Aristotle calls simple, the terms 'musical man' and 'unmusical man' he calls complex. Now, the paradox about coming to be (becoming) will always arise unless we describe the change by the appropriate simple terms. For description 1 seems to present us with something coming to be out of nothing (musicality comes to be out of what is not musical and thus may as well be nothing for these purposes), while the complex description 3 only adds to 1 that the man remains a man, which is not a case of coming to be at all. Description 2, however, reveals that in this case, as in all cases, of change there is both something that remains and something that is replaced. As Aristotle puts it, the thing that remains is numerically single, but formally plural. The very same thing, the man, differs in description before and after the change (190^a12–22).

The example of the man becoming musical is an example of what Aristotle calls alteration, when a primary substance changes in regard to a quality or some item in one of the other categories. This is the sort of case in which a substance comes to be X. But there are also cases where substances simply come to be, where they, as we say, come into existence or are generated. Since Aristotle holds that it is only substances that can come to be in this way ($^a32$–6), this sort of change is usually called substantial generation. In the *Physics*, Aristotle explains substantial generation on precise analogy with alteration, but this, as we shall see, causes severe problems for his ontology. The main difference between generation and alteration concerns what persists through the change, the continuant. In the case of alteration, the continuant is unproblematically the primary substance that is undergoing the change. But in the case of generation, in which a primary substance is coming into existence, it is profoundly obscure what persists.

Aristotle elucidates this problem once more by scrutiny of ordinary language ($^a23$–31). In describing change, we often use the pronouns 'from' or 'out of' (*ek*). However, we only use this pronoun in some cases. We say that the man becomes musical from being unmusical but not that the musical comes to be out of the man. In this case, the 'thing-out-of-which' is replaced. But in other cases, it is the thing-out-of-which that survives. For instance, we talk of a statue coming to be out of bronze, and in this case the bronze is the continuant. It is such changes that are cases of substantial generation, since Aristotle would regard the statue as a primary substance. In these cases, then, the continuant is the thing-out-of-which, which is effectively Aristotle's most general term for matter. So we arrive at the first clear statement of the doctrine of immanent form, the doctrine that ordinary objects of our experience are composites of forms and underlying matter (190^{b}1–191^{a}22). This doctrine is often called 'hylomorphism' in modern discussions, from Aristotle's word for matter (*hulē*) and one of his words for form (*morphē*).[18]

Aristotle has provided, in the first book of the *Physics*, an ingenious solution to the difficulties in both concepts of change, and in the last two chapters he favourably contrasts his approach with that of the Pre-Socratics and of the Academy. However, there is a high price to be paid in the treatment of primary substances as composites which the analysis of generation requires. Aristotle came to doubt whether the same entities could be both primary and composite, and he attempts to resolve this problem, as we shall see, in the central books of the *Metaphysics*. The composite character of ordinary objects, especially natural objects such as plants and animals, also raised difficulties, however, for the methodology of science. On which of the two aspects of these entities should the scientist concentrate, or can he aspire to explain both? It is to this question and its ramifications that Aristotle devotes the second book of the *Physics*.

2.2. Scientific Explanation (Book 2)

2.2.1. *Natures and Science (2. 1–2)*

The arguments in the first book of the *Physics* have shown that it is possible to have genuine scientific understanding of a pluralistic world in a constant state of change. However, there remains the task of outlining the key concepts under which the explanation of the world will actually proceed. This task falls to the second book of the *Physics*, in which Aristotle presents his two central scientific concepts, those of *phusis* and *aition*, the meaning of both of which will emerge as we proceed.

The conventional translation of *phusis* is 'nature', which is connected with the Latin word for birth. This has the advantage of suggesting, as does the Greek term, that the character of anything is determined to some extent by what it is originated as. On the other hand, it is common to use the word 'nature' to refer, in English, to the totality of things, effectively as a synonym for 'the universe' or 'the world'. Aristotle does sometimes use the word in this sense, but what he has primarily in mind is something different, namely the indwelling character that belongs to particular items in our experience, the primary substances of the

---

[18] *Physics* 1. 7 is one of the most important chapters in the whole corpus, and it is impossible to do it full justice in the space available. There are many excellent discussions in the literature, and the reader is referred esp. to *Aristotle's Physics Books I and II*, trans. Charlton, Waterlow, *Nature, Change and Agency in Aristotle's Physics*, ch. 1, Ackrill, *Aristotle the Philosopher*, ch. 3, Graham, *Aristotle's Two Systems*, ch. 5, and J. Lear, *Aristotle: The Desire to Understand* (Cambridge, 1988), ch. 3.1–2.

Categories, and which shapes and guides the behaviour of that item. In this sense, *phusis* is the focal point of Aristotelian science, a science that is pluralistic in approach, assuming as given a broad diversity among natural things. It is a piece of irony that he should have used the term *phusika* to describe a science that is essentially the same as what we would call biology. What he provides in the second book is the conceptual underpinning of such a science.

The concept of a nature is introduced in a dialectical manner by being contrasted with that of an artefact (192^b9–32). Appeal is made to the ways in which we talk about both sorts of things in ordinary language. The crucial distinction is that a nature is the source of its own changes and developments, whereas with an artefact these are imposed from without. Aristotle stresses the point that the way in which a nature acts upon itself cannot be accidental. The possibility of accidental self-modification is illustrated by the case of a doctor who treats himself. He acts upon himself, but it is only an accidental matter that the same person is both agent and patient. He could equally easily have cured someone else, and someone else could equally easily have cured him. It is not in this sort of a way that natures are the patients of their own agencies. A nature cannot but act on itself, nor can anything else perform the appropriate actions on it. The appropriate source of change could never be external (192^b21–7). A nature is thus both an active and a passive thing, but it is essentially acted on only by itself and it is essentially active only on itself. The character of its action, apart from these two restrictions, is, however, very like that of an artefact in all other respects, and Aristotle is notoriously willing to illustrate points about the natural world by reference to the apparently simpler case of artefacts. He insists, in any case, that his formal introduction of the concept of a nature is not empty of empirical application, since there very evidently are items that satisfy the conceptual constraints. Someone discussing the behaviour of natures is not in the position of a blind man discussing colour (193^a2–9).

In the first chapter, Aristotle concentrates on connecting the notion of a nature, which he has just introduced, with the distinction between form and matter, which he has drawn in the previous book. He poses the question whether a thing's nature is rather given to it by its form or by its matter. It is a question that he treats in a characteristically dialectical manner, discussing the locutions in ordinary language by which we talk about both the formal and the material aspects of natures (193^a9–$^b22$). He accepts that there are many ways in which we describe the behaviour of things on the basis of their material properties, citing the point made by Antiphon that if a bed is put in the earth, then what eventually comes up is not a bed but its matter, wood. This would suggest that it is the matter which is really the nature of the bed ($^a12$–17). Aristotle, however, turns this point by saying that a man, or other natural organism, reproduces not his matter, flesh and bone, but another man. This strongly suggests that it is a man's form that is his nature ($^b8$–12).

In the second chapter, Aristotle is more concerned with methodology than with conceptual clarification. Given that formal properties of natures do fall within the ambit of physical science, he wishes to determine the distinction between this sort of inquiry and the purely formal inquiries of the mathematician, which is the question with which the chapter begins. The difference between the natural scientist and the mathematician is that the latter studies the mathematical properties of natural objects in abstraction from those objects, while the natural scientist studies them as properties, with explanatory relevance, of those natures. The abstraction that the mathematician thus performs is, however, wholly legitimate, since the properties that he studies can be studied in a way that makes no allowance for change. Those, on the other hand, such as adherents of the theory of Forms, who separate and abstract other, non-mathematical, aspects of natural substances are performing a quite improper separation, inasmuch as those properties cannot be genuinely understood in abstraction from the physical things to which they belong (193^b22–194^a12).

The claim that geometrical features are separable from the process of change, in a way that non-mathematical physical features are not, is one that turns on the special character of the latter, a character which is consistent with all that we have so far heard about the formal properties of natures. The formal properties of natures are linked conceptually with the entities in which they are realized. Aristotle is fond of illustrating this point in a rather idiosyncratic way. He considers, as in this passage, the ordinary notion of a *snub* (nose). A snub is not something that could be without being a nose. A snub is concavity *in a nose*—something quite different from either concavity in general or noses in general. It is therefore highly misleading to talk of the characteristic concavity of the snub in separation from the discussion of the whole snub; and this homely example illustrates the general difficulty of abstracting non-mathematical, change-sensitive characteristics from the objects of natural science, in just the way that the theory of Forms encourages. We cannot meaningfully study snubness without considering noses, whereas we can perfectly easily have a quite general and abstract theory of concavity.[19] The central problem of Platonism, as presumably still practised by many in the Academy, was to look on all the properties of natural things, especially their functional properties, as being essentially like their geometrical properties (194^a12–15).

The second half of the second chapter is devoted to those who make the contrary error of supposing that the formal aspects of a nature are irrelevant to its explanation. This is, of course, the position of the materialists, including the Atomists (although Aristotle does not have much to say in opposition to atomism at this stage of the *Physics*). He again uses the illustration of the snub. This must be explained in terms of noses, but cannot be explained exclusively in

---

[19] Cf. *Aristotle's* Physics *Books I and II*, trans. Charlton.

terms of noses. Similarly, although we cannot explain natural organisms without adverting to their material composition, yet we cannot hope to explain them exhaustively in terms of the latter. The two must be combined for the purposes of explanation. Aristotle begins his case against materialism by some informal arguments, such as those suggesting that explanation in theory should follow the path of medicine in practice (194^{a}21–7). He then moves on to the key point that a thing's organization can be explained in terms either of what is involved in making it or of what is involved in using it. In the case of natural organisms, only the latter style of explanation is possible—which suggests that it is their function that holds the key to their organization (194^{a}33–^{b}8). The chapter ends, accordingly, with the conclusion that the natural scientist must investigate both the matter and the form of natures, but that his primary interest will be in the latter (194^{b}10–15).

2.2.2. *The Varieties of Explanation (2. 3 and 7)*

In the central chapters of the second book Aristotle puts forward his theory of causal explanation, which is at the heart of his account of the scientific project. The principal account of causation takes place in chapters 3 and 7, which are punctuated by what is formally a digression on chance and luck in chapters 4 to 6. These chapters, however, in fact present material that is vital for the defence of teleological explanation with which the book ends. A teleological theory seeks to explain phenomena as effects of inherent or external purpose, and Aristotle is usually considered to be a leading advocate of such an approach.

The third chapter opens with the list of Aristotle's much discussed four *aitia* (194^{b}24–195^{a}3), and it is important to see how this connects with the discussion of the formal and material aspects of natures. Unfortunately, the traditional translation of *aition* as 'cause' is potentially misleading—and, no doubt, has often misled. A better translation would be 'explanatory factor', since the term covers all those things to which any event or process can be ascribed, anything in the light of which it can be said to make sense. Considered in this light, the four *aitia* are much less baffling. The first *aition* is the 'material cause', which explains why things are as they are in terms of the stuff of which they are made. For instance, if a chest can be burned, the reason for this is that it is made of wood, which is a combustible stuff. The second *aition* is the 'formal cause', which explains why something's taking on a particular organization is to be ascribed to the realization of its predetermined function. For instance, we might explain the growth of feet in an animal by saying that it is part of the form of that animal that it be able to walk. The third *aition* is that which corresponds to the source of a change or process. This is the cause that is closest to the modern notion of an 'efficient cause', but is still very different, as is shown by the example that a man can be considered the cause, in this sense, of a child by begetting it. The fourth *aition*, the 'final cause', is the most controversial, that in terms of the purpose for which something has been designed. It is unclear how this can apply to natural entities, but the most satisfactory way of treating the difficulty is to think of the fourth cause as being an invitation to look to the contribution that each part of an organism makes to the life of the organism as a whole. This is a perfectly reasonable and sober way to use the idea of indwelling purpose as a kind of regulatory guide-line for the special science of biology.[20]

It is characteristic of Aristotle to introduce lists, as we have already seen with the *Categories*, and these are prone to disguise the underlying nature of his thought behind an architectonic façade. This is very much the case with the doctrine of the four *aitia*. It is pointless to speculate in what sense Aristotle felt that the list that he had provided was exhaustive of all forms of scientific explanation and, if so, what this showed. It is more useful to try to make sense of the list in modern terms and to harmonize our interpretation with the doctrine of form and matter. This can be done if we take the foursome to reflect two underlying ways of explaining the world.[21] On the one hand we have a purely mechanical conception, that of a world entirely dominated by pure necessity, which is reflected in the first type of causation, the material. On the other hand, we have a world in which various levels of organization are constantly emerging, the full importance of which cannot be explained in a purely reductivist way. It is the point of introducing the formal and final *aitia* to insist on the explanatory autonomy of this dimension of the world. (We should perhaps say of the efficient *aition* that it hovers somewhat uneasily between these two styles of explanation.) Thus, underlying the fourfold division we find a more fundamental dichotomy between these two ways of explaining the world. This explanatory dichotomy, in turn, corresponds to the two aspects of a nature. So that the doctrine of the four *aitia*, so far from being a fresh start, should be seen as an amplification of the foregoing discussion of natures.

It is characteristic of Aristotle as a philosopher of science that, while not denying the importance of the mechanical level, he also insists on the ineliminability of the level of explanation which works in terms of embodied functional roles.

2.2.3. Purpose, Chance, and Necessity (2. 4–6 and 8–9)

It is in the light of these considerations that we should look on Aristotle's teleology. The defence of teleology in chapters 8 and 9 of the second book draws heavily on the subtle distinctions introduced in connection with the investigation of chance and luck. These in turn depend on the notion of accidental

---

[20] A defence of this construal of Aristotle's teleology is offered in W. Wieland, *Die aristotelische* Physik (Göttingen, 1970) and in the two chapters excerpted from it in Barnes *et al.* (eds.), *Articles on Aristotle*, i.

[21] *Aristotle's* Physics Books I and II, trans. Charlton, 114–20.

causation: something may be a cause or explanation of something else under one description but irrelevant to it under another. Aristotle would say that it is its proper cause under the appropriate description but only an accidental one under the inappropriate one. It is thus that a statue is made by a sculptor as its proper cause but only accidentally by Polyclitus (195ª32–ᵇ6). This is a quite general statement of the crucial insight that causal explanation is relative to a description.

He uses this insight to give his account of chance developments, which he divides into two kinds, luck and what he calls 'the automatic'. Both cases are ones in which something happens that might have been an intended outcome. For instance, if a stone falls in such a way that someone can sit on it, then that is a case of something's happening by chance which might also have been brought about by intentional effort on the part of some agent. What caused the stone to fall in that way was, in the proper sense, mere necessity, but from an accidental perspective it can be viewed as something that might have been done on purpose and so can be considered a matter of chance, in this case good chance (196ᵇ17–197ª8). Within the category of chance things, Aristotle also recognizes a subdivision of those that are lucky. It is the distinguishing feature of these that they happen to rational agents, who are, so to speak, in a position to regard them as lucky or otherwise. A characteristic example is that of a man who goes into the market for some other purpose and happens to meet there a debtor from whom he collects his money. He might have gone for that purpose, but in fact he did not. In this sort of way, Aristotle hopes that our dialectical intuitions about luck and chance can be preserved. Above all, he wants to show that the notion of chance is parasitic on that of cause (ᵇ32–ª5).

It is this same notion of the accidental character of chance occurrences that Aristotle uses, in the eighth chapter, to establish the rationality of teleological explanations of the more complicated aspects of nature. He presents a classic argument against those who would seek to offer an exhaustively mechanistic account of all natural processes (198ᵇ17–199ᵇ34).[22] He first states such an account, in which the beneficial character of such things as the organic parts of animals are dismissed as being no more really purposive than the fall of rain in the spring which helps crops to grow (198ᵇ17–32). In the case of animal parts, at any rate, this cannot be the appropriate explanation. He gives several reasons for this conclusion, but the most important is the argument from regularity. He starts with the assumption that the parts of animals are, as a matter of fact, beneficial to them. They are thus among those things that are beneficial. This class of things divides into those that are purposive and those that are a matter of chance, as we have seen. If, then, with the mechanists, we suppose that, in the case of the parts of animals, their being beneficial is a matter of chance, which

---

[22] See esp. the article by J. M. Cooper, 'Hypothetical Necessity and Natural Teleology', in A. Gotthelf and J. G. Lennox (eds.), *Philosophical Issues in Aristotle's Biology* (Cambridge, 1987).

is to say that their beneficiality is unrelated to their proper cause, then we have to accept that they must comply with something that we have seen to be a crucial element in all chance occurrences, namely that they be exceptional. Chance events are by definition exceptional. The fortuitous cannot be the norm. But, of course, it is not the case that the beneficiality of animal parts to their possessors is in any sense exceptional. Rather, it is one of the most striking regularities in nature. Therefore it cannot be the case that these parts are, as the mechanists allege, a matter of chance (198ᵇ33–199ᵃ8).

This is usually thought to be Aristotle's strongest argument against a non-teleological biology. It is, however, bolstered by others, of which the most important are those which exploit the parallels between natural organisms and artefacts, which are a central feature of Aristotle's whole scheme of explanation. Given the utility of both artefacts and the parts of organisms, it is reasonable to assume that they are produced in analogous ways, which requires us to talk in at least some sense of the purposiveness of the organs (199ᵃ8–12). Aristotle also has a fascinating argument against the assumption that purposiveness requires deliberation and therefore a kind of mental state (199ᵃ20–33). He shows an awareness that this is not so, even though it would be a mistake to take him as saying merely that we should adopt a teleological stance towards natural organisms by treating them *as though* they were the products of purposive processes. Such a pragmatic and heuristic view of scientific explanation is much too modern for Aristotle, who certainly believes that the formal and final causes are as much real features of nature as are the material and efficient ones.[23]

Indeed, in the final chapter of the second book, he seeks to show that, far from having to give up the notion of indwelling form in favour of that of blind natural necessity, we can retain the notion of form and reshape that of necessity in the light of it. It is the notion of necessity that is secondary to talk of form, not the other way round (199ᵇ34–200ᵃ31). The reason for this is that necessity is always something that has to be assessed in terms of the purpose for which a thing is to be used or the function that it is intended to serve. Just as we cannot say what matter is without specifying in relation to what we are asking the question, so we cannot say what necessity is in some sort of absolute way in abstraction from any particular purpose which that thing is supposed to subserve. Necessity, at least in so far as it affects the biological sciences, is always conditional, or, as Aristotle puts it, hypothetical. Questions about necessity are always of the form of a question why a saw has to be made of iron. It must be of iron, because (formal cause) only so can it carry out its function of cutting wood. The necessity is clearly determined by the function. Were the function of a saw quite different, then the necessity would cease to apply to it. Aristotle is, of course, aware that iron's being itself hard is a matter of unconditioned

---

[23] But see Wieland, *Die aristotelische* Physik, for the contrary view.

material necessity, but his point is that this is not the sort of necessity that needs to be invoked in science, that it is not an explanatory necessity. If we wish to use the notion of necessity to explain, then we must do so in a hypothetical way. We must show, for instance, how it is that, given the function that something has to serve and given the material that it is made from, it must be arranged in the way in which it is (200^{a}32–^{b}9).

The achievement of the first two books of the *Physics* is to establish the logical incoherence of any kind of absolute monism and the logical coherence of the conventional concept of change on which a natural science must be built, as well as introducing the central concepts of such a science, namely those of nature and *aition*. On the question whether forms or matter are the proper object of science, we have seen that there is a deep ambivalence running through the argument in the second book, which is apparent in both discussions. Aristotle leaves open two questions, which are really two aspects of the same problem: Is the nature of a substance given to it by its form or its matter? And is a substance to be explained in terms of its material or of its formal properties? His answer in the second book, that natures must be explained in both material and formal ways, is an uneasy compromise. In many ways, the logic of his position is that nature is really form and that the non-material modes of explanation are the philosophically and scientifically more basic, but he is reluctant to abandon matter entirely. The reason for this is that he is rightly aware that, if he now claimed that a thing's *nature* was given to it entirely by its formal *and thus general* properties and that it was in terms of these that it was to be explained, then he would endanger the ontology of the *Categories*, with its ascription of priority to particulars. Given that it has emerged that the fundamental particulars of the early metaphysics are in fact composites of matter and form, and therefore fundamentally divided entities, their status as ontologically basic entities is seriously compromised. Aristotle is not prepared to bite this bullet in the *Physics*, but it develops into the central problem of his later metaphysical programme—how to reconcile the scientific priority of formal explanation with the intuitive pull of common-sense ontological particularism?

3. THE *METAPHYSICS*

3.1. The Solution of Zeta: Species as Form

The problems bequeathed by the *Physics* are taken up in the *Metaphysics*. The traditional explanation of the title of this work is that it is the treatise that came after (*meta*) the *Physics* in the order of Aristotle's writings, but a more reasonable way to take the traditional story might be to regard the *Metaphysics* as coming after the *Physics* in the sense of being primarily addressed to the questions that the *Physics* raises but leaves unanswered. It is, in a sense, the philosophical sequel to the *Physics*. At least this can be said of its central four books, vii–x, or, as they are often known, Zeta, Eta, Theta, and Iota. The work as a whole is, on any construal, a compilation of treatises rather than a single one. By common consent, however, the most important group is that formed by Zeta–Iota, in which the central problems of ontology are addressed and a position is defended that seems to contradict the conclusions reached in the *Categories*. This, however, is modified in Eta to one more conformable with the early doctrine, in a way made possible by the introduction of conceptual refinements that are made more explicit in book Theta.

3.1.1. The Problem of Substance (Zeta 1–3)

The first chapter of Zeta clearly tells us that the central problem of metaphysics is that of substance. This is an important revision and clarification of the traditional metaphysical problem. Early philosophers had persistently asked 'What is being?' (*ti to on*), but, freed from confusion about the complexity of being, we can see that the question that they were really trying to ask was 'What is substance?' (*tis h-e ousia*). If we could get clear about substance, then all the other aspects of metaphysics would fall into place, and we would know what the world really contains (1028^{b}3–8). We are given a brief summary of the arguments for thinking that all other modes of being are dependent on substance and that substance has three types of priority, namely definitional, epistemic, and temporal (28^{a}31–^{b}3). In the second chapter, as usual in Aristotle, the received opinions of other philosophers, what Aristotle calls the *endoxa*, are reviewed and various candidates for substantial status are examined. The most popular candidates are the sensible substances, which include both animals and their parts, and the simple substances, such as the elements (28^{b}8–16). There are, however, some thinkers who hold that there are also non-sensible substances, such as mathematical objects and separable (i.e. Platonic) Forms (28^{b}16–26). The inquiry must, therefore, clarify which of these claims, if any, is justified.

The real work begins in the third chapter. If we are to decide what things are substances, we must have some criterion of substantiality. There are, we are told, four candidate criteria for substantiality: subject, essence, universal, and genus (28^{b}32–7). In fact, in Zeta, the universal and genus are taken together and effectively equated with separable, Platonic Forms, so that three criteria are discussed, subjecthood (chapter 3), essence (chapters 4–12), and the universal (chapters 13–16).

The second half of the third chapter provides a brisk rejection of the pure subject criterion. If substance is that which underlies all other properties, the ultimate bearer of properties, then it in itself will have to be wholly without characteristics. This will in turn mean that it is unknowable, so that the metaphysical grounding of the whole world will be necessarily beyond our understanding (29ᵃ7–26). This Aristotle regarded as a *reductio ad absurdum*. It simply cannot be the case that we cannot know the ontologically basic particulars. We must therefore either reject or amend the subject criterion. (It is in rejecting what we might call the naïve subject criterion for substance that the discussion in Zeta most obviously departs from the perspective of the *Categories*, in which particulars are primary substances precisely because they are always subjects in this sense.)

What is more, Aristotle has, he thinks, the explanation of what has gone wrong. The subject criterion, unamended, fails to contain the crucial notion of 'thisness'. Thisness is something that featureless matter cannot have, so that a subject which also has thisness may, after all, turn out to be an intelligible substance. Even, however, if we supplement the subject criterion with the requirement of thisness, it is still left open what things might qualify to have it. Even matter, appropriately conceived, might have the necessary thisness.²⁴ However, the discussion in the next chapter turns to consider the merits of form as substance, and does so at the same time as considering the second candidate criterion, that of essence.

It is clearly the position of Zeta 3, then, that the naïve subject criterion of the *Categories* (being never either in or said of) must now be rejected. Aristotle now wants to stress two important and closely related constraints on subjecthood: separation and thisness (29ᵇ27–9).²⁵ Unfortunately, he never makes clear what he here means by these two crucial notions, nor how their application affects the claims to substantiality of the composite particulars introduced by the *Physics* or their constituents, matter and form. Two items are separate spatially if they occur apart from one another, ontologically if they do not depend on each other for their existence, and conceptually if they can be defined without reference one to another. And an item constitutes a this (*tode ti*) either by being a particular individual or by having a certain determinateness, such that it is always clear whether that item is present.²⁶ Now on none of these readings do either of these constraints rule out the claims of any of the three physical candidates, matter, form, and the composite, to be substance. The conception of matter under which it might be separate and a this is that of ordinary matter such as bronze, not that of the completely featureless ultimate stuff that has just been rejected as a candidate for substantiality. The composite seems to satisfy the criteria of sub-

---

²⁴ For the whole discussion of the subject criterion and especially for the notions of thisness and, closely connected, separation, see Gill, *Aristotle on Substance*, ch. 1.

²⁵ Cf. *Categories* 3ᵇ10–23. The translation in *The Complete Works of Aristotle*, ed. J. Barnes (Princeton, NJ, 1984), also included in *A New Aristotle Reader*, ed. J. L. Ackrill (Oxford, 1987), for the term that I translate as 'thisness' is 'individuality'.

²⁶ For a full discussion of the subject criterion, thisness, and separation, see Gill, *Aristotle on Substance*, ch. 1, and *Aristotle:* Metaphysics *Books Zeta and Eta*, trans. with notes by D. Bostock (Oxford, 1994).

jecthood, separation and thisness, but it is ruled out because it is now known not to be a mere subject since it is posterior to its components, form and matter. Form is not excluded by the subject criterion from being substance, but it is highly problematic how the Aristotelian notion of form meets the constraints of separation and thisness, as the subsequent discussion discovers.

3.1.2. *Definition and Essence (Zeta 4–6)*

We do not, however, at the start of Zeta 4 pass to a discussion of the separation and thisness of form. Rather, chapters 4–6 constitute the initial investigation of the essence criterion. As we shall see, the notion of essence is central to the position adopted in Zeta. However, Aristotle has no simple abstract noun for this notion. Rather he uses the obscure phrase *ti en einai*, literally 'what it was to be'. Chapter 4 opens by introducing this notion, in a highly compressed style which is by no means easy to follow. We must first dialectically clarify the notion of essence and then see what light it throws on substantiality (29^b12–13). Essence, then, is something which a thing is said to be in virtue of itself, its *per se* being. So, to use Aristotle's example, a man cannot be essentially musical, since it cannot be just in virtue of his being what he is, a man, that he is musical (29^b13–15). This much might seem straightforward, but Aristotle then goes on to insist, obscurely, that essence is not even all of that which a thing is *per se*. The difficult sentence at 29^b16–18 must be taken[27] to be about the essence of whiteness, not that of surface. The point is that, even though whiteness must always be realized in some surface so that surface can be called the proper subject of whiteness, nevertheless surface is not part of the essence of whiteness. Whiteness is in a surface *per se*, but not essentially. We might distinguish accidental, *per se* properties as follows: if I am told just that something is a man, then I have no idea whether it possesses the accidental property of musicality, whereas if I am told that something is an instance of whiteness then I know that it must have the *per se* property of being realized in a surface, but my mere knowledge of that does not mean that I grasp the essence of whiteness as opposed to any other colour, that I know what it is to be white. So, as Aristotle puts it, being a surface is not being white (29^b17). For the same reason, 'white surface' cannot figure in the formula of the essence of whiteness, since this formula is not allowed to make reference to anything beyond that of which it gives the essence (29^b18–20). (It will, indeed, turn out that it is the definition that gives the formula of the essence, but Aristotle is refraining from making that connection at this point.)[28]

---

[27] See Gill, *Aristotle on Substance*, 116–20, and M. Frede and G. Patzig, *Aristoteles: Metaphysik Z* (Munich, 1988).

[28] Unfortunately, not all scholars accept that it is the essence of whiteness rather than of surface that is here being discussed, and the translation in *The Complete Works of Aristotle*, trans. Barnes (and *A New Aristotle Reader*,

An example of the right sort of formula of the essence would be a scientific theory which said that it is of the essence of white to be smooth ($29^{b}20-1$). Now whiteness is an item in the category of quality, not in that of substance, but the comparable point about a substance is that, although a man, say, is realized in flesh and bones *per se*, he is not realized in them essentially. It is paradoxical that Aristotle should choose to illustrate the notion of essence in a category other than substance, given that he holds that only substances really have essences in the strictest sense, but he presumably thinks that the idea of essence can be more easily conveyed in terms of a quality than of a substance.

We have so far concentrated on the central case of a substantial essence, such as that of man, but it is a legitimate question whether the notion of essence can be extended more widely, both to cover items in the other categories and to cover items with elements of more than one category, usually known as 'cross-categorial compounds'. Strangely, Aristotle discusses the latter ($29^{b}22-30^{a}18$) before the former ($30^{a}18-^{b}13$). He is in fact ready to allow that items in the other categories can be defined, though only in a secondary way. He is, however, not prepared to countenance the definition of, and ascription of essence to, cross-categorial compounds. He considers the fact that such compounds often have a single term. We might think of a case like 'bachelor', which means an unmarried man, but Aristotle in fact gives an artificial example. Suppose that we assign to some arbitrary word, say 'cloak', the meaning 'white man'. Then the question arises whether 'cloak' in this sense is definable and has an essence. Aristotle wishes to return a negative answer to this question on the grounds that 'cloak' cannot have an essence, since it lacks the necessary thisness, which is in fact confined to the category of substance. This reason for denying the essentiality of cross-categorial compounds would seem to be in tension with the ascription to items of the non-substantial categories of a kind of secondary essentiality in the second half of the present chapter, but the intuitive point is that a thing like 'cloak' is not really a single thing—it is a combination of a really single thing and a property, and it could still be the thing that it is if it lost the property in question ($29^{b}26-30^{a}6$).[29]

Aristotle is now in a position to add a further requirement for a thing's having an essence. To have an essence a thing must indeed be strictly definable, but we now see more clearly that there are many items of which an account, but not a strict definition, can be given. Anything, then, which is strictly definable and so can have an essence must also be primary, in the *Categories* sense of not being said of anything ($30^{a}7-11$). And the only things that actually meet this

---

ed. Ackrill) only makes sense in terms of the latter interpretation. More helpful versions can be found in Gill, *Aristotle on Substance*, 117–18, and *Aristotle: Metaphysics Books Zeta and Eta*, trans. Bostock.

[29] The structure of this paragraph is much more obscure and complex than this intuitive summary suggests. Anyone wishing to grapple with it must consult the reconstruction in *Aristotle: Metaphysics Books Zeta and Eta*, trans. Bostock.

requirement are species, which are now proclaimed to be the unique possessors of substantiality (30ª11–18). The details of this position are obscure, but the intuitive idea is that only species have all their properties essentially. Any individual member will have some of its properties accidentally, so that there will be more to the account of it than its definition. It will exceed its essence. This passage is crucial for establishing that only species have essence and thus substance (the doctrine of special substance), but it rests on two premises that are, to say the least, underdefended. The first is that only primary things (and thus not compounds of any sort) are strictly definable, the second that species are the only examples of such primary things.

In the last part of the chapter (ª18–ᵇ6), Aristotle allows essence in a non-strict way to the other categories, reminding us of the way in which they are said to be by homonymy with substance. His remarks on meaning at this point clearly show how he is thinking in terms of what Owen has called 'focal meaning'.[30] The chapter ends by stressing the importance of the unity of essence, which is similar to the requirement of thisness (30ᵇ6–13). The problem of the unity of essence is one of the central themes of chapters 10–12.

In chapter 5, Aristotle turns to another difficulty for his formal theory of definition. We have seen that he rejects the possibility of defining cross-categorial compounds, but there remains the task of dealing with what are usually called 'coupled terms'. These are terms that involve items from more than one category, but in a way that seems to make them more intimately connected than is the case with compounds. The distinguishing feature of the coupled term is that the qualification is one that can only be used of the thing in question. For instance, as we have seen, white man is not something that is capable of definition, because it is perfectly possible for things to be white without any men being so. On the other hand, although an animal does not have to be female to be an animal, only animals can be female, so that the connection between female and animal is somehow closer than that between white and man. We can say that animal is the proper subject of female while man is not the proper subject of white. Aristotle's paradigm example of a coupled term is snub nose. Nose is the proper subject of snub. So are such terms as snub or female susceptible of definition? Aristotle wants to insist that if this is the case it can only be so in a secondary way, as with the definitions of the non-substantial categories (ᵇ14–27). Coupled terms, like cross-categorial compounds, can only be given an account with an addition, as Aristotle puts it, an account that makes reference to something other than themselves and cannot thus be a strict definition.

The impossibility of strictly ascribing essence to coupled terms is also suggested by the use of an infinite regress. If the snub were to have a definition,

---

[30] G. E. L. Owen, 'Logic and Metaphysics in Some Earlier Works of Aristotle', in Barnes *et al.* (eds.), *Articles on Aristotle*, iii.

then it would presumably have to be 'concave nose', but then there would already be a difficulty in that a snub nose would be a concave nose nose. If one then, further, wants to say that a snub thing is a snub nose, then one has to say that a snub nose is a snub nose nose and that a snub nose nose is a snub nose nose nose, and so on.[31] For Aristotle, this shows that snub itself is not definable and therefore does not have an essence ([b]27–34). The importance of this is that, as will later appear, ordinary composites of form and matter, particular individual species members, will turn out to be ontologically in the same position as snubs. The snub is, as it were, a dialectical place-holder for the sorts of entity in science whose compositional nature denies them the possibility of being defined.

Aristotle ends the chapter by restating the point that the concepts of definition and essence have double applications. In their strict use, they apply only to substances, but they can loosely be applied also to things in the other categories and even to coupled terms, the account of which involves addition. There cannot, however, even in the loose sense, be a definition of a cross-categorial complex. Thus the chapter succeeds in reinforcing the conclusion of its predecessor that only species can truly be defined (31^a1–14).

The essentiality of species is again approached at the start of chapter 6, this time by the inquiry whether there are things that are identical with their essences. We have in fact already seen that there are such things and that the only ones of which we have certain knowledge are species. So this discussion will, once again, assert the claims of species to be substances, if, that is, the essence criterion for substance is upheld. It is, however, allowed that, if there were Platonic Forms, then these would also have to coincide with their essence. Unless they did so, neither could there be participation in them by individual instances nor could they be knowable, on the plausible assumption that to know something is to know its essence. The fact, of course, that if there were Forms, then their essence would have to coincide with them is not something that can be used to establish that there are in fact any such things (31^a15–$^b11$).

There is also a review of what has been said about the secondary senses of essence and how this connects with the question whether things coincide with their own essences (31^b22–8). It turns out that with accidental characteristics, such as whiteness in a man, the characteristic is in one way identical with its essence and in another not (31^b27–8). It is also the case that the account of the thing and of its essence will always coincide, so that there can be no question of essences of essences, nor can we draw a sophistical divide between Socrates and to-be-Socrates and ask whether their essences coincide. Thus by the end of the chapter, Aristotle has told us the ways in which essences are to be identified with their bearers and those in which they are not (32^a6–11).

---

[31] See *Aristotle*, Metaphysics *Books Zeta and Eta*, trans. Bostock.

The discussion in these chapters is obscure and incomplete, but the central arguments are clear and crucial for the whole metaphysical position of Zeta. The notion of essence, which has already been claimed to be a possible criterion of substantiality, is dialectically examined and found to coincide with those *per se* properties of a thing that are caught by its definition. We are then told that only primary things, which are substances by the modified subjecthood criterion, can be strictly defined, though items in the other categories can be defined and thus have essences in a looser manner of speech. Cross-categorial compounds are completely indefinable, but coupled terms can, it seems, be loosely defined. It thus turns out that the only items that can both be strictly defined and be subjects with the necessary separability and thisness are species, and their claim to be the baseline substances is reinforced by the argument that a genuine substance will be identical with the thing of which it is the substance. The substance of the species man, for instance, just is the species man, or perhaps its formal aspect, whereas the substance of any individual man, such as Socrates, always falls short of being his whole nature, since he will have some non-substantial, because non-essential, characteristics.

3.1.3. Substantial Form (Zeta 7–9)

The discussion of the essence criterion, which has concluded that essence is indeed the criterion for substance and that by this criterion species turn out to be substances, has been dialectical in character. The substantiality of species is now approached from a scientific angle, in terms, that is, of the substantiality of form, on which the following three chapters (7–9) constitute in effect a separate treatise, which, however, is appropriately inserted at this point.[32] The discussion of form as substance is, in a sense, the scientific version of the discussion of species as substance. Aristotle uses the same word, *eidos*, for both form and species, and he similarly runs together the claims to substantiality (which he rejects) of the dialectical concept of a universal and the scientific concept of a genus. After this, there follows a purely philosophical discussion of the most important questions arising out of the theory of definition, namely those of the unity of the definition and of the relative priority of parts and whole (chapters 10–12).

Chapter 7 begins with a recapitulation of the general features of all natural and artificial changes more or less as they are presented in the *Physics*. In all cases, there is that out of which the change occurs, the matter, that by which the change is produced, the formal cause, and that which comes to be, the composite of form and matter. The thing that thus comes to be is also known as

---

[32] See the discussion of chapters 7–9 by S. Mansion, 'The Ontological Composition of Sensible Substances in Aristotle (*Metaphysics* VII. 7–9)', in Barnes *et al.* (eds.), *Articles on Aristotle*, iii. The whole structure of Zeta is also thoroughly investigated in Felix Grayef, *Aristotle and his School* (London, 1974).

nature, but so, in a manner reminiscent of the doctrine of the *Physics*, are both the matter and the form. In the case of artefacts, the form is in the mind of the operator, be he doctor, sculptor, or whatever, whereas in the case of natural changes the formal cause is within the seed of the generating animal (32ª11–33ª6). As for the matter, it continues to be in one way and in another does not. Mention of it must be made in any account of the composite, but in ordinary language we refer to the composite's material in a way which suggests that it is not simply its usual self so long as it is participating in the composite. This shows that the primary substance of the composite is its form and not its matter, and this is entirely in harmony with the dialectical conclusions reached in the preceding section (33ª6–23).

In chapter 8, Aristotle draws on the model of change that he has reviewed in order to establish the point that form is never the product of a process. Bringing things to be, in either of the two possible ways, is a case of bringing a form into a matter (33ª30–4). So, for instance, we might bring the form of sphericality into the matter of bronze and thus produce a bronze sphere. What we have produced would be the bronze sphere, the composite of form and matter, and not either the bronze itself or the sphere (33ᵇ1–10). The difference between the two uncreated ingredients is that the matter might have been itself the product of some antecedent creation—in the case of bronze, it too must at some point have been made out of earth—whereas this can never be the case with the form. There can necessarily never be a case of making a form. For, Aristotle argues, if we were to make a form, it would have to be in the same way in which we make a composite, so that we would have to be able to speak of both the matter and the form of the form. It is doubtful whether this is coherent at all, but even if it is, it very obviously threatens us with a regress, since at each stage there would have to be some prior production of form for the production itself to occur. So forms can never be products, and this also points to their status as primary substances (33ᵇ16–19).

In the second half of the chapter, Aristotle asks whether in the light of the foregoing analysis we have any need to postulate separate Forms (33ᵇ20–34ª9). He concludes, in line with his general doctrine, that we do not, and that doing so is not explanatory of the actual process of change. For the formal cause to be operative it must not be remotely located in some Platonic heaven but be immanent in the immediate creator, whether by art or reproduction, of the new bearer of the form (33ᵇ20–9). Thus we are reminded that the substantiality of form does not require its separability, whereas its separability would preclude its causal efficacy.

Chapter 9 is an appendage to the inserted treatise on immanent form. Aristotle begins by addressing the puzzle of why it is that some things can be produced either by art or by chance while others cannot (34ª9–22). The explanation lies in the notion of accidental causality, which has already been discussed in the *Physics*. The general conclusion is that, with the exception of chance cases, the relation between the cause and the effect is an internal one—causal necessity is relative to a description of the process in question. This provides another perspective on the fundamental causal and metaphysical role of form. All production requires the potential pre-existence of the form to be realized, as the form of man is in the seed, but substantial forms themselves cannot be produced, as we have seen, and neither, as we are now told, can the forms in any of the other categories (34^b8–19).

The whole section—presumably, as we have said, a separate treatise that has been inserted at this point—is intended to give us scientific grounds for taking the substantiality of form seriously. That substantiality has first been posited on the strength of dialectical considerations connected with the assessment of the essence criterion, and it is characteristic of Aristotle's maturity to seek to bolster these with an account of the operation of form in the natural world. The scientific doctrine of immanent form seems to fit well with the dialectical doctrine of special substance. At this point, therefore, of the discussion, Aristotle appears to have taken up a position diametrically opposed to that which he adopted in the *Categories*, and this impression is not diminished by the rest of Zeta, which consists of two things, a philosophical defence of the coherence of the notions of definition and essence and a polemical attack on the postulation of separable Forms.

Despite the fact that it is strongly supported by both dialectical and scientific considerations, many scholars have found the doctrine of special substance problematic. In fact, it represents a compromise between the naïve ontology of the *Categories* and the extreme Platonism of the theory of Forms. Its intuitive appeal rests on the notion that what underlie the patterns that we observe in the world are not mere particulars which cannot be fully explained and understood but particular kinds. A man, for instance, is not a metaphysically fundamental thing but part of the species man, which is fundamental. The accidental properties of the individual man, moreover, are also accidental properties of the species. It is the species, basic kinds, that form the fundamental furniture of the world and account for the systematic regularity of what appears. The species can themselves be grouped into larger kinds in the light of shared characteristics, but these kinds are classificatory entities, metaphysically posterior to the species that they include. Even if Aristotle eventually reverts to an ontology of particulars, the power and attraction of the doctrine of special substance is not to be denied.

3.1.4. The Philosophy of Definition (Zeta 10–12)

Chapters 4–6 have given us a formal theory of definition, in the light of which we are to conclude that essence is indeed the key to substance and that species are clearly the primary substances. Chapters 7–9 have reinforced this conclusion by pointing to the special role of immanent forms in natural and artificial production. The central questions posed in the first and third chapters would therefore seem to have been answered. There remain, however, certain profound problems about the whole notion of definition and essence, and these Aristotle tackles in the very difficult chapters 10–12, which should be regarded as the first sustained discussion in philosophical logic.

It is impossible even to summarize this discussion in the available space. Aristotle certainly holds that the logical problems connected with definition can be solved, so that the doctrine of special substance can be saved. The treatment of definition thus amounts to an exercise in 'logical hygiene', whereas the intuitive philosophical motivations for the doctrine of special substance are presented dialectically in chapters 4–6 and scientifically in chapters 7–9. Thus the appeal and flavour of the doctrine can be appreciated without close consideration of the logical problems of definition.[33]

3.2. The Refutation of Platonism and the Restoration of Particulars

3.2.1. The Rejection of Universal Substance (Zeta 13–16)

So far, Aristotle has been concerned to show that the crucial determinant of substantiality is essence and that, if it is adopted, species turns out to be substance. He has thus completed his review of the first two criteria of substantiality, and he now considers the last two of the four candidates, which are in effect run together. The ontological status of the universal, the Platonic detached Form, and the genus are the same, and they are all now shown by a series of arguments not to be substance.

The first set of arguments are presented in Zeta, chapter 13. The first of these shows that if the universal were substance, then it would have to coincide with either all or none of its instances. It would be absurd to suppose that it was somehow closer to someone than any other of its instantiations (38^b8–14). The point is also taken over from the *Categories*, that the universal is always the predicate and never the subject term (38^b15–16). It is then stressed that if there were universal substances, then they would both have and not have identity with their instances (38^b17–33). In general, the universal is always what Aristotle calls a *toionde*, a such-and-such, and never a *tode*, a this (38^b34–39^a2). These considerations are bolstered by the observation that substance is always actually, though not potentially, indivisible (39^a3–14). The chapter ends with an aporia on the possibility of definition given the monadic nature of substance (39^a14–22). A resolution of this is promised but not provided in our text. The

---

[33] Those interested are strongly advised to begin with the extensive discussion of these chapters in *Aristotle: Metaphysics Books Zeta and Eta*, trans. Bostock.

main thrust of the chapter is to reject the claim of universals (tacitly equated with separable Forms) to be substance. Since there is a clear sense in which species could be considered universal rather than particular entities, there is an evident tension with Aristotle's own position.[34]

Unfortunately, Aristotle's arguments against universal or general substance seem to work equally well against the notion of special substance. He does not really succeed in this chapter in spelling out within his own conceptual framework how it is that Socrates and Callias have the same substance, while a man and a horse do not. It is arguable that the problem stems from his reliance on dialectic at this point rather than on scientific reasoning.

In chapter 14, various other absurd consequences of postulating really existent separate Forms are introduced. These are no doubt for the most part commonplaces of the Lyceum. Typical of them is the point that, if there were separable Forms, then there would be an absurd abundance of substances within a single entity, such as a man. There would be Forms corresponding to each of his parts and therefore each one would have to be a substance. This would also have the consequence that he would be a different thing from his parts (39^a24–$^b19$). In chapter 15, the further point is made that separable Forms would also fall foul of the ban on individual substances, since they too, if genuinely separable, would be individual entities. This would have the consequence that they would be unknowable, which is clearly an absurdity for a Platonic Form, which is literally nothing if it is not knowable (39^b20–40^a22). (There is also an interesting subsidiary discussion of the status of species with only one member, such as the species of the sun or the moon. Aristotle shows that in such cases it is still the species and not the individual that is the substance (40^a28–$^b3$).)

By chapter 16, Aristotle feels that he has demonstrated that there can be no separately existing Forms and no universal substance. It remains for him to review in the light of the conclusions that have been reached the list of candidate substances that was originally introduced in chapter 2. Four candidates can be eliminated in the light of the inquiry. Elements are banned as being too material. The parts of animals are dependent upon the substances to which they belong (40^b5–16). The Pythagorean One and Being, which were probably favoured by Speusippus and his followers as by the later Neoplatonists, are excluded (40^b17–27), as, of course, are Platonic Forms (40^b27–41^a5). This still leaves on the list both individual animals and their species, but, of course, the whole tenor of the discussion has been to favour the latter at the expense of the former.

Aristotle has thus succeeded in steering a middle way between the materialists and Platonists. However, he has done so at the expense of abandoning the

---

[34] An attempt to resolve this is made by M. J. Woods, 'Problems in *Metaphysics* Z, chapter 13', in Moravcsik (ed.), *Aristotle*.

common-sense ontology of the *Categories*. It seems clear that Aristotle was disturbed by the thought that hylomorphism and the concomitant doctrine of special substance meant that particular entities had to be regarded as metaphysical disunities. The problem that Aristotle needed to solve, therefore, in order to reconcile the doctrine of special substance with a particularist ontology was that of showing that the individual composites could, after all, have what Gill has called 'vertical unity'.[35] Upon this depended the coherence of the defence of change that had been provided in the *Physics*. It is this task that Aristotle attempted in book Eta of the *Metaphysics*, drawing on a crucial distinction that is outlined in Theta.

3.2.2. Substance, Form, and Matter (Zeta 17, Eta 6, and Theta 7)

We have seen that in the bulk of book Zeta the adoption of definable essence as the criterion for unity and thus substantiality has meant that species or perhaps species-forms, rather than composite individuals, are now to be treated as primary substances. However, we have also seen how, in Zeta 16, the list of those candidates for substantiality that have been ruled out does not include composite individual animals. There is, in fact, good reason to think that Aristotle was not content to rest with the conclusions to which he had been driven in Zeta. In the last chapter of that book he begins a quite new approach to substantiality, the consideration of substance as the cause of unity for composites, and this approach will, at the end of book Eta, when he returns to the topic of definable unity, enable him to allow that composite individuals are also possessors of definable unity. Vindicating this claim will rely heavily on the distinction between potential and actual existence, which it is the primary business of book Theta to clarify.

Zeta 17, then, sets out to show that composite individuals need some principle of unity that will keep together their constituents, which would otherwise tend to split apart. This principle cannot, in its turn, merely be one of the elements, since there would in that case be no reason to think that it would not also naturally be disjoined from the other elements. Rather it must be something over and above the elements, which is responsible both for their entering into, and for their remaining in, their observed arrangement (41^b11–33). It is reasonable, chapter 17 concludes, to think that the essential form, whose substantiality has been underlined by the discussion in Zeta, should play this role (41^b27–9). Book Eta seeks to examine how this happens, how unity is imposed on the various types of matter that go to make up an organic whole. The surprising conclusion at the end is that the composite organic whole is itself a definable unity, no less than the substantial essence which is responsible for its organization. Thus the composite too is a substance.

[35] *Aristotle on Substance.*

These conclusions are reached in Eta 6. The chapter opens with a discussion of the unity of genus and differentia, a topic that has already been handled in Zeta 12. For the Platonist, there is a real problem about the definition of man as biped animal, since this seems to suggest the participation in him of two Forms, animal and biped (45^a15–20). The solution in Zeta 12 is to treat the subgenera and their accompanying differentiae as contained within the last differentia. It is not clear that this solution will deal with the difficulty of the coexistence in the species of the genus itself with the last differentia. This problem is, however, now addressed here in Eta 6, and it is solved with reference to the distinction between potentiality and actuality (45^a21–$^b8$). Aristotle describes the genus as being the material of the definition, which is, at first sight, a strange notion, but this is explicated to mean that the genus is only potentially present in the species. The species is to be seen as the imposition of the actual form of the last differentia on the matter of the genus. So the genus only potentially exists in the species and thus, since potential existence is non-existence, the species is, after all, a single thing (45^a28–9).

The invocation of potentiality has therefore solved the problem of the unity of definition by genus and differentia, but this is in fact a much simpler problem than that of the unity of hylomorphic definition, the sort of definition that would apply, if any could, to the individual composite of form and matter. However, it is precisely this problem that Eta 6 goes on to consider, and it is clear that the two problems are supposed to be treated in parallel, that the use of potentiality and actuality to illumine the difficulty about genus and differentia is supposed to be a paradigm for the use of the same distinction to solve the problem of ascribing essence and therefore substance to composites of form and matter.

Aristotle takes as his example the familiar case of a bronze sphere (45^a26–7). By the doctrine of Zeta 12, this is just the sort of thing that cannot be a single definable unity, but is rather a this-in-this. Now Aristotle wants to say that it is after all a unity, since the bronze only exists in the sphere potentially, so that it no more divides it than does the genus divide the definition of a species by genus and differentia (45^b8–23). But the analogy between the bronze and the genus is awkward, since there is already a genus of sphericality, namely shape, and, as Gill points out, whereas in saying that a biped is an animal we are saying something that is analytic, we are by no means being so uninformative in saying that a sphere is bronze.[36] It is no part of our mere grasp of the concept of a sphere that we think that it is realized in bronze, or any other specific material. Thus the extension of the potential–actual distinction to cover the hylomorphic case is far from being obviously coherent.

These difficulties are resolved by the account of potentiality in Theta. What

---

[36] Ibid.

Aristotle requires is that the matter of the composite should be potentially existent in it but not actually so. How this can be is demonstrated in Theta 7. The
crucial idea that is introduced here is that the wood of a box, to take the example used, only survives in the actual composite in that it contributes properties
to it (49ª19–ᵇ2). The wood, before being the constituent of the box, had, of
course, properties of its own, and it is these that it contributes now to the box.
However, for it to make this contribution, there is no need for the previous
bearer of the properties, the wood itself, to be present at all, except potentially.
It performs its crucial task as continuant not by being actually present itself in
the composite whose unity it would thereby destroy, but by contributing its
non-substantial features to it, which features would revert to being those of
wood in the event of the destruction of the box. It is the possession of those features that has made the wood potentially material for the box, and it is only the
features that need to survive to deal with the Parmenidean problem about the
logical absurdity of coming into existence out of nothing.[37]

Thus the distinction between potentiality and actuality, which is the topic of
the whole of Theta and especially clearly treated in Theta 7, makes possible the
claim advanced at the end of Eta that composite individuals are substantial uni-
ties. Despite the sophisticated defence in Zeta of the doctrine of special substance, Aristotle finally returns to the common-sense particularism of the
Categories. He is thus able to satisfy two requirements which he cherishes. On
the one hand, the world turns out to be constituted by things broadly in line
with what common sense and the reflections of serious people take to be fundamental. On the other hand, there is no bar, after all, to the full scientific
understanding of these things. They are as conceptually coherent as they are
intuitively fundamental, and science is not at odds with our everyday thinking
but at all points continues and enriches it.[38]

BIBLIOGRAPHY

References to the Aristolelian corpus follow the current standard procedure. The title
of the work is followed by the page numbers and page subdivisions (ª or ᵇ) of the first
modern edition of the entire Greek text by I. Bekker (Berlin, 1831). Since the page divisions are fewer and larger than with Plato, line references are also always given. Thus
the beginning of the first book of the *Physics* is at 1028ª10. The first one or two numerals are sometimes omitted for brevity, but any translation that does not include the
Bekker page numbers in the margin should be regarded with suspicion.

[37] Gill develops this sort of interpretation in great detail in *Aristotle on Substance*, 149–61.
[38] Cf. Lear, *Aristotle*, ch. 1.

ESSENTIAL READING

A New Aristotle Reader, ed. J. L. Ackrill (Oxford, 1987). It is crucial to read the text of Aristotle in a reliable and authoritative translation. Ackrill's version is the so-called Oxford translation updated and represents the state of the art of Aristotle translation.

The Basic Works of Aristotle, trans. R. McKeon (New York, 1941). This is the next-best translation to that collected by Ackrill, since it is also the Oxford version, though rather less updated. Both collections contain all the key texts, though they do not entirely overlap in content.

The Complete Works of Aristotle: The Revised Oxford Translation, ed. J. Barnes, 2 vols. (Princeton, NJ, 1984). This is the most authoritative current translation, but only a relatively small part of Aristotle's total output is covered in our book, so that Ackrill's condensed collection is quite adequate for our purposes.

RECOMMENDED READING

There is, of course, a huge secondary literature on Aristotle, both popular and more specialist. The following are all excellent introductory texts:

ACKRILL, J. L., *Aristotle the Philosopher* (Oxford, 1981). Ackrill seeks to give an impression of the way in which Aristotle addresses philosophical problems, rather than present a straightforward exposition of his doctrines.

ALLAN, D. J., *The Philosophy of Aristotle* (Oxford, 1970). This presents a very clear and comprehensive account of Aristotle's system that relatively downplays the developmental perspective.

BARNES, J., *Aristotle*, Past Masters (Oxford, 1982). This is a readable and perspicacious survey of Aristotle's central arguments. It will appeal to those already familiar with Barnes's scholarly style.

GRAHAM, D., *Aristotle's Two Systems* (Oxford, 1987). Graham presents an account of Aristotle which sees him as evolving through definably systematic phases.

IRWIN, T. H., *Aristotle's First Principles* (Oxford, 1988). Irwin sees the central theme of Aristotle's development as being the refinement of the notion of dialectic and brings the central works magisterially within the scope of this interpretation.

LEAR, J., *Aristotle: The Desire to Understand* (Cambridge, 1988).

LLOYD, G. E., *Aristotle: The Growth and Structure of his Thought* (Cambridge, 1968). This is a relatively straightforward account of Aristotle's development along lines close to those originally proposed by Jaeger.

ADDITIONAL READING

BARNES, J., SORABJI, R., and SCHOFIELD, M. (eds.), *Articles on Aristotle*, i–iv (London, 1975). This is a central collection of both recent and classic articles on Aristotle. The four volumes cover, in order, science, ethics, metaphysics, and psychology (with aesthetics).

MORAVCSIK, J. M. E. (ed.), *Aristotle* (London, 1968). This is another important collection of articles, mostly pertaining to the subject-matter covered by this chapter.

The *Categories*

Aristotle's Categories *and* De Interpretatione, trans. with notes by J. L. Ackrill (Oxford, 1963). This item in the Clarendon Aristotle series remains the standard modern commentary on an English version of the text. It is advisable to use Ackrill's notes in conjunction with the translation cited (in the Barnes and McKeon collections).

ALLEN, R. E., 'Substance and Predication in Aristotle's *Categories*', *Exegesis and Argument, Phronesis*, supp. vol. 1 (1973).

FREDE, MICHAEL, 'Individuen bei Aristoteles', *Antike und Abendland*, 24 (1978), 16–39; trans. in Frede, *Essays in Ancient Philosophy* (Oxford, 1987). This offers an unorthodox interpretation.

GRAHAM, D., *Aristotle's Two Systems* (Oxford, 1987), ch. 2.1.

IRWIN, T. H., *Aristotle's First Principles* (Oxford, 1988), sects. 26–43.

JONES, B., 'An Introduction to the First Five Chapters of Aristotle's *Categories*', *Phronesis*, 20 (1975), 146–72. This and the next two are useful, but relatively technical articles.

MORAVCSIK, J. M. E., 'Aristotle's Theory of *Categories*', in *Aristotle* (London, 1968). This is the best general survey of recent interpretations of the work. Moravcsik's conclusions are to a considerable extent in sympathy with Ackrill's.

OWEN, G. E. L., 'Inherence', *Phronesis*, 10 (1965), 97–105.

The *Physics*

Aristotle's Physics *Books I and II*, trans. with notes by W. A. Charlton (Oxford, 1970). This is the first instalment of the Clarendon edition of the *Physics*. Charlton has updated it with a survey of recent work.

ACKRILL, J. L., *Aristotle the Philosopher* (Oxford, 1981), ch. 3. This gives a particularly clear 'walk-through' of the crucial argument in book 1.

GRAHAM, D., *Aristotle's Two Systems* (Oxford, 1987), ch. 5.

IRWIN, T. H., *Aristotle's First Principles* (Oxford, 1988), sects. 45–9.

WATERLOW, S., *Nature, Change and Agency in Aristotle's* Physics (Oxford, 1982). Particularly strong on connecting the first two books together into a more or less continuous argument.

There are three major collections of articles and essays on Aristotelian science:

GOTTHELF, A. (ed.), *Aristotle on Nature and Living Things* (Pittsburgh, 1985).

—— and LENNOX, J. G. (eds.), *Philosophical Issues in Aristotle's Biology* (Cambridge, 1987).

JUDSON, L. (ed.), *Aristotle's* Physics : *A Collection of Essays* (Oxford, 1991).

Two highly influential general books on Aristotle's conception of scientific explanation are:

BALME, D. M., *Aristotle's Use of Teleological Explanation* (London, 1965).

SOLMSEN, F., *Aristotle's System of the Physical World* (Ithaca, NY, 1960).

ALLAN, D. J., 'Causality Ancient and Modern', *Proceedings of the Aristotelian Society*, supp. vol. 39 (1965), 1–18. Contains an excellent discussion of the notion of *aition*.

MOURELATOS, A. P. D., 'Aristotle's "Powers" and Modern Empiricism', *Ratio*, 9 (1967), 97–104. Contains an excellent discussion of the notion of *phusis*.

WIELAND, W., *Die aristotelische* Physik (Göttingen, 1970) (of which two important chapters appear in translation in J. Barnes, R. Sorabji, and M. Schofield, *Articles on Aristotle*, i (London, 1975)) is a seminal work for German-readers.

The *Metaphysics*

Aristotle: Metaphysics *Books Zeta and Eta*, trans. with notes by D. Bostock (Oxford, 1994). Contains much new and valuable material on the central books of the *Metaphysics*.

Aristotle: Metaphysics *Books Zeta, Eta, Theta, Iota*, trans. M. Furth (Indianapolis, 1985). Furth's commentary is a kind of explanatory translation which may be helpful with the most arid parts of book Z in particular.

FREDE, MICHAEL, *Essays in Ancient Philosophy* (Oxford, 1987) is a collection of the works of a particularly important student of Aristotle.

—— and PATZIG, G., *Aristoteles*: Metaphysik Z (Munich, 1988). This is the most important commentary on book Z perhaps ever to have appeared. Unfortunately, it is only available in German.

FURTH, M., *Substance, Form and Psyche: An Aristotelian Metaphysics* (Cambridge, 1988). A little speculative, but highly readable.

GILL, M. L., *Aristotle on Substance: The Paradox of Unity* (Princeton, NJ, 1989). Very sound guide to the tensions between the *Categories* and the *Metaphysics* as well as an interesting proposed solution.

GRAYEF, FELIX, *Aristotle and his School* (London, 1974). This unusual book combines an entertaining account of Aristotle's life and of the fate of the Lyceum after his death with a detailed analysis of the structure of the central books of the *Metaphysics*, especially book Z.

KIRWAN, C. A., 'How Strong are the Objections to Essence?', *Theoria*, 37 (1971), 43–59. This deals with the introduction of the essence criterion in Z. 4.

LEAR, J., *Aristotle: The Desire to Understand* (Cambridge, 1988), ch. 6.5–6. This is an engaging 'guided tour'.

LLOYD, A. C., *Form and Universal in Aristotle* (Liverpool, 1981).

OWENS, J., *The Doctrine of Being in the Aristotelian Metaphysics* (Toronto, 1963). A little out of date, but an extremely clear and influential introductory text.

SCHOFIELD, M., 'Metaph. Z 3: Some Suggestions', *Phronesis*, 17 (1972), 97–101. This is primarily a consideration of the issue whether Aristotle is committed to the postulation of wholly formless prime matter by his discussion of the subject criterion in Z. 3.

SELLARS, W., 'Substance and Form in Aristotle', *Journal of Philosophy*, 54 (1957), 688–99. On the doctrine of form in the 'physical' treatise (chs. 7–9) which interrupts the course of book Z.

WITT, C., *Substance and Essence in Aristotle* (Ithaca, NY, 1989).

WOODS, M. J., 'Problems in *Metaphysics Zeta*, chapter 13', in J. M. E. Moravcsik, *Aristotle* (London, 1968). This clarifies the difficult arguments for the rejection of universal substance.

8

MODERN PHILOSOPHY I:
THE RATIONALISTS AND KANT

Roger Scruton

INTRODUCTION

The 'modern' period in the history of philosophy is conventionally supposed to begin in the seventeenth century, with the *Novum Organon* (1620) of Sir Francis Bacon (*c.*1561–1626) and the *Discourse on the Method* (1637) of René Descartes (1596–1650). Bacon and Descartes were not isolated thinkers, and their writings are everywhere influenced by the work of their predecessors and contemporaries. Nevertheless, it is not arbitrary to credit them with initiating modern philosophy, since between them they destroyed the assumptions, the methods, and the language which had been the common property of philosophers since the early Middle Ages.

It is usual to follow Kant in dividing the philosophers of the seventeenth and eighteenth centuries into 'rationalists' and 'empiricists', Descartes being an example of the first, and Bacon of the second. This division is frequently questioned, and some writers would reject it entirely. Nevertheless, it has proved useful in drawing a preliminary map of the terrain, and has become incorporated, for better or worse, into the study and teaching of the subject. The normal practice, therefore, is to divide the history of modern philosophy into three sections: empiricists (Bacon, Locke, Berkeley, and Hume); rationalists (Descartes, Spinoza, and Leibniz); and Kant, whose conscious rejection of the two rival traditions has led to him being considered independently. Very roughly, empiricists believe that all knowledge is derived from, and justified by, sensory experience; rationalists hold that knowledge is obtained only through rational thought; while Kant argues that knowledge involves a synthesis, in which the faculties of sensation and thought come together.

The history of philosophy is a branch of *philosophy*. It consists in the exposition and criticism of arguments, lifted from their historical context and assessed for their validity. Ideas are studied for the light that they cast on questions that still concern us. The history of philosophy is therefore distinct from the history of ideas, which is a branch of *history*. A historian of ideas is interested in the origin and influence of an idea; but he may be indifferent to its truth or validity. Most people cannot think clearly or consistently; hence absurd conceptions tend to have more historical impact than serious arguments, and minor thinkers occupy the foreground of the history of ideas. But life is short and philosophy arduous; hence only major thinkers are studied in the history of philosophy. That is one reason why we consider only Descartes, Spinoza, Leibniz, and Kant, and ignore their many fascinating contemporaries—including Malebranche, Pascal, Wolff, and Baumgarten, to name but four.

The distinction between the history of philosophy and the history of ideas is not as clear-cut as I have just implied. Many writers doubt that you *can* lift an idea from its historical context without changing it into something else. They maintain, for example, that you can understand an argument only by studying the debates from which it grew, and the contemporary meaning of the terms used to express it. Such writers pay great attention to historical detail, and to the tracing of influences. Others, by contrast, lay hold of the great dead philosophers and shake them to life, impiously interrogating them as though they were our contemporaries. The second kind of commentator will be more useful to the student; but the first is not to be despised, and is beginning to have considerable influence on the subject.

1. DESCARTES

Descartes was born at La Haye, near Tours, in 1596, attended a Jesuit college in Anjou, took a doctorate in law from the University of Poitiers in 1616, and in 1618 embarked on a military career, travelling to Holland to join the army of Prince Maurice of Nassau. He made no mark as a soldier and in 1619, while campaigning in Germany, discovered his vocation as a thinker. After a few unsettled years he returned in 1628 to Holland, where he lived for twenty-one years, composing works of cosmology, mathematics, physics, optics, meteorology, and philosophy, and becoming celebrated as one of the greatest savants of his day. In 1649 he travelled to Sweden at the invitation of Queen Christina, whose exacting demands were partly responsible for his death in the following year. (The adjective 'Cartesian' records the fact that Descartes's name is condensed from 'Des Cartes'.)

Descartes wrote in French and Latin. The works that are of particular importance to the student of modern philosophy are *The Discourse on the Method*, published in French in 1637, the *Meditations on First Philosophy*, published in Latin in 1641, and the *Principles of Philosophy*, published in Latin in 1644. Although the *Principles* contains the most comprehensive statement of the Cartesian position, the *Meditations* is the key text, not only because of its relentless and concentrated argument, but also because it represents Descartes's attempt to show the originality and importance of his philosophical method. Several sets of objections to this work were published in Descartes's lifetime, together with his replies, and these too should be studied. As for the other works, the selections contained in Cottingham's edition (see the Bibliography) are adequate.

Descartes was an accomplished scientist and mathematician, who laid the foundations for Newtonian mechanics, and revolutionized both number theory and geometry. It is worth bearing Descartes's scientific and mathematical achievements in mind, since they exerted a strong influence over his philosophy. Descartes believed that mathematics is a realm of 'eternal truth', revealed to the intellect without reference to experience. He also believed that scientific theories aim in the same direction, towards abstract and universal principles. By what method, however, can we justify these claims to certain knowledge, and to knowledge of necessary and universal truths? This question plunges us into the heart of Descartes's philosophy, and to his ruling principle, which he formulated in these words: 'For right philosophizing . . . the greatest care must be taken not to admit anything as true which we cannot prove to be true' (*Fifth Set of Objections and Replies*).

His quest for a method, therefore, was a quest for proof—and at the same time for a philosophy on which our many claims to knowledge could be founded.

1.1. The Method of Doubt

Descartes believed that he must demolish all his beliefs and opinions, and begin again from the foundations if he were to be sure of anything 'in the sciences' (i.e. in the recognized fields of inquiry) (Meditation 1, 17).[1] To this end he proposed his method of doubt: not to accept anything as true if he could give a reason for thinking it might be false. Two arguments persuade him that he can doubt virtually all his normal beliefs:

1. The dreaming argument. I believe that I am sitting by the fire with a piece of paper in my hand. Why? Because my senses tell me so. But could I not be dreaming? In dreams my senses present me with information of the same kind as I receive when waking. So how do I know that I am not dreaming now?

There are beliefs that are not shaken by this argument—beliefs about what is most general, such as we encounter in mathematics: 'whether I am awake or asleep, two and three added together are five, and a square has no more than four sides. It seems impossible that such transparent truths should incur any suspicion of being false' (Meditation 1, 20).

2. The demon argument. I imagine that I was made, not by a good God, but by an evil demon of the utmost power and cunning, who employs all his energies in order to deceive me. Thus the demon produces in me the experiences that tell me that I am sitting by the fire—although there is no fire, and no body to be sitting there. He produces my memories, images, and thoughts, even though nothing in the world corresponds to them. He even deceives me 'in those matters which seem to us supremely evident', such as mathematics (*Principles*, 1. 5. 6).

This argument is immensely powerful, especially if it is true, as Descartes maintains, that we could be deceived even in that which seems to us most evident. For this casts doubt on Descartes's own solution to the problem of knowledge. (See below, Section 1.7.)

---

[1] Page references are to the *Œuvres de Descartes*, i–xii, plus supplement, ed. Charles Adam and Paul Tannery (Paris, 1897–1913). Good English editions will quote the page numbering of this edition in the margins of the translated text.

The two arguments have the effect of transforming our local doubts about this or that into a global doubt about everything—and this is the result that Descartes requires.

1.2. The Cogito

So how is doubt overcome? The answer is contained in the famous phrase 'Cogito, ergo sum', 'I think, therefore I am'. 'I saw . . . that from the mere fact that I thought of doubting the truth of other things, it followed quite evidently and certainly that I existed' (*Discourse on the Method*, 32). Descartes's way of putting the point was later amended: 'this proposition, *I am, I exist*, is necessarily true whenever it is put forward by me or conceived in my mind'.

The following observations should be noted:

1. The original statement of the Cogito, as it is known, makes it look like an inference. The premiss is 'I think', and the conclusion is 'I am': in which case we need another premiss if the inference is to be valid, namely: 'Everything that thinks exists'. But that is precisely what Descartes has to prove.

2. The statement in the *Meditations* is therefore often preferred: it is not that I infer my existence from the premiss that I think. It is rather that I cannot think that I exist without it being true that I exist. The statement that I exist is 'self-verifying'.

Hintikka describes the statement that I do not exist as 'existentially inconsistent'. It is not that it is necessarily false—I might not have existed. Rather, the statement cannot be correctly made, except in circumstances that automatically refute it. It is the *performance* of making the statement that defeats it. And this applies also when the performance is carried out 'internally', when I merely *think* that I do not exist, without overtly stating it. The attempt to think one's own non-existence is necessarily self-defeating.

3. Descartes says '*I am, I exist*, is necessarily true whenever it is put forward by me'. But it is not, in itself, necessarily true. The proposition that I exist expresses a *contingent* truth, one that might have been false.

The Cogito is interesting for many reasons. Recent commentators have been particularly impressed by the role of the word 'I' (or the 'first-person case') in establishing Descartes's desired conclusion. It seems that many sentences formulated in the first person are immune to error—or at least to certain kinds of error. One is 'I exist'; another is 'I think'; another is 'I am in pain'. Are these immune to error for the *same reason*, or in the *same respect*? At times Descartes seems to answer in the affirmative: 'I ask [my readers] to reflect on their own mind, and all its attributes. They will find that they cannot be in doubt about these, even though they suppose that everything they have ever acquired from their senses is false' (*Objections and Replies*, 162; see also *Principles*, 1. 8. 9 and 11. 7–9).

1.3. The Theory of Ideas

Descartes takes the Cogito as proof of several things: first, that he exists, secondly that he exists as a 'thinking thing', and thirdly that he has a criterion
whereby to recognize a true belief. This is the criterion of 'clear and distinct perception'. This phrase marks a point of great difficulty and controversy in
Descartes's argument, and the student should approach the matter with care.

1. All mental activity, for Descartes, is a form of thinking (*cogitatio*)
(Meditation 2, 28–9). Thinking always involves 'ideas', which come before the
mind, and are the immediate objects of thought. Thus when I think of a horse,
an idea of a horse is before my mind; when I decide to go home, an idea of going
home is before my mind; when I see a green field, an idea of a green field is
before my mind. These ideas are the 'matter', so to speak, of thinking, and are
organized by the various activities of the mind (believing, desiring, doubting,
imagining, etc.).

Descartes was probably the first philosopher to use the word 'idea' in this
way, although the usage caught on, and was made common by Locke and
Berkeley.

2. 'All the modes of thinking that we experience within ourselves can be
brought under two general headings: perception, or the operation of the intellect, and volition, or the operation of the will' (*Principles*, 1. 32. 17). Operations
of the intellect include sense perception and imagination, and involve the direct
confrontation with an idea, and the attempt to understand it. When I go on to
affirm or deny the idea, then this involves an act of will in addition to the perception.

3. I perceive my ideas more or less 'clearly and distinctly'. Alternatively, ideas
themselves may be more or less 'clear and distinct'. What is meant by 'clear and
distinct'? Descartes gives the following definition: 'I call a perception "clear"
when it is present and accessible to the attentive mind . . . I call a perception "distinct" if, as well as being clear, it is so sharply separated from all other perceptions that it contains within itself only what is clear' (*Principles*, 1. 45. 22). That
definition is certainly neither clear nor distinct. Immense controversy therefore
surrounds the question what Descartes means by clear and distinct perception,
or a clear and distinct idea, and why he should have regarded clarity and distinctness as marks of truth.

4. What he seems to have in mind is the idea of a *self-evident* proposition.
Certain things that come before my mind simply cannot be doubted—and in
that sense bear an intrinsic mark of their own truth. The Cogito is one of them,
and by studying it we come to see that any other proposition that is perceived
as clearly and distinctly as this one must also be true. Its truth is revealed to the
'natural light' of reason.

Descartes is trying to give an account of a priori knowledge. But it is a very unsatisfactory account.

5. Descartes also refers to adequate and inadequate ideas: an idea can be clear and distinct without containing a full account of the essence of something: i.e. without being 'adequate' to its subject-matter. The notion of an 'adequate' idea or conception was to play a vital part in the philosophy of Spinoza.

6. Descartes also introduced into philosophy the concept of an innate idea, which was to play an important role in the thought of Leibniz. Sometimes he writes as though *all* ideas are innate in us, and that we derive no ideas from experience at all. (See *Comments on a Certain Broadsheet*, 358–9.)

The upshot of the theory of ideas is rationalism. Knowledge comes through reflecting on our own ideas, and so arriving at a clear and distinct perception of the essences of things. Our guide in this exercise is the 'natural light' of reason; the senses, which provide only obscure and confused perceptions, can at best show the world as it seems, but are silent concerning the world as it is.

1.4. The 'Real Distinction'

Having established his own existence, Descartes goes on to examine his nature. It is clear from the Cogito that I am a thinking thing. Moreover, I cannot conceive myself except as thinking: any conception of myself that is available to me is a conception of myself thinking. Hence it is of my essence to think. However hard I try, I can find nothing else that belongs to my essence. For example, it seems to me that I have a body which I can move at will; but I can readily conceive of this body as not existing, without supposing my own non-existence.

Descartes then goes on to reflect upon the nature of physical things (bodies). Consider this lump of wax: it has a certain shape, size, colour, perfume—qualities which I can perceive through the senses. Yet approach it to the fire and it changes in all these respects, while remaining the same piece of wax. Those sensory qualities do not therefore belong to the essence of the piece of wax. Indeed, no sensory experience enables me to perceive the essential nature of the wax or of any other corporeal thing: only by reasoning will I obtain the clear and distinct perception which reveals the essence of the wax that I hold before me. And this reasoning tells me that, while the wax may change in respect of its shape, size, colour, perfume, or any other sensory 'mode', it cannot cease to be extended in space without ceasing to be. Extension belongs to its essence; but I can find nothing else that belongs to its essence. And the same is true of all physical (corporeal) things.

Those two arguments occur in Meditation 2; in Meditation 6 Descartes adds the following observation: 'I know that everything which I clearly and distinctly understand is capable of being created by God so as to correspond exactly with my understanding of it. Hence the fact that I can clearly and distinctly understand one thing apart from another is enough to make me certain that the two things are distinct, since they are capable of being separated, at least by God.' (See also *Principles*, 1. 60. 28–9.) Since I clearly and distinctly perceive that thought is of the essence of mind, and extension of the essence of body, and nothing else is of the essence of either, I clearly and distinctly perceive that mind is essentially distinct from the body and therefore in principle separable from it. There is a 'real distinction' between mind and body.

The details of the argument are set out again in the sixth set of Descartes's *Replies to Objections*, and many are the fallacies that have been discerned, rightly or wrongly, in this immensely subtle piece of reasoning. The following points should be noted:

1. Mind, for Descartes, is a thinking substance, in the specific sense common to the rationalist philosophers: it is a bearer of properties, which depends for its existence on no other thing besides God (*Principles*, 1. 51. 24).

2. The body is not a substance in that sense, since it depends for its existence on other things besides God. Nevertheless, Descartes writes of 'extended substance', meaning matter in general, and also of corporeal substances, meaning individual physical things.

3. Thought and extension are 'principal attributes', through which the substances that possess them may be completely or adequately conceived (*Principles*, 1. 53. 25; see Section 2 below).

4. Given the truth of (1), (2), and (3), there is a problem as to how mind and body interact: reflection on this problem was one of the main motives behind Spinoza's philosophy.

1.5. The Cartesian Theory of the Mind

Descartes begins from the question 'How can *I* know, be certain of, the things that I claim to know?' Immediately his thought is turned inwards, to the contents of his own mind and the certainties which attach to them. Although the peculiarity of the Cogito lies in its self-verifying nature, there lurks behind it a host of other certainties. (See *Principles*, 1. 8. 9 and 11. 7.) I am able to know what I think, feel, experience, desire, with an authority that you could never match. The first-person case is not merely a paradigm of certainty; it seems to show the essence of the mind—what it really and essentially is—through the inner awareness of 'ideas'.

Certainty about my own mind goes hand-in-hand with uncertainty about the external world. My mind is more immediately present to me than any physical thing, and I can have knowledge of it while presupposing nothing about a physical reality. It seems as though my subjective viewpoint is a viewpoint on another realm—a realm that is no part of physical reality, an 'inner' realm, connected only contingently with 'outer' things.

Such is the picture associated with 'Cartesian dualism'. Is it coherent? Many philosophers deny that it is.

1.6. God

Descartes was a pious Christian. But it was not only for this reason that he sought to prove the existence of God. Without such a proof, he argued, there would be no way of refuting scepticism: nothing would be certain beyond a handful of truths about myself. By establishing the existence of a supremely good and wise God we destroy the hypothesis of the evil demon. We obtain an absolute guarantee that the world is as we take it to be, when correctly using our God-given powers.

In the Third and Fifth Meditations and elsewhere, Descartes gives two arguments for the existence of God:

1. I have the idea of a most perfect being. Whence came this idea? Not from me, since I am imperfect. There must be as much reality (perfection) in the cause of an idea as is contained in it 'objectively' (i.e. in the object that it represents). Hence there must be a cause of my idea of God which is as great as God. This argument is very strange and difficult, and adds a new twist to the theory of ideas. It is not helped by Descartes's use of scholastic terminology ('formal' and 'objective'), nor by his disposition to regard the most difficult step in the argument (sentence 4 in the preceding paragraph) as self-evident. (Descartes's best explanation of his meaning is at *Principles*, 1. 17. 11.)

2. A version of the ontological argument. I have an idea of a most perfect being; I clearly and distinctly perceive that such a being contains all perfections, and hence reality in every degree. Hence this idea contains existence, which means that God's essence is to exist. (Of no other thing, Descartes adds, can this be said.)

The ontological argument is still highly controversial; most philosophers think there is something wrong with it—but what exactly?

Since God is no deceiver, it follows that my faculties, properly employed, will lead to truth rather than error. God underwrites my claims to knowledge.

1.7. The Cartesian Circle

We now encounter what is generally considered to be the greatest stumbling-block in Descartes's philosophical enterprise. If I can rely on my cognitive powers only on the assumption that God exists, then do I not need to assume God's existence in order to prove it? In other words, is not Descartes's argument viciously circular?

The Cartesian circle, as it is known, can be expressed in many ways. It was first diagnosed by Arnauld, in his objections to the *Meditations*, and Descartes replies to it (*Second Objections and Replies*, 125–6, 140–6). In effect the objection is saying the following: either clear and distinct perception is a guarantee of truth, in which case we can know what is true without invoking God; or else it is not, in which case we cannot prove God's existence.

Matters are made difficult by Descartes's admission that the demon could deceive me even about those truths that seem most certain, including the truths of mathematics. For is not mathematics a realm of clear and distinct ideas?

One way out of the circle is suggested by Descartes's own reply (and also by *Principles*, 1. 13. 9–10): we *can* doubt our clear and distinct ideas, but only in retrospect, when doubt concerns the reliability of memory. Truths that have to be proved by a series of steps may be doubted, in so far as we rely on our memory to assure us that the proof was carried out. But when a proof is before our mind in its entirety, we can be sure of it; we are granted an 'intuition' of its validity, and this we cannot doubt. The idea of intuition was to play an important part in Spinoza's theory of knowledge.

Even so, the circle points to a peculiar feature of Descartes's philosophy. His criterion of truth is *internal* to ideas. Locked within the realm of ideas, he none the less supposes that he can choose the true from the false among them. And his test of this is that there are some that he cannot doubt. He then builds a bridge to God, and calls on God to guarantee his other claims to knowledge. But why does Descartes's inability to doubt that *p* show that *p* is true?

1.8. The Absolute Perspective

One way of looking at Descartes's philosophy is suggested by Bernard Williams, in his stimulating commentary. Descartes's professed aim is to seek foundations for his claims to knowledge. And the only place in which these foundations could be found is his own mind—among the ideas which are before his mind when thinking. His very method leads him into the subjective realm.

But his subjective point of view is unreliable: it is that of a sensuous being, the majority of whose beliefs arise through sensory experience. To justify any claim to knowledge he must rise to another perspective, in which he can confront things as they *are*, and not as they *seem*. This means acquiring an 'absolute' viewpoint, which does not merely reflect the world as it appears, but which shows it as it is. Only reason can provide that viewpoint. To put it another way, things really *are* as they *seem* to reason. That is the hidden meaning of the doctrine of 'clear and distinct' ideas. (Hence the argument about the wax—precursor of so much later philosophy, from Locke's discussion of primary and secondary qualities, to Saul Kripke and Hilary Putnam on 'natural kinds'.)

But can we reach this absolute viewpoint, starting as Descartes does, from the narrow perspective of a self-conscious and doubting individual? Maybe we could reach it, if we could prove the existence of God, whose perspective it is.

The suspicion is, however, that no proof of God's existence is available from *our* perspective. Any proof must covertly assume that we have already obtained that 'absolute conception' of reality to which we are in fact merely aspiring.

1.9. Other Matters

The following should be borne in mind by those who wish to make a special study of Descartes:

1. Descartes's theory of the will, and of the distinction between entertaining an idea and assenting to it. (See Meditation 4, 59–60; *Principles*, 1. 33–5. 17–18.)

2. Descartes's theory of substance, and of the dependency of finite substances on God. (See next section.)

3. Descartes's theory of 'common notions', and his attempt at an axiomatization of his system. (See Appendix to the *Second Replies*, and next section.)

2. SPINOZA

Benedict (Baruch) de Spinoza (1632–77) lived in Holland, where his family, who were Spanish Jews, had come as refugees from the Inquisition. He was brought up in the Jewish faith, but was anathematized and cast out from the synagogue on account of his heretical views. These views had been acquired through his study of Descartes, and through friendships with Christian and Cartesian thinkers. His defence of freedom of conscience, in the anonymously published *Theologico-Political Treatise* (1670), caused him to fall out with the synod of the Calvinist Church, and hence with the civil authorities. As a result of these troubles, Spinoza withheld his masterpiece, the *Ethics*, from the press, and lived in retirement, refusing the offer of a professorship at Heidelberg, and developing his philosophy through correspondence with other scientific and philosophical thinkers. Spinoza had wide-ranging interests, in politics, law, biblical scholarship, and painting, as well as mathematics and physical science. He carried out experiments in optics, and the grinding of lenses for these experiments may have exacerbated the consumption which brought him to an early death.

An earlier treatment of some of the themes of the *Ethics* is contained in the short and unfinished *Treatise on the Emendation of the Intellect*. In addition to those two works, Spinoza wrote the *Theologico-Political Treatise* referred to above, an unfinished *Political Treatise*, and an exposition of the philosophical system of Descartes (*Descartes's Principles of Philosophy*, published in 1663). However, despite Spinoza's enormous importance as a political philosopher, we shall be concerned solely with his metaphysical theories and their ethical consequences.[2]

---

[2] Spinoza wrote in Latin; the available translations are described in the Bibliography.

2.1. Cartesian Rationalism and the Geometrical Method

The impact of Descartes on Spinoza's thinking was enormous. The principal terms, subjects, and arguments of Descartes's philosophy all appear in Spinoza, sometimes affirmed, sometimes denied, but always treated with reverence. At the same time, those aspects of Descartes which are of most interest to philosophers today were not necessarily of most interest to Spinoza. For example, Spinoza was largely indifferent to the sceptical arguments from which the *Meditations* begin, and had no special use for the Cogito. He was far more impressed by the great rationalist design that he discerned in Descartes, and which Descartes, in Spinoza's opinion, had failed to carry through. Spinoza's philosophy is an attempt to complete the method of 'clear and distinct ideas' and to describe the nature of the world through reflecting on the idea of it.

To this end Spinoza deployed the 'geometrical method', which Descartes had toyed with in his *Replies to Objections*, while believing it to be more suited to mathematical than to metaphysical argument. By 'geometrical method' was meant the systematic exposition of a subject, through the presentation of all the relevant truths in the form of theorems deduced from a set of axioms and definitions. The model was Euclid's geometry, the axioms of which purport to be self-evident, and the proofs of which therefore establish the theorems *conclusively*. If there is such a thing as a method of 'clear and distinct' ideas, then this surely must be it. The secret is to find the self-evident axioms from which the rest of metaphysics could be derived. That was the task that Spinoza set himself in the *Ethics*, each of the five parts of which begins from axioms and definitions, and proceeds by mathematical proof towards its conclusions. As the title indicates, the book was not intended simply as a treatise of metaphysics. Of equal importance for Spinoza were the problems of human nature, human conduct, and human destiny. These too, he believed, could be treated in geometrical fashion, and the resulting answers would have the certainty, necessity, and universality of the laws of mathematics.

This geometrical method presents a formidable obstacle to the modern reader. Many commentators (e.g. Edwin Curley) try to 'go behind' it, and reconstruct Spinoza's real intellectual agenda in other terms. At any rate, it is almost impossible to understand Spinoza if you take his proofs entirely at face value, accepting those which are valid and rejecting the remainder. For often the most shaky argument may be given for a proposition upon which the whole system depends for its force and plausibility.

Because of the difficulties presented by the *Ethics*, many students of philosophy pay scant attention to Spinoza. This is a mistake. A knowledge of Spinoza's philosophy is essential to obtaining a full grasp of the significance of Descartes, whose thoughts become clear through the interrogation contained in Spinoza.

And it is precisely the geometrical method that enables Spinoza to bring out the fundamental character of Cartesian rationalism: namely, its dependence upon the method of 'clear and distinct ideas'. Spinoza takes over the term 'idea', and also the theory of 'clear and distinct' perception. He assumes, therefore, that there are self-evident truths, and that these are the corner-stone of knowledge. But he is more interested in the distinction made by Descartes between 'adequate' and 'inadequate' ideas. The idea of X is adequate if the nature of X can be deduced from it. Adequate ideas show us the essences of things. Knowledge consists in replacing our inadequate conceptions with their more adequate versions; and this is done by refining away the sensory component in our thinking (the ideas of 'imagination') and deriving an account of the world which proceeds deductively from axioms in which nothing is contained that is not evident to the natural light of reason. If we cannot complete that deduction, then we have no proof that the ideas that we entertain of things really *are* adequate; and it is by providing that proof that we show the imperfection of the Cartesian system.

So what exactly happens in the *Ethics*? To put the matter simply: Spinoza takes over the key concepts that Descartes had introduced—the theory of ideas, the concepts of substance, attribute, and mode, the idea of God, defined through the ontological argument, the a priori theory of thought and extension, and so on—and builds them into a consistent system, in which nothing is assumed that is not, in Spinoza's view, self-evident. The result is something entirely surprising, which shows not only the untenability of Descartes's philosophy, but also, Spinoza thinks, the clear and unique alternative which is destined to replace it.

2.2. Substance, Attribute, and Mode

There is an important section in Descartes's *Principles* (1. 51–6. 24–6), in which the key notions of Spinoza's metaphysics make a preliminary appearance: substance, attribute, and mode. Descartes seems to mean three different things by 'substance':

1. Anything that depends upon nothing outside itself for its existence. He says that only God is a substance in this sense.

2. Ordinary individual things in the world, whether bodies or minds. (This is the traditional idea of substance, as the 'bearer of properties' or 'attributes'.)

3. That which is defined by an 'essence': as mind and matter are defined (the one by thought, the other by extension). In this sense a substance is not an individual thing, but either a kind of things, or a systematic whole of things.

Descartes also distinguishes the 'principal attribute' from the other attributes of a substance. This principal attribute defines or constitutes the essence of the substance: as thought constitutes the essence of mind.

Finally, Descartes writes of the ordinary properties of things as 'modifications' or 'modes'—ways of being, in respect of which a substance may be affected or 'modified', and which cannot exist without the substance on which they depend (the redness in the book, the fragrance in the wax, and so on).

Spinoza thought long and hard about these technicalities, and concluded that the world can be described using one concept of substance, provided that we clearly distinguished attributes from modes. For Spinoza a substance is defined by the fact that it depends for its nature and existence on nothing outside itself: it is 'in itself and conceived through itself' (part 1, def. 3).[3] The definition has two parts: 'in itself'—i.e. substance is dependent on nothing; and 'conceived through itself'—i.e. substance can be fully understood without reference to anything outside our idea of it.

An attribute is defined as Descartes defines 'principal attribute': it is 'what the intellect perceives of a substance, as constituting its essence' (def. 4). In other words, it is not a property, in any ordinary sense, but the very nature of the thing that possesses it. And this too is something of which we have an adequate idea.

Finally the 'modes' of a substance are those 'modifications' of it that are not self-dependent. They are accidental properties, or local configurations, which owe their nature and being to the substance in which they inhere. Consider Descartes's wax, for example: it is not a substance, since it depends for its existence on the entire system of physical objects of which it is a part. Moreover, it can evaporate, undergo a chemical transformation, vanish into the ether, yet still its *essential* being remains—nothing real 'goes out of existence' in these transformations. Yet the particular physical object *has* gone out of existence. It was, in short, a modification of a true substance, namely, the substance whose essence is extension and which is extended everywhere (what we should now call physical matter).

So here is what Spinoza makes of Descartes's original three meanings of 'substance': properly speaking, only the first meaning captures a clear and adequate idea of substance. Substances in the second sense are modes of substance in the first sense, while in the third sense 'substance' is just another way of talking about the attributes through which substances are known to the intellect.

2.3. God

The first part of the *Ethics* is devoted to God, defined as 'a substance consisting of infinite attributes, each one of which expresses an eternal and infinite essence' (part 1, def. 6). Spinoza follows Descartes in giving a version of the

---

[3] References in the text have two numerals: the first refers to a part of the *Ethics*, the second to a proposition within that part (unless it makes explicit that the number is that of a definition or axiom). Thus 5. 14 means part 5, proposition 14. There are now standardly accepted page numberings.

ontological argument. However, the proof has an interesting twist to it. Spinoza believes that all substances exist necessarily, since it 'belongs to the nature of substance to exist' (1. 7). But he also argues that there 'cannot be two or more substances with the same nature or attribute' (1. 5). That is, substances cannot share their attributes. Since God possesses all attributes, there cannot be another substance in the world—if it existed, it would have to share an attribute of God's, in which case it would be identical with God. It follows that there is only one substance, namely God, and that everything that exists is either an attribute or a mode of God. Everything that exists exists 'in' God, in the sense of being dependent on God for its existence and nature.

The word 'in' creates difficulties. Here is an analogy: a group of people join to form a club, which then does things, owns things, organizes things. When I say that the club bought a house, I really mean that the members did various things with a specific legal result. But none of the members bought a house. Hence it looks as though the club is an independent entity, whereas it is dependent for its existence and nature on the activities of its members: it is 'in' the members in Spinoza's sense. And when X is 'in' Y, X can be understood fully (adequately) only *through* Y, as the club, in my example, can be understood and explained only in terms of its members. Another way of putting this is to say that Y is 'prior to' X, since we cannot understand X without prior conception of Y. It is in this sense that a 'substance is prior in nature to its affections (i.e. its modes)' (1. 1).

God has 'infinite attributes'. Does this mean infinitely many? The point is disputed, but it is hard to interpret Spinoza in any other way. Nevertheless, it seems that we know only two of them: thought and extension. But since an attribute is 'what the intellect perceives' as constituting the essence of whatever possesses it, we can obtain adequate knowledge of God, under the two attributes that we know.

What then *is* God? Known in one way, he is the system of extended things—the natural world understood as the physicist understands it. Known in another way he is the all-embracing mind, of which our own minds are modes. The world can be described as 'God or nature', and is one and the same, however we conceive it. It follows that God is not outside creation, but identical with it: he is the 'immanent', and not the 'transeunt' cause of everything (1. 18). Moreover, since all the truths about God follow necessarily from his essence, and since everything happens 'in' God, everything happens by necessity: things could have been otherwise only if God had been otherwise; and that is impossible. Spinoza, therefore, is a strict determinist.

In fact, when we speak of things 'happening', of process and change, there is a sense in which our conceptions are less than adequate to the reality. These descriptions attach only to the modes of God, and not to his eternal and infinite essence. From these ideas of finite modes we can, indeed, advance to a more adequate knowledge, by coming to understand the 'infinite modes' of God—modes which are true of him everywhere and everywhen. Nevertheless, to explain things ultimately, we must not relate them to what precedes them in time, since that is merely to explain one mode in terms of another. We must show their timeless dependence on the eternal essence of God. An ideal science would aim to see the world 'under the aspect of eternity' (*sub specie aeternitatis*), in the manner of a mathematical proof, and not under the aspect of duration.

2.4. Mind and its Place in Nature

The theory of the attributes was partly intended by Spinoza to solve an outstanding question raised by Descartes's philosophy of mind. If the mind is a separate substance from the body, then how do mind and body interact? What mechanism can join one substance to another, so that changes in the one are explained by changes in the other? On Spinoza's reading of 'substance' the suggestion is a nonsense, and his reading, he thought, is the only consistent one.

Spinoza's solution to the problem of mind and body is ingenious, if hard to understand in its entirety. 'The mind and the body are one and the same thing, which is conceived now under the attribute of thought, now under the attribute of extension' (2. 21, scholium). Spinoza thinks that his theory of the attributes enables him to say this, since it implies not only that the one substance can be known in two ways, but that the same two ways of knowing apply to the modes of that substance. The mind is a finite mode of the infinite substance conceived as thought; the body is a finite mode of the infinite substance conceived as extension. And the mind is 'the idea of' the body (2. 13)—meaning that the two modes are in fact one and the same mode, conceived in two different ways.

In a similar way every idea is 'of' some *ideatum*, which is the physical object with which it is identical. However, when we describe a mode of thought, we situate it in the system of ideas, and no explanation of an idea can be formulated except in terms of other ideas (in terms of the attribute of thought). Similarly, when we describe a mode of extension, we situate it in the system of physical things, and explain it accordingly. Mind and body are one *thing*; but they are conceptualized under rival and incommensurable systems. Hence, while we can assert in the abstract that they are identical, we can never *explain* a physical process in terms of a mental one, or a mental process in terms of a physical. (See the discussion in 3. 2.) This combination of doctrines has proved, not surprisingly, immensely puzzling to Spinoza's commentators. On the one hand, he seems to be a monist, believing that there is only *one* ultimate reality, of which everything is a part (or 'mode'); on the other hand, he remains a kind of dualist, reaffirming the separateness of mind and body in the very act of denying it. Certainly, it can hardly be said that he has produced a clear and satisfactory answer to the Cartesian problem of the relation between the mental and the physical.

2.5. *Conatus*

If there is only one substance, how do we account for the many apparent *individuals* in the world? Even if my mind is a 'mode' of God, it is not the same thing as your mind, and it has an individuality and uniqueness that are not only precious to me, but also recognized in all our ways of referring to it. Strictly speaking, of course, only God is 'one and single', since only God is 'in himself'—i.e. self-dependent and self-sustaining. However, finite things may have a lesser version of this divine characteristic, being more or less able to maintain themselves in existence, more or less 'in themselves' (see, for example, 3. 6). This is illustrated by organisms. Consider animals: unlike stones they avoid injury, resist it when it is threatened, and even restore themselves when it is inflicted. They are more self-dependent, more 'in themselves' than stones. They have more of what Spinoza calls *conatus*, or 'endeavour': they endeavour to persist in their own being. It is *conatus* that constitutes the individuality of finite things, and enables us to speak of them as though they were substances.

Spinoza attributes a parallel *conatus* to body and mind, the latter being the idea of the former.

2.6. Spinoza's Theory of Knowledge

Spinoza's theory of knowledge is an extension and refinement of the Cartesian theory of clear and distinct perception. For every idea there is an *ideatum*—an object conceived under the attribute of extension, which exactly corresponds to the idea in the system of the world. Every idea is 'of' its *ideatum*, and therefore every idea displays what Spinoza calls the 'extrinsic' mark of truth, namely an exact and necessary correspondence to its *ideatum* (part 2, def. 4). Error is possible, however, since many ideas fail to possess the 'intrinsic' marks of truth, which are present only in 'adequate' ideas (part 2, def. 4). Although the term 'adequate' comes from Descartes, it effectively replaces the notion of a 'clear and distinct' perception, as Descartes had discussed this.

Spinoza's theory of knowledge is very intricate, and is designed more as a theory of error than as a theory of truth. Every adequate idea is self-evident to the one who grasps it (2. 43), and 'falsity consists in privation of knowledge, resulting from inadequate or mutilated and confused ideas' (2. 35). A prime example of this inadequacy is sensory perception. My image of the sun is of a small red disc in a sea of blue: this is an 'idea', but its *ideatum* is not what I take it to be (namely, the sun); rather, it is some process in me, in my brain perhaps. By referring this idea to the *sun* as its *ideatum* I naturally fall into error.

Knowledge gained through sense perception is assigned, in the *Ethics*, to the lowest of three levels of cognition: the level which Spinoza calls imagination or opinion. Such cognition can never reach adequacy, since the ideas of imagination do not come to us in their intrinsic logical order, but in the order of our bodily processes. By the steady accumulation of confused ideas we can arrive at a grasp of what is common to them—a 'universal notion', such as we have of man, tree, or dog (2. 40, scholium). But these are not in themselves adequate ideas, even if they constitute the meaning of our everyday general terms.

The second level of cognition, exemplified by science and mathematics, comes from the attempt to gain a full (adequate) conception of the essence of the thing studied. This involves adequate ideas and 'common notions', since 'those things which are common to all and which are equally in a part and in the whole can only be conceived adequately' (2. 39). All human beings possess these common notions, since they too participate in the universal nature expressed in them.

The third level of knowledge is intuition, or *scientia intuitiva*. 'This kind of cognition proceeds from an adequate idea of the formal essence of certain attributes of God to the adequate knowledge of the essence of things' (2. 40, scholium 2). Spinoza seems to mean by intuition the comprehensive understanding of the truth of a proposition that is granted to the person who grasps it together with a valid proof of it from self-evident premisses, in a single mental act.

'Cognition of the first kind is the only cause of falsity . . . while cognition of the second and third kinds is necessarily true' (2. 41). From our point of view, therefore, the truth of an idea consists in, and is understood through, its logical connection to the system of adequate ideas; the advance of knowledge consists in the replacement of confused and inadequate ideas by adequate conceptions, until, at the limit, all that we think follows inexorably from a self-evident conception of the essence of God. We then see things 'under the aspect of eternity' (2. 44, cor. 2), which is how God sees them too.

Man's condition is one of conflict: reason aspires towards the eternal totality, while the concerns of sensuous existence persist only so long as we see things temporally and partially.

2.7. Freedom

Spinoza had a distinctive and highly influential theory of freedom. According to 2. 35, scholium, 'men are mistaken in thinking themselves free, and this opinion consists in this alone, that they are conscious of their actions and ignorant of the causes whereby they are determined'. However, this deterministic doctrine is by no means the end of the matter; there is another sense in which we can achieve freedom, and freedom, so understood, is the most valuable of our possessions.

Spinoza distinguished 'active' from 'passive' states of mind (3. 1): 'our mind acts certain things and suffers others: namely in so far as it has adequate ideas, thus far it necessarily acts certain things, and in so far as it has inadequate ideas, thus far it necessarily suffers things'. This distinction between doing things and suffering things is a distinction of degree, and, since only God is the full and originating cause of anything, only he acts without being acted upon—so only he is free in the metaphysical sense.

Nevertheless, we can advance from the passive to the active state, and this is what freedom means for us. And it is precisely by possessing adequate ideas that we become active. The 'actions of the mind' arise through adequate ideas alone (3. 3); for in having such ideas, the mind participates in the self-determining nature of the divine mind, and is freed from the influence of external causes.

Adequacy of ideas is tantamount to power; the more my ideas are adequate, the more am I independent. This independence from external causes is what Spinoza calls virtue, and 'by virtue and power I understand the same thing' (part 4, def. 8). Virtue is perfection, and perfection and reality are also one and the same. Pleasure is defined as 'the passion with which the mind passes to a higher state of perfection' (3. 11). So Spinoza advances quickly to his philosophy of life, according to which it is in our nature constantly to increase our power. Moreover, this is the source of all pleasure, and the process whereby we obtain pleasure is the very same 'emendation of the intellect' that leads us to adequate ideas, and therefore to freedom.

2.8. The Theory of the Passions

Spinoza's theory of freedom should be understood in terms of his account of the passions, which he delivers in the astonishing third part of the *Ethics*, in the preface to which he argues that 'such emotions as hate, wrath, envy etc. . . . follow from the same necessity and ability of nature as other individual things: and therefore they acknowledge certain causes through which they are understood'. He therefore proposes to treat the emotions exactly as he had treated God and the natural world, by the geometrical method, regarding 'human actions and desires as though I were dealing with lines, planes and bodies'.

He defines emotion as 'a confused idea wherewith the mind affirms a greater or less power of existing of its body or of any part of it than before, and which, being granted, the mind is thereby determined to think one thing rather than another' (part 3, appendix).

He has in mind two fundamental truths about the emotions: first that they arise from our life as embodied creatures, propelled by forces which we do not wholly understand or control; secondly, that they are mental 'affirmations' or judgements. And emotion is therefore a confused form of understanding, which reflects the inadequacy of our ideas, and the degree of our servitude to things external to us. Emotions can therefore be arranged on a scale, from the extreme of passion, in which the mind is the helpless victim of processes which it does not understand, to the extreme of mental action, in which, through serene contemplation of the truth of things, the mind asserts its perfection and its power.

Hence there is a process whereby the passions may be emended, like the intellect, in order to pass from passion to action. 'An emotion which is a passion ceases to be a passion as soon as we form a clear and distinct idea of it' (5. 3); from which it follows that 'the more an emotion becomes known to us, the more it is within our power, and the less the mind is passive towards it' (5. 3, cor.).

Stuart Hampshire[4] finds in such ideas a precursuor of Freudian analysis, a metaphysical grounding for Freud's dictum that 'where there was *id* there shall be *ego*'. He praises Spinoza for recognizing the extent to which our emotional life is hidden from us by its dependence on our bodily history, and also for his attempt to show that freedom in respect of the emotions comes only with self-knowledge—the acquisition of more 'adequate' ideas of the causes of our actions. Whether or not we agree with this interpretation, we can see Spinoza's theory as part of an attempt to reconstruct the notion of freedom, so as to reconcile it with the necessity that rules the universe.

Briefly, Spinoza's solution to the paradox of freedom is this: the more we know of the causality of our actions, the less room do we have for ideas of possibility and contingency (which merely reflect our ignorance: part 4, defs. 3 and 4). However, the knowledge of causality does not cancel our belief in freedom, but vindicates it. It is the *illusory* idea of freedom, rising from imagination, that creates our bondage, for we believe in the contingency of things only in so far as our mind is passive in respect of them. The more we see things as necessary, through obtaining adequate ideas of them, the more do we increase our power over them, and so the more are we free (5. 6). Freedom is not freedom from necessity, but the consciousness of necessity. In a mathematical proof our mind is wholly determined by logical necessity, and at the same time wholly in control: and this, for Spinoza, is our paradigm of freedom.

2.9. The Intellectual Love of God

Spinoza's metaphysics culminates, like Plato's, in a vision of man's salvation through reason. 'He who understands himself and his emotions loves God, and the more so the more he understands himself and his emotions' (5. 15). This

---

[4] 'Spinoza and the Idea of Freedom', in S. Paul Kashap (ed.), *Studies in Spinoza* (Los Angeles, 1972).

love, which stems necessarily from the pursuit of knowledge, is an intellectual love. The mind is wholly active in loving God, and hence rejoices constantly, though without passion, in the object of its contemplation. God himself is free from passion, from pleasure, and from emotion: he loves and hates no one, and he who loves God not only understands and accepts this fact, but 'cannot endeavour to bring it about that God should love him in return' (5. 19). This disinterested love is the very love with which God loves himself, and by participating in it we are one with God and blessed with his tranquillity and happiness (5. 36).

Spinoza includes in his discussion of man's salvation a singular proof of the immortality of the soul, or at least of the rational part of it. 'The human mind cannot be absolutely destroyed with the human body, but something of it remains which is eternal' (5. 23). The idea is roughly this: adequate ideas show the world under the aspect of eternity: and such ideas are themselves eternal—i.e. outside time and change. Hence, in entertaining them we are emancipated from the chains of duration, and released into the eternal.

The force of this 'proof' depends upon persuading the reader to grant less reality to time than our life spontaneously requires. In a sense Spinoza did not take time seriously. Duration exists for him only as a condition of the modes of God; substance conceived in itself is timeless. Time is, as it were, our way of perceiving what is essentially outside time, an aid to the imagination with which reason can ultimately dispense.

Such ideas anticipate Kantian idealism, and help to explain the enthusiasm for Spinoza's philosophy among Kant's immediate successors—Schelling and Hegel especially. But they are seldom found persuasive by modern commentators, who pass over this aspect of Spinoza's system as quickly as they can.

3. LEIBNIZ

Gottfried Wilhelm von Leibniz (1646–1716) was probably the greatest intellectual genius of his age. He shared with Newton the discovery of calculus, and contributed the concept of kinetic energy to mechanics. He was accomplished in history, law, chemistry, geology, and mechanics, to all of which he made original and important contributions. He was a tireless politician and diplomat, who, among other public achievements, founded the Academy of Berlin. He wrote fluently in French, German, and Latin, corresponded extensively with the intellectual giants of his age, and produced a philosophical system that was to be the basis of German academic philosophy for a century.

Leibniz wrote extensively and continuously. But with interests so diverse, and energies so easily engaged, it is not surprising that he prepared little for publication, and left no single work that is truly definitive of his position. Many of his manuscripts remain unpublished, and the student must put together an understanding of Leibniz from fragmentary or hasty productions, many of which were not designed for publication, and none of which contains the whole of Leibniz's philosophy.

Matters are made worse by the fact that Leibniz clearly changed his mind about certain of his doctrines during the course of his life, while remaining obstinately attached to them, and unable overtly to reject them. The picture to be obtained from reading his earlier *Discourse on Metaphysics* is therefore different from that contained in the mature *Monadology*, though it is not immediately clear where the difference lies. The following summary tends more in the direction of the later Leibniz, though I draw on other sources.

3.1. Substances and Individuals

Spinoza's conclusion, that all apparent individuals are merely 'modes' of the one substance, is inherently paradoxical. For the distinction between substance and mode derives from the ancient attempt to understand subject and predicate in logic, and to distinguish individuals from their properties. Spinoza seems to have abolished individuals from his world-view, reducing them to properties of something which is neither individual nor universal but a strange metaphysical hybrid. Leibniz's philosophy arose from the attempt to provide a concept of the individual substance, and to use it to describe a plural universe—indeed, a universe in which there is not one substance, but infinitely many.

Spinoza argues for human immortality; but he concludes that we survive only in part, dispersed in the infinite mind of God. Leibniz also believed in human immortality, but immortality would be worthless, he thought, if it were not immortality of the soul. The soul, for Leibniz, is an individual, something which is numerically the same at one time as it was or will be at other times. But what exactly *is* an individual? What is the distinction between the individual and its properties, and what do we mean by saying that this individual is identical with the one I saw last week? These are the deep and difficult questions that Leibniz placed on the agenda of modern philosophy.

3.2. Monads

Every entity is either composite or simple; and simple entities do not contain parts. It is the simple entities that are the true substances, from which all other things are composed. These simple entities cannot be extended in space, since everything extended is also divisible. They are not to be confused, therefore, with the atoms of physical theory, and can best be understood in terms of their one accessible instance—the human soul, which is neither extended nor divisible, and which seems to be self-contained, substantial, and durable in exactly the way that a substance must be. Such simple individuals Leibniz called 'monads'; and, although the soul is our clearest example, there are and must be other kinds of monad, which do not share our distinguishing attributes of rationality and self-consciousness.

Leibniz's monadology contains three parts: the theory of the monad, the theory of the aggregates of monads, and the theory of the appearances of monads. These tend in three separate directions, and much ingenuity was required in order to attempt a reconciliation. Very roughly, the theory of the monad goes as follows:

1. Monads are not extended in space.

2. Monads are distinguished from each other by their properties or 'predicates'.

3. No monad can come into being or pass away in the natural course of things; a monad is created or annihilated only by a 'miracle'—i.e. an event that is unaccountable in natural terms.

4. The properties of a monad are 'perceptions'—i.e. mental states—and the objects of these mental states are ideas. Even stones are aggregates of monads and owe their nature to the minute perceptions which are predicated of those monads.

5. Not all perceptions are conscious. The conscious perceptions, or apperceptions, are characteristic of rational souls, but not of lesser beings. And even rational souls have states of which they are not conscious.

6. 'Monads have no windows'—that is, nothing is passed to them from outside; each of their states is generated from their own inner principle, according to their individual nature. This does not mean that they do not interact; but it does mean that certain theories of *how* individual substances interact are untenable.

Such conclusions follow, according to Leibniz, from the very idea of an individual substance; but they are also borne out by metaphysical principles which he defended independently.

3.3. Principles

There are two principles which Leibniz proposed as the supreme principles of rational thought, and which he defended throughout his intellectual career:

1. The principle of contradiction, 'in virtue of which we judge that which involves a contradiction to be false, and that which is opposed or contradictory to the false to be true' (*Monadology*, sect. 31; *Theodicy*, sects. 44, 169);

2. The principle of sufficient reason, 'by virtue of which we consider that we can find no true or existent fact, no true assertion, without there being a sufficient reason why it is thus and not otherwise, although most of the time

these reasons cannot be known to us' (*Monadology*, sect. 32; *Theodicy*, sects. 44, 196).

Corresponding to those two principles, there are also two kinds of truth: truths of reason and truths of fact. The first are necessary and their opposite impossible, whereas truths of fact are contingent and their opposite possible. Leibniz's rationalism derives from his belief that for every truth of fact there is a sufficient reason, so that there is no *bare* contingency in the world.

In earlier writings, Leibniz was disposed to emphasize another principle:

3. The predicate-in-subject principle. This is stated in various ways, for instance: 'when a proposition is not an identity, that is, when the predicate is not explicitly contained in the subject, it must be contained in it virtually . . . Thus the subject term must always contain the predicate term, so that one who understands perfectly the notion of the subject would also know that the predicate belongs to it' (*Discourse on Metaphysics*, sect. 8). More succinctly: 'In every true proposition, necessary or contingent, universal or particular, the concept of the predicate is in a sense included in that of the subject, *praedicatum in est subjecto*, or I know not what truth is' (Letter to Arnauld, 4 July 1686; Gerhardt, ii. 56).[5]

The third principle has posed many difficulties to commentators, and Leibniz himself was aware of the objections to it: in particular, its inability to deal with negative propositions ('No good person is unhappy'), or propositions involving quantity and existence. He had intended the principle as a general theory of truth. The truth of a proposition consists in the fact that it attributes to a subject a predicate the concept of which is already contained in that of the subject. Whether or not Leibniz still believed in this principle when he wrote the *Monadology* is a moot point. But it should be understood in terms of what follows in Section 3.4.

3.4. The Complete Notion

To every individual substance there corresponds a 'complete notion', which is given by the complete list of its predications. This notion identifies the substance as the individual that it is, and is the conception given in God's mind when he chooses to create it. Since there is no truth about a substance that is not a predication of it, substances must be distinguished by their predications. And having enumerated all those predications, one has given the *whole* truth about the individual to which they apply. Moreover, anything less than the whole truth will not suffice to identify the individual as the individual that it is: for an individual may share any of its predications with another individual, and only the totality can be guaranteed to individuate it. If God is to have a reason

---

[5] In *Leibniz: Philosophical Papers and Letters*, ed. Leroy E. Loemker, 2nd edn. (Dordrecht, 1969), 377.

to create some individual, therefore, it can only be because he has a complete notion of that individual, so as to determine which individual it is that he is creating. The principle of sufficient reason—which implies that there is a sufficient reason for the existence of each contingent thing—requires that there be a complete notion for every substance.

If that is so, however, then the predicate-in-subject principle is true, even if we could not ourselves apply it. For God, at least, the truth of every subject–predicate proposition consists in the fact that the concept of the predicate is contained in the complete notion of the subject. One consequence of this, which is also an application of the principle of sufficient reason, is another famous Leibnizian principle:

4. The identity of indiscernibles. If two putative individuals have all their properties in common, then they are not two individuals but one. There cannot be two individuals which are exactly alike. There will always be *some* respect in which *a* differs from *b*, if *a* and *b* are not identical.

The converse of this principle holds that if *a* and *b* are identical, everything true of *a* is true of *b* and vice versa: it is sometimes known as Leibniz's law, and is rarely disputed by modern philosophers. The identity of indiscernibles, however, is highly controversial, since it is used by Leibniz to prove the relativity of space and time, and to establish a metaphysical distinction between the world of substances and the world of their appearances. (See below, Section 3.10.)

3.5. God

Like the other rationalists, Leibniz accepted a version of the ontological argument for God's existence. However, the proof works only on the assumption that the concept of God contains no contradiction—an assumption that we are entitled to make, according to Leibniz, since the concept of a being with all perfections (including existence) contains nothing negative which would contradict any of the positive predications. (*Monadology*, sect. 45.)

But Leibniz arrives at the existence of God in a more interesting way, through the principle of sufficient reason. The sufficient reason for the existence of contingent things cannot be found in other contingent things, which always demand an explanation for their existence. This explanation is forthcoming only on the assumption of a necessary being, a being which 'carries the reason for its existence within itself'. 'And this ultimate reason for the existence of things is called *God*' (*Principles of Nature and Grace*, sect. 8).

Being supremely good, God must have created the best of all possible worlds. Hence the truth of another famous Leibnizian principle:

5. The principle of the best. The actual world is the best of all possible worlds. 'Best' means 'simplest in hypotheses, richest in phenomena' (*Discourse on*

Metaphysics, sect. 6): in other words, containing the greatest variety and extent of substances compatible with the greatest simplicity of laws.

The concept of a 'possible world' entered philosophy for the first time with Leibniz. It enabled him to formulate in a new way those intuitions about necessity and contingency which the rationalists made fundamental to their worldview. In particular, it enabled him to give an account of contingency.

3.6. Contingency

The truth of the proposition that Caesar crossed the Rubicon consists in the fact that the predicate 'crosses the Rubicon' is contained in the complete notion of Caesar. But in that case, someone might object, it is necessarily true that Caesar crossed the Rubicon. Anyone who did not cross the Rubicon would be someone whose complete notion did not contain this particular predicate; and such a one could not be Caesar. What, then, is the distinction between a necessary and a contingent truth?

Leibniz's solution to this problem is not entirely clear. Here is one possibility: There is a sense in which it is necessarily true, of Caesar, that he crossed the Rubicon: anyone who did not do that thing would not be Caesar. But still, Caesar might not have crossed the Rubicon: for there might have been no such individual as this Caesar. His existence is a contingent fact, dependent upon the will of God. There are possible worlds in which there is no such person, and in which the event that we describe as 'Caesar crossing the Rubicon' does not occur. In that sense the proposition that Caesar crossed the Rubicon might have been false. A necessary truth, by contrast, is one that is true in all possible worlds: and the marks of a necessary truth are that it is universal and knowable a priori to us. Only God can know a *contingent* truth a priori, since only he possesses the complete notions of contingent things. We must know them a posteriori, if we are to know them at all. The terms 'a priori' and 'a posteriori' did not have the same resonance for Leibniz as they do today. Nevertheless, they indicated a radical division in his metaphysics between God's view of the world and our view. God knows everything a priori, and it is this a priori aspect of things that is captured by the 'predicate-in-notion' principle. But it follows from this that every contingent thing exists because of the world which contains it—the world which God has chosen and of which this very individual is an indispensable part. But this suggested to Leibniz an idea that was to assume ever greater importance in his thinking: the 'mirroring' thesis, according to which each substance mirrors the world that contains it: 'every substance is like a whole world, and like a mirror of God or of all the universe which each expresses after its own fashion' (*Discourse on Metaphysics*, sect. 9).

What, then, is a contingent truth for Leibniz? It is a truth of which God possesses an a priori proof, but which we cannot demonstrate as necessary (as following from the principle of contradiction) but only as contingent, in accordance with the principle of the best (*Discourse on Metaphysics*, sect. 13).

3.7. Freedom and Necessity

It is in some such way that Leibniz tries to reconcile his philosophy with the belief in human freedom. In *Discourse on Metaphysics*, sect. 13, he writes as follows:

We must distinguish between what is certain and what is necessary. Everyone grants that future contingents are certain, since God foresees them, but we do not concede that they are necessary on that account. But (someone will say) if a conclusion can be deduced infallibly from a definition or notion, it is necessary. And it is true that we are maintaining that everything that must happen to a person is already contained virtually in his nature or notion, just as the properties of a circle are contained in its definition . . .

Yet, he argues, human freedom is a reality, since, although it is necessary in *this* sense that Caesar should cross the Rubicon, it is still not impossible that the event should not happen. God chose the best of possible worlds, and in that world, just such an event indeed happens. But there is no contradiction in supposing that God had chosen differently.

But surely God, being supremely good, *must* choose the best of all possible worlds? And in what sense am I, created according to God's complete notion of me, free to do other than I do, when what I do is contained in my notion from the start?

Leibniz seems to say that there are two kinds of necessity, corresponding to two kinds of reason. In a mathematical proof, reasoning necessitates the conclusion. In reasoning about what is best to do, however, our reasons 'incline without necessitating' (*New Essays*, 175; *Correspondence with Arnauld*). Such are God's reasons for creating the actual world (the best); and such, presumably, are our reasons for behaving as we do.

Most commentators have found Leibniz's treatment of free will obscure at best; part of the problem lies in the fact that Leibniz has two contrasting ways of envisaging the individuality of monads (see Section 3.8).

3.8. Activity and the *Vis Viva*

Monads are individuated in God's mind by their complete notions. But the complete notion merely lists the predicates of a monad, and says nothing about the link between them. Looked at in another way, each monad can be seen as a centre of activity, whose perceptions are generated by a single perduring force. Like Spinoza, Leibniz was impressed by the substantial unity of organic beings, and believed that we observe in them, from another perspective, the individuality that is revealed in a timeless way to God. He sometimes writes of the *conatus* of individual substances, and defends a theory of dynamics which gives pride of place to what he calls the *vis viva*, or 'living force', in things, as opposed to the 'dead force', or momentum, that features in the Cartesian physics. (Leibniz's defence of the *vis viva* initiated one of the most important scientific controversies of the day.)

The active principle in monads enables us to individuate monads without relying on their complete notions. I can identify the individual substance who is Caesar, without already predicating of him that he will cross the Rubicon. But the active principle that binds the predicates of this substance together inclines him already in that very direction—inclines, but does not necessitate.

Leibniz also refers to the activity of monads in another sense, familiar from Spinoza: a monad is active to the extent that its ideas are 'distinct', passive to the extent that they are 'confused'. But to understand this aspect of Leibniz we must attend to his theory of aggregates.

3.9. Aggregates of Monads

In speaking of organic things we are not as a rule talking of individual monads. Every living organism is an aggregate of many monads. What binds them together, and what enables us to speak of *one* organism, when we have a plurality of simple individuals? It seems that the original problem that motivated Leibniz—the problem of accounting for the actual individuals in our world—remains with him.

First, Leibniz makes use of the theory of ideas, which he inherits from Descartes. Each monad has perceptions or knowledge, which may be more or less clear and distinct, and more or less adequate.

When I can recognize a thing from among others without being able to say what its differences or properties consist in, the knowledge is *confused*. It is in this way that we sometimes know something *clearly*, without being in any doubt whether a poem or a picture is done well or badly, simply because it has a certain something, I know not what, that satisfies or offends us. But when I can explain the marks which I have, the knowledge is called *distinct*. And such is the knowledge of an assayer, who discerns the true from the false by means of certain tests or marks which make up the definition of gold.

But distinct knowledge has degrees, for ordinarily the notions that enter into the definition would themselves need definition and are known only confusedly. But when everything that enters into a distinct definition . . . is known distinctly . . . I call this knowledge *adequate*. (*Discourse on Metaphysics*, sect. 24)

What, then, is the relation between an idea and its object? For example, what happens when I perceive something? Nothing is passed to me from the thing perceived; nevertheless, there is a sense in which all my perceptions represent the world around me. They do this because the predicates of other monads unfold in harmony with mine: each of my perceptions corresponds to perceptions in the surrounding monads, and enables me to infer, with more or less confusion, what is going on in them. This is possible, however, only on the assumption of another Leibnizian principle:

6. The principle of pre-established harmony. Each monad has a 'point of view' on the world, defined by the totality of its perceptions; and because our perceptions evolve in harmony with each other, my perceptions can be treated as perceptions of the surrounding world.

Another way of putting this is to say that each monad 'mirrors' the universe from its own point of view. The 'interconnection or accommodation of all created things to each other, and each to all the others, brings it about that each simple substance has relations that express all the others, and consequently, that each simple substance is a perpetual living mirror of the universe' (*Monadology*, sect. 56).

How then are monads related? Such influence as there is between monads is only 'ideal', an effect of God's constant intervention (*Monadology*, sect. 51). Nevertheless, monads can have a more or less clear idea of each other, or of their situation—as I have a clear idea of my body (without knowing how it is composed—i.e. without having a distinct idea). Through the greater or less clarity and distinctness of our ideas, we are connected to surrounding monads more or less closely. We can speak of being 'affected' by them, to the extent that our perceptions represent more or less clearly what is going on in them.

In each organism, there is a 'dominant monad', distinguished by the clarity of its perceptions of the others, which is the true source of the organism's unity. This dominant monad is the 'entelechy' of the body: the animating principle, or soul. In some way that Leibniz does not manage to explain, it binds the aggregate of monads into a substantial unity: it provides a *vinculum substantiale*, or 'substantial chain', making a new quasi-individual out of the simple individuals of the body. (*Monadology*, sects. 61–5.)

3.10. The Appearance of Monads

That is confusing enough. But matters are made worse by Leibniz's growing conviction that the appearance of the world is organized and understood in ways that do not represent the reality. The familiar world around us appears ordered in space and time; it contains extended and durable things, which interact and obey causal laws. Yet monads are not extended—perhaps they are not 'in time' in quite the way that physical objects are. ('Time is no more nor less a thing of reason than space is': Letter to de Volder, 24 March/3 April

1699.)[6] Moreover, they do not interact in the way that physical objects appear to interact, but only through their all-embracing power of representation. As for causal laws, these are established a posteriori, by observation of the physical world: how can we use them to describe the activities of monads, which are not really part of that world at all?

The attempt to reconcile the truths of physics with the extraordinary theory of composite monads pushed Leibniz in a direction that was to be followed by Kant. The ordinary physical world, he suggested, is a 'well-founded phenomenon'—i.e. an appearance that does not deceive us, since its regularity and order reflect the underlying order of the monads themselves. Space is not really real: it is an order in which the monads appear to our point of view, a system of apparent relations between things which, in themselves, possess no spatial properties at all. (Hence Leibniz's attack on Newton, in the *Correspondence with Clarke*.) Causal laws are systematic regularities in the world of appearance: but they do not describe the real principles of activity in the world of monads.

The interesting result is that, having tried to reconcile the rationalist concept of substance with the common-sense concept of an individual, Leibniz ends by saying that the apparent individuals in our world are for the most part not individuals at all. Moreover, he is able to give no coherent account of the fact that they nevertheless appear to be individuals. No example of a monad presents itself, save the individual soul: and yet the soul is as much outside the natural order (the order of well-founded phenomena) as anything else.

4. KANT

Immanuel Kant (1724–1804) was the greatest philosopher of modern times, and the most influential thinker of the German Enlightenment. He spent his entire life in the city of Königsberg, then a centre of civilization, but since devastated by war and by forcible incorporation into the former Soviet Union. (It remains part of Russia, though entirely cut off from the rest of that country.) He was a Christian of the pietist school, and his life reflected the habits in which he had been brought up: chaste, dutiful, cheerful, and studious. His early interest in mathematics and physics left an abiding mark on his thinking, as did his lifelong delight in poetry. His masterwork, the *Critique of Pure Reason*, was composed when he was Professor of Philosophy in the University of Königsberg, and appeared in 1781, when Kant was 57. It was followed by a *Critique of Practical Reason*, dealing with ethics, and a *Critique of Judgement*, dealing with aesthetics and theology.

This survey does not cover the second or third of those Critiques. It is

---

[6] In *Leibniz: Philosophical Papers and Letters*, ed. Loemker.

devoted solely to the *Critique of Pure Reason*, and in particular to the first two parts of it, in which Kant mounts his great criticism of empiricism and scepticism, and tries to lay the foundations for an objective science. There were two editions of this first Critique in Kant's lifetime, the second substantially different from the first. Standard translations include both texts, referred to as A and B respectively.

It is unwise to study the *Critique of Pure Reason* without first acquiring some knowledge of Leibniz and Hume—if only the introduction provided by this chapter and the companion to it written by Anthony Grayling. Kant was brought up in the Leibnizian system, as this had been expounded by Wolff and Baumgarten, and his philosophy began as a reaction against it. The reaction was precipitated by a reading of Hume, whose scepticism about causation awoke Kant 'from his dogmatic slumbers'. The Kantian system is at one and the same time a critique of the pretensions of Leibnizian rationalism, and an answer to the corrosive scepticism of Hume.

In the following summary I depart from my previous practice, and include no direct quotations from Kant: relevant quotations can be found in my short introduction;[7] to include them here would make the already difficult task of condensation totally impossible.

4.1. The Structure of the *Critique of Pure Reason*

As its title implies, the first Critique was originally conceived as a critique of rationalism—specifically, of the view that we can know how the world is, and how it must be, by a priori reflection which makes no reference to experience: by 'pure reason'. Kant perceived that, for all their attempts to give firm foundations to their systems, the rationalists were driven to assume that reason is sufficient in itself to produce objective knowledge. (Hence the Cartesian circle: see Section 1.7.) Such knowledge would be a priori and also 'synthetic'. The term 'synthetic' is to be understood in contrast to 'analytic', where an analytic judgement is one whose truth follows merely from the meaning of the words used to express it—in Kant's terms, a judgement in which the concept of the predicate is 'included' in that of the subject. (Notice the influence here of Leibniz's predicate-in-subject principle.)

Thus 'All bodies are extended' is analytic: it follows from the meanings that we give to 'body' and 'extended' that the second term applies to everything that falls under the first. If a priori knowledge were merely of analytic truths, Kant argues, then it would be trivial and uninformative, as the empiricists tended to claim, and reason could advance to no substantial (synthetic) conclusions about the nature of reality. In effect the rationalists had neglected to answer (and also

---

[7] *Kant* (Oxford, 1982).

to ask) the fundamental question on which their enterprise depends: namely, how is synthetic a priori knowledge possible?

Kant aims to answer that question in the first two parts of the Critique, before moving on to his negative assessment of traditional rationalist philosophy. Briefly, his answer is that synthetic a priori knowledge *is* possible, but only from the point of view of 'possible experience'—the point of view of sensory awareness. The rationalists' attempt to free reason from the senses, and to know the world as it is in itself, independently of how it appears to us, is vain, and leads only to contradictions, fallacies, and paradoxes.

Kant's answer to his question is couched in technical terms, and his genius for inventing or adapting these terms and giving to them a lasting resonance produced a new philosophical vocabulary. Here are some examples, with which the student of Kant should make himself familiar:

1. 'Faculty'. According to Kant, our knowledge comes to us through the exercise of certain 'faculties'—mental capacities—which, while radically different in kind, do not operate in isolation, but are bound by a mutual dependence. One faculty is that of sensibility, through which we obtain 'intuitions' (the raw material of experience). Another faculty is that of reason, which is deployed in several ways, through various subfaculties, some of which are legitimate, others of which are not. Thus we need reason in order to bring our intuitions under 'concepts', and so to make judgements about how the world seems. This legitimate deployment of reason is also called 'understanding', which is the faculty of concepts, just as sensibility is the faculty of intuitions. We deploy reason in inference, and in thinking about what to do. Both of those are legitimate exercises, and the second, called practical reason by Kant, is the subject of his second Critique, in which he deals with morality. We may also try to deploy reason in pure speculation about the world, without reference to the 'conditions' which make experience possible. This is pure reason, the illegitimate employment of our reasoning powers from which all the vain systems of the rationalists derive.

2. 'Empirical' and 'transcendental'. To prove a proposition empirically is to derive it by valid reasoning from the data of experience. Such empirical proof lies outside the domain of philosophy, whose arguments are really 'transcendental'. In a transcendental 'deduction' I transcend the limits of empirical inquiry, so as to establish a priori the conditions which make experience possible. I may deduce from my present experience that I am seeing a sheep: that is an empirical deduction. But I may also deduce that I am a conscious subject of experience, who endures through time and change—for that is a presupposition of my having any experience at all. This second deduction is a priori and also transcendental.

3. 'Aesthetic' and 'logic'. From the Greek words for sensation and reason, these terms are used by Kant in order to distinguish the study of sensibility from that of our reasoning powers.

The *Critique of Pure Reason* is organized as follows: an introduction poses the general question of synthetic a priori knowledge: how is it possible? The answer is given in the Transcendental Doctrine of Elements, which divides into two parts: the Transcendental Aesthetic, which deals with sensibility, and which justifies those claims to synthetic a priori knowledge that depend upon the 'forms of intuition' alone; and the Transcendental Logic, which deals with those claims to synthetic a priori knowledge which depend upon concepts. The Transcendental Logic itself divides into two parts: the Analytic, which justifies the legitimate employment of reason (reason as understanding), and the Dialectic, which criticizes the illegitimate excesses of 'pure' reason.

For simplicity's sake, the Critique is normally divided into three parts: the Aesthetic, the Analytic, and the Dialectic, ignoring Kant's own elaborate architecture, much of which seems irrelevant to his intellectual purpose.

4.2. The Aesthetic

Kant noticed that there are at least two kinds of a priori knowledge, apart from the knowledge of analytic truths: mathematics and metaphysics. (At certain points, Kant proposes natural science as containing, or deriving from, a third kind of a priori knowledge.) It seems unlikely that mathematics and metaphysics could be justified in the same way. For one thing, mathematical truth is the property of all rational beings, an area of immediate certainty and agreement, which seems to proceed untroubled from discovery to discovery. Metaphysics, by contrast, is an area of doubt and confusion, whose every claim is disputed. In explaining the a priori nature of mathematics, we must also explain its 'immediacy', and its intuitive obviousness.

Some philosophers—Leibniz included—had tried to show that mathematical propositions are analytic ('true by definition'). But their efforts end, Kant thinks, in inevitable failure. Every mathematical judgement—even so simple a judgement as 2 + 2 = 4—requires a 'synthesis', an advance in thought from premiss to conclusion. Plato's theory of mathematics, as a sphere of eternal truth concerning entities (the numbers) that exist outside space and time, renders our knowledge of mathematics mysterious: for how could finite and experience-bound creatures ever ascend to such a sphere, and how could numbers act on us to produce our knowledge of them? We need to show how creatures like us can gain access to this fertile realm of a priori truth, by means of the faculties that we employ, and must employ, in gaining knowledge.

There are two kinds of mathematical truth: geometry and arithmetic. According to Kant, these are not reducible to each other, and you can have full knowledge of the one with only an imperfect grasp of the other. So two explanations are needed, if mathematics is to be fully accounted for:

1. Geometry. According to Kant, geometry gives us a priori knowledge of space. And by space, he means what is now called Euclidean space: the space described in Euclid's *Elements*. How is it that we can have a priori knowledge of space? Not implausibly, Kant suggests that we *perceive* objects as arranged in space, and that this is a fundamental truth about the faculty of 'intuition'. If we are to have an experience in which something is represented as objective (i.e. independent of our mental processes), it must also be represented as being *somewhere* in relation to us. Hence the very process whereby we come to see the world as objective inscribes a spatial arrangement upon it. Space is the 'form' of our intuition of objective items, or the 'form of outer sense'. Hence we can have a priori knowledge of space, since the properties of space are reproduced in our own sensibility.

Kant goes on to argue that there is only one space, that space is absolute, Euclidean, and given to us through an 'a priori intuition'.

2. Arithmetic. Having derived geometry from 'outer sense'—i.e. the faculty whereby we refer our sensory states to an objective world—Kant goes on to make obscure remarks about the derivation of the other branches of mathematics. At certain points he seems to suggest that arithmetic derives from 'inner sense'—the faculty whereby we refer perceptions and experiences to ourselves, as the subjects of them. He assimilates arithmetic to counting, which is the general science of 'succession'. This 'order of succession', as Leibniz had called it, is the order of experience itself, which is also the order of time. This suggestion, which would make arithmetic the a priori science of time, just as geometry, for Kant, is the a priori science of space, is, however, never confidently endorsed by Kant. It would imply that, just as we have a priori knowledge of space through geometry, so do we have a priori knowledge of time through arithmetic. In the end Kant passes over the question of arithmetic, contenting himself with examples (such as addition) which show, he thinks, that the truths of arithmetic cannot be analytic, since there is always a 'synthesis' involved in drawing any arithmetical conclusion.

Despite its obscurity, Kant's theory of space and time as forms of intuition (i.e. pre-conceptual orders of experience) was extremely influential. And it suggested to him a general theory of a priori knowledge: we can know the world a priori because the world 'conforms to' our faculties. We know a priori that the world is knowable (otherwise we should not even have the *question* of knowledge). It is knowable, however, only if it conforms to the conditions which make knowledge possible. One is that it should mirror the forms of intuition—i.e. it should be arranged in space and time. And that explains not only the a priori nature of mathematics, but also its immediacy (being connected with intuition, rather than concept).

4.3. The Analytic

The Analytic contains Kant's positive theory of metaphysics. First, he argues that knowledge in general, and experience in particular, cannot be derived from intuition (i.e. pure sensory intake) alone: it requires a 'synthesis' of intuition and concept. Intuitions lead to knowledge only if they are brought under concepts: intuitions are the matter to which concepts provide the form.

Concepts are of two kinds: a posteriori and a priori. The former are also empirical concepts: concepts, like that of a horse, which we derive from our experience. But not all concepts are like that. If we are to derive concepts from experience we must first of all interpret our experience in the appropriate way, for instance, as an experience of an object. The concept of an object is not itself empirical, since it is presupposed in the very attempt to obtain empirical knowledge. It is an a priori concept—the Kantian equivalent of Leibniz's 'innate idea'. In their 'pure' form (the form in which they are separated entirely from space and time, and therefore from intuition) the a priori concepts are called 'categories'. (The term comes from Aristotle.)

Kant draws up a table of twelve categories, which he believes give the fundamental forms of thought—the mental operations without which the understanding could not bring intuitions under concepts at all. This Table of Categories is a hodgepodge; but it contains several items—notably the concepts of substance and cause—which lead to much interesting discussion at a later point.

If we are to uphold our claims to synthetic a priori knowledge, Kant argues, we must provide a 'deduction' of these categories—a proof that we are entitled to use them, that the world 'conforms to' them, and that therefore the pre-conditions for their use are in fact fulfilled. This deduction cannot be empirical, since an empirical deduction would already require us to use the categories in order that our experience should be described; it must therefore be transcendental. Thus we arrive at the most important and most obscure chapter of the *Critique of Pure Reason*: 'The Transcendental Deduction of the Categories'.

Very roughly, the Transcendental Deduction attempts to show that experience is possible only under a certain general condition, which we might describe as 'objectivity'. If there is to be experience at all, the world must be objective in relation to the perceiver—there must be a real distinction between how the world seems to him and how it is. And the categories are justified, in so far as they tell us what that distinction amounts to. They tell us that an objective world is one containing substances (i.e. enduring objects), organized by causal laws, in a constant state of interaction, and that we are part of its all-embracing order. If that is so, then the sceptic has been refuted: his arguments make no sense, except on the understanding that he has experience; but experience presupposes the very things that he doubts—his existence as part of an objective order, obedient to causal laws.

But what is the argument? No commentator seems to agree with any other, and the darkness of Kant's prose does nothing to abate the confusion. The premiss seems to be contained in the proposition which Kant summarizes as 'the transcendental unity of apperception': the unity of the self, which enables me to say that this thought that I have, and this sensation, belong to *one* thing. I know this unity on no basis, without doubt or the need for discovery (i.e. with a 'transcendental' rather than an empirical guarantee). What makes such a transcendental unity possible? Only my awareness of my own existence and identity through time. But how is that awareness possible, if I do not situate myself in a world of enduring things—things which can be other than they seem to me, and which therefore exist objectively? In some such way Kant advances to the astonishing conclusion that subjective experience is possible only in an objective world, a world which 'conforms to the categories'.

But, he adds, this justification of the categories renders them legitimate only on the supposition that they are applied in experience, and to the world as experienced. We can use them to obtain synthetic a priori knowledge, but only of the world construed as an object of 'possible experience'. Any other use of the categories, for example to obtain knowledge of the world as it is in itself, and from no empirical viewpoint, would be illegitimate.

So what is the nature and extent of our synthetic a priori knowledge? In a chapter devoted to 'principles', Kant goes through the categories one by one, and tries to show that each of them can be applied only on the assumption that a certain principle holds true of the world as we encounter it. For example, the concept of cause can be applied only on the general assumption that every event has a cause (the law of causality, which Kant takes to be a special case of the principle of sufficient reason). This assumption could never be proved empirically, since it has the two marks of an a priori truth: it is both universal, and necessary. But it can be proved 'transcendentally', by the following steps:

(1) I have experience.
(2) Therefore experience is possible.
(3) Experience is possible only if the category of cause can be applied to the world of experience.
(4) The category of cause can be applied only if the world of experience 'conforms to' it.
(5) Therefore the world of experience conforms to the a priori condition of the category of cause: namely, it obeys the principle, that every event has a cause.

Of course, Kant needs to show that the principle that every event has a cause really *is* assumed in the application of the concept of cause. Most commentators doubt that he succeeds in proving this in the section (the second Analogy) in which he tries to do so.

4.4. Appearance and Thing-in-itself

The vindication of the a priori applies only to the world as we experience it—the 'world of appearance' or 'appearances'. Kant makes a distinction between appearance and thing-in-itself, and suggests that the attempt to know the thing-in-itself is doomed to failure. What exactly does he mean by 'thing-in-itself'?

One way of looking at the matter is through Descartes's search for the 'absolute conception' (see Section 1.8). We know the world through our sensory experience and the conceptions that we derive from it. But can we know it as God knows it, as it really is, unpolluted by our finite viewpoint? Kant's answer is that we cannot, and that the idea of an absolute view of things—while it persists as a kind of after-image of pure reason—is no more than an idea, and corresponds to no actual or possible knowledge. Kant made another distinction in this connection, between phenomenon and noumenon. A phenomenon is an object of possible experience. This does not mean merely something that can be seen, heard, or touched: it means anything that is part of the system of the world, as experience reveals it—anything that is postulated by an empirically based science. A noumenon is an object of pure thought, which has no counterpart in the world of experience (the world of science). Many of the entities postulated by philosophers are noumena: they have no reality in the world of appearance but exist, like the monads of Leibniz (on Kant's interpretation), outside the conditions of sensibility (outside space and time), and unconnected with anything observable. Of such things, Kant argues, we can have no positive conception, since the categories do not apply to them—they violate the condition of 'possible experience'. Nevertheless, we seem to have the concept of a noumenon. It is therefore a concept that we can employ only 'negatively', and not in positive judgements. The negative employment of the concept of a noumenon is essentially critical: it sounds a warning, saying in effect that here our knowledge stops, and to attempt to know this thing is to pass beyond 'the bounds of sense'.

The distinction between appearance and thing-in-itself is a metaphysical version of the epistemological distinction between phenomenon and noumenon. All our knowledge is of the empirical world; and even that which we know a priori merely describes the form and structure of the empirical world, and our place within it.

4.5. The Dialectic

While reason, circumscribed by the concepts of the understanding, yields genuine knowledge, it also contains a temptation to illusion. The Dialectic presents a diagnosis of this illusion, by exploring the common views of rationalist philosophers, and showing that each incorporates a fallacy. Concepts, divorced from their 'empirical conditions', are empty; and this means that they can never be used as the rationalists wish to use them, in order to give a description of the world from no point of view within it. The attempt to obtain such a description is also a search for 'unconditioned' knowledge. At the same time, it seems to lie in the nature of reason that it should seek to transcend the conditions of sensibility, and to see the world as it is in itself. The 'unconditioned' is not a concept, but an 'idea of reason'. For Kant, ideas of reason are permanent parts of our mental equipment, inevitable by-products of our understanding, which also tempt us away from it.

Three such ideas dominate traditional metaphysics: God, freedom, and immortality. These correspond (in reverse order) to the three principal divisions of the Dialectic:

1. The Paralogisms. In this chapter Kant argues vigorously against the rationalist and Cartesian conception of the soul, as a simple, indivisible, and indestructible substance. In every case, he argues, the rationalists commit a fallacy, arguing from the 'transcendental unity' of apperception, which is merely formal, to a 'substantial unity'. They begin from a true premiss: that I am immediately acquainted in my thinking with a unity of consciousness; but they proceed to a false conclusion: that therefore I am a substance, an enduring and simple thing, independent of the physical world. No such conclusion can be drawn.

2. The Antinomies. In addition to discussing (in the third Antinomy) the problem of freedom, and Kant's highly influential and original solution to it, this chapter is devoted to the entire field of rational cosmology. The questions considered are these: Did the world have a beginning in time? Is the world limited or unlimited in space? Is matter infinitely divisible? And so on. The argument proceeds by an 'antinomy': a contradiction is derived from a certain assumption, and the assumption thereby shown to be illegitimate. For example, we suppose that we can understand the world as a whole in both space and time: this is part of what is assumed by the rationalist conception of knowledge. If that is so, we could meaningfully ask whether the world has a beginning in time. We can prove that it must have; but also that it cannot have (these are the thesis and the antithesis of the first Antinomy). There must be something wrong, therefore, with the assumption: the point of view on the world that is presupposed by the rationalist cosmology is unobtainable.

3. The Ideal of Reason. This chapter deals with 'natural theology', and consists in a systematic demolition of the traditional arguments for the existence of God, which Kant divides into three kinds: teleological, cosmological, and ontological. The first (the argument from design) argues that the world exhibits such an order that only a creator could have caused it; the second argues that there must be a 'first cause' if there is to be a cause of anything; the third argues, as

we have seen, that God, defined as a being containing all perfections, must exist, since existence is a perfection.

Kant famously dismisses the ontological argument with his assertion that existence is not a 'true predicate': it adds nothing to the subject. Hence it is not a perfection, and cannot be 'part of the concept' of anything, as the rationalists supposed. Although this reply has not satisfied everyone, it can fairly be said that Kant's attack on the ontological argument was the final nail in the coffin of rationalism—a coffin which Kant himself had designed.

BIBLIOGRAPHY

A suitable brief introduction is Roger Scruton, *A Short History of Modern Philosophy* (London, 1981).

DESCARTES

EDITIONS

The standard edition of Descartes's works is the *Œuvres de Descartes*, i–xii, plus supplement, ed. Charles Adam and Paul Tannery (Paris, 1897–1913).

The following English editions are satisfactory: *The Philosophical Works of Descartes*, trans. E. S. Haldane and G. R. T. Ross, 2 vols. (Cambridge, 1911). *Descartes: Philosophical Writings*, a selection trans. and ed. Elizabeth Anscombe and P. T. Geach (Sunbury-on-Thames, 1954; rev. 1970). *The Philosophical Writings of Descartes*, trans. John Cottingham, Robert Stoothoff, and Dugald Murdoch, 2 vols. (Cambridge, 1985). *Descartes: Selected Philosophical Writings*, trans. John Cottingham, Robert Stoothoff, and Dugald Murdoch, ed. John Cottingham (Cambridge, 1988). This is a one-volume abridgement of the previously cited work and has been brilliantly edited to meet student needs. It contains marginal page reference to Adam and Tannery's edition, and presents a clearly translated text with the minimum of distracting apparatus.

COMMENTATORS

These are legion, but the following deserve special mention: Anthony Kenny, *Descartes: A Study of his Philosophy* (New York, 1968). This is an unexciting work, which is a useful (if not wholly reliable) guide to Descartes's central argument. Bernard Williams, *Descartes: The Project of Pure Enquiry* (Harmondsworth, 1978). An imaginative work, which—though difficult in parts—conveys an unmatched sense of the importance of Descartes and his philosophical project. Margaret Wilson, *Descartes*, Arguments of the Philosophers (London, 1983). A dull but dutiful book, which will neither interest nor mislead.

In addition there is a valuable collection of articles, which should be read if at all possible: Willis Doney, *Descartes: A Collection of Critical Essays* (London, 1968). The essays in this collection are frequently difficult, and to a measure out of date.

Nevertheless, those by Williams, Hintikka, Kenny, and Gewirth are important. The volume also contains a valuable bibliography, although confined to material published before 1968.

SPINOZA

EDITIONS

Spinoza wrote in Latin; the standard edition of his works in the original is *Spinoza Opera*, ed. C. Gebhardt, 4 vols. (Heidelberg, 1925). There are several translations of the major metaphysical works available. Undeniably the best, in what will surely become the standard English-language edition of Spinoza, is that by Edwin Curley: *The Collected Works of Spinoza*, i (Princeton, NJ, 1985). (Volume ii, containing the political works and the remainder of Spinoza's correspondence, has yet to appear.) This magisterial edition, containing everything one needs, is complete with glossary, index, and editorial apparatus, and makes the works fully accessible for the first time. Unfortunately, however, it is expensive, and not very easy to obtain. An acceptable alternative is the translation of the *Ethics* rev. and ed. G. H. R. Parkinson, Everyman (London, 1989). However, this does not contain two other works that should, if possible, be consulted: the *Treatise on the Emendation of the Intellect*, and the *Correspondence*. The first is available in the original Everyman edition, trans. Andrew Boyle (London, 1910); the second is available in a translation edited by A. Wolf (London, 1928; reissued 1966). The correspondence relating to the metaphysical works also occurs in Curley, where it is illuminatingly introduced by the translator. The correspondence should not be neglected, since it contains Spinoza's own attempts to make his system clear and accessible to puzzled or sceptical readers. It should be said that Boyle's translation is far from adequate, even in Parkinson's revision. Rather better is the translation of Samuel Shirley, which is available in a volume that contains both the *Ethics* and the *Treatise on the Emendation of the Intellect*, together with a selection from the *Correspondence*, edited, with a lively introduction, by Seymour Feldman (Indianapolis, 1991). This is the edition that the student should use, if it is available.

COMMENTATORS

There has been surprisingly little useful commentary on Spinoza's philosophy, although in recent years the literature has begun to expand, with a professional journal devoted entirely to Spinoza studies, and many often highly abstruse and technical papers in that and other academic publications. Most useful are: R. Scruton, *Spinoza*, Past Masters (Oxford, 1986), available in paperback. This is very short, and intended merely as a map of the territory. It is no substitute for a proper commentary in which specific arguments are explored in depth. Stuart Hampshire, *Spinoza* (Harmondsworth, 1951; repr. 1981). This path-breaking book introduced Spinoza to analytical philosophers, and remains a valuable source of ideas, even if many of its readings of the text would now be regarded as eccentric. Jonathan Bennett, *A Study of Spinoza's Ethics* (Cambridge, 1984). This is a difficult and strenuous book, which unrelentingly explores the detail of Spinoza's arguments. It is a useful antidote to the classical commentators, most of whom did not see the trees for the wood. Edwin Curley, *Behind the Geometrical*

Method: *A Reading of Spinoza's* Ethics (Princeton, NJ, 1988). This, a reworking of a previous commentary by the same writer, is also a response to Bennett's book. But it can be read on its own, and is perhaps the most readable and accessible of the shorter commentaries currently available. Also useful is: Henry Allison, *Benedict de Spinoza: An Introduction* (New Haven, Conn., 1987).

Among the collections of articles now available, S. Paul Kashap (ed.), *Studies in Spinoza: Critical and Interpretive Essays* (Los Angeles, 1972), is the most useful. It contains the important essay, 'Spinoza and the Idea of Freedom', by Stuart Hampshire, to which I refer in the text, and an essay by G. H. R. Parkinson which is an adequate substitute for the same author's dull but reliable book *Spinoza's Theory of Knowledge* (Oxford, 1954).

LEIBNIZ

EDITIONS

Leibniz's works (the majority of them unpublished in his lifetime) are being published in scholarly editions by the German Academy, which Leibniz himself founded. Moving with exemplary slowness (due in part to the political divisions of Germany in recent times) the Academy has done little to replace the previous standard edition in German, ed. C. I. Gerhardt (Berlin, 1875–90). As a result, the Gerhardt edition is still widely referred to as the leading text.

In addition there is the famous collection of Leibniz's unpublished writings by the French mathematician Louis Couturat, *Opuscules et fragments inédits de Leibniz* (Paris, 1903). This was highly influential in emphasizing the role that logical theory played in shaping Leibniz's metaphysics.

The works that the student should pay special attention to are the *Discourse on Metaphysics* and the *Monadology* (both extremely short), together with the *Principles of Nature and Grace* (also short), and the *New Essays on Human Understanding*, a lengthy dialogue with Locke which Leibniz never published. The standard selections contain important correspondence, which should not be neglected since the letters are often the clearest guides to Leibniz's ideas. Available editions are described below.

There have been two widely used English-language editions of the more important works, both including correspondence, fragments, etc.: *Leibniz: Philosophical Papers and Letters*, ed. Leroy E. Loemker, 2nd edn. (Dordrecht, 1969). *Leibniz Selections*, ed. Philip P. Wiener, 2nd edn. (New York, 1986). (Do not use the first edition if you can avoid it.)

There is now, however, a selection which is of far more use than either of those, since it is shorter, more clearly edited, and better translated. This is: G. W. Leibniz, *Philosophical Essays*, trans. and ed. Roger Ariew and Daniel Garber (Indianapolis, 1989), especially the *Discourse on Metaphysics*, the *Principles of Nature and Grace*, and the Letter to de Volder, as well as the *Monadology*, all of which are contained in it.

Among other works which are particularly important, the following are recommended: *The Leibniz–Arnauld Correspondence*, trans. H. T. Mason (Manchester, 1967). *The Leibniz–Clarke Correspondence*, trans. Samuel Clarke, ed. H. G. Alexanders (Manchester, 1956). G. W. Leibniz, *New Essays on Human Understanding*, abridged, trans., and ed. Peter Remnant and Jonathan Bennett (Cambridge, 1982). The last is an extremely useful paperback, with a succinct introduction by the editors which gives a brief biography of Leibniz, a summary of several of his more important theories, and a map of the *New Essays*. It also has an up-to-date and lucid bibliography.

The above reading list may seem long; but in fact it is very short, since all the works recommended, with the exception of the *New Essays*, are minuscule.

COMMENTATORS

I would recommend the following: G. H. R. Parkinson, *Logic and Reality in Leibniz's Metaphysics* (Oxford, 1965). A dry, scholarly work, but reliable. C. D. Broad, *Leibniz: An Introduction* (Cambridge, 1975). Thorough, straightforward, and comprehensive, if a little out of date. (These are posthumously published lecture notes.) Hidé Ishiguro, *Leibniz's Philosophy of Logic and Language* (London, 1972; 2nd edn. (much to be preferred) Cambridge, 1991). A difficult and sometimes tortuous work, which nevertheless repays study. Benson Mates, *The Philosophy of Leibniz* (Oxford, 1986). Probably the best and most accessible commentary.

There is also a famous book by Bertrand Russell, *A Critical Exposition of the Philosophy of Leibniz*, 2nd edn. (London, 1937). This tried to show that Leibniz's metaphysics (which Russell did not admire) was motivated by his logic (which he did). The interpretation offered was very influential, though now largely rejected.

Among collections of articles, the following can be recommended: Michael Hooker (ed.), *Leibniz: Critical and Interpretive Essays* (Minneapolis, 1983). R. S. Woolhouse (ed.), *Leibniz: Metaphysics and Philosophy of Science*, Oxford Readings (Oxford, 1981). This contains a good, if undiscriminating, bibliography.

KANT

EDITIONS

There is only one acceptable edition of the *Critique of Pure Reason* in English, which is that translated by Norman Kemp Smith (London, 1929). This translates both editions and contains marginal page references to each of them. Abridged editions of this work should be avoided. Kant himself wrote a kind of introduction to his metaphysical views in the *Prolegomena to Any Future Metaphysic*, trans. P. G. Lucas (Manchester, 1953). There is also available in English a useful selection from Kant's 'pre-Critical' writings (those written before the first Critique): *Kant: Selected Pre-Critical Writings*, ed. G. B. Kerferd, D. K. E. Walford, and P. G. Lucas (Manchester, 1968).

COMMENTATORS

For a short survey of Kant's philosophy, the student could consult: Roger Scruton, *Kant*, Past Masters (Oxford, 1982). This is as short a commentary as is decent, but would give a preliminary map of the territory. For more detailed analysis, the following should be consulted: P. F. Strawson, *The Bounds of Sense* (London, 1966). A thorough exposition and partial defence of the argument of the *Critique of Pure Reason*. Ralph Walker, *Kant*, Arguments of the Philosophers (London, 1979). This is in part a reply to Strawson, and is somewhat easier to read. There are two vigorous and combative commentaries by

Jonathan Bennett: *Kant's Analytic* (Cambridge, 1966), and *Kant's Dialectic* (Cambridge, 1974), which are difficult but highly stimulating.

Among collections of articles, the most useful is: Ralph Walker (ed.), *Kant on Pure Reason*, Oxford Readings in Philosophy (Oxford, 1987).

9

MODERN PHILOSOPHY II: THE EMPIRICISTS

A. C. Grayling

INTRODUCTION

Among empiricist philosophers of the early modern period three especially stand out: John Locke (1632–1704), George Berkeley (1685–1753), and David Hume (1711–76). The sections that follow discuss each in turn. Between them they addressed a wide range of philosophical questions, but the principal focus of attention here is their contributions to the theory of knowledge. Despite having a shared commitment to empiricism there are significant differences of view between them, a fact which use of the collective label 'the British empiricists' should not be allowed to obscure. Their importance is great; much in contemporary debate about epistemology and associated pursuits owes itself to their work.

Characterized generally, empiricism is the view that the source and test of contingent knowledge is experience. 'Experience' chiefly means sensory experience, that is, the use of the five senses, aided when necessary by such instruments as telescopes and microscopes. But it also includes introspective awareness of the contents and operations of the experiencer's own mind.

In the somewhat simplified way usual in introductory histories of philosophy, empiricism is opposed to rationalism, the epistemological doctrine stating that the chief route to knowledge is intellectual rather than sensory. Rationalism is typically characterized as follows. The proper object of knowledge is eternal and immutable truth. Anything less would not be a fit target of knowledge, but of mere opinion or belief. Experience cannot make such truth accessible to us, for the most it can offer is more or less probable belief about how things happen to be in our part of the universe at this point in its history. To grasp unconditional truth we must transcend the limits of experience or have available to us resources that lie outside them. Therefore only the exercise of reason, or innate endowment, or both, can furnish us with knowledge.

The paradigm of knowledge for rationalists is accordingly the formal deductive system, like geometry or logic, where excogitation from first principles, self-evident truths, or definitions leads to bodies of wholly certain knowledge.

Empiricists, by contrast, argue that knowledge cannot come from armchair speculation, but only from going and looking. Use of our senses (and instruments that extend their range) can alone inform us about contingent matters of fact. It is a mistake, they argue, to regard formal deductive systems as paradigms of knowledge, for they are not bodies of knowledge in the same sense at all, but are merely 'analytic', that is, true just in virtue of the definitions of the terms in which they are expressed. (An example is afforded by tautological statements. Tautologies are a species of analytic statement, differing from their fellows only in being obvious. 'A bachelor is an unmarried man' is an analytic statement, 'An unmarried man is a man' is a tautologously analytic statement; in both cases the analyticity consists in the fact—to state the traditional view summarily—that what is being predicated of the subject is already implicit in the subject. It is important to note that the question whether there really is such a feature as analyticity is controversial.)

The paradigm of knowledge for empiricists is natural science. Here observation and experiment constitute both the source of knowledge and the means of legitimizing it. Empiricists take the practical success of science to be a vindication of their view.

This sketch of the two schools of thought ignores important questions, such as what account rationalists might give of perception, and what empiricists might say about a priori knowledge. None of the three thinkers considered in what follows conforms exactly to the picture given of an empiricist. But they agree with it, and therefore with one another, in premising the fundamental role of experience.

The empiricist view has, as one might expect, some problematic consequences. One is that concepts have content—or: the expressions of language have meaning—only if experience in one or another way confers it upon them. To stray beyond what experience legitimizes is, empiricists claim, to involve oneself in either vacuity or nonsense. (This suggests a distinction between two kinds of empiricism: one in which experience is said to be the source of concepts, the other in which it is said to be the guarantee of their legitimacy. But there are, as aspects of the following discussions show, close connections between them, so the distinction is not laboured here.) One can immediately see a difficulty: if one accepts 'realism' in respect of the physical world, which in philosophical terms is the view—again speaking summarily—that the world exists independently of experience, one seems to be in conflict with empiricism, which cannot allow sense to claims about what transcends experience. This is not a tension which the first of the British empiricists, John Locke, was able to resolve. His two successors attempted to deal with the problem in highly distinctive ways.

1. JOHN LOCKE

1.1. Life and Work

'Others', Voltaire said, 'have written romances of the soul, but Locke—the Hercules of metaphysics—has written its history.' This high praise is a measure of Locke's impact on his own age and the one that followed it, in which his work was required reading for all educated people. He and Newton were bracketed together as the intellectual eminences of their time, and without question they altered, in their respective ways, the course of subsequent intellectual history.

Locke was born in Somerset, the son of a lawyer who favoured the Parliamentary cause in the Civil War. Through political connections his father was able to get him a place at Westminster School, then the best in the country, where he studied Greek, Latin, and Hebrew. From there he went to Christ Church, Oxford. Like Hobbes before him he found the scholastic education offered at the university unprofitable. Upon graduating he therefore turned his attention elsewhere: to politics, and to science and medicine.

This choice determined the direction of his life. Because of it he established friendships with some of the leading scientists of the time, among them Robert Boyle and Thomas Sydenham, and met the future Lord Shaftesbury, whose private secretary and physician he became. Shaftesbury introduced Locke to the turbulent political activity of the day, his experience of which motivated and informed his political writings. For political reasons he was obliged to live for a time in exile in Holland. He was an active supporter of the 'Glorious Revolution' of 1688; he sailed from Holland in the fleet bringing Mary, wife of William of Orange, to England.

1.2. Locke's Aims

Locke and a group of his friends made a regular practice of meeting to discuss science and politics. Early in its discussions the group found itself in difficulties over questions about the nature and extent of human knowledge. Locke volunteered to look into the matter, intending to write a short essay on the subject. The endeavour resulted in his chief work, the *Essay Concerning Human Understanding*. It took him twenty years to complete, mainly because his life was crowded with practical affairs, but also because the task proved far more difficult than he expected.

That task was 'to examine our Abilities, and see what Objects our Understandings are, or are not fitted to deal with'. This implied a detailed project of inquiry into 'the Original, Certainty, and Extent of humane Knowledge, together with the Grounds and Degrees of Belief, Opinion and Assent' (*Essay*, I. i. 2).[1]

The fourth and final book of the *Essay* sets out the result of that inquiry. It is that we have knowledge when we are justifiably certain of what we claim to know: 'What we once *know*, we are certain is so; and we may be secure, that there are no latent Proofs undiscovered, which may overturn our Knowledge or bring it into doubt' (IV. xvi. 3). Anything short of this is not knowledge properly so called, but judgement, belief, opinion, or faith. Most of what we ordinarily claim to know does not amount to knowledge in this austere sense. Does that matter? No, says Locke, for 'the Candle, that is set up in us, shines bright

---

[1] All references to Locke's work in what follows are to the *Essay*, giving book, chapter, and section numbers.

enough for all our Purposes'; by which he means that, used properly, our minds can provide us with beliefs adequate to our needs (I. i. 5). The chief practical purpose of the *Essay* is to show us what we can and cannot expect from our epistemic capacities, so that we can direct our attention to acquiring well-founded beliefs about matters we are competent to investigate.

The point of Locke's endeavour is illuminated by his motive for undertaking it. He lived in the century which saw the first flourishing of modern natural science—the century of Galileo, Newton, Boyle, and others. Inspired by science's achievements, he wished to see its empiricist methodology defended against the weight of philosophical tradition, which was rationalist in temper. The *Essay* is Locke's contribution to that task. In its 'Epistle to the Reader' he describes himself as an 'Underlabourer' serving science by 'clearing Ground a little, and removing some of the Rubbish, that lies in the way to Knowledge', the rubbish in question being the outdated, jargon-laden abstractions of scholastic and rationalist theories.

Rationalism, as noted above, is the view that since the only proper objects for knowledge are changeless truths, and since empirical inquiry can only inform us about contingent matters, the intellect alone is capable of yielding knowledge. Some important versions of this view consist in commitment to a doctrine of innate ideas. This doctrine states that we are born with a significant quantum of knowledge, in particular about the fundamentals of theology, morality, and logic. Rationalists took this view in order to escape the difficulty that if we do not learn ultimate truths by experience, and yet both need and seem to have access to a number of them—not least, they claim, ideas about goodness, reason, and God—there must be an explanation of how it is we have them. So they adopted from Plato the idea that such knowledge is in some way already present in our minds before birth.

This view is in sharp conflict with the empiricists' defining commitment to the primacy of experience in the acquisition of knowledge. Locke accordingly begins his *Essay* by attacking it. But this negative task is only a first step. In order to make out the claim that knowledge comes primarily from experience, it is necessary to specify the nature of experience, and to show what we can know by its means and with what degree of assurance. It was Locke's chief aim to address these questions.

1.3. Innate Ideas

Locke's argument against innate ideas occupies most of the first book of the *Essay*. He begins by attacking the claim that we innately know such principles as that *what is, is*, that *nothing contradicts itself*, and that *a whole is greater than its parts*. The 'great Argument' for the innateness of these principles is that everyone agrees with them. Locke's reply is that even if such universal agreement existed, it would not prove knowledge of the principles to be innate; but that anyway there is no such universal agreement, for they are not present in the minds of children and many adults.

If the argument is that we are born with the capacity to recognize these principles, Locke has no complaint; nor does he object to the claim that they are in some sense self-evidently true to anyone capable of understanding them. For both views are true, but neither entails innatism.

Arguments against the innateness of logical principles apply also in the case of practical and moral principles, although here Locke adds a further counter-argument, namely, that if any principles are innate then so must be their constituent ideas, which is obviously not so: he remarks, '*It is impossible for the same thing to be and not to be* is certainly (if there be any such) an innate Principle. But can any one think, or will any one say, that *Impossibility* and *Identity* are two innate *Ideas*?' (I. iv. 3).

Although a chief reason for Locke's assault on innatism is his opposing commitment to empiricism, he had other reasons besides. One is that innatist doctrines buttressed certain political claims that he found objectionable. For example, some argued that we cannot oppose royal authority because we know innately that kings rule by divine right. Locke rejected such views and their more general correlative that there are ideas which are not open to criticism.

1.4. Two Concepts of Innateness

It is not difficult to agree with Locke about the implausibility of claiming that we are born with knowledge of specific logical, theological, and moral principles. But it is equally implausible that the mind literally begins as a 'blank slate', for if so it would be incapable of receiving and processing the inputs of experience upon which, on the empiricist view, knowledge is built. The mind must have capacities suited to the task of receiving data from experience, working upon them, storing them in memory, comparing, contrasting, and reasoning about them. Locke indeed accepts this, as we shall see, and later in the *Essay* makes important use of the fact.

These reflections prompt the need for a distinction between stronger and weaker forms of innatism. The stronger form, exemplified by Plato's views, has it that we are born with knowledge. It might be more accurate to rephrase this as the claim that we are born knowing a number of propositions—perhaps many—to be true. (Plato further held that we forget them all at or before birth, and that what we call learning is in fact the process of recalling them.) The weaker claim is that we are born with capacities for acquiring knowledge, just as in normal circumstances we are born with the capacity to digest, see, walk, and learn language, all of which we come to do if we develop in the normal way. This latter view is consistent with the claim that Locke was especially concerned to support, namely that all knowledge is ultimately based on experience.

The controversy over innate ideas is closely allied to the important question of a priori knowledge. Russell was by no means the first to conclude—in his case reluctantly—that if we do not know something independently of experience we cannot know anything at all.[2] Just this view was the corner-stone of Kant's *Critique of Pure Reason*. Locke did not use the expression 'a priori', nor did he countenance a distinction between the *independence* and the *antecedence* of knowledge in relation to experience (a priori knowledge can be independent of experience without literally coming into the mind before experience) for his official line is that all ideas, and hence knowledge, are dependent upon because they ultimately derive from experience—that is, are entirely a posteriori. (Strictly speaking, his finished view is that our *concepts* derive from experience, and knowledge consists in grasp of relations between them; but this is a refinement to be noted and for the moment postponed.) Nevertheless he had, as we shall see, an account of intuition and demonstration as furnishing the highest forms of knowledge available to us.

In his *New Essays* Leibniz attempted to defend innatism against Locke's criticisms. His argument turns on a question of priority; it seems that because the principle of identity—*everything is identical with itself*—is logically prior to any of its instances, we must grasp it in advance of recognizing any of its instances—e.g. *that tree is identical with itself*—for otherwise we would not recognize this latter for the truth it is. Locke anticipated such a move by remarking that logical and psychological priority are different things; the fact that a principle is 'logically prior' to its instances does not mean that we have to know it before we know its instances. (Note that this is not the same distinction as the one just mentioned between the independence of knowledge from, and the antecedence of knowledge to, experience.) On the contrary, says Locke, it is just a fact about our psychological histories that we learn them by one or another commonplace route, chiefly by being taught them (I. iii. 22–6); but the basis of any grasp of them is recognition of their embodiment in their instances. They have, in other words, an empirical origin. How we come by principles is simply therefore part of the way we come by our ideas in general.

'How do we come by our ideas?' is the crucial question for Locke, and he therefore immediately turns to an account of it.

1.5. The Doctrine of Signs

In the final chapter of the *Essay* Locke states that everything that comes within the compass of human knowledge falls under one of three heads, for which he

---

[2] See Russell, *Human Knowledge* (London, 1948), 524.

employs the Greek originals of the expressions 'physics', 'practics', and 'semi-otics'. By 'physics' he means inquiry into the 'Nature of Things', not only 'Matter, and Body, but Spirits also'; in short, everything that exists. By 'practics' he means chiefly ethics, the inquiry—as he describes it—into conduct which leads to what is good and useful in the promotion of happiness. And by 'semi-otics' or the 'doctrine of signs'—'aptly enough termed also *logikē*'—he means the study of the 'signs' which 'the Mind makes use of for the understanding of Things, or conveying its Knowledge to others' (iv. xxi. 1–4).

It is 'the doctrine of signs' with which the two central books of the *Essay* are concerned. There are two kinds of signs: *ideas* and the *words* used to communi-cate them. These are 'the great Instruments of Knowledge', and therefore it is a necessary preliminary to the account given of the nature and extent of knowl-edge in book iv that ideas and words be thoroughly investigated. As regards ideas, the task is to be clear about their nature and origins; this Locke under-takes in book ii. By its end he has found that 'there is so close a connexion between *Ideas* and Words' that before turning to the question of knowledge it is necessary to consider 'the Nature, Use and Signification of Language'. This he undertakes in book iii.

1.6. The Origin of Ideas

Locke begins book ii by tackling the fundamental question of how we come by our ideas, by 'ideas' meaning 'whatever it is, which the Mind can be employ'd about in thinking' (i. i. 8). His answer is that they come from experience, which takes two forms: observation of external sensible objects, and internal observa-tion of the operations of one's own mind. The former he calls 'sensation', the latter 'reflection'. 'These two are the Fountains of Knowledge, from whence all the *Ideas* we have, or can naturally have, do spring' (ii. i. 2). On this apparently slender basis, not helped—as we shall shortly see—by ambiguities in the word 'idea', Locke erects a theory of knowledge.

Sensation is, he says, caused by the action of external objects on our sense organs, which are thereby stimulated to 'convey into the Mind' perceptions of the sensible qualities of the things which caused the sensation—such as their shape, texture, colour, and scent. Reflection is introspective awareness of the activities of the mind as it busies itself with the ideas it contains—comparing, remembering, believing, and the like.

Locke needs to explain how the variety and elaboration of knowledge can derive from these two sources alone. He does so by distinguishing between 'simple' and 'complex' ideas. The former are, so to speak, the atoms of expe-rience, the building-blocks out of which complex ideas are formed by com-bination. Typical examples of simple ideas are colours and tastes, passively received by the mind in sensation. But there are also simple ideas of

reflection, these being ideas of the mind's operations upon its other ideas
(II. vi. 1).

This is one part of the combinatorial picture. The other relates to the mind's
capacities. The mind has, says Locke, 'the power to repeat, compare and unite'
simple ideas 'even to an almost infinite Variety, and so can make at Pleasure new
complex *Ideas*. But it is not in the Power of the most exalted Wit, or enlarged
Understanding, by any quickness or variety of Thought, to *invent or frame one
new simple* idea in the mind, not taken in the way before mentioned' (II. ii. 2).

On its first appearance this simple–complex distinction is an experiential one.
A simple idea is 'one uniform Appearance, or Conception, in the Mind', and
cannot be distinguished into component ideas (II. ii. 1). But Locke also employs
a logical or semantic criterion, describing simple ideas as those whose names
are not capable of being defined (III. iv. 4). These are not equivalent definitions,
but neither are they inconsistent, and indeed there is arguably a natural connection. (The connection has been exploited to advantage by other philosophers: G. E. Moore in *Principia Ethica* and Wittgenstein in the *Tractatus* are
salient examples.)

In the first edition of the *Essay* Locke classified complex ideas under the three
heads 'substance', 'modes', and 'relations'. In ordinary ways of thinking this
denotes an arrangement into ideas of things, ideas of their properties, and ideas
of the relations in which they stand to one another. Roughly speaking, this is
what Locke intended; with the difficulty that 'things' here is ambiguous
between concrete particulars (individual substances) and other possible objects
of reference, including abstractions. But it is implicitly an advantage of the theory that ideas can be as *complex* as they need to be, allowing experience to be
sufficient to underlie their variety and elaboration in the form of simple ideas
alone.

In the fourth and final edition of the *Essay* Locke added another way of
classifying complex ideas, a psychological account given in terms of the mind's
ability to *combine, compare*, and *abstract*. Combination produces complexity,
comparison produces relation, and abstraction produces general ideas (such as
man, dog, whiteness). There is some strain between the original classification and
this one, so it is worth noting that most of the *Essay* draws chiefly on the
former.

1.7. Representation and Qualities

The function of ideas is, as noted, to serve as signs. The function of a sign, in
turn, is to stand for or represent something other than itself. Locke espoused a
view which for a long time enjoyed currency in philosophy, namely that sensory
ideas are intermediaries between the mind and whatever the mind is related to
in experience. This view came to be called 'the veil of perception doctrine'. Its

apparent plausibility arises from consideration of such simple perceptual cases as when one looks at an object—say, a table—from different points of view, different distances, and in different circumstances, and notes that it appears to have different sizes, shapes, and colours accordingly, while still (we take it) being the same thing. So ideas of it can vary while the thing remains the same; and therefore our perception of it is indirect, mediated by the ideas it produces in our minds.

Among the questions this view prompts is one about what relation obtains between ideas and the things to which we thus mediately refer them. In line with corpuscularian theory, Locke took a causal view, holding that there are powers in objects to produce ideas in our minds. 'Whatsoever the Mind perceives in itself or is the immediate object of Perception, Thought, or Understanding,' says Locke, 'that I call *Idea*; and the Power to produce any *Idea* in our Mind, I call *Quality* of the Subject wherein the power is' (II. viii. 8).

Here Locke introduces a crucial notion, that of *qualities*. They come in three types. First, there are five *primary* qualities, namely extension, shape, motion or rest, number, and solidity. They are 'in' objects themselves, 'utterly inseparable from the Body, in what estate soever it be' (II. viii. 9).

Next there are five *secondary* qualities, namely colour, sound, taste, smell, and texture—one corresponding to each of the five senses—which Locke says 'are nothing in the Objects themselves, but Powers to produce the various sensations in us by their primary Qualities' (II. viii. 10).

Finally, there are those powers by whose means things act on one another, for example the power in fire to melt wax (ibid.).

An important difference for Locke between primary and secondary qualities is that the former resemble their causes in external objects, but the latter do not: 'the *Ideas of primary Qualities* of Bodies, *are Resemblances* of them, and their Patterns do really exist in the Bodies themselves; but the *Ideas, produced* in us *by* these *Secondary Qualities, have no resemblance of them* at all. There is nothing like our *Ideas*, existing in the Bodies themselves' (II. viii. 15).

It seems clear that the theory of perception to which Locke thus commits himself is an indirect representative realist theory. He sums it up thus: 'For since the Things, the Mind contemplates, are none of them, besides it self, present to the Understanding, 'tis necessary that something else, as a Sign or Representation or the thing it considers, should be present to it; And these are *Ideas*' (IV. xxi. 4).

It is possible at one level to see Locke's account, at least so far, as having a deep simplicity of structure. The account gives us ideas, their taxonomy, and a view of their origins, and from this basis Locke proposes to launch his investigation into the nature of knowledge. But already there are problems, as the following points suggest.

1.8. Some Difficulties: Ideas

One of the more obvious difficulties arises from the imprecision of the term *idea* itself. Critics castigate Locke for using it in a number of different senses, variously denoting some or all of (1) states of mind such as feelings and sensations, (2) acts of thinking such as considering and paying attention, (3) images or pictures in the mind's eye, (4) concepts—Locke sometimes appears to mean the act of conceiving and sometimes the concept itself, and finally (5)—the 'most notorious use'—intermediaries between minds and objects. The simple–complex distinction might help abate the problem that at times 'idea' denotes the content of a sense-experience and at other times the complex idea of a particular substance; for example: in the former use, 'idea' might denote any of the particular brown, smooth, solid sensations I have when seeing and touching a table, while in the latter it denotes the idea of the table itself. But that touches only part of the difficulty; the risk of confusion remains.

Locke was aware that not all ideas represent in the same way, as we see from his saying that whereas sensory ideas of primary qualities resemble their causes, those of secondary qualities do not. But there are further differences. When ideas are images they represent not qualities or things but other ideas. And ideas as general concepts such as 'dog' and 'man' obviously do not represent in the same way as ideas of particular substances, such as the ideas of this individual dog Fido or that individual man Fred.

One explanation of how these difficulties arise is that Locke was trying to achieve different aims at the same time and on the same basis. For one thing, he was attempting to give an account of mind and its operations, in which ideas can be treated as constituents of thoughts. This imposes a demand for a classification of them suitable for an explanation of how they are combined and (for the purposes later of defining knowledge) compared. It also imposes a demand for some account of the mental processes they accordingly undergo. But secondly, Locke's empiricist premiss—the principle that all our ideas ultimately derive from experience and owe their content to it—obliges him to address, in a fresh way, questions about the relation of knowledge and its objects in order to accord with corpuscularian science, which, in its causal story about sensory experience, does not allow any Cartesian certainties about the world and our theories of it.

The question whether either aim interferes with the other is answerable only by looking at the detail of Locke's case. But two obvious problems are these: If we restrict attention to considerations about sensory and introspective awareness, do we have an adequate basis for a general theory of mind and knowledge, which is no less than Locke aspires to give? And, what are the implications of a restriction to that basis for an understanding of a priori knowledge and—a point taken up again shortly—the nature and degree of the mind's contribution to experience?

1.9. Further Difficulties: Perception and Qualities

Any theory which places the source of knowledge in perceptual experience implicitly or otherwise claims that something substantial is acquired in perception that is antecedent to our reasonings and theories, and indeed provides their basis. It therefore matters crucially what account is given of perception and what it conveys. Locke held such a theory, but its interpretation is a matter of controversy.

On the standard view, Locke's account is representational. Sensory ideas are pictures of their originals in the world, conveying information about them to the mind by serving as their intermediaries. Given the claim that primary qualities resemble what causes them whereas secondary qualities do not, we have to accept that these pictures are partly drawn by the receiving mind. We should ignore, Locke say, any sceptical scruples this might prompt.

From this theory—which critics regard as an unattractive one, among other things because of the problematic 'veil of perception' commitment and the open invitation to scepticism—some commentators have attempted to rescue Locke by denying that he saw sensory ideas as intermediaries between things and minds. The solution, they suggest, is to see Locke as exploiting the ambiguity of 'idea' sometimes to denote 'a thought of an object' and sometimes 'an object of thought', and never as an intermediary between them.

This suggestion does not, however, appear to be supported by the *Essay* itself. There Locke writes, 'How shall the Mind, when it perceives nothing but its own *Ideas*, know that they agree with the Things themselves?' His answer is to appeal to the causal origin of simple ideas, 'which', he says, 'the Mind can by no means make to itself', so therefore they 'must necessarily be the product of Things operating on the Mind in a natural way' (IV. iv. 4). It is the 'must' that troubles critics, because only certain assumptions—discussed in the next paragraph—can license it; but they require independent defence, which Locke does not provide.

An alternative to rescuing Locke from a representational theory is to defend his commitment to it. This has to be done by showing that there are ways in which representations can be treated as reliable even though we cannot break out of the circle of ideas in which the theory places us. The most effective way, it is claimed, is to assume as true the realist view that there is a world of physical things, among which causal relations obtain. On this assumption a representational theory makes sense (and the 'must' above gets its support). And this indeed is just the assumption Locke makes. But it is also just this that his critics do not grant, on the ground that a large part of epistemology's task is to find a way of defending this very assumption. If one can simply help oneself to it, they say, anything goes.

If Locke's account of perception invites discussion, so does his associated view of the primary–secondary quality distinction. Here what attracted Locke, as it did some of his predecessors, was that because primary qualities are 'in the things themselves' we are in closest touch with things when we perceive, describe, and measure their primary qualities. The distinction is integral to the corpuscularian physics of the day, and indeed Locke adopted the terminology of qualities and powers from Robert Boyle.

But is there such a distinction? The first thing to note is that to draw it one must already have accepted a view of perception as indirect and representative, in which sensory ideas convey information about something other than themselves—namely, material things in the world—but only partly as those things intrinsically are. Any problems for such a theory undermine the primary–secondary quality distinction.

It might be supposed that, by the same token, anything that supports the existence of such a distinction could be used to support a representative theory of perception. Consider the phenomenon of colour-blindness. Here the same external factors (the surfaces of physical objects reflect light, etc.) give rise to sensory ideas of different colours in different perceivers. Such examples can be multiplied, all lending credence to the existence of a distinction between properties that objects have in themselves and those that are attributed to them by us as a result of ways we interact with them (or indeed as a result of other, perhaps interfering factors not intrinsic either to them or to us). If these considerations support the distinction, do they thereby support the representative theory of perception?

Berkeley, for one, did not think so. He argued that both kinds of qualities, for all that they are distinguishable on other grounds (primary qualities are available to more than one sense, secondary qualities only to one; primary qualities are measurable, secondary qualities are not), are importantly alike in being *sensible*, that is, objects of sensory awareness; so that all the considerations—made familiar by scepticism—aimed at showing that secondary qualities are not properties of objects but are mind-dependent artefacts of perception, apply to primary properties also. The implications of this notion, if it is half-way plausible, are radical, as we shall see in connection with Berkeley's views.

Another problem with Locke's account is that he describes secondary but not primary qualities as powers. Secondary qualities, recall, are 'powers in objects' to produce in us ideas of colour, taste, and the rest. So when we are not looking at the red flag, the flag is not red, although it has the power to make us see red if we care to look. Primary qualities are properties of the objects which are there whether we perceive them or not. But clearly, on Locke's theory, some power in the object is responsible for causing us to have ideas of primary qualities. The best suggestion seems to be that primary qualities are in some sense the *grounds* of those powers. If so, Locke's theory asks us to accept something odd: that perceptions of, for example, shape are *resemblances of the grounds of a power* to produce in us an idea of a certain shape. The problem surely lies with the notion of powers itself, a notion required for the causally indirect story, but otherwise not at all clear.

These remarks merely brush the surface of debates prompted by Locke's views in book II of the *Essay*. Everything turns on whether his account of ideas holds water, for it is the crucial part of his case.

1.10. Words

Locke's concern in book II, as we have just seen, is to identify and classify the basic materials of knowledge, namely, *ideas*. At first, he remarks, he thought that after doing this he could proceed directly to an account of knowledge. But he then saw a need to investigate how 'names' are applied to things, not least because, with the exception of 'proper names' like 'Tom' and 'Dick', they are *general*, that is, stand not for individuals but for classes or kinds of things (III. i. 6); and knowledge chiefly consists in conversance about kinds.

The significance of an investigation into language, he says, is that it will 'lead us a little towards the Original of all our Notions and Knowledge, if we remark, how great a dependence our *Words* have on common sensible *Ideas*' (III. i. 5). What is in the offing is a theory of meaning, a crude and partial one, to be sure, but Locke makes a highly original contribution in recognizing the importance of such theory to philosophy. In brief, the theory is that words have meaning by denoting ideas, which in turn originate in experience, so that the meaning of words—and relatedly, the content of concepts—is empirically derived and controlled.

Thought, Locke observes, is private, so when men first wished to convey their thoughts to each other they needed something external and visible to stand for them. This is the origin of words, which are sounds or marks arbitrarily chosen as signs of ideas, by whose use men can record their thoughts and communicate them to others. '*Words in their primary or immediate Signification, stand for nothing, but the* Ideas *in the Mind of him that uses them*, how imperfectly soever, or carelessly those *Ideas* are collected from the Things, which they are supposed to represent' (III. ii. 2).

Two assumptions, according to Locke, accompany the use of words. The first is that the words men use as marks of their own ideas stand for the same ideas in the minds of others, for otherwise—obviously—they would fail to communicate. The second is that 'Because *Men* would not be thought to talk barely of their own Imaginations, but of Things as they really are; therefore they *often suppose their Words to stand also for the reality of Things*' (III. ii. 4–5). Locke regards the first assumption as important and right because the very possibility of communication rests upon it (III. vi. 28). He comments that we are insufficiently careful to check whether it holds in practice, for problems often arise from mis-understandings. But the second assumption is in his view a serious mistake: 'it is a perverting the use of Words, and brings unavoidable Obscurity and Confusion into their Signification, whenever we make them stand for any thing, but those *Ideas* we have in our own Minds' (III. ii. 5). Words denote ideas, and ideas are signs of things; reference to things is therefore mediated by ideas, just as is perception of them.

An acute observation on Locke's part is that although things are particular, the 'far *greatest part of Words*, that make all Languages, *are General terms*: which has not been the Effect of Neglect, or Chance, but of Reason, and Necessity' (III. iii. 1; examples of general terms are *man*, *dog*, *tree*, that is, expressions which denote sorts or kinds of things). This is because it would be impossible for each of the many things in the world to have its own individual name, since if this were so, language would be useless for communication (III. iii. 2–3).

But how do names come to be general in signification? Locke's answer is notorious: 'Words become general, by being made the signs of general *Ideas*: and *Ideas* become general, by separating from them the circumstances of Time, and Place, and any other *Ideas*, that may determine them to this or that partic-ular Existence.' This Locke calls 'the way of abstraction' (III. iii. 6). Thus general ideas are arrived at by abstraction from acquaintance with particulars, by not-ing what is common to them (III. iii. 7), and they and the general terms that sig-nify them 'belong not to the real existence of things; but *are the Inventions and Creatures of the Understanding*, made by it for its own use, *and concern only Signs*, whether Words, or *Ideas*' (III. iii. 11; Locke's emphases).

1.11. Difficulties about Words

There are a number of problems with Locke's account of language. The most obvious is this: if words signify ideas and ideas are mental entities private to their possessors, what ensures that they rouse the same ideas in one user's mind as in the mind of another? How does anyone come to learn to use words in con-formity with others' uses if what they signify is hidden within the minds of each? Expressions in a language must have public and relatively stable senses to fulfil their communicative function. On the face of it, Locke's theory seems inconsistent with this minimum requirement.

Locke in fact recognizes the requirement well enough. In one passage he urges people to '*apply their Words*, as near as may be, *to such* Ideas *as common use has annexed them*' (III. xi. 11). This advice contains an important implicit assump-tion, namely, that meaning is related in some way to 'common use'. This antic-ipates later views having it that the meanings of expressions in natural languages are functions of the uses speakers make of them. But Locke's view is not that use determines meaning, only—more weakly—that it constrains it; for he also recognizes that there is no non-circular way of saying what common use is, which means that disputes and negotiations about the signification of words always remain possible (III. ix. 8). Moreover, words change in meaning, and new words are coined, as knowledge develops; so 'common use' is not always, Locke suggests, an infallible guide.

But Locke assumes that language is separate from thought, arriving after it to encode it—he talks of men coming to feel a need for communication, and devising language accordingly. This was a commonplace among Locke's contemporaries, but it is no longer plausible to think this way. It can be argued that thought, at least above a rudimentary level, is impossible without language; that indeed thought and language are the same thing, even if it is not ordinary natural language like English or French, but a deep-structure mental language ('mentalese' in the jargon of the philosophy of mind where these matters are debated) which carries the identity. One brief consideration to illustrate the point is as follows. One can say of a dog that *he expects his master home soon*—and so attribute the relevant thoughts to him—but if his master is, say, a painter called Tom, we cannot say that *he expects a painter called Tom home soon*, for it would seem that he would need to be a language-using creature to master concepts of that complexity. It is not just that language-possession is a necessary condition for the relevant concept-possession, on this view; it is that *what it is to have* the concept consists in having the relevant linguistic competence. On some versions of the view, this condition is claimed to be equivalent to saying that a third party only has grounds to ascribe possession of concepts if the only behaviour capable of manifesting them—the relevant linguistic behaviour—is available. Accordingly, the notion that people could have concepts of this elaboration and only later feel the need of a public encoding of them in order to communicate, looks deeply implausible. And even if it were not, questions remain, among them: what is the encoding relation, and how do different speakers come to share the same one?

One of the most serious criticisms of Locke's account is that it confuses two different things: the sense of a term, which is a public or shared feature of it, and the psychological associations which it might contingently arouse in the mind of an individual hearer or user. For example: both you and I mean the same thing by the expression 'ice-cream', but on hearing it I might invariably think of summertime in Bognor, whereas you might think of dinner at Tiffany's. Subjective associations cannot constitute the meaning of expressions in a shared language. Therefore, whatever constitutes meaning, it cannot be a relation of signification of private ideas. This is a lesson which, in more recent philosophy, Gottlob Frege (1848–1925) was especially concerned to teach.

Controversy almost immediately surrounded Locke's account of abstraction and general ideas. Berkeley attacked him on the ground that general terms function by standing indifferently for any of the particular things that fall under them—that is, by having a particular *use*, again anticipating later views—not by denoting an indeterminate 'general idea' which is an amalgam of the things it signifies. In one passage particularly criticized by Berkeley, Locke says that the abstract idea of a triangle is of a figure 'neither Oblique, nor Rectangle, neither Equilateral, Equicrural, nor Scalenon; but all and none of these at once. In effect, it is something imperfect, that cannot exist, an *Idea* wherein some parts of several and inconsistent *Ideas* are put together' (IV. vii. 9). Apart from the inadequacy of the account itself, it is clear that Locke is here a victim of the excessive reliance, over which criticism is especially made, on visual imagery as the model for ideas.

Locke's theory has been called 'semantic individualism' because it depicts language as a flexible and mutable medium which individual speakers employ in order to—so to speak—negotiate communication with one another. On this view, language is not a unified public instrument but a network of interconnecting private paroles. As noted, the chief argument against this is that meaning cannot be exclusively or even largely a function of the contingently different private psychologies of speakers, but must be a public property of our signs. What this in turn means is an actively debated matter, but the general point is persuasive: it invites us to think of language as a social construct, shared among speakers on the basis of a common repository of theories and beliefs. Arguably, Locke's aim of examining and defending empirical inquiry is far better served by this view of language than by his own.

1.12. Knowledge

Locke at last turns to the question of knowledge in the fourth and final book of the *Essay*. Among his chief aims, one recalls, is that of contesting, on behalf of science, the epistemological view that we can arrive at knowledge properly so called by rational means alone, and that experience at best yields only opinion or defeasible belief. His strategy is to agree with rationalism that certainty is primarily a property of intuitive and demonstrative knowledge, and then to assert the right of 'sensitive knowledge'—knowledge acquired by the senses—to be taken with equal seriousness. His argument is as follows.

Because our minds have no other object than their ideas, knowledge can be 'nothing but *the perception of the connexion and agreement, or disagreement and repugnancy of any of our Ideas*. In this alone it consists' (IV. i. 2). When the agreement or disagreement of two ideas is immediately obvious, Locke calls it 'intuitive knowledge' (IV. ii. 1). When reasoning is required to make the agreement or otherwise plain, so that one does not instantly grasp the relation but comes to it by steps of inference, Locke calls it 'demonstrative knowledge' (IV. ii. 2–4).

Whatever falls short of intuition or demonstration is not, strictly speaking, knowledge (IV. ii. 14). This is the point which Locke appears to surrender to rationalism. But then—the crucial step—he adds that there 'is, indeed, another *Perception* of the Mind, employ'd about *the particular existence of finite Beings without us*; which going beyond bare probability, and yet not reaching perfectly to either of the foregoing degrees of certainty, passes under the name of Knowledge' (ibid.). Here he deals—almost for the only time with any seriousness—with the problem of scepticism. 'But whether there be anything more than barely that *Idea* in our minds, whether we can thence certainly inferr the existence of any thing without us, which corresponds to that *Idea*, is that, whereof some Men think there may be a question made' (ibid.). His answer is a robust dismissal of such doubt; we are 'invincibly conscious' of the effects on us of the external world, and the supposition that it might all be a dream is either pointless or manifestly improbable (ibid.); 'So that, I think, we may add to the two former sorts of *Knowledge*, this also, of the existence of particular external Objects, by that perception and Consciousness we have of the actual entrance of *Ideas* from them, and allow these *three degrees of Knowledge*, viz. *Intuitive, Demonstrative, and Sensitive*: in each of which, there are different degrees and ways of evidence and certainty' (ibid., and see Locke's account of the 'reality' of knowledge later at IV. iv. 1 ff.).

Knowledge has limits, Locke observes; we can go no further than our ideas, and even with respect to our ideas we have many unresolved 'Doubts and Enquiries', not least concerning the inner constitution and nature of things, which is the particular province of the new science otherwise making such impressive contemporary progress (IV. iii. 1–6, 12). Locke takes the limitations of our knowledge to be well illustrated by the extent of our ignorance, which arises from lack of ideas, lack of discoverable connections between them, and failure on our part properly to trace and examine them (IV. iii. 22). But still there is much we can know, not least if we are judicious about such things as faith, (religious) enthusiasm, error, and other matters; to which Locke devotes a number of concluding chapters.

What Locke says here amounts to a forcible statement of the common-sense view. It anticipates a line of argument from Hume and Kant to Wittgenstein (leaving differences aside) which says that there are bare facts with respect to which we have no option about what to believe and how to think. In later arguments, especially in Kant and those influenced by him, a case is made for the important 'no option' clause—since this is the one which, if it works, helps to defeat scepticism—by examining in detail the structure and basis of the scheme of concepts we employ. Locke's tactic, however, is simply to reject outright the idea that sceptical challenges over 'sensitive knowledge' are worth considering. He accepts that there are lesser sceptical anxieties about whether science can penetrate to the inner nature of things, but does not accept that sceptical considerations pose a threat to empirical knowledge in general.

It is natural to feel sympathy with this robust line. But an appeal to native convictions is not, critics say, by itself philosophically compelling, for it can be used to justify almost any set of beliefs. Locke's claim that we have an 'invincible consciousness' that the senses deliver reliable knowledge says no more than that *we just feel sure* that they do. If 'just feeling sure' were enough, it could be used to justify anything from astrology to Zoroastrianism.

It must, in reply, be acknowledged that Locke's refusal to address scepticism has a practical rather than a theoretical basis; the strength of his case lies in the fact that there is assuredly no way one could live as if scepticism were true, that is, as if we have no knowledge or justified beliefs. But the point for Locke's critics is that our epistemological aim must surely be to find a theoretical basis for that practical commitment, for it is at least unsatisfying to have the empirical basis for knowledge itself rest upon an act of faith in its validity, which is in effect what Locke seems to do in book IV.

But again a defender of Locke might respond that this overlooks two key points: his attack on innate ideas and his account of simple sensory ideas. The point of his attack on innatism is that all our knowledge *can* come from experience (book I does not say that it in fact does, only that it can). The doctrine of simple ideas of sense—which, Locke is anxious to stress, arise in ways uncontrolled by our wills and as if from external sources—provides us with a notion of the 'empirically given', intended as a foundation for the rest of our cognitive structure. In combination, these points suggest theory rather than faith.

But at this juncture critics might refocus their charge in order to lay it against the idea of an 'empirically given'. Our 'invincible consciousness' applies, after all, to what we believe on the basis of combining simple ideas of sense and reflection, but it is precisely here—over the origin, nature, and security of simple ideas of sense, and the constructions we are entitled to place on them—that sceptical problems arise; so it is only by brushing these aside, as Locke does—and there lies the act of faith after all—that one can allow oneself to feel secure about them.

1.13. Substance and Essence

The account so far given traces the outlines of Locke's theory only. Its detail contains much that requires fuller discussion, much of which, in turn, is of great philosophical interest. Three topics that especially demand mention are substance, essence, and (discussed in the next section) identity.

Locke found it difficult to articulate a satisfactory notion of substance, one of the three types (with modes and relations) of complex ideas. Intuitively a substance is an individual self-subsisting thing, and Locke wished to defend the common-sense idea that the world contains a plurality of such things, thus opposing the Cartesian identification of substance with stuff ('extended stuff' and 'thinking stuff') to which is annexed an unsatisfactory account of individuality. But given that simple ideas are general in character, as the products in our minds of powers in objects to produce ideas in us, it is difficult to see how one should characterize a notion of their bearers. One certainly does not succeed by merely aggregating simple ideas, nor is it satisfactory to rest with a purely negative conception—nothing being sayable about bearers other than that they are the bare substrata or 'support' of qualities.

The problem is to know how to specify the nature of an individual. Locke attempted to make some sense of these matters by means of a distinction between real and nominal essence. Real essence, in Locke's definition, is 'the real internal, but generally in Substances, unknown Constitution of Things, whereon their discoverable Qualities depend' (III. iii. 15). Nominal essences are the collections of properties by which we sort things into kinds for our own theoretical and practical convenience, and which we denote by general terms (ibid.). For example: the nominal essence of gold consists in its yellowness, heaviness, and malleability, the manifest properties by whose means we recognize it in practice. But its real essence is whatever is the actual internal constitution which makes it what it is and gives rise to its appearing that way to us (we might now say: its real essence consists in its being the element having 79 protons in the nucleus).

In simple ideas, and in the complex ideas of modes and relations, real and nominal essence always coincide. But they never do so in complex ideas of substances (III. iii. 18). A good reason might be that essences do not relate, as the foregoing shows, to individuals but to *kinds of thing*. As an aggregation of simple ideas, a substance *qua* individual therefore has a nominal essence only, given by specifying the complex of simple ideas constituting it. Locke does not put matters this way, but doing so would have been an option if another concern were not troubling him: namely, that he could find no satisfactory way of reconciling the two facts—as he saw them—that some of our ideas are manufactured by us, and do not answer to things as they really are out there (as with mixed modes), and that some of our ideas *should* be, if we are to maintain a realist view, the products of impingement by external things upon our minds. Individual substances should *par excellence* be such things.

It is arguably a feature of Locke's failure to sustain the internally unstable combination of realism and empiricism which generates the problem here. Realism asserts the independence of the objects of experience from experience of them; empiricism asserts the fundamental dependence upon experience of anything we can say or think about its objects. Locke held both views, and in forms which make it difficult to reconcile them. There are questions of great interest and importance here which defy summary treatment: it must suffice to say that they are the subject of lively contemporary debate, most of the contributors to which, recognizing that Locke's commitments cannot both be held together, argue for abandoning one or the other.

This difficulty is related to other reasons Locke had for problems over substance. One, already suggested, is that he is the uneasy inheritor of two conceptions: Cartesian philosophy's use of a notion of underlying substance-as-stuff, and a quite separate notion of individual essence. These sit uneasily together. Yet given the need to explain a crucial cluster of notions—identity, individuality, and being—some version of a notion of substance seems necessary to philosophy. Locke accordingly groped for an answer. The incomplete and unsatisfactory nature of his attempt, some critics say, has to be blamed on his empiricism: witness how he speaks of 'the *Idea of Substance*, which we neither have, nor can have, by *Sensation* or *Reflection* . . . We have no such *clear Idea* at all, and therefore signify nothing by the word *Substance*, but only an uncertain supposition of we know not what . . . which we take to be the *substratum*, or support, of those *Ideas* we do know' (I. iv. 18). He is saying that the concept of substance is not empirically well grounded, and this way with the matter explains much about the view of his successors in the tradition, especially Berkeley.

1.14. Personal Identity

If there are no individual essences, what makes a person the same individual over time, despite the various changes—including growth and ageing—that affect him? One of Locke's correspondents, William Molyneux, suggested that he should include a discussion of personal identity in the second edition of the *Essay*. This Locke did, with momentous consequences.

The view current in Locke's day, in so far as religious beliefs constituted an orthodoxy on the question, was that a person consists of a material body and an immaterial immortal soul, which, despite accidental changes, remains essentially the same from the time of its creation onwards (here 'accidental' and 'essential' have their strict philosophical senses). It is the soul rather than the body which carries personhood, for on this view bodily death does not end a person's existence, which supposedly continues in some non-physical realm.

This view implies something Locke accepts, namely, that a human being, considered as a physical thing, is distinct from a person. The concept of a person is a forensic one, that is, is the concept of an intelligent, rational being responsible in morality and law for what he does, and correspondingly aware of and rationally concerned for himself as himself (II. xvii. 25–6). The difference can be made plain by remarking that we are born human beings, but become persons.

But the agreement between Locke and orthodoxy is restricted to denying identity of body and person; for whereas the orthodox commitment was to the existence of an immaterial substance as what underpins identity over time, Locke argues that it is something radically different: namely, the consciousness a person has of being himself, and of being the same self now as at earlier times, in which identity consists (ibid.). This psychological basis for identity had, for espousers of the orthodox view, too many uncomfortable implications to pass without controversy; which it duly attracted.

The argument is as follows. The identity of simple physical entities—Locke uses the idea of an 'atom' as then understood—consists simply in its spatio-temporal continuity (II. xxvii. 3). The identity of living things like oak trees or horses is more complex, because many different atoms come and go as such things grow and change; so here identity consists in their being 'the same Organization of Parts in one coherent Body, partaking of one Common Life' (II. xxvii. 4).

The same applies to humans considered as physical things (II. xxvii. 6). But since a person as a thinking rational being could occupy different bodies at different times while still being the same person—that is, still with the same consciousness of self as a persisting unity of memories and projects—and since a single body could have a plurality of such consciousnesses associated with it, a person is not identical with a body (II. xxvii. 10–24).

This view—that personal identity is 'consciousness of self' alone—ignited the fury of Churchmen and initiated a debate which rumbled for years. In 1712 a leading article in the *Spectator* magazine said that the question of personal identity is so vexed that all the learned men of the kingdom should get together to resolve it. Fifty years after publication of the second edition of the *Essay*, Hume was able to argue that so far as there is any empirical ground for a concept of a self, it is merely a contingent bundle of fleetingly occurrent impressions.

A considerable difficulty with Locke's account is that it is not clear how consciousness—'consciousness of self' as a somewhat sketchily defined compound of self-awareness, memory, and interest in the future—performs its uniting task. It has to do so as constituting the person both at a time as well as across time. There are several *different* accounts in Locke of this, arising from his having at least two interests in play: a view of the self on the one hand as a thing, and on the other hand as a purely forensic item—the moral as opposed to the ontological entity.

Early objections to Locke's view took two basic forms. One is that, as Joseph Butler put it, 'consciousness of personal identity presupposes, and therefore cannot constitute, personal identity'.[3] The other is that if a person forgets, he is on Locke's view no longer identical with his earlier self; and this seems

---

[3] *The Works of Joseph Butler*, ed. Samuel Halifax, 2 vols. (Oxford, 1807), i. 385.

paradoxical, because we wish to say that the boy who stole an apple is the same person who later, as a young subaltern, performed a heroic deed on the battlefield; who in turn later became the old general in retirement. But the general might remember the heroic deed, and the subaltern the felonious deed, without the general remembering the felonious deed; and therefore on Locke's principles the general is not the same person as the boy, despite *ex hypothesi* being so.

Locke's insistence on the forensic character of personhood has led some commentators to think that he meant to nominate the moral link of responsibility rather than the cognitive link of memory as fundamental to identity. On such a view, a person *P* is identical with an earlier self for whose actions, debts, and the rest *P* accepts responsibility. There are glaring difficulties with this view (for example, parents accept responsibility for what their young children do without being identical with them) which could be abated with refinements; but it seems unnecessary to discuss them in this connection at least, because the text makes Locke unequivocal in identifying memory as the link (II. xxvii. 9). (Note that a forensic link does not depend on a memory link: *P* could take responsibility for an earlier self's actions without remembering that he performed them, whether or not he did so. This does not rule out some psychological link other than consciousness of self or memory; but saying this does not aid Locke's purposes.)

In contemporary debates over personal identity a common strategy is to devise thought experiments to see whether a person would still be the same person after the occurrence of some eventuality—loss of memory, a split-brain operation, transfer of one man's brain to another's body, and so on with greater elaboration and whimsy—which might on the face of it seem to interrupt continuity or render it ambiguous. Locke's memory criterion looks vulnerable to the kind of example in which, say, a child suffers total amnesia, but still has major claims on its parents to be treated in most relevant respects as the same person as before. This thought suggests a first crack in Locke's view: that whether or not it can be sufficient for personal identity, memory is not necessary for it. And argument can proceed from there.

1.15. Concluding Remarks

The continuing vigour of debates such as that over personal identity testifies to the enduring importance of Locke's contribution. His influence on his immediate successors, to whom we now turn, was great. One aspect of his influence is well worth mentioning. It is that he accepted from Descartes, and transmitted to the empiricist tradition, the assumption that the right place to start an inquiry into the nature and extent of knowledge is the private contents of individual consciousness. The empiricist twist is to place reliance on data of sense, whose significance rationalists like Descartes subordinated to self-evident principles or innate ideas.

Beginning with the private data of sense and reflection, says the Lockean empiricist, we are to work outwards to knowledge of an external world. The sceptical difficulties which this invites, and the inconsistency of the project with a realist metaphysics, were obvious to Berkeley and Hume. They accepted Locke's Cartesian starting-point, but with the intention of constructing a better empiricist account of knowledge from it. This project is essentially shared by later thinkers such as Mill, Russell, and Ayer.

A related assumption accepted from Locke by his successors is that the solution to the problem of knowledge, or at very least the beginnings of a solution, rest on correctly identifying its source. Beliefs formed by experience have an authority or validity which they would lack if they derived from other sources such as hearsay, visions, dreams, fantasies, or the teachings of one or another dogma. The idea of an authoritative source in experience is crucial. For all that he is the first major proponent of the principle in modern philosophy, Locke was by no means as thoroughgoing in his application of it as were his successors, whose views, as we shall now see, turn much more sharply upon it.

2. GEORGE BERKELEY

2.1. Life and Work

Berkeley was born in Ireland in 1685 and educated at Trinity College Dublin, where he took orders in the Church of Ireland, later becoming Bishop of Cloyne. His major philosophical work was accomplished early in life; the *Principles of Human Knowledge* was published in 1710, and the *Three Dialogues between Hylas and Philonous* in 1713, when he was aged 25 and 28 respectively. He wrote much thereafter, expanding on the theory of vision he had published in 1709, writing about motion, and engaging among other things in polemics against agnosticism and atheism; but he did not change the philosophical position articulated in his chief early works. His prose, it is worth remarking, is beautiful.

Berkeley travelled in Europe, and lived for a while in the American colony of Rhode Island while hoping to see the fruition of a scheme for a university in the New World. When he assumed the bishopric of Cloyne he turned his attention to the medical condition of the poor in his diocese, and wrote upon the virtues of tar-water as a panacea. He died in Oxford in 1753 and is buried in Christ Church.

His views were misunderstood in his own day and frequently still are. To the discomfiture of his contemporaries they seemed neither refutable nor believable, and were therefore ignored; but philosophers otherwise very different in temper, in particular the phenomenalists and positivists of the twentieth century, have been considerably influenced by him.

In what follows the arguments of the *Principles*, *Three Dialogues*, and Berkeley's philosophical notebooks, the *Commentaries*, are the principal focus of attention.

2.2. Aims

Berkeley's philosophical aims were two: to attack scepticism and thereby to defend common sense, and to attack atheism and thereby to defend religion. In the process he hoped to eradicate 'causes of error and difficulty in the sciences'. The second aim is approached on a metaphysical rather than doctrinal level in the *Principles* and *Three Dialogues*; doctrinal questions receive more attention in later writings like *Alciphron*. In one important respect Berkeley saw his views as a contribution to natural theology (that is, study of the concept of deity which proceeds independently of revelation or dogma), in that he thought they furnished a new and powerful proof of the existence of God. This argument is central to his whole enterprise, and is discussed in its due place.

Achieving the first aim—the refutation of scepticism—and the metaphysical version of the second aim go together for Berkeley. He takes the root of scepticism to be the opening of a gap between experience and the world, forced by theories of ideas like Locke's which involve 'supposing a twofold existence of the objects of sense, the one *intelligible*, or in the mind, the other real and without the mind' (*Principles*, 86).[4] Scepticism arises because 'for so long as men thought that *real* things subsisted without the mind, and that their knowledge was only so far forth *real* as it was conformable to *real things*, it follows, they could not be certain they had any real knowledge at all. For how can it be known, that the things which are perceived, are conformable to those which are not perceived, or exist without the mind?' (ibid.). The nub of the problem is that if we are only ever acquainted with our own perceptions, and never with the things which are supposed to lie inaccessibly beyond them, how can we hope for knowledge of them, or even be justified in asserting their existence?

Berkeley's predecessors had talked of *qualities* inhering in *matter* and causing ideas in us which *represent* or even (but how could we know?) *resemble* those qualities. The concept of *matter*, a technical philosophical notion denoting the corporeal substratum of the qualities of things, particularly troubled Berkeley. If we are to be consistent in our empiricist principles, he asked, how can we tolerate the concept of something which by definition is empirically undetectable,

---

[4] References for the *Principles* and the *Commentaries* are to paragraph numbers.

lying hidden behind the perceptible qualities of things as their supposed basis or support? If the concept of matter cannot be defended, we must understand experience and knowledge in other terms.

Berkeley's theory is an account of these other terms. He summarizes his diagnosis of the source of scepticism, and signals the positive theory he has in response to it, in a pregnant remark in the *Commentaries*: 'the supposition that things are distinct from Ideas takes away all real Truth, & consequently brings in a Universal Scepticism, since all our knowledge is confin'd barely to our own Ideas' (*Commentaries* 606).

One thing must be clearly grasped at the outset. Berkeley denies the existence of matter, for which reason his view is sometimes called 'immaterialism'. But he does not deny the existence of the external world and the physical objects it contains, such as tables and chairs, mountains and trees. Superficial misunderstandings of Berkeley result from thinking that a denial of the existence of matter is the same thing as a denial of the existence of the physical world. As we shall see, Berkeley holds no such view.

Nor—by way of advance warning—does Berkeley hold that the world exists only because it is thought of by me or you or any one or more finite minds. His views are better appreciated if the phrase he often uses, 'in the mind', is understood more precisely as 'with reference to mind' or better still 'with reference to thought or experience'. The point of this caveat becomes clear very shortly.

2.3. The New Principle

Berkeley's answer to scepticism is to deny that there is a gap between experience and the world—in his and Locke's terminology: between ideas and things—by asserting that ideas and things are the same. The whole of his argument is summarized in the first six paragraphs of the *Principles*, with the conclusion stated in the first sentence of the seventh paragraph. The rest of the *Principles*—and *Three Dialogues*, which was written to state Berkeley's arguments more accessibly because of the incomprehension that greeted them upon publication of the *Principles*—is devoted to spelling out the argument's details and meeting objections.

Berkeley begins in a way reminiscent of Locke: the 'objects of human knowledge' are 'either ideas actually imprinted on the senses, or such as are perceived by attending to the passions and operations of the mind, or lastly ideas formed by help of memory and imagination, either compounding, dividing, or barely representing those originally perceived in the aforesaid ways'. Ideas of sense—colours, shapes, and the rest—are 'observed to accompany each other' in certain ways; 'collections' of them 'come to be marked by one name, and so to be reputed one thing', for example an apple or tree (*Principles*, 1).

Besides these ideas there is 'something which knows or perceives them'; this 'perceiving, active being is what I call *mind, spirit, soul* or *myself*', and it is 'entirely distinct' from the ideas it perceives (*Principles*, 2).

It is, says Berkeley, universally allowed that our thoughts, passions, and ideas of imagination do not 'exist without the mind'. But it is 'no less evident that the various sensations or ideas imprinted on the sense, however blended or combined together (that is, whatever objects they compose) cannot exist otherwise than in a mind perceiving them' (*Principles*, 3).

From these claims it immediately follows that the gap between things and ideas vanishes; for if things are collections of qualities, and qualities are sensible ideas, and sensible ideas exist only in mind, then what it is for a thing to exist is for it to be perceived—in Berkeley's phrase: to be is to be perceived: *esse est percipi*. 'For what is said of the absolute [i.e. mind-independent] existence of unthinking things [i.e. ideas or collections of ideas] without any relation to their being perceived, that seems perfectly unintelligible. Their *esse* is *percipi*, nor is it possible that they should have any existence, out of the minds or thinking things which perceive them' (*Principles*, 3).

Berkeley is well aware that this claim appears startling, and therefore remarks that it is the common opinion that sensible objects like mountains and houses have an 'absolute', that is, perception-independent, existence; but that if one reflects on the points just made, this belief turns out to be a contradiction. 'For what', he asks, 'are the forementioned objects but the things we perceive by sense, and what do we perceive besides our own ideas or sensations; and is it not plainly repugnant [illogical, contradictory] that any of these or any combination of them should exist unperceived?' (*Principles*, 4).

The source of the belief that things can exist apart from perception of them is the doctrine of 'abstract ideas', which Berkeley attacks in his introduction to the *Principles*. Abstraction consists in treating separately things which can only be separated in thought but not in reality, for example the colour and the extension of a surface; or involves noting a feature common to many different things, and attending only to that feature and not its particular instantiations—thus do we come by the 'abstract idea' of, say, redness, apart from any particular red object (*Principles*, Introduction, 6–17). Abstraction is a falsifying move, in Berkeley's view. What gives rise to the 'common opinion' about houses and mountains is that we abstract existence from perception, and thus come to hold that things can exist unperceived. But since things are ideas, and ideas only exist if perceived by minds, the notion of 'absolute existence without [i.e. without reference to] the mind' is a contradiction (*Principles*, 5).

So, says Berkeley, to say that things exist is to say that they are perceived, and therefore 'so long as they are not perceived by me, or do not exist in my mind or that of any created spirit, they must either have no existence at all, or else subsist in the mind of some eternal spirit', that is, God (*Principles*, 6). And from this the conclusion follows, that 'there is not any other substance than *spirit*, or that which perceives' (*Principles*, 7). Berkeley's new philosophical notion, his 'New Principle', is that because the *esse* of sensible things is to be perceived (or, correlatively, to be a perceiver, that is, a mind or 'spirit'), and because whatever is perceived is an idea, it follows that the universe consists of minds and their ideas; which is to say that the only substance—that is, the ultimate reality, the ultimate nature of the universe—is mind.

2.4. Ideas, Perception, and Mind

By the 'New Principle', with its conclusion about the nature of substance, the refutation of scepticism is achieved. For if there is and can only be spiritual substance or mind, there is no use for a concept of corporeal substance or matter; and therefore no gap between perception and a material world supposed to lie hidden behind a veil of ideas; and therefore no occasion for scepticism: 'the reverse of the Principle introduced Scepticism' (*Commentaries*, 304).

Berkeley's argument, as the foregoing sketch of it shows, proceeds very quickly. As a first step in investigating it in more detail, some of the key terms require comment.

Berkeley uses 'idea' to mean 'any immediate object of sense or understanding', but he is careful to distinguish this from what, in the second paragraph of the *Principles*, he had described as 'such as are perceived by attending to the passions and operations of the mind', for these are what he later calls *notions*. The distinction is as follows. Ideas are always *sensory*; they are either the content of states of sensory awareness, or the copies of these in memory and imagination. *Notions*, on the other hand, are concepts principally of self, mind, and God, and do not have their origin in sense experience but, as regards one's own mind, in immediate intuition and, as regards God, in 'reflexion and reasoning' (*Principles*, 42, 140–2; *Three Dialogues*,[5] 232). And Berkeley gives the name *perception* to any way of having ideas and notions before the mind, in sensing, conceiving, imagining, remembering, reasoning, and the rest.

Two features of ideas are crucial for Berkeley: their *inertness* and their *mind-dependence*. They are the latter simply in virtue of being ideas. Their being the former is a more intricate matter. Anticipating Hume, Berkeley argues that there are no necessary connections between ideas; they are individual entities 'with no power or agency included in them. So that one idea or object of thought cannot produce or make an alteration in another' (*Principles*, 25). To verify this we are simply asked to introspect, doing which, says Berkeley, reveals that 'there is nothing in [ideas] but what we perceive', and we perceive no power or activity in them (ibid.). We have a 'continual succession' of ideas, some

---

[5] References to the *Three Dialogues* are to page numbers of the original edition, preserved in the margins of Ayers's edition.

arising and others disappearing; but since they are causally inert, they are not themselves responsible for these changes, so there must be some other cause of them (*Principles*, 26). The only candidate remaining for this role is spirit or mind. Since my mind is causally responsible for very few ideas and their changes, there must be 'some other spirit that produces them' (*Principles*, 29).

Any inference to the nature of the spirit that is causally responsible for ideas and their changes must start from the nature of those ideas and their changes. 'The ideas of sense', says Berkeley, again anticipating Hume, 'are more strong, lively, and distinct than those of imagination; they have likewise a steadiness, order, and coherence, and are not excited at random, as those which are the effects of human wills often are, but in a regular train or series' (*Principles*, 30). These 'set rules or methods' we call '*Laws of Nature*'; and these we learn by experience, which teaches us that such and such ideas are attended with such and such other ideas, in the ordinary course of things' (ibid.). From this Berkeley concludes that God, the 'Author of Nature', is the ultimate source of ideas and their connections.

From this in turn it follows that although everything that exists is mind-dependent, it is not dependent on particular or finite minds, but has an objective source and structure, namely, the eternal, ubiquitous, and lawlike perceiving of an infinite mind. In this sense Berkeley is a realist; the world exists independently of the thought and experience of finite minds (*Three Dialogues*, 166–7), and this explains what he means by claiming to defend common sense, for common sense holds that grass is green and the sky is blue whether or not any of us happen to be looking at either, whereas Locke and the corpuscularians held otherwise—grass has powers to make us see green, but it is not itself green; indeed, on the Lockean view the world is colourless, odourless, and silent until a perceiver chances by, when it produces in him visual, olfactory, and auditory experiences. But for Berkeley the world is just as we perceive it to be even when we are not perceiving it, because it is always and everywhere perceived by the infinite mind of a deity.

The deity perceives the universe by thinking it, that is, causing it to exist by conceiving it. In a letter to the American Dr Samuel Johnson Berkeley remarked that his view differs only verbally from the theological doctrine that God sustains the universe in being by an act of continual creation. So the ideas which constitute the world are caused by the deity, and appear in our consciousnesses as the effects of his causal activity: this is the *metaphysical* way of describing what, in ordinary terminology, we describe as seeing trees, tasting ice-cream, and so forth. It is not that the latter way of describing the facts is wrong, for it is not; the ordinary and the metaphysical ways of describing reality are alternative descriptions, Berkeley holds, of the same thing.

A significant feature of this account is its view of causality. Locke had argued that the empirical basis for our concept of causality comes from our own felt powers as agents, able to initiate and intervene in trains of events in the world. This sense of our own efficacy we 'project' on to the world to explain chains of events in it, imputing to events we describe as 'causes' an agency or power on analogy with our own. For Berkeley the projective move is empirically ungrounded. We indeed have experience of causal agency as spirits, which are the only active things we know. But although it is a convenience to impute causal agency to things—to ideas—in our ordinary way of talking, things (ideas) are inert, and apparent causal connections between them are in fact and ultimately owed to the causal activity of God. So: we say the heat of the flame causes the water in the pot to boil. This way of talking is unexceptionable for ordinary purposes. But at the metaphysical level the explanation is that the succession of ideas in which this event consists are caused in lawlike fashion by the infinite mind of the deity.

2.5. Objections

It is immediately clear that Berkeley's theory rests upon a vital assumption, borrowed unquestioningly from Locke, who equally unquestioningly borrowed it from the Cartesians, namely, that the place to begin one's inquiry is among the private data of individual consciousness, that is, among the ideas constituting an individual's experience. Once started from there, there is a certain persuasiveness about the early steps of Berkeley's argument, as can be seen by looking at a proposed objection to it.

Berkeley's argument is that the sensible qualities of objects—their colours, shapes, and the rest—are sensory ideas; objects are collections of such; therefore objects exist 'in the mind', that is, as essentially mind-dependent entities. A standard objection to this is that Berkeley makes an elementary error in identifying sensible qualities and sensory ideas, for—says the objection—there is a large difference between 'The table is brown' and 'The table looks brown to me', since the truth-conditions of the two statements differ. The table could be brown without it seeming so to me—and vice versa. So Berkeley's argument collapses.

But this argument begs the question against Berkeley by assuming that claims about what qualities an object possesses are independent of claims about how they can be known to possess them; which amounts to the claim that there are observation-independent facts about the qualities of objects which can be stated without any reference to experience of them. But this claim is exactly what Berkeley denies has sense, on the grounds that any characterization of a sensible quality has to make essential reference to how it appears to some actual or possible perceiver. For how does one explain redness, smoothness, and other sensible qualities independently of how they appear? So the objection fails by premising a seems–is distinction, which is precisely what Berkeley is rejecting on the grounds that it leads straight to scepticism.

To deny that there is a seems–is distinction is just another way of asserting that sensible objects (things in the world) are collections of sensible qualities, and hence of ideas. So Berkeley takes the contrast he wishes to resist to be one between (1) sensible objects, which as collections of sensible qualities are what is immediately perceived, and (2) objects existing independently of perception but causing it. This is not the same contrast as between (3) sense-data, in the sense of uninterpreted contents of sensory states, and (1) sensible objects. It is important to note this because for Berkeley what is immediately present in experience is the sensible object, not some mediating representative item (or collection of such items) different from the object. We do not, he says, infer from colour-patches and other sense-data in our sensory experience to the existence, in a world beyond them, of books and trees; what we see (and touch etc.) are, immediately, books and trees.

This seems to create a problem for Berkeley, because he seems to be having things both ways: we immediately perceive such familiar objects of sense experience as books and trees, while at the same time what we immediately perceive are colours and textures. To see what is involved here, consider an argument offered in more recent philosophy. This says that books and trees are interpretations of, or inferences from, the sensory data of experience, and that in speaking of books rather than colour-patches we are going beyond what is strictly licensed by talk of colour-patches. This is because we take physical objects to exist independently of particular perceivings of them, and to be publicly available to more than one perceiver at a time, and so on—none of which is true of the sensory ideas from which they are inferred. So we have to keep (1) and (3) strictly separate.

Berkeley can be defended against this objection by noting that he is careful to distinguish between what can be called 'phenomenal' and 'phenomenological' levels of explanation. The phenomenal level concerns the things we encounter in ordinary experience—books and trees—while the phenomenological level concerns facts about sensory experience considered strictly from the viewpoint of the experiencer's apprehension of sensible qualities. Given the distinction, Berkeley argues, we can say that at the phenomenological level what are immediately perceived are colours and textures, while at the phenomenal level what are immediately perceived are books and trees. The latter consist wholly of the former, and it is only if one disregards the distinction of levels that one might fall into the mistake of thinking that when one perceives a book, one perceives redness and smoothness *and* a book, as if the book were something additional to the sensible qualities constituting it. Just such a view is forced by the materialist position, in which something inaccessible to sensory awareness constitutes the underlying causal origin of the sensible qualities we perceive.

Some critics urge the objection that having thus argued that all perception is immediate, Berkeley promptly proceeds to admit a species of *mediate* perception by inference or 'suggestion'. The passage cited is the one where Berkeley says, 'when I hear a coach drive along the streets, immediately I perceive only the sound; but from the experience I have had that such a sound is connected with a coach, I am said to hear the coach' (*Three Dialogues*, 204). This might count as a case of mediate perception if Berkeley did not immediately add, 'It is nevertheless evident, that in truth and strictness, nothing can be *heard* but *sound*: and the coach is not then properly perceived by sense, but suggested from experience.' The same applies to our practice of saying elliptically that one sees that the poker is hot; again, one does not see heat, one sees *that* something is hot, that is, one infers on the basis of experience that when something looks like that, it will feel a certain way if you touch it. These are not cases of mediate perception, but of experience-based inference, to which Berkeley gives the name 'suggestion': the ideas of one sense *suggest* the ideas of another.

As long as certain of Berkeley's premises are accepted, and as long as discussion of the main plank of his views (the notion of God and his metaphysical activity) is deferred, his views remain resilient to objections. If we reject the Cartesian super-premiss on which his project is grounded, namely, that the place to start is among the data of individual experience, his views are not so resilient. But it must be said, in relation to this strategy, that in adopting such an approach one is well advised to keep sight of the subjective perspective, for any account of the nature of experience and its relation to knowledge has to be sensitive to the fact—for fact it is—that each subject of experience is to some degree in the solipsistic and finitary predicament which the Cartesian tradition emphasizes. This remains so even if we argue, as we doubtless should, that assumptions about shared language and therefore a shared world, on which we have a participant rather than a merely passive perspective, provide material for a better account.

These remarks touch upon one set of objections to Berkeley's views. Others, as remarked, more threatening to his position, concern its underpinning, namely, the deity to whom a central metaphysical role is allotted. This is discussed below.

2.6. Matter and 'Immaterialism'

The concept of matter is redundant, Berkeley's argument purports to demonstrate, because everything required to explain the world and experience of it is available in recognizing that minds and ideas are all there can be. But Berkeley adds to this argument-by-exclusion a set of positive anti-materialist considerations.

An important argument for materialism is that use of a concept of matter explains much in science. Berkeley eloquently summarizes the view: 'there have been a great many things explained by matter and motion: take away these, and you destroy the whole corpuscular philosophy, and undermine those mechanical principles which have been applied with such success to account for the phenomena. In short, whatever advances have been made . . . in the study of nature, do all proceed on the supposition that corporeal substance or matter doth really exist' (*Principles*, 50). One of Berkeley's replies to this argument had considerable influence on Ernst Mach and other more recent positivists. It is that science's explanatory power and practical utility neither entail the truth of, nor depend upon, the materialist hypothesis, for these can equally if not better (because more economically) be explained in instrumentalist terms. Instrumentalism is the view that scientific theories are instruments or tools, and as such are not candidates for assessment as literally true or false, but rather as more or less useful. One does not ask whether a gardening utensil such as a spade is true, but whether it does its intended job well—and not only well, but as simply and economically as possible; here 'Occam's razor' applies, namely, the principle that one should not postulate the existence of more than is absolutely necessary for adequate explanation.

Berkeley expresses his early version of instrumentalism in terms of a 'doctrine of signs', in which the regularity and order among our ideas reflect the steady will of God, which is so reliable that we can represent the connections we observe as laws. He writes, 'the steady, consistent methods of Nature, may not unfitly be styled the *language* of its Author, whereby he . . . directs us how to act for the convenience and felicity of life' (*Principles*, 109). Science is thus a convenient summary, for sublunary purposes, of what at the metaphysical level of explanation would be described in terms of the activity of infinite spirit.

This is a rejoinder to an attempted 'appeal to the best explanation' on behalf of the materialist hypothesis. It is at the same time a rejoinder to a closely allied argument, an 'appeal to the simplest explanation'. This says that postulating the existence of matter simplifies the account we give of the world. The rejoinder consists in the same slash of Occam's razor; it is that since experience could be exactly as it is without matter existing independently of it, the materialist hypothesis is not the simplest explanation after all.

But the key point for Berkeley is that whatever else matter or corporeal substance is, by definition (1) it is non-mental, and as such cannot be the substrate or support of qualities, because qualities are ideas, and ideas can only exist in a thinking substrate or support, namely minds; and (2) it is inert, that is, causally inactive, and so cannot produce change, motion, or ideas.

For Locke and others among Berkeley's predecessors the concept of primary qualities was important because, they held, experience of them puts us most closely in touch with independent reality. Berkeley therefore examines their argument. Materialists, he says, hold that primary qualities are 'resemblances' of 'things which exist without the mind, in an unthinking substance which they call *matter*' (*Principles*, 9); but since primary qualities are ideas, and since 'nothing can be like an idea but an idea' (*Principles*, 8), it follows that 'neither they nor their archetypes can be in an unperceiving substance' (*Principles*, 9). Moreover, the primary–secondary quality distinction, understood in terms of a supposed difference between the way each kind of quality relates to mind, involves a specious abstraction of one kind from the other; for since one cannot conceive such primary qualities as motion or number apart from such secondary qualities as colour, both are on a par in the way they relate to mind, namely by being essentially dependent upon mind for their existence as ideas.

Some of Berkeley's critics think he failed to separate the question of material substance from that of the primary–secondary quality distinction, since one can reject materialism while retaining the distinction. But this in fact is what Berkeley does, for he does not deny that there is a distinction between primary and secondary qualities—he recognizes that the former are available to more than one sense at a time, the latter available to one sense only; that the former are measurable, the latter not (or not so straightforwardly); and so on—but he points out that in the *crucial* respect of their relation to mind, they are on a par in both being *sensible* and hence mind-dependent.

2.7. The Mind–Idea Relation

One charge levelled at Berkeley is that his account of the crucial relation between minds and ideas is contradictory or at very least confused. In the *Principles* he says that the mind 'is a thing *entirely distinct* from [ideas], *wherein they exist*, or, which is the same thing, whereby they are perceived' (para. 2; my emphases). Three paragraphs later he adds that it is not possible to conceive 'any sensible thing or object *distinct from* the sensation or perception of it' and in the same paragraph he remarks, 'is it possible to separate, even in thought, my ideas from perception? For my part, I might as easily divide a thing from itself.' These assertions appear to commit him to three principles which are together inconsistent, but which each play an important part in the rest of what he is concerned to argue.

The three principles have been called the *Distinction Principle*, asserting that minds and ideas are distinct from one another (*Principles*, 2, 27, 80, 142), the *Inherence Principle*, asserting that ideas exist only in the mind (*Principles*, 2, 3, and *passim*), and the *Identity Principle*, asserting that ideas are not distinct from perceivings of them (*Principles*, 5; *Three Dialogues*, 195 ff.). The second and third are consistent; the first and third appear to contradict each other; and the relation between the first two at very least demands explanation.

Most critics think that the easiest solution is to drop the Distinction Principle. One reason is that it seems to commit Berkeley to an *act–object* analysis of perception, whereas the Identity Principle commits him to an *adverbial* analysis.

The first describes perceiving as an act of mind directed upon an object, rather like the beam of a torch shining upon a tree; the object is independent of the act, which can be repeated with different objects (the act of looking can have as its objects the bookshelf, the cat, the desk, and so forth). The adverbial analysis has it that perception is a modification of the mind, so that, for example, to see a cat is to 'see catly', so to speak; hence the label 'adverbial'; the mind is shaped or modified into a catly-perceiving state. Here there is one event—the modification of one's mental states in a certain way—whereas on the act–object analysis there is the mental act and something independent of it, its object. Since this analysis demands the *independence* of the objects of perception, which on Berkeley's theory are ideas and hence incapable of independence from mind, the Distinction Principle seems to be the obvious candidate for rejection.

But the principle is crucial to Berkeley; the very plan of the *Principles* depends on it: 'Human knowledge [reduces] to two heads, that of *ideas* and that of *spirits*' (*Principles*, 86). And this is no surprise, since if the principle were rejected, minds would be identical with their ideas, but this cannot be, for Berkeley insists on the differences: minds are active, ideas inert; ideas are dependent entities, minds substantial. In the *Commentaries* Berkeley had considered and rejected the notion that minds are just bundles of ideas, on the good ground that 'a colour cannot perceive a sound, nor a sound a colour . . . therefore I am one individual principle, distinct from colour and sound; and, for the same reason, from all other sensible things and inert ideas' (*Three Dialogues*, 234).

The Distinction Principle, therefore, cannot be abandoned. But neither can the others; the Inherence Principle, after all, is simply a version of *esse est percipi*, and the Identity Principle follows from the attack on abstraction, which tells us that we cannot abstract ideas from perception of them. Is there a solution?

There is; and it is to be found in recognizing that the expressions 'Inherence' and 'Identity' are misleading. For Berkeley does not hold that ideas 'inhere' in the mind, as attributes are said to inhere in substance, nor that ideas and perception of them are identical. I take each point in turn.

The 'Inherence' Principle states that 'ideas exist in the mind'. The formula 'in the mind', as already noted, is to be understood as 'with essential reference to mind', in the sense that the existence of an idea is dependent upon its being perceived—*actually*, not just *possibly*, perceived: for in Berkeley's theory everything is always actually perceived by an infinite mind, so ideas are only possibilities of perception relative to finite minds. The sense of 'dependence' here is that in which (to adapt an obstetric example of Plato's) an embryo is dependent on a womb: it exists in it, and cannot exist without it, but it is nevertheless distinct from it. 'Inherence' is an adverbial notion: it is the relation of a wave to the sea; the wave is a 'mode' of the sea. Berkeley writes, 'there can be no substratum of . . . qualities but spirit, in which they exist, not by way of mode or property, but as a thing perceived in that which perceives it' (*Three Dialogues*, 237).

As for the 'Identity' Principle, it is a simple mistake to construe Berkeley's anti-abstractionist view—namely, that any account of ideas cannot be abstracted from an account of perception—as amounting to an assertion of the identity of ideas with perception of them. The assertion that one cannot 'conceive apart' any 'sensible thing or object distinct from the perception of it' (*Principles*, 5) is not a claim that these are numerically the same thing. Consider an example: bread and the process by which it is baked are internally related; there cannot be one without the other; but bread is not numerically identical with the baking of it. The same kind of internality characterizes the relation of perception and ideas.

The question of the mind–idea relation is important because it is the only major threat to the internal coherence of Berkeley's theory. These comments show that there is not after all a threat. As before, it remains that the Cartesian basis of the project, and its linchpin metaphysical thesis that an infinite mind perceives everything always, are the two real problems with Berkeley's theory. It is time to consider the second of these.

2.8. Spirit as Substance

Given the Cartesian super-premiss, Berkeley's argument is highly consistent and tightly knit, and rests on a single major foundation: the thesis that there is an infinite mind which perceives (conceives; and thus causes) everything always. If this thesis cannot be sustained, either the whole edifice collapses or some alternative metaphysical underpinning is required.

Berkeley took his arguments to amount to a new and powerful argument for God's existence. As such, as noted, they are a contribution to natural theology; nothing turns on revelation or traditional conceptions of deity, beyond that such a being has to be infinite and omnipotent. Indeed Berkeley's arguments require no more than a metaphysical god thus conceived. Whether such a being is a person, or much interested in the universe or the finite minds in it, is neither here nor there, so long as it fulfils its function of making the universe exist.

The nub of Berkeley's argument for God is that since everything that exists is either mind or ideas, and since finite minds, even in concert, could not perceive all the ideas that constitute the universe, there must be an infinite mind which perceives everything always and thereby keeps it in being.

The classic statement of the argument occurs in the second of the *Three Dialogues* (212–14). From the proposition 'that sensible things cannot exist otherwise than in a mind or spirit', Berkeley concludes 'not that they have no real existence, but that seeing they depend not on my thought, and have an existence distinct from being perceived by me, *there must be some other mind wherein they exist*'. This conclusion is a weaker one than that there is a single infinite mind which perceives everything always; it establishes no more than that there is 'some other mind'—who might for all we know be the next-door neighbour. But in the very next sentence Berkeley adds, 'As sure therefore as the sensible world really exists, so sure is there an infinite omnipresent spirit who contains and supports it.' This is quite a leap. The missing step is provided later (*Three Dialogues*, 215):

I perceive numberless ideas; and by an act of my Will can form a great variety of them, and raise them up in my imagination: though it must be confessed, these creatures of the fancy are not altogether so distinct, so strong, vivid, permanent, as those perceived by my senses, which latter are called *real things*. From all which I conclude, *there is a mind which affects me every moment with all the sensible impressions I perceive.* And from the variety, order and manner of these, I conclude the Author of them to be *wise, powerful, and good beyond comprehension.*

This 'Author' Berkeley a few lines later describes as 'God the Supreme and Universal Cause of all things'. The missing step is a version of the teleological argument for the existence of a god.

The argument in fact has two stages. The first argues that things are causally dependent on mind for their existence, and therefore, since I cannot think of everything always, there must be mental activity elsewhere carrying out the task. The second stage says that one can infer the character of that mind by inspecting the nature of its ideas: since the universe is so huge, beautiful, intricate, and the rest, it must be a 'wise, powerful', and so forth mind.

The first thing to note is the inadequacy of the teleological argument here coopted as the second stage. The appearance of design, purpose, or beauty in the universe does not entail that it was designed; and even if it did entail this, it does not thereby entail that it was designed by a single mind, or an infinite mind, or a good mind. (What if—regarding this last point—we concentrated upon the violence and bloodshed in nature, and the disease, waste, and other evils flourishing there? What picture of the creating mind would this suggest?) In any case there are more economical ways to explain the teleological appearance of the universe, the best being evolutionary theory.

What of the first stage? The most it establishes is the bare conclusion that what exists can do so only in relation to mind. The relation in question needs to be explained; Berkeley is committed to saying that it is a *causal* relation, but it is exactly this which pushes him to the unpersuasive second stage of the argument for an infinite mind. An alternative resource might be to say that there is no account to be given of the world which does not make essential reference to facts about thought or experience of it, and this might furnish the starting-point for views like Kant's or those of certain contemporary 'anti-realists'.

Although Berkeley does not need the God of traditional theology but only a metaphysical being causally competent for its task, his employment of teleological considerations mixes tradition with metaphysics to the injury of the latter. There is certainly no shadow of an argument why the mental activity to which the existence of the whole universe is to be referred has to be unitary or infinite. A committee of finite minds might seem an even less palatable option, but nothing in the argument excludes it.

Upon inspection, accordingly, the argument for the metaphysical linchpin of Berkeley's theory does not pass muster. As remarked, if this does not entail the collapse of the project, it will be because there is some other way of making out the idea that what exists stands in an internal relation to thought or experience of it. On that score, philosophy is not without resources.

2.9. Concluding Remarks

There are other points in Berkeley's views which repay examination, for example his concept of conceivability, his finitary realism, the sense in which it is correct to call his views 'idealist', his views of time, and—as just suggested—the metaphysical implications of his arguments considered independently of their theistic basis. But enough has been said to suggest reasons for his influence on later thinkers, not least among them the phenomenalists—including Russell and Ayer—and the Logical Positivists. It is in particular both interesting and philosophically important to understand why phenomenalism, as a version of Berkeley's theory in which the bare concept of 'possibilities of perception'— 'possibilia'—has been substituted for the concept of a deity, is arguably less cogent than the original, because it demands that we accept their existence as what objects consist in when they are not currently being perceived. From the point of view of unacceptability there may not be much to choose between a metaphysics of possibilia and a theological basis for the universe, but, at least in Berkeley's version of the latter, everything that exists does so actually.

Berkeley was a more thoroughgoing empiricist than Locke. He started from the data of experience and strictly observed them as the touchstone in what can be accounted meaningful—including, although his account of the point is sketchy and unclear—the 'intuitive' and 'reflexive' experience which gives us 'notions'.

But the most austere and rigorous empiricist of the three—indeed of any to whom the label can be applied—is Hume, to whose views we now turn.

3. DAVID HUME

3.1. Life and Work

Hume was born at Edinburgh in 1711 and educated there. He read law at the university, but his first interest was philosophy, to which he early devoted himself. For a reason connected with his intensive studying he suffered a nervous breakdown. His family sent him to work in the office of a Bristol merchant, in the hope that the experience would prove an antidote to poring over books; but he found the life deeply uncongenial. In 1734 he went to France and resumed his philosophical work, the result appearing five years later in the form of books i and ii of his major philosophical work, the *Treatise of Human Nature*. Its reception was exceedingly disappointing; Hume described it as 'falling dead-born from the press'. It had no readers and only one reviewer, who was anyway one of those who did not read it, so Hume himself wrote an anonymous review, the *Abstract*, which is an excellent short introduction to his views. Despite the disappointing reception of the first two books, Hume published the third and final book of the *Treatise* two years later. It too met with indifference.

Determined to communicate his hard-won insights to the public, Hume a decade later rewrote the *Treatise* as two separate works, the *Enquiry Concerning Human Understanding* and the *Enquiry Concerning the Principles of Morals*, the first *Enquiry* corresponding to the *Treatise*'s first book, 'Of the Understanding', and the second *Enquiry* to its third book, 'Of Morals'. Hume wrote them in an easier style in the hope of finding readers among the general public. He said to a friend, '*addo dum minuo*; I add by subtracting', that is, he had improved the presentation of his ideas by cutting out technicalities and details. Although the two *Enquiries* are works of great value, and indeed—despite Hume's claim—add material to his original arguments, the *Treatise* remains his prime philosophical achievement.

Hume, like Berkeley, did his philosophical work young, and turned his attention later to the writing of history and essays, producing works of distinguished literary merit. He held diplomatic appointments in Europe, chiefly Paris, where he consorted with many of the leaders of the French Enlightenment, and earned the sobriquet 'le bon David' because he was much loved among his friends. He retired to Edinburgh to pass the remainder of his life as a scholar-gentleman in the sinecure position of Librarian to the city's Faculty of Advocates. He died in 1776, visited in his last illness by James Boswell, who was eager to see how death was faced by one known to be an atheist. To the surprise of the superstitiously anxious Boswell, Hume did so with equanimity and good cheer.

3.2. Aims and Method

The discussion in book i of the *Treatise* and the first *Enquiry* is the chief concern in what follows. In these works Hume addresses some of the same problems as had exercised Locke and Berkeley, but with different emphases and two important differences of approach. Locke had sought to articulate a general epistemological theory; Berkeley, more narrowly, had sought to establish a special thesis about the nature of knowledge and its objects. Hume saw that their views turned crucially upon accounts of the nature of the human mind, and accordingly set himself the task of giving what we might now call a 'philosophical psychology', and which he described as a theory of human nature.

The other difference is that Hume's account of human nature in book I is offered not only for its intrinsic importance, but as a preface also to a further crucial matter, namely, discussion of the principles of morality. It is implicit in the structure of the *Treatise* that the argument of book I, 'Of the Understanding', is required in order that the conclusions of book III, 'Of Morals', can be derived. As a framework for Hume's discussion 'of the Understanding' it helps to consider these two points more fully.

That the theory of the mind is, in Hume's view, the basis for a theory of morals, can be illustrated—roughly and very briefly—as follows. Debate about the foundations of ethics was minimal between the time that Christianity became the official ideology (so to say) of Europe—in what are misleadingly called the 'Dark Ages'—and the seventeenth century. Such questions had been vigorously debated in the ancient world, as witness the thought of Plato, Aristotle, and the later schools, among which Stoicism was for a long period particularly influential. But after the rise to dominance of Christianity there was little debate about ethical principles, the main form of moral discussion instead consisting in interpretation of Scripture and Church teaching, an enterprise known as 'casuistry'. But with the development of Renaissance and Enlightenment ideas, discussion returned from casuistry to the foundations of morality.

Among the reasons for this was recognition of the following point. One cannot answer the moral sceptic's question 'Why ought I to do so-and-so?' by saying that a deity requires it, not even if it is added that the deity supports the requirement with a threat of punishment; for neither the mere fact that any being—deity or not—desires that someone else should think or behave in a certain way, nor the fact that he proffers threats to back this desire, constitute logically adequate reasons why anyone should act in accordance with them. It might be *prudent* to act in accordance with them, if one wished to avoid, say, eternal punishment; but they are not otherwise compelling.

Further, if there indeed exist good reasons why one should act one way rather than another, those reasons would be as binding on a deity as they are on any other agent. So whatever constitutes the basis, if there is such a thing, of morality, it cannot be found in the will of a deity, but must be independently sought.

Freed from constraints of dogma, discussion of the principles of ethics resumed in the early modern era, returning to its proper place among philosophy's central concerns. Among those who contributed significantly to that debate in the eighteenth century were Joseph Butler, Bernard Mandeville,

Francis Hutcheson, Lord Shaftesbury—and Hume. They all, but especially Hume, were occupied by the great question of 'the general foundation of Morals; whether they be derived from Reason, or from Sentiment; whether we attain the knowledge of them by a chain of argument and induction, or by an immediate feeling and finer internal sense; whether, like all sound judgement of truth and falsehood, they should be the same to every rational intelligent being; or whether, like the perception of beauty and deformity, they be founded entirely on the particular fabric and constitution of the human species' (second *Enquiry*, sect. 134).

In Hume's view, the answer is that morality is founded 'entirely on the particular fabric and constitution of the human species'. For this reason he took it that the need for an adequate 'science of human nature' is pressing. He described this science as falling under three heads: *logic, morals and criticism*, and *politics*. 'The sole end of logic', he wrote, 'is to explain the principles and operations of our reasoning faculty, and the nature of our ideas: morals and criticism regard our tastes and sentiments: and politics consider men as united in society, and dependent on each other' (*Treatise*, I, introduction). Hume proposed to develop a science of human nature by introducing 'the experimental method of reasoning into moral subjects'—that is, by basing the investigation firmly on empiricist principles.

The starting-point for a science of human nature is 'logic' as just described, for it concerns the 'operations of the understanding', about which Hume proposes a distinctive thesis: that our fundamental beliefs about the world, ourselves, and morality rest not upon the operations of reason, but upon contingent facts about human nature.

Speaking of himself in the third person in the *Abstract*, Hume describes his aim thus: he 'proposes to anatomize human nature in a regular manner, and promises to draw no conclusions but where he is authorized by experience'. The second part of this statement asserts Hume's empiricism, which he applies rigorously: nothing we say or think is legitimate unless it can be traced to its origin in experience. This deceptively simple principle, rigorously applied, has far-reaching consequences. It is based on Hume's account of the mind's contents and operations, which is the chief premiss of his theory. He saw himself as doing for 'moral philosophy' what Newton had done for 'natural philosophy': Newton had stated a principle, the principle of gravitation, which explains much about the constitution and workings of the physical world. Hume offers a principle—the 'principle of the association of ideas'—to serve as a corresponding basis for a science of human nature, by giving explanations of experience, belief, the nature of knowledge, and the place and limits of reason.

3.3. Hume and Scepticism

The philosophical conclusions Hume drew from his theory of human nature prompted many of his successors to describe him as a sceptic. Many commentators still do. In the following sketch of Hume's philosophy reasons are given for thinking that this portrayal of him is not straightforwardly correct.

The standard story about Hume's place in the empiricist tradition runs somewhat as follows. Locke attempted to construct a theory of knowledge which would both accord with and validate the new corpuscularian science. It depended on a theory of perception which seemed to his successors, not least Berkeley, to turn on a problematic separation between what lies immediately before the mind in perception—namely, ideas—and what are supposed to be their independent causes in the external world. Berkeley denied the existence of material substance, and argued that the universe consists of minds and their ideas alone. Hume—so this view goes—went further, arguing that there is as little reason to assert the existence of substantial minds (that is, individual mental beings persisting through time; and this includes God) as there is to assert the existence of matter. Further still: whereas in their different ways Locke and Berkeley accepted the existence of causality—Locke holding that causal relations operate between physical things, Berkeley that only minds are capable of causal agency—Hume argued that the common notion of causation as a necessary connection between distinct entities is a myth.

Taken in sum, Hume's view accordingly seems to be that on the basis of experience—the only acceptable basis, in the empiricist view, for investigation of these questions—all we are entitled to say is that there are briefly lived perceptions, with neither cause nor object in an outer world, nor persisting subject to which they belong, nor any kind of necessary bond between them.

This austerely sceptical, not to say incoherent, conclusion was attributed to Hume by the fiercest of his early critics, the Scottish philosopher Thomas Reid (1710–96), founder of the school of 'Common Sense Philosophy'. Reid argued that the scepticism into which, on his interpretation, Hume's view collapses is the result of taking empiricism to its logical conclusion, thus demonstrating the falsity of one of its chief premises, namely the theory of ideas. This theory, one recalls, assumes that what is immediately perceived—the idea—exists only as an object of perception, and is distinct from whatever, if anything, is postulated as its independent cause. Reid argued that we should start instead by just accepting that there are experiencing subjects, that they are directly acquainted with things in the world, and that these things exist independently of our perceiving them. (This indeed is the common-sense view of the matter; but Reid entirely misses the point of what Hume and his predecessors were trying to do, which was to examine and, as far as possible, support the credentials of that common-sense view.)

Reid's view of Hume, portraying him as a radical sceptic who effects a *reductio ad absurdum* of the work of Locke and Berkeley, has continued to colour perceptions of Hume's work. It runs oddly counter to Hume's own declared intention in the introduction to the *Treatise*: 'In pretending therefore to explain the principles of human nature,' he there writes, 'we in effect propose a compleat system of the sciences, built on a foundation almost entirely new, and the only one upon which they can stand with any security' (*Treatise*, p. xiv). Elsewhere Hume accuses Berkeley of having produced 'merely sceptical' arguments, by which he means 'that they admit of no answer and produce no conviction. Their only effect is to cause that momentary amazement and irresolution, which is the result of scepticism' (first *Enquiry*, sect. 155). These are not the remarks of someone bent upon producing a sceptical system of his own.

Those who interpret Hume as a sceptic like to quote his remark at the end of *Treatise*, book I, where he claims that his arguments show that 'the understanding, when it acts alone, and according to its most general principles, entirely subverts itself and leaves not the lowest degree of evidence in any proposition, either in philosophy or common life' (*Treatise*, I. 267–8). But a careful reading of this and the arguments of which it is the conclusion show that Hume's conclusions are far from sceptical. He argues that human nature is so constituted that we cannot help but believe in such fundamental matters as causality, the reliability of inductive reasoning, and the existence both of selves and of an external world. What he is indeed sceptical about—and this is a quite different matter—is the claim of *rationalist* philosophy to give proofs of the truth or falsity of these commitments.

These claims about Hume's view receive support from the account of his thought offered in what follows.

3.4. The Furniture of the Mind

Hume begins by describing the contents of the mind. All our perceptions, says Hume, are of two kinds, *impressions* and *ideas*. The difference between them is wholly qualitative; the former are more forceful and lively when they appear in consciousness, while the latter are 'the faint images of these' in thinking and reasoning (*Treatise*, I. i. 1). Each kind is also distinguished into simple and complex, simple impressions and ideas constituting the building-blocks of complex ones.

Every simple impression has a simple idea corresponding to it, and vice versa, but this is not the case with complex ideas, because these can be built—as when we use our powers of imagination—out of simple perceptions in ways that do not correspond to any one of them. 'I can imagine to myself', Hume says by way of example, 'such a city as the *New Jerusalem*, whose pavement is gold and walls are rubies, tho I never saw any such' (ibid.).

And now comes the key point for Hume: *'all our simple ideas in their first appearance are deriv'd from simple impressions, which are correspondent to them, and which they exactly represent'* (ibid.). Simple impressions come first in experience, and one only has an idea if it derives from that original impression. 'To give a child an idea of scarlet or orange or sweet or bitter, I present the objects, or in other words convey to him the impressions; but proceed not so absurdly, as to endeavour to produce the impressions by exciting the ideas' (ibid.).

These are the basic ingredients of mind. But there are important distinctions still to be noted. Impressions come in two varieties: those of *sense* and those of *reflexion*. The former 'arise in the soul originally, from unknown causes' (*Treatise*, I. i. 2), by which Hume means that at this early stage of the inquiry we cannot make assumptions about the existence of an external world which causes our sense impressions by acting on our sensory organs; so we have to begin by accepting that we just possess *givens*.

Impressions of reflexion arise in the following way. An idea is produced in us as the copy of a sense impression of, say, heat or cold, pleasure or pain. When the idea returns in memory it prompts a new impression of desire or aversion, hope or fear; from which yet new ideas are in turn copied. Such ideas of the emotions are important to Hume because they provide him with the chief material for his account of human nature, especially in relation to the passions (*Treatise*, book II) and morals (*Treatise*, book III), so the impressions of reflexion which give rise to them play a key part in his theory (*Treatise*, I. i. 2).

Ideas also are of two sorts: those of memory, and those of imagination. The former are more lively and strong than the latter, and whereas memories retain the form in which they originated, ideas of imagination can be rearranged at will, allowing us to invent 'winged horses, fiery dragons and monstrous giants' (*Treatise*, I. i. 3).

It is immediately noticeable that Hume's model for the contents of mind is an imagist one. Ideas (leaving aside for the moment impressions and ideas of reflexion) are copies of sense impressions, and are therefore mental pictures: if after looking at someone's face you close your eyes and think of it, the resulting mental picture is a complex idea constructed out of component simple ideas themselves derived from simple impressions. This raises questions about Hume's view of *thought*, for it would seem that he wishes to view ideas as components of thoughts. On this view, if ideas are images, it follows that thoughts are too. But this does not on the face of it look plausible. Thought might be accompanied by mental images, but need not be, and many thoughts are such that we would be hard pressed to nominate a certain mental picture, or series of them, that could embody and fully express their content. One way of seeing this is to think of thoughts as propositions. The thought that 'the Corn Laws were largely responsible for the Irish famine in the 1840s' might evoke mental images of certain kinds, but only contingently so, and in a way wholly subjective to different thinkers of the thought. Moreover, the structural complexity of thoughts involves irreducible logical features which are simply not imageable. One immediate question, therefore, is whether Hume has other things to say that will yield an adequate conception of thought.

Hume wished to postulate a simple experiential test for distinguishing impressions from ideas by their intrinsic features alone, namely, their differing degrees of force and liveliness, and their temporal ordering. This is forced on him by the fact, already emphasized, that he cannot separate them by saying that impressions are the effects of external objects currently interacting with our senses. But a difficulty this creates is that ideas can at times seem to have richer content than impressions, as when we become aware in recollection of more than we actually noticed at the time of, say, looking at something. Someone might reply that this additional content was indeed present in the impression, but not noticed because some other salience held one's attention. It is a question worth exploring whether a notion of latent content is consistent with Hume's account of impressions.

These points recur shortly in connection with some more general questions about Hume's argument.

3.5. Association and Belief

With his basic inventory of the mind in place, Hume turns to an account of its operations. Among the reasons he felt it important to give such an account is that impressions are *atomic*, that is, there are no logical connections between any of them; they are each independent and self-standing. Yet despite this, the simple ideas to which they give rise combine into complex ideas in a regular and orderly way, which they would not do unless there were 'some bond of union among them, some associating quality, by which one idea naturally introduces another' (*Treatise*, I. i. 4). This uniting principle cannot be considered an inseparable or necessary connection, for, if so, the recombining activities of imagination would be impossible. Rather, the associative force 'is a gentle force, which commonly prevails . . . nature in a manner pointing out to every one those simple ideas, which are the most proper to be united into a complex one' (ibid.).

Three relations explain how ideas associate: *resemblance, contiguity in place and time*, and *cause and effect*. If one idea resembles another, the imagination easily runs from the one to the other. As to contiguity: 'the senses, in changing their objects, are necessitated to change them regularly, and take them as they lie *contiguous* to one another, the imagination must by long custom acquire the same method of thinking, and run along the parts of space and time in conceiving its objects' (ibid.).

But the most powerful, important, and extensive associating relation is cause and effect, to which Hume devotes special attention, as we shall shortly see. These three are 'the only tie of all our thoughts, they are really *to us* the cement of the universe, and all the operations of the mind must, in great measure, depend on them' (*Abstract*).

Apart from explaining how simple ideas uniformly combine, the principle of association also explains the nature of belief. In Hume's view, to believe something is to entertain the idea of it with a special strength and liveliness arising from its association with a present impression. The mechanism is this: '*when any impression becomes present to us, it not only transports the mind to such ideas as are related to it, but likewise communicates to them a share of its force and vivacity*' (*Treatise*, I. iii. 8). This account is significant for Hume's theory of the main associating relation, causation, which is the chief ground of all 'knowledge and probability' because it is the only relation that 'can be trac'd beyond our senses, and informs us of existences and objects, which we do not see or feel' (*Treatise*, I. iii. 2).

It is important to note that Hume does not expect the principle of association to explain everything. Consider the example of general ideas. For anyone who thinks, as Hume in common with his two predecessors thought, that ideas are distinct individual entities in consciousness, there is a need to explain how they can ever be general, that is, stand for a multiplicity of things. Hume agreed with Berkeley that Locke's proposal will not do, and offered instead an account of how general terms come to be applicable to many individuals on the basis of resemblances we notice between them, there being a 'custom' that licenses the use of such expressions to denote indifferently any one of the individuals in question. It is significant that Hume's resource in explaining general *ideas* is an account of the use we make of general *terms*, but it well illustrates the fact that he was not confined to thinking that everything must fit the principle of association. It is obvious that if general ideas were to be explained on associationist lines, there would be a problem about how, given the finite nature of our experience, any individual user of the expression 'dog' could understand that it applies to every dog there has been or ever could be.

In introducing his account of association Hume describes it as a 'gentle force' uniting logically independent perceptions as a result of experience-formed habits. But the metaphor appears misleading when one sees—as in the case of causality, discussed shortly—that the links thus forged can feel to us like iron necessities. Moreover, the analogy with Newton's principle of gravitation is misleading also, for in coming to be associated, perceptions act not upon one another but upon the mind.

Hume's account leaves a number of points unexplained. Contiguity and resemblance are observed, but how do they give rise to association? Why is it that among all the contiguous and resembling perceptions we have—and what counts as 'resembling' might be a matter of degree or even taste for different perceivers—some come to be associated and others not? Why do these associations form in more or less the same way in almost all minds?—for surely it is more than possible that for some minds certain regularities will be salient, and for other minds others, with the possibility that different and even opposing associations might be formed.

It has been argued that Hume's view of association is in fact more elaborate than it at first appears, and is accordingly well able to deal with these questions. What does the work, so this view goes, is an implicit theory of 'propensities', or 'dispositions to form dispositions' (where a 'disposition' is a readiness or aptness to behave or perform in certain ways in certain conditions). The suggestion has Hume saying that the mind has propensities to develop conceptual habits in the course of experience, chief among them the linking of perceptions which are contiguous or resembling; and part of this is a propensity to impute the link to something in the world—to project it on to the objects themselves.

The idea that there are innate propensities seems to be stated by Hume in this passage: 'I must distinguish in the imagination betwixt the principles which are permanent, irresistible, and universal; such as the customary transition from causes to effects, and from effects to causes: And the principles, which are changeable, weak, and irregular . . . the former are the foundation of all our thoughts and actions, so that upon their removal human nature must immediately perish and go to ruin' (*Treatise*, I. iv. 4).

This is an interesting suggestion, and it would make Hume an even closer anticipator of Kant than is already acknowledged. But it has to be admitted that he does not stress the idea of innate structural propensities of mind, preferring to place greatest weight on experience. This he is bound to do, as a scrupulous empiricist relying only on 'the experimental method of reasoning' in his account of human nature. Still, at every point in the discussion of belief, causality, and our belief in an external world, Hume insists that it is human nature that makes us feel and judge as we do, and a theory of propensities could figure comfortably in an account of this kind. But to distance such a conception from weaker forms of innatism consistent with rationalism, Hume has to be careful to insist that there is something one might variously describe as natural, automatic, unwitting, or pre-reflective about our believing and judging as we do in the relevant respects, *and* that nothing thus believed or judged would figure at all unless prompted by experience. This too is consistent with a propensity theory, but it keeps attention fixed where Hume wants it, namely on what can be justified by reference to originating impressions.

There is one large fly in the ointment of the propensity theory, however, and that is that 'permanent, irresistible and universal' principles could be formed by experience, not inherited as structural features of mind; and if one is to choose between these interpretations on the basis of what Hume is officially committed to as an empiricist, this less plausible view would have to be given official status too. The question is open.

If it were possible to bolster the theory of association by appealing to a propensity psychology in this way, it would be a good deal less implausible. It would not, however, render much less unconvincing Hume's analysis of belief, to which I return after another central piece of Hume's jigsaw is in place.

3.6. Causality and Induction

In conformity with his strict empiricism Hume begins his investigation of causation by inquiring 'from what origin it is deriv'd', that is, by looking for the primary impression that gave rise to it (*Treatise*, I. iv. 4). Two relations immediately appear to him to be involved in the concept of causation: the *contiguity* of causes and their effect in time and place, and the *succession* in time of effects upon their causes—it being, in Hume's view, necessary that a cause should precede its effect, despite the view of some that causes and effects can be contemporaneous, which Hume thinks threatens the very idea of time (ibid.).

But these two relations are insufficient to give us our concept of causation, for many events are contiguous and successive without counting as instances of causal connection. There is, says Hume, a far more important relation to be taken into consideration: *necessary connection*. To think of A as the *cause* of B—and not simply as something that chanced to happen just before B and close to it in space—we have to think of A as somehow *producing B* or *making B happen*, such that B might not have happened without the occurrence of A. In short, we think of there being some special tie between A and B which constitutes the causal link, with which the terms '*efficacy, agency, power, force, energy, necessity, connexion*, and *productive quality*'—'all nearly synonymous'—are variously associated (*Treatise*, I. iii. 14). It is this special tie we must investigate if we are to understand causation.

What then is 'necessary connexion'? This is such a difficult question, Hume says, that it has to be approached circuitously; which he does by 'beating the neighbouring fields' to clarify related matters such as the nature of inference from impressions to ideas, belief, habit, and the nature of probability (*Treatise*, I. iii. 3–13). On the lessons thus learned he bases his theory.

Bear in mind Hume's main points so far. Impressions always precede ideas; possession of an idea is legitimate only if it can be traced to its originating impression; perceptions (impressions and ideas) are logically distinct, but associate together as a result of three main kinds of relation—resemblance, contiguity, and causation; belief consists in the vivacity which a present impression attaches to an associated idea. To these points Hume now adds another. To say that perceptions are logically distinct or 'atomic' is, as already noted, to say that none of them implies or is in any way necessarily linked to others, so that the mere contemplation of any one of them would not lead the mind to associate it with another. But, as we know, the mind nevertheless forms associations between ideas, and moves from one to another with great frequency and ease (*Treatise*, I. iii. 6). What explains this? The answer is of course *experience*; not just of one or a few juxtapositions of ideas, but of many such. It is the *constant conjunctions* of ideas in our experience which lead us to form habits of mind in relation to them—rather as if the repeated passage from one idea to another established a groove in the mind, making it all the easier for thought to move from one to another, as if there were a necessary tie between them. *And this is the key to causation*: the habitual transition of thought between perceptions *feels like* a necessitation or determination, as if the mind were obliged to go from one to another; and this internal impression of necessity is the origin of the idea of necessary connection (*Treatise*, I. iii. 14).

Two points of moment follow from this analysis. One is that it explains what underlies belief in the existence of things not present to the mind. A present perception associated in this habitual way with another will bring that other into consciousness; all inference from the perceived to the unperceived, whether in the present, past, or future, consists in this. In this therefore lies 'all our reasonings in the conduct of life'; everything we think about the world, and all our inductive reasonings from past to future, or from the observed to the unobserved, thus involves inference from cause to effect.

The second is that these reasonings are founded entirely on experience, not on rational principles or innate ideas. There is nothing in the nature of our ideas which determines their connections; their connections, and our use of them in drawing inferences, are the result of custom and experience alone. One such habit of thought is pivotal in our causal reasonings: it is the belief in the uniformity of nature, that is, the belief that the world will continue in future to be much as it has been in the past (*Treatise*, I. iii. 8).

Summarizing his own argument, Hume says that he has shown that the tie of necessary connection 'lies in ourselves, and is nothing but the determination of the mind, which is acquir'd by custom, and causes us to make a transition from an object to its usual attendant, and from the impression of one to the lively idea of the other' (*Treatise*, I. iv. 7). The necessary connection is not discovered in the world, but is contributed by the way our minds are constituted—it is *projected onto* the world.

Exactly this kind of analysis is intended by Hume to apply to other central philosophical problems: our belief in an external world, and our belief in the existence of a self which is the bearer of personal identity over time. And it forms the basis of his proposal in book III and the second *Enquiry* about the principles of morals.

It is now high time to consider some objections to Hume's arguments.

3.7. A General Objection

A general objection to Hume's project is that in proposing a 'science of human nature' based on 'experimental method' Hume is attempting not philosophy but psychology. This would not be a problem, say the objectors, if he were to go about it in the right way, that is, by truly experimental means; but instead he assumes that introspection and armchair observations about how minds work is sufficient as a basis for the task, which clearly it is not.

In response it must be acknowledged that Hume, and Locke before him, were attempting to construct theories of psychology. They were among the first to do so systematically, and suffered all the difficulties usual for pioneers. But they were not, as the objection implies, engaged in a primitive form of what we now think of as scientific psychology. Psychology now examines specific phenomena of learning and development, memory, perception, behaviour, and related matters, and does so as scientifically as the subjective nature of some of the data allow. The empiricists, very differently, were concerned with more general conceptual questions. It is no part of current psychology's brief, for example, to investigate such concepts as belief, knowledge, truth, identity, reason, and probability; and although it might aim to tell us what we think about the world, it does not aim to tell us whether we are justified in doing so, or whether the concepts we thus employ are consistent with one another and legitimate by some general criterion. These are philosophical matters, and Hume's chief concern, as did Locke's, lay with them.

The charge that Hume was attempting a priori scientific psychology distorts his intentions. Agreeing with Frances Hutcheson that our moral and aesthetic valuations spring from sentiment rather than reason, Hume wished to extend that view generally, and show that all our beliefs are a product 'more properly of the sensitive than of the cogitative part of our natures', that is, arise from experience rather than reason (*Treatise*, i. iv. 1). This view has a determinate polemical thrust: it is aimed at confuting rationalism, by showing that reason cannot explain causation, or prove the existence of an external world or of persisting selves; at best and most, reason can only serve as 'the slave of the passions, and can never pretend to any other office than to serve and obey them' (*Treatise*, ii. iii. 3). Hume is not a sceptic about the external world, causation, or the self; nor is he a sceptic about reason, which after all is important to us as an aid in everything our human nature makes us believe and do. Rather, he is a sceptic about the claims of rationalism, the doctrine that reason is the principal route to truth. If one keeps in mind the longer objective—making the case in ethics that the 'foundations of morals' lie in human nature, and are not objectively discoverable by reason—one sees the point of the argument in the *Treatise*, book i.

3.8. Difficulties about Impressions and Ideas

The charge about armchair psychology is not, however, without point, for it prompts recognition of certain difficulties in Hume's account. An important one relates to the distinction between impressions and ideas. The distinction is central to Hume's theory, yet it is not, upon inspection, clear.

As noted, Hume says that impressions and ideas are distinguished by the *degree* of forcefulness with which they appear in consciousness—look at something, then close your eyes and think of it; there is the difference made manifest—yet Hume concedes that impressions can be faint (as when one is sleepy) and ideas vivid (as when one is fevered). The problem is, as we have seen, that the qualitative difference Hume specifies is meant to mark a difference between experience and thought; but is this the same difference? To assess this we should need to be clearer about the qualitative features which some perceptions have and others lack, thereby constituting a purely internal mark by which the possessor of them can categorize them appropriately. Despite the insecurity of the distinction—as the concession reported above shows—Hume says little beyond inviting us to introspect and just *see* the difference for ourselves. But can we thus just *see* the difference between experience and thought?

The general question of the relation of experience to thought is too large for discussion here, but one tangential comment is relevant. It is sometimes forcefully argued that sense-experience cannot be regarded as possible in the absence of beliefs about the realm over which it ranges. The point is sometimes put by saying that perception is 'theory-laden'; it is soaked through with beliefs and concepts without which it would not amount to perception at all, but mere uninterpreted stimulation of the sensory pathways. Now, it is clear that Hume wished to regard impressions as inputs of data, the content of which, replicated in the having of ideas, will amount to knowledge. True to his empiricism, he held that the content of ideas is exhausted by the content of the impressions they derive from. This leaves no room for questions about what contributions are made by the mind to experience beyond such operations as associating; and it does not lend itself to assessment from the perspective of views of theory-ladenness of the kind just described. It is hard to see this as an advantage of Hume's theory, for both raise matters of importance.

Some of what Hume says suggests that the priority consideration—the claim that impressions arrive in consciousness before ideas—constitutes a different criterion for distinguishing the two. But if so the view threatens to be question-begging, for it is precisely Hume's empiricist method to challenge the legitimacy of ideas (*qua* concepts, beliefs) by asking for their pedigree in the impressions (experiences) which gave rise to them. On the view that temporal priority amounts to epistemological privilege, to find a justification for some idea one need only link it to another perception which entered consciousness earlier. But some ideas (as *opposed* to impressions, on the *qualitative* criterion for distinguishing them) entered the mind before other ideas, and yet cannot on that fact alone be allowed to serve as their empirical ground. Temporal priority therefore seems to be insufficient, even if it is necessary, for something to serve as an empirical basis for justification.

These problems about the criterion of difference between impressions and ideas arise because, as we saw, Hume cannot assume what philosophy must explain, namely, our belief in an external world (compare Locke's view of this matter), and therefore he cannot attribute the source of impressions to the activity of objects in an external world affecting our senses. Therefore he has to say that impressions 'arise in the soul originally, from unknown causes' (*Treatise*, I. i. 2), and later writes, 'As to those *impressions*, which arise from the *senses*, their ultimate cause is, in my opinion, perfectly inexplicable by human reason, and 'twill always be impossible to decide with certainty, whether they arise immediately from the object, or are produc'd by the creative power of the mind, or are deriv'd from the author of our being' (*Treatise*, I. iii. 5). His view is, of course, that our human nature simply makes us believe, without a real sense of option, that there is an external world from which our impressions of sense derive ('Nature, by an uncontroulable necessity has determin'd us to judge as well as to breathe and feel': *Treatise*, I. iv. 1); and these passages are sallies against rationalism. But by the same token, since there is nothing beyond our involuntary belief in this regard, and since experience—which is all we have—by itself does not select for us among the three options Hume offers, namely Locke ('immediately from the object') or Berkeley ('from the author of our being') or a radical subjective idealism ('by the creative power of one's own mind'), we seem to be in the familiar difficulty created by accepting what I earlier labelled 'the Cartesian super-premiss', namely, the belief that the right starting-place for inquiry is among the private contents of an individual mind.

Locke's 'invincible consciousness' that sensory perception is in order as a means to knowledge is similar to Hume's view that we just have to believe what we do. But there is a difference: Hume offers us an account of why this is so, which is that human nature is constructed that way. The advance lies in the thought that a systematic account of the nature and functionings of mind can reveal that certain fundamental commitments are, so to speak, structural to it. It was this hint which Kant developed in the *Critique of Pure Reason*.

3.9. Difficulties about Belief

An immediate problem with Hume's account of belief is that it conflicts with ordinary experience. Consider, for example, the fact that there is a large difference between reading a book as a work of fiction and reading it as a work of history. In the latter case, one believes what one reads (if one trusts the author), in the former, one treats the work as make-believe, and in so far as it purveys truths one does not treat them as typically of the factual kind. (Of course novels can contain factual truths, for example about places; but the point is clear.) On Hume's theory, anyone reading the book as history would have to have a 'more lively conception' than the person who reads it as fiction. But exactly the reverse can be true. It would occasion little surprise, although some regret, to find after an opinion poll that, among the generality of readers, fictional books regularly produce livelier conceptions than history books.

Hume was himself dissatisfied with his theory of belief, and says as much in the Appendix to the *Treatise*. What led him to adopt it was the parsimony of his account of the mind's contents, and the fact that the only way distinctions can be drawn among them is in terms of the difference in their manner of appearing to the mind—that is, in terms of their degrees of force and liveliness. Accordingly Hume's account of the difference between believing an idea and merely considering it (let alone disbelieving it) had to be couched in the same terms.

What seems to be right in his attempt is that a belief possesses, from the point of view of the believer, something a mere idea lacks. It is not open to Hume to think that a believed idea is one that comes in tandem with another idea, namely, the idea of the first idea's truth, because there is no 'impression of truth' from which such an idea could be derived (compare his response to the notion that there might be an impression of 'existence' accompanying every other impression: *Treatise*, I. ii. 6). Hume could have concluded something different from the line he took; he could have concluded that belief consists in the mind's having a particular attitude towards an idea—having towards it a distinctive readiness to act upon it, or to license certain inferences from it which it would not license otherwise, for example. Or he might have considered describing belief as a combination of an idea and an appropriate emotion. But he elected to characterize belief in terms of a property of the *ideas*—their degree of force or liveliness—which they borrow from associated impressions.

If, despite its unpersuasiveness, there is another advantage of Hume's account of belief, it is that it allows a sharp separation between the content of an idea and whether or not it is believed, disbelieved, or merely entertained. This is important because any change of content makes the idea a different idea, which is a matter of its history (its connections with originating impressions) and not a matter of whether it is believed or not. The property which marks it as a believed idea, if it has that property, does not affect or influence it otherwise. But this advantage is shared with the alternative view suggested, namely that belief is a mental attitude.

One diagnosis of Hume's difficulties about belief is that he was trying to explain it from the believer's viewpoint and not from the viewpoint of giving an independent specification of the concept of belief as such. It seems natural to do the latter in terms of dispositions to action, license to draw inferences, and the like, but none of these notions relate to the phenomenology of belief, that is, to what it is like to believe something from the subjective standpoint. Hume's attention was fixed exclusively on this latter.

3.10. Difficulties about Causation

In the economy of the *Treatise*, book I, the discussion of causation is vitally important, because it is the only relation that can take us beyond present experience to what lies in the world beyond. It is the crucial notion for the argument, and Hume was careful to give it detailed attention.

In his discussion Hume offers two definitions of 'cause'. As a 'philosophical relation' a cause is (1) 'An object precedent and contiguous to another, and where all objects resembling the former are placed in like relations of precedency and contiguity to those objects that resemble the latter'; while as a 'natural relation' a cause is (2) 'an object precedent and contiguous to another, and so united with it that the idea of the one determines the mind to form the idea of the other, and the impression of the one to form a more lively idea of the other' (*Treatise*, I. iii. 14). These definitions have given rise to controversy, critics variously objecting that the two definitions are not equivalent, that the classes of 'objects' referred to in (1) and (2) are not the same, and that only one of the two can serve as a definition—some argue that (1) is so, with (2) as merely a psychological aside. Moreover, they point out, the two notions of 'relation' are unclear.

Hume himself claims that the two definitions present 'a different view of the same object', and explains 'philosophical relation' as 'a comparison of ideas' and 'natural relation' as 'an association betwixt ideas' (ibid.). One way to gloss the definitions in line with this distinction is to say that contiguity, temporal order, and constant conjunction constitute the 'philosophical' relation of causation, while the 'natural' relation is contiguity, temporal order, and the association of our perceptions of the objects between which the 'philosophical' relation holds—that is, the accustomed link which invites thought and expectation to move from one to the other as if necessitated. But does this gloss preserve Hume's claim that (1) and (2) are different definitions of the *same* thing?

Given the analysis Hume offers of the origin of the notion of necessary connection, the definition which best captures his intention would seem to be (2), incorporating as it does reference to the psychological basis for our view of the causal link, whereas no mention is made of this in (1). And whereas (2) speaks of ideas of objects, (1) confines itself to reference to objects. The difference cannot be insignificant. According priority to (2) troubles some commentators because it makes Hume's account fundamentally psychologistic, but it is hard to see how it can be construed otherwise, given that the *kind* of analysis which explains the source of the idea of necessary connection is crucial, for it applies to other important questions also.

But such critics are disinclined to leave matters there, since it means that 'necessity' becomes subjective necessity, and the view seems to open the way to thinking that causal nexuses cease to hold in nature in the absence of observers. Their resource is to describe the drafting of (2) as careless and to assert that (1) gives the better picture. A passage they cite in support has Hume saying, 'As to what may be said, that the operations of nature are independent of our thought and reasoning, I allow it; and have accordingly observed, that objects bear to each other the relations of contiguity and succession . . . independent of, and antecedent to our understanding' (*Treatise*, I. iii. 14). This looks realist enough, and lends support to the thesis that (1) is the main definition. But unfortunately for those who adopt this line he immediately adds, in the continuation of the passage just cited, 'But if we go any farther, and ascribe a power of necessary connexion to these objects; this is what we can never observe in them, but must draw the idea of it from what we feel internally in contemplating them.' Here (2) comes into its own again.

Another response is to deny that the definitions are really definitions, upon the grounds that Hume himself says 'it is impossible to give any just definition of cause, except what is drawn from something extraneous and foreign to it' (first *Enquiry*, sect. 60). But this leaves their status mysterious, and accords ill with Hume's offering them as 'exact' ways of seeing the same thing under different descriptions (ibid.). Matters are not helped by noticing that Hume later offers two parallel definitions of *necessity* in a way that threatens a regress in his account of causation: he says, 'I define necessity two ways, conformable to the two definitions of *cause*, of which it makes an essential part. I place it either in the constant union and conjunction of like objects, or in the inference of the mind from the one to the other' (*Treatise*, II. iii. 2). Here Hume says that necessity is an essential part of causation, definition (1) of which is couched in terms of regularity; but now it transpires that necessity is to be defined in terms of regularity also—'the constant union and conjunction of like objects'. But how is *this* regularity to be defined, if not by a further appeal to necessity? And so regress looms.

Among the objections that have been urged against Hume's view is that it is itself a causal theory—we are caused to believe in causality by experiential regularities giving rise in us to habits of mind. Therefore, says the criticism, the account is circular. In reply one can grant that it is, but deny that it is viciously so. For suppose we are indeed caused to believe in causality; surely this fact does the reverse of making the account we are caused to give of it false. It is, instead, the very evidence we have for asserting it.

Another, and more troubling, objection is that Hume's theory provides no way of distinguishing between some connection's being causal and its being a completely coincidental but unfailing constant conjunction. We are, oddly enough, familiar with such things; darkness falls every evening (away from the polar regions) and not long thereafter one blinks an eyelid; but one does not regard this as a case of causality. On Hume's view it should be thought of as a case of causation on the grounds that the required invariant psychological link should have forged the projective link of necessity between them. Hume argues that our inferences from the observed to the unobserved travel along the highways laid by constant conjunctions. But if his theory rules out the mere possibility that there should be constant conjunctions which do not sustain such inferences, then it is highly counter-intuitive.

There is a great deal to be said about Hume on causality, and a copious literature says some of it. Here the surface of the discussion has been skimmed merely. Hume is the source of the debate about causality in recent and contemporary philosophy, and therefore study of his views on the matter is important.

3.11. Personal Identity

The interest generated by Locke's views on personal identity could be effectively ignored by Berkeley, who premised the existence of substantial selves, but not by Hume, for whom a scrupulous adherence to empirical principles meant that the notion of a self requires the same treatment as the other central notions he discusses.

Intuitively, 'selves' are supposed to be the entities which persist through time and change, despite other, presumably non-essential changes that happen to a person. They are also supposed to be the substrate or support of our thinking, perceiving, memory, and the like—the ultimate 'bearers' of our psychological properties.

Hume argues that the concept of the self has no empirical basis (*Treatise*, I. iv. 6, from which all quotations in this section are taken). All we need do, he says, is introspect: we will find 'nothing but a bundle or collection of different perceptions' in a state of continual change. No single persisting thing over and above particular occurrent perceptions can be discerned among them. It immediately follows, says Hume, that we are mistaken if we 'suppose ourselves possessed of an invariable and uninterrupted existence through the whole course of our lives'.

And yet this is exactly what we indeed suppose. If we are mistaken about the matter, how can the mistake have arisen? Hume claims that it rests on our confusing the notions of *identity* and *diversity*. The former is the idea of something persisting through time uninterruptedly and changelessly. The latter is the idea of a succession of related objects. The confusion arises—and here is the familiar Humean move—because the experience of diversity is the experience of *related* objects succeeding each other; and this feels to the mind like an experience of a single, persisting, unchanging thing. So we project identity on to what is in fact a succession. All disputes about identity are therefore, says Hume, merely verbal.

Hume's view makes an individual an impermanent bundle of occurrent impressions and ideas. But what do we mean by 'individual' here? Or to put it another way, what makes this bundle a bundle? How does one individuate a bundle in such a way as to distinguish it from a different bundle? If bundles had no boundaries it would not only be hard to do this, but it would leave it open that what we normally think of as different people could, so to speak, blend into each other, any number at a time.

Hume's reply is to say that the bundles are kept together by the familiar trio of resemblance, contiguity, and—chiefly—causation. That, to begin with, looks like the right reply for Hume to make; but a little reflection suggests that these relations might be insufficient for individuation, for there is no obvious reason why there cannot be causal links between perceptions in one bundle and those in another, or resemblance, or even contiguity. And if so, we have our original problem, which is that we are without not only a principle of identity, but a principle of individuation.

The central point to be made about Hume's account, however, is that it rests on the charge that it is a mistake to call something that changes the 'same thing'. Is this indeed a mistake? To show that it is not, one needs to note first that there are different ways of counting entities. An individual man might count as one; fifteen men together might count as one rugby team; thirty men might count as one set in 'the set of players in a rugby match'; and so on. Now it is clear that anything which consists of parts counts as one thing or as many things, depending on whether you count it or its parts. And it might undergo change to some of its parts while still being the same thing, as when one man is substituted for another in the team, or cells are replaced in the human body. So one can allow identity over time to an entity considered as the same thing despite its changes, since its changes occur to parts or aspects of it. And that identity can be preserved even if, at two distantly separated points in the time continuum, none of the parts or aspects are any longer numerically the same.

Hume's mistake is to think that since we characterize something as identical if it continues for a period without alteration, and since we recognize a succession of objects as a case of diversity, we cannot apply the former characterization to a case of the latter. But given that a self is not any one of its component perceptions, this thought suggests that there is no reason not to count a given bundle of perceptions as one, and to continue to do so even when one or some of its component perceptions change. If the idea of a history of a bundle's changes makes sense, as this further implies it does, then it suggests another line of resistance to Hume's argument, namely, that something needs to be postulated as the subject of those changes, without appeal to which the very idea of change itself might fail to make sense.

3.12. Concluding Remarks

Hume's thesis is that our beliefs about the existence of body (i.e. the external world), personal identity, and causation—and therefore the reliability of inductive inference, which wholly rests on the relation of cause and effect—are not derived from or established by reason, but are a function of human nature: we are, he tells us, just made that way. For this reason Hume is frequently described as a 'naturalist'. ('Naturalism' as applied to Hume's theory should be distinguished from its use to describe contemporary views such as those of Quine, where it means the claim that philosophers should premise the deliverances of the natural sciences in their work.) Kant claims to have been woken from his 'dogmatic slumbers' by Hume, in recognizing that facts about the constitution of our minds play a central role in giving us the beliefs and experience we enjoy. The difference is that Kant was not content merely to gesture towards human nature as the basis of our beliefs, but tried to give the idea a systematic statement.

In the course of working out his views Hume relied on an important distinction between (in his terminology) 'matters of fact' and 'relations of ideas': 'the operations of human understanding divide themselves into two kinds, the comparing of ideas, and the inferring of matter of fact' (*Treatise*, III. i. 1). Relations of ideas are discovered either by intuition, as when we see that $1 + 1 = 2$, or by demonstration, as when one proves a theorem or deductively infers a conclusion from its premisses. The arenas where reasoning about relations of ideas takes place are paradigmatically mathematics and logic. 'Matters of fact' are discovered by observation and causal inference, and concern how things are in the world. This distinction would now be marked as one between necessary and contingent propositions, a criterion of the difference between them being that to deny a true necessary proposition is to contradict oneself, whereas to deny a true contingent proposition is merely to say something false, not contradictory, because it might have been true in other circumstances.

Exploiting this distinction, Hume famously ends the first *Enquiry* by claiming that if his views are correct they are highly consequential. 'When we run over libraries, persuaded of these principles, what havoc must we make? If we take in our hand any volume; of divinity or school metaphysics, for instance; let us ask, *Does it contain any abstract reasoning concerning quantity or number?* No. *Does it contain any experimental reasoning concerning matter of fact and existence?* No. Commit it then to the flames, for it can contain nothing but sophistry and illusion' (first *Enquiry*, sect. 132). 'Divinity' and 'school metaphysics' (scholasticism) are the natural homes of the rationalist views Hume contests; here we see how his 'science of human nature' confronts them.

This resounding conclusion was one of the reasons why earlier commentators on Hume took the view, as noted earlier, that he was a thoroughgoing sceptic and had effected a *reductio ad absurdum* of the empiricist project. This, as we can now see, is a misperception; Hume is not a sceptic but a 'naturalist'; his scepticism is reserved for the claims of rationalist philosophy to offer a priori proofs of our most fundamental concepts.

Later commentators emphasize the enormous influence Hume's views have exercised on analytic philosophy, partly in his own right and partly through his influence on empirically minded philosophers in the earlier twentieth century, not least Russell.

Among the matters mentioned but not taken up in the foregoing are Hume's accounts of abstract ideas, substance, space and time, and probability—all of which, but especially this last, is germane to the main thrust of his argument. On these as on the other topics discussed Hume richly repays study.

BIBLIOGRAPHY

LOCKE

The best edition of Locke, unabridged, is: John Locke, *An Essay Concerning Human Understanding*, ed. P. H. Nidditch (Oxford, 1975). A detailed and philosophically interesting commentary is provided by Michael Ayers, *Locke*, 2 vols. (London, 1991). An influential discussion of themes in Locke well worth reading is: J. L. Mackie, *Problems from Locke* (Oxford, 1976).

Other works to be consulted:

AARON, R. I. *John Locke* (Oxford, 1963).
ALEXANDER, P., *Ideas, Qualities and Corpuscles* (Cambridge, 1985).
GIBSON, J., *Locke's Theory of Knowledge and its Historical Relations* (Cambridge, 1968).
O'CONNOR, D. J., *John Locke* (New York, 1967).
TIPTON, I. C. (ed.), *Locke on Human Understanding* (Oxford, 1977).
YOLTON, J. W., *Locke and the Way of Ideas* (Bristol, 1993).

Also helpful for reference purposes are:

CHAPPELL, V. C. (ed.), *The Cambridge Companion to Locke* (Cambridge, 1994).
YOLTON, J. W., *A Locke Dictionary* (Oxford, 1993).

BERKELEY

The best edition of Berkeley's works containing the *Principles, Three Dialogues,* and *Notebooks* is: George Berkeley, *Philosophical Works*, ed. M. R. Ayers (London, 1975). Recent commentaries include A. C. Grayling, *Berkeley: The Central Arguments* (London, 1986) and Jonathan Dancy, *Berkeley: An Introduction* (Oxford, 1987). A good collection of essays is Colin Turbayne (ed.), *Berkeley: Critical and Interpretative Essays* (Manchester, 1982).

Other works to consult are:

ARMSTRONG, D. M., *Berkeley's Theory of Vision* (Melbourne, 1960).

FOSTER, J., and ROBINSON, H., *Essays on Berkeley: A Tercentennial Celebration* (Oxford, 1985).

MARTIN, C. B., and ARMSTRONG, D. M. (eds.), *Locke and Berkeley: A Collection of Critical Essays* (London, 1968).

PITCHER, G., *Berkeley* (London, 1977).

STEINKRAUS, W. E., *New Studies in Berkeley's Philosophy* (New York, 1966).

TIPTON, I. C., *Berkeley: The Philosophy of Immaterialism* (London, 1974).

WINKLER, K. P., *Berkeley: An Interpretation* (Oxford, 1989).

HUME

The editions of Hume's work to be used are David Hume, *A Treatise of Human Nature*, 2nd edn., ed. P. H. Nidditch (Oxford, 1978). David Hume, *Enquiries Concerning Human Understanding and Concerning the Principles of Morals*, ed. P. H. Nidditch, 3rd edn. (Oxford, 1975). The main commentaries are D. F. Pears, *Hume's System* (Oxford, 1990) and Barry Stroud, *Hume* (London, 1977).

Other works are:

CHAPPELL, V. C. (ed.), *Hume* (London, 1966).

FOGELIN, R. J., *Hume's Skepticism* (London, 1985).

KEMP SMITH, N., *The Philosophy of David Hume*, 2nd edn. (London, 1949).

PASSMORE, JOHN, *Hume's Intentions*, 3rd edn. (London, 1980).

PRICE, H. H., *Hume's Theory of the External World* (Oxford, 1940).

STRAWSON, G., *The Secret Connexion: Realism and David Hume* (Oxford, 1989).

10

ETHICS

Bernard Williams

INTRODUCTION:
WHAT THE SUBJECT IS ABOUT

Moral philosophy is the philosophical, reflective study of certain values that concern human beings. A sense of ethical values informs people's lives, directly in deciding what to do, and in their comments and judgements on people and actions, including their own. People try, in varying degrees, to shape their lives by reference to such values: they think, even if not very explicitly, that some kinds of life are more worth living than others, and try to bring up their children to share their outlook, or perhaps to develop another which equally they hope to be able to respect. Most, unless life is desperate, also accept moral constraints on what they do, refusing (most of the time) to lie or cheat and (almost all the time) to kill or maim in order to advance what they want. In virtue of this, moral philosophy tries to understand certain kinds of reasons for action. Decisions about action ('What ought I to do?') are not the only concern of moral philosophy, but they are one important focus of its interest, as are the kinds of comment or assessment or judgement that we make about ourselves and other people in the moral or ethical style.

The subject is called, indifferently, 'moral philosophy' or 'ethics', but the terms 'moral' and 'ethical' do have slightly different resonances. 'Ethical' (derived from a Greek word for personal character) carries a broader conception, including a concern with the value of different kinds of life and activity; 'moral' (derived from a Latin word for social custom) tends to narrow its interest to rules and obligations, and to the experiences and considerations most closely related to those. 'Moral' is often used (though it does not have to be) in such a way that it is supposed to make an important difference whether a given consideration or feeling is or is not of the moral kind: remorse, for instance, may be sharply contrasted with other forms of regret as being a properly moral reaction, and it can become a matter of anxiety which personal characteristics have strictly moral value, as contrasted with such qualities as wit or sexual attractiveness. There is some basis for such distinctions in everyday experience, but they cannot be taken too far: intelligence, sensitivity, a sympathetic imagination, a certain toughness can all have their relevance to the moral life without being exclusively 'moral' qualities. A sharp exaggeration of the distinction is likely to be the product of a theory of moral value, in particular one that places great emphasis on the will.

There is a particularly sharp contrast on this point between Hume and Kant, well brought out with reference to Hume by Baier (1991). On the significance of the contrast, see Williams (1985, ch. 10).

I am grateful to Nora Freed for help in preparing this chapter.

Both 'ethical' and 'moral' do stand in contrast to some other kinds of consideration, even if the boundaries are often (and interestingly) rough. There is an important contrast with *self-interested* concerns, though the contrast can, of course, be drawn in different places, depending on the 'self' in question. The claims of my family may represent an ethical demand on me as against my purely selfish interests, but, in face of some wider demand of society or the community, the interests of my family may themselves be seen as a matter of our self-interest. At a rather different level, ethical considerations may be contrasted with aesthetic, economic, political, or religious considerations. This does not mean that these various considerations necessarily conflict or pull in different directions, but only that the kinds of reasons, sentiments, or interests involved are typically different.

It is to an even greater extent true of moral philosophy than it is of other areas of philosophy that it cannot keep itself sharply apart from other philosophical studies, or from subjects outside philosophy. Moral experience involves many of one's deepest thoughts and feelings about one's own life and one's relations to others, while at the same time moral rules and expectations constitute one way, a very significant one, in which society is controlled and the relations of one citizen to another are formed. Interesting moral philosophy is likely to sustain lively relations with subjects such as political philosophy, the philosophy of law, and philosophical psychology, as well as with various parts of the social sciences. Moreover, a constant tendency of moral philosophy to become abstract and unreal needs to be counterbalanced by imaginative literature and history, to remind one both that actual life is morally complex, and also that it can be notably, and sometimes fruitfully, resistant to morality. The present study, granted its purpose, will present the subject in its most unyieldingly theoretical form, but it should be read with the thought that moral philosophy must get its interest ultimately from its relation to actual experience, not all of which is either philosophical or moral.

Rawls (1971) relates moral and political philosophy at a deep level; Nozick (1974) is a maverick but very stimulating contribution in a different direction. The work of Sen (1982 and other) joins philosophy to economic and other social scientific concerns. On relations to the law, see below, Section 2.3. Nussbaum (1990) is among those who have emphasized the continuities of moral philosophy and literature; Wollheim (1984, ch. 7) illuminates psychoanalytic connections.

1. ETHICS AND META-ETHICS

Philosophical studies are often understood as being *higher-order*, in the sense that natural science, for instance, will study natural phenomena, while the philosophy of science will study, from some particular points of view, the operations of science. Some of moral philosophy is certainly a higher-order study. It discusses such things as the nature of moral judgements, and asks whether they express genuine beliefs, whether they can be objectively true, and so forth. Such higher-order questions are the concern of *meta-ethics*. At one time (thirty to fifty years ago) it was widely thought in analytical philosophy that ethics consisted only of meta-ethics. A powerful source of this conception was a belief in a firm distinction between fact and value, or, as it was also put, between 'is' and 'ought' (though to equate these two distinctions requires some very disputable theory, to the effect that all value can be expressed in terms of 'ought'). To arrive at this idea of ethics from the distinction between fact and value required two further assumptions. One was that philosophy itself should be in the business of 'fact' (which, for the purposes of the distinction, included theory) and not of value. This was connected with a certain conception of philosophy, still current, in which it is taken to derive its authority from its theoretical stance as an abstract intellectual inquiry. Some earlier philosophers (e.g. Moore 1903; Ross 1930) had believed in the distinction between fact and value, but had supposed that philosophers, in one way or another, could have quite a lot to say about values. The journey from the fact–value distinction to a view of ethics as only meta-ethics involved the assumption that this was impossible or inappropriate.

The second assumption involved in the journey was that meta-ethics itself could be value-neutral, that the study of the nature of ethical thought did not commit one to any substantive moral conclusions. A yet further assumption, which was not necessary to the journey but did often accompany it, was that meta-ethics should be linguistic in style, and its study should be 'the language of morals'. That phrase was the title of an influential book by a leading philosopher in this style, R. M. Hare (Hare 1952). Hare has always held the meta-ethical view that a moral outlook consists of moral principles and that principles are universal prescriptions (where a prescription is something like an imperative). He also believes that this conclusion can be drawn from an analysis of moral language. Earlier he thought that this could not commit one to any substantive moral view, but now he believes that a correct analysis will show that the use of moral language commits one to a certain kind of moral outlook, which, given the facts of what the world is like, will yield substantive moral conclusions (Hare 1981). This still does not mean, in Hare's view, that values follow from facts or theories alone; rather, what philosophical theory shows is that if one commits oneself to using moral language (something with regard to which one is thought to have an option), one commits oneself to having one specific kind of moral outlook. Philosophy can address itself to working out that outlook, so philosophy can yield some substantive moral conclusions. Ethics is not, after all, just meta-ethics.

For discussion of Hare's positions, see Fotion and Seanor (1988).

Almost all philosophers would now agree with this conclusion, but most of them have abandoned more of the original assumptions than Hare has. It is doubted that meta-ethics can be value-neutral, and, even apart from that, philosophers simply feel freer in making their own ethical commitments clear (a straightforward example is Singer 1986). Meta-ethics remains a part of ethics, but most writings in philosophical ethics now will declare substantive moral positions, either in close association with some meta-ethical outlook or in a more free-standing manner.

However, one thing that typically remains from the earlier set of assumptions is that the authority of philosophy consists in its being a theoretical subject. If philosophers are going to offer moral opinions, they need to have some claim to attention. They are not, as philosophers, necessarily gifted with unusual insight or imagination, and they may not have a significantly wide experience or knowledge of the world. Their claim to attention rests on their capacity for drawing distinctions, seeing the consequences of assumptions, and so forth: in general, on their ability to develop and control a theoretical structure. Their special contribution to substantive ethical issues, then, is likely to be found in a theoretical approach to them, and one of the most common enterprises in moral philosophy at the present time is the development of various ethical theories.

2. ETHICAL THEORIES

2.1. Methodology

The aim of ethical theory is to cast the content of an ethical outlook into a theoretical form. An ethical theory must contain some meta-ethics, since it takes one view rather than another of what the structure and the central concepts of ethical thought must be, though it need not have an opinion on every meta-ethical issue: it may not even commit itself on the extent to which ethical outlooks can claim objectivity. However, it is committed to putting forward, in a theoretical form, a substantive ethical outlook. In doing this, ethical theories are to different degrees revisionary. Some start with a supposedly undeniable basis for ethics, and reject everyday moral conclusions that conflict with it (an extreme example is Kagan 1989). Others claim, rather, to arrive at conclusions about the proper form of ethical thought by considering the moral conclusions that would be delivered by conflicting outlooks and deciding which outlook makes the most coherent systematic sense of those conclusions that we (that is to say, the author and those of his readers who agree with him) find most convincing. Unsystematized but carefully considered judgements about what we would think it right to do in a certain situation, or would be prepared to say in approval or criticism of people and their actions, are often called in the context of such a method 'moral intuitions', where the expression 'intuition' has a purely methodological force: it means only that these judgements seem to us, after consideration, pre-theoretically convincing, not that they are derived from a supposed faculty of intuiting moral truths.

A preferred method of proceeding for the less dogmatic kind of moral theorist is to seek what John Rawls has called a 'reflective equilibrium' between theory and intuitions, modifying the theory to accommodate robust intuitions, and discarding some intuitions which clash with the theory, particularly if one can see how they might be the product of prejudice or confusion (Rawls 1951, 1971 ch. 1, sects. 4 and 9; Daniels 1979). The method may be applied to a particular area of moral thought. It does seem, for instance, that many of us share intuitions about cases where the distinction between what may be done and what may not turns on the difference between positively intervening and allowing things to happen, or (differently) between intervening in a way that directly aggresses on someone else and intervening in a way that does not. A number of writers in recent years have tried to uncover a shared structure of thought about such distinctions and their effects on rights and obligations. From the point of view strictly of ethical theory, the aim of such work will be to see whether such distinctions are rational and legitimate. At the same time, the inquiry can be understood as a kind of moral psychology, uncovering inexplicit principles that form the shared intuitions. In this role, the work faces serious methodological questions (reminiscent of some familiar in linguistics), notably of how far the intuitions are an artefact of the way in which the examples that trigger the intuitions are presented.

A focus of this type of work has been the so-called 'trolley problem', introduced in Foot (1967). A long and meticulous work on this is Kamm (1993, 1994); see also her (1989). Works on related issues include Bennett (1966, 1983) and Quinn (1989a, b); see also Steinbock (1980), a useful anthology, and Thomson (1976).

More usually the method of reflective equilibrium is applied to the structure of our ethical outlook as a whole. The approach, in its general outline, goes back to Aristotle, but the pioneer of it in its modern form was perhaps Sidgwick, who tried to make the utilitarianism which he had inherited from Mill more acceptable by systematically exploring its relations to what he saw as common sense. Sidgwick led the way in offering the rationale for practising ethical theory that it will help to make our moral beliefs more rational and to defend them against corruption by mere prejudice. It is seriously disputed by others that appealing to a model of theory is the best way of making our ethical outlook rationally coherent.

The indispensable guide to Aristotle's ethics is Broadie (1991). Schneewind (1977) provides valuable historical background to Sidgwick (1907). Critics of ethical theory in the present sense include Stocker (1990, chs. 6 and 8), Williams (1985).

Moral theories are standardly presented as falling into three basic types, centring respectively on *consequences*, *rights*, and *virtues*. The first are unsurprisingly called 'consequentialist', and the last 'virtue' theories. The second are often called 'deontological', which means that they are centred on duty or obligation, but this is a cross-classification, since consequentialist theories also give prominence to an obligation, that of bringing about the best consequences. In terms of obligations, the difference is rather that pure consequentialist theories present only one basic obligation, while the second type of theory has many. But a more distinctive mark of difference is to be found in the idea of a right: the second type of theory grounds many of an agent's obligations in the rights of others to expect certain behaviour from that agent, a kind of consideration that utilitarians and other consequentialists regard as at best derivative and at worst totally spurious. (Bentham, the founder of utilitarianism, famously called rights 'nonsense on stilts'.)

Another way of understanding the division into three is in terms of what each theory sees as most basically bearing ethical value. For the first type of theory, it is *good states of affairs*, and right action is understood as action tending to bring about good states of affairs. For the second, it is *right action*; sometimes what makes an action right is a fact about its consequences, but often it is not—its rightness is determined rather by respect for others' rights or other obligations that the agent may have. Virtue theory, last, puts most emphasis on the idea of a *good person*, someone who could be described also as an ethically admirable person. This is an important emphasis, and the notion of a virtue is important in ethics, but once the types of theory are distinguished in this way, it is hard to see them as all in the same line of business. Consequentialist and rights theories can each aim to systematize our principles or rules of action in ways that will, supposedly, help us to see what to do or recommend in particular cases. A theory of the virtues can hardly do that: the theory itself, after all, is going to say that what you basically need in order to do and recommend the right things are virtues, not a theory about virtues. Moreover, the thoughts of a virtuous person do not consist entirely, or even mainly, of thoughts about virtues or about paradigms of virtuous people. Indeed, they may consist, sometimes, of thoughts about rights or good consequences, and this makes it clear that thoughts about the good person cannot displace these other ethical concepts, since a good person will have to use some such concepts. It is clear that 'virtue theory' cannot be on the same level as the other two types of theory. Those two types will now be treated by themselves, leaving the virtues for discussion later.

2.2. Consequentialism

Consequentialism is distinguished, as has been said, by taking the basic bearer of ethical value to be good states of affairs, and the worth of actions is basically assessed in terms of their tendency to bring about such states of affairs. (In fact, this cannot be quite right, since some valuable states of affairs are not caused by, but consist of, certain actions being performed: this is typically true of enjoyable actions, for instance. But this complication can be ignored.) This says nothing, so far, about what makes states of affairs valuable. Some consequentialists, notably Moore (1903), have had a pluralist view about the sources of value, supposing that pleasure, friendship, and other things could have value independently of one another. Anyone who thinks about the value of states of affairs as most of us do, as one kind of ethical consideration among others, is likely to agree with this. Theorists, however, who are anxious to isolate as basic just one type of ethical consideration—the valuable state of affairs—are likely to be keen to isolate just one source of value as well, and the most popular form of consequentialism, utilitarianism, tells one to maximize one value, 'welfare' (itself sometimes called 'utility').

Modern utilitarians claim, in fact, that while their theory formally holds that only one kind of thing is valuable, this is not really so, since 'welfare' and 'utility' stand only for agents' getting what they want or prefer (or, in most versions, what they would want or prefer if they were well informed). The actual content of people's preferences may be very various, and, in particular, it may include altruistic objects as well as egoistic or selfish ones; if someone wants her loved one to flourish, then his flourishing will contribute to her welfare. Structurally and psychologically, modern utilitarianism is more flexible than the earlier versions, which represented the item to be maximized in terms of 'pleasure and the absence of pain' or 'the greatest happiness of the greatest number'.

Utilitarianism does, nevertheless, put strong constraints on the ways in which its basic value can be realized, since it requires the welfare of different people to be the kind of thing that can be added together, so that total states can be compared with each other. Utilitarianism can thus be defined as 'sum-ranking welfarist consequentialism'. Each element in this definition has laid utilitarianism open to criticism. Its very strong demand that outcomes can always be ranked in terms of the sum of welfare they contain runs into technical objections (which concern economics and rational decision theory as well as philosophy). It also gives rise to ethical problems, such as the objection that utilitarianism ignores the separateness of persons, and is prepared illegitimately to sacrifice the interests of any given person with the aim, not just of protecting, but even of increasing, the aggregate welfare. This objection is urged by those who believe in rights; it can also be seen as an objection to utilitarianism's character as a form of consequentialism.

Another kind of objection to the consequentialism of utilitarianism is that the utilitarian agent is related to the world simply as a producer of states of affairs: all that matters is what state of affairs is produced. Because of this, utilitarianism (and consequentialism in general) has no place for a type of thought familiar to many people, that each of us is specially responsible for his or her own actions; for this reason, it has a problem in making sense of qualities such as integrity. Last, objections to utilitarianism may focus on its welfarism: the attempt to reduce all human values and objectives to something like preference satisfaction has been reasonably argued to be implausible and at the limit unintelligible. Apart from questions of whose preferences are at issue (a matter of particular importance when utilitarianism addresses problems of population control), it seems notably false to certain aesthetic and (differently) environmental values to reduce them to matters of what people happen to like or prefer.

The simplest form of utilitarianism applies its criterion of welfare maximization directly to individual actions. The moral value of an action is understood as calculated in terms of its specific results. It perhaps does not follow necessarily from this that agents are enjoined to deliberate in utilitarian terms, but it seems impossible to avoid that conclusion, in particular because the utilitarian results of an action can be calculated only in relation to its alternatives, and what counts as an *alternative* must be relative to the agent and his deliberations. But utilitarian calculation of each action has serious disadvantages in utilitarian terms themselves. If each agent in a group tries to bring about the best result overall without there being any co-ordination between them, the outcome is likely to be inefficient. Moreover, individual agents are likely to be ignorant about the consequences of their actions, and they are also likely to suffer from bias, giving too much weight to their own or their friends' welfare. Act-utilitarianism, or, as it is also called, direct utilitarianism, further tends in various cases to give what common-sense morality would regard as the wrong answer, typically giving too low a weight to considerations of justice.

There are other forms of utilitarianism which try to deal with these problems by applying the welfarist criterion to some item more general than particular actions, such as rules, institutions, or dispositions. This is indirect utilitarianism. One difficulty with such accounts lies in their relation to the agent's motivation. If agents are supposed to be themselves aware of the theory, it is not clear how it is possible for them both to stick with values of justice, loyalty, and so forth in cases where this goes against the balance of welfare—which is what the two-level structure is supposed to deliver—and at the same time be aware that these values (rather, their and others' acceptance of these values) are just a device to increase welfare. In fact, there is a utilitarian tradition, explicit in Sidgwick, of assuming that the people who stick strongly with the first-level values and the people who understand their utilitarian rationale are not the same people. The style of theory that introduces this type of alienation has been called 'Government House utilitarianism'.

The literature relating to utilitarianism is enormous, both in philosophy and in economic theory. A clear exposition of direct utilitarianism is Smart in Smart and Williams

(1973); of a version of indirect utilitarianism, Hare (1981). Brandt (1979), while not presenting an unqualified utilitarian theory, pays serious attention to the correction of preferences; on this and other questions about welfare, see Griffin (1986). Parfit (1986) discusses many central issues, including consequences for population theory. Scheffler (1982) carefully assesses objections to consequentialism. Collections of papers for and against include Sen and Williams (1982), the introduction to which offers a critical overview, and Scheffler (1988), which includes Railton (1988), defending consequentialism against the objection in terms of alienation, one of the criticisms made in Williams (1973, 1985).

2.3. Rights and Contractualism

The belief in rights holds, contrary to at least direct consequentialism, that the interests of separate agents are not fungible, and that the rights of one person can make a categorical requirement on the actions of another. The requirements on *A*'s action imposed by *B*'s rights are most frequently negative: there are many things that *A* cannot do to *B*, even in the interests of the general welfare, such as kill him (secretly) to distribute his organs among five worthy people who need organ transplants. In other cases, *B* has a claim right against *A*, and it can be demanded that *A* act in certain ways on *B*'s behalf. The right of people to receive help in emergencies is of this kind.

Most theorists agree that there can be conflicts of rights, but there is disagreement (representing a familiar difference in ethical outlook) on the question whether rights can be violated to avoid some large disaster, even if the disaster does not involve anyone's rights being violated. Rigorists will insist, correctly, that the whole point of rights is that they do not simply enter into a maximizing calculation—in Ronald Dworkin's phrase, 'rights are trumps'. Pragmatists will say, also correctly, that a point comes at which purism becomes moral frivolity. A further turn in the question is revealed if the disaster does involve someone's rights being violated, by someone other than the agent who is making this deliberation. It is part of the point of rights that we should not simply think in terms of maximizing or minimizing, even when it is a matter of rights violations: if I know, for some reason, that if I keep my promise, two other promises will be broken by others, this is not supposed to give me a reason for breaking my promise. This is related to the idea, mentioned in criticism of utilitarianism, that each of us is specially responsible for his or her own actions. Pragmatists, again, will point out that to exaggerate this principle can introduce a priggishness which itself can represent a kind of irresponsibility.

Among moral concepts, that of rights is closest to law and also to politics, and philosophical discussions of them often cross those boundaries. It is also not surprising, given these relations, that the kind of theory most often constructed to articulate the idea of moral rights is contractualist, invoking the idea of an agreement that might be rationally arrived at by parties in some hypothetical situation in which they are required to make rules by which they can live together. Rights, or at any rate the belief in rights, can be supported by other styles of theory. Indirect consequentialism may possibly argue for a belief in rights on the basis of the good consequences of such a belief, but it is likely to find, once again, that the actions and thoughts it licenses at the ground level are remote from the consequentialist spirit that is supposed ultimately to justify them. Conversely, there are contractualist theories that have consequentialist results: Harsanyi's (1982) contractualist model supports utilitarianism. However, the association between contractualism and rights theory is a strong one, both because actual legal contracts generate rights, and because the contractual model emphasizes at the ground level the separateness of the parties and their several interests.

The inspiration of such theories goes back, in particular, to Kant. Although he does not express himself in moral philosophy explicitly in terms of a contract, his conception of a notional republic of moral agents ('the Kingdom of Ends', in his phrase), each of whom can see himself as laying down laws for everyone including himself, embodies the basic idea. It is very important, too, that Kant's theory is 'constructivist' in spirit. Kant rejected any dogmatic foundation of ethics which was supposedly derived from religion or from a priori knowledge of some realm of values. In part, he was concerned with the distinction between fact and value, but his insistence on the 'autonomy' of ethics involves a wider metaphysical conception, movingly expressed in his essay 'What is Enlightenment?', to the effect that humanity had now reached a point of self-conscious development at which it must realize that it is, so to speak, on its own and must construct its own values, and not expect them to be delivered by some higher authority.

Kant's own construction relies on some ideas which are not shared by many modern theorists, in particular that a commitment to the basic principle of morality (the so-called 'Categorical Imperative') is presupposed by the very activity of a rational agent. It also involves a very obscure doctrine of freedom. The modern theories inspired by Kantian ideas are less committed than Kant was to showing that morality is ultimate rationality, and they allow also more empirical material into the construction than Kant did. The leading example of such a theory is that of John Rawls (1971, 1980). His model of a set of contracting parties reaching an agreement behind 'a veil of ignorance' was designed for a purpose in political philosophy of constructing a theory of social justice, but it has had an immense influence on thinking about morality. In Rawls's theory, the veil of ignorance is introduced to disguise from each contractor his own particular advantages and disadvantages and his own eventual position in the society that is being designed. Any contractualist theory of morality has to introduce some way or other of distancing the parties' thoughts from their actual situation; otherwise one would have a contract merely serving the contingent interests of the parties and this could not model the impartiality and general application that is associated with principles of morality. In versions of contractualism less formal than Rawls's, the same result may be achieved by appealing to the idea of people's general interests. T. J. Scanlon has suggested that one might think of acceptable rules as those that could not be 'reasonably rejected' by parties seeking a basis for uncoerced coexistence, and here the notion of what is reasonable is connected with what we can understand as basic human interests, an idea which is of course closely associated with what are thought to be fundamental human rights.

A contrasting type of contractualist model, more in the lineage of Hobbes than of Kant, has been proposed by Gauthier (1986). Appealing to results in rational decision theory, this tries to show that it is in each egoistic agent's interest to become what he calls 'a constrained maximizer', someone who limits his pursuit of self-interest by respect for the interests of others. This is different from Rawlsian and similar theories, which try to model morality on a contract between parties who are already committed to some shared moral life. Those theories offer a rational morality to people who are already prepared to live under morality, but Gauthier tries to give an argument in purely self-interested terms in favour of the moral life. Few are convinced that this is possible. It is revealing that Gauthier has to make occasional use of specific empirical hypotheses, not all of which are universally correct, notably that people's motives are moderately transparent to each other. The obvious objection is that if one is going to open the account to empirical considerations, one should open it to many more, and admit from the beginning that human beings have many rational motivations besides pure egoism on the one hand and morality on the other.

A brief but fundamental account of the differences between consequentialism and contractualism is Scanlon (1980). Works that discuss rights in ways that relate morality and the law include Dworkin (1977), Raz (1986), and Waldron (1993). Scholarly commentaries on Kant are not the present concern, but O'Neill (1989) should be mentioned as giving a revealing account of a basic Kantian motivation. Defenders of the Kantian enterprise in a fairly strong form include Nagel (1970, and cf. 1986, 1991). Gewirth (1977) has a Kantian project, of deriving a supreme moral principle from the nature of rational action. Donagan (1977) and Darwall (1983) offer rationalist theories with some Kantian affinities. Herman (1983) defends Kantian morality against the charge (cf. Williams 1981, ch. 1) that it emphasizes impartiality at the expense of the personal.

3. META-ETHICS

3.1. Truth and Objectivity

A major preoccupation of meta-ethics has been a set of questions about the objectivity, in some sense, of ethical outlooks. In this connection, 'moral judgements' are often grouped together and compared with everyday statements of fact or with scientific statements. Some theories claim that moral judgements lack some desirable property which factual statements can attain, such as objectivity or truth, while other theories claim that they can have this property. These debates, particularly those conducted under the influence of positivism, have tended to assimilate two different issues. One concerns the prospects of *rational agreement* in ethical matters. The other concerns the *semantic status* of moral judgements: whether they are, typically, statements at all (as opposed, for instance, to prescriptions), and whether they aim at truth.

Objectivity is best understood in terms of the first kind of question. There are, manifestly, substantive and indeed systematic disagreements about ethical questions, both between different societies or cultures and within one society (particularly when, as now, the culture of one society may be highly pluralist). Some of these disagreements may turn out to be due to misunderstanding or bad interpretation and dissolve when local practices are better understood, but this is not true of all of them. Since ancient times it has been suggested that these disagreements have a status different from disagreements about facts or about the explanation of natural phenomena. With the latter, if the parties understand the question at issue, they understand in principle how the question might be answered. They see how after further inquiry they may end up in one of several positions: they may come to rational agreement on one answer or another, they may recognize that such evidence as they can obtain underdetermines the answer and leaves them with intelligible room for continued disagreement, or they may advance in understanding to a point at which they see that the question in its original form cannot be answered, for instance because it was based on a false presupposition.

By contrast, it is suggested that we can understand an ethical dispute perfectly well, and it be clear that it need not come out in any of these ways. In a dispute about an ethical matter, the parties may radically disagree about the kinds of consideration that would settle the question. In some cases, another kind of disagreement may be involved: disputes between secular and religious moralities may turn on conflicting views about the existence and nature of God (the sceptical side may say, in fact, that this issue itself is simply an ethical disagreement, but the other side is unlikely to agree). But most usually the difference is one in ethical outlook, and then the suggestion will be that there is at the end of the line no rational way of arriving at agreement. This is the suggestion that ethical claims lack objectivity.

Some theories have associated this position with a view about the semantic status of moral utterances. Emotivism, a theory closely associated with positivism, held that moral utterances were merely expressions of emotion, not far removed from expletives, and it took this, reasonably enough, not to be an objectivist theory. In fact, some more sophisticated views of the moral emotions can leave some room for ideas of objectivity even at the emotional level (we shall come back to this point), but in emotivism's case the semantic account and the denial of objectivity went closely together. However, it is a mistake to think that the two issues are in general simply related to one another.

The classic account of simple emotivism is Ayer (1936, ch. 1); a more complex theory (not so tied in with positivism) in Stevenson (1937).

A clear illustration of this is Kant's theory. Kant supposed that moral statements, or at any rate the most basic of them, were actually prescriptions, and he understood the fundamental principle of morality as literally an imperative. However, when the issue is expressed in terms of rational agreement or disagreement, Kant is quite certainly an objectivist: the Categorical Imperative, together in some cases with empirical information, determines for any rational agent what morality requires, and all rational agents are in a position to agree on it. Rather similarly, in the latest version of Hare's theory, informed and rational agents who have committed themselves to morality should in principle be able to agree what morality requires, up to unresolved disagreements about matters of fact. Hare is also a prescriptivist, so that neither he nor Kant has a semantic account that allows for agreement in *belief*, but they nevertheless in the present terms are objectivists.

It is of course true that both Kant and Hare propose (different) tests for the acceptability of a moral prescription. In considering the idea of objectivity, one has to consider the relations between, on the one hand, rational agreement on a moral prescription, say 'killing is wrong', and, on the other, rational agreement on a belief to the effect that 'killing is wrong' passes the test. Under the idea of objectivity, the two kinds of rational agreement seem very similar. However, the content of the belief that 'killing is wrong' passes the test cannot, for obvious reasons, itself be the content of 'killing is wrong'. Moreover, unphilosophical agents can rationally agree that killing is wrong without having any thoughts about such tests.

Another example of objectivity which is at least non-committal about the semantics involved comes from virtue theory. Aristotle believed that experienced and discriminating agents who had been properly brought up would reach rational agreement in action, feeling, judgement, and interpretation. He believed, further, that this was grounded in the best development and expression of human nature, and that views about what counted as the best human development could themselves command rational agreement. This certainly offered a kind of objectivity, but there was no particular emphasis on agreement in belief; no doubt some agreement in belief will matter, but so equally will agreement in feeling and in practical decision.

A less clear, but revealing, example is provided by Hume. He strongly plays down the status of moral judgements as reporting any matter of fact or truth of reason, insists that morality is a matter of feeling and sentiment, and occasionally makes provocative remarks which imply that there is just as much virtue or vice in anything as each of us cares to find in it. But he just as strongly claims that nothing counts as a moral judgement or reaction unless the sentiments involved in it are based on a 'steady and general view' of the situation, something that involves the correction of our feelings by judgement, as when we realize that we are not really entitled to the view that this is a bad man, but only to the more personal or partisan reaction that he is, for instance, a nuisance to us and our friends. Hume thought, moreover, to a rather surprising degree, that the *general* sentiments of mankind about moral matters were very much the same at all times and places (though, like many Enlightenment thinkers, he had to have a theory of distortion and prejudice, particularly religious prejudice, to explain why his own benevolent and reasonable views were not universally accepted). It is no doubt paradoxical to describe Hume's theory as objectivist, but in terms of rational agreement it offers more objectivity than its own formulations invite one to expect.

However, even if objectivity need not imply rational agreement in belief, it may be argued that the converse holds: that a theory which represents moral judgements as basically expressing beliefs must be committed to objectivity. Beliefs, this argument goes, are true or false. If moral judgements express beliefs, then some of them are true and there is such a thing as truth in morality. So if people disagree about what to believe, someone must be wrong. This certainly sounds as though there must be objectivity. The difficulty with this argument is that it seems to be too easy to agree that moral judgements admit of truth or falsehood. They are certainly called 'true' and 'false', as even the emotivists had to concede, and the claim that nevertheless they are not really true or false needs some deciphering. An alternative semantic analysis which showed such judgements not really to be statements would give some content to the claim, but such analyses run into difficulty precisely because the statemental air of moral judgements is not merely superficial—they behave syntactically just as other kinds of statements do.

There is a basic problem with non-statemental analyses of moral sentences, deriving from a point made by Frege: they cannot explain how such sentences can be embedded, conditionalized, etc. On this see Geach (1958, 1965); Searle (1962). Blackburn (1984: 189–96) responds to Geach's argument; Gibbard (1990, ch. 5) gives a semantic theory to overcome the problem.

An alternative is to argue that moral judgements can indeed be true or false, but that nothing interesting follows from this. On some theories of truth, sometimes called 'redundancy' theories, to claim that '*P*' is true is to do no more than to assert that *P*. Any theory of truth must accept the equivalence ' "*P*" is true if and only if *P*'; the peculiarity of redundancy theories is to claim that this is all there is to the nature of truth. If this is correct, then the truth or falsehood of moral judgements will follow simply from their taking a statemental form, which allows them to be asserted or denied. Objectivity will then either be understood as something that necessarily goes along with truth and falsehood, in which case, on the redundancy theory, it will be no more interesting or substantive than truth; or it will be more interesting and substantive—implying, for instance, the possibility of rational agreement—in which case, on the redundancy view, it will not follow just from the fact that moral judgements can be true or false.

It is widely, though not universally, agreed that an adequate theory of truth needs to go beyond the redundancy view, but it is disputed how far it needs to go. Wiggins has argued that if one takes seriously the claim that a proposition is true, this does imply the idea that there could be convergence in belief in the proposition under favourable circumstances, and this brings the idea of truth itself nearer to that of objectivity as that has been introduced here. Wright, on the other hand, holds that a properly 'minimalist' theory of truth need not bring in such a strong condition. Without trying to resolve the debate here, one point to be made is that a lot turns on how strongly we take the idea that disagreement on moral issues can be rationally resolved, and what will count as 'favourable circumstances' for resolving it. Perhaps every serious moral claim allows for the possibility of rationally resolving disagreements within a certain range of circumstances, but for some of them, at least, there is a limit to the range of circumstances, not simply because there is (for instance) a shortage of relevant information, but because of the nature of the disagreement. Thus a dispute over a given moral claim might be rationally resolvable between some disputants but not between others, because the disagreements would be too deep and would involve too wide an ethical divide. In considering to what extent this might be possible, it will be necessary to drop a very limiting assumption which has been made up to this point in the discussion, that all 'moral judgements' are essentially of the same kind and stand in the same relation to such matters as truth and objectivity. In doing this, it will be helpful to turn to another concept in the same general area, realism.

A detailed survey of the issues concerning truth (including questions about realism which are addressed in the following section), and of the literature, is Darwall *et al.* (1992). Several articles in Wiggins (1987) set out his position on truth; Wright (1992) develops minimalism.

3.2. Realism and Cognitivism

If objectivism and the mere truth of moral statements are often assimilated in meta-ethical discussion, realism is equally assimilated to one or both of them. Yet we should expect realism, if it is an issue at all, to be a further issue. Elsewhere in philosophy, for instance in the philosophy of mathematics or the philosophy of science, it can be agreed that statements of a certain kind (about numbers, or about subatomic particles) are capable of truth, and also that they can command rational agreement, and yet it is thought by many philosophers that this does not answer the question whether those statements should be interpreted *realistically*, where this means (very roughly indeed) that the statements are taken to refer to objects that exist independently of our thoughts about them. It is, admittedly, not at all easy to give a determinate sense to this kind of question. In the philosophy of science, for instance, the standard contrast with realism about theoretical entities such as atomic particles is operationalism: accepting the theory, on that view, commits one only to using it as a predictive device. But if one accepts the theory, and the theory claims that there are protons, it is unclear (and it has been much discussed in the philosophy of science) exactly what more is being claimed by one who says, against the operationalist, 'protons do exist—really'. There are parallel, though different, problems in interpreting realism in moral philosophy, but at any rate one would not expect realism to follow trivially from the claim that moral statements can be true or false.

It is clear enough that realism implies that such statements can be true: it implies, further, that there is something for them to be true *of*. It is not entirely clear whether it implies objectivism (it may depend on how sceptical one is about realism's reality being grasped by us). However that may be, objectivism does not imply realism, if only because, as we have already seen, objectivism (of a Kantian kind, for instance) need not even imply that at the most basic level moral positions consist of statements.

One way of understanding realism in ethics and its denial is in terms of explanation: moral 'facts' it has been claimed, in particular by Harman (1977, ch. 1), have no independent explanatory power. Part of Harman's argument is that some phenomena are of course explained by our moral beliefs, but we would have the same beliefs even if there were no moral facts; this is criticized by Sturgeon (1988). Railton (1986) argues that moral facts are constituted by natural facts (of a kind congenial to utilitarianism), and it follows from this that they can be explanatory (see also Boyd 1988). This debate gives the question of realism a distinct focus, but it can be objected that even if Harman is right, this shows only that moral facts do not have the causal powers of ordinary empirical facts, and that there is no reason to expect that they should.

A different approach to the question is offered by Blackburn (1984, ch. 6,

1993), who, following Mackie (1977, ch. 1) and in the line of Hume, claims that the moral properties of people, actions, and so forth, are not 'in the world' but are 'projected' on to it from our feelings and reactions. Blackburn offers, in addition, an account of moral language to explain why language does not make this truth obvious, but rather tends to make us think that there is moral truth independent of our experiences, and so encourages realist and objectivist theories. This account is part of a more general position which Blackburn calls 'quasi-realism'.

According to quasi-realism, secondary qualities such as colours are also projected on to the world, and this raises the question whether the metaphor has not mislocated the most significant issues about moral properties. An anti-realism that gives moral properties much the same status as colours will probably satisfy many moral realists. Analogies and disanalogies between moral properties and secondary qualities have been explored in this literature. A pressing question for the metaphor of 'projection' is: on to what kind of world are moral properties supposedly projected? The position with regard to secondary qualities seems to imply that it is a world characterized merely in terms of physical theory. This does imply, presumably, that ethical outlooks are 'perspectival' or related to human experience in ways in which physical theory is not. This claim is not empty. Some, such as Kant, deny that ethics is perspectival, while others, such as Putnam in more recent work (e.g. 1990, chs. 9 and 11), would claim on the other hand that physics, too, is perspectival. But even if this contrast is correct, it does not take us very far. It will not tell us anything very distinctive about ethical realism to know only that ethical concepts are perspectival in a sense in which colour concepts, or psychological concepts, are also perspectival. Many of the most interesting questions about moral realism—indeed, more generally, about moral objectivism—come into view when one asks questions which the metaphor of projection does not itself encourage us to ask. How far can the moral concepts and outlooks of various human groups intelligibly differ while the rest of their ways of describing the world, in particular their psychological concepts for describing people's behaviour, remain the same? How far can their psychological concepts themselves intelligibly vary, and how should we understand those variations?

Wright (1988a, b) criticizes the analogy with secondary qualities; for a subtle discussion, see McDowell (1985, 1987). Wiggins (1987) addresses closely related questions.

Here it is important to distinguish, as we have not distinguished up to now, between different kinds of ethical statements. Many discussions concentrate, explicitly or by implication, on statements expressed in terms of 'right', 'ought', or 'good'. Some such 'thin' ethical concepts, as they may be called, are used in any culture, and just for this reason, if attention is concentrated on them, the ethical differences between cultures will emerge as differences of content, not as differences in concepts. Moreover, the truth-conditions of such statements, considered just in themselves, are very elusive (with 'good' this is particularly so when it is used 'predicatively', as in 'It is a good thing that . . .'). However, there are also 'thick' ethical concepts, such as (to take examples from our own culture) 'betrayal', 'brutality', 'cowardice', and so forth, which have a higher descriptive content (Williams 1985, ch. 8). Whether a given use of a thick concept yields a true or false statement seems to be determined to a great extent by the state of the world. (They come in various thicknesses: 'justice' cannot apply to any laudable characteristic one likes, but its content displays significant, and usually explicable, differences between cultures and indeed between political traditions.)

It is a mistake to suppose that thin concepts are more basic than thick ones, and that the latter are simply thin concepts with some useful package of descriptive features attached to them. (This false position is what Hurley (1990, ch. 2) calls 'centralism'. Hurley, however, holds that conclusions using thin concepts, to be intelligible, must always supervene on judgements using thick ones. This underestimates the extent to which thin concepts can be used autonomously, as they often are in modern societies and in modern ethical theories such as utilitarianism.) It may well be the case, as McDowell has argued (1978, 1979), that one cannot grasp the sense of a thick ethical concept without grasping its evaluative point. Judgements using such concepts are certainly action-guiding or reason-giving; at the same time, their correct application is strongly constrained by states of the world, and while there is no doubt often room for conflicting interpretations and variations in the weight given to different criteria, this may be no more so than with other, less obviously evaluative, parts of the psychological vocabulary. Here there seems to be, in favourable cases, clear applications for ideas of truth and objectivity. It may be that their use also supports some version of realism, but we shall see later that this is not straightforward.

A final notion that may be added to the list of meta-ethical concepts is *knowledge*. 'Cognitivism', which by its derivation of course refers to the possibility of knowledge, is yet another term that is often used more or less interchangeably with 'objectivism' and 'realism', and sometimes, like them, is equated with the mere possibility that moral statements can be true or false. However, the question whether there can be moral knowledge clearly raises further issues.

It seems hard to deny that there can be knowledge under thick ethical concepts: all the time, we take ourselves to know such things as that a certain action was cruel or that a certain person is dishonest. It has often been argued against the possibility of moral knowledge that if there were such a thing, there would be moral experts, but the idea of a moral expert is very suspect, for reasons that do not seem merely to reflect a modern belief in liberal autonomy. However, this objection has most force against a conception of moral knowledge as theoretical. A more recognizable picture (which has an Aristotelian provenance) is that of a person who is good at understanding situations which raise moral questions, can helpfully suggest the moral light in which a problem can be seen, and so forth. This is the model of ethical knowledge in terms of a person who can be a good ethical adviser (which he or she will assuredly be only if a good practical adviser more generally). This model respects a general feature of the concept of knowledge, that a principal interest we have in using it is to locate informants, people who can help us to come to know the answers to questions we have. (For the development of this idea about knowledge in general, see Craig 1990.) In the ethical case the idea of an informant yields rather to that of an adviser; to become convinced of an ethical conclusion involves more than one's being authoritatively informed of it (which is why the idea of a theoretical expert about morality is so unconvincing). However, an informant and an adviser importantly share the feature that we seek them because we want to resolve some question, and we think that in virtue of things that they know or understand they can help us do so. This model ties up helpfully with the idea of knowledge under thick concepts, since one of the most helpful activities of ethical advisers is to suggest ways in which a situation falls or fails to fall under such concepts.

However, such an adviser will be no help to someone who does not share the same thick ethical concepts. This is just one aspect of a general point about these concepts, that they are by no means constant across cultures or times (it is instructive to reflect what has happened in the past century or so to the concept of chastity). Assured and shared use of thick concepts in a given culture may well provide, to a greater extent than anywhere else in ethics, examples of truth, objectivity, and knowledge, but that advantage is rarely shared by discussions between cultures, groups, traditions, or generations on questions of what thick concepts to use. That is why it does not go far enough to point out that, relative to a given concept such as cruelty, there may be 'no alternative' to thinking that a given act was cruel; this overlooks the alternative of not thinking in terms of cruelty at all.

This consideration does not in itself undermine the claim made by judgements using thick concepts to be true, to express knowledge, or to be objective—different individuals or groups who use the same concept can reach reasoned agreement. However, it does cast doubt on some larger claims of moral cognitivism, which imply that ethical inquiry might lead to an agreement about what concepts should be used in our ethical dealings with the world, as scientific inquiry, on the more optimistic descriptions of it, may result in agreement on what scientific concepts best fit the requirements of theory and explanation.

The variation in ethical concepts may also raise some doubts about realism. The demands of realism seem to go beyond those of truth, objectivity, and knowledge in suggesting that the different ethical conceptual systems of different groups are all perspectives on one ethical reality. It is not clear exactly what this means, but it seems to imply at least that there is some common basis, a universal ethical structure, in terms of which the different local systems could be comprehensibly fitted together, and we could come to see how their differences constituted intelligibly different versions or aspects of that one structure. We do not know that this is possible. Its possibility certainly does not follow merely from the fact that various groups can use their own concepts to make true ethical statements of which, in those local terms, they have knowledge. It is reasonable to think that we do not know, either, that such a unified picture is impossible. However, it is important, in making meta-ethical claims about the possibility of ethical truth, objectivity, and knowledge, that we should not adopt theories which presuppose that this ambitious unified picture is already to hand.

3.3. Relativism

One reaction which, since ancient times, has been elicited by the fact that different cultures vary in their ethical practice is relativism. It is indeed more recognizable as a reaction than as a theory. Its general spirit is to the effect that each outlook is appropriate in its own place, or that other people's practices are right 'for them', but it is hard to turn this into a theory which will not either lose the relativist spirit, on the one hand, or become incoherent, on the other. It is not enough for the relativist spirit that there should be an absolute morality which makes allowance, in its content, for local variations. Someone might think, for instance, that certain rules governing sexuality are appropriate in some social and technological circumstances and not others, but this is not strictly relativism. Rather, it is an outlook which claims that sexual behaviour should be appropriate to its context, and this itself is not a relativized claim, but a universal, absolute one. It is no more relativist than the principle that each person should look after his or her own elderly parents: the content of this involves a relation to each agent, but the principle is meant to apply, non-relativistically, to everyone.

To get to relativism, it has to be the case that the all-important relation governs the *application* of the rule or practice, and, moreover, that the relevant groups, to whom the relativization is made, are picked out by reference to their being the people who have this rule or practice. The structure of relativism is given by there being two outlooks (sets of rules, moral codes, etc.), and two groups (societies, cultures) which are distinguished from one another by the fact that they have respectively those two outlooks. Relativism claims that each outlook applies to or binds only its own group. What does this mean? If it were simply the statement that each group possesses its own outlook, this would be vacuously true by definition. Relativism goes beyond this, and does so by trying to find something to say about the attitude that it is appropriate for one ethical outlook to have towards another. Its difficulty is to find something that it can consistently, coherently, and helpfully say. In some forms, it seems to say that the right attitude to different outlooks is to leave them and those who hold them alone. This can be fine in some circumstances (though hardly in all), but this principle itself is manifestly not relativist, but rather an absolute principle of toleration, or something like it. (Only something like it, perhaps, because relativism is aiming at an attitude by which one does not see the other group's outlook as wrong, but toleration has traditionally been understood as an attitude that one extends to outlooks which one thinks are wrong.) The relativist who expresses the view in this form is not a relativist, but rather someone who believes absolutely in toleration.

This looks like a particular version of a general problem, that in formulating an attitude that can be appropriately taken by one outlook towards others, relativism must commit itself to a normative position, and any normative position it can take must, it seems, offend against its own restrictions. It looks as though it must be always either too early or too late for relativism to say anything. It is too early if the two different outlooks have never encountered each other; in that case, there is no room yet for a question about their relations to each other. If they have encountered each other, then it is too late, for there is already a question to be answered of how they, or rather the human beings who have the outlooks, should treat each other, and relativism provides no materials to help the parties with that question, unless it departs from its stance, as we have seen, and advocates toleration or some other non-relativist principle.

It is important that once it is too late, and two groups impinge on one another, toleration or non-interference does involve an ethical attitude towards the other people, and cannot merely register the absence of any ethical attitude. This point is obvious when relativism is extended from differences between cultures to differences between individuals, as it often is in everyday arguments. Relativism in that case usually stands for peaceable coexistence, a preference for people more like oneself, and a disinclination to argue about anything, and this may pass simply as an absence of an attitude. But once the question has arrived, 'What should I do when they do these things to me?', the supposed absence of an attitude can be clearly seen to represent an attitude—one that is likely to break down if the other's attitudes are disagreeable or threatening.

The 'too early or too late' point comes out also in this, that it very soon becomes too late to go on speaking of two societies or cultures. Once the groups have encountered one another, questions arise of their negotiating ways of living together, negotiations which may mean that they are moving towards forming one society. Relativism can contribute, by definition, nothing to such a process. Either it is made inapplicable by the very fact that the process has started, or else it is applicable at the beginning and inapplicable at the end; but even if it is applicable at the beginning, it seems that all it has to say is that there is no basis for the negotiations, and it is doubtful whether it can say that much coherently. The relativist seems doomed to being a peculiarly passive and discouraging spectator of social change.

A peculiar application of this point is to Harman's (1975) semantic relativism. Harman thinks that an important class of moral statements (roughly, those involving 'ought') have as part of their semantic content a reference to a society to which the morality in question, and hence the statement, is relativized. This formulation raises some interesting questions: for instance, whether in the case of second-person statements, the reference should be to the utterer's society or the hearer's. There is also a question whether the references should be presented through names of societies or cultures, or indexically. If the first, then the negotiations between societies that break out when they encounter each other will require the meaning of some moral statements to change in the course of the process, as a new name takes the place of the old ones. If the relativization is achieved indexically, the reference will have to move, in the course of the process, from 'my' and 'your' to 'our'. But, once again, relativization is too late, because one needs to be able to say and think 'our' before one has got as far as creating an actual society which will be 'ours'.

The basic problem with relativism is that there is almost no serious ethical issue for which 'other than mine' forms an interesting class of societies or cultures. Cultures bear all sorts of relations to one's own, being more or less distant, similar, congenial, threatening, interesting, to hand, overlapping, and so on, and relativism can do nothing with these important distinctions. Nevertheless, there is perhaps something coherent that relativism is trying to say. It is saying something to the effect that one's moral comments about the other should be restrained, that the wish of one's morality to have something to say about everyone everywhere should be tempered by a modest consciousness that we are only one lot of people among others and our moral outlook only one contingent product among others. As we have already seen, this attitude cannot serve to regulate all our attitudes to everyone other than ourselves, if only because each group encounters people other than themselves and may merge with them. But there is perhaps some room for the attitude, and, if so, philosophy should make room for it, and not rule it out a priori.

In order to do so we shall have to find possibilities that have been overlooked by the 'too early or too late' argument. We must recognize that there is more than one thing that can count as an outlook's 'encountering' another. The argument assumed that if one group encounters another, there must be real questions of how one is to treat the other. This is true of some encounters, 'real encounters', and in their case relativism indeed has nothing it can coherently offer. However, it is not true that the only alternative to this is that the groups have never heard of each other. It may be merely that at least one group has heard of the other, without their having to live together. This may be called a 'notional' encounter, and it does provide relativism with something intelligible to say. If we are in this relation to another culture, relativism says something to the effect that since there is no question of how we should live in relation to this other ethical life, we should question it rather than judge it, learn about it rather than tell it what we think about it. This has been called 'the relativism of distance'. In fact, in the modern world there are no longer any occasions for this attitude; all encounters on this planet, now, are real. So the only effect of this attitude, probably, would be to restrain moral comment about past societies. It will have no effect on them, but it might possibly have some good effects on us.

Points made here are developed in Williams (1972) and (1985). An extended discussion is Wong (1984); Meiland and Krausz (1982) is a helpful collection.

4. MORAL PSYCHOLOGY

'Moral psychology' here means the philosophical psychology of morality. Some issues central to moral philosophy either are issues in the philosophy of mind, or immediately involve such issues; indeed, one important constraint on theories in moral philosophy is that they should be consistent with a plausible psychology. Here we shall take up three areas that involve psychological issues.

Flanagan (1991) surveys a good deal of psychological literature, and argues that moral philosophy needs to be more psychologically realistic. He puts this, however, in terms of ethical theory; it can be asked whether any ethical *theory* can be psychologically realistic. Psychoanalysis also offers an approach to ethical issues; an interesting representative is Wollheim (1984, ch. 7).

4.1. Internal and External Reasons

There are two different questions that have been discussed under the heading of a disagreement between 'externalism' and 'internalism' with regard to moral reasons and action. One (raised by Frankena 1958) is a question specifically about moral beliefs and their connection to motivation. The second (raised by Williams 1981) is a general question, which has some implications for ethics, about what it is to have a reason for action: it asks what the connections are between having a reason to do a certain thing and being motivated to do that thing.

Let us assume that if an agent *acknowledges that* he has a reason to act in a certain way, he will be motivated to act in that way (though not, of course, conclusively: he may have stronger reason to do something else). The first of the two questions about internalism might then be put by asking whether every moral belief is such that if an agent holds it, he must acknowledge that he has a reason to act in a certain way, and so (granted the assumption) be motivated to act in that way. The answer to the question in this form is too obviously 'no'. My belief that the Roman emperor Heliogabalus was a spectacularly nasty man is presumably some kind of moral belief, but it does not give me any reasons for action (except perhaps, once in a while, to announce it). We might ask, instead, whether there are some moral beliefs which are such that an agent who accepts the belief must acknowledge a reason to act. The answer now is too obviously 'yes': one kind of moral belief, presumably, is 'I have a moral reason to act in this way'.

If the first question is to be interesting, it has to take the form of asking about specific kinds of moral belief and their connections with reasons for action and motivation. The case of thick ethical concepts is particularly relevant. At first sight, it might seem that people could apply such concepts without at all thinking that they provided them with prima-facie reasons for action. Cannot someone see that a certain act of his would be generous, without supposing that this gives him a reason to do it, or that another act would be disloyal or unkind, without necessarily thinking that he has a reason to avoid it? The answer seems to be 'yes', and so, with regard to these moral beliefs, externalism seems to be true. But in the light of what was said earlier about the learning of such concepts, and the fact that their application to new cases is guided by their evaluative interest, we shall expect that someone who really uses such a concept to structure his experience, as opposed to simply mimicking other people's use, will have a pattern of evaluations, reactions, and sentiments which are signs of his genuinely using the concept, and which are indeed tied in various ways to action and to having specific reasons for action. If we do not concentrate on tight entailments, but, more helpfully, look for necessities on a larger scale, internalism on this issue seems to be correct.

Another case that can make externalism look plausible is that of obligations. It seems obvious that cynical people can agree that they are under an obligation to do a certain thing (because they promised, for instance), and yet not think that this gives them a reason to do it. They are not contradicting themselves, and in this narrow sense externalism about obligations and motivation is correct. However, we can understand these people because we and they understand a general practice in terms of which obligations are moral considerations with certain kinds of content (that they stem, for instance, from promises). The cynic can admit that such a consideration is present (and also recognize that certain social consequences may follow from that fact) though he is not committed to the practice. But there cannot be such a practice unless in general people are committed to it, and those who are committed to it will acknowledge an obligation as a kind of reason for action. At the more general level, then, there is an internalist connection between obligations and motivation.

This leads us to the second question that is discussed under the title of 'internalism', the general question about what it is to have a reason for action. We keep the assumption which was made earlier, that an agent who acknowledges that he has a reason to act in a certain way is motivated (other things being equal) to act in that way. The question concerns the claim, made by one agent, that another agent has a reason to do a certain thing, when the latter does *not* acknowledge that he has that reason. What is the first agent saying? What are the truth-conditions of such a claim? The internalist answer to this question is (roughly) that *A* has a reason to do *X* only if he could arrive at a decision to do *X* by a sound deliberative route from his existing motivational state, where the idea of a 'sound deliberative route' includes the idea that any errors in relevant factual information are corrected. What *A* has reason to do is thus conceived of as a projection of *A*'s actual psychology, with improvements to the extent that *A* is interested in such improvements (as he almost always will be with respect to relevant factual information). The externalist takes a broader view, and thinks that we can often truly say that *A* has a reason to do *X*, for instance if *X* is the decent thing to do, even if there is nothing in *A*'s psychology that constitutes a motivation to do things of this sort.

The chief problem with externalism is that it makes it hard to distinguish statements about *A*'s reasons from other kinds of statements which we certainly are entitled to make, but which seem on the face of it to be different: for instance, that we have reason to want *A* to do this thing; or *A* would act well if he did it; or this is what a decent person would do in these circumstances. The last kind of statement can scarcely say the same as the statement that *A* has a reason to do this thing, since there are things that a decent (good, sensible, virtuous) person would have reason to do in these circumstances, but which *A* has reason not to do, because, not being virtuous, he could not bring them off. Once we start trying to correct for such limitations of *A*'s psychology, we may find it hard to stop before we are back with *A*'s actual psychology, and so with internalism.

This last point illustrates one way in which this second debate about internalism is relevant to ethics. Its major relevance, however, is to statements of obligation and other second-person or third-person uses of 'ought'. If *A* says to *B* that *B ought* to do a certain thing (for instance, because he has promised), is *A* saying that *B* has a reason to do it? If so, it seems that internalism must be wrong, since *A* can say this while quite aware that *B* has no motivation, even potentially, to do it. If not, what is he saying? Indeed, if he is saying that *B* has a reason, but not in an internalist sense, what is he saying? This is not a question to which there is a very satisfactory answer. Some philosophers have claimed that *A* in such a case is merely telling *B* a fact of how things stand in the realm of values, but, apart from its obscurity, this leaves us with a version of the same problem, since we can still ask why *B* might have any interest in this piece of information. We need a more naturalistic account, one that can perhaps borrow something, in more sophisticated form, from emotivism. It need not take as sceptical a form as Nietzsche's (1887) account in terms of *ressentiment*, or at any rate should not confine itself to those materials.

It is important to start from the primitive case, in which the content of certain obligations is jointly recognized among a group who also share the idea that obligations will give their members reason (typically, overriding reason) to act. In these circumstances, the claim that one party ought to do a certain thing will be a contribution to a shared discussion about what that party has internal reason to do (as it might come from an adviser, of the kind we considered in the discussion of knowledge). As the scene gradually changes to circumstances in which not everyone has the same view of what obligations there are, and some recognize no obligations at all, and some are undermotivated to perform the obligations they recognize, the statements about what others have reason to do take on a more persuasive or pre-emptive aspect. Instead of simply stating what the person has reason to do, they may hope to bring it about that he has a reason to do it, by mobilizing sentiments which will support others' expectations, expectations which are signalled to him, among other ways, by this very utterance. Statements about what others ought to do can often be understood as part of a general disposition to recruit and sustain them in a shared practice of having internal reason to do what others expect them to do. It would follow from this that if a given person is seen as too hard a case, too recalcitrant to any moral persuasion or recruitment, others would give up using the 'ought' of obligation to him or about him. This is indeed what we find: others give up on him altogether, or if they do not give up on him, they approach him with something other than 'ought'.

Hume and Gibbard (1990) both speak to these issues of interpersonal dynamics. Korsgaard (1986) interestingly relates the question of internal reasons to Kantian considerations about practical reason.

4.2. Virtues

It has already been argued that so-called 'virtue theory' does not offer an ethical theory in the sense in which utilitarianism does so, but the virtues do provide an important reference point in ethical thinking, and their nature is a significant question for moral psychology.

The classical account of the virtues is that of Aristotle, but just because of its power and its influence, it is easy to overlook the extent to which a modern theory may need to distance itself from it. A modern account is likely to agree with Aristotle that virtues are dispositions of character, acquired by ethical training, displayed not just in action but in patterns of emotional reaction. It will agree, too, that virtues are not rigid habits, but are flexible under the application of practical reason. But there are at least four matters on which it may well disagree with Aristotle, which may be labelled *ground, content, unity,* and *reality*.

4.2.1. Ground

Aristotle held that the virtues (for which the word in his language means only 'excellences') had a teleological ground, in the sense that they represented the fullest development of a certain kind of natural creature, a non-defective male human being. No one now is going to agree with Aristotle that there are creatures which are biologically human beings but who are excluded from this full development by their nature as women or as people he called 'natural slaves'. There is a question of how much, when this is corrected, modern thought is going to be able to share with Aristotle about the natural basis of the virtues, and this in turn raises the question of how strongly Aristotle's own teleological view should be taken. On one interpretation, he had an overall teleological conception of the contents of the universe, with each kind of creature fitting into a discoverable overall pattern. On such a conception, substantial parts of the theory of the virtues will be discoverable by top-down systematic inquiry which will tell us what sort of creature human beings are, and hence what their best life will be. Other interpreters give a much more moderate account of Aristotle's enterprise, by which it will be honoured by a hermeneutical inquiry into what we, now, regard as the most basic and valuable aspects of human beings.

4.2.2. Content

What is undeniably lacking from Aristotle's thought, as from that of other ancient thinkers, is a historical dimension. It is surprising that modern virtue theorists often fail to notice this lack: an exception is MacIntyre, who tries to give an evaluative account of the history of virtue ethics by appealing to its development within various traditions. Aristotle's account is in several respects different from any account of the virtues one would give now, both in what it puts in and in what it leaves out. A modern person, asked for the principal virtues, might well mention kindness and fairness. Fairness bears a relation to an important Aristotelian virtue, justice, but the latter is defined to an important extent in political and civic terms, and gives a fairly restricted account of fairness as a personal characteristic. Kindness is not an Aristotelian virtue at all. Moreover, there is no account of an important modern virtue, truthfulness; what Aristotle calls the virtue of truth is concerned exclusively with boasting and modesty.

Historical variation in the content of the virtues is obvious. Aquinas, who notably developed Aristotle's account, of course modified it to accommodate

Christianity, and Hume used it (and other pagan sources) to produce an ethics that would, in turn, exclude Christianity. The historical variation raises wider issues of how theories of the virtues are to be understood, since it seems that the ideas of human nature and human circumstances which underlie such theories are open to wide reinterpretation in the face of changing values, and the Aristotelian presupposition (however strongly exactly it is interpreted) that an understanding of human nature could yield a determinate account of the virtues does look unrealistic. There are of course some constants of human psychology that make some version of some virtues ubiquitous: everyone is likely to need (something like) courage, (something like) self-control with regard to anger and sexual desire, and some version of prudence. These platitudes, however, do severely underdetermine what the list of the virtues may be like, as is shown by the very simple consideration that the constant features of human life are indeed constant, but the virtues that have been recognized vary considerably.

4.2.3. Unity

Aristotle inherited from Socrates an interest in the unity of the virtues. Socrates seems to have held that there might be only one virtue, a kind of normative sense, the conventional distinction between the virtues referring only to different fields of application of this sense. Aristotle did think that there were separate virtues, but his view came almost to the same thing, since he thought that one could not have one virtue without having them all. This conclusion followed because one could not properly possess even one virtue unless one had the central capacity to make sense of what one is doing, in Aristotle's language *phronesis* (which is often translated as 'practical reason', but might be better rendered as 'judgement' or 'good sense'); but if one had this quality, then one had all the virtues.

It is not hard to see the general idea underlying this position. For example, if you have no sense of justice, you cannot really be generous, since generosity requires you to give more than someone is entitled to. Similar points can be made about the interrelations of some other virtues. However, it is important to the theory of the virtues that they provide psychological explanations as well as normative descriptions, and from a realistic psychological point of view it is hard to deny (as many ancient Greeks other than Socrates and Aristotle found it hard to deny) that someone can have some virtues while lacking others. In particular, the so-called 'executive virtues' of courage and self-control can surely be deployed in the interests of wicked projects. The refusal to acknowledge this may simply represent an ethical reluctance to give moral accolades to bad people. In Aristotle's case, it is the product of a substantial ethical ideal in favour of a balanced and moderate character, something that is expressed also in the perhaps not very helpful doctrine of the Mean.

On the contrary, the fact that the virtues can, to some degree, be separated from one another itself helps to give point to virtue theory. Some modern ethical theories do imply that there is basically only one moral disposition. Utilitarianism, at least in its direct form, places everything on benevolence; and though Kant himself did have a theory of the virtues, Kantianism insists on the primacy of a sense of duty. Other theories may conceive the best ethical state in terms of something like an all-purpose normative ability. One advantage of virtue theory is that it allows for interesting psychological connections between the ethical and other aspects of character, accepting that a person's temperament will have something to do with how he conducts himself ethically. For the same reason, virtue theory is implicitly opposed to sharp boundaries between the moral and the non-moral, and is likely to acknowledge that there is a spectrum of desirable characteristics, and that no firm or helpful line can be drawn round those that are of specially moral significance. Aristotle did not even try to draw such a line: his own terminology distinguishes only between excellences of character and intellectual excellences, and one of the latter, *phronesis*, is itself necessary to the excellences of character. Hume, who was very aware of moralists who wanted to draw such a line, goes out of his way to mock the attempt to draw it, and his deliberately offensive treatment of the subject is still very instructive.

4.2.4. Reality

Aristotle conceived of the virtues realistically, as dispositional characteristics of people which they possess in at least as substantial a sense as that in which a magnet possesses the power to attract metals, though people, unlike magnets, have of course acquired the dispositions in the way appropriate to such things, by habituation. Modern scepticism, however, to some extent supported by social and cognitive psychology, questions whether we can take such a naïvely robust view of what it is for someone to have a virtue. There are at least two different sources of doubt. One is the extent to which people's reactions depend on situation: it is claimed that they will act in ways that express a given virtue only within a rather narrow range of recognized contexts, and if the usual expectations are suspended or even, in some cases, slightly shifted, agents may not act in their usual style. The other doubt concerns ascription. When we understand people's behaviour in terms of virtues and vices, or indeed other concepts of character, we are selecting in a highly interpretative way from their behaviour as we experience it, and the way in which we do this (as, indeed, we understand many other things) is in terms of stereotypes or standard images, which may range from crude 'characters' to sophisticated and more individuated outlines constructed with the help of types drawn, often, from fiction. The available range of such images forms part of the shifting history of the virtues.

At different times there have been pattern books of virtue and vice, and one of the first was the *Characters* written by Theophrastus, who was a pupil of Aristotle's.

Even assuming such ideas to be correct, it is not clear exactly how much impact on virtue theory they should have. Everyone knows that virtues do not express themselves under all circumstances, and also that agents may be very rigid in their ability to understand how a situation is to be seen in terms of virtues (here again the role of the adviser is relevant). Again, with regard to ascription, it is very important that if we form our interpretations of an agent's character in terms of a stock of images, so equally does the agent. The point is not so much that there is a gap between interpreter and agent, but rather that all of us, as interpreters of ourselves and of others, use shared materials that have a history. There are lessons in such ideas for ethics generally and for virtue theory, but they need not be entirely sceptical. They alert us to the important theme that our ethical ideas do indeed have a history. Moreover, the points about the situational character of the virtues and about their ascription both serve to remind us that an agent's virtues depend in many different ways on his or her relations to society: not simply in being acquired and in being necessary, but in being constantly shaped, interpreted, and either reinforced or weakened. In this, there is something of an analogue to the point made earlier about reasons and the 'ought' of obligation, that social interaction can help to keep morality and the ethical dispositions going, through others proleptically ascribing to an agent what they ethically expect of him, and his reacting positively through recognizing that this is what they expect.

On Aristotle see, as above, Broadie (1991). Foot (1978) and MacIntyre (1981, 1988) are among works that have revived interest in virtue theory; see also Wallace (1978). Nussbaum (1993) seeks to shape Aristotle's account to modern requirements.

4.3. Free Will

There is a point (which will emerge in the course of the discussion) in considering free will as a topic in moral psychology and not as a purely metaphysical question. It has been traditionally seen as a question about the relation between two items: moral thought and practice on the one hand, and, on the other hand, some proposition about the universe which, if true, seems to threaten the possibility of moral thought or some vital part of it. The aspect of moral thought at the centre of the question is that people are typically taken to act freely, in a sense that has something to do with their holding themselves and each other responsible for what they do (what the exact content of this can be is of course an important part of the question). The question arises when some proposition about the universe which is taken to be true, or at least as possibly true, seems to threaten this freedom. The proposition has not always been the same, and the location of the question has correspondingly varied, but it has always been, in a broad sense, metaphysical.

Some versions of the free-will question have been part of Christian theology. In this case, the proposition has concerned the nature of God, and the question has been, for instance, whether human beings can act freely and responsibly if an omniscient God eternally knows, as he must, their actions and thoughts. At least, this is the version of the Christian problem best known to philosophers, though in fact it is not the version that is historically most important to the Christian tradition: that concerns, rather, the necessity for grace, and the ways in which we could conceive the relation between our actions and our salvation. That problem is also ethically more interesting, and it has deep secular analogues, above all in a Kantian conception of moral merit, but it is not the present concern.

In contemporary philosophy, the question has concerned, rather, the relations of freedom to determinism, which is understood (roughly) as claiming that each state of the world, including therefore our actions, is a strict causal product of earlier states of the world. (A version of this question was discussed already by Epicureans and others in antiquity.) In fact, there is no reason to take the obscure and over-ambitious doctrine of determinism, which few now believe, as setting the question. It was traditionally taken to do so because it was only at such a general level that there was reason to think that our thoughts and actions had strong causal explanations. With increasing knowledge of the brain, we have stronger reason to believe that there are such explanations of our thoughts than that the universe is a deterministic system, and the question should now be taken to be set by the relations between freedom and the strongest version we can imagine of psychophysical science, a version which would represent our experience as a function of brain-states explained as products of earlier brain-states. We need a label to replace 'determinism' in the free-will question; let us (begging many questions) call the item that possibly conflicts with freedom 'the strong scientific claim'.

The question in this form still recognizably has the traditional form: is the universe such as to leave room for moral thought as we understand it, above all with respect to freedom and responsibility? It allows, also, for traditional distinctions between ways in which that question is answered. Some say that we can have the freedom that morality requires even if the strong scientific claim is true, and try to show how this is possible; they are 'compatibilists'. Others, incompatibilists, say that we cannot; and they then divide into those who think that we rightly believe in freedom, and hence that the strong scientific claim is baseless (libertarians), and those who think that the strong scientific claim is probably true, and hence that our belief in freedom is probably wrong (antilibertarians). In fact, each of the incompatibilist parties recognizes or should recognize that it has more work to do than this suggests. The anti-libertarians need to explain what the illusion of freedom is, while the libertarians have the hard task of making clear how a conviction about moral freedom could tell us in advance about the prospects for psychophysical science. It is obvious, in fact, that there must be something to be said about these matters, because if there were not, incompatibilists would not know whether to belong to the libertarian or the anti-libertarian party.

When these matters are more carefully considered, we can begin to see that it is too simple to formulate the free-will question in terms of the possible conflict between just two items. It involves, rather, three items: our moral beliefs, above all a belief in freedom and responsibility; some proposition about the world, now identified as the strong scientific claim; and the psychology that is relevant to morality, in particular our use of concepts such as choice, intention, and trying. Let us call these respectively the moral, the metaphysical, and the psychological elements of the question. Some of the traditional problems concern the relations between the metaphysical and the psychological. If this is the incompatibilist's concern, he is likely to say that the strong scientific claim is incompatible with our choosing, or, perhaps, really choosing. The conflict with morality then comes out as a consequence: the psychology of freedom requires real choosing, and on this showing there is no such thing if the strong scientific claim is true.

On a different emphasis, the conflict that matters is at the boundary between morality and psychology. In this case, incompatibilism threatens because our thoughts about freedom, or some of them, seem not to square with our best psychological understanding, where this may well have nothing to do at all with the causal claims of some strong psychophysical science (the descendant of determinism). The troubling understandings may come from depth psychology, or merely from an observant and disabused conception of what people are like. Here it is important to bear in mind the extent to which the more extravagant claims of moralists about freedom and responsibility have always encountered scepticism based on psychological interpretation, quite apart from large issues at the metaphysical level.

The first set of questions, which arise at the metaphysical–psychological border, are not questions for moral philosophy as such, but for the philosophy of mind. It is important to recognize this point, since once they are seen in that light and the inquiry is freed from the pressures of moral anxiety, it is very plausible to think that the supposed conflicts will turn out to be illusory. There are immense, perhaps even insoluble, problems in understanding the relations between conscious experience and processes in the brain, but they have nothing specially to do with morality or freedom: they arise just as much with the experiences that everyone, libertarian or anti-libertarian, agrees to exist. The psychological concepts that come closest to moral experience, choice and trying, do raise some special difficulties, but those difficulties are not concerned particularly with morality or responsibility: they apply as much to any choice at all. Moreover, it is now quite hard to believe (though the question is still disputed) that there is any real problem with such concepts; recent work suggests that their application is compatible with the strongest assumptions about psychophysical explanation. In considering this, it is important to bear in mind the risk of running into an ancient confusion, between determinism and fatalism. Some arguments designed to show that there is a conflict between choice and determinism (or its modern surrogate) offer the conclusion that if determinism is true, then nothing that happens depends on our actions, or none of our actions depends on our thoughts, or some such manifest fatalistic untruth, and this, certainly, must show that something has gone wrong with the argument. But these, once again, are questions for metaphysics and the philosophy of mind.

Nowadays, we can understand the traditional problem of free will, a conflict between the metaphysical and morality, only as running through consequences which the metaphysical position supposedly has for our psychology. So if it is correct that there are no fundamental conflicts on the metaphysical–psychological border, then the problem of free will, as traditionally understood, is over. However, this does not mean that compatibilism has won. Compatibilism, as usually understood, implies that when we properly grasp morality's relations to metaphysics, we shall see that our morality, including its beliefs about freedom, works perfectly well. But there is no reason to accept this, since there are problems on the border between morality and a realistic psychology. As has already been said, these are not problems that rest on metaphysics or on large claims about psychophysical science, and they need not necessarily involve very new ideas. They may rest simply on quite well-known grounds for thinking that our conceptions of freedom, responsibility, and blame are often not what they seem, and are variously exaggerated, self-deceiving, sentimental, or vindictive (epithets which themselves, it should be noticed, largely belong to an ethical vocabulary). If this is so, it does not necessarily mean that the existing language of voluntariness, in particular, needs to be abandoned; it may mean that it turns out to be useful but incurably superficial, not designed to sustain the deep implications that it has been given in the past.

The implications of this, and many other related questions, remain to be discussed. Those discussions will belong with the psychological understanding of morality—one may also say, the ethical understanding of the ethical—and will have little to do with the traditional metaphysical threats to freedom. Those metaphysical debates may well turn out to have been a distraction from the important task, perhaps an evasion of it: the task which provides the principal aim of all moral philosophy, of truthfully understanding what our ethical values are and how they are related to our psychology, and making, in the light of that understanding, a valuation of those values.

Chisholm (1964) is an incompatibilist who describes free action in terms of 'agent causation'; van Inwagen (1978, 1983) offers a classical style of anti-determinist argument. Wiggins (1973, revised 1987) proposes a more moderate libertarian line. On the other side, Dennett (1984) is a robust compatibilist; Frankfurt (1971) construes free action in terms of second-order desires; Strawson (1962) argues that our moral attitudes are not going be unseated by causal discoveries. Hampshire (1959) tries to blunt the edge of causal theories of action by arguing that they must be predictively incomplete. O'Shaughnessy (1980, vol. i, ch. 4, vol. ii, ch. 17) powerfully argues that causal theory is compatible with concepts such as choice and trying. Honderich (1973) and Watson (1982) are useful collections.

BIBLIOGRAPHY

AYER, A. J. (1936), *Language, Truth and Logic* (London).

BAIER, A. (1991), *A Progress of Sentiments* (Cambridge, Mass.).

BENNETT, J. (1966), 'Whatever the Consequences', *Analysis*, 26: 83–102.

—— (1983), 'Positive and Negative Relevance', *American Philosophical Quarterly*, 20: 185–94.

BLACKBURN, S. (1984), *Spreading the Word* (Oxford).

—— (1993), *Essays in Quasi-Realism* (New York).

BOYD, R. (1988), 'How to be a Moral Realist', in G. Sayre-McCord (ed.), *Moral Realism* (Ithaca, NY).

BRANDT, R. B. (1979), *A Theory of the Good and the Right* (New York).

BROADIE, S. (1991), *Ethics with Aristotle* (New York).

CHISHOLM, R. (1964), 'Human Freedom and the Self', The Lindley Lecture (Lawrence, Kan.).

CRAIG, E. (1990), *Knowledge and the State of Nature* (Oxford).

DANIELS, NORMAN (1979), 'Wide Reflective Equilibrium and Theory Acceptance in Ethics', *Journal of Philosophy*, 76: 256–82.

DARWALL, S. (1983), *Impartial Reason* (Ithaca, NY).

—— GIBBARD, A., and RAILTON, P. (1992), 'Toward "Fin de Siècle" Ethics: Some Trends', *Philosophical Review*, 101: 115–89.

DENNETT, D. (1984), *Elbow Room* (Cambridge, Mass.).

DONAGAN, A. (1977), *The Theory of Morality* (Chicago).

DWORKIN, R. (1977), *Taking Rights Seriously* (Cambridge, Mass.).

FLANAGAN, O. (1991), *Varieties of Moral Personality: Ethics and Psychological Realism* (Cambridge, Mass.).

FOOT, P. (1967), 'The Problem of Abortion and the Doctrine of the Double Effect', *Journal of Medical Philosophy*, 3: 253–5; repr. in Foot (1978).

—— (1978), *Virtues and Vices* (Berkeley, Calif.).

FOTION, N., and SEANOR, D. (eds.) (1988), *Hare and Critics: Essays on 'Moral Thinking'* (New York).

FRANKENA, W. K. (1958), 'Obligation and Motivation in Recent Moral Philosophy', in A. I. Melden (ed.), *Essays on Moral Philosophy* (Seattle).

FRANKFURT, H. (1971), 'Freedom of the Will and the Concept of a Person', *Journal of Philosophy*, 67: 5–20; repr. in Watson (1982).

GAUTHIER, D. (1986), *Morals by Agreement* (Oxford).

GEACH, P. (1958), 'Imperative and Deontic Logic', *Analysis*, 18: 49–56.

——— (1965), 'Assertion', *Philosophical Review*, 74: 449–65.

GEWIRTH, A. (1977), *Reason and Morality* (Chicago).

GIBBARD, A. (1990), *Wise Choices, Apt Feelings: A Theory of Normative Judgment* (Cambridge, Mass.).

GRIFFIN, J. (1986), *Well-Being: Its Meaning, Measurement, and Moral Importance* (Oxford).

HAMPSHIRE, S. (1959), *Freedom of the Individual* (New York).

HARE, R. M. (1952), *The Language of Morals* (Oxford).

——— (1981), *Moral Thinking* (New York).

HARMAN, G. (1975), 'Moral Relativism Defended', *Philosophical Review*, 84: 3–22.

——— (1977), *The Nature of Morality* (New York).

HARSANYI, J. (1982), 'Morality and the Theory of Rational Behavior', repr. in Sen and Williams (1982).

HERMAN, B. (1983), 'Integrity and Impartiality', *Monist*, 66: 233–50.

HONDERICH, T. (ed.) (1973), *Essays on Freedom of Action* (London).

——— (ed.) (1985), *Morality and Objectivity: A Tribute to J. L. Mackie* (London).

HUME, D. (1777), *An Enquiry Concerning the Principles of Morals*; repr. ed. E. Steinberg (Indianapolis, 1993).

HURLEY, S. (1990), *Natural Reasons: Personality and Polity* (New York).

KAGAN, S. (1989), *The Limits of Morality* (Oxford).

KAMM, F. (1989), 'Harming Some to Save Others', *Philosophical Studies*, 57: 227–60.

——— (1993), *Morality and Mortality*, i: *Death and Whom to Save from It* (New York).

——— (1994), *Morality and Mortality*, ii: *Rights, Duties, and Value* (New York).

KANT, I. (1785), *Groundwork of the Metaphysic of Morals*; repr. trans. and ed. H. J. Paton (New York, 1964).

KORSGAARD, C. (1986), 'Skepticism about Practical Reason', *Journal of Philosophy*, 83: 5–25.

McDOWELL, J. (1978), 'Are Moral Requirements Hypothetical Imperatives?' *Proceedings of the Aristotelian Society*, supp. vol. 52: 13–29.

——— (1979), 'Virtue and Reason', *Monist*, 62: 331–50.

——— (1985), 'Values and Secondary Qualities', in Honderich (1985).

——— (1987), 'Projection and Truth in Ethics', The Lindley Lecture (Lawrence, Kan.).

MACINTYRE, A. (1981), *After Virtue* (Notre Dame, Ind.).

——— (1988), *Whose Justice, Which Rationality?* (Notre Dame, Ind.).

MACKIE, J. (1977), *Ethics: Inventing Right and Wrong* (New York).

MEILAND, J., and KRAUSZ, M. (1982), *Relativism, Cognitive and Moral* (Notre Dame, Ind.).

MOORE, G. E. (1903), *Principia Ethica* (Cambridge).

NAGEL, T. (1970), *The Possibility of Altruism* (Oxford).

——— (1986), *The View from Nowhere* (New York).

——— (1991), *Equality and Partiality* (New York).

NIETZSCHE, F. (1887), 'On the Genealogy of Morality'; repr. in K. Ansell-Pearson and C. Diethe (eds.), *On the Genealogy of Morality and Other Writings* (Cambridge, 1994).

NOZICK, R. (1974), *Anarchy, State and Utopia* (New York).

NUSSBAUM, M. (1990), *Love's Knowledge: Essays on Philosophy and Literature* (New York).

—— (1993), 'Non-relative Virtues: An Aristotelian Approach'; repr. in M. Nussbaum and A. Sen (eds.), *The Quality of Life* (New York).

O'NEILL, O. (1989), *Constructions of Reason: Explorations of Kant's Practical Philosophy* (New York).

O'SHAUGHNESSY, B. (1980), *The Will: A Dual Aspect Theory*, 2 vols. (Cambridge).

PARFIT, D. (1986), *Reasons and Persons* (New York).

PUTNAM, H. (1990), *Realism with a Human Face* (Cambridge).

QUINN, W. (1989a), 'Actions, Intentions and Consequences: The Doctrine of Double Effect', *Philosophical Review*, 98.

—— (1989b), 'Actions, Intentions and Consequences: The Doctrine of Doing and Allowing', *Philosophical Review*, 98.

RAILTON, P. (1986), 'Moral Realism', *Philosophical Review*, 95: 163–207.

—— (1988), 'Alienation, Consequentialism, and the Demands of Morality', in Scheffler (1988).

RAWLS, J. (1951), 'Outline of a Decision Procedure for Ethics', *Philosophical Review*, 60: 177–97.

—— (1971), *A Theory of Justice* (Cambridge, Mass.).

—— (1980), 'Kantian Constructivism in Moral Theory', *Journal of Philosophy*, 77: 515–72.

RAZ, J. (1986), *The Morality of Freedom* (Oxford).

ROSS, W. D. (1930), *The Right and the Good* (Oxford).

SCANLON, T. M. (1982), 'Contractualism and Utilitarianism', in Sen and Williams (1982).

SCHEFFLER, S. (1982), *The Rejection of Consequentialism* (Oxford).

—— (ed.) (1988), *Consequentialism and its Critics* (New York).

SCHNEEWIND, J. (1977), *Sidgwick's Ethics and Victorian Moral Philosophy* (Oxford).

SEARLE, J. (1962), 'Meaning and Speech Acts', *Philosophical Review*, 71: 423–32.

SEN, A. (1982), *Choice, Welfare and Measurement* (Oxford).

—— and WILLIAMS, B. (eds.) (1982), *Utilitarianism and Beyond* (Cambridge).

SIDGWICK, H. (1907), *The Methods of Ethics*, 7th edn. (London).

SINGER, P. (1986), *Practical Ethics* (Cambridge).

SMART, J. J. C., and WILLIAMS, B. (1973), *Utilitarianism: For and Against* (Cambridge).

STEINBOCK, B. (ed.) (1980), *Killing and Letting Die* (Englewood Cliffs, NJ).

STEVENSON, C. L. (1937), 'The Emotive Meaning of Ethical Terms', *Mind*, 46: 14–31.

STOCKER, M. (1990), *Plural and Conflicting Values* (New York).

STRAWSON, P. (1962), 'Freedom and Resentment', *Proceedings of the British Academy*, 48; repr. in Watson (1982).

STURGEON, N. (1988), 'Moral Explanations', in G. Sayre-McCord (ed.), *Moral Realism* (Ithaca, NY).

THOMSON, J. (1976), 'Killing, Letting Die and the Trolley Problem', *Monist*, 59: 204–17.

VAN INWAGEN, P. (1978), 'The Incompatibility of Free Will and Determinism', *Philosophical Studies*, 27: 185–99; repr. in Watson (1982).

—— (1983), *An Essay on Free Will* (Oxford).

WALDRON, J. (1993), *Liberal Rights: Collected Papers 1981–1991* (New York).

WALLACE, J. W. (1978), *Virtues and Vices* (Ithaca, NY).

WATSON, G. (ed.) (1982), *Free Will* (New York).

WIGGINS, D. (1973), 'Towards a Reasonable Libertarianism', in Honderich (1973).

—— (1987), *Needs, Values, Truth* (Oxford).

WILLIAMS, B. (1972), *Morality* (New York).

—— (1973), 'A Critique of Utilitarianism', in Smart and Williams (1973).

—— (1981), *Moral Luck* (Cambridge).

—— (1985), *Ethics and the Limits of Philosophy* (Cambridge, Mass.).

WOLLHEIM, R. (1984), *The Thread of Life* (Cambridge, Mass.).

WONG, D. (1984), *Moral Relativity* (Berkeley, Calif.).

WRIGHT, C. (1988*a*), 'Realism, Antirealism, Irrealism, Quasi-realism', *Midwest Studies in Philosophy*, 12: 25–49.

—— (1988*b*), 'Moral Values, Projection and Secondary Qualities', *Proceedings of the Aristotelian Society*, supp. vol. 62: 1–26.

—— (1992), *Truth and Objectivity* (Cambridge, Mass.).

11

AESTHETICS

Sebastian Gardner

INTRODUCTION:
THE SCOPE OF PHILOSOPHICAL AESTHETICS

Aesthetics may be divided into the *philosophy of the aesthetic*, which is concerned with aesthetic experience and judgement in general, and in former times concentrated on the concept of beauty; and the *philosophy of art*. Aesthetics in contemporary analytical philosophy is centred firmly on the philosophy of art and encompasses a wide range of issues which intersect with topics in metaphysics, ethics, the philosophy of mind, and the philosophy of language.

Philosophical aesthetics, as it has been traditionally conceived, may be regarded as resting on two fundamental presuppositions. Spelling these out gives some idea of its goals.

The first is that there is a distinctive form of experience which is common to the appreciation of art and natural beauty, which has, typically, a pleasurable and contemplative character, involves a sense of release from the practical concerns of life, and leads us to describe its objects—works of art and natural scenes and objects—in a distinctive vocabulary, as graceful, beautiful, inspiring, and so on. Philosophy refers to this kind of experience, and the judgements which it leads us to make, as 'aesthetic'.

The second presupposition is that art has an essence or some sort of underlying unity. This would seem to be the common-sense view. Although the various forms of art—music, literature, painting, and so on—are at one level highly dissimilar, we apply to all of them the concept of art, which we regard as more than an arbitrary term of classification. The traditional goals of philosophical aesthetics have been, therefore, to account for the nature of aesthetic experience and judgement, and the unity of art.

Although, as most would agree, art provides the most complex and intense form of aesthetic experience, in which everyday practical life recedes into the background and gives way to complete imaginative involvement, aesthetic awareness suffuses to some degree our ordinary perception of the world. Architecture exerts a quiet but constant influence on our feelings. The choices that we make daily in designing our environment manifest aesthetic preferences. We ask for the instruments and materials that we employ in daily life— everything from clothes to cutlery—to be not merely functional but designed in ways that we find agreeable. Plausibly, the ability to respond to the world aesthetically is necessary for full or normal personal development, and the opportunity to appreciate art is a necessary component of human well-being. A society that had no agreed aesthetic standards and measured the worth of things purely in terms of their utility—if imaginable—would lack a culture. All of which shows, as again most would agree, that we set value on art and aesthetic experience, and that such value is not practical.

In spite of the pervasiveness of aesthetic concern in human life, aesthetic experience and judgement can come on reflection to seem mysterious and in some respects even paradoxical. What explains the special character of aesthetic experience? How can a judgement that an object is beautiful both, as would appear to be the case, report a fact about the object and express a feeling of the subject's? Why do we bother arguing about the aesthetic merits of objects, given that there seems to be no way of resolving such disagreement? What kind of thing is beauty? The concept of art exhibits on reflection a similar lack of philosophical perspicuity. What makes an object a work of art? How can art, as is often supposed, put us in touch with the mind of the artist? How can music have meaning and express human feeling? What are we to think when critics disagree about the meaning of a work of art? Why do we attach an importance to art that we deny to sport and cuisine? And so on.

Section 1 below describes the issues surrounding the nature of aesthetic experience and judgement in general and focuses on the seminal writings of two historical figures, Hume and Kant. The philosophy of art occupies the next two sections. Section 2 concentrates on the concepts which are fundamental to a philosophical understanding of art, such as representation and expression. These concepts concern the logically basic dimensions of works of art, and present-day analytical philosophy focuses closely on these. Section 3 sets out some of the most important attempts in the history of aesthetics to provide an account of the nature and value of art, and draws attention to the place of aesthetics in some of the great philosophical systems.

1. AESTHETIC EXPERIENCE AND JUDGEMENT

1.1. Aesthetic Judgement and Taste

Contemporary discussions of the nature of aesthetic judgement derive from a view of the topic formulated by thinkers in the eighteenth century, above all Hume and Kant. The relevant writings are Hume, 'Of the Standard of Taste' (1757), and—a difficult work—Kant, 'The Critique of Aesthetic Judgement', which forms part 1 of his *Critique of Judgement* (1790) (especially the Analytic of the Beautiful, sects. 1–22).

The aesthetic theories of Hume and Kant did not solve all of the problems raised by aesthetic judgement, but provided a framework outlining its basic features. The framework inspired by Hume and Kant involves two key claims: that aesthetic judgement presupposes taste, and that aesthetic qualities are subjective.

By an aesthetic judgement is meant, simply, a judgement such as that a sunset, or vase of flowers, or painting is beautiful. The traditional term 'beautiful'—which is only one of the many terms in ordinary language for ascribing aesthetic qualities—is not important in this context. What is important is the idea that in an aesthetic judgement the object is said to be, simply by virtue of its appearance, an intrinsically rewarding object of attention. According to Hume and Kant, aesthetic judgements exemplify *taste*. Taste, in eighteenth-century aesthetics, refers to the special mental faculty (or special mode of employment of ordinary mental faculties) which is exercised in aesthetic judgement. The two crucial logical features of judgements identified by Hume and Kant which show them to presuppose taste are:

1. *The condition of felt response.* Aesthetic judgement rests fundamentally on a felt response to its object and personal acquaintance with it (Kant 1790, sect. 1). The condition of felt response is reflected in the fact that an aesthetic judgement, like an avowal of emotion, can be made sincerely or insincerely, depending on whether or not a person really has, or merely feigns, the appropriate inner response.

Behind the condition of felt response lies the more logically basic condition of direct personal acquaintance with the object of aesthetic judgement. We reject the idea that aesthetic judgements can be passed second-hand on objects: the testimony and descriptions of others may make me confident that I will find a certain object beautiful, but I am not within my rights to declare it to be so until I have seen it myself. To see the force of this point, aesthetic judgement may be compared with moral judgement, which (arguably) does not presuppose in the same sense either a felt response or personal acquaintance. That aesthetic judgement presupposes personal experience of its object agrees with the plain fact that objects of aesthetic judgement must be sensory (works of art must exist in some medium or other).

2. *The absence of rules.* Rules play no role in aesthetic judgement (see Kant 1790, sect. 8). This claim is expressed in various ways, sometimes by saying that there are no principles or standards of taste, or that there are no criteria for aesthetic judgements. An aesthetic rule would be a general proposition that enabled aesthetic judgements to be *inferred* on the basis of information about the formal, sensory, or other non-aesthetic properties of an object: it would have the form 'Everything that is F is G', where F is a non-aesthetic property and G is an aesthetic quality. With the aid of such a rule one could infer, syllogistically, that x has aesthetic quality G from the premiss that x is F, and so arrive at the judgement 'x is G'. Thus one could know that a piece of music is rapturous simply because it is in a particular key and orchestrated for certain instruments; or that a painting is dynamic because the form of its composition exemplifies a certain geometric pattern. Fairly obviously, no such rules are in fact recognized. The much stronger claim of Hume and Kant is that such rules *could not* exist,

for a judgement could not logically be aesthetic and based on a rule: if it were based on a rule, it would fail to qualify as an *aesthetic* judgement.

Note that what is denied here is the role of general propositions in *justifying* aesthetic judgements: it is a completely different question whether or not there may be lawlike generalizations (furnished by psychology or sociology), to which our aesthetic judgements conform, or that provide causal, empirical explanations for our aesthetic preferences. Note also that the question of whether there are aesthetic rules is not the same as that of whether aesthetic judgements have or lack justifications, since it is possible that aesthetic judgements may be justified on some basis other than rules (this is in fact what Hume and Kant—having disposed of aesthetic rules—go on to claim).

It has not, it should be stressed, always been agreed that there are no aesthetic rules. On the contrary, the view which prevailed up until Hume and Kant was that aesthetic rules, hard though they might be to find, must indeed exist. This is in one way unsurprising, for it is a standard part of the notion of 'making a judgement' that one should do so on some basis, i.e. with criteria of some sort in play. Baumgarten, Kant's immediate precursor in the history of aesthetics, held that there are rules constituting beauty and defined aesthetics as the 'science of the beautiful' (an idea that Wittgenstein, who carried forward the approach of Hume and Kant, dismissed as 'too ridiculous for words'). Attempts to draw up specific rules for aesthetic judgement crop up in many places in the history of aesthetics: Joshua Reynolds's Seventh Discourse on Art (1797) is a prime example. Some contemporary writers hold to the existence of aesthetic rules (for example, Beardsley 1982).

A great number of reasons have been given for the absence of aesthetic rules, which it is important to grasp: (1) the absence of aesthetic generalizations that we can all rationally agree on; (2) the unjustifiability, in cases of aesthetic disagreement, of asking another person to relinquish her aesthetic judgement on the grounds that it conflicts with some aesthetic rule; (3) the logical impossibility of translating whatever inductive truths about aesthetic preferences may exist into aesthetic rules; (4) the irrelevance of rules to the engendering of aesthetic responses, and their consequent epistemological redundancy; (5) the highly circumscribed role of conformity to rules in the creation of works of art; (6) the highly limited application of the notion of consistency in the aesthetic sphere. In most of these contexts, comparisons with moral judgement are illuminating.

What explains the absence of aesthetic rules? The explanation must make reference to the conditions of felt response and personal acquaintance. Of equal importance is the fact that aesthetic interest is directed essentially towards *particular* objects, appreciated for their own sake and grasped in their uniqueness. The condition of particularity is sometimes expressed by saying that the features of objects that support aesthetic judgements are themselves particular, in the following sense: what may legitimately be cited in support of the judgement that Caravaggio's *Conversion of St Paul* is dramatic is the *particular* use that Caravaggio makes of chiaroscuro in that painting—not the general method of alternating light and dark, some applications of which may result in wholly undramatic paintings.

Note that to say that aesthetic judgement is independent of rules and that it is directed towards particulars is not to say that the critical history of art is mistaken in aiming at general propositions: undoubtedly, there are valid generalizations to be made about the development of Renaissance painting and the nineteenth-century novel. This historically orientated interest is, however, pitched at a level distinct from that of aesthetic judgement. Nor does the stress on particularity mean that all forms of aesthetic comparison between objects are illegitimate: both Hume and Kant assert the importance, in a fully developed culture, of *exemplary* aesthetic objects, 'established models', as Hume calls them, which serve as touchstones of aesthetic value.

The foregoing points are assembled in the writings of Sibley, whose lucid account of the logic of aesthetic judgement is widely referred to in analytical aesthetics. The logic of aesthetic discourse described by Sibley is relatively straightforward and largely uncontroversial, and may be broken down into the following key claims (Sibley's arguments for each merit close examination). (1) Ordinary language allows us to draw a sharp distinction between aesthetic and non-aesthetic qualities. (2) Although there is a very weak sort of dependency of aesthetic on non-aesthetic qualities, aesthetic qualities are not 'condition-governed', meaning that no logical relations of any kind hold between attributions of non-aesthetic and aesthetic qualities. (3) From this it follows that no rules for aesthetic judgement can be provided: such rules would only be possible if aesthetic qualities were condition-governed. (4) Sibley's positive thesis is that aesthetic judgement requires an exercise of taste or 'sensitivity', conceived on the model of perception.

1.2. Aesthetic Objectivism and Subjectivism

In addition to affirming that aesthetic judgements presuppose taste, Hume and Kant both reject the view—which is found in classical aesthetics and the aesthetics of the rationalists—that aesthetic qualities are objective.

The contrast of objectivism and subjectivism occurs in many philosophical contexts; in particular, many of the arguments about objectivity and subjectivity in ethics carry over to aesthetics. Aesthetic objectivism is the doctrine that aesthetic qualities are genuine properties which inhere in objects independently of the subject's awareness. (Note that what is here called aesthetic objectivism is sometimes called aesthetic 'realism'.) Aesthetic subjectivism is the doctrine that aesthetic qualities do not inhere in objects and that what it is for an object to have some aesthetic quality is for it to produce a certain response in the subject.

This is a *metaphysical* distinction. Questions of agreement and disagreement, by contrast, are epistemological: so the question of whether aesthetic qualities are objective or subjective is not the same as that of whether or not there can be agreement in aesthetic matters, even though this epistemological issue is relevant to the metaphysical question.

1.2.1. Aesthetic Objectivism

According to aesthetic objectivism, aesthetic experience consists in acquiring knowledge of its object's properties through perception. Aesthetic objectivists take different views of the nature of aesthetic properties. (1) They may be identified with an object's formal properties, such as 'unity', 'balance', 'ideal proportion', 'uniformity amidst variety', 'conformity to the Golden Section', or with its 'perfection'. (2) Other objectivists regard aesthetic properties as *sui generis* and irreducible to the object's formal or other non-aesthetic properties (see Moore 1903 and McDowell 1983). (These two varieties of aesthetic objectivism correspond to, and are illuminated by, comparison with ethical naturalism and ethical intuitionism respectively.)

Historically, aesthetic objectivism has been associated with rationalism. Why this should be is not hard to understand. Rationalism, which regards all the mind's ideas as cognitions, looks on an idea such as beauty as a cognition of a real property shared by all beautiful objects; it claims that aesthetic cognition is distinguished from intellectual cognition by its relative indistinctness. It was natural for the rationalists, in view of their neo-classical cultural heritage, to identify the property in question with perfection. Leibniz accordingly identified beauty with intellectual perfection. The rationalist Baumgarten by contrast identified beauty with a distinct type of perfection, which is sensory rather than intellectual and concerns the perceptual individuality of the object.

1.2.2. Aesthetic Subjectivism

According to aesthetic subjectivism, in aesthetic experience I am *affected* by the object, and my response—the effect that the object has on me—does not consist in perception of its properties. The aesthetic subjectivist may grant that in order to produce an aesthetic response an object must have certain formal or other non-aesthetic properties, but for the subjectivist these properties are merely what causes the response: the response itself is something over and above a perception of the properties. Aesthetic subjectivism comes in various degrees of sophistication (its varieties correspond to varieties of subjectivism in ethics).

Historically, aesthetic subjectivism is associated with empiricism. Empiricism, treating the mind as a passive container of sensory ideas, inclines to a view of beauty and other aesthetic qualities as simple semi-sensory ideas caused in the mind by certain combinations of perceptible features in objects. As Hume says, beauty 'is no quality in things themselves; it exists merely in the mind which contemplates them'. (Other empiricist aestheticians whose writings are of interest are Hutcheson, Addison, Shaftesbury, Reid, and Burke.)

1.2.3. *Arguments for Aesthetic Subjectivism*

Some central arguments for aesthetic subjectivism are the following.

1. The considerable variation between the tastes of different individuals and cultures, which Hume's essay (1757) begins by stressing, counts in favour of aesthetic subjectivism: the fact of aesthetic divergence and lack of agreed methods for bringing divergent judgements into line implies that aesthetic qualities do not inhere in objects. The aesthetic objectivist may respond that divergence is present in all spheres (Sibley, in Sibley and Tanner 1968), and add that aesthetic qualities are *elusive*: that is, observers have to meet special conditions in order to discern aesthetic properties (in the case of works of art, observers must have an appropriate cultural background) (see Pettit 1983). The subjectivist will ask why, if aesthetic qualities are objective, special conditions should be required in order to 'discern' them. The upshot of these points is unclear: plausibly, divergence gives strong but not conclusive reason for the subjectivity of aesthetic judgements.

2. Kant spells out (1790, sect. 1) the significance of the fact that pleasure is essential to the experience which grounds an aesthetic judgement (this is part of the 'felt response' condition referred to in Section 1.1). Pleasure, like pain, is a feeling and not a cognitive mental state: as Kant says, pleasure 'designates nothing whatsoever in the object'. The aesthetic objectivist consequently faces the difficulty of accounting for the fact that pleasure is necessary for, and not just a contingent accompaniment to, aesthetic response. The subjectivist by contrast has no problem explaining this connection: for the subjectivist, pleasure is part of what makes a response aesthetic. The subjectivist will argue that the idea of properties which inhere in objects but *necessarily* generate pleasure when apprehended makes no sense: such 'properties' are too metaphysically queer to be counted into the fabric of reality.

3. The aesthetic subjectivist may argue that aesthetic objectivism, because it thinks of aesthetic judgements as cognitive, misconstrues the nature of aesthetic interest. Cognition aims to fit reality and implies a distinction between reality and experience. How appropriate is each of these features to aesthetic experience and judgement? The aesthetic subjectivist will argue that it does not matter whether or not aesthetic experience puts us in touch with the world as

it really is (what we want is to have rewarding relations with aesthetic objects, as we do with people), and that the distinction between how things are and how they merely seem is either non-existent in aesthetic contexts or very different from how it is in cognitive contexts (successful 'appearances' of aesthetic quality are as good as, indeed they are the same as, the real thing, for aesthetic 'reality' precisely consists in appearances).

1.3. The Problem of Taste

If, however, aesthetic subjectivism is philosophically cogent and to a large extent commonsensical, it appears to carry an implication that is unwelcome. If aesthetic quality does not inhere in objects, what is to prevent the same object being viewed as beautiful by one person and as ugly by another—both being justified, to an equal degree, in their pronouncements? Because aesthetic subjectivism appears to deny that aesthetic matters can be argued about, it seems to prescribe that each individual should simply, as Hume says, 'acquiesce in his own sentiment, without pretending to relegate those of others'. This would amount to all-out, *unqualified* subjectivism, in which there is no logical difference between aesthetic taste and gustatory taste.

Unqualified aesthetic subjectivism holds that a person who passes a favourable aesthetic judgement on a piece of music does no more than report, or give expression to, their own mental state. It is therefore the equivalent of emotivism in ethics. So we find the emotivist Ayer saying: 'Such aesthetic words as "beautiful" and "hideous" are employed, as ethical words are employed, not to make statements of fact, but simply to express certain feelings and evoke a certain response. It follows that there is no sense in attributing objective validity to aesthetic judgements' (1976). For Ayer, aesthetic judgements are equivalent to avowals of like and dislike: they have no richer meaning than exclamations like 'boo!' and 'hurrah!'

1.3.1. The Incompatibility of Unqualified Subjectivism with Common Sense

It is crucial to recognize that unqualified subjectivism clashes with common sense (Kant 1790, sect. 7). Common sense is unequivocal that 'the music is beautiful' means more than, even if it presupposes, 'the music gives me pleasure'. If those two thoughts were the same, one could not regard one's aesthetic judgement as something that another person might take issue with, and in support of which reasons—other than the fact of one's liking it—may be given. But we *do* think that a judgement that the music is beautiful clashes with the judgement that it is ugly or sentimental: it does so because—as its grammatical form suggests—it aims to say something about the music, not about oneself. Someone who makes an aesthetic judgement therefore supposes that others will or ought to concur, and that any failure to do so indicates some sort of blindness or deficiency of taste.

Hume and Kant each bring out the incompatibility of unqualified subjectivism with common sense.

1. Hume (1757) recognizes the force of, and spells out the case for, unqualified subjectivism. Hume grants that it has, to some degree, 'the sanction of common sense'. However, Hume then makes the anthropological observation that it is 'natural for us to seek a Standard of Taste: a rule, by which the various sentiments of men may be reconciled; at least, a decision afforded, confirming one sentiment, and condemning another'. Adherence to a standard of taste is therefore also part of common sense. This means, not that common sense contradicts itself, but that it tends to 'modify and restrain' its subjectivism.

2. A subtle but powerful demonstration that unqualified aesthetic subjectivism is indeed at odds with common sense is provided by Kant, who calls it the 'antinomy of taste' (1790, sect. 56). Kant's argument hinges on the idea that when aesthetic judgements diverge, common sense supposes that there is at least something at issue between them, even though there may not be reason for engaging in argument.

Because it contradicts common sense, unqualified aesthetic subjectivism is equivalent to *scepticism*: it denies the rationality of a kind of judgement (aesthetic judgement) that common sense supposes to be rational.

Thus the *problem of taste*: how to maintain the subjective character of aesthetic judgements without collapsing into scepticism? It is at this point that the theories of Hume and Kant are best appreciated. Each responds to the problem of taste in a different way.

1.4. Hume

Hume (1757) contends that a 'standard of taste'—that is, a basis for accepting some judgements of taste as correct and rejecting others as incorrect, and thus a source of rationality in aesthetic judgement—is at work in our aesthetic practice and philosophically defensible. The standard of taste lies not in the object but in the sensibility of the subject. Hume's account encompasses five key claims. (1) There are certain relations 'which nature has placed between the form and the sentiment': 'Some particular forms or qualities, from the original structure of the internal fabric, are calculated to please, and others to displease.' (2) The aesthetic sensibility of individuals varies in its quality or 'delicacy'. (3) Because we recognize certain individuals—the 'critics'—as having superior, i.e. more delicate, sensibilities, we defer to their judgement. (4) A correct aesthetic judgement is one that issues from a delicate sensibility operating under ideal conditions. (5) Although aesthetic judgements do not identify aesthetic properties inhering in objects, nor do they simply report the subject's experiences. An object's possession of an aesthetic quality consists in its being 'fitted' to generate a certain response in us.

In Hume's exposition of these ideas, the following deserve attention: Hume's account of the features that constitute an ideal sensibility, and of the characteristics of the critic; the analogy that Hume draws between aesthetic qualities and colours (secondary qualities); the role of exemplars; Hume's appeal at one point to the notion of an ideal observer; and Hume's concluding admission of the limits of convergence of aesthetic judgement.

Hume's solution to the problem of taste rests on two, ultimately contingent, facts of nature: that some 'particular forms or qualities [in objects] are calculated to please, and others to displease'; and the contingent uniformity of human sensibility, the sameness in 'the original structure of the internal fabric' of our minds.

Hume's achievement—if his account is accepted—is to endorse the subjectivist and 'sentimentalist' view that aesthetic judgement is a matter of feeling, and yet show that we do not need to abandon the application of notions of correctness and incorrectness to aesthetic judgements. In this way Hume qualifies aesthetic subjectivism and separates it from aesthetic scepticism, thus reconciling the two strands in common sense, its subjectivism and its adherence to a standard of taste.

1.4.1. Assessing Hume

A potentially deep problem for Hume concerns what may be called the *normative* dimension of aesthetic judgement. It may be asked what in Hume's account grounds the authority of the critic. Granted that, as Hume says, there are, as a matter of psychological fact, differences of internal fabric between my mind and that of the critic, and that, as a matter of sociological fact, people go around deferring to the critic—still, why *ought* I to give precedence to the judgement of the critic? I myself am not the critic, and his responses are not my responses. What sense is there then in my regarding his pronouncements as having a stronger claim to correctness than my own? Hume appears to offer only a causal, psychological explanation of why we do, as a matter of fact, defer to the judgements of critics: he does not say why we *ought* to do so, and so does not take us far enough. (In a similar vein, it may be asked if Hume has provided a sense in which an object may be said to *merit* an aesthetic response, a point taken up in Wiggins 1987.)

This objection is one that a Kantian will press. On a Kantian diagnosis, Hume's shortfalling is due to his not having told us what the relation of 'conformity' between certain objects and the fabric of our minds consists in, other than a bare causal relation; Hume therefore fails to explain how aesthetic experience can be taken as providing the ground for a genuine *judgement* of the object (see Stroud 1977).

1.5. Kant

To understand Kant's theory of aesthetic judgement, it helps to think of it as divided into three main parts. (Kant's text itself does not, however, distinguish these sharply as such.)

1. *Kant's solution to the normative problem of aesthetic judgement.* Kant interprets the demand for agreement implicit in aesthetic judgement—that others ought to concur—very strongly, as applying to all other persons without exception. His solution to the normative problem—what Kant calls the 'deduction of pure judgements of taste'—is in essence fairly simple, although his presentation of it extremely intricate.

Suppose that in making an aesthetic judgement we abstract from everything that might pertain to our contingent, natural, individually variable constitutions, and base our judgements solely on conditions which are 'strictly universal', in the sense of being necessarily available and common to all persons. According to Kant, this would mean basing our aesthetic judgement on (*a*) the bare perceptual form of the object, and (*b*) its interaction with our basic, universally shared mental powers of perception and understanding. (Kant's reasoning here recapitulates his analysis of moral judgement in terms of the categorical imperative.) Kant argues that this 'universal' standpoint can be achieved through freeing our awareness of the object from desire and practical concern—what he calls 'disinterestedness'—and from our conceptual understanding of it. When these stringent conditions are met, the judgement that we make is valid for everyone and we have what Kant calls a 'pure judgement of taste', which has 'strict universal validity'. Such judgements are grounded in the supposition that we share a 'common sense', i.e. that our capacities for felt response are the same. (Kant grants that this supposition is not actually realized, and holds that it must be worked towards.)

Kant's argument for the above is detailed, and supplemented by the solution that he offers to the antinomy of taste referred to in Section 1.3.1.

2. *Kant's theory of aesthetic response.* Kant argues that it is indeed possible for the mere form of an object to please us: certain perceptual forms stimulate our mental faculties optimally, by engendering in us a 'harmonious free play of imagination and understanding', awareness of which is pleasurable. Two judgements are according to Kant involved implicitly when an object is pronounced beautiful: (*a*) a judgement *of the object* (that its form is such-and-such), and (*b*) a judgement *of the pleasure* given by the object, that it is valid for everyone.

3. *The metaphysical and moral significance of aesthetic experience.* Kant also advances a metaphysical interpretation of aesthetic experience: it makes us

conscious of a connection that we have with the world, and with one another, which lies beyond the empirical world (it concerns what Kant calls the 'super-sensible'). Kant argues that the frame of mind involved in the appreciation of beauty is analogous to that involved in awareness of moral obligation. Beauty therefore has a moral significance for Kant, and he calls it 'the symbol of the good'.

There is disagreement between commentators as to whether or not Kant's deduction of judgements of taste—his postulation of a 'common sense'—depends upon the connection that he draws with morality.

The two other main components of Kant's aesthetic theory are his accounts of the sublime and of art.

The sublime, an aesthetic phenomenon that Kant distinguishes from beauty, does not have for Kant quite the same importance as beauty, but he regards it too as metaphysically significant, and offers in the Analytic of the Sublime a complex account of how judgements of the sublime are arrived at. In understanding Kant's account of the sublime and how it differs from beauty, it is helpful to read Burke (1757).

Kant's theory of aesthetic judgement is elaborated with respect to natural beauty. Extending his theory to art demands some adjustments, and there is a prima-facie problem of some sort here for Kant: his account of aesthetic judgement requires everything but the form of the object to be eliminated, whereas in art content too is clearly essential (arguably, it is inseparable from form). Consequently, in accounting for art, Kant introduces the notions of 'aesthetic ideas' and 'genius'.

1.5.1. Assessing Kant

There is of course enormous scope for examining the fine grain of Kant's arguments for each of his claims, for which Crawford (1974) is perhaps the most useful text.

Crucial questions to be raised about Kant's aesthetic theory include: the correctness of Kant's assumption that a judgement of beauty is universal in its scope; the cogency of Kant's theory of aesthetic response; the tenability of Kant's solution to the antinomy of taste; and the validity of the connections that Kant draws with morality. The last of these has special importance if, as some interpreters maintain, Kant's deduction of judgements of taste depends upon an appeal to moral interest. But the most important and interesting question is perhaps the degree to which Kant's theory makes an advance on that of Hume.

Hume and Kant offer the same *kind* of solution to the problem of taste: both maintain that aesthetic judgements are *logically dependent* on pleasure and liking, but deny that aesthetic judgements are reducible to, or analysable into, judgements of pleasure or liking, and so maintain that aesthetic judgements *transcend* judgements of pleasure or liking. Thereafter, the theories of Hume and Kant point in opposite directions. Hume grounds aesthetic response on the natural, and thus *contingent*, constitution of our minds, Kant on the metaphysical, and thus *necessary*, aspects of our minds. The arguable weakness of Hume's account was indicated above. Kant's theory appears to solve the normative problem, but a cost nevertheless attaches to his austere solution: purifying aesthetic judgement in the way that Kant requires excludes from aesthetic experience everything in our psychological and cultural constitutions that is not strictly universal. The Humean will argue that this leaves us with an intolerably impoverished view of aesthetic experience.

1.6. Contemporary Accounts of the Aesthetic

Against the background of Hume and Kant, contemporary accounts of aesthetic experience, judgement, and qualities may be explored. Many of these show the influence of Wittgenstein, whose 'Lectures on Aesthetics' (1978) extends and elaborates the framework bequeathed by Hume and Kant. Wittgenstein's text is fragmentary but replete with insights.

Four writers who take different stands on the meaning of aesthetic judgements and the degree to which they are subjective are Sibley, Hungerland, Meager, and Scruton. It is difficult to decide between these theories, but rewarding to at least explore the differences between them.

Sibley claims that aesthetic qualities are no more subjective than colours. Being on a par with colours is the *least* subjective status that aesthetic qualities can be accorded within the Humean–Kantian framework. This claim of Sibley's has been criticized on the grounds that aesthetic disagreement is more extensive and different in kind from disagreement about the colours of objects (Tanner, in Sibley and Tanner 1968).

Hungerland (1968) rejects Sibley's claim that taste involves a special kind of perception and argues that aesthetic qualities are better compared to the aspects that Wittgenstein discusses (as exemplified by the famous duck–rabbit picture) or the 'looks' that objects are said to have (as when one says of someone that 'she looks as if she could run a four-minute mile').

Meager (1970) goes further in the direction of subjectivity by stressing the way in which aesthetic awareness is defined by an interest in having a certain sort of experience, and rejects the idea that aesthetic qualities are 'features' of objects in any sense. Meager nevertheless hangs on to the idea that the logical role of aesthetic judgements is descriptive and so expresses her thesis by saying that the role of aesthetic judgements is to ascribe powers to objects—powers to induce experiences in us.

Scruton (1974), in opposition to Sibley, Hungerland, and Meager, denies that aesthetic judgements are descriptive and claims that their logical function is, as

Wittgenstein suggests, closer logically to that of gestures and exclamations—it is to 'put across' or convey a certain kind of experience. On Scruton's 'affective theory', we should not really speak of aesthetic qualities at all, as opposed to aesthetic experiences or responses. Scruton's (1974) development of this theory is complex but comprehensive and rewarding.

1.7. Aesthetic Reasons and Criticism

Contemporary discussion of aesthetic judgement focuses also on the logical nature of reasons given in aesthetic contexts and, relatedly, on the role of criticism in the arts. Aesthetic reason-giving differs in fundamental ways from reason-giving in other contexts and has a number of peculiarities which make it hard to understand: it does not consist in inferring one proposition from another, and makes no use of rules, criteria, induction, or generalization. It seems therefore that aesthetic reasons operate independently from all of the conditions that are integral to the very concept of a reason. And yet, if aesthetic judgements are to remain distinct from mere likings and qualify as, in a broad sense, rational, they must in some sense be open to justification. Much discussion of this problem is bound up with Wittgenstein's treatment of the distinction between reasons and causes.

The question of what it is to reason about aesthetic matters has ramifications for how we are to conceive the job of the critic. The critic can be regarded as (1) identifying the sources of a work's aesthetic qualities (an explanatory function), and thereby (2) determining what responses are appropriate (a normative function). These go hand in hand with the function of (3) deepening and intensifying our aesthetic responses (the critic 'puts across' or conveys her experience, which has interest for us because the critic's sensibility has the virtue of Humean 'delicacy'). Finally the critic must (4) provide an interpretation of the work and identify its meaning (a notion discussed in Section 2.5).

1.8. The Aesthetic Attitude

The claim that there is such a thing as the *aesthetic attitude*—a notion bequeathed by Kant's notion of disinterestedness—and that it constitutes the essence of aesthetic experience has had considerable traditional importance. It remains controversial. The distinctive phenomenology of aesthetic experience makes the idea alluring, but the question (which is difficult) is whether enough can be said about the aesthetic attitude to make it philosophically explanatory.

Aesthetic experience, proponents of the aesthetic attitude claim, consists essentially in the adoption of a special, non-cognitive, and non-practical attitude or stance, in which objects are attended to dispassionately and for their own sake. On this basis, theorists make further claims about the aesthetic attitude. Schopenhauer (1819) identifies aesthetic contemplation with a state of metaphysical liberation from selfhood (see Section 3.6.3). Bell's (1914) 'metaphysical hypothesis' claims that in 'aesthetic emotion' we are confronted with 'Reality'. Something similar is involved in Heidegger's (1950) conception of poetry as thought which 'discloses Being'. Bullough's (1957) version of the theory is psychological rather than metaphysical and makes use of the idea of mental 'distancing'.

Against the aesthetic attitude, it is claimed that specifications of the aesthetic attitude remain fundamentally negative (saying that an object is enjoyed 'for its own sake' really means just that it is not enjoyed for any ulterior end). It is then urged that if nothing can be said about the attitude *other than* that it differs from and precludes practical and cognitive attitudes, then this is not enough: the attitude fails to be explanatory. Dickie (1964) objects that there is no genuine distinction between 'interested' and 'disinterested' ways of attending to an object: so long as one does attend to an object, one does so interestedly; to attend 'disinterestedly' can only mean attending poorly or distractedly. The notion of the aesthetic attitude therefore reduces to the meagre notion of attending to an object with full and proper attention.

It should be considered whether Dickie's deflation of the aesthetic attitude is justified: proponents of the attitude will counter that the 'full and proper attention' given to aesthetic objects is different from that accorded to practical tasks. Wollheim (1980, sects. 40–1) offers a subtle resolution to the question, suggesting that there is indeed such a thing as an aesthetic attitude but that its importance for aesthetics is limited.

1.9. Beauty

A final issue concerns the concept of beauty, which has undergone a dramatic reversal of fortunes in the history of aesthetics. Classical aesthetics takes it for granted that beauty is the only, or at least the fundamental, aesthetic quality. Some modern writers propose by contrast either that 'beautiful' is a mere catch-all term, roughly equivalent to 'aesthetically commendable'; or that there is, as ordinary language suggests, a limitless plurality of aesthetic qualities (encompassing elegance, grace, poignancy, etc.) of which beauty is only one. The modern devaluation of the concept of beauty is sometimes supported by the argument that the objects deemed beautiful are so radically dissimilar (especially across the ontologically different contexts of nature and art) that there cannot be a simple quality common to them all.

The traditional view that beauty is not just one aesthetic quality among many but somehow pre-eminent accounts for the unity of aesthetic experience. The 'pluralist' view is consequently challenged to find an alternative account of the unity of the aesthetic (see Mothersill's (1984) defence of the concept of beauty).

2. FUNDAMENTAL CONCEPTS IN THE PHILOSOPHY OF ART

2.1. Art and the Aesthetic

The philosophy of art can be regarded as proceeding at three levels (although formally distinct, these overlap to an enormous extent): (1) an examination of the various basic dimensions of works of art which aims to analyse the *fundamental concepts* that enter into our understanding of individual works of art and the various forms of art; (2) a *definition of art*, which attempts to give necessary and sufficient conditions for an object to qualify as a work of art, i.e. a criterion for discriminating art from non-art; (3) a *theory of art* is considerably more ambitious than a definition of art and aims to provide a deep, explanatory account of art, which goes at least some way towards accounting for the importance that art has for us. Theories of art assume that the concept of art picks out more than a merely nominal or historically accidental phenomenon: they assume, in short, that art has some sort of essence. Theories of art characteristically focus on a single concept—such as form or expression—which they claim encapsulates its essence.

This section is concerned with (1), and Section 3 with (2) and (3). Contemporary analytical aesthetics, by and large suspicious of attempts to construct monolithic 'grand theories' of art, has tended to adopt instead a piecemeal approach to the philosophy of art and concentrated on clarifying its fundamental concepts, in the belief that an accurate picture of art as a whole will emerge out of a proper understanding of its parts. Of the several concepts which are fundamental to our understanding of art, those which stand out as of particular importance, and have been most intensively discussed, are representation, expression, and interpretation and intention. Each of these is most strongly associated with a particular form of art: representation with painting, expression with music, and interpretation and intention with literature.

2.1.1. The Question of Priority

It is worth noting that the division of aesthetics into the philosophy of art and the philosophy of the aesthetic raises a substantial and important philosophical question. Given that aesthetic experience occurs both in the context of art and in that of nature, which has conceptual priority? On one view (that of Kant), art is just a special, more complex instance of aesthetic experience in general, and we should therefore accord conceptual priority to the aesthetic experience of nature, where it occurs in its purest form. The opposite view—that of Hegel— that art has conceptual priority, is less straightforward. It does not of course mean to deny that it is possible to respond aesthetically to nature without having ever been exposed to a work of art: what it maintains is rather that the aesthetic capacities exercised in responding to nature are ones which can be exercised fully only in relation to works of art. So it may be said that in responding aesthetically to nature, we are (implicitly) regarding nature somewhat as if it were a (rudimentary) work of art. On this view, the best way of understanding the aesthetic in general is via the concept of art. Hegel's aesthetic theory (see Section 3.6.2) provides a deep metaphysical rationale for the priority of art; Wollheim (1980) and Strawson (1974) also hold to the priority of art, but for non-metaphysical reasons. Scruton (1974) defends and explores the opposite, Kantian approach.

2.1.2. Aesthetic and Artistic Properties

A further issue in this context that needs to be understood concerns the distinction between aesthetic and artistic properties. The theories of the aesthetic considered in Section 1 (especially Section 1.6) have bearing on the distinction between aesthetic and non-aesthetic properties. It is a further question what makes a property artistic, and how artistic properties relate to aesthetic properties.

2.2. Ontology

Perhaps the most basic question of the philosophy of art is: What kind of thing is a work of art? This is described as a question of ontology (it is concerned with that in which the being of a work of art consists), or of identity and individuation (it is concerned with the criteria by which works of art are distinguished from one another and counted as one and the same across different contexts). Little reflection is needed to see that the issues here are many and deep. Your copy of *Ulysses* and my copy are not the same, although they are copies of the same novel; so a literary work cannot, it seems, be a physical object. Nor can a piece of music be identified with a particular sequence of sounds; otherwise, the same musical work could never be performed twice. Paintings and sculptures by contrast must, surely, be identified with physical particulars (this underpins our notion of forgery). This seems to mean that there is no one, general answer to the question of what kind of thing a work of art is. All sorts of further complications are introduced by such familiar facts as that an artist may paint the 'same' painting twice, or revise a work extensively at a later date, and that a (musical or dramatic) work may be performed in ways that depart radically from the original.

Ontological questions are discussed illuminatingly by Wollheim (1980), who stresses their importance for other issues in aesthetics. There is considerable philosophical motivation for thinking that the criteria of identity for works of art must differ in logical ways from those for other, more humdrum objects. In this spirit Strawson (1974) claims that 'the *criterion of identity* of a work of art is the sum of features which are relevant to its aesthetical appraisal'. There is also a strong tradition in aesthetics that regards works of art as existing originally in the artist's mind and the appreciation of art as a matter of re-creating the artist's mental object. This 'idealist' view is advanced by Collingwood and Croce (see Section 3.4). Similar refusals to identify works of art plainly with physical entities appear in phenomenological aesthetics: Sartre (1940) describes works of art as 'unreal objects', which, he argues, means that to the extent that art is confined to the world of imagination, its values cannot intersect with, or contribute to, those of the real world.

2.3. Representation

The question of what it is for a painting to represent something has been considered in depth by analytical philosophers. Understanding the issue of pictorial representation (or, as it is also called, depiction) may be broken down into two stages: understanding the problem, and adjudicating between the several, sophisticated solutions that have been proposed.

2.3.1. *The Problem*

That paintings represent things is plain enough. When we look at Monet's *Haystacks, Sunset* we do not see, or do not just see, pigments spread on a two-dimensional surface: we see a haystack in a field at sunset. The things that paintings represent may, but need not, exist: portraits represent real people, paintings of unicorns represent imaginary objects. The question is: How do paintings represent objects? How can a pigmented canvas present us with a 'visual object' such as a haystack? This question is evidently more basic than questions about the iconographic (symbolic) meanings carried by the things represented in paintings.

Common sense would say that pictorial representation consists in *resemblance*: a painting represents O by *looking like* O; paintings are realistic to the extent that they resemble their objects. A little reflection shows that this claim is, however, simply false. Canvases marked with pigments do not resemble the things that they represent: Monet's painting does not even begin to share the physical dimensions of the scene that it represents! In fact, each canvas resembles nothing so much as other canvases—but it does not of course represent them.

It may be thought that what the common-sense, resemblance view means is that a painting P represents an object O when P is looked at, not as a mere physical object, but *as a picture*. This, however, merely restates the problem, for the question now becomes: What is it for a pigmented canvas to be looked at as a picture? Also unhelpful is the notion of an image. It is often said that a painting P represents O by giving us an 'image' of O. But this proposal just translates the problem of how pictures represent objects into that of explaining how pigmented canvases give rise to images.

Theorists such as Goodman (1976) and Gombrich (1977) have argued vigorously against the notion of resemblance, arguing that resemblance is neither sufficient nor necessary for representation. Gombrich attacks in particular the assumption that there is such a thing as an 'innocent eye' and that an artist can simply 'copy what he sees' by attending to his visual experience.

2.3.2. Solutions

Theorists turn away from resemblance to other, less commonsensical notions. At the opposite extreme, there is the view that pictorial representation has nothing to do with perception and that it is entirely conventional: knowing what a painting represents is logically like understanding a sentence in a natural language. This is Goodman's (1976) account, on which pictorial representation is a species of denotation: knowing what a picture represents is a matter of interpretation, which requires a grasp of the 'symbol system' to which the painting belongs. For Goodman, 'realism' in painting is just a function of the viewer's familiarity with a particular pictorial symbol system, the facility with which the painting imparts information to the spectator.

Goodman's view is highly counter-intuitive. Common sense would say that paintings differ from prose descriptions, and from maps, road signs, and other visual symbols, by virtue of the visual experiences that they give us. Maps, like descriptive passages in novels, need to be read and do not enable us to see the areas of land that they represent. Landscapes by contrast give us visual experiences of scenes in nature. Goodman's theory denies these differences.

Gombrich, unlike Goodman, does not assimilate pictorial representation outright to interpretation. On his account, pictorial representation does involve a visual experience: a painting represents O by giving us an *illusion* of O. How illusions are created is explained in terms of the representational practices which have evolved in the history of art, a process of 'making and matching' in which visual 'schemata' are established in order to represent objects, without resemblance playing any role.

Gombrich's theory is not, like Goodman's, at odds with common sense, but it has difficulties of its own. Some visual representations—such as Escher's *trompe l'œil* drawings—do create illusions, but most paintings do not: in looking at a painting we do not normally find ourselves having to correct a tendency to *mistake* its content for reality, as the concept of illusion implies (we do not find ourselves trying to step up to Monet's haystacks). The illusion theory entails furthermore that as the illusion induced by a painting takes hold of us, we lose awareness of the material canvas. But this contradicts the fact that appreciation of a painting normally involves simultaneous awareness of its brushwork and the object that it represents (see Wollheim 1974, ch. 13).

Wollheim's theory (1980, 1987) seeks to respect the intuitively correct idea that pictorial representation crucially involves visual experience, whilst rejecting the idea that resemblance provides its explanation. It does this by proposing that pictorial representation engages a species of perception that is inherently imaginative. This Wollheim calls *seeing-in*. Wollheim explains and argues for this claim as follows. A clue to the underlying nature of the experience of painting lies in the fact that paintings give us experiences of absent or non-existent objects. Now this is something that occurs also in dreams, daydreams, and hallucination. It may be ventured that pictorial representation exploits and cultivates a power that the mind possesses innately: its power to generate visual experiences out of itself. Seeing-in occurs when this capacity is exercised in the course of perceiving the external world, in such a way that the visual experience generated by the mind is fused with perception of an external object. This happens in numerous everyday contexts: things are seen-in Rorschach ink-blots, clouds, and damp-stained walls. Seeing-in does not presuppose resemblance, and it is not involved in reading maps or other visual symbols. On Wollheim's account, a painting P represents O if P is marked in such a way that (when viewed in accordance with the artist's intentions) O is seen-in it.

Wollheim's theory may be considered in relation to two other recently advanced theories of interest. Walton's (1990) theory of 'make-believe' holds that to look at a painting is to participate in a fiction: what it is for a painting P to represent O is for P to enable one to make-believe that one's perception of P is a perception of O. Peacocke (1987) by contrast returns to the idea of visual resemblance, but this he understands in a theoretically refined way (Peacocke's key theoretical concepts are 'experienced resemblance', 'experienced shape', and 'visual field'). It may be asked if Walton or Peacocke's theories are incompatible with that of Wollheim and, if so, which theory has the greatest explanatory power.

2.4. Expression

Passages in musical works are described, by critics and ordinary listeners, in such terms as 'frozen with grief', 'calm', 'triumphant in consummation', 'collapsing into despondency', 'sweetly melancholic', 'resolute', and so on. Such descriptions are distinguished by the employment of terms whose primary use lies in describing people's emotional states. These—the expressive qualities of works of art—are a subclass of their aesthetic qualities. Expressive qualities appear to be integral to the beauty, meaning, and value of music. The pre-eminence among the arts accorded to music in the nineteenth century was grounded on its incomparable power of expression. Again, studying this topic involves grasping first the depth of the problem, and then the strengths and weaknesses of the solutions that have been proposed.

2.4.1. The Problem

The philosophical problem of expression comes about because we apply emotional terms to works of art without believing or meaning to imply that works of art *have* emotions. A musical work is at one level just a sequence of sound (just as a painting is at one level nothing but a pigmented canvas), and a sequence of sounds cannot have emotional or any other psychological states. The fundamental question of expression in art, which music brings out most sharply, is: How is it possible for a work of art to express emotion? In virtue of what in our experience of a work of art is it appropriately describable in emotional terms?

One commonsensical answer to the question is that musical works have expressive qualities because they serve as vehicles for expressing the emotions of the composer (this anticipates the expression theory of art: see Section 3.4). This, however, is no answer to the present problem, for it does not explain how it is possible for a composer to use patterns of sound to express emotion: it merely takes that fact for granted.

If it does not help to locate the emotion expressed by music in the mind of the composer, nor does it help to locate it in the mind of the listener. The analysis of a musical work's expression of an emotion in terms of its power to induce that emotion in the listener (sometimes called the 'arousal theory') is directly falsified by the fact that we are not ourselves made melancholic or frozen with grief by music that we describe in such terms; if we were, we would not listen to it. The listener does not herself *have* the emotion expressed by music in the same sense as she has the emotions of real life. The problem, therefore, is to understand how emotion can be ascribed neither to the composer nor to the listener, but rather hover suspended between them, as a sort of aura surrounding the work.

2.4.2. Solutions

In view of these difficulties, one strategy is to relocate the problem of musical expression at the level of language. Thus Goodman (1976) advances a purely logical characterization of how terms are used in the ascription of expressive qualities (in terms of what he calls 'metaphoric exemplification'). It is far from clear, however, that Goodman's theory addresses the true explanandum of the problem of musical expression, since it does not take account of the emotion-ally charged experience that we have in listening to music, which is what makes the use of emotional terms in describing music more than a metaphor.

An alternative and much more plausible way out of the problem is the for-malist position defended by Hanslick (1854). Hanslick grants that music has emotional *effects* on listeners, but denies that there is any genuine sense in which music *expresses* emotion. This combination of claims may sound peculiar, but what Hanslick means is that although music may cause certain feelings in us, this cannot amount to more than a personal association. Hanslick has both (1) an argument for denying that music can express emotion (based on the fact that emotional states, unlike music, have objects and involve thoughts and con-cepts), and (2) an explanation (in terms of the dynamic properties shared by music and episodes of emotion) for why we suppose falsely that it can. Hanslick maintains that it is an illusion that a particular piece of music expresses a par-ticular emotion, and that the proper object of musical appreciation is the beauty of musical form.

Arguably, Hanslick's repudiation of emotion should not be welcomed, since it proscribes the expressive descriptions of musical works that seem to be indis-pensable for our estimates of their value. Two avenues that may then be explored are the 'human analogy' theory and Langer's 'presentational symbol' theory.

The first of these (Kivy 1989) proposes an analogy between the recognition of emotion in music and in people. It asserts that music derives its expressive power from its resemblance to emotionally expressive features of human bod-ily behaviour, physiognomy, and speech; hence the phenomenological similar-ity between hearing emotion in music, and perceiving emotion in the body or voice of another person. The human analogy theory faces, however, the diffi-culty of locating relevant resemblances. It may be asked, What exactly are the features shared by music and human bodies or voices? It is true that both tempo and bodily movement or speech can be slow, but properties such as slowness are emotionally indefinite: so, if a sad piece of music is slow, what makes its slow-ness that of sadness rather than serenity? Objectors to the human analogy the-ory say that only after music has been experienced as expressive can it be modelled imaginatively on the human figure.

On Langer's (1942) theory too, there is a resemblance between music and emotion, but for Langer it is the inner aspect of emotion, rather than its outer bodily expression, which music mirrors. This makes musical works symbols of a special kind: unlike the discursive symbolism of language, they share the 'logical form' of emotion, which allows them to *present* emotion, as language cannot. Problems, however, confront Langer's theory. In what non-metaphorical sense does emotion have 'logical form'? And, arguably, the formal similarity between music and emotion alleged by Langer is either non-existent or insufficiently definite to explain musical expression.

One further possibility is to suppose that the connection of music with emotion is direct and does not take, as Kivy and Langer suppose, a detour via resemblance. Wollheim pursues the Humean idea that the mind has a natural propensity to spread itself on to the world and that certain objects in the world are fitted by nature to serve as recipients for the projection of specific emotional states. Arguably, if Hanslick's repudiation of emotion is to be avoided, some such assumption—that there are natural, innately established 'correspondences' between emotions and external objects—is necessary, whether or not it is sufficient, to account for musical expression.

2.5. Interpretation and Intention

Interpretation is the function of criticism that aims to identify the meaning of a work of art. That works of art have meaning, over and above their representational content and their aesthetic and expressive qualities, is implied by the fact that works of art allow for and call for *understanding*. Questions of interpretation arise in all the arts, but it is literature, and literary criticism, which put the issues surrounding interpretation in sharpest focus.

The first point to be appreciated is that different interpretations have been proposed for all great literary works and that there is usually no straightforward way of deciding between them. For example: Is *Paradise Lost* a Christian work, or does it represent Satan as a moral being 'far superior to his God', as Shelley claimed? Are Kafka's writings religious or political parables, or articulations of the personal *Angst* evident in his diaries and letters? Differences in interpretation force two questions on us: (1) Can biographical information concerning the author serve as legitimate evidence for or against a given interpretation? (2) Can we talk of one interpretation as being the correct interpretation of a work? (The questions are closely interrelated and arguments about the one issue invariably refer to the other.)

2.5.1. Intentionalism and Anti-intentionalism

The starting-point for the first question is the famous attack made by Wimsatt and Beardsley (1954) on what they call the 'intentional fallacy'. The fallacy, Wimsatt and Beardsley say, is committed by critics who suppose that information about the author—or any kind of evidence 'external' to a poetic text, such as information about the culture in which it was created—can elucidate the meaning of a literary work. Everything that is pertinent to the meaning of a poem can be gleaned by careful attention to the words on the page; to suppose otherwise, according to Wimsatt and Beardsley, is to commit the fallacy of seeking to infer a fact about a poem from a psychological fact about its author.

In this light, two opposing views of the relation between the meaning of a literary work (textual meaning) and the intentions of the author (authorial meaning) can be spelled out. What may be called *intentionalism* identifies textual meaning with authorial meaning: what the text means is what the author meant. *Anti-intentionalism* denies that textual meaning is authorial meaning and asserts that textual meaning is autonomous: it resides objectively in the work and has nothing to do, conceptually, with what the author may have meant. (These positions are connected with the theories of art referred to in Section 3: the expression theory is straightforwardly committed to intentionalism, and formalism to anti-intentionalism.)

There is much to be said on this issue, and the arguments of Wimsatt and Beardsley require careful examination. Some of the most important points are the following. It seems right to say that a literary work, considered as a work of art, should be judged in terms of the experience of reading it: it stands or falls on its own merits, and if certain meanings do not show up in an optimally sensitive reading of the work then, whatever the author may have meant and wanted the work to mean, they have not been concretely realized and so do not form part of its meaning. The intentionalist will say, however, that when a work *is* artistically successful, then intentionalism is true and what we grasp is the author's meaning. The intentionalist may add that although 'external' evidence cannot transform an artistic failure into a success, attention to such evidence can make it easier to see what meaning is contained in the words on the page; and that, since we rarely approach a literary work without some conception of its historical circumstances, the author's other writings, and so on, there is in reality no hard-and-fast distinction between internal and external evidence. Intentionalists also draw attention to the fact that estimates of sincerity, maturity, and perceptiveness are important for our responses to literary works, and that these seem to be attributes of the author, in so far as her moral personality is manifested in her work.

A further anti-intentionalist strategy is to argue that literary interpretation should serve the kind of interest appropriate to literary works, and that literary interest, as a case of aesthetic interest, centres on response, not cognition (Dworkin 1985), from which it follows that the proper goal of interpretation is to enhance our experience of the work: an interpretation must offer a reading which makes the work mean as much as possible and 'speak to us'. Facts about authorial meaning are irrelevant to this enterprise.

Wimsatt and Beardsley did not establish that intentionalism involves a logical fallacy. They did, however, define anti-intentionalism as a theoretical option, and indicated the methodological repercussions of the issue: if intentionalism is true, then the study of literature is licensed to cast its net wide and draw on, in addition to literary biography, whatever other disciplines (such as history, psychology, anthropology) are concerned with factors which may be thought to contribute, either consciously or unconsciously, to the author's meaning; whereas, if anti-intentionalism is true, such external information ought to be bracketed out.

2.5.2. Monism and Pluralism

The second question raised by differences of interpretation, which concerns the notion of correctness, again takes the form of a sharp opposition. On what may be called the *monistic* view, there is for each work a uniquely correct interpretation, whether or not it can be identified conclusively. On the *pluralist* view, there is not even in principle a uniquely correct interpretation for each work: rather a number of different interpretations can meet the condition of legitimacy.

Again, the issue requires careful adjudication. In the arguments between monism and pluralism, the notion of *determinacy* figures prominently. The pluralist points out that the notion of correctness of interpretation presupposes that literary works have objective and therefore determinate meanings. But the monist can be challenged to say where this determinacy comes from. Even if the meaning of each individual word in a text is determinate (a claim which is in any case rendered doubtful by the ubiquity of metaphor in literature) the meaning of the work as a whole is far from being a straightforward function of the dictionary meanings of the words composing it. The meaning of the whole leaves room for interpretation, and this, according to the pluralist, means that room is left for a *number* of interpretations. This forceful point drives most monists to embrace intentionalism since, if intentionalism is true, a source of determinacy is supplied by the author's intention, and external evidence can decide between interpretations whose correctness remains undecidable on the basis of the text alone. The assumption that authorial meaning itself is determinate can, of course, be queried in turn by the pluralist.

A second argument advanced in favour of pluralism should be assessed. If (as suggested above) it is the function of literary interpretation to make literary works 'speak to us', then, because the perspectives of different readers differ, and because each reader may entertain a variety of perspectives, it would seem that there need not be a single optimal interpretation. The monist objects that, if this is so, it follows that 'anything goes' in interpretation, an implication which the monist claims reduces pluralism to absurdity.

2.5.3. Literary Theory

These philosophical issues have great relevance to the present situation of literary studies, where theoretical and ideological commitments are explicitly appealed to in interpreting texts, and literary theory has replaced the older conception of literary criticism (of, for example, Leavis). The conception of literary meaning which is presently dominant among literary theorists—known as deconstruction or post-structuralism—is an extreme form of anti-intentionalist pluralism. This position is adopted on wholly general philosophical grounds: it is held that the notion of determinate meaning should be rejected in all (not just literary) contexts. Such literary theorists reverse the common-sense conception of the relation between meaning and interpretation: they hold that the meaning of a literary work is created rather than grasped through interpretation. On this conception, there is a sense in which literature exists for the sake of interpretation, rather than the other way round.

2.6. Fiction

Fictional discourse presents a philosophical problem for our understanding of literature: What is it to employ language in such a way as to make a fictional statement? Is it to make a genuine statement about a world which happens to be fictional, or is it to merely seem or pretend to make a statement? Lewis (1978) brings out the main considerations. The question has implications for the sense in which a literary work generates a 'world' of its own (in the sense in which one speaks of the world of Sherlock Holmes or of Balzac's *comédie humaine*).

It is usually assumed that each form of artistic representation requires its own independent solution, but Walton's (1990) theory of make-believe is a recent attempt to provide a single theory with application to all of the representational arts.

2.7. Emotional Response to Fiction

Distinct from the question (in metaphysics and philosophy of language) of what it is to make a fictional statement, there is the question (in the philosophy of mind) of how we can be moved by fictional events and characters that we know to be unreal. The problem is that emotion seems to presuppose belief: in order to be afraid I must believe that I am threatened, in order to feel grief I must believe that a great loss has occurred. At least, *genuine* emotion seems to presuppose belief. Yet in reading a novel or watching a play we know that what we are presented with is fictional and not real. Why then does this knowledge not cancel out the emotion? Given that we do respond emotionally to fiction, it appears to follow either that (1) we believe in the worlds of the fictions that move us in the same way that we believe in the existence of the real world (Coleridge's proposal that we must undertake or undergo a 'willing suspension of disbelief for the moment, which constitutes poetic faith' assumes that this is so); or (2) in fictional contexts what we feel is not genuine emotion. Neither of these options is appealing: the first seems to be contradicted by the fact that enjoyment of fiction is not a pathological state, the second by common sense and the evidence of introspection. Solutions to the problem of emotional response to fiction generally seek to dispel the appearance of contradiction between belief and emotion by taking refined views of the nature of the belief and/or emotion involved when we participate in fiction.

2.7.1. Tragedy

A special, aggravated case of the problem of emotional response to fiction is presented by tragedy. Tragedy is a category of art in which events that are terrible and painful are represented. The problem here is not how we can be moved at all, but why we should wish to return to representations of events of a kind that we would strive to avoid experiencing in real life. Aristotle's (1987) account centres on the claim that the combination of terror and pity inspired by tragedy is 'cathartic', an idea that requires elaboration if it is to yield a full solution to the problem of tragedy. Nietzsche's *The Birth of Tragedy* (1871) confronts more directly the question of the *meaning* of tragic experience, which Nietzsche attempts to articulate in metaphysical terms; the unclarity of Nietzsche's account reflects the difficulty of the task.

2.8. Metaphor

Describing laughter as hot, man as a wolf, or the sun as remorseless are all instances of the distinctive employment of language that we call metaphorical. Metaphorical language is something that we set value on. This requires explanation, since on the face of it metaphors are either false or meaningless—laughter does not have a temperature, *Homo sapiens* is not lupine, the sun cannot feel or fail to feel remorse—and so ought to be found pointless. A theory of metaphor should tell us what kind of meaning metaphors have (is there a special kind of metaphorical meaning, or do words used metaphorically have only their ordinary kind of meaning?) and what their value consists in (do metaphors give us new information, or merely engender psychological experiences?). A theory of metaphor ought to account for its ubiquity and importance in art (in painting and the other arts as well as literature), and thus contribute to our understanding of art.

2.9. The Particular Forms of Art

The fundamental concepts in the philosophy of art most discussed are common to several, if not all, of the forms of art: all works of art allow for interpretation, and most works of art have some expressive qualities. There is, however, also a distinct philosophical literature that aims to identify and elucidate the philosophical issues that are specific to each particular form of art. The philosophy of literature has been developed most extensively. The questions arise then, with respect to literature, whether it may communicate moral knowledge, and whether its enjoyment presupposes sharing any of the author's moral, religious, political, or other beliefs; with respect to photography, whether it qualifies as an art at all and if so on what grounds; with respect to music, how instrumental music compares with choral music, whether music may represent, what it means to describe music as deep or profound, and what kind of meaning music has; with respect to painting, what defines the concepts of forgery, authenticity, and style, what 'abstract' and 'conceptual' art amount to, and what kind of meaning paintings have; with respect to architecture, by virtue of what an architectural work may qualify as a work of art, and how its artistic value is related to its function; and so on.

3. THEORIES OF ART

3.1. Definitions of Art

As said in Section 2.1, the job of defining art is done when the principle on the basis of which art is sorted from non-art is given. Traditional approaches to this question took it that works of art are distinguished by something intrinsic to them: examples are Batteaux's definition of art as 'the imitation of beautiful nature' and Tolstoy's definition of art as the communication of feeling. It is fairly clear that any such simple definition is wide open to counter-examples: many works of art (most literature) cannot be said to imitate nature, let alone beautiful nature, in any ordinary sense; many things that convey feelings are not art (propaganda, for instance). Definitions of art must also tackle the complications introduced by objects which, it may be argued, count as art but are either not artefacts (say, a piece of driftwood discovered on a beach and exhibited as art by an artist), or not produced with the intention of qualifying as art (such as prehistoric cave-painting, 'primitive' art, Russian icons, medieval sculpture and architecture).

One response to the failure of traditional definitions is scepticism: it has been claimed that the difficulty of defining art is a reflection of there simply *not being* anything in common to all works of art. Some proponents of this view (discussed in Tilghman 1984) appeal to Wittgenstein's notion that a network of loose 'family resemblances' between instances of a given concept is often all that ties them together. On this view, art's lack of an essence makes it no different from other concepts.

Alternatively, the evident inadequacy of traditional definitions may lead to the revisionary approach, now often explored, which defines art not in terms of anything intrinsic to the work of art, but in terms of the circumstances in which the object finds itself, i.e. its social or historical context. Of these, Dickie's *institutional theory* of art is the principal contender and has been most discussed. It says that something is a work of art if and only if it has had that status conferred on it by a competent member of the artworld. The artworld is a nebulous entity that includes artists, critics, gallery staff, and some portion of the general public. 'Work of art', on this theory, is an 'honorific' term, which denotes a certain status, and being a work of art is a 'non-exhibited' property, one which cannot be discerned on the basis of a mere sensory inspection of an object; to recognize art, one must know an object's place in a cultural network (analogous with the property of 'being a £1 coin').

The institutional theory is intended to accord with the open-endedness of art, especially avant-garde art: Duchamp's *Fountain*, a factory-produced 'ready-made' urinal, is the favourite example. In favour of the institutional theory, it explains how it is possible for only one of many perceptually indistinguishable objects—the particular urinal displayed by Duchamp, and not its less privileged mass-produced counterparts—to qualify as a work of art, and thus how it may differ from them in other of its properties (Duchamp's urinal, unlike its counterparts, may be described as 'audacious', 'shocking', or 'revolutionary').

The institutional theory confronts, however, the following problem. For what *reason* does a member of the artworld bestow the status of art on some objects rather than others? The institutional theory tells us that this happens, but not why it happens. It therefore leaves out of account something that, arguably, ought to figure centrally in any treatment of a concept, namely its connection with the understanding of those who employ it, their grasp of themselves as justified in applying it on some occasions and not others (see Wollheim 1980, essay 1). The institutional theory, it is objected, mistakes a sociological account of the parameters of the concept of art for a philosophical account.

Proponents of the institutional theory seek to deflect this criticism by saying that what they are concerned with is art in the 'classificatory' sense, not the 'evaluative' sense in which to describe something as a work of art is to recommend it for appreciation. But it is unclear that this response does not merely beg the question. Opponents of the institutional theory say that it is impossible to dissociate the two aspects, classificatory and evaluative, of the concept of art: we do not first classify objects as art, and then discover that they happen to be aesthetically rewarding; rather, evaluation is integral to classification.

It cannot be ruled out that a formula can be found adequate to account for the line that we draw between art and non-art: a wide variety of (functional, procedural, historical, and other) definitions are set out and explored in Davies

(1991). But, plausibly, a moral to be drawn from the difficulty of finding a definition of art is that no definition can be expected to succeed independently of a theory of art. A theory of art does not require there to be a single *manifest* property—either intrinsic or contextual—shared by each and every work of art: it allows that what unifies art may not be visible at its surface, and probes beneath the surface to locate the essence of art. (Note that this is not to say that art is itself a theoretical concept, like 'atomic structure', which it is clearly not.)

There are two ways in which one may proceed to construct a theory of art. The first is to work, as analytic aesthetics has tended to do and as Section 2 described, through the fundamental concepts of art, and to integrate the analyses of each. Proceeding in this way, Wollheim, Goodman, and Scruton may be held to have produced theories of art. The second is to aim directly and more speculatively at a single concept designed to capture the essence of art. This is the traditional undertaking of aesthetics, and the rest of this section will look at some of the central theories. Section 3 of Hegel (1820–9) gives a sense of the range of theories of art, and questions that they raise.

3.2. Art as Mimesis

The concept of representation, as ordinarily understood, does not provide a ready definition of art, since instrumental music ('programme music' aside), architecture, and abstract painting and sculpture are all, it would seem, non-representational. It may be, however, that the concept of representation can be extended beyond its ordinary scope. This is in effect the claim of the *mimetic theory* (from the Greek term 'mimesis', which is rendered approximately by 'representation', 'imitation', or 'copying') (Plato 1974; Aristotle 1987). The mimetic theory, it should be noted, dominated thinking about art right up to the eighteenth century, and continues to have adherents.

The object of mimesis is usually identified with nature, by which is meant not only physical nature, and includes human nature. Although some art appears to be non-representational, the mimetic theorist may contend otherwise: in antiquity it was thought, for example, that music imitates the harmony and order of the cosmos and the soul. It is open to the mimetic theory to include moral truths, conceived as part of the natural order, as objects of imitation (Sidney (1595) defends mimesis as a means to moral improvement). A contemporary aesthetic theorist who has sought to show the breadth and unexplored potential of the concept of mimesis is Gadamer (1991).

Even if the concept of representation can be extended, and even if we accept that it is natural to enjoy imitation and the skill exhibited therein (Aristotle argues that imitation is a component of learning, which is generally pleasurable), the mimetic theory is open to the objection (Hegel 1820–9, sects. 61–7) that it leaves it unexplained why we should find imitation valuable in the particular way that art is found valuable. The values connected conceptually with representation are cognitive, truth-orientated values such as accuracy and comprehensiveness. These have an important role in art—verisimilitude of plot and characterization evidently matter greatly in literature—but it is hard to see that truth encapsulates the interest of art. We want works of art to figure in our experience as objects with a character of their own, and not to function as mere transparent windows on to the world or vehicles for communicating truths.

These pressures oblige the mimetic theory to lay emphasis on factors other than the bare function of representation. Mimetic theorists accordingly tend to say that representation which is *artistic* must be circumscribed in subject-matter: it must be of particular kinds of things. The mimetic theory is consequently closely associated with the idea that the subjects represented by art should be either ideal (such as perfect human figures) or typical (according to Aristotle, the poetic arts are superior to history in that they represent universals, free from arbitrary and distracting contingent features). The question, however, remains: Can the mimetic say what it is about art that enables it to represent its (ideal, typical) subjects in a way that is *aesthetically* rewarding?

3.3. Art as Form

Where the mimetic theory ties art down to the real world, *formalism* allows the work of art to float free by claiming that only form—the complex arrangement of parts unique to each individual work—has artistic significance. Only what is internal to the work is relevant to its status as art: works of art are 'autonomous', answering only to themselves. Any outward references, to a real, fictional, or imaginary world, are irrelevant. The concept of form can be made more or less narrow, and the distinction of formal from non-formal features will be drawn differently for each artistic medium (evidently the formal properties of literature will need to be identified in a very different way from those of painting or music).

Formalists differ over the continuity of form in art with form in nature: Kant holds that artistic form must be recognizably of a kind with natural form, whereas Bell (1914)—perhaps the most forthright exponent of formalism since Hanslick (see Section 2.4.2)—regards artistic form, which he calls 'significant form', as exclusive to art (Bell thinks that only artists can discern significant form directly in the natural world, and that all others must look to art for significant form). Appreciation of art consists, for the formalist, not in merely recognizing artistic form, but in responding to it: Kant's theory of mental harmony, referred to in Section 1.5, seeks to explain what the response consists in; Bell posits a unique kind of 'artistic emotion' which accompanies the recognition of significant form. According to formalism, works of art exercise to a heightened degree the mind's power of ordering sensory data in perception.

A frequently indicated weakness of formalism concerns the concept of form, which is arguably too indefinite to play the role asked of it. In specifying the kind of form that matters in art, the formalist uses notions like 'balance' or 'uniformity amidst variety', but it is very difficult to define these in a way that prevents them from applying to anything and everything—some sort of balance and uniformity amidst variety can, surely, be found in all objects. The formalist may consequently be pushed to declare that artistic form is indefinable. Bell cheerfully embraces this result, but it exposes his theory to the charge of emptiness: significant form is explained by Bell in terms of the 'artistic emotion' that it induces, but we are then referred back to 'significant form' for our understanding of artistic emotion.

It is not clear that this circularity is so serious as to reduce Bell's theory to vacuousness, as often alleged, but there is another, more substantial objection which is commonly pressed against formalism. This is that our interest in form is not in fact as uncontaminated with extra-formal, worldly concerns as the formalist supposes. Sometimes formal values are of self-sufficient aesthetic interest, but much more often they serve non-formal ends: plausibly, form in art is the vehicle through which a work articulates its non-formal meaning. Unless form has at least an indirect connection with the world, it tends to become artistically uninteresting and reduces to mere decoration. In other terms, the attempt to disentangle form from content leaves nothing much on the side of form, which means that the essence of art cannot be identified with form.

3.4. Art as Expression

Formalism has been found attractive by some aestheticians and has served the interests of some artistic movements (such as post-impressionism, championed by Bell), but it has not dominated cultural thought in the manner of the mimetic theory. By contrast, the *expression theory* of art, since its inception early in the nineteenth century, has effectively displaced the mimetic theory and conditions most deeply our present common-sense conception of art. The concept of expression is paired with that of emotion, and although connection of art with feeling cannot consist in a straightforward equation of art with the communication of emotion (see Section 3.1), the expression theory of art seeks to offer a sophisticated and persuasive account of the central place of emotion in art.

The expression theory may be regarded as originating in writings of the English and European romantic poets (see, for instance, Wordsworth's Preface to the *Lyrical Ballads*), and its rudiments were first set out by Tolstoy, for whom art serves as a vehicle for transmitting morally purposive emotion. The first philosophically informed formulation of the expression theory is that of Croce (1902), who bound it up with the tenets of German idealism. Croce employs a technical notion of 'intuition'—as a non-conceptual, form-giving mode of knowledge, which Croce says is identical with expressive activity—and arrives at the formula art = intuition = expression. Collingwood (1937) provides a more accessible version of the expression theory which detaches it from explicit metaphysical commitments, and the expression theory is now mostly discussed in terms of his exposition of it.

Collingwood regards artistic expression as a special form of self-expression. The artist's motive for self-expression contains both an affective element (the artist seeks relief from the pressure of feeling) and a cognitive element (the artist seeks self-understanding). Artistic expression is a process in which the artist begins with an indefinite and inchoate emotional state, for which he seeks to find a uniquely appropriate concrete articulation, and in so doing transforms his mental state into something definite, tangible, and intelligible. The work created by the artist does not describe his state of mind so much as incorporate it, somewhat in the way that bodily expressions such as smiles and grimaces embody mental life. Since the product of expression cannot be known in advance of the creative process that gives rise to it, expression cannot consist in merely exercising an already mastered technique: it must take whatever specific form is dictated by the particular emotion in the artist's mind. Because expression is not undertaken with any further end in view—it is, so to speak, its own end—artistic creation contrasts with instrumental activities, in which means and ends are distinct, which Collingwood calls 'craft' and opposes to 'art proper' (a distinction that requires careful examination). Collingwood holds that mistaken, 'technical' conceptions of art—which include the conceptions of art as mimesis and as a means for communicating feeling—arise from a failure to grasp this distinction. By giving primacy to the perspective of the artist rather than (as on the mimetic and formalist theories) that of the audience, the expression theory offers an interpretation of Hegel's intriguing and attractive claim (see Section 3.6.2) that the mind 'recognizes itself' in works of art: according to the expression theory, works of art do not merely exhibit mental features, they, as it were, contain mind. The expression theory allows the understanding of art to draw on the resources of psychological theory (see Wollheim 1987), and an ultimate verdict on the theory may be thought to depend in part on the success of psychologically orientated approaches in elucidating the meaning of particular works.

On the side of artistic appreciation, although Collingwood's account leaves this underdeveloped, a natural development of his view is to say that the expression theory regards the audience as retracing the route pursued by the artist: the audience's appreciation re-enacts the artist's creative process and thereby 'retrieves' his psychological state (see Elliott 1967; Wollheim 1980, essay 4). The audience's relation to the work of art is thus symmetrical with the artist's relation to his own mind. The capacity of a work of art to transmit the artist's psychological state is, although not the artist's goal, not a fortuitous, accidental side-effect of self-expression, but a necessary consequence of successful expression.

A number of objections are standardly made to the expression theory.

1. The expression theory, in both Croce and Collingwood, is associated with the highly questionable ontological claim that works of art are mental objects (see Section 2.2), an association which has rendered the theory philosophically vulnerable (see Wollheim 1974, ch. 12). Arguably, the expression theory can be freed from that ontological claim, and the artist's activity of self-expression regarded as routed instead through a public, physical object.

2. The theory's apparent emphasis on personal psychology exposes it to criticism. It may be objected that impersonal ideas, as much as emotions, can be expressed by art, whose legitimate subject-matter is not restricted to the contents of the artist's own mind. But again the expression theorist can plausibly meet this objection by saying that although an emotional component is necessary, the content of artistic expression need not be exclusively emotional: mental states permeated by concepts and thoughts—including moral and spiritual views of the worlds and conceptions of life—are proper material for expression. What a work of art expresses is not therefore confined to merely biographical material.

3. Those who are sympathetic to formalism will challenge the expression theory's emphasis on psychology from a different angle. How can such a supremely self-contained and self-sustaining work as a Ming vase be construed as a product of personal expression? This objection cannot really be met by including formal values in the content of artistic expression, since this risks trivializing the theory. In which case, the expression theorist is obliged to declare that objects which possess only formal virtues fail to qualify as full-blooded works of art, as opposed to aesthetically valuable artefacts. It should be considered whether such a move is acceptable: the formalist will say that this stipulative measure betrays the theory's fundamentally parochial, pro-Romantic bias. In all, it seems fair to say that the expression theory has a strong claim to capture one central component of art as we conceive it; what remains open to question is its claim to capture *all* that is essential to art.

3.5. Art as Language

A fourth theory, which is not traditional but dominates a great deal of contemporary discourse about art, should also be understood and considered critically. This is the *semiotic theory* of art, which proposes to analyse works and forms of art in terms of linguistic and logical categories, such as signification, reference, denotation, syntactic and semantic rules, and so on. On the semiotic theory, art is, like natural language, a fully fledged symbol system: calling it a language is not just a metaphor (formalists and expression theorists, for example, might grant that there is a metaphorical sense in which art is a 'language of form' or 'language of emotion'), nor is the claim just that there is an analogy between art and language (a claim explored in Wollheim 1980). Goodman (1976), the principal exponent in analytical aesthetics of the semiotic theory, analyses representation and expression in logico-linguistic terms (see Sections 2.3 and 2.4). The semiotic conception of art is also endorsed by structuralist and post-structuralist or deconstructionist literary theorists, who graft linguistic science and philosophical theories of language on to the study of literature (see Section 2.5).

The three principal sources of the semiotic theory of art are the following: (1) a rejection of the primacy of psychological and subjective or experiential concepts; proponents of the semiotic theory claim that these concepts are not autonomous and need to be understood in terms of language and signification; (2) a confidence in the superior clarity and fruitfulness of linguistic and logical concepts; (3) a belief in the radically conventional nature of art, often coupled with and grounded on a general rejection of philosophical realism. All these claims are explicit in structuralism and post-structuralism or deconstruction, and in Goodman (1976, especially ch. 6).

The semiotic theory's perspective on art is austere and it appears to offer a certain kind of precision. The theory will, however, be rejected by anyone sympathetic to the Kantian or Humean approach to aesthetics. The Kantian will maintain that art cannot be understood apart from certain forms of aesthetic experience, the nature of which cannot be reduced to logico-linguistic terms; the Humean, that human psychology sets universal, non-conventional parameters to art.

Langer's theory that works of art are 'presentational symbols' (see Section 2.4.2) is also sometimes ranked under the heading of the semiotic theory, but care is needed here, for Langer's account has features that make it in many ways closer to the expression theory of art.

3.6. Post-Kantian Aesthetics

There remain, of course, a large number of philosophically well-developed theories of art that either do not fall into the four categories of mimesis, form, expression, and language, or offer versions of those theories so distinctive as to require wholly independent study and evaluation. The writers indicated below—all post-Kantian German philosophers—present theories of art in the context of general philosophical systems. For this reason it is not easy to evaluate their theories, but each has a strong claim to address and illuminate some features of our experience of art.

3.6.1. *Schiller*

Schiller's aesthetics (1793–5) can only be understood against the background of
Kant's aesthetics and ethics. Schiller seeks to show that only through what he
calls aesthetic education (which includes art) is it possible to achieve wholeness
and full humanity: aesthetic experience alone enables the metaphysical contradictions in human nature (between freedom and necessity) to be overcome, and
the relation of the individual to society to be harmonized.

3.6.2. *Hegel*

Hegel (1820–9) asserts that art 'pervades what is sensuous with mind', and that
art accordingly has 'a higher rank than anything produced by nature, which has
not sustained this passage through the mind'. Hegel's conception of art as a synthesis of mind with something other than itself, by means of which the mind
comes to 'recognize itself'—which underpins his view of the superiority of art
over nature—is a powerful and attractive claim, which arguably may be
detached from his metaphysical system. Of importance are Hegel's comprehensive critical review of theories of art and the aesthetic; his division of art into
three phases (a division which is better regarded as logical than historical); and
his assertion that art has already fulfilled its historical role and ceded to philosophy, and so is in some sense presently redundant (a strange claim, which
requires careful interpretation).

3.6.3. *Schopenhauer*

Schopenhauer (1819) takes over Kant's notion that disinterestedness is the foundation of aesthetic experience and welds it to elements in his own metaphysics,
which are very different from those of Kant. For Schopenhauer, the point of art
lies in the metaphysical liberation from selfhood that will-less aesthetic contemplation induces. Transcendence of selfhood is metaphysically sanctioned,
since according to Schopenhauer individuality is a metaphysical illusion and the
source of all suffering: reality consists of a single, undifferentiated world-will
(music takes us closest to this reality, and so has a privileged place in
Schopenhauer's system). Also important, though not clearly connected with
the rest of his account, is Schopenhauer's view that Platonic Ideas are the
objects of aesthetic contemplation.

3.6.4. *Nietzsche*

Nietzsche's principal contribution to aesthetics is his early book (1871), *The
Birth of Tragedy*, an account of Greek tragic drama (and Wagnerian opera).

Profoundly influenced by Schopenhauer, Nietzsche introduces a fundamental distinction between the Dionysian (concerned with immersion in the underlying, collective, undifferentiated, painful oneness of the world) and the Apolline (concerned with the realm of appearances, separation, and idealization). This distinction has proved inspirational for artists and writers on art, but remains philosophically obscure: it has been much discussed whether Nietzsche intends the distinction to be one between different forms of experience, different kinds of art, or different but equally necessary aspects of all works of art. Nietzsche may be regarded as seeking to answer the question, What must the world be like if tragedy is to be, as it is felt to be, our deepest experience of life? In this light, Nietzsche offers a metaphysical answer to the question about tragedy raised in Section 2.7.1. Also important is 'The will to power as art' (1901), which contains in condensed form Nietzsche's later ideas on art.

3.7. The Value of Art

There remains the question, What value does art have? (What is the point of art?) There is no need, and indeed no room, to provide a 'justification' of art in quite the same sense as a philosophical justification of morality, since the appreciation of art does not share the necessity of moral obligation. There is nevertheless a question as to whether we can articulate and defend our sense of the importance of art. This question is not a mere coda to the philosophy of art: on the assumption that art is an evaluative concept (see Section 3.1), any adequate theory of art must carry the implication that art has value and tell us what this value consists in (in Section 3.2 it was suggested that the mimetic theory faces difficulties in accounting for the value of art).

It is not beyond dispute that art has value, or that the kind of value that it has is any higher than that of what we consider mere 'forms of entertainment'. Positive reasons for scepticism about the value of art are not hard to identify: they derive from art's essential connections with pleasure, play, and imagination, and its freedom from reason and practical purposes. Plato's critique of art in book 10 of the *Republic* (1974) goes further, by suggesting that art's preoccupation with appearances weakens our awareness of reality, and that its effects may be psychologically detrimental and morally pernicious.

Most discussions of the point of art make use of the distinction between ends and means, which they employ critically: some accounts are rejected on the grounds that they reduce art to a 'mere means', and others said to recognize correctly that art is an end.

Care is needed, however, in applying the means–end distinction to art, for two reasons. First, so long as art has some value of some kind, it can always be redescribed trivially as a means to whatever value it realizes. Second, it is far from clear what can be meant by describing art, or its appreciation, as an end.

Of course, individual works of art have to be approached in their own terms and contemplated 'for their own sake', but it would be a mistake to infer from this—which simply expresses the requirement that aesthetic attention be sharply focused—that art or its appreciation *is* its own point and kind of value. If formalists such as Bell and Hanslick, who describe works of art as ends in themselves and identify the point of art with artistic form, do not quite make this mistake, they come very close to doing so.

Arguably, what is meant by saying that art is 'not merely a means' is not that the value of art is of a kind that is unique and cannot be realized in any other sphere, but that its value cannot be realized *in the same way* by anything else. Interpreted in this way, the claim that art is not a mere means seems plausible, for we do in fact recoil from views that suggest that other things could be substituted for art without loss, and that the complexity of art is in principle redundant: hedonistic, moral, or didactic views that regard art as an instrument for creating pleasure or virtue, or as educative, clash with common sense. Tolstoy's (1898) theory of art as the transmission of moral feeling, for example, makes little effort to distinguish art from other, more efficient ways of achieving that end.

It follows that so long as art is viewed as having a necessary role in relation to the kind of value that it realizes, and that its complexity is not regarded as redundant, there is nothing necessarily objectionable about assigning a hedonistic, moral, didactic, or other goal to art. For instance, the goal assigned to art by Schiller—namely, realizing full humanity (see Section 3.6.1)—is 'extra-aesthetic', but Schiller regards aesthetic education as the only way in which it can be achieved.

Having clarified the terms of the question of the value of art, it may be considered what accounts of the value of art are available. It is helpful to bear in mind two broad divisions between kinds of account:

1. Accounts may be divided in the first place according to how closely they relate the value of art to the values of life. In the perspective of the literary critic Leavis, art is inextricably bound up with and subordinate to the values of life: the '*raison d'être* of the work' is to 'have its due effect and play its part in life' (1986: 286). At the other extreme, Bell holds that art is autonomous and that it has value only to the extent that it distances us from life: 'to appreciate a work of art we need bring with us nothing from life, no knowledge of its ideas and affairs, no familiarity with its emotions . . . It is a world with emotions of its own' (1914).

2. A second distinction is between naturalistic and metaphysical accounts of the value of art, foreshadowed by the contrast of Hume and Kant in Section 1. Naturalistic accounts ground art in human nature: starting with the contingent fittedness by nature of certain objects to our minds proposed by Hume, the naturalist proposes to exhibit the point of art by showing how art engages with

fundamental, natural human mental processes. On such accounts, art has a point because it is natural for us to create and appreciate it: it responds to human psychological needs, and the functions which it performs could not be fulfilled through other means. In this spirit Wollheim (1980) describes art as a 'form of life'. Naturalism is the approach of the American pragmatist Dewey (1934), and of psychoanalytic accounts of art (see Wollheim 1987). The naturalistic view qualifies as a theory of art in the sense described earlier: it accounts for the unity of art in terms of the unity of the mind.

Metaphysical accounts of the point of art tend to be more speculative and less closely grounded on the empirical or 'surface' features of art. They also depend explicitly on a general philosophical outlook, which naturalistic accounts need not. A metaphysical theory of the value of art should not, however, simply force art into place in a preformed metaphysical system: it should illuminate aspects of art that would otherwise remain mysterious. Optimally, art should be granted a role in forming the metaphysical system itself, and this is what we find to some extent, and in different ways, in Kant, Hegel, Schiller, Schopenhauer, and Nietzsche (see Section 3.6: German idealism has been notably more hospitable to art than any other philosophical tradition).

3.8. Art, Culture, and Politics

A final set of issues, not well defined philosophically but important and closely related to the question of the point of art, concerns the relation of art to culture and to politics. The overarching question is both explanatory and normative: What is the actual relation of art to the cultural and political life of a society, and how ought it to be so related? Material on the social and cultural dimension of art can be found in many of the writings already referred to. Questions of how art may reflect—and potentially contribute to transforming—the political realm are taken up in Marxist literary theory. Very different is the view of the English tradition, articulated by Arnold (1869) and forcibly reasserted by Leavis (1986), which associates art and the humanities with predominantly liberal ideals of individual and social flourishing.

BIBLIOGRAPHY

Books especially recommended are asterisked. By far the best work giving an overview of aesthetics is Wollheim (1980).* Sometimes Wollheim proves difficult, but his view of aesthetics is broad and deep, and his book is useful in studying particular topics. An alternative to Wollheim, also a stimulating introduction, is Danto (1981). Other, plainer introductions are Sheppard (1987) and Eaton (1988) (very elementary). Older and out-of-print introductions are Charlton (1970) and Aldrich (1963).

A text that is certain to prove extremely useful is Hanfling (1992).* This contains a series of essays specifically written so as to comprise a unified introduction to aesthetics, but of sufficient length for many arguments to be set out in detail. It too may be read through profitably at the outset of studying aesthetics. Another way into the subject— either in place of or in addition to the others just recommended—is to read the detailed entries under 'Aesthetics, problems of', 'Aesthetics, history of', and 'Beauty', in Edwards (1972).

A first-rate currently available anthology of classic writings that will be found useful is Hofstadter and Kuhns (1976).* Of the individual classic writings on aesthetics, the one that it makes most sense to purchase is Kant's *Critique of Judgement* (1790)* (by far the best edition is that of Hackett 1987). An older and out-of-print but useful selection of short extracts from classic writings is Carritt (1976). Two further anthologies (unfortunately out of print) which are excellent and intersperse selections from the classics with modern writings are Dickie and Sclafani (1977) and Rader (1979). Both are organized thematically and contain helpful bibliographies, as does Wollheim (1980). A very clear account of the historical development of aesthetics is Beardsley (1966), which may also serve as a reference book when studying historical figures. A second reference book that it is helpful to have access to, although not all of its entries are of high quality, is Cooper (1992).

Some of the works of analytical aesthetics that will be referred to at particular points may be singled out in advance as especially important. They include: Beardsley (1982) and Mothersill (1984), which reflect systematically on the nature of aesthetic experience and judgement; Danto (1981), where the accent is firmly on contemporary art; Budd (1985), which gives detailed and lucid analytical treatment of several central aesthetic theories; Wollheim (1974), which brings issues in aesthetics in relation to the philosophy of mind; Scruton (1974), which emphasizes the contribution of philosophy of language together with that of philosophy of mind; Scruton (1983), which relates aesthetics to cultural issues; and Goodman (1976), which has been highly influential in developing the view of art as a species of language.

The following collections (most, unfortunately, out of print) contain papers of high quality: Dickie and Sclafani (1977), Barrett (1965), Elton (1954), Margolis (1987), Osborne (1972), Rader (1979), Schaper (1983b), and Vesey (1973).

Works that are either classics of central importance, or strongly recommended contemporary writings, are asterisked.

ALDRICH, V. (1963), *Philosophy of Art* (Englewood Cliffs, NJ).
ARISTOTLE (1987), *Poetics, trans. S. Halliwell (London).
ARNOLD, M. (1869), *Culture and Anarchy* (Cambridge, 1988).
AYER, A. J. (1976), *Language, Truth and Logic* (Harmondsworth).
BARRETT, C. (ed.) (1965), *Collected Papers on Aesthetics* (Oxford).
BEARDSLEY, M. C. (1966), *Aesthetics from Classical Greece to the Present* (Tuscaloosa, Ala.).
—— (1982), *The Aesthetic Point of View* (Ithaca, NY).
BELL, C. (1914), *Art* (London, 1958).
BLACK, M. (1962), 'Metaphor', in *Models and Metaphors* (Ithaca, NY).
BUDD, M. (1985), *Music and the Emotions* (London).

BUNGAY, S. (1987), *Beauty and Truth: A Study of Hegel's Aesthetics* (Oxford).

BURKE, E. (1757), *A Philosophical Enquiry into the Origin of Our Ideas of the Sublime and the Beautiful* (London, 1968).

CARRITT, E. F. (ed.) (1976), *Philosophies of Beauty* (Westport, Conn.).

CASEY, J. (1966), *The Language of Criticism* (London).

CHARLTON, W. (1970), *Aesthetics* (London).

COLLINGWOOD, R. G. (1937), **The Principles of Art* (Oxford, 1958).

COOPER, D. (1986), *Metaphor* (Oxford).

—— (ed.) (1992), **The Blackwell Companion to Aesthetics* (Oxford).

CRAWFORD, D. (1974), *Kant's Aesthetic Theory* (London).

CROCE, B. (1902), **The Aesthetic as the Science of Expression and of the Linguistic in General*, trans. C. Lyas (Cambridge, 1992).

CURRY, G. (1990), *The Nature of Fiction* (Cambridge).

DANTO, A. (1981), **The Transfiguration of the Commonplace* (Cambridge, Mass.).

DAVIDSON, D. (1984), 'What Metaphors Mean', in *Inquiries into Truth and Interpretation* (Oxford).

DAVIES, S. (1991), *Definitions of Art* (Ithaca, NY).

DEWEY, J. (1934), *Art and Experience* (New York, 1958).

DICKIE, G. (1964), 'The Myth of the Aesthetic Attitude', in Hospers (1969).

—— (1984), *The Art Circle* (New York).

—— and SCLAFANI, R. J. (eds.) (1977), *Aesthetics: A Critical Anthology* (New York).

DUFRENNE, M. (1973), *The Phenomenology of Aesthetic Experience* (Evanston, Ill.).

DWORKIN, R. (1985), *A Matter of Principle* (Cambridge, Mass.).

EAGLETON, T. (1990), *The Ideology of the Aesthetic* (Oxford).

EATON, M. (1988), *Basic Issues in Aesthetics* (Belmont, Calif.).

EDWARDS, P. (ed.) (1972), *The Encyclopedia of Philosophy* (New York).

ELLIOTT, R. K. (1967), 'Aesthetic Theory and the Experience of Art', in Osborne (1972).

ELTON, W. (ed.) (1954), *Aesthetics and Language* (Oxford).

ENRIGHT, D. J., and DE CHICKERA, E. (eds.) (1987), *English Critical Texts* (Oxford).

FUBINI, E. (1990), *A History of Music Aesthetics*, trans. M. Hatwell (London).

GADAMER, H.-G. (1991), *The Relevance of the Beautiful and Other Essays* (Cambridge).

GOMBRICH, E. H. (1977), *Art and Illusion*, 5th edn. (Oxford).

GOODMAN, N. (1976), **Languages of Art* (Indianapolis).

HALLIWELL, S. (1986), *Aristotle's Poetics* (London).

HAMPSHIRE, S. (1954), 'Logic and Appreciation', in Elton (1954).

HANFLING, O. (ed.) (1992), **Philosophical Aesthetics* (Oxford).

HANSLICK, E. (1854), *On the Musically Beautiful*, trans. G. Payzant (Indianapolis, 1986).

HEGEL, G. W. F. (1820–9), **Introductory Lectures on Aesthetics*, trans. B. Bosanquet (Harmondsworth, 1993).

HEIDEGGER, M. (1950), 'The Origin of the Work of Art', in Hofstadter and Kuhns (1976).

HIRSCH, E. D. (1976), *The Aims of Interpretation* (Chicago).

HOFSTADTER, A., and KUHNS, R. (eds.) (1976), **Philosophies of Art and Beauty* (New York).

HOSPERS, J. (ed.) (1969), *Introductory Readings in Aesthetics* (New York).

HUME, D. (1757), **'Of the Standard of Taste', in 'Of the Standard of Taste' and Other Essays* (Indianapolis, 1965).

HUNGERLAND, I. C. (1968), 'Once Again, Aesthetic and Non-aesthetic', in Osborne (1972).

INGARDEN, R. (1964), 'Artistic and Aesthetic Values', in Osborne (1972).

JANAWAY, C. (1995), *Images of Excellence: Plato's Critique of the Arts* (Oxford).

JEFFERSON, A., and ROBEY, B. (1986), *Modern Literary Theory*, 2nd edn. (London).

KANT, I. (1790), **Critique of Judgement*, trans. W. S. Pluhar (Indianapolis, 1987).

KIVY, P. (1989), *The Corded Shell*, repr. in *Sound Sentiment*, pt. 1 (Philadelphia).

—— (1990), *Music Alone* (Ithaca, NY).

KRAUSZ, M. (ed.) (1993), *The Interpretation of Music* (Oxford).

LANGER, S. (1942), *Philosophy in a New Key* (Cambridge, Mass.).

LEAVIS, F. R. (1986), *Valuation in Criticism and Other Essays* (Cambridge).

LEWIS, D. (1978), 'Truth in Fiction', *American Philosophical Quarterly*, 15/1: 37–46.

LODGE, D. (1972), *Twentieth Century Literary Criticism* (London).

—— (1988), *Modern Criticism and Theory* (London).

McCLOSKEY, M. (1987), *Kant's Aesthetics* (London).

McDOWELL, J. (1983), 'Aesthetic Value, Objectivity and the Fabric of the World', in Schaper (1983).

MACKIE, J. L. (1977), *Ethics* (Harmondsworth).

MARCUSE, H. (1979), *The Aesthetic Dimension* (London).

MARGOLIS, J. (ed.) (1987), *Philosophy Looks at the Arts*, 3rd edn. (Philadelphia).

MEAGER, R. (1970), 'Aesthetic Concepts', *British Journal of Aesthetics*, 10: 303–22.

MOORE, G. E. (1903), *Principia Ethica* (Cambridge, 1984).

MORAVCSIK, J., and TEMKO, P. (eds.) (1982), *Plato on Beauty, Wisdom and the Arts* (Totowa, NJ).

MOTHERSILL, M. (1984), **Beauty Restored* (Oxford).

NEWTON-DE MOLINA, D. (ed.) (1976), *On Literary Intention* (Edinburgh).

NIETZSCHE, F. (1871), *The Birth of Tragedy*, trans. S. Whiteside (Harmondsworth, 1993).

—— (1901), 'The Will to Power as Art', in *The Will to Power*, trans. W. Kaufmann and R. Hollingdale (New York, 1968).

NUSSBAUM, M. (1990), *Love's Knowledge* (Oxford).

OSBORNE, H. (ed.) (1972), *Aesthetics* (Oxford).

PASSMORE, J. (1991), *Serious Art* (London).

PEACOCKE, C. (1987), 'Depiction', *Philosophical Review*, 96: 383–409.

PETTIT, P. (1983), 'The Possibility of Aesthetic Realism', in Schaper (1983).

PLATO (1974), **Republic*, trans. H. D. P. Lee (Harmondsworth).

RADER, M. (ed.) (1979), *A Modern Book of Esthetics*, 5th edn. (New York).

REYNOLDS, J. (1797), *Discourses on Art* (London, 1988).

SARTRE, J.-P. (1940), *The Psychology of Imagination* (London, 1972).

—— (1967), *What is Literature?*, trans. B. Frechtman (London).

SAVILE, A. (1982), *The Test of Time* (Oxford).

—— (1987), *Aesthetic Reconstructions: The Seminal Writings of Lessing, Kant and Schiller* (Oxford).

SCHAPER, E. (1960), 'Significant Form', *British Journal of Aesthetics*, 1: 33–43.

—— (1964), 'The Art Symbol', *British Journal of Aesthetics*, 4: 228–39.

—— (1978), 'Fiction and the Suspension of Disbelief', *British Journal of Aesthetics*, 18: 31–44.

—— (1983*a*), 'The Pleasures of Taste', in Schaper (1983*b*).

—— (ed.) (1983*b*), *Pleasure, Preference and Value* (Cambridge).

SCHIER, F. (1986), *Deeper into Pictures* (Cambridge).

SCHILLER, F. (1793–5), *[Letters] On the Aesthetic Education of Man*, trans. E. Wilkinson and L. A. Willoughby (Oxford, 1989).

SCHOPENHAUER, A. (1819), *The World as Will and Representation*, vol. I, trans. E. F. J. Payne (New York, 1969).

SCRUTON, R. (1974), *Art and Imagination* (London).

—— (1979), *The Aesthetics of Architecture* (London).

—— (1983), *The Aesthetic Understanding* (London).

SHEPPARD, A. (1987), *Aesthetics* (Oxford).

SIBLEY, F. (1959), *'Aesthetic Concepts', *Philosophical Review*, 68: 421–50.

—— (1965), *'Aesthetic and Non-aesthetic', *Philosophical Review*, 74: 135–59.

—— and TANNER, M. (1968), *'Objectivity and Aesthetics', *Proceedings of the Aristotelian Society*, supp. vol. 42: 31–72.

SIDNEY, SIR PHILIP (1595), *An Apology for Poetry*, in Enright and de Chickera (1987).

SILK, M. S., and STERN, J. P. (1983), *Nietzsche on Tragedy* (Cambridge).

SIRCELLO, G. (1968), 'Subjectivity and Justification in Aesthetic Judgements', *Journal of Aesthetics and Art Criticism*, 27: 3–12.

—— (1972), *Mind and Art* (Princeton, NJ).

STOLNITZ, J. (1960), 'The Aesthetic Attitude', in Hospers (1969).

STRAWSON, P. F. (1974), 'Aesthetic Appraisal and Works of Art', in *Freedom and Resentment and Other Essays* (London).

STROUD, B. (1977), *Hume* (London).

TAYLOR, R. (ed.) (1980), *Aesthetics and Politics* (London).

TILGHMAN, B. R. (1984), *But is it Art?* (Oxford).

TOLSTOY, L. (1898), *What is Art?*, trans. A. Maude (Oxford, 1930).

VESEY, G. (ed.) (1973), *Philosophy and the Arts* (London).

WALTON, K. (1978), 'Fearing Fictions', *Journal of Philosophy*, 75: 5–27.

—— (1990), *Mimesis and Make-Believe* (Cambridge, Mass.).

WIGGINS, D. (1987), 'A Sensible Subjectivism?', in *Needs, Values, Truth* (Oxford).

WIMSATT, W. K., and BEARDSLEY, M. C. (1954), 'The Intentional Fallacy', in Newton-de Molina (1976).

WITTGENSTEIN, L. (1978), *'Lectures on Aesthetics', in *Lectures and Conversations on Aesthetics, Psychology and Religious Belief* (Oxford).

WOLLHEIM, R. (1974), *On Art and the Mind* (Cambridge, Mass.).

—— (1980), *Art and its Objects*, 2nd edn. (Cambridge).

—— (1987), *Painting as an Art* (London).

—— (1993), *The Mind and its Depths* (Cambridge, Mass.).

YOUNG, J. (1992), *Nietzsche's Philosophy of Art* (Cambridge).

Index

Index compiled by Frank Pert